A War of Empires

OSPREY
PUBLISHING

'When the day comes that man gives to peace what he has given to war, then the circle can close, and the Indian Army may yet appear to be an imperfect and flawed but brilliant jewel in the now-fallen crown of empire, most valuable as a symbol of better things to come.'

Roger Beaumont

A War of
Empires

JAPAN, INDIA, BURMA &
BRITAIN 1941–45

ROBERT LYMAN

OSPREY PUBLISHING
Bloomsbury Publishing Plc
Kemp House, Chawley Park, Cumnor Hill, Oxford OX2 9PH, UK
29 Earlsfort Terrace, Dublin 2, Ireland
1385 Broadway, 5th Floor, New York, NY 10018, USA
E-mail: info@ospreypublishing.com
www.ospreypublishing.com

OSPREY is a trademark of Osprey Publishing Ltd

First published in Great Britain in 2021

A catalogue record for this book is available from the British Library.

ISBN: HB 978 1 4728 4714 0; PB 978 1 4728 4715 7; eBook 978 1 4728 4713 3;
ePDF 978 1 4728 4711 9; XML 978 1 4728 4712 6

21 22 23 24 25 10 9 8 7 6 5 4 3 2 1

Plate section image credits are given in full in the List of Maps and Illustrations (pages 9–10).

Maps by www.bounford.com
Index by Zoe Ross

Typeset by Deanta Global Publishing Services, Chennai, India
Printed and bound in Great Britain by CPI (Group) UK Ltd, Croydon CR0 4YY

This book is for Hannah.

It is dedicated to all those who those who fought and died in Burma and India between 1941 and 1945 for the 'four freedoms' of the August 1941 Atlantic Charter – freedom of speech and expression, freedom of worship, freedom from want and freedom from fear.

Contents

List of Maps

List of Illustrations

Japanese troops on a bridge in Burma. (Getty Images)

Chinese soldier in Burmese jungle. (Hulton-Deutsch Collection/ CORBIS/Corbis via Getty Images)

Men of the 17 Dogras bayonet training in 1943. (Image courtesy of the National Army Museum, London)

Men of the 81 West African Division, Kaladan Valley. (Image courtesy of the National Army Museum, London)

Bombay Sappers and Miners men maintaining the Imphal–Tamu road. (Image courtesy of the National Army Museum, London)

US medics tend British wounded in the northern railway corridor, 1944. (NARA)

Supplies being dropped to 81 West African Division in the Kaladan Valley. (Image courtesy of the National Army Museum, London)

Japanese sniper captured by British troops. (Keystone/Getty Images)

Gurkhas swim their mules across the Irrawaddy above Mandalay in January 1945. (Photo by Sgt. A Stubbs/ Imperial War Museums via Getty Images)

Japanese bunker on Garrison Hill, Kohima. (MH33898 IWM)

Indian infantry hitching a ride on Sherman tanks, Meiktila, 1945. (Pen and Sword Books/Universal Images Group via Getty Images)

An Indian infantry 3-inch mortar platoon in central Burma, 1945. (Image courtesy of the National Army Museum, London)

Indian infantry advancing through a burning village, Burma, 1945. (Image courtesy of the National Army Museum, London)

USAAF C46 flying across the mountains between Upper Assam and Yunnan Province, China. (PhotoQuest/Getty Images)

Troops of the 14 Army wash close to the Irrawaddy, Burma, 1944. (Image courtesy of the National Army Museum, London)

Indian sappers rebuild a bridge, Burma, 1945. (Image courtesy of the National Army Museum, London)

An RAF Lysander aircraft flies from an airstrip in the Burmese jungle. (Dr Richard Duckett – Courtesy of Simon Leney, Sergeant Roger Leney's son)

17 Indian Division advance through Pyawbe, south of Mandalay, April 1945. (AFP via Getty Images)

17 Indian Light Division nearing Rangoon, April 1945. (Image courtesy of the National Army Museum, London)

Author's Note

This is a military history, telling the story of the Burma campaign. In it I return to subjects I have written about elsewhere, although for the first time I have been able to bring these themes and subjects into a single account of the longest British campaign of the Second World War. As I have undertaken the writing process, I have been reminded once more that no account can ever hope to be comprehensive. This book does not pretend to be encyclopaedic. Given the vast array of subject matter (the notion of the Forgotten Army is now an exaggeration, so far as the written record is concerned), parts of any account can only be general in nature.[1] The *story* of the Burma campaign includes a vast corpus of subjects and events, not all of which, for reasons of space, can be covered comprehensively. Some parts of this vast canvas must be limited therefore to simple brushstrokes. Unfortunately, little of this has been written by the Indian and African soldiers who fought in the campaign, and not much is available in English from either Chinese or Japanese perspectives.[2] The brushstrokes of *my* story are therefore reflective, sadly, of all these realities. If, because of my choice of emphasis some aspects of the story are more general than readers might wish, or do not tarry long on areas of personal interest, I beg their indulgence. This is, after all, my story. Readers are free to take up their pens and do likewise.

My primary interest lies in the collision of armies on land in 1942 in Burma – primarily British, Burmese, Indian and Japanese, but tangentially also Chinese and American – and the course of their relationship in battle during the nearly four years that followed. It's the story in the main of the nexus between military strategy (the mechanism by which countries translate their grand strategies into military action) and military command, especially in its strategic and operational aspects, because while soldiers fight battles, it's the generals who prepare, train, equip, lead and motivate soldiers, and who direct and command the forces that are engaged in the fighting. However, even in military histories such as this one, the *meaning* of war requires exploration, even if briefly. What did this war mean for the nations that fought it? For India, which started the war as a colonial supplicant of the British Empire, and yet which ended it as a soon-to-be-independent regional and industrial superpower? Of a militaristic Japan, which had foolishly gambled – and lost – its future for short-term, hubristic gains in 1941? Of Britain, which paid for the military unpreparedness and impoverishment of its empire with repeated humiliations at the hands of the Imperial Japanese Army and then helped to bring about the defeat of its enemy – irony of ironies – by virtue of the commitment of 2.5 million Indians who flocked to join not the Japanese Army, or even the Indian National Army, but the *Indian* Army of the Raj? Of Burma, lost to Japan and a dramatic groundswell of popular anti-British support in 1942? Ironically, Burma saw no fruits of this alliance with Japan until the Japanese were defeated in 1945 and independence gained – from Britain, the old colonial power – in January 1948. Of China, who fought itself as well as the Japanese, at the same time as keeping at arm's length the despised but necessary British ally, while holding in a close embrace the United States, its most fervent, energetic and deep-pocketed supporter?

All these subjects are examined insofar as they impinge on what was happening on the battlefield. Primarily this is an account of how the Japanese Army and Air Force swamped Burma in 1942, what the British in India were forced to do in the two years that followed to redress the military balance, and how the Japanese found themselves, in 1944 and 1945, ill-equipped on the battlefields of Assam, Manipur and Burma to deal with the consequences of the war they had so ill-advisedly and egregiously unleashed.

Writing a book is a solitary exercise. It is dependent, however, on the help and support of many people. In my case, the list of acknowledgements for this book is very long. The librarians and custodians of various libraries and manuscript repositories in the United Kingdom were unfailing in their patience, despite the ravages of COVID. I am grateful to the Keeper of the National Archives at Kew; the British Library; the Trustees of the Liddell Hart Centre for Military Archives at King's College, London; the John Ryland Library at the University of Manchester; the Master, Fellows and Scholars of Churchill College, Cambridge University; the Controller of Her Majesty's Stationery Office; the National Army Museum; the Imperial War Museum; and the Trustees of the Broadlands Archive at the Hartley Library, University of Southampton, for access to material and for permission to quote from the documents and manuscripts in their charge. Likewise, I am grateful to the copyright holders who have allowed me use of their material. I wish especially to thank Mark Slim for allowing me permission to quote from *Defeat into Victory*; Chris Twells for allowing me to quote the passage from his father's (John Twells) memory of listening in December 1943 to Slim's plans for the defeat of the Japanese; and Penguin Random House to quote from John Master's incomparable *The Road Past Mandalay*.

Many people assisted in various ways as I made my way through the issues and arguments contained in these pages. I cannot hope to acknowledge the full extent of their support and collaboration here, but to the following, for both small and large favours, I am truly grateful: Kyoichi Tachikawa, Rana Chhina, Sylvia May, Catriona Child, Utpal Borpujari, Phyobemo Ngully, The Countess Mountbatten of Burma, Robin Rowlands, Ann Powley, Oliver Backhouse, Mandeep Bajwa, Paul Barnes, David Fraser, David Jervis, George Lee, George Pritchard, Alex Bescoby, Bertie Lawson, Helen Blake, Ian Price, James Wells, John MacKinlay, Jonathan Maquire, Keith Rigby, Luke Parker, Patrick Moberly, Neal Staniland, Pamela Hamer, Pamela Hervey, Michael Matthews, Philip Grant, Phillip Moss, Simon Sole, Timothy Sharp, Vanessa Davis, William Franklin, Kirsty Done, George Pritchard, Vincent Oliverio, Ian Trollope, Roger Brooks, S. Jagdish, Margaret Sainsbury, Zulfiqar Ali, Steve Rothwell and Xandra Kendall. I am grateful to Tom Donovan, Ben Brownless and Clive and Jeff Pettigrew for permission to use material in each of the prologues.

My heart pauses gratefully to acknowledge the many hundreds of veterans, few who are with us now, who have helped me over the years, in the UK and India. This book is my tribute to them. For conversations specifically about aspects in this book I wish to thank Ted Maslen-Jones, Philip Brownless, John Slim, David Rooney, John Nunnely, Michael Demetriadi, Mike Ball, Khriezotijo Sachü, Khoienuo Keretsü, Ketsoü Sekhose, Shürhosielie Pienyü, Aviü ('Mari'), Gordon Graham, John Nunneley, Ian Lyall Grant, James Lunt, Michael Lowry, John McCann, David Wilton, George Macdonald Fraser, John Henslow, Terence Molloy, John Hamilton, David Atkins, John Hudson, John Randle, John Leyin, Arthur Freer and Raymond Street.

During my research a number of authors, either by means of their books or correspondence (or both) have become firm friends. I am grateful to them all for helping me understand better this kaleidoscopic war: Tim Moreman, Easterine Iralu, K. S. Nair, Khrienuo Ltu, Hemant Katoch, Liz Lockhart-Muir, Simon Anglim, Edith Mirante, Andrew Muldoon, Ian W. Toll, Richard Frank, Keggie Carew, John Dower, Jonathan Fennell, Yasmin Khan, Srinath Raghavan, Douglas Delaney, Ralph and David Tanner, Kaushik Roy, Peter Harmsen, Andrew Lownie, Thant Myint-U, George Wilton, Niall Barr, Ian McGill, Alan Macfarlane, Mark Simner, Charles Chasie, Harry Fecitt, Daniel Todman, Mark Felton, Karl James, David Edgerton, Frank McLynn, Jon Latimer, Philip Woods, Graham

Dunlop, Chandar Sundaram, Stephen P. Cohen, Annabel Venning, Ashley Jackson, Richard Duckett, Daniel Marston, Ray Callahan, Andrew Bird, Cat Wilson, Walter Reid, Alan Jeffreys, George Forty, Tarak Barkawi, David Omissi, Francis Pike, Roderick Matthews and Rana Mitter.

I am especially grateful to friends who have gone the extra mile by reading parts or all of the manuscript, or by allowing me to discuss aspects of it with them. To James Holland, with whom I have walked many of the battlefields described in this book; Dr Sumantra Maitra; Yaiphaba (Yai) Meetei Kangjam, Dr Alan Jeffreys; General The Lord Dannatt; Subimal Bhattacharjee, Utpal Borpujari, Dr Zareer Masani; Professor Ray Callahan; Professor Saul David; Professor Ian Beckett and Dr Walter Reid. My especial thanks goes to Professor Kate Venables whose skilful eye and pen, in addition to her expertise in medical matters in India and Burma during the war, saved me from several errors and many infelicities. I remain responsible, of course, for any remaining errors of judgement or fact.

It has been my great pleasure over the years to work with superb editors in a variety of publishing houses. The experience of working with the Osprey team of Marcus Cowper, Kate Moore and Julie Frederick has been among the best. Thank you for making the process of transcribing my scribbled notes into such a beautiful end product so enjoyable.

Timeline

1937

7 July	Full-scale Japanese invasion of China
13 December	Nanking Massacre ('Rape of Nanking') begins

1939

1 September	Germany invades Poland
3 September	Britain and France declare war on Germany

1940

26 September	Japan invades French Indochina (Vietnam)
27 September	Japan signs Tripartite Pact with Germany and Italy

1941

22 June	Germany invades the Soviet Union
26 July	US and Britain impose oil embargo and other sanctions on Japan
July	Japanese occupy Saigon and enter Cambodia
August	Atlantic Charter
7 December	Japan attacks Pearl Harbor and shells US military base on Midway Island
8 December	US declares war on Japan, entering Second World War
	Japan attacks Hong Kong, Wake Island, Malaya, Thailand and the Philippines

10 December	Japanese sink British warships *Prince of Wales* and *Repulse* off Malaya
	Japanese capture US military base Guam and begin landing on Luzon, Philippines
11 December	Germany and Italy declare war against the US and the US declares war on Japan and Italy
15 December	Japan attacks Dutch East Indies
16 December	Japanese land in Borneo
22 December	Japanese land at Lingayen, Philippines, beginning the main attack on the Philippines
23 December	Japanese seize US base Wake Island and bomb Rangoon
25 December	Hong Kong falls

1942

15 February	Fall of Singapore
27 February	Japanese victorious at the Battle of the Java Sea
8 March	Fall of Rangoon
2 May	Japanese take Mandalay
4 May	US naval victory at the Battle of the Coral Sea
23 May	British forces complete withdrawal from Burma
4 June	US naval victory at the Battle of Midway
September	Launch of First Arakan campaign

1943

13 February	First Chindit operation launched into Burma
May	Defeat of First Arakan campaign
	Trident Conference, Washington
1 August	Japanese declare Burma independent

August	Mountbatten becomes Allied Supreme Commander in South East Asia
	Quadrant Conference, Quebec
September	Stilwell's Northern Combat Area Command begins advance into Upper Burma
October	Completion of the Thai–Burma railway
	Japanese declare the Philippines independent
November	Creation of South East Asia Command (SEAC) under Admiral Lord Louis Mountbatten

1944

February	Japanese feint begins in Arakan (Operation *Ha-Go*)
	Second Chindit operation launched in support of Stilwell in Upper Burma
March	Start of Japanese Imphal–Kohima offensive (Operation *U-Go*)
31 May	Japanese begin withdrawal from Kohima
6 June	D-Day in Europe
18 July	Japanese begin retreat from Imphal
August	Stilwell's NCAC captures Myitkyina
December	Slim's 14 Army crosses Chindwin into Burma

1945

11 January	14 Army begins to cross the Irrawaddy
19 February	US Marines land on Iwo Jima
2 March	14 Army advances to Meiktila
10 March	Large US bombing raid on Tokyo
20 March	14 Army captures Mandalay
1 April	US forces attack Okinawa

3 May	14 Army enters Rangoon
8 May	Victory in Europe (VE) Day
6 August	Atomic bomb dropped on Hiroshima
8 August	Soviet Union declares war on Japan
9 August	Atomic bomb dropped on Nagasaki
15 August	Victory over Japan (VJ) Day – Japan announces its surrender
2 September	Japan signs the formal surrender agreement at Tokyo Bay

Introduction

A variety of empires, for some the vestiges or remnants of empires, the fortunes of some declining and others rising, collided in Burma in 1942. The sickly, inbred, thousand-year-old Konbaung Empire of Burma had finally been deposed by the British Raj in 1885, but a renaissance in the idea of Burmese identity tugged at the heartstrings of some among the British-educated Burmese elite during the 1930s. British rule, they urged themselves to believe, was a transitory state: it had, one day or another, to end, and in its place arise the purity not just of self-government, but of a national sense of 'self', a feeling of belonging to this ancient Burmese soil.[1] It should be noted that this identity was one of racial essentialism; it was primarily a 'Burman' one, excluding for the most part the identity of some Burmese who claimed a different ethnicity – Karens, Shans, Nagas and Chins for example, or a religion different to the dominant Buddhism of the plains.[2]

At the time of the cataclysm in Asia in 1941, the British governed the country from the Colonial Office in far-off London, through a Governor and a civil service built on the model of the Indian Civil Service, by which Burma had been governed since being formally detached from India in 1937. For many Burmans, being treated as a province of India for much of the previous 56 years was a national humiliation. Limited self-government had been in place since 1932, with a Burmese Prime Minister appointed by means of a system of party-based popular suffrage from 1937. But the forced marriage with India had been an unhappy affair: neither spoke each other's language, they did not share a religion and enjoyed widely divergent histories and cultural appetites, not to mention centuries of martial animosities. They shared a colonial master, true, but that wasn't a voluntary state of affairs, and in all other respects India and Burma were very different. In London they shared a Secretary of State, Leo Amery. Britain's Empire was delivered on the cheap, and without much allowance, from London at least, for the peculiar nuances of race,* religious or national identity. Most

---

*'Martial races' was a term applied by the post 1857 Raj to categorise those ethnic groups the Government of India considered best for recruitment into the Indian Army. The idea was that those from martial races were better soldiers than those from less military-minded, or

Britons shared this ambivalence. In London, Indians were Indians, not Punjabis, Baluchis, Dogras, Madrassis, Garhwalis, Sikhs, Rajputs, Jats, Kumaonis and Pakhtuns (Pathans) or Assamese. The fact that the map was red was what mattered most, if indeed it was given much thought at all.

In neighbouring China, the Great Qing dynasty, which had ruled since 1644, had finally ended in 1912, ushering in the Republic of China which fought thereafter to survive warlordism, the rise of communism and the aggressive interests of the Empire of Japan. Japan, which had occupied Manchuria in 1931, established a puppet head of state, before invading China properly in 1937, initiating a two-pronged war, first against the legitimate state of China, and second against the Communist Party, itself vying for national authority in what had since 1927 become a bitter civil war. Long forgotten under the weight of other 20th-century horrors, the Japanese war in China was 'the most inhuman, the most brutal, the most devastating war in Asia's history.'[3] It was also unwinnable. The Japanese Army slaughtered Chinese civilians and soldiers in huge numbers to achieve a strategy that had at its heart nothing more than militaristic aggrandizement. This was itself a product of its own developing sense of self and self-worth in a world where 'might was right' and achieved for countries what talk or friendly coexistence alone never could. Why else was the world so full of competing empires? Better to be one, thought Tokyo, than not. Except that, unattached to political, social or economic vision, such policies rarely flourish outside of the bellicosity of the parade ground or beer hall.[4] In the anaemic desperation of its blood loss, it was the interests of the Republic of China in resisting the Empire of Japan that helped attract 1930s America to Asia, beginning to provide massive quantities of state aid through the Lend Lease Bill to China from 1941. The focal point for American resistance to Japanese expansionism in China happened to run from Rangoon through to Kunming, as it was the so-called Burma Road, completed in 1938, that allowed the start of billions of dollars' worth of American investment to flow into the Chinese treasury and to keep its resistance alive. Perversely, it was this lifeline that brought Burma into the sphere of Japanese war planning for the expansion of its empire into the Pacific and South East Asia, the so-called *Dai Toa Kyoeiken*, the Greater East Asian Co-Prosperity Sphere.

Burma was, therefore, the historic fulcrum on which the imperial interests of Britain, Japan and the United States coalesced in 1942. The backdrop was

---

'non-martial' groups. Tribes from the north east were preferred. The Second World War and the mass participation of Indians in the war effort demonstrated the inherent hollowness of this concept.

MAP I: Assam Province in 1936

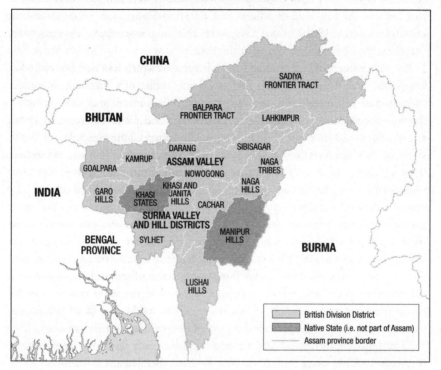

provided by the ambitions (for some) for an independent Burma, together with a Republic of China that was suffering the twin hardships of invasion at the hands of Japan, and civil war.

Before we start, some clarifications are necessary. First, 'Raj' was the common name given to British rule in India (Raj means 'rule' in Hindi) between the end of the Mutiny in 1857 and Independence in 1947. It included areas administered directly by Britain ('British India') as well as the princely states ruled by individual rulers under the 'paramountcy' of the British Crown. The region was less commonly also called the 'Indian Empire', the 'Federation of India' and 'Empire of India'. Incidentally, most British officers in the Indian Army did not use the word, preferring 'Sirak' – government – instead, as they did not consider themselves rulers.[5]

Second, there was no such thing as the 'British-Indian' or 'British Indian' Army. In respect to post-mutiny India, there were only ever two armies, the British Army and the Indian Army. Both were, quite separately, the legally constituted armies of their respective governments. Confusion naturally arises in part because the vast bulk of officers in the Indian Army until the Indianization initiatives of the 1920s and 1930s were British. These men, however, were commissioned into and served with the Indian Army, not the British Army. The Indian government had long accepted that these officers needed to be trained at Sandhurst and Woolwich, in order to achieve consistent standards of officer training and education, and to ensure compatibility between the two armies – the role for most of the Indian Army's history until 1942 was as an imperial reserve, able to support the British Army with trained manpower – which allows some to consider that the Indian Army was a British one. But the differences between them are more than nuance, and must remain separate if one is to understand the relationship between India and its armed forces in the late colonial period.[6] Equally, a political narrative sometimes insists that because of the colonial paradigm, the Indian Army wasn't truly Indian, and therefore the 'British-Indian' label is appropriate. I do not dispute the political sense of this argument, except to say that in purely legal terms it is incorrect, and to use it in the context of the Second World War confuses the purpose, role, history and achievements of the *actual* Indian Army, as opposed to the politicized view of the Army that some elements of opinion have subsequently manufactured. At the time, the distinction was preserved by use of the term 'armies in India'.

Third, during the period under discussion, the north-eastern Indian province of 'Assam', where, along with Manipur, the battle for India was fought in 1944, denotes Assam Province as it was constituted between 1912 and 1947 (see Map 1), encompassing the entire part of India from the Brahmaputra to the Chindwin, and included the territory of the Naga Hills and Naga Tribes in what is today Nagaland. It did not include the Princely State of Manipur, bordering Burma to its east along the Chindwin, nor too that of the Princely State of Tripura that lies sandwiched between Bengal (in the west) and the Lushai Hills in the east.

Fourth, the war in the Far East is defined as that occurring in the theatre of operations that in November 1943 was overseen by South East Asia Command (SEAC). Its neighbouring theatre of war was the Pacific, commanded by General Douglas MacArthur. Unsurprisingly, the terms 'Far East' and the 'Burma campaign' have become synonymous, because in the period from May 1942 to 15 August 1945, Burma was the object of strategic attention in the region. The defence of India in 1944, therefore, was part of the Burma campaign.

Finally, the army and its subordinate corps that was deployed against the Japanese in Assam and Burma from late 1943, namely 14 Army, with its integral IV and XV Corps, was Indian, not British. This distinction has long been forgotten in the consideration of the British Empire and the Indian Army. Two subordinate British formations – 2 and 36 Divisions,[7] together with 3 Commando Brigade, alongside many separate British units (i.e. infantry battalions, armoured and artillery regiments) and brigades, posted as integral parts of Indian divisions – served within this Indian Army, as did large numbers of individual officers, such as those in the Royal Army Medical Corps, serving alongside their Indian colleagues.[8] For a period of time 36 Division was part of the Northern Combat Area Command (NCAC), led by the American, Lieutenant General Joseph 'Vinegar Joe' Stilwell. 14 Army was subordinate to 11 Army Group, the commander of which was, until it became Allied Land Forces South East Asia (ALFSEA) in November 1944, General Sir George Giffard. Occasionally in the text I use the catch-all 'British' to include British, Indian and African troops, but the reader should always be alert to the difference.

By 1939 India was a creaking political, economic and social enterprise in which some 100,000 Britons ruled, largely by consensus and within a widely accepted interpretation of the rule of law – albeit on British terms – a variety of Indian nations, ethnicities and states numbering some 350 million people.[9] It was a state of affairs that the British (and Indian) taxpayer had inherited from 'John Company' – the East India Company – after the Great Rebellion (or 'Mutiny', depending on one's political perspective), in 1858. The Indian Army was an essential component in the coercive power of the Raj, existing primarily to 'defend the internal security of the colonial order'.[10] By 1941 this shaky imperial edifice was tottering. Noisy political elites in India were loudly proclaiming their right to self-determination and pressing their case with a British public increasingly conscious of the moral arguments against imperialism and wearied of the expense. Given the political trajectory on which India was already travelling it isn't fanciful to see, if the war had not occurred, an independent, free and democratic India coming to fruition in the 1950s, or perhaps even earlier were a Labour government to find itself in power in Westminster. The war certainly hastened Britain's return of the fabled jewel in Britain's imperial crown to its own people, and probably exacerbated its most catastrophic impacts, particularly relating to Partition in 1947, although as much blame can be placed for this on communal and religious partisanship – especially the Muslim versus Hindu versus Sikh partisanship, as it can be on the haste with which a war-exhausted Britain exited its imperial commitment.[11] For all its undoubted deprivations and indignities, colonial India nevertheless benefited from a drag effect of the development of democratic, constitutional and politically liberal government from Britain. This was of necessity a gradual process; the vote in Britain itself didn't reach all adults, for example, until 1928.[12] Colonialism it might have been, but imperialism nevertheless established in India a tradition of and desire for democracy that is the truest legacy of its otherwise extra-national incarceration until 1947. This sense of itself, of what it was and what it could be, was inherited from its imperial progenitor. India desired independence, because it saw this as the natural state of a free society. By the time the Japanese war – which had begun in China in 1937 – was lapping against India's shores in 1942, Britain had come to understand this every bit as much as Indian nationalists. The debate, therefore, was not about when India would become detached from Britain but how – or indeed whether – the *new* India would fit within the British Commonwealth of Nations. Would it be – initially, perhaps – a Dominion, like Canada or Australia had been – or fully independent from the outset?

The war transformed the Indian Army. It had always been a unique institution, not really British (although overwhelmingly officered by Britons) and not truly Indian either, reflective of its origins as one of three mercenary armies (Bengal, Madras and Bombay) in the pay of the East India Company. It formed almost a sub-state within the Raj, with sworn loyalty to the Queen-Empress and her successors, and trained and deployed to protect India's borders, while British battalions on long-service rotation in India (in 1939 some 48 infantry battalions, four cavalry regiments and nearly all of the artillery in India) maintained 'military aid to the civil power'. It had traditionally recruited from races the British had considered the most martial – Sikhs, Rajput, Jats from the north, north-west and western regions – whose sturdy resilience was melded with battlefield toughness and a fearsome fighting reputation allied to an unquestioning loyalty to their salt.* Equally, most recruits were landholders; indeed, in previous generations retiring soldiers were given grants of land in recompense for their service. It was often the progeny of these families that provided men for military service. It was these men – Dogras, Gurkhas, Garhwalis, Sikhs, Rajputs, Jats, Kumaons and Pathans among them – who had helped put down the Mutiny in 1857. Other races were recruited into the army, but in supporting roles. The divisional history of 23 Indian Division described the composition of the division in 1942 in terms that reflected the make-up of the old (pre-1939) imperial army:

---

*This phrase was widely used at the time to describe the loyalty of Indian troops to the Raj, in contrast to those during the Mutiny of 1857 and after the fall of Singapore, who did not.

We were, from the outset, predominantly, a division of Indian troops, volunteers one and all. Punjabis, Gurkhas from the hills of Nepal, Mahrattas from the Western Ghats, these were some of the races that had made the name of the Indian soldier famous and they were to be found in our ranks. Equally well known for their fighting qualities were the Rajputs, Patialas and Kumaons who joined us in Assam; nor must we omit the Bengalis and Madrasis who, if they could point to no such distinguished past, under the stress of war rendered fine service in the engineer, signal and administrative units.[13]

The result was that in 1939 two-thirds of the army was sourced from within one-third of India's ethnic groups. The ambiguity of its status meant that the Indian Army reacted in part to instructions from London and in part from India, responding to events without being able much to control them.[14] As a mercenary army and a tool first of John Company and then of the Raj, it hadn't ever been necessary to ensure that it was Indian-officered. This only began to change after the First World War, when it began to develop a more nationally based identity, and long-range political forecasts suggested that India one day might become a self-governing dominion like Canada, Australia or New Zealand, if not fully independent. Consequently, the Indianization of its officer ranks was a painfully slow affair. If the Indian Army was 'the bedrock of British power' it stood to reason that the imperial power would allow only gradual, carefully chauffeured change.[15] The Second World War changed all that. By 1943 the army already looked very different, and by the end of the war it was no longer the carefully managed organism of imperialism, but the fully national flowering of an entirely new sentiment. Now, in addition to those traditionally recruited from the peasant communities of the north, such as the Sikhs and the Rajputs, every area of India, even those purposefully neglected in the past for being insufficiently 'martial' in background, joined the army in large numbers. Consequently, in a few short years the entire racial makeup of the Indian Army was transformed, and some ancient shibboleths were rapidly shelved. Indian commissioned officers were eligible from June 1940 to serve anywhere in the Indian Army. Untouchables and men from previously non-martial races were recruited for the first time in ever increasing numbers, a process begun in the 1920s following the 1917 House of Commons commitment by Britain eventually to give India what it called 'responsible government'. For the first time, remarked the historian Byron Farwell, 'Sikhs from different parts of the Punjab were mixed; Jats and non-Jats were mixed as well; and Dogras served with various Punjabi Hindus. All Madrasis, whether Hindu, Muslim or Christian, served together.'[16] By 1943 the two largest religious groups represented in the army were Hindus with 50 per cent and Muslims with 34 per cent. About half of the army came from the Punjab, but significant minorities now came from United Provinces (15 per cent), Madras (10 per cent), Bombay (10 per cent), North West Frontier Province (5 per cent), Central Provinces (5 per cent), Ajmere and Merwara (3 per cent) and Bengal (2 per cent). Fifteen- and 16-year-old boys were recruited following the British pattern, in which they were trained and educated, and deployed into combat only when they had reached their 18th year. Similarly, the young British officers now arriving under commissions that required them to serve for the duration of the current emergency ('Emergency Commissioned Officers') were on the whole a different breed to those who, before the war, had sought a life of colonial service and whose views and attitudes perhaps were tailored by the context and demands of historic colonial endeavour. The war had removed the will of most people in Britain to manage an empire. One, 24-year-old medical officer Captain Harry Walker, was angered when in late 1943 he saw India for the first time, writing home in high dudgeon about what he considered to be British double standards. He had purchased a copy of Nehru's *Glimpses of World History* and found himself agreeing with the man who would one day become post-partition India's first Prime Minister:

> I feel ashamed, almost, to be British when I read of the things we have done and are doing here to the country and its people. We were so very pious and holy – holding up our hands in horror at the things the Nazis did. Yet all the time we had India in a perfect Fascist grip. People were thrown in jail in their thousands, without trial, for merely holding some political views the government disliked, and were kept there for years. In peacetime, Government here had far wider powers than it has at home in wartime under 33(b). Floggings, hangings, shootings, were all too common. It's my opinion that we must give India absolute and complete freedom as soon as the war is over. Otherwise I am fairly certain there will be another Mutiny – and I would be all in favour of the Indians. The more I see of British overseas policy the more I am disgusted – perfidious Albion – what an apt description that is![17]

Since its more recent reorganization in 1921–22, the Indian Army had been built on the need to defend India's borders and provide aid to the civil power in times of disturbance or a threat to law and order. It was not built on a warfighting basis, designed to prosecute a modern war with modern equipment against a modern enemy. It had, therefore, no armour and very little artillery. Its cavalry was horsed. Its inter-war preoccupation was the Great Game against Russia in its recent

Soviet incarnation on the North West Frontier with Afghanistan. It was only in 1933 that the role of acting as the empire's strategic manpower reserve, in order to relieve the pressure on the fast-dwindling and cash-strapped British Army, was revived as a cheap way of populating British overseas garrisons. It was only in 1935 that artillery was reintroduced to the Indian Army as an Indian combat arm. With the war clouds gathering over Europe in 1938 a modernization programme sought to bring the Indian Army rapidly into the modern age, designed to fight alongside and against a so-called 'first-class' opponent. Doing nothing would mean that the army would 'fall behind the forces of such minor States as Egypt, Iraq and Afghanistan'.[18] A deployable force was created, later to be designated 4 Indian Division, but the journey to change the Indian Army into a modern force, trained to fight confidently abroad, with all the equipment and materiel necessary to enable success, was clearly going to take considerable time and effort. As the Chatfield Committee concluded in 1938, the Indian Army's equipment was poor, relying on the cast-offs of the British Army.[19] For example, Indian battalions at the time possessed only 12 Vickers-Berthier light machine guns, one per platoon of 40 men.[20] By contrast, the Japanese had a light machine gun in each section of 12 men. The shocking state of the (dis)armament of the deployable Indian Army in 1941 and 1942 is only now vaguely recalled, but is of paramount importance in assessing the fighting effectiveness of units when facing the Japanese juggernaut in 1942. Nevertheless, the modernization programme, led by the Commander-in-Chief, General Sir Claude Auchinleck, was to have an unexpected bonus, for it established the mechanisms for the rapid growth of the Indian Army when the requirement came at the outset of war.[21] Within a year of the declaration of war, the army had grown four-fold, volunteers flocking to the call to arms from a far wider section of the population than had been the traditional recruiting ground of the Indian Army but at a rate that far outstripped the ability of India to produce the weapons and warlike stores necessary to equip them, or the instructors necessary to train them. Newly formed infantry battalions could expect to receive just about enough rifles to issue to recruits, but only a fraction of the automatic weapons required and no mortars, grenades, Bren guns or Boys anti-tank rifles. General Archibald Wavell, Commander-in-Chief India, re-emphasized this running sore with a note to London on 11 September 1941 that India only possessed 20 2-pounder anti-tank guns. The fact was that Britain didn't have many more, and couldn't equip its own army, let alone India's. After Dunkirk, Britain remained critically short of every kind of weapon: 12,200 artillery pieces, 1,350 anti-aircraft and anti-tank guns, 6,400 anti-tank rifles, 11,000 machine guns, 75,000 vehicles and virtually all its tanks had been left in France in 1940.

This unprecedented expansion also created enormous problems for the quality of units, which in all armies rely on experienced junior leaders to maintain cohesion and discipline in battle, as more experienced junior officers and NCOs were taken from their units to form the basis of new ones being created in a process known as 'milking'. The Indian Army grew from 194,373 in 1939 (not including the 75,311 soldiers of the Indian Princely States) to 900,000 12 months later (a third of whom were in training) and 2,000,000 in mid-1943.[22] The immediate impact of this dramatic expansion lay in an equally dramatic reduction in the Indian Army's preparation for war. A year after the start of this expansion, the Indian Army was far less capable than it had been before the growth had begun.[23] The requirement to train the new army acted to remove the NCO structure that formed the bedrock of the army, so that for the most part the units despatched to serve in Burma were raw, inexperienced and only partially trained. But there was much more to it than this. The vast, rapid and unprecedented expansion of the Indian Army broke the golden thread of the old regimental system, one in which men joined and served their whole careers in a family tradition, in regiments sourced from specific areas of the country with proud and long-held traditions of military service, in which regimental commitment, discipline and loyalty were more important than anything else other than religious observance. With it also went the bonds of loyalty to their British officers who from the age of 18 until retirement nearly 40 years later would expend their lives in the service of their regimental family. At a stroke the recruitment effort in India that began following the shock of Dunkirk in 1940 created a new army, with increasingly fragile connections to the old, and by virtue of its youthfulness lacking the experience, discipline or emotional bonds of the loyal elements of the army that the Raj had inherited in 1857.[24] In addition, the mix of races in the old regiments was forced to change, further impacting the nature of the newly developing army. But the bigger problem was that the old army that was recruiting the new had no idea about these dynamics. Indeed, in 1940 GHQ India was trying to expand the army by growing it on the model of the pre-war army. But as GHQ was itself to quickly discover, this was now impossible. The historian Tarak Barkawi has described how the old *imperial* (i.e. pre-1939) army was built on a couple of centuries of mainly European perceptions of military effectiveness in the army, combined with a fine nuance for maintaining control on a potential socially and politically fractious environment that made up the totality of colonial India. Martial ethnicities were recruited, trained and managed by British officers in regiments that held local affinities. No attempt was made to 'convert' recruits to a uniform Indian identity; indeed, the peculiarities of race, creed, language, diet and culture were jealously maintained. It was held as an article of faith by many that it was this carefully managed set of sub-identities that kept the Indian Army loyal. In the massive expansion of the army, however, this set of laws would have to be broken. How would recruits manage in a new army where these old distinctions were much less evident? Could Viceroy's commissioned officers and NCOs command soldiers of different races to their own? The result in fact seemed to be that the army had by this time a unique identity of its own that surpassed those of the tribal affiliations of its recruits, and it was the intra-army bond that brought people of widely divergent backgrounds, races and creeds together into a happy melting pot. Indeed, as Barkawi concludes, it 'was not essential, it turned out, to segregate the classes in the army because of the communal bigotry of Indian populations.'[25] Nor, too, did they require the type of patrician man-management of the kind that the British believed was essential to leadership of Indian soldiers before the war. The discovery was that even so-called 'pseudo-sahibs', Indian or British, could command Indian soldiers as effectively as their pre-war predecessors just so long as they displayed the characteristics of true combat leadership, pulling their polyglot troops into teams of warriors based on natural 'followership' and military competence.

Above all, few were to recognize this at the time, but the order to expand the Indian Army to meet the exigencies of the new war in 1939 was a watershed moment for India as a nation. For the first time its army would reflect the primary imperative of government – the protection and security of its subjects. In 1939 it might have been true that the Indian Army fought because it was a supremely professional and disciplined army, and in the manner of all good armies, it went where it was sent, did what it was told and did it well. It didn't particularly matter one way or another whether a soldier had strong nationalist opinions, because they were professional soldiers first and foremost: their regiment was their family, not India. Indeed, in Malaya in 1941 the British concluded that only about 6 per cent of soldiers were nationalistically inclined.[26] The fundamental deceit of the pre-war Indian Army was that it was not truly Indian.[27] It did not reflect the fact of *Indian* nationhood, and stood in contradistinction to the imperatives of India's mass independence movement.[28] By serving the needs of its British masters, it did not represent a national Indian identity, fully representative of the people from whom it recruited, but rather the needs of the British for internal security, domestic order and the somewhat fractious border with Afghanistan on the North West Frontier. Indeed, the modern army was created as part of the merger under the Kitchener Reforms in 1903 from the restructuring of the three previous armies of the presidencies (Bengal, Bombay and Madras), which had themselves been inherited directly from the East India Company. Its command and control mechanisms were not Indian – indeed the first steps towards the 'Indianization' of the officer corps did not begin until 1919 when ten places annually were reserved for Indians at the Royal Military Academy Sandhurst.[29] The process was hesitant and, because it involved the principle of reducing the number of non-Indian officers in the Indian Army, overtly political. Nationalists demanded that the army move from being an instrument of colonial coercion to an embryonic national force, representing 'Indian' rather than 'imperial' interests. The British recognized that it could 'hardly maintain a permanent monopoly over the management of violence without eventually harming the legitimacy of the Raj', which meant that some mollification of nationalist demands was required.[30] It was only the dramatic expansion of the army in 1940 and its recruitment for the first time from other than the martial races that was to make it a truly Indian one. Indian officers commissioned at the three officer training schools and the Indian Military Academy, Dehra Dun ('Indian Commissioned Officers', ICOs) became open to employment across any regiment or unit in the Indian Army, rather than limited to the segregated units that had been allocated to them prior to June 1940 and for the first time could command British troops. Capacity was increased and courses shortened, and two new officer schools opened, to cater for the rapidly increasing number of British and Indian Emergency Commissioned Officers (ECOs). By 1945 there were 8,300 ICOs and ECOs in military service, a number that would have been far greater had the process of Indianization been taken seriously in the 1930s. Nineteen per cent of officers in the Indian Army in 1939 were Indian (rising to 43 per cent in 1945), so progress of a sort had been made, although the lateness of this change meant that by 1945 there was only one Indian brigade commander, Brigader Kodandera Subayya Thimayya, in the Indian Army.[31]

When in 1958 the editor of the *Official Indian History of the Second World War*, Dr Bisheshwar Prasad, who had raised ire in London because of his perceived anti-British bias, asserted that during the war 'the Indian Army was not serving its own people, nor the interests of the people across whose territory the war was fought', he was making an argument that questioned the motivations of the several millions of his countrymen who had decided to fight the Japanese threat to the peace and security of Asia.[32] When the tide of the fascist war lapped against India's shores in 1939, many hundreds of thousands of young Indians flocked to join the Indian Army, despite its proximity in time to the horror of the Amritsar

Massacre, when Brigadier-General Dyer outrageously used live ammunition to exercise crowd control in the city in April 1919, a disaster that resulted in the deaths of at least 379 people, and the compelling noise of pro-independence agitation across the country.[33] They joined for many reasons, ranging from altruism, familial loyalty, the lure of regimental glory in the context of India's long martial traditions – not forgetting the fact that 'many men enjoy soldiering' – to material need; it was a well-paying job after all.[34] A handful joined to do their 'bit to fight the Nazis'.[35] Communists and working-class activists feared the Japanese expression of fascism and temporarily supported the British in the war against the Japanese in order to preserve their freedom so as to continue to advocate for collectivization and the eradication of capitalism.[36] A few joined because they considered loyalty to the British-led government at this moment of existential crisis for India the right thing to do, and some – a few perhaps – were unashamedly loyal to the King-Emperor.[37] In the mountain frontier with Burma, large numbers of Naga and Chin tribesmen, some of whom had fought the British in 1879 but who now found common cause against the invader, were to join forces with the British to eject the Japanese when they invaded in 1944.[38] Despite the political opposition in many quarters in India to the continuance of British rule, and of being dragged into a war not of India's making, it cannot be said that these young men were enlisting to perpetuate the Raj. At least one of the motivations in what can only be described as a complex array was a determination to fight for the defence of India, whose independence was vouchsafed not merely by the various independence movements in India, but by a rapidly changing political culture in Britain, where the empire had begun to be seen by many as 'irrelevant, even rather embarrassing'.[39] Then as now people don't tend to fight for 'governments' but for 'their' country, however they perceive it. It seems clear that issues of ultimate governance were trumped in India by a simple desire by men and women to serve 'their' country.

In this sense those who joined the Indian armed forces after December 1941 made a personal choice to support the government in the war against Japan. In so doing they were rejecting the offer of a competing model for India based on the racial essentialism, violence and barbarism they were able to witness, by virtue of the Indian press, in neighbouring, Japanese-occupied China. Indeed, it appears rational to suggest that Indians in very large numbers considered that the Raj offered India precisely the sort of protection it needed at the time from the militaristic adventurism of Japan, and were content to grant to the Indian government their military labour to see off this threat, without removing their desire for independence or self-government at a more propitious time or in any other way obviating their ability to think or act as autonomous political agents. Many of the democratic principles succinctly articulated in the Rooseveltian 'Four Freedoms' of the August 1941 Atlantic Charter (freedom of speech and expression, freedom of worship, freedom from want and freedom from fear), offered Indians a surety of the type of future they wished to fight and die for. That they did so in their millions offers a counter to Prasad's claim. Most Indians who thought about these things, and who made a conscious choice to join the Indian Army, including politically conscious nationalists, were more than capable of differentiating between the imperialism to which they were subject by Britain and that on offer from Japan.[40] In February 1945 Auchinleck remarked that 'every Indian officer worth his salt today is a nationalist.'[41] An anonymous Indian soldier, quizzed on the subject in Burma in 1945, asserted simply, "I have joined the army to serve my country… This is a people's war.'[42] Realists in the Indian National Congress loudly proclaimed their opposition to fascism in all its guises (including that of Japan), although some members, such as the soon-to-be ex-member, Subhas Chandra Bose, saw in the Japanese an opportunity to advance their own political cause[43] and idealists – and pacifists especially – like Gandhi never really understood the malevolent intent that lay behind the ambitions of the racist leaders of countries like Germany and Japan.[44] Many nationalists were prepared to put on uniforms to fight the Japanese, although they were not prepared while in uniform to undertake the oppression of their own people by means of crowd control.[45] Any assessment of the motivation of Indians joining the Indian Army after 1939 must recognize an essential duality at play – that men and women in colonial India were perfectly capable of having strong nationalistic aspirations while at the same time wishing to join the Indian armed forces because they accepted the immediate physical threat to their own lives to be an existential one, one that threatened their conception of what India should, could and one day would be.

Even when the British Empire in India received its most crushing blow, the loss of Malaya and Singapore in February 1942, Indian determination to resist the onrush of Japanese fascism never once threatened the Raj.[46] Indeed, shortages of recruits from the old martial races were so acute by 1944 that the composition of units had to be changed, such as Punjabi Mussalmen being drafted into battalions of the Sikh Regiment, something unheard of in the pre-war army. These statistics deflate the claim that by this time the government of India was somehow diminished, or otherwise failing. Instead, what it demonstrated was that many Indians wanted to preserve India and its government, although (perhaps) under a different ownership. The growth of the armed forces, numerically and qualitatively, served to strengthen the idea of a capable and effective India, independent of British rule.[47]

In 1942 it cannot be said that the several millions who had joined both to fight and to carry out war work after the loss to the British Empire of Malaya, Singapore and Burma didn't do so to maintain the political status quo ante in India, but because (in part) they hoped for a new, independent and democratic future. That they did so in a social, cultural, economic and political environment in which they were not yet *primus inter pares* with their British masters – the substantive criticism of the Indian Army is that its men weren't equal in human status to their British overlords – they knew they soon would be. As the army increased dramatically in size after 1940, there were many in India, of all political stripes, 'who saw in the building and expansion of the Army the most practical steps towards the building of a new, free India.'[48] It is for this – the future, not the past, nor even the present – that they fought.

For many generations, young Indian men had contrived to allow themselves to join the army, and sacrifice their lives in combat, for something other than imperial coercion. Indian recruits to the army had, from its inception, done so on the basis of an 'active choice', and one in which the strongest bonds of loyalty and commitment to the regiment, and the army, were established.[49] Once in uniform, it was their honour, and that of their family and regiment – their *izzat* – that counted above everything else for the loyalty and commitment. This continued, in spectacular fashion, with the onset of the war with Japan, regardless of their political sentiments. In fact, it was noticeable how, as the war progressed in intensity and acuteness, and as the army recruited massively from new strands of Indian sentiment, that political dissent did not feature. The journalist D.F. Karaka asked himself the question in 1945: 'What motivated the Indians in this fight?'

> It is true that in wartime British soldiers are conscripted. It is equally true that the Indian soldier often joins because the Army offers him a job. But there is something more in it than that. In the minds of those British and Indian Servicemen who can think and feel, there are, generally speaking, two ideas that have taken root. To most men they have become essential to ordinary, decent living. The first is the idea that a soldier must fight for his *izzat. Izzat* does not necessarily imply loyalty and patriotism… A man fighting for *izzat* fights as he thinks a man of his country is expected to fight. *Izzat* implies both self-respect and one's respect in the eyes of his fellow men.[50]

By and large Indians loyally served the army, regardless of political opinion or perspective, if they were treated fairly. 'Crucial to discipline in the Indian Army, it turns out, were the conditions, not the politics of service.'[51]

As the war turned through its bloody revolutions, more dramatic, unforeseen changes came with it. The critical year was 1942, when war encroached against India's eastern frontier and coastline. For the first time India's physical geography was threatened, and not from the long-anticipated push by the Soviet Union into Afghanistan in the north-west. The USSR was now a friend of sorts, or at the very least a 'pacific enemy'. The military humiliations suffered at the hands of the Japanese in 1942, the capture of large numbers of Indian POWs, the conversion of a significant number of these men (as many as 60 per cent) into a Japanese-sponsored anti-British army – the Indian National Army (INA) – should have seen the demise not merely of the Indian Army, but arguably, with nothing to defend its vast and open borders, India as well. A widespread and sophisticated nationalist movement was in place, loudly articulating a popular demand for a free and independent India. This movement instigated a dangerous challenge to the British that autumn through the Quit India campaign, when violence burst onto streets in towns and cities across the country. The British had offered independence when the war was over (see Chapter 14) when many – not just in India – were uncertain that Britain would even last long enough to cash what Nehru called 'a post-dated cheque drawn on a crashing bank'.[52] A devastating famine across Bengal that cost the lives of perhaps as many as 3 million innocents, could have been avoided with better preparation and civil administration, in accordance with the existing Famine Codes that had helped reduce the human cost of famine in previous decades.[53] Why and how did India survive? More importantly, how did a discredited army in 1942 revitalize itself to conquer its foes and establish in the army that exited the Second World War something that was very different to that which had entered it? The reality is that while 'the Second World War saw the unmaking of an imperial Indian Army, it was not the undoing of the army as such.'[54] The opposite seems to have been the case: the Second World War was to see the army's greatest flowering.

PART ONE

Hubris, 1942

Prologue

Major John Hedley, 4 Burma Rifles[*]

*Recollections of his first battle, Kawkareik, on the border
between Siam (Thailand) and Burma, January 1942*

Moulmein was under our old brigadier, Bourke by name. The new brigadier decided to pull us back into reserve, in the Kawkareik area, and to bring up the new battalions onto the hill. He was also going to change over units of these battalions with units of ours which were blocking the small tracks north and south of the main road. Actually, the change-over was about half completed when the Japanese struck and the number of separate units dotted about the countryside ran to about ten. Suffice it here to say that most of the 1/7 Gurkhas were on the hill, most of the Jats were still in the Kawkareik area, one company of the Jats was east of the hills guarding the track to the south, and the Burma Rifles were spread all over the place. I have said, and I have heard said, more bitter things about the so-called battle of Kawkareik than any other subject in the course of the war. Certainly when I got back to Moulmein I told Brig. Bourke and his staff what I thought of Kawkareik and its brigadier in terms – mostly beginning with the consonant 'b' – for which I could have been put under arrest on the spot. But by then I was so fighting mad I didn't care about anything…

---

*John Hedley, a pre-war employee of the Bombay Burmah Trading Corporation, received a commission in the Burma Rifles in 1940 and served as both a Chindit in 1944 and a member of Force 136 in 1945. In January 1942 two Indian and one Burmese battalions – 1/9 Jat, 1/7 Gurkha and 4 Burma Rifles – were formed into a new brigade, 16 Indian Brigade, under the command of Brigadier J.K. 'Jonah' Jones. The hills east of Kawkareik overlooked the Thoung-yin River, running parallel with the Thai border. The brigade's task was to repel the Japanese if they crossed into Burma. This is an abridged version of the original account in John Hedley, *Jungle Fighter* (Brighton: Tom Donovan Publishing, 1996). Quoted with permission.

Now I'm NOT, repeat NOT, going to go to the extent of saying I think the brigadier did right, which I do NOT, but I will admit that there were extenuations. One was the fact that the Japs had by then got Tavoy: so sooner or later would be able to cut our lines of communication. A second was that the Jats had 50 per cent recruits and as a result were not reliable – no real fault of theirs. The last, however, and by far the greatest, was the old story: the Japs were trained in jungle fighting: we were not. Everything they did was a surprise, and it was this sense of doubt and confusion in the brigadier's mind, I'm sure, which produced his hasty and ill-conceived plan. And, mark you, this was only the first time. The Japanese tactics of encirclement through the jungle were destined to bring about – during the campaign – one bloodless withdrawal after another: and it was that fact – their tactics being right and ours wrong – which would have lost us the Burma campaign no matter what aircraft we had. The bravest men are useless in battle if wrongly trained...

When the Japanese struck there was a company of the 1/7 Gurkha Rifles at Myawadi, a company of the 1/9 Jats on the track to the south – the rest of the Jats were at Kawkareik – and the 4 Burma Rifles and 1/7 Gurkha Rifles were divided between the main positions in the Sukli area, Kawkareik and the track to the north. Kyondo was our dump, and had been and was being stocked by river, and from Kyondo the supplies were lorried up to the troops. The road through Kya-In was the road to Moulmein, and at Kya-In there was one of the two ferries.

As can be seen, all the Japanese had to do was to bomb Kya-In and Kyondo and our line of communication became pretty well hopeless. This they did and it did. They got a direct hit on the Kya-In ferry, and that was the end of any chance of getting lorries across there. They then hit the unloading jetty at Kyondo and, although that would not have been an insuperable objection, their air superiority would in a short time have made it impossible for us to get river steamers up with supplies. So the supply position was soon hopeless. However, we had quite large supplies at Kyondo, and could have held out for some time as far as food etc. was concerned.

The Japanese attacked at dawn on 20 January 1942. They surrounded the company at Myawadi, as it was also obvious that they would, but the company fought its way out and got back to the main positions in the Sukli area. Simultaneously they attacked and dispersed the company of the 1/9 Jats on the southern track. Lt.-Col. White of the 1/7 Gurkha Rifles went forward to see what had happened, and was ambushed. He was reported missing but subsequently turned up. Unfortunately, however, Raymond Hall was killed in this ambush. He had been Steels' forest representative in this area, and had been taken on as an intelligence officer.* He was absolutely invaluable, as he not only knew the area backwards, but also was greatly beloved and respected by the villagers. He was a fine man and his death in action was a great blow. Lt.-Col. White having been reported missing, my colonel, Lt.-Col. Abernethy was ordered up to Sukli to take over the forward positions, and as his adjutant I went with him.

So passed the night of 20/21 January. Up to this time there had been some bombing of the main positions, but no attacks of any sort.

On the 21st Lt.-Col. White turned up once more: so Abernethy and I went back to the Kawkareik area – actually we were about 5 miles north of Kawkareik. The position then was that there had been no attack on the main position, but the narrow 12 mile-track leading through the hills and coming up south of Kawkareik was in the hands of the Japs. On the other hand, this track was very difficult, and had been blocked by us – so far as possible, and I don't suppose even mules could have got through, there didn't, therefore, really seem to be any reason for particular alarm.

Nothing much happened on the 21st, apart from some bombing of the Sukli positions, and then came 22 January – a date I shall not easily forget. At about noon we received orders that on the night of 22/23 January all stores would be destroyed, the demolitions on the road would be blown, and the brigade would march back to Moulmein with what it could carry! I don't ever remember feeling more utterly bewildered during the whole of my life. There is one type of defence only – the last man and the last round; that had been drummed into us in training at the Officer Cadet Training Unit, so that it was a completely accepted axiom. Yet, here we were, proposing to pull out of a superb defensive position without firing a shot, and abandoning all our equipment. We couldn't believe it – it couldn't be true. Needless to say, Abernethy was not a man to take that lying down, so off he went to brigade headquarters and was told that the right flank was gone, the Japs were 'getting round us' – how often we were to hear that during the Burma war, and usually on utterly flimsy or non-existent evidence, and that as the line of communication was cut for all motor transport – which was true – we had no option. Abernethy argued for all he was worth, but to no avail, and at about 2100 hours on 22 January the retreat was due to start. I don't ever remember spending a glummer day – a day spent in reflecting that after one and a half years of really hard work with one's battalion, and we had worked hard in that time – the whole thing was going to be thrown to the winds at 9 o'clock

---

*Steels was a pre-war British-owned firm in Burma, with a wide range of commercial interests.

that night. I've had some bad moments in this war, but I still look back to that as the worst of all…

We started at about 2 a.m., and as the mules would be slower than we who were in lorries, the mules were sent ahead. We followed at about 0400 hours, to catch them up about half a mile north of Kawkareik, not as might be expected going towards Kawkareik, but coming out of it as fast as the mules could gallop, having been shot up on approaching the village. Helter skelter they went up the road, into the jungle, anywhere. It was heart breaking but by then it was useless trying to chase them. We soon found out that the people who shot us up were the 1/9 Jats – this happened over and over again in Burma – and in other theatres too for that matter – but the CO had to assume that it was the Japs who were in Kawkareik, so we had to abandon our mules, and, without going through Kawkareik, began our march back to Moulmein. The Japs were not, I know, in Kawkareik until the following afternoon, as at eight o'clock that morning one of our men walked through Kawkareik, and at 11.15 we saw the Japs bombing the lorries which we had left 2 miles north of the village. The Jats reported large numbers of Japs – at NIGHT, of course, in the paddy south of Kawkareik, and fired a good many thousands of rounds at these nebulous samurai…

Sick at heart we marched back to Moulmein. Kawkareik was the result of people losing their heads when flustered by utterly new tactics employed by a new enemy, and the situation was further aggravated by certainly exaggerated, and possibly quite untrue, reports of enemy encirclement from the right flank…

So ended my first battle. The effect on British officers was bad enough, and the effect on the native troops can well be imagined. It was my first real insight into the state of uncertainty one can get into by the confusion of battle, and while I can't agree the commander was right, I can at least sympathise with him. After Kawkareik I was prepared to bet nothing could surprise me – but it did not take long to dispel that juvenile illusion.

1

Burma at the Intersection of History

The heat was almost unbearable. The thermometer at midday registered a sweltering 111 degrees Fahrenheit, too hot for mad dogs or Englishmen. It was two days before Christmas, 1941. The streets of this city of some half a million souls were busy, although most sensible people would soon be inside and abed, taking the opportunity at the hottest part of the day to stretch out under some shade, or an electric ceiling fan for the very privileged, for the few hours it took for the sun to pass its zenith. That was what Leland Stowe, the white-haired 42-year-old Pulitzer-winning journalist, who was in Rangoon on behalf of the *Chicago Daily News*, hoped to do. He was there to investigate what he was later to describe as 'the greatest racket in the Far East', Chinese graft on the Burma Road.[1] He glanced up. A distant humming far above alerted him to a swarm of silvery shapes approaching the city at a great height. *British planes*, he thought, and proceeded on his way, the thought of the fan in the hotel bedroom inviting him to hurry.

Seventeen miles to the north of the city at Mingaladon airfield, Rangoon's joint military and civil air terminus – and home to one of the two British infantry battalions in Burma – Chuck Baisden, an armament technician in the American Volunteer Group (AVG), stared into the sky in surprise. He too had heard the distinctive, distant drone of massed aircraft, but knew immediately that they weren't from Mingaladon. The AVG had just arrived, a month before, operating 14 American P40B Tomahawk fighters with their distinctive tiger teeth painted on the engine cowlings, flown by mercenaries operating on behalf of the Chinese Army. The Burma Road ran from Lashio for 770 long, twisting, dusty and dangerous miles to Kunming in distant Yunnan. It had been scratched, as one American engineer observed, by

Chinese villagers along the route, 'out of the mountain with their fingernails'.[2] The American presence in Burma came about in 1941 because Washington had been persuaded – by virtue of sophisticated and relentless lobbying by Chiang Kai-shek (through his plausible, American-educated wife and her brother T. V. Soong, a banker and the Chinese government's smooth-talking ambassador to Washington) – that America had a significant role to play in supporting Chinese efforts to engage and perhaps restrain Japanese ambitions in the region. The United States had agreed to despatch $5 billion of 'Lend Lease' supplies to China, through Burma, to bolster Chinese efforts to defend themselves against the Japanese. Supplies arrived by ship in Rangoon port, after which they were transported by rail to Lashio, and thence to Kunming by truck along the rickety nail-scratched road. The Hollywood-dubbed 'Flying Tigers', commanded by the superannuated Colonel Claire Chennault and his American pilots – who were paid a bonus of $500 for each aircraft they destroyed – were to protect the road from attack by Japanese aircraft flying from occupied China.

The arrival of the Americans had caused something of a stir: it was well known that colonial Burma did not have any modern fighters allocated to its defence. It hadn't been thought necessary: Burma lay sandwiched protectively between Mother India and the Super Fortress of Singapore. In October 1940 a British study concluded that 280 modern aircraft would be necessary to protect this critical part of the air route between India and Singapore, if it were required.[3] Securing such an armada was a pipe dream: the massive rearmament programme underway in Britain had a far more immediate priority. At the end of 1940 Wavell told Far East Command that he had but four bombers in India available to assist in the regional defence effort.[4] In early 1942 the newly reinforced inventory boasted a single Royal Air Force (RAF) Squadron of 16 fat-bodied Brewster Buffaloes, under-powered and rejected by the United States Army Air Force, and no match for modern Japanese fighters. In any case, on this day all the aircraft were accounted for, parked on the strip or in the workshops. In the city, anyone who paid attention to the aircraft simply thought they were British. Probably reinforcements from India, given the shocking news two weeks back that the Japanese had launched overwhelming attacks against the US Pacific Fleet at Pearl Harbor, at the same time as undertaking simultaneous invasions of British Hong Kong, Malaya and Borneo; the American Philippines and Dutch-run Sumatra and Java. The Japanese had even occupied a point on the distant, southern tip of Burma at Victoria Point, the deputy governor scurrying back to Rangoon with his tail between his legs, mortified at the abject loss of British prestige this event entailed. The recently appointed British Governor – Sir Reginald Dorman-Smith – had assured the population that there was nothing to be worried about. The country was well protected. The great fortress of Singapore was nearby and would provide military aid in the unlikely event that it was required.[5]

His comments reflected the widespread inertia in the country. The European war was far distant. The prospect of war with Japan was widely dismissed. In any case the Japanese were 'little yellow men with prominent teeth, peering myopically through thick glasses', and 'one white soldier was more than capable of seeing off two or three coloured ones.'[6] On reflection (because we know how the story ends), British military failure in 1941 and 1942 lay in not measuring the capabilities of its potential enemies, and countering them with effective stratagems – military and political – of their own. The concomitant British political failure (for the two were intimately entwined) lay in pretending that those risks didn't exist, or would never materialize. When they did, a degree of emotional discombobulation – dissonance even – accompanied the physical lack of preparation and readiness for war. The journalist Eve Curie, daughter of the physicist Marie Curie, visiting in February 1942, observed the obvious lack of enthusiasm among the British colonial elite to die for Burma in a way their countrymen at home had been prepared to do during the Blitz.[7] Old England stirred the blood; old Burma did not. Despite some political noise before the war, there was no threat of internal rebellion. Now, in 1941, nationalist opinion was growing stronger by the day and many people were hostile to British rule, but there was no obvious internal threat to the security of the country. The Raj had quickly and efficiently emasculated the old ruling family, removing it from its old centre of power in Mandalay and exiling its remnants – poverty-stricken and powerless – to India half a century before. The removal of the *ancien régime* after its final defeat in 1885 had been surgical and complete, its life – cultural, political and social – quickly and expertly terminated. Or not quite. The vestiges of the old culture were deep-rooted and had enough life in them to become the wellspring of a renewed nationalism. Thereafter, revolution would only come to Burma as the handmaiden of Japanese rule which, the young hotheads of the anti-British movement didn't fully appreciate, would merely be another, more ruthless form of colonialism.

The government, conscious of the need to maintain civilian morale, insisted on repeating publicly the line that all was well, that Burma was prepared for any eventuality and that in any case Japan was not the threat the rumourmongers claimed it to be. Duff Cooper, resident British Cabinet Minister in Singapore, had told Whitehall a month before that he could 'find no support for the theory that war in Burma is imminent.'[8] In London, the Joint Planning Staff dismissed the idea that the Japanese were a threat, on the basis that the Asian upstarts had 'never fought against a first-class Power.'[9] Britain didn't have to work hard to persuade itself that the Japanese wouldn't be stupid enough to invade. It would be hard to do so, they told themselves. Burma had few roads. Only one, the famous Burma Road, ran into China. Another, likewise, ran into northern Thailand, from the Shan States. There was no road to India: vociferous lobbying by the coastal steamship trade with India had made sure of that. A single road ran south into Tenasserim to Moulmein and beyond, although the bridge over the Sittang was for rail traffic only. Otherwise, the few tracks that existed were not suitable for all-weather use, particularly by vehicles, and were frequently interrupted by floods and landslides during the six-month monsoon that lashed the country in the months between April and October. The best way of getting around Burma, when the weather allowed, was by aeroplane or, around the coast, by boat. The quiet tempo of life had continued throughout 1941 as it had done since the onset of the European war, despite the emerging signs of war in the Far East. Even the formal mobilization of the army on 7 December 1941, just hours before the Japanese attack on Malaya, had brought no change to the preparations for war.

Suddenly, at Mingaladon, one of Chuck Baisden's colleagues started counting the planes. When he got to 27, he shouted, 'Hell they are not ours, we don't have that many.' Reality dawned. The 80 bombers and 30 accompanying fighters – a vast number for these usually quiescent skies – were Japanese.[10] In the entirely unprotected, defenceless city, loud explosions began to reverberate, shockwaves billowing through the low-rise wooden structures of the suburbs, damaging those buildings not destroyed by direct blast. Clouds of smoke and debris rose lazily into the sky, black and sooty where the bombs had hit the oil tanks around the docks. The inaccuracy of dropping bombs from moving aircraft from a great height meant that it wasn't just the docks that were hit, where 85,000 tons of American Lend-Lease supplies awaited transport to China, but residential and city centre locations also. With no expectation of attack, complacency by the authorities and no public air raid shelters, the population was both un-warned and unprotected. If the primary duty of government is the active protection of its citizens – and one of the claims made by imperialism was that it conferred security on its subject peoples – the colonial authorities failed completely in Burma in 1941. Estimates of the civilian casualties on that first day were staggering – as many as 3,000 dead and wounded. But physical casualties were the least of Dorman-Smith's problems, for with the first whistle of Japanese bombs came the evaporation of confidence by the population in the government's ability to protect them. By the end of the day vast numbers were clogging the roads north on foot to escape the horror with whatever meagre possessions they could carry.

A second attack was launched two days later, 25 December, there being no irony in the Japanese attack falling on the Christian day-of-goodwill-to-all-men, as this was a deliberate part of the plan. Holidays are always a good day on which to launch a surprise attack, as Pearl Harbor had demonstrated. Equally, it sent a message: Japan's god – the Sun King, and his living descendant, Emperor Hirohito – was demonstrably more powerful than the Christian god, and was in the ascendant. Fear him! One of those caught in this attack was Wavell, returning from a flight to Chungking – the provisional capital of Chiang Kai-shek's Kuomintang government – on Christmas Day, who found himself sheltering in a trench at Mingaladon as 17 bombs exploded only yards away. Dorman-Smith was surprised at Wavell's sangfroid that night, as he took his gimlet without the least sign of a tremor.[11] Whatever his other delinquencies in Burma in 1942, Wavell was a brave man. The shock caused by these unexpected attacks was incalculable. The workforce – mainly indentured Indian labour, which constituted about half of Rangoon's population – fled. Many vital civil and administrative functions ceased with immediate effect and a paralysis in government and administration set in. The city's labour force, on which it relied for its civic functions, from rubbish removal to labourers of every type, was on the road, tramping north in what came to be called 'the Walkout'. Many Indians, seeing the writing on the wall – for Indians were unloved in colonial Burma – began heading for Arakan, via Taungup and the An Pass which led across the Arakan Yomas from Prome on the Irrawaddy, 150 miles north of Rangoon. All essential services ceased. Railway and bus services, electricity, telephones, water and sanitation, post, mortuaries, as well as private enterprise, especially food supply, never recovered from those two devastating air raids. With the cessation of vital civil and administrative functions, hysteria and, ultimately, widespread lawlessness, set in. Many read the runes far better than their colonial masters, and started trying to leave the country, on foot if they had to, the Chinese heading for China and the Indians, in far larger numbers, for distant India. By the end of Christmas Day the journalist O'Dowd Gallagher estimated that 300,000 men, women and children were in the process of fleeing the smoke-shrouded capital, seeking sanctuary in the countryside, taking with them whatever they could carry or push.[12] On the same day Hong Kong fell.

Desperate to retain control of information and deny intelligence to the enemy, the British refused to advertise the full horror of the attacks to the world. Try as they might, no correspondent could get the magnitude of the disaster past the British government censors, so the world remained largely unaware of Burma's predicament. 'Damage was slight and casualties few' reported the few newspapers across America on 1 January 1942 who bothered to run the story. Much bigger things, they thought – the infamy of Pearl Harbor was, after all, barely three weeks old – were happening elsewhere.

The largest constituency of sufferers from Britain's dereliction of Burma's security were the hundreds of thousands of poor expatriate Indian workers, many of them Tamils from southern India, who had followed the British rupee into Burma to fulfil the menial but essential jobs in an economy dependent on large-scale manual labour, because (at least according to the British) the 'Burman has not shown himself to be particularly keen on industrial or manual labour'.[13] The distinctive darkness of their skin marked them out indelibly as aliens. They had followed the British in the good times as the empire had expanded, in Burma's case since the British had occupied parts of the country – Arakan and Tenasserim – following the first (of three) Anglo Burmese Wars in 1824–26 (the others followed in 1852 and 1885).[14] A small but significant proportion of the Indian community were money lenders, financiers and entrepreneurs, joining with 300,000 or so Chinese, mainly middle class, shopkeepers and traders. Over time, Indian investments controlled significant parts of the Burmese economy, from agriculture to railways. The mortgages of large numbers of Burmans were provided by Indians. Money lenders are regarded as pariahs in many societies, and Burma was no different. From the perspective of the subjugated Burmese – their rulers, identity, culture and history erased – these foreigners helped maintain British rule and prevented native-born Burmese from fully enjoying their birthright. The end of British protection therefore meant extreme danger for this large Indian – and smaller Chinese – diaspora, against whom the more militant sections of Burmese nationalist opinion had been violently opposed for some time.

During the 1930s three groups competed to consider how best to foster the revival of Burmese identity, culture and politics by securing independence from Britain. An educated group calling themselves the Thakins – a deliberate reversal of the word meaning 'master' used by Burmese to refer to the British: the Burmese were the masters now – met to calculate a route to freedom, as did Ba Maw's Sinyetha Party and the Myochit Party under U Saw, Ba Maw's political enemy. Ba Maw, an energetic barrister and anti-colonialist, had cut his political teeth as Prime Minister of the British Crown Colony of Burma between 1937 and 1939. All debated how best to harness sources of foreign assistance. Some looked to Thailand, some to China and others to Japan. U Saw, Prime Minister between 1940 and 1942, a Janus-like creature who wafted with every change of the political breeze (and who was eventually to be executed for his assassination of the Burmese leader and his rival Aung San in 1947), travelled to London in 1940 to converse with Churchill. From 1940 the Thakins were extensively groomed by the Japanese, although Aung San's Ba Sein faction was initially regarded by Tokyo as too communistic in leaning to receive support. The Thakins determined to piggyback on impending war to achieve their political aims. A group – the Thirty Comrades – now a founding myth of the Republic of the Union of Myanmar – were provided with intensive military training on Hainan Island to prepare them for battle. By contrast many (but not all) of the hill people tended to be anti-Burman, increasingly Christian and, consequently, inclined to support the British. For generations little love had been lost between the 10 million indigenous Burmese, who tended to populate the coastline and the lowland plains of the Irrawaddy delta, and the 7 million of the various tribes who occupied the hill country away from the river valleys – the Shans, Arakanese, Karens, Chins, Kachins, Mons and Nagas. The Shans, for instance, had never been part of the Third Burmese Empire, although they had paid it tribute. Racial intolerance was a significant feature of relations between tribe, nation and country not just in Burma, but across the entire region, and far beyond. The idea that Western colonialism was primarily a racial venture, and that the colonized were united in rejecting rules based on the prerogatives of race, is an ahistorical deceit. It was nevertheless a convenient one, then and now, and allowed in 1941 for the Japanese lie: 'Asia for the Asiatics'.

Japan went to war on 8 December 1941, representing the end of an intense debate within Japan as to the virtues and viability of war.[15] It was an argument that the 'war is inevitable' zealots had won, led by General Tōjō Hideki and supported enthusiastically by Emperor Hirohito. In Japan, the military in its various guises – army and navy – ran politics, rather than the other way around. But its declaration of war – Tokyo's diplomats fluffed delivering formal notification of war, required under the terms of international law, which meant that war was declared de facto rather than de jure – was an act of collective suicide. The navy had long wanted to recover power lost to the army in its domination of domestic politics by virtue of its operations in Manchuria and China, pushing its 'Southward Advance Doctrine' (*Nanshinon*) into government policy in August 1936. Despite the efforts of both Britain and the United States to persuade Japan to desist from the follies of rampant militarism,[16] an influential party of politicians and a sizeable proportion of the population – persuaded by aggressive, militaristic gallivanting that had its roots in colonial adventurism in Korea as far back as 1894 – believed that war was the only way Japan could consolidate power in China and give permanent effect to what was fast considered the Empire of Japan.[17] But the totalitarian mindset in Tokyo entirely discounted the potential *human* reaction in a noisily democratic United States when popular sentiment was faced with what was universally regarded as an act of perfidy. Pearl Harbor lit the touch paper of American exceptionalism which, unlike that of Japan, was linked irrevocably to unheard of stores of human potential and industrial power. It wasn't the Battle of Midway in June 1942 that saw the start of a reversal in Japanese fortunes in the Second World War, but Pearl Harbor itself.

In the decades since the end of the First World War, a sense of military and cultural uniqueness had combined to create an ardour for adventurism that changed the political face of Japan. In many respects it was the result of Japan's attempt to secure international self-respect in the years since the Meiji Restoration in 1867, one that had taken a decidedly aggressive, military path. The country otherwise had been a natural ally of Great Britain as a counter to American interests across the Pacific, only Britain's pragmatic commitment to an ongoing friendship with the United States in the 1930s trumping that which it had with Japan. Indeed, until the early 1930s the United States Navy had been fearful enough of British sympathies to retain plans to counter either a war with the Royal Navy in Asia (Plan Red), or a war against an Anglo–Japanese alliance (Plan Red-Orange).[18] The modern notion of a British–American 'Special Relationship' was a (British) concoction built on expediency as a result of the Second World War: such a concept, especially insofar as Asia was concerned, would, before 1939, have been considered ludicrous. But by 1937 Japan had changed out of all recognition. As fast as it had advanced out of pre-industrial antiquity, it had just as rapidly fallen for the false prophetess of racial exceptionalism, dangerously entwined with national assertiveness built on the power of its disciplined, modern armed forces. Japan's sense of what it wanted to be was of an up-to-date, industrialized trading nation, able to exert its influence – politically, culturally and militarily – wherever and howsoever it wished, in pursuance of its interests.[19]

Japan's reach into mainland Asia had rapidly become an important concomitant of this sense of rightful power, a mighty nation rising fast from the depths of medievalism to enjoy the benefits of its increasingly dominant status in east Asia, concerned to protect itself from the depredations of its powerful neighbour, the Soviet Union.

By 1941 the idea of China was to many in Japan an existential issue. Without China, Japan would not have an empire, and thus be unable to give full expression to its manifest destiny as first among equals in Asia. The problem for Japan, however, was that to win its slogging war against the resisting Kuomintang and Communist armies principally required oil – rubber, rice, bauxite and steel were useful too – none of which it could provide itself in the quantities necessary to wage the warfare necessary to overcome China. But neither, too, in 1941 were the European (and American) colonial powers in Asia prepared to sell their resources to an increasingly ultra-nationalist Japan (where they had once done so, with commercial alacrity). They knew that these riches merely fed militarism's voracious appetite, and would be used for the brutal subjugation of China and possibly the rising threat to their own commercial domination of Asia and the Pacific. Japanese involvement in China had already produced well-publicized events such as the Rape of Nanking and other, dreadful examples of Japanese rapine that built upon the terror the Japanese military had exercised in its subjugation of Korea.[20] The world looked on in horror at the Japanese Army as it trampled knee deep in the blood of hundreds of thousands of Chinese after 1937, behaving like 'a looting and raping expedition in the traditions of the Huns and the Spanish Conquistadores'.[21]

What was to be done with Japan? How could its aspirations for an empire, to be the dominant non-white power in Asia, be managed short of all-out war? Between 1937 and 1939 the general policy of both Britain and the United States was to limit Japan's excesses while protecting their own imperial interests in Asia. From 1939 and the onset of war, British policy could best be described as 'Waiting for F.D.R.' Britain, recognizing its military weakness in the region now that it was involved in a war for its survival on the other side of the world, couldn't spare the fleet (nine capital ships, three aircraft carriers and 19 cruisers), aircraft and other military resources that planners had otherwise committed to the defence of its South East Asian possessions. It wanted the USA to take on the bulk of the security commitments on behalf of both powers, while Britain took the lead in fighting Germany and Italy in Europe and the Mediterranean. The level of American support for China, however, was a significant feature propelling Japanese hostility to the USA. Indeed, Churchill's government, desperate not to rile Japan into precipitate military action against Britain's colonial possessions in Asia at a time when London was under direct attack by the Luftwaffe, had undertaken the appeasement of Tokyo in 1940 by temporarily closing the Burma Road, terrified of offending Japan in case it determined to go to war. The Japanese had threatened to blockade Hong Kong and had long threatened British interests in Shanghai and the Yangtse Valley. Britain's frosty relationship with China didn't help. The bad blood that had lain at the heart of the Anglo–Sino relationship in the decades before Japan invaded China in 1937 was a conspicuous feature of the relationship between Britain and China in 1941. America's biggest fear was that it would in some way end up protecting the British Empire, anathema to most Americans in 1939, for whom the only righteous empire was their own. The big question was, 'what would an increasingly friendless Japan do to assert its prerogatives?' Japan's options were threefold. It could continue to wage an infantry-based war in China, seeking the resources it needed where it could for this increasingly resource-hungry and potentially unending struggle (China's population at the time was 600 million, compared with Japan's 70 million). Alternatively, it could, from June 1941, join in Operation *Barbarossa* by striking Siberia, applying an eastern, Axis pincer against the Soviet Union. The Soviet Union was, after all, the first and primary enemy. Or, finally, it could throw caution to the wind and lash out at the American and European colonial possessions in Asia. The German attack on the Soviet Union relieved Japan of any immediate concern from this quarter and allowed it to consider an attack to the south unthreatened on its northern flank. Nevertheless, ostrichitis continued to dominate diplomacy. Even until the last minute, despite the possibilities for war, the general opinion in Western capitals was that, because a simultaneous attack against all the Western interests in Asia was inconceivable, its possibility was considered extremely low. There was, therefore, despite the noise, little real concern for alarm.

During the late 1930s the United States had come to view China through the lens of its own kind of imperialism at the hands of Christian missionaries, and a romantic contrast between psalm-singing Chinese orphans and bayonet-wielding Japanese samurai was firmly fixed in the American popular mind. It was a notion that marched hand-in-glove with hostility to the British Empire as it manifested itself in Asia, a prejudice that had deep roots in parts of America's own historic Anglophobic psyche. Roosevelt himself was not immune to the emotional tug of China, feelings that came possibly from the knowledge that his businessman grandfather had made his fortune in China.[22] Whatever its origin, American feelings for China came at the expense of any for Japan. The more Japan threatened China, the more hostile America became, and the less willing it was to consider efforts by others, such as Britain, for rapprochement with Japan in the interests of peace. Indeed, the American-funded back door route to feed the Kuomintang from Rangoon was all the evidence Tokyo needed to prove that the United States was deliberately attempting to prevent Japan from achieving its legitimate national goals. Empire (to the minds of the existing imperial powers) was one thing, a historic fact that for better or worse could not be gainsaid; acquiring it by means of war in the modern age was another. Consequently, the United States, the Netherlands and Great Britain in 1941 refused, by means of sanctions and embargoes on oil, to allow Japan free access to the resources it needed if the Chinese component of Japanese self-expression was to continue. For its part, Tokyo had determined in 1938 to prepare plans to attack and seize for itself the resource-rich European and American colonial possessions in Asia, and for their part Britain, France and the Netherlands were only too aware of the hungry glances thrown their way by an increasingly assertive Japan. When, following the fall of France in June 1940, the Japanese demanded its dividend in the form of northern Indochina, the alarming precedent was set. By continuing to frustrate Japanese efforts to win this war, Tokyo increasingly considered both Washington and London its mortal enemy. By 1940, Tokyo had come to believe that the German (and Italian) war in Europe and North Africa had weakened the British, French and the Dutch to such an extent that their Asian colonial possessions would be ripe for the picking, and that these would provide all the natural resources the country needed to pursue its China policy.

The primary interest Japan had in 1941 in Burma, was the Burma Road. This now famous trail, part rail and part road, was the lifeline for Chiang Kai-shek's beleaguered government in Yunnan, which had been engaged in an imperial adventure in Manchuria since 1931 and fighting the Japanese since the start of the Sino–Japanese War in 1937. Chinese military resistance, both nationalist and communist, was at the time tying down some 600,000 Japanese troops. By the end of 1940 the road was the only external source of supplies into China, and a considerable hindrance to Japanese ambitions, even though, because of theft and corruption, perhaps only a third of all the American Lend-Lease supplies arriving in Rangoon, so Leland Stowe calculated, ever reached Chungking. The most effective way for the Japanese to halt United States support to the Chinese was to seize Rangoon, and thus close the road. From the moment construction of the road began in 1938, spies trained in the Nakano intelligence school began gathering information that would be helpful in the preparations for a military offensive against Burma.[23] Not only did they garner military information, but under the auspices of Major Keiji Suzuki, they began to work with the Thakins to build a cadre to help support wider Japanese war aims in the region, which included an eye on the possibility of an independent Burma aligned with Japan.[24]

2

Defending Burma (Badly)

When the Japanese bombs were falling on Rangoon on Christmas Day, 1941, the confusion in the city was no less than that in respect of the arrangements for Burma's defence. Although Burma had become independent from India in 1937 (with limited self-government starting in 1932), the Burma Army continued to be a subordinate command of GHQ India in New Delhi, although policy direction came from the War Office in London. Burma Army HQ, in Rangoon, exercised day-to-day responsibility of the forces in the country. The confusion had been exacerbated by the changing policy in London towards Malaya and Singapore at the outset of war, especially as it had become uncomfortably clear that Britain did not have the resources to operate a two-fleet deployment, one based in Singapore securing its Asian colonies, and the other in the northern hemisphere fighting Germany and Italy. To the protestations of India Command, which had long seen Burma as a guardian of the security of its Assamese, Manipuri and Bengali borders, not to mention its eastern, Indian Ocean seaboard – the primary reason after all for India being in Burma in the first place was the demand for security against the repeated depredations of the Mandalay kings – the defence of Burma was handed over to the new Singapore-based Far East Command in October 1940. In a structure that could very well have been designed by the Mad Hatter himself, the General Officer Commanding Burma (appointed by the C-in-C India) had to report to Singapore on military matters, to Whitehall on administrative matters, and to the Governor of Burma on all other civil issues. The historian Raymond Callahan observed acutely: It was nobody's child.'[1]

This structural dysfunction is understandable perhaps in the context of the almost complete inconsequentiality of Burma to British strategy. Prior to the rise of militarism in Japan, the country had no known enemies except, perhaps, the latent threat posed by China's territorial claims in the Hukawng ('Death') Valley, the source in the far north of the country of the mighty Chindwin. Burma was a place where officers came to spend the sunset of their careers in colonial comfort; where British battalions could be habitually undermanned because their only real responsibility was to beat the drum and show the flag, to give hundreds of thousands of expatriate Indians a sense of security, and to provide the threat of menace to any Burman who was foolish enough to upset the colonial apple-cart. There was no need for land defences, or aircraft for that matter, as these could be provided if China, or Thailand – the only possible, but hardly credible, potential enemies – decided to threaten British hegemony. It was, in retrospect, as Wavell's official despatch complained, an absurd set of conclusions:

> The vital importance of Burma, in a war against Japan, to the Allied cause in general and to the defence of India is obvious. Through Burma lay the only route by which the Chinese armies could be kept supplied, and bases stocked for Allied air attack on Japan itself. From India's point of view, so long as Burma was in our possession, Calcutta and the great industrial centres of North-East India were practically immune from air attack, and her eastern land frontiers were secure from the threat of invasion.[2]

Events in Burma in 1942 are a reminder to risk managers the world over that worst case scenarios do happen. Indeed, the allocation of British strategic priorities in Asia meant that Burma never received what it required for its defence. Singapore was the strategic linchpin of the region. On 28 April 1941, Churchill directed that because he considered the threat to the Far Eastern colonies to be minimal, and because of the enormity of the pressures facing Britain in the months before the USA entered the war, no further effort was to be taken to prepare Malaya and Singapore for war 'beyond those modest arrangements which are in progress…'.[3] This decision meant that Burma could hope for no extra resources to defend it above what it already had. Churchill could hardly feign surprise when, in the event, ten months later, Burma appeared distinctly ill-prepared for invasion.

To make matters worse, within days of the onset of hostilities on 8 December 1941, London transferred operational responsibility for Burma back to India Command, under the ultimate command of Wavell. Wavell's own star had waned dramatically by mid-1941, with the near loss of Egypt, the dramatic defeats in Greece and Crete and the long and rancorous disputes with the Prime Minister over military strategy in Iraq and Syria. Churchill believed that Wavell's 'general's luck' had turned, and sacked him as Commander-in-Chief Middle East, sending him to New Delhi to sit 'under a pagoda tree'.[4] One of Wavell's greatest weaknesses, a leitmotif of his command during 1942, was to underestimate his enemy. He failed adequately to comprehend Japanese strategy or the capabilities either of Japanese generalship or of its soldiers. During his time in command he never really shifted far from his judgement in November 1940 that 'I should be most doubtful if the Japs ever tried to make an attack on Malaya and I am sure they will get it in the neck if they do so.'[5] Wavell subscribed to the view that as the Japanese had been held in a form of stalemate for over four years by rag-tag Chinese armies, they could not be much good. Wavell's underestimation of the Japanese, together with his persistent overestimation of the strengths of his own forces, combined to form a potentially fatal mixture of mistaken prejudices that were to contribute in substantial measure to the eventual British defeat.[6]

So it was that when he was given responsibility for the country, Wavell had no detailed knowledge of the situation in Burma. He had visited Rangoon fleetingly two days before the first Japanese air raid, and even then, a week and a half after the landings in northern Malaya, he was shocked by its obvious somnolence. The only military forces worthy of the name comprised Major General Bruce Scott's 1 Burma Division, based at Toungoo in the southern Shan States. This consisted of the two locally raised 1 and 2 Burma Brigades, together with the weak 13 Indian Brigade, which had arrived from India in April 1941. The entire division was poorly equipped. It had no 'artillery, engineers, signals, transport and provost staff,' recalled Lieutenant James Lunt, a young British officer seconded to 4 Burma Rifles; 'there were no light aircraft, helicopters or other modern means of covering great distances rapidly'.[7] Brigadier John Bourke's 2 Burma Brigade comprised two Burma Rifles battalions and one of the two British battalions in Burma, the half-strength 2 Battalion, King's Own Yorkshire Light Infantry (KOYLI). Wavell reported to London of what he had found:

At present time Burma is very far from secure. From lack of aircraft and breakdown in intelligence system... [knowledge of] Japanese moves and intentions is completely lacking. At present moment G.O.C. Burma is working blindfold. Little has been done to make defensive works on main line approach. Fighting qualities of great proportion of forces available are quite unknown quality. Defensive plan seems to have been based largely on hope that our air forces would make enemy approach difficult or impossible by bombing. This is contrary to all experience of this war and anyway we have now no bombers.

He further emphasized deficiencies in administration, repair and medical facilities and added at the end, 'I am sending Burma seven Bofors which are only mobile A.A. guns available in India'.[8]

Wavell immediately sacked the aging local military commander and replaced him with Lieutenant General Thomas Hutton, who arrived in Rangoon to take up the post at the end of the month. Even at this stage the prospect, to Wavell at least, of a Japanese attack on Burma was a remote one. He still thought he had plenty of time to put into effect a suitable defensive plan for the country, which was why he had chosen Hutton, who had built for himself a reputation in India as a solid administrator.[9] Just to complicate matters, Wavell travelled to Java in January 1942 to take command of the well-meaning though ill-fated attempt at strategic unity, the American-British-Dutch-Australian Command (ABDACOM), which stretched from Burma to Java. He left his deputy, General Alan Hartley, to hold the reins in Delhi. ABDACOM was a piece of foolish impracticality (for the time) dreamt up by Roosevelt and Churchill at the Arcadia Conference in Washington as an attempt to coordinate the command of the disparate Allied armies, navies and air forces across an impossibly large area of Asia and the south-west Pacific. The distance between his left (New Delhi) and his right (Lembang, in Java) was about 2,000 miles, with Rangoon lying approximately midway between the two. ABDACOM had run its course in six weeks, after which responsibility for Burma's security was returned to India. Foolish it might have been in practical terms, ABDACOM pointed to the prospect, entirely unforeseen in Japanese planning, that the United States and Great Britain would become a single, common enemy, joining together their planning and resource functions in a coordinated fashion, so as to fight the Axis powers strategically. The practical outworking of the new combined effort was the creation of the Combined Chiefs of Staff.[10]

Although Burma had been made responsible for its own defence since 1937, there was a period of transition while units of the Indian Army were sent back to India and indigenous units of the Burma Army were trained to take their place, a process known as 'Burmanization'. By 1939 all that remained in Burma of the Indian Army were a field company of Madras sappers and miners together with a battery of ancient but accurate 3.7-inch screw guns of the Indian Mountain Artillery. Some expansion of Burma's defences had taken place between 1939 and 1941. The three regular battalions of the Burma Rifles ('Burifs'), together with a training battalion, were rapidly expanded to eight during this period, a dilution of experienced men, to create the new units resulting in a noticeable reduction in their operational effectiveness. The seven part-time Burma Military Police battalions, lightly armed with rifles and Lewis guns, were scattered around Burma's periphery with a largely paramilitary and border-surveillance role. These battalions were converted, in 1941, into the Burma Frontier Force. A decision made in 1927 (later repealed in 1940) prevented ethnic Burmese (as opposed to hill people) from joining the Burma Army, for reasons of supposed loyalty. On reflection it was hardly sensible to exclude the largest proportion of the population from one of the few civic structures able to allow the coalescing of national identity. By 1939 only 472 of the 3,669 soldiers in the Burma Army were Burmese.[11]

The two British resident battalions attached to the Burma Army in 1941, 1 Battalion, Gloucestershire Regiment and the KOYLI, were hardly fit for war.[12] The former, based at Mingaladon airfield, was primarily responsible for the maintenance of law and order in the capital. By the end of 1941 it could muster about half of its authorized war establishment of some 600. The KOYLI, in Maymyo since 1935, with a company detached in Mandalay, was in no better position. When the battalion deployed into Tenasserim in February 1942, it did so with a total strength of about 250, which amounted to little more than two rifle companies. Both battalions were as short of equipment as they were of trained soldiers. The lack of an obvious enemy had been enough justification for the Burmese exchequer to keep military expenditure on a tight rein. Very little was spent on defence. There were insufficient reserves of vehicles, weapons or ammunition. Basic stores for engineering and defensive purposes did not exist, neither did key equipment such as anti-tank and anti-aircraft guns. The Rangoon arsenal was virtually bare. 'There were some 13-pounder horse artillery in the Rangoon arsenal,' recalled Lunt, 'and a few anti-aircraft pieces.' There was very little training ammunition, scarcely any grenades and defence and engineering stores such as barbed wire and sandbags were scarce. However, there did appear 'to be plenty of horseshoes, as I recall, but an absence of horses for the fitting of them. There were also plenty of topis [sun helmets].'[13] In any case, with no expectation of having to fight a war in Burma, the army busied itself in preparing for the requirements of desert warfare, reflecting the fact that the Indian Army had been geared, since 1940, to providing formations for service in the Middle East.

Because no one expected ever to fight in Burma, no consideration had ever formally been given to the subject of jungle training, a failure subsequently described by Wavell as 'incomprehensible'.[14] Indeed, the jungle – to many a frightening, primeval place – remained a no-go area for most Europeans in

Burma. When Lieutenant John Randle arrived in Burma in January 1942 with his inexperienced, war-raised battalion, 7/10 Baluch, a senior staff officer from Burma Army headquarters, on being asked a question about training areas, replied, 'You can't do much training here, it's all bloody jungle!'[15] This wasn't just a problem afflicting Burma: few if any troops ever trained in jungle or 'forest' conditions before the war. It was just too difficult, the all-pervasive excuse being that thick forest or jungle was 'impenetrable' and therefore dismissed as irrelevant. When Brigadier Francis 'Gertie' Tuker, the Director Military Training at GHQ India, prepared an 11-page pamphlet on the subject in October 1940 for troops serving in Malaya – Military Training Pamphlet No. 9 (MTP 9), based on Tuker's experience in Assam in 1919, and on his time commanding the 1/2 Gurkha Rifles in the mid-1930s[16] – there is no evidence that they did anything other than accumulate in piles in headquarters buildings.[17] The assumption seemed to be that the principles of war outlined in the British Army's latest (1935) iteration of its Field Service Regulations (written in part by the then Major General Archibald Wavell), which framed British tactical approaches to warfare, 'were unchanging and could be applied by trained officers and NCOs to all military situations.'[18]

Before 1937 it might be said that Britain, because of its long history of commercial aggrandizement in the region, was China's enemy Number One. As a result of war with Japan after 1937 it was demoted to Number Two. After the Japanese attack on its country, China and Britain became allies of a kind. The marriage of convenience was consummated in late 1941 as a result of Japan's declaration of war on Britain and its empire. The facts of realpolitik underpinned the Anglo–Sino relationship in the years that followed. Generalissimo Chiang Kai-shek was delighted with the expansion of the war, playing 'Ave Maria' on his gramophone in Chunking when he heard news of the Japanese strike on Pearl Harbor.[19] In a public broadcast some weeks later he told his people that the Allies were resisting barbarism. It was something, of course, about which the Chinese knew much. But it was an unusual public admission for someone who hated Britain as much as he did. 'I despise them,' he admitted, 'but I also respect them.'[20] Far away in London Winston Churchill also celebrated Pearl Harbor: at a stroke the Japanese action irrevocably committed the world's largest democracy to the war against the Axis powers. The strategy of 'Waiting for F.D.R.' had worked. Persuading by fair means or foul a reluctant and strongly isolationist USA directly into the fray had been one of the British Prime Minister's war aims since the beginning of hostilities in Europe. Arguably for Churchill, the losses of Malaya, Singapore and Burma that then followed, unexpected and undesirable as they were, were perhaps a price worth paying for America's full-blooded commitment to war on Britain's side, even if that meant a long war on two fronts. Chiang Kai-shek's delight was equally grounded in the reality that by means of this single action, after years of US assistance to China and sanctions against Japan, Tokyo 'finally melded China's struggle with that of the most powerful nation on earth.'[21] From 8 December 1941 all three parties – Britain, America and China – were involved in an involuntary military and political ménage à trois that fundamentally shaped the future of the war in the Far East.

The complexity of this three-way relationship at the grand strategic and military strategic levels of war in the first half of 1942, as all parties attempted to develop a modus vivendi in the face of the fast-developing Japanese threat, was built on the wages of failure. Britain lost Burma, as it did Hong Kong, Malaya, Singapore and Borneo, through incompetence, ill-preparedness, inefficiency and hubris, in the face of a superbly prepared, organized and energetic enemy. America suffered the same fate in the Philippines and the Pacific, as did the Netherlands in the Dutch East Indies.[22] Turning the table on the victorious Japanese was a tall order.

Britain therefore joined the Sino–Japanese War only as part of the widening of the war brought about by Japanese aggrandizement in December 1941, content in the past to observe what was going on inside China but, for several decades following its acquisition of Hong Kong in 1898, only interested in the country from a perspective that was limited to this, tiny, horizon. China was remote therefore in British policy, consideration or imagination before late 1941, and there was certainly no 'forward' policy with respect to the country in the way that there was from New York. When the Sino–Japanese War began in 1937 Britain simply did not have the resources to do anything but watch, even if it had the inclination to intervene in affairs in which it had no compelling interest. In any case, it was hard to conceive of Britain supporting the leader of the Kuomintang who had repeatedly articulated public antagonism towards British imperialism in neighbouring Burma, Hong Kong and India and made common cause with those in India conspiring to topple the Raj. Chiang Kai-shek's hostility to Britain – or at least its empire – was well known, and visceral. In any case, British military capability in the Far East in the 1930s, following savage cuts in defence spending in London in the 1920s and attempts to satisfy the requirements of naval disarmament, together with an equally parsimonious Indian government in the 1930s, was paper thin. Little practical support could have been given even if there had been the political will to so. At the time the Nazi regime was supporting the Kuomintang with military assistance.[23] In November 1940 Chiang Kai-shek had asked Britain for a $50–75 million loan. Britain could only afford a credit of £10 million. This was for no other reason than poverty. Britain was emerging from economic depression and trying to rearm to confront a rapidly emerging threat in Europe. It didn't help that it oversaw an empire it could not afford to defend.[24]

In November 1940, No. 204 British Military Mission was appointed to Chungking, under an Indian Army officer, Major General Lancelot Dennys.[25] London had considered that the relations so established were satisfactory and included a visit in April 1941 by a Chinese military mission to Burma and Singapore. However, when war began for real in December 1941, engagement between the British and Chinese became quickly strained. This was partly because cross-cultural communication was difficult, but it was also because the unexpected need to work closely together brought into conflict both sides' competing strategic imperatives. Widely divergent grand strategic goals created the opportunity for mutual suspicion and incomprehension. In addition, the military practices of both sides diverged widely in respect of logistics and administration. For instance, whereas British operations were based on maintaining an elaborate logistical 'tail' and could not move without protecting it, the Chinese tried as much as they could to forage for food locally. The only common factor between them was their shared enemy. When Britain began losing its Asian colonies to Japan, following on from their repeated defeats in Europe, North Africa and the Mediterranean, Chiang Kai-shek's antipathy towards perfidious Albion became stronger. In the view of the Chinese leader Britain did not deserve to keep its empire; nor did it deserve Chinese help. It was only the threat of western encirclement by the Japanese, and the cutting of the Burma Road, that forced his hand.

On 22 December 1941, when Wavell had concluded that a land-based invasion of Burma was not imminent, he flew from Rangoon to Chungking, with the US representative Major General George Brett, to confer with Chiang Kai-shek. Without prejudicing British sovereignty in Burma, especially that which might come about by the presence on Burmese territory of Chinese troops, Wavell sought to secure specific Chinese support for the defence of Burma. He had in mind the use of one of the three AVG squadrons for the defence of Rangoon; the diversion of some of the Lead-Lease supplies in Rangoon docks for the temporary relief of a variety of the most serious deficiencies in the Burma Army; and for the reinforcement of the Chinese division at Wanting – inside the

Chinese frontier – to act as a general reserve, together with an additional division nominated for service in Burma, should they be required.

The background to Wavell's meeting was the commitment made to General Dennys on 8 December 1941 – the day war broke out – by Chiang Kai-shek:

> [In effect] all China's manpower, armed forces and resources were unreservedly placed at the disposal of the British and United States Governments for the prosecution of the war; that China was very anxious to give direct assistance to Burma; that one regiment of 93 Chinese Division which was in the Puerh area could be increased to a full division, if Burma could supply rice; and that troops could be made available for service in northern Burma, if Burma could supply rations.[26]

Chiang Kai-shek immediately formed the Chinese Expeditionary Force, comprising troops of the experienced and relatively well-equipped Fifth, Sixth and Sixty-Sixth Armies from Szechwan and Kwangsi, and ordered its movement towards Yunnan.[27] It was clear that this was a significant offer of assistance: Burma, and the Burma Road was, after all, of prime strategic importance to China. But London's response was half-hearted. It replied in the language of diplomacy: it was grateful to China for the offer and instructed Wavell to open negotiations to see 'how British and Chinese forces could best cooperate in the common cause.' It wasn't a warm, open-arms welcome, merely the prelude to negotiations in which the British would attempt to keep Chinese involvement in Burma to a minimum. Behind the polite diplomatic language, both Chiang Kai-shek and London both knew very well what was at stake: namely residual Chinese claims on Burmese sovereignty to the Hukawng Valley, locked from Chinese claim by the Anglo–Sino Treaty of 1886. London's nightmare scenario was the presence in Burma of Chinese soldiers using support to the British as a pretext for exerting their own claims on the country. In the chaos of war, anything was possible.[28]

But Wavell's supposedly careful protection of London's position was not understood by the Americans present at the meeting, and if Chiang Kai-shek did recognize the reasons for British reticence he pretended not to, making the most of Wavell's apparent refusal to generate political capital in Washington. The message the Chinese leader wanted to portray – perhaps with a deep metaphorical sigh of frustration – was just how difficult it was to deal openly with the British. He never fully trusted his new British allies, a message he wanted to emphasize to the undoubtedly sympathetic Americans. Deep suspicion ran throughout the

Sino–Anglo–American relationship in 1942. Chiang Kai-shek believed Wavell to be naïve about the problems facing him, and in this he was undoubtedly right. Wavell believed that he would not need Chinese troops, not comprehending the speed with which the Japanese would invade Burma and topple the imperial edifice they found there, considering that he had more than enough time to bring in reinforcements to see off the Japanese. He viewed the offer of the Fifth and Sixth Chinese Armies as akin to a fire brigade: he would ask for them only when, and if, the conflagration threatened to get out of hand.[29]

Wavell reported his nuanced response back to London. The Americans meanwhile reported to Washington that the British had flatly rejected Chinese offers of military assistance. Whatever Wavell's intentions and clumsy diplomacy, the Americans with him interpreted Wavell's refusal as 'inconsistent with the picture of Burma's defenceless state, presented to justify requests for the transfer of China's lend-lease. The Chinese thought it a refusal and were bitterly angry.'[30] A British Foreign Office official minuted at the end of 1942, 'Where our relations with China are important is in their very great potentiality to affect, for better or worse, our relations with America. The Americans are pathological about China, and keenly suspicious of any possible unfriendliness towards it on the part of others.'[31]

Wavell could have done this much better, by proffering a warm diplomatic response to Chiang Kai-shek's offer. Wavell's reasons would have been sound *if* he had all the time in the world. This was his mistake, because clearly time was never on his side. At this stage Wavell still expected substantial reinforcements from Britain, India and Australia. Equally, he knew that the British would have to be administratively responsible for any Chinese forces deployed into Burma, which would place an even greater logistic burden on a weak Burma Command. Nevertheless, Wavell's apparent half-heartedness in the face of what appeared to be Chinese generosity caused the Chinese great offence and acted significantly to irritate the United States, where there resided a feeling among some that Britain was attempting to fight a political war, one that put the survival of its empire above that of defeating the Japanese. These attitudes continued to plague the Anglo-American relationship in the years ahead.

Whether Wavell liked it or not, the Chinese armies of Chiang Kai-shek were to play a key role in the drama that unfolded in Burma in the first five months of 1942. It seems likely that Wavell's failure to get the Generalissimo on side irritated Churchill, who saw all too clearly the importance of China to the Americans, and of America to Britain. Now was not the time to fuss over the small 'p' of politics, but rather to bind Britain and China together in a joint effort to defend Britain's Asian Empire against the greatest threat it had ever faced, and to keep the United States agreeable. With the Chinese holding down perhaps as much as half of the deployable Imperial Japanese Army, it was in London's and Washington's interests not merely to continue, but to accelerate the work of Lend-Lease through the Burma Road. Churchill told Wavell on 22 January 1942 following the Arcadia Conference, 'If I can epitomise in one word the lesson I learned in the United States, it was "China".'[32] Roosevelt added some extra puff to the relationship by elevating Chiang Kai-shek to Supreme Commander of the China War Theatre. It was this new relationship that Wavell had naïvely transgressed. This dimension grew new and disquieting legs for the British, as Chiang Kai-shek began to engage directly with nationalist leaders in India. The conundrum for both the Chinese leader and his Indian interlocutors such as 'Mahatma' Gandhi, Jawaharlal Nehru and Maulana Azad (Chiang Kai-shek visited New Delhi in mid-February 1942) was to balance his strident anti-imperialism with his urgent *cri de coeur* for India to support the Allies – and ironically, Britain – in the fight against Japanese fascism. Clearly imperialism was bad, but Japanese military imperialism was in an entirely different league to that of Britain. The Chinese leader's speech on 21 February 1942 during his visit to India was broadcast in English from Calcutta. While reminding his listeners of the danger of a rapacious Japan, the author of such horrors as Nanking, he urged Britain to give India its independence in exchange for its goodwill in fighting their common enemy. 'I completely support the liberation of India,' he wrote in his diary. 'The British may not understand this, but I deeply believe it may be of advantage to Britain.'[33] It was a prescient and intelligent observation. Those in Britain with eyes to see could see the political trajectory on which the new military realities could take India. Only three weeks before, on 2 February 1942, Secretary of State for India and Burma Leo Amery warned his cabinet colleagues to recognize and respond to a new dimension developing in imperial politics. Reverses at the hands of the Japanese allowed Indians to ask obvious questions about why they needed to continue in a state of colonial subservience.[34] And despite Roosevelt's noisy complaints about British imperialism (he had no problems with the American variety), it wouldn't be good for London if the empire was seen to be propped up by American weapons and industrial power. Britain had to find a way to satisfy China, build up its forces in India to be perceived as serious about contributing to the defeat of the Japanese not just in the eyes of the United States but for reasons of its own prestige, while retaining stability in India to allow the immediate challenge – the defeat of Japan – to be achieved as quickly as was practically possible. For the Americans, pressure from the British in Burma would also reduce the fighting power of the Japanese in the south-west Pacific and was increasingly seen as a measure of Britain's commitment to the defeat of the Japanese. Those in Washington of an Anglophobic bent (and there were many) never strayed far from the suspicion that Britain, in order to ensure the preservation of its dastardly empire, would be happy to fight to the last American.

3

A Hurried and Ill-Considered Plan

On his arrival in Rangoon at the end of December 1941, amid the smoking ruins of the capital city, Hutton undertook a rapid assessment of Burma's strategic situation. His conclusions mirrored those made by his predecessor, the now forcibly retired Major General Donald McLeod. Rangoon was the key to the defence of Burma, as the port provided the only practical means of reinforcing the country given the time and resources available. To prevent its loss, he needed to concentrate his forces to block the two entry routes from Thailand, first in the southern Shan States and second in the area between Moulmein and the Sittang River. He needed also to protect the road that ran from Rangoon to Moulmein and protect the forward air bases in Tenasserim that provided the Burmese legs in the air route between India and Singapore.

He judged that, if they attacked, the Japanese would seek the shortest route to Rangoon. This was through the area of the southern Shan States opposite Chang Rai in Thailand in the area of Toungoo, where good roads would enable the Japanese to congregate on the Thai side of the border. They would probably launch a secondary attack on Moulmein in the south but would limit their activities in the long southward-looking finger of southern Burma to seizing the airfields. They would continue to launch paralysing air attacks against the port of Rangoon and on road and rail communications.[1] Hutton expected that they would advance rapidly, be lightly equipped and live off the country. His task in Tenasserim, therefore, was to hold ground, denying the Japanese the opportunity of establishing themselves in the region in strength. If an attack developed, it would most likely occur before the onset of the monsoon in mid-May.

The best way to defend Rangoon, he concluded, with the limited resources at his disposal, was to accept Chiang Kai-shek's offer of the Fifth and Sixth Chinese

MAP 2 The Retreat from Burma

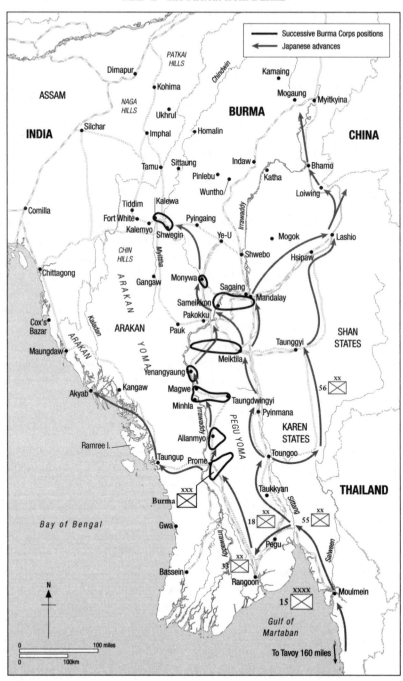

Armies, deploying them in the Shan States to block the direct route from Thailand. This would allow Hutton to concentrate 1 Burma Division, at the time centred on Toungoo, for the protection of both Rangoon and Tenasserim. Furthermore, his report recommended taking over – with Chinese permission of course – quantities of American Lend-Lease equipment piling up in the Rangoon docks, in order to fill some of the most obvious of gaps – for vehicles and machine guns, for instance, in the Burma Army.[2]

For all its logic, Hutton's rapid assessment was wrong. In this, he erred in common with all previous British estimates, which discounted the possibility of the Japanese using Tenasserim as the focus of their attack. This heavily jungled region was considered by the British rather lazily as an impediment to a modern army which, they assumed, would be entirely dependent – as the highly mechanized British Army now was – on roads. In fact, General Iida Shōjirō's plan was to advance with his two experienced infantry divisions (33 and 55) on Rangoon from the south, through Tenasserim, precisely where Hutton had discounted the primary attack. Once Rangoon had been captured, he would head into central Burma to capture the key oilfields at Yenangyaung and the city of Mandalay, using forces made available following the campaign in Malaya and brought into Rangoon by sea. Hutton, not knowing anything of this – indeed his and British intelligence of Japanese plans through the 1942 campaign remained precisely zero – led him to conclude that his primary forces, weak as they were, should be placed in the Shan States, blocking entry from Thailand, and only secondary forces allocated to Tenasserim. Hutton determined – again, quite logically – that to protect Rangoon from air attack he needed to deploy these secondary forces in Tenasserim well forward, to protect its air bases as well as block the frontier crossings, denying bridges and roads to the enemy as far away from Rangoon as possible. The idea was that the advancing Japanese forces would be degraded by constant harrying attacks so that they would run out of steam long before the capital city was reached. This would serve also to buy time to allow reinforcements to land at Rangoon and for any Chinese formations to make their way south to Toungoo.[3] The plan presupposed the forward deployment of forces capable of undertaking long fighting withdrawal through the construction of a series of defensive positions. The alternative, to concentrate his forces closer to Rangoon, such as at the bridge over the Sittang River, was considered too risky, principally because it would entail giving up too much ground too early, allowing the enemy to get close to Rangoon before they were engaged in decisive battle. Wavell agreed with Hutton's assessment, although he considered that Hutton's view of Japanese capabilities was unduly pessimistic.

The Japanese could not possibly be as capable as they were being made out. Wavell counselled Hutton not to fall prey to his fears.

Accordingly, when its first elements landed in the Rangoon docks in January 1942, Hutton sent Major General Jackie Smyth VC's 17 Indian Division to Tenasserim. It arrived with only one weak brigade: its other two (44 and 45 Brigades) had been sent to Malaya, where they had been lost to the Japanese onslaught. The brigade that did arrive – Brigadier Roger Ekin's 46 Brigade – was judged to be 'not really fit for active operations without further training and it had no experience in jungle warfare.'[4] Tenasserim, in Hutton's logic, was the best place for the brigade, where it wouldn't have to face the full ferocity of a Japanese onslaught (he supposed) in the (unlikely) event of an invasion. Smyth was temporarily allotted 2 Burma Brigade and 16 Indian Brigade to bring his division back up to strength. His fourth brigade, the all-Gurkha 48 Indian Brigade,[5] arrived in Rangoon on 31 January 1942. From this point, while ostensibly well manned, the division was nevertheless seriously deficient in artillery, signals and engineer support. It 'had no pack transport, no pack rations and no pack wireless,' recalled Smyth. 'There wasn't even any mepacrine, the anti-malaria drug which, in the later Burma campaign, was considered almost more essential than ammunition.'[6] Nor had it been trained for war, resembling an administrative amalgam of disparate units with no collective training, identity or ethos to hold it together under the strain of battle. The good news nevertheless was that a slew of antiquated fighter aircraft – Blenheims, Hurricanes and a handful of Tomahawks – many oiled in crates, arrived at Rangoon docks to bolster the numbers of RAF and AVG aircraft responsible for defending Burma's skies. A few dozen more, ancient Hurricane Mk 1's – veterans of the battles over southern England in 1940 – lumbered all the way from Egypt in a painful series of hops and jumps, at the end of the month. They were all that the fabled British Empire had to spare. In terms of air transport, the whole of India only boasted a single squadron of 25 RAF C47s.[7]

Smyth's divisional area in Tenasserim stretched for some 400 miles. The front line ran from Moulmein, where he initially placed his headquarters, 50 miles up the Salween River to Pa-an, and thence a further 100 miles to Papun. The insistence on forward defence filled him with disquiet. If the Japanese did advance into Tenasserim, his division was far too small, too badly prepared and far too widely dispersed to offer an effective counter to an attack, even though the Salween River was a formidable obstacle to any attacker. The problem, he realized, was that he would struggle to defend the major crossing points, let alone every potential crossing area. And when he did place his main defences, what would stop an attacker from simply bypassing them? It was obvious to him that the long, narrow finger of the Tenasserim coastline presented almost insoluble problems for defence. It was not defensible in depth and presented many advantages to the Japanese. Its seizure would cut the chain of airfields linking India with Malaya, and it formed the shortest route to Rangoon from Japanese-held Thailand. Its only road was essential for the resupply of his division but it could be cut at will. Lying across this extended line of communication were two huge rivers, the Salween and the Sittang, with a smaller one, the Bilin, between them. Of these three the Salween and the Sittang were the most formidable, the latter holding the strategic key to Rangoon. The Salween, on the southern bank of which was located Moulmein, was 7,000 yards wide and impossible to defend properly – certainly not by a comprehensive form of linear defence – with only the single, weak brigade he had available. Fifty miles farther west lay the Bilin and a further 50 miles west lay the Sittang. The latter was crossed at Mokpalin, where the estuary collapses to form the neck of the river, by a railway bridge half a mile long and not designed to carry wheeled traffic. It had recently been boarded for this purpose but little else had been done to prepare the Tenasserim line of communication for war.

Smyth was, accordingly, strongly opposed to Hutton's plan. A man of strong opinions, he sought, much to his superior's irritation, to have it changed. Smyth believed that placing troops well forward invited defeat in detail. In fact, it served to weaken the security of the capital, because it placed his weak division in a position where it could be easily bypassed. With his battalions and brigades spread in penny packets across the wild and sieve-like Tenasserim front, often up to 40 miles apart and with little or no coverage between them, unable to support each other, he would be unable to concentrate enough force to bring decisive action against the main thrusts of the Japanese advance as and where they developed. He proposed, instead, to prepare positions on the Sittang where he could fight a concentrated divisional battle at the end of a much shorter line of communication.[8]

The Christmas bombing of Rangoon had, rather unfortunately, the effect of seemingly bearing out the British high command's assessment of likely Japanese actions, which were that the Japanese would attack Rangoon from the air, rather than attempt a land invasion.[9] The Japanese had occupied Thailand in December 1941 (after having seized the French colony of northern Indochina the previous July and occupied the south in July 1941), and the likeliest threat to Burma appeared to be an aerial attack on Rangoon to cut the road to China.

This misapprehension was rudely dispelled on 19 January 1942, when a battalion of 55 Division crossed the border from eastern Thailand to seize the town and airfield of Tavoy. This cut off Mergui to the south, which Hutton was forced to evacuate a day or so later for fear that the tiny garrison would be isolated and destroyed. Both towns had been weakly defended in any case and had no artillery or engineer stores necessary to develop the area for defence. At a stroke the Japanese had gained control of the key Tenasserim airfields, increasing substantially Rangoon's vulnerability to air attack.

The following day the main body of General Iida's 30,000-strong 15 Army[10] crossed the border into Burma at Myawaddy and Pauk. Two days later, Iida broadcast to the Burmese people that he was there 'to sweep away British power which has been exploiting and oppressing you for a hundred years [sic], and to liberate all Burmese people and support your aspirations for independence.'[11] Iida was a career infantry officer with a steady if unexciting reputation. He had commanded both 4 Guards Regiment and 2 Guards Division and had seen service in Formosa and Indochina. Described as a 'serious-minded person' who had been responsible for the first two months of planning for the Malaya operation (from July 1941), but who was replaced as commander by Yamashita, he was given what was considered to be the less demanding task of capturing Burma with 15 Army instead.[12]

Iida's first objective was the rail bridge over the Sittang at Mokpalin. His plan was for Lieutenant General Takeuchi Yakuta's experienced, 14,000-strong 55 Division to drive westwards towards Moulmein, forcing Smyth to draw reserves south to support the town, while the 16,000 China-war veterans of Lieutenant General Sakurai's aggressive 33 Division would thrust across the Salween at Pa-an. Sakurai would maintain a parallel advance to Takeuchi, marching through the jungle and behind the defenders, in order to threaten the flanks and rear of 17 Indian Division. Both divisions were entirely self-sufficient and carried with them all the weapons, rations and equipment they required to reach the Sittang without resupply.

4

The First Shots

The farthest forward of Smyth's brigades in mid-January 1942 was Brigadier J.K. 'Jonah' Jones' 16 Indian Brigade, tasked with covering the hilly border area in the region between Kawkareik along the road that led into Burma from the town of Rahaeng in Thailand. The road ran for about 80 miles through the jungle from Moulmein across 'about 40 wooden rickety bridges on it, at many of which even the 30 cwt [hundredweight] lorries... had to be unloaded; furthermore, there were two river crossings, at each of which there was a single ferry, capable of taking one lorry only.'[1] Forward of Kawkareik the border followed the Dawna Hills – a tangled web of jungle-clad hills running due north–south, over which the brigade, in order to cover a multitude of tracks and hamlets, was widely dispersed. Local commanders had no prior intelligence that might have told them about the routes the Japanese planned to use, and they were thus forced to place their forces widely to counter every eventuality. This enforced dispersion would have been a demanding task for a well-trained, battle-hardened formation, but Jones' brigade – given its inexperience and lack of training – was in no state to present a viable defence of Kawkareik. Most men in 4 Burma Rifles, for example, were malaria casualties.[2] The initial Japanese infiltration attacks on 20 January sowed confusion among inexperienced Indian and Burmese soldiers – many of them raw recruits – leading in some cases to rumour and panic.[3] Fast Japanese columns, moving rapidly through the jungle, hidden by the canopy of trees and using all the tracks available to them, forced decision-making confusion on junior commanders. What tracks should they defend? What happened when they chose one, and the enemy simply melted into the jungle, bypassing them, and continued advancing far to the rear? A new shock awaited. When action was engaged, the phenomenal weight of firepower deployed by the Japanese took everyone by surprise. Whereas Indian units at this time did not have automatic weapons at company level, each Japanese section had a 6.5mm Type 96 ('Nambu') light machine gun, and plentiful 8mm Type 100 machine carbines. The Nambu was subsequently credited with causing 'more Allied casualties in the Pacific and Far East theatres than any other weapon.'[4] Few Indian soldiers in Burma had ever seen or heard an automatic weapon before, let alone prepared themselves for coming under its sustained fire. All these new terrors led to countless battlefield errors, such as when, as Captain John Hedley reported in the prologue, 1/9 Jats fired on 4 Burma Rifles one night south of Kawkareik, mistaking them for Japanese.

A fear of being encircled led to a precipitate withdrawal being ordered to Moulmein. Withdrawals in contact with the enemy are the most difficult operations of war, even with well-trained, professional soldiers. 16 Indian Brigade was not such. The evacuation from Kawkareik on 22 January, and the subsequent withdrawal to Moulmein over the following days, proved to be hurried and disorganized. 'The net result was [the] loss of all transport and equipment... somehow orders were passed to destroy arms and equipment. Even rifles were thrown away... The men were thoroughly shaken and the Brigade thoroughly disorganised.'[5] Losses to enemy action were not overly significant, but the morale of the brigade had plummeted, and a dangerous precedent had been established. In particular, the energy and dynamism of the Japanese came as a considerable shock to many.

In their ignorance of what was happening on a far-off battlefield, Rangoon and New Delhi remained hopelessly optimistic in the face of this bad news. Wavell cabled London on 21 January to the effect that 'large scale effort against Burma seems improbable at present'. Likewise, Hutton reported to Wavell the following day that 'Attack on Tavoy and Kawkareik may have been isolated operation and not first stage of general offensive'.[6] Four days later Wavell visited Hutton in Rangoon and reported to London after the visit that he did not regard Rangoon as being in any immediate danger. He was, however, surprised at how quickly 16 Indian Brigade had been overcome and apportioned the blame for these collective failures on poor leadership. 'It is quite clear', he wrote in his despatch, 'that the enemy were allowed to gain cheap initial successes through bad handling of local commanders, lack of training and in some cases lack of fighting spirit on the part of our troops. It was an unfortunate beginning to the campaign and had serious results in raising the morale of the enemy and depressing that of our own troops.'[7] 'I have issued instructions for offensive action and for measures to meet Japanese tactics', he wrote to General

Alan Brooke, the Chief of the Imperial General Staff in London, on 26 January 1942. Wavell's ill-founded optimism (and anger at the overly pessimistic reports emanating from the commanders on the ground) was revealed in a closing comment to this message: 'Governor, Hutton and Stevenson cooperating closely and all full of fight though I think their recent cables pictured situation too gloomily.'[8]

They would have been gloomier still had they known that with the Japanese marched 300 Burmans of the newly formed Burma Independence Army (BIA), based on a small core of committed Thakin supporters. In Japanese uniform, carrying Japanese weapons, some having undergone training on Hainan Island, the 'Minami Organ' represented the aspirations of those Burmese who desired their country for themselves, and who had naïvely accepted the Japanese blandishments at face value.[9] The role of the BIA fighters – in truth a 'motley, undisciplined array, officered only by untrained Thakins and including a considerable proportion of criminal riffraff bent on looting and other forms of self-aggrandizement' – was to act as guides, interpreters, saboteurs and intelligencers rather than fighters.[10] In this role they were very effective, particularly in mobilizing large numbers of local Buddhist monks (*pongyis*), many of them militantly racist and eager to join the fray against the hated *kala-phyu* (Caucasians), Chinese and Indians who had long sullied the country with their presence. Within a few weeks perhaps as many as 5,000 – both dacoits and hardened anti-British militants – had swollen the ranks of the BIA. Many accounts among the withdrawing British in 1942 attest to the work of dacoits and dark-red-robed priests in taking part in the fighting and in fomenting violence against any whom they considered their enemy. The bodies of murdered Indian refugees littering the 250-mile trail across the Arakan Yomas and into the sanctuary of India marked the true depths of the hatred bubbling up from within these self-appointed protectors of Burmese exceptionalism.

The creation of the BIA in Thailand only a few months before in December 1941 was, nevertheless, a remarkable achievement, providing an inkling as to what could be achieved if the revolutionary independence movement could garner large-scale, popular support, and if it were sustained by a sympathetic sponsor. Perhaps the mass turning of Burmese villagers against the British could be a pattern for something similar in India? At the time, however, the idea of an operation against India was on nobody's mind, although the seed of an idea had been planted. An officer in the Intelligence Section of Field Marshal Terauchi's headquarters in Saigon, Major Fujiwara Iwaichi, was despatched to Burma at the end of the fighting to look at ways in which this dramatic popular support could be harnessed for Japan's benefit. Fujiwara had been instrumental in looking at ways in which expatriate Indians, including those captured in Malaya and Singapore, could be harnessed in support of Japanese interests, but when he investigated the BIA, he was dismissive of using them further.[11] The war in Burma was now over; what possible use could this ragtag army offer Japan? It had played its part and should be stood down and replaced with a much smaller, professional army under the control of the Japanese. Major Keiji Suzuki, a Kurtz-like ideologue, who believed passionately in Japan's decolonizing mission and had nurtured the relationship with the Thakins since 1940, was outraged at the suggestion. He was overruled. The BIA was accordingly disbanded and replaced in July 1942 with a new, smaller Burma Defence Army (BDA), under the command of Aung San. A year later the BDA boasted a strength of 55,000 men.

Not all nationalists in the pre-war years had sought salvation at the hands of the Japanese. The communists remained resolutely hostile. Certainly, Chiang Kai-shek had assiduously warned the Burmese to be wary of them. Nevertheless, significant numbers of Thakins were prepared to throw caution to the wind in 1941 and accept Japanese liberation claims at face value. In December 1941, those Burmans dressed in Japanese uniforms prepared to accompany Iida into Burma were the chrysalis of actual anti-British rebellion, the agents for converting academic conversations about political theory into physical, militant, action. The fact that the vehicle for achieving independence had a distinctly fascistic bent did not prove a hindrance to the Thakin argument for 'action now', at any cost. The ends justified the means. Time would, nevertheless, demonstrate painfully that the Thakins were in 1942 the cheerleaders of a movement that represented the triumph of hope over political reality. Japan was to behave in Burma as a feudal tyrant, establishing not independence but suzerainty. At the end of the campaign, when it began to establish its own puppet regime, the Japanese released Ba Maw from jail in Mogok, where he had been imprisoned for sedition, and appointed him *Adipati* or Head of State, in May 1942.[12] The Japanese didn't think that Aung San was impressive looking enough for the job, and appointed Ba Maw as their puppet instead.[13] In totalitarian regimes, looks (and therefore uniforms) matter. The Thakins were aghast that Japan could so quickly turn its back on them and appoint a member of a rival political group to the most senior Burmese position in the new Japanese dispensation, but the appointment demonstrated Japan's essential lack of commitment to any single nationalist faction or group in Burma. Ultimately, it would do what it considered best for Japan's interests. For his part, Ba Maw rose to the challenge in magnificently Goebbels-like style, revealing his attraction to gaudy pomp and ceremony unrivalled since the time of King Thibaw, removed by the British in 1885. His totalitarian instincts were laid bare with the promulgation of the regime's new motto: 'One Blood, One Voice, One Command'.[14] In truth, Japan's military and economic priorities trumped any sentimentality about the achievement of local political freedom, although it is true that many Japanese, Iida included, regretted that 'Burmese independence was only used as a means for carrying out Japan's war.'[15] Japan's policy was not so much Asia for the Asiatics as it was Asia for Japan.[16] By failing to nurture Burmese aspirations for genuine nationhood, Japan demonstrated the hollowness of its redemptive claims.

The next domino in the Tenasserim defences was Moulmein, situated on the southern bank of the Salween Estuary. From the outset Smyth believed that the task of holding the town was hopeless. He was right, and the instructions to defend the ferry town demonstrated the foolishness of attempting to hold ground that was irrelevant to an enemy determined on a very different objective. From the outset, therefore, the short struggle to defend Moulmein was an unnecessary battle. Smyth had only Brigadier John Bourke's locally raised 2 Burma Brigade available to protect the town. His original intention – to use its four weak battalions to live off the country and harass the advancing Japanese – was, according to Smyth, denied permission by Hutton to use them thus. Accordingly, he was forced to employ them in a conventional role, for which they were unsuited. The result, he claimed, was 'great chance was lost'.[17] Furthermore, the brigade had no artillery apart from a troop of Bofors anti-aircraft guns (which in the event did sterling work in the ground role), nor did it possess any engineer stores sufficient to prepare the town for defence. Indeed, Moulmein had its back to the Salween: it would be easy for a superior enemy either to drive the defenders into the sea or to bypass them as an irrelevance.

Although Hutton recognized the weakness of the Moulmein area and sought reinforcements from Wavell, he was not prepared to countenance a precipitate withdrawal from the town. He was determined to resist the Japanese, to cause them casualties and to delay and disrupt their advance in accordance with his forward strategy. He continued to believe, at this stage, that they did not intend to carry through their attack to Rangoon. On 22 January, Wavell replied to Hutton's requests for more infantry to the effect that he had no resources to spare. 'Cannot understand', he wrote, 'why with troops at your disposal you should be unable to hold Moulmein and trust you will do so. Nature of country and resources must limit Japanese effort.'[18] He flew to Rangoon on 23 January to say as much to his face. Wavell – and Hutton for that matter – were both wrong.

The size and scale of the Japanese attack and its ultimate intent was still not recognized for what it was. Holding the town with inadequate forces risked losing all the defenders to Japanese envelopment over the Salween, the loss of which would be catastrophic to the defence of Burma as a whole. The political pressure on Wavell not to withdraw in the face of Japanese aggression in Malaya and Burma was undoubtedly considerable. The war in Europe and North Africa was not going well, and the recognition that the units in place in Malaya and Burma were unsuited to the task of fighting the Japanese was insufficient an excuse to consider retreat. As the Director of Military Operations in London observed, 'A withdrawal would have been difficult to justify in the eyes of the world, especially while MacArthur was fighting on in the Philippines; and it would have been hard to meet the criticism that we could have held the place had we tried.'[19]

Over the three days to 29 January, Takeuchi secretly infiltrated his units through the jungle to surround Moulmein's feeble perimeter, allowing Bourke's troops no advance knowledge of their intentions. On the morning of 30 January, five infantry battalions and two troops of cavalry of 55 Division attacked. The weakened brigade stood no real chance, although the defence of Moulmein was in fact conducted creditably by 2 Burma Brigade, the Japanese war diaries speaking of the 'fierce hand-to-hand fighting on all sides of Moulmein' and 'the resistance of a determined enemy.'[20] In order to prevent what remained of the brigade being unnecessarily destroyed, Smyth authorized its evacuation by ferry to Martaban on 31 January after a battle lasting only 24 hours. Smyth now had the best part of two brigades (16 Indian and 2 Burma Brigades) seriously shaken in piecemeal actions far from the vital ground of the Sittang.

Once he had his troops behind the Salween, Hutton ordered 17 Indian Division to hold the line of the river, and to yield no ground. Wavell insisted that the river be defended by mobile and offensive action, that the invader be contacted boldly, watched continuously and attacked vigorously. But such laudably aggressive aspirations were simply not capable of being delivered by the troops available. Nor were they properly equipped for the type of warfare in which they were now engaged. The KOYLI, for instance, arrived at Martaban in early February still wearing their peacetime tropical uniforms, complete with sun helmets (topis). Information on the Japanese was non-existent. There was no air support. Eve Curie, visiting the front for a few days in mid-February, noted the dark quips offered by soldiers about the almost complete absence above the battlefield of the RAF, and the domination of the air by the Japanese.[21] Confidence had already received a sharp knock at Kawkareik and Moulmein, both encounters of which had a damaging effect on the morale of the locally enlisted men of the Burma Rifles. Worse still, the idea of 'holding the Salween' suggested that the line of the river from Moulmein to Pa-an and beyond could be defended in the manner of something from the linear battlefield of an earlier war. It could not. The vast distances to be covered, and the many places across which the Japanese could cross unopposed (even though it remained a significant obstacle), meant that the very idea of holding 'lines' in the face of an enemy whose primary tactic was infiltration around and beyond fixed defences, was nonsense.

The problem was that Hutton's plans were strangely divorced from the complexity of Burma's topography and the enormous distances Smyth was expected to defend. One might conclude that they were dictated solely by the imperative not to give up ground, or by a desktop exercise involving maps. Smyth simply did not have enough troops to cover all approaches in such a vast area, making it relatively easy for Iida to identify the main points of British defence, and make his way around them. For the most part the country was rugged and jungle clad. The remnants of 16 Indian Brigade, now reinforced by the understrength KOYLI, were given responsibility for about a thousand square miles of dense jungle, including a 70-mile stretch of the Salween running from Martaban in the south to Kamamaung in the north. The road from Naunglon east of the Salween that ran through Pa-an and Duyinzeik to Thaton bisected the brigade area in half.

Although putting on a relaxed and confident front to visitors such as Eve Curie, Smyth was infuriated by orders that bore no relation to the reality that he faced on the ground. What he wanted above all was to get back to the Sittang to turn it into a formidable defensive position. It is difficult not to acknowledge that Smyth was given a task far beyond the capacity of his weakened and widely dispersed brigades. He nevertheless attempted faithfully to carry out Hutton's instructions at the Salween, and desperately spread his forces across the huge territory allotted to him. 46 Indian Brigade was positioned to the rear and north of 16 Indian Brigade, with an even larger area of responsibility covering both the Bilin and Salween Rivers north to Papun. In similar fashion to the other newly arrived units of 17 Indian Division, this brigade consisted in the main of new recruits, milked heavily of their experienced NCOs in the rapid expansion of the Indian Army and suffering a poor standard of individual and collective training.[22] 48 Indian Brigade was tasked to cover the coast running from Martaban to the Sittang Bridge, while the shaken 2 Burma Brigade was placed between the Sittang and the Bilin, with its headquarters at Kyaikto.

On 6 February 1942 Wavell and Hutton visited Smyth at his divisional headquarters. Wavell impressed on Smyth that he could not withdraw without Hutton's express permission, but to Smyth's recollection offered nothing more positive than the unhelpful advice that the Japanese were overrated. On a positive note, Wavell decided to divert to Burma the battle-experienced 7 Armoured Brigade, at that time on the high seas and intended for operations in Java. But more bad news came from the Japanese. By the end of the first week of February 1942, Sakurai's 33 Division crossed from Thailand and secured the northern flank of 55 Division. Smyth immediately recognized the danger that this posed to his division, for if he were to be outflanked to the north and east, he would be cut off from his only escape route over the Sittang: the bridge at Mokpalin.

Over the period 9 and 10 February, 55 Division probed Martaban, but when they finally bypassed the town and threatened it from the north-west the commander of the small garrison withdrew his forces to prevent being cut off entirely. At the same time, on 11 February, the full weight of 33 Division was thrown against the Pa-an positions, and despite some gallant and effective resistance the weakened defenders of 46 Indian Brigade were slowly crushed. On that and the two days that followed, the Japanese mounted a three-battalion attack against the key town of Kuzeik, sitting on the Salween on the single road running back to the Bilin River. The town was defended by 7/10 Baluch Regiment which, although it fought stubbornly, was overwhelmed. The survivors, numbering about 70 all ranks, escaped through the jungle to Thaton. By 13 February the Japanese had begun crossing the Salween at many points, and together with the opening at Kuzeik they acted now to force their way relentlessly towards the towns of Duyinzeik and Thaton. Constant air attacks and sabotage by fifth columnists acted severely to disrupt the defence.

Looking back, Smyth regarded 12 February as the day in which Burma's fate was decided. The widely spread out 16 and 46 Indian Brigades on the Salween were brigades in name only. Both being each the strength of a battalion, were further weakened by their dispersion, allowing the Japanese to infiltrate through them at several points. He sent back the newly arrived Brigadier David 'Punch' Cowan from 17 Indian Division Headquarters at Kyaikto to Rangoon, to represent personally to Hutton his fears about being outflanked, requesting permission to hold the Bilin only for as long as he could withdraw to proper defensive positions on the Sittang.[23] With only Brigadier Hugh-Jones' 48 Indian Brigade left intact, Smyth asked to withdraw to a better defensive position with a less extended front so as to prevent the division from being 'eaten up in penny packets before it was able to fight a real battle at all.'[24] He told Eve Curie on 15 February, the day that Singapore fell, that his concern was 'the necessity of shortening the front by withdrawing steadily before making a stand.'[25] Remembering all too well similar, overly confident briefings in France in 1940, her heart sank.

Cowan's request fell on deaf ears. Hutton refused to countenance another withdrawal. Smyth was ordered to hold the line of the Bilin. The performance of 17 Indian Division was nevertheless worrying him. The next day he told General Sir Alan Hartley (Wavell was preoccupied with his ABDACOM responsibilities) that though the Burma Army 'had every intention of fighting it out east of the river Sittang it was possible that exhaustion of the troops and continued infiltration might eventually drive them back to the river Sittang.'[26] He was also honest about the potential fate of Rangoon, stating that if Pegu were lost Rangoon's fate would be more or less certain. The starkness of this message came as a shock to Dorman-Smith, who until now had been assured that there was no land threat against his capital emanating from Tenasserim.

Despite Hutton's determination to hold the Salween, he nevertheless gave Smyth permission on 13 February to withdraw to the Bilin when he felt it necessary to do so. By this time, however, Ekin was convinced that 33 Division had entirely bypassed Thaton and was moving around the eastern flank to cut off his brigade. Smyth, never convinced of Hutton's strategy, and interpreting his superior's orders in the most liberal sense possible, the following day ordered his scattered division to withdraw from its positions on the Salween to a new, concentrated position behind the Bilin.

Although Hutton censured Smyth severely for withdrawing so precipitately (although not in direct contravention of the letter of his orders, the withdrawal was most definitely in violation of their spirit), there seems little doubt that Smyth's actions were necessary.[27] The withdrawal was 'carried out in the nick of time', as Sakurai's 33 Division launched its first attacks against Smyth on the Bilin on 16 February.[28] Wavell, and Hutton with him it seems, appreciated none of these certainties at the time, not least of which was the fact that on the Bilin Smyth faced the combined might of the whole of Iida's 15 Army. Holding an extended line along the Bilin was a non-starter, given the enemy's penchant for infiltrating through British defences. A 'concentrated position' at the Bilin was in any case only of use if it sat on or astride ground important to the enemy. This wasn't the case. Iida simply wanted to get to Rangoon as fast as he could: it would be relatively easy to fix the British on the Bilin with 55 Division while making all haste for Rangoon with 33 Division.

The confidence of Smyth's division was by now, in any case, irreparably damaged. Eve Curie saw this half-heartedness in its leaders. 'The British leaders,' she observed, 'were still asking their men to make the gestures of war, but they were doing so without faith.'[29] News of Smyth's withdrawal provoked ire when it reached new Delhi. On 21 February, two days after Hutton had authorized the withdrawal to the Sittang, three of the angriest signals ever to come from Wavell's pen arrived at his HQ in quick succession. They were wildly inaccurate and must have caused consternation at their destination. 'There seems on surface no reason whatsoever for decision practically to abandon fight for Rangoon and continue retrograde movement', Wavell wrote in one. 'You have checked enemy and he must be tired and have suffered heavy casualties. No sign that he is in superior strength. You must stop all further withdrawal and counterattack whenever possible. Whole face of war in far east depends on most resolute and determined action. You have little air opposition at present and should attack enemy with all air forces available.'[30] In another he instructed Hutton to organize a counter-offensive with all available troops, east of the Sittang. 'In any event plans must be made to hit enemy and hit him hard if he ever succeeds in crossing. He will go back quickly in face of determined attack.' His advice to Hutton included suggestions for using an armoured train for the railway and coloured umbrellas for coordinating air strikes on enemy targets in the jungle. In any case, he insisted, the instruction to hold Rangoon was inviolate.[31] The messages indicated Wavell's continuing lack of comprehension about the situation on the ground in Burma, and bewilderment that Hutton and Smyth were seemingly unable to stop the onward march of the Japanese.

In accordance with Smyth's instructions, Brigadier Roger Ekin's 46 Indian Brigade began to withdraw to Kyaikto to form a defensive line on the Bilin over the period 14 and 15 February. In the absence of permission for a full-scale withdrawal to the Sittang, Smyth had little choice but to do Hutton's bidding, at least for the time being. The Bilin itself presented a most unsatisfactory position for defence. It isn't a wide river, and was easily fordable for most of its length at that time of year. Smyth exaggerated only slightly when he described it as 'a wet ditch in thick jungle which anyone could jump across. As a defensive position on which to fight a battle it could not have been more unsuitable'.[32] His battalions had virtually nothing in the way of stores such as barbed wire and mines to develop a proper position, and the appalling state of communications meant that units could keep in touch with each other only with the greatest of difficulty. In the event it seems clear that Hutton's insistence that the Bilin be defended guaranteed only that the Sittang position would be occupied too quickly to allow enough time to prepare the bridgehead for defence. The action delayed the

Japanese for four days but came at the price of the further exhausting and wearing down of 17 Indian Division and of preventing the Sittang position from being properly prepared for defence.

The Japanese pressed home attacks across the whole Bilin sector from 16 February. The summer heat was intense, and an acute lack of drinking water added to the agonies of the exhausted troops. The Japanese themselves seemed to have inexhaustible supplies of men. Some of Smyth's units fought extremely well, even bringing the Japanese to a halt in very tough fighting of a kind they had not hitherto experienced in Burma. Other units, however, fared less well. At least one battalion withdrew from its position on 17 February 'in complete disorder', recorded their Regimental History, 'without rifles, automatic weapons and in some cases boots.'[33] Elements of another battalion disintegrated on the Bilin. By 18 February panic was widespread. In one instance Japanese 'jitter' parties* at night frightened whole battalions of 16 Indian Brigade into firing off 15,000 rounds of machine gun and rifle fire, doing little or no damage apart from revealing the battalion positions to the watching Japanese.

The pressure on Hutton at this time, together with the prospect of a greatly expanded span of command with the arrival of new formations from India, prompted him to write on 13 February to General Hartley requesting the creation of a corps headquarters.[34] Even without the arrival of extra reinforcements Hutton's span of command was already too great. He was to comment later that the Army HQ in Burma was simultaneously a War Office, a General HQ, a Corps HQ and a Line of Communication (LOC) HQ. 'This organisation, or lack of it clogged the whole machine. It also imposed an intolerable burden on the GOC. It was impossible for me with my vast responsibilities to keep detailed control of operations on [the] 17 Division front and it was necessary to allow wide discretion to the Divisional Commander... A Corps HQ was essential from the first'.[35]

Amid this exhausting battle Hutton was forced to expend time and energy replying to criticism of his decisions from both London and New Delhi. In one riposte Hutton laid out the stark realities of Burma's pre-war defences. 'Through no fault of GOC', he wrote to the Director of Military Operations in London, 'Burma was totally unprepared for defence on outbreak of war. Few infantry battalions available, had little transport and were very short of equipment.

---

*Jitter parties were small patrols designed to sow confusion and consternation among the enemy, troops often throwing firecrackers, shouting threats, orders and abuse in English.

Headquarters, anti-aircraft, intelligence, engineers, signals, base, Line of Communications, transportation and medical services, were practically non-existent. This was, I believe, reported by Burma and certainly was by India over a period of twelve months before outbreak of war.'[36]

To add to Hutton's burden a sharp signal arrived from Wavell in Java on 17 February. 'I do not know what consideration caused withdrawal behind Bilin River without further fighting. I have every confidence in judgement and fighting spirit of you and Smyth but bear in mind that continual withdrawal… is most damaging to morale of troops… Time can often be gained as effectively and less expensively by bold counter-offensive. This is especially so against Japanese.'[37]

The battle for the Bilin dragged on for four tiring, and in Smyth's eyes, wholly unnecessary, days. At 6 p.m. on 18 February Smyth's appreciation of the situation was that in 48 Indian Brigade he had lost all but a few platoons of two whole battalions, and that 16 Indian Brigade, which had done most of the fighting, had been fought to a standstill. Hutton now appeared wholly seized by the difficulties in which Smyth had long been submerged. On the same day he told Wavell that he could not be certain of holding the so-called 'Bilin Line'. Furthermore, he warned, 'if this battle should go badly enemy might penetrate line of River Sittang without much difficulty and evacuation of Rangoon would become imminent possibility.'[38] Wavell was shocked and angered. On 19 February Hutton visited Smyth, and in view of the grave danger of not being able to disengage the troops from contact, instructed him to prepare for a withdrawal to the Sittang, and to begin it when Smyth believed it was necessary. It was only too clear, as Hutton admitted later, that the only alternative in the circumstances was the destruction of 17 Indian Division and the immediate loss of Rangoon.[39] Smyth rather bitterly commented that this permission was given seven days after he had first asked for it.[40]

It is interesting to see how the relationship between Wavell, Hutton and Smyth informed their view of the best strategy to adopt for the defence of Burma. Smyth's constant withdrawals infuriated Wavell and Hutton, neither of whom could understand why he wasn't able to hold the Japanese at bay. Hutton suspected that Smyth was scuttling back to the Sittang to suit his own plan, paying lip service to his orders. For his part, Wavell suspected that Hutton was not impressing his will firmly enough on Smyth, and because his soldiers didn't seem capable of stopping the Japanese, that his leadership was in some way deficient.

17 Indian Division, although in close contact with the enemy, immediately began to break contact to get back to the Sittang Bridge. But as Smyth's tired and battered brigades sought to disengage, disaster struck. Sakurai, seeing that his left flank was well covered by 55 Division and therefore relatively secure from British

counterattack, decided to make a dash to seize the bridge at Mokpalin before Smyth had the chance to organize its defence. His decision was made easier by an instruction to withdraw being passed in clear over the radio by a British unit. There now developed a race for the Sittang, which by an inexplicable error by Smyth, the Japanese won by a whisker. Despite the obvious imperative to get back as quickly as possible, Smyth instructed his freshest brigade, Roger Ekin's 46 Indian Brigade, to remain where they were to cover the withdrawal of the remnants of 48 and 16 Indian Brigades. Ekin was aghast, urging Smyth to allow him to withdraw at best speed to secure the bridge. Smyth demurred. Smyth was convinced that the primary requirement was to withdraw his division in an orderly fashion given the exhausted state of his troops. Ekin, however, considered that the opportunity for an ordered withdrawal had long since disappeared and that the absolute requirement at this stage of the battle for the Sittang was to secure the Mokpalin bridge. In the event no defensive position at the bridge was prepared.[41] Nor too, despite Smyth being convinced to the contrary, was the bridge prepared for demolition.[42]

Accordingly, the division wasted a further 24 hours, resting in the region of Kyaikto over the period 21 and 22 February, instead of withdrawing with all speed to the Sittang. In the event Sakurai's battalions made the journey through the jungle in 56 hours, marginally ahead of 17 Indian Division but enough to pip Smyth to the post. It was a major blunder and cost the British not just the bridge, but the campaign.

There seems little doubt that even after the Salween had been evacuated, in some disorder, Hutton continued to deceive himself, and his superiors, about the rapidly collapsing situation. On 18 February Dorman-Smith reported to London that he had just met Hutton, who was 'quietly optimistic'.[43] On the following day, however, this had been replaced with such a gloomy assessment of the situation that it took the Governor, until now used to receiving nothing but positive reports, by surprise. Hutton said that there was now only a 50 per cent chance of holding Rangoon. The troops were very tired, there were no reserves, and the Japanese seemed to be daily injecting fresh troops into the battle.[44]

5

'We Could at Any Rate Send a Man'

During this time Smyth was in agony, unable to walk for long periods, suffering regular injections of strychnine to treat a painful and debilitating fissure of the anus. While he never subsequently admitted to any impairment in his ability to make rational command decisions, his ability to think clearly during the Sittang Bridge debacle was undoubtedly diminished.[1] Ekin for one believed that 'Smyth's physical condition was the cause of some of the mistakes he found otherwise hard to explain.'[2]

By 20 February the withdrawal to the Sittang was fully underway, the retreating units of 17 Indian Division under constant pressure from the advancing Japanese, with Smyth reporting that he was being enveloped on both flanks and that his front had been penetrated south of Bilin. Smyth was faced with the problem of getting his three brigades, and their transport, back to Mokpalin along a single dusty track, now jammed with vehicles, and thence over a railway bridge that had been hastily boarded to take wheeled vehicles.

The organization of the withdrawal and the defence of the Sittang was little more than disastrous. The troops had been withdrawing for a month under pressure of the inexorable Japanese advance, in ferocious heat amid considerable confusion and uncertainty. Communications were virtually non-existent and restricted largely to word of mouth. Smyth's tactical HQ was attacked by a jitter party in the early hours of 21 February, 'achieving little but adding to the general feeling of alarm and despondency.'[3] All accounts speak of almost total confusion for 40 hours as units, small groups of men and individuals trudged exhaustingly back towards Mokpalin and the promise of safety. At the bridgehead itself elements of 48 Indian Brigade fought hard to retain possession of high ground on the east bank. Along the road from Kyaikto the withdrawing units of 17 Indian

Division were involved in confusing engagements with elements of 33 Division, who launched attacks on the slow-moving road-bound columns of troops as they struggled towards the Sittang.

Even well-trained units were affected. By a series of poor decisions, 2 Battalion, The Duke of Wellington's Regiment (DWR), which had been sent up from Rangoon on 19 February, was inexplicably sent forward to Kyaikto rather than being used to dig in around the Sittang Bridge when it had arrived at the Sittang. The battalion was then forced to withdraw back to the Sittang 48 hours later, having 'lost most of their weapons, all their transport, all their kit and upwards of 300 well-trained and well-officered troops' in the process.[4] The Regimental History of the KOYLI talks of near panic stalking the battalion during these two fateful days. The enforced delay on the Bilin meant that when 17 Indian Division was given permission to withdraw, on 19 February, it did so in contact with the Japanese. To add to the sense of desperation and frustration amid the heat, dust and confusion, the retreating division, congesting the tracks leading to the river, was repeatedly, though mistakenly, attacked by aircraft of the RAF and AVG on 21 February. These attacks caused considerable casualties, especially to transport, and added to the crisis in morale that was acting to tear apart the remnants of Smyth's division.[5]

By 22 February divisional headquarters and 48 Indian Brigade began to cross the bridge, but by nightfall only a small part of the brigade was across. Sakurai's 33 Division had kept up pressure on the weak bridgehead all day, during which time confusion had reigned on the east bank. That night, believing that he could not protect the bridge for another day, and that all who could be saved had crossed the bridge, Smyth – who was asleep in his rear headquarters at the railway station at Abya, 8 miles away – was awakened and advised that the bridge was in imminent danger of capture. 'Blow it,' he ordered. In the early dawn of 23 February witnesses on both sides of the bridgehead stood stunned as the enormous strength of explosions caused by recently rigged demolitions took away the central spars of the bridge and threw them into the river. Unknown to Smyth, nearly two-thirds of his division was on the far bank. Most of the 300 boats which normally crowded the riverbanks had been destroyed to prevent their use by the Japanese. The only option was to swim or to build a raft. It was a disaster of considerable magnitude, although the Japanese immediately desisted from follow up, moving north to find a more convenient crossing point. Although some 3,500 officers and men were saved (from 16,000), many swimming the river, only 1,400 rifles accompanied the survivors. The division was left with no equipment or heavy weapons. Many had no boots, helmets or personal weapons.

Those who were unable to flee across the Sittang fell into Japanese hands. Of all the POWs captured by the Japanese in the years to 1945, the vast majority were captured at the Sittang. Men died of exhaustion, of drowning, at the hands of the Japanese and, in some cases, at the hands of Burmese villagers and red-robed *pongyis*. 17 Indian Division was shattered and Rangoon – and the rest of Burma – lay open to the Japanese. The only good to come out of what was undoubtedly a disaster was the fact that Iida had been denied the opportunity to strike an immediate blow against Rangoon, and a further ten days' grace was bought for Smyth's battered troops.

The shockwave that followed the destruction of the bridge reverberated as far as London: the recriminations went equally as far and lasted for decades. Hutton reported to Hartley and Wavell that the enemy had got around both flanks of 17 Indian Division and occupied dominant positions in the centre. There were no reserves. Troops were tired and unprotected, although they had fought well and killed a great deal of the enemy. Air reconnaissance had indicated that the enemy had been greatly reinforced. Thick jungle had prevented the detection of the fresh Japanese 33 Division. In a vain attempt to deflect blame from Smyth, Hutton added, 'I accept full responsibility for decisions taken and Smyth is not in any way to blame.'[6] This was unnecessarily magnanimous. They shared the blame, although Hutton was in no way responsible for the parlous state of the defences he found on his arrival a few short months before. Little good can be said of Smyth's performance in those last few days before the debacle at the Sittang, although of course he realized at the outset the foolishness of Hutton's defensive plans. His organizational and command performance was poor. There was no defence plan, nor any attempt to manage the administration and logistics of an orderly withdrawal across the bridge. He failed to take control of a confusing battle, to build and garrison a dug-in defensive position (something which he had long insisted he be allowed to do) and allowed confusion to determine the moment the charges were fired.

Wavell was to complain, with some justification, that the withdrawal to the Sittang had been badly managed by HQ 17 Indian Division. There is no doubt that the whole period amounted to little more than a succession of blunders, many of which were avoidable but which nevertheless all need to be seen in the context of defeat and withdrawal. It wasn't all 17 Indian Division's fault. Wavell and Hutton both insisted on a forward defensive strategy that played into Japanese hands, enabling them to bypass and infiltrate, while denying Smyth the opportunity to concentrate his forces and build a proper defensive position, at the Sittang Bridge. This concept of 'fighting forward', in which the enemy was able to concentrate its strength and retain the operational and tactical initiative, could only have worked if Hutton and Smyth had found a way of preventing the repeated confusion and disorientation caused by the Japanese tactics of infiltration. Likewise, the enforced delay on the Bilin meant that when 17 Indian Division was given permission to withdraw, on 19 February, it did so in contact with the enemy, and was unable to disentangle itself to make a clean, unmolested withdrawal.

The situation was further complicated by the fact that on 22 February ABDACOM was dissolved and Wavell began the long and tiring journey back to India. He arrived home on 28 February. Responsibility for Burma was thereafter transferred back to India. During this period, communication with Wavell was all but lost and Hartley in New Delhi had for six days the added responsibility for the disintegrating defences in Burma.

Even before the Sittang Bridge was blown Rangoon had begun to collapse. As early as 22 February, Dorman-Smith told Lord Linlithgow, Viceroy of India, 'Fires are raging here, and looting has begun on a considerable scale. City is as pathetic as it is smelly. Only 70 police remain and military are too few to take real charge though they are now happily shooting looters and convicts (who) have been prematurely released without order.'[7] On 28 February, in what he later described as a 'rather shamedly emotional telegram', Dorman-Smith reported to Leo Amery in London that 'nothing short of seasoned Army Corps could retrieve Sittang situation. Our troops have fought well but are outnumbered… I appreciate fact that any decision I make will probably be wrong, but it is now essential to make decision… I take full responsibility for this most distressing decision to abandon Rangoon.'[8] With the loss of Moulmein, Major General 'Taffy' Davies, Hutton's Chief of Staff, reported that the civil police in Rangoon disintegrated. 'Prisons and lunatic asylums were opened and the inmates loosed on the unhappy town.' Likewise, many animals had escaped from the zoo, and an injured orangutan 'lurked in the darkness attacking unsuspecting passers-by. Large numbers of poisonous snakes turned up in odd places at inappropriate moments. It became necessary to enclose Army H.Q.s. with barbed wire against depredations by gangs of cut-throats and criminal lunatics.'[9] These were all metaphors for the rapid, uncontrolled and unexpected (by the British, at least) collapse of their comfortable colonial civilization.

Hutton's appreciation of 18 February suggesting that Rangoon might fall to the Japanese had astonished Wavell and came as a shock to London and New Delhi. After this, however, the warnings became more frequent. 'Certain Indian battalions, Burma Rifles and Frontier Force have failed', Hutton reported on 21 February. 'Few units still in condition to fight effectively without reorganisation.'[10] The reports from Hutton prophesying disaster, however, had seemed to come out of the blue. Linlithgow complained to Leo Amery the same day, 'What little we have heard from Hutton over the last two days presents a depressing picture of progressive deterioration with prospect of all organised resistance breaking down under growing enemy pressure with apparently little prospect of an orderly withdrawal to northern Burma.'[11] He concluded from the Delhi gossip that the reason was 'in great part due to lack of drive and inspiration from the top.' He castigated Hutton's performance. Churchill responded by suggesting that Hutton be replaced by Alexander.[12] 'No troops in our control could reach Burma in time to save it. But if we could not send an army', he later wrote, 'we could at any rate send a man'.[13] On 22 February Hutton was told that Wavell had agreed to Churchill's suggestion to send Alexander to Burma to take command of the army. The suggestion of failure must undoubtedly have come as something of a shock to Hutton; Wavell had thus far given him no indication that he had lost faith in his ability successfully to hold Burma. Hutton's humiliation was very public and could not have come at a worse time for him personally, or for the Burma Army. He was undoubtedly under enormous pressure from Wavell, he profoundly disagreed with Smyth's plans for, and the conduct of, the Tenasserim campaign, and he had worked hard to keep a tight rein on his opinionated subordinate. Even worse, Hartley and Linlithgow had launched a ferocious sniping offensive at him from the comfort of New Delhi, the ultimate and savage effect of which was his removal from post.

The truth is that Hutton was an honest and intelligent man, asked to make bricks without straw. When the stark implications of the withdrawal to the Sittang became clear, he immediately reported his fears to Wavell. He cannot be accused of failing to impress upon Wavell the direness of 17 Indian Division's position, even though Wavell regarded his reports to be unduly pessimistic. On 23 February Hutton reported that the division had 'counter-attacked and fought to point of exhaustion. Withdrawal behind River Sittang inevitable but still doubtful how many units will be fit to fight... Have no intention of abandoning Rangoon and nobody is panicking but it is my considered opinion that prospects of holding it are not good.'[14] In response to comments by Hartley in New Delhi on 23 February[15] about his intention to give up Rangoon, Hutton rather testily responded that the 'possibility of offensive action has always been in mind, but it is impossible to ignore the realities of the situation of the sort which have so far been concerned with active defence against superior numbers with very limited resources pending reinforcement. Practically everything I have said has been actually borne out by events, but the unpleasant truth is never popular.'[16] Like Wavell, Hartley – far to the rear and without an inkling of the situation in which Hutton was enmeshed – consistently ignored the military poverty of Burma in his assessments of Hutton and Smyth's conduct of the campaign.[17]

There was no respite for the beleaguered Burma Army, or for its embattled commanders, after the loss of the Sittang Bridge. 33 and 55 Divisions began to infiltrate across the Sittang on 27 February, occupying villages in the area of Waw, north-east of Pegu. The Japanese goal was the capture of Rangoon, which they naturally expected the British to defend robustly, as its loss would prevent the British from further reinforcing their forces in Burma. They knew, if the British didn't, that the loss of Rangoon meant the loss of Burma. At this stage there was no plan to do other than cut the head off the snake that succoured Chungking. Accordingly, 55 Division crossed the Sittang on 3 March with the intention of turning south and encircling the shattered 17 Indian Division at Pegu, while 33 Division crossed the Rangoon–Prome Road before turning south to seize Rangoon from the north-west. Iida intended to exploit the 40-mile gap that had emerged between 17 Indian Division and the scattered and weak brigades of 1 Burma Division spread along the Sittang to the north, having just been relieved in the southern Shan States by the Chinese Sixth Army. The gloom was mitigated by the appearance of the newly arrived 7 Armoured Brigade with its 115 precious Stuart Light Tanks, a battery of the Essex Yeomanry (104 Royal Horse Artillery) with its twenty-four 25-pounder guns, and a battalion of the Cameronians.[18] Hard fighting, some of the fiercest of the entire campaign, now developed as 7 Armoured and 48 Indian Brigades fought to hold Pegu.

Hutton, recognizing the threat to Rangoon posed by the potential exploitation of this gap by the whole of 15 Army, and acknowledging Burma Army's inability to prevent it, ordered 17 Indian Division and 7 Armoured Brigade to withdraw to a concentration north of Rangoon, prior to the evacuation of the city. The division reformed around 16 and 48 Indian Brigades. With just under 7,000 troops, it had less than half its normal establishment, but 'Punch' Cowan achieved miracles to pull the reconstituted division into fighting trim.[19] Many units had been completely shattered and were patched up as best they could for the next stage of the campaign. 46 Indian Brigade was broken up and the remnants of the KOYLI, about 200 strong, were amalgamated with the DWR.

Thereafter, a general withdrawal was to be conducted northwards to the Irrawaddy. Hutton told Hartley on 27 February that, unless he had instructions to the contrary, he intended to complete the evacuation of Rangoon and fire the demolitions. He also instructed a 17-ship convoy containing the raw 63 Indian Infantry Brigade heading for Rangoon, to return to India. He feared that the arrival of an untrained brigade would offer nothing tangible to the defence of Burma and would make the scale of the impending defeat greater than it needed to be.

However, when Wavell arrived back in New Delhi on 28 February, he was aghast at what he regarded as Hutton's pessimism, and immediately instructed him by cable to take no action until he could visit Burma in person. It was an angry Wavell who landed at Magwe airfield on the Irrawaddy on 1 March. Dorman-Smith had already left Rangoon. Hutton and Smyth met Wavell on the tarmac of the airfield. Furiously, Wavell berated Hutton for failing to stem the tide of the Japanese advance. To this humiliation Hutton made no reply, observing later that had Wavell 'had his way the whole Army and a large number of civilians would have been captured in Rangoon by the Japanese.'[20] Turning to Smyth, he sacked him from command of his division, reduced him in rank and dismissed him from the army. It was the ultimate humiliation for a commander who was punished for failing to succeed in following through a flawed policy, and one that he knew would fail. The strategy was Wavell's, but both Hutton and Smyth suffered for its failure.

Wavell's baneful influence on events continued.[21] He attempted to take charge of operations on the Burma front himself, despite knowing nothing of the detailed situation, instructing 7 Armoured Brigade to attack northwards to reoccupy the village of Waw, having already reversed Hutton's decision to turn back 63 Indian Brigade from Rangoon. With its imminent arrival it was now imperative to hold the city until the brigade could be unloaded from its ships, with no port labour or functioning dockyard apparatus. After giving these instructions, Wavell then flew to Chungking on 2 March for an audience with Chiang Kai-shek. As Hutton predicted would happen, the attacks ordered by Wavell failed entirely to recover the ground that had been steadily lost to Japanese encroachment during the previous week. Wavell returned to India after this short trip still blissfully ignorant of the critical nature of Hutton's predicament. He could not accept both Hutton and Dorman-Smith's advice that with the destruction of 17 Indian Division on the Sittang, Rangoon was no longer defensible. In a telegram to General Alan Brooke on 5 March, he asserted that while the troops in Burma were 'somewhat disorganised and short of equipment after the Sittang River battle their morale was nevertheless sound.'[22] This was categorically untrue. Nevertheless, faced with the imminent threat of Japanese breakthrough to Rangoon, Hutton belatedly, and with considerable moral courage, ignored Wavell's instructions on the morning of 5 March and ordered the evacuation of Pegu.

It is hard to understand why Wavell failed to trust, or support, Hutton, the commander on the spot. He refused to believe that the forces at Hutton's disposal could not stop the Japanese. The weakened state of the Burma Army – the failure of a peacetime administration that had entirely discounted the need for adequate defensive preparations for the country – had proved wholly unable to meet the challenges posed by the Japanese attack through Tenasserim and across the Sittang. The poorly thought-out command arrangements in the Far East and Burma placed unnecessary complications in the way of both Hutton and Smyth and contributed significantly to the rapid demise of Burma's defences in early 1942. The grievous lack of planning prior to the Japanese invasion could not be placed at Hutton's door.

The decision to evacuate Rangoon when necessary to do so was taken by Hutton and Dorman-Smith in fact on 20 February.[23] The fateful day came eight days later. If they didn't go now, Dorman-Smith had told Wavell, they risked 'going into the bag', the unfortunate experience of Percival and his staff at Singapore only days before. On their last day in the now empty Governor's residence, Dorman-Smith and his small staff found themselves playing billiards after drinking the last bottles in the cellar. Eric Battersby, his aide-de-camp, decided to prevent the pictures of the past governors of British Burma from falling into the hands of the enemy. Picking up the billiard balls, the younger men vented their frustration by throwing them at the paintings in turn. 'It was a massacre,' noted Dorman-Smith drily. The ripped canvases seemed an appropriate metaphor for the way in which 53 years of British rule were coming to an unexpected and violent end.[24]

6

A Slim Chance to Save Burma

Alexander flew into Magwe airfield on 4 March 1942. A day later he flew into Rangoon in the last plane to land before it fell. He hurried forward to 17 Indian Division HQ at Hlegu where he met both Cowan and Hutton. En route he had stopped over in Calcutta, to meet Wavell. The C-in-C had impressed on him the absolute need to hold Rangoon. Without the port the Burma Army could not be reinforced or re-supplied until a land route could be pushed through from India, something that would not be complete for many months. The retention of Burma was important to maintain the connection with China, to protect north-eastern India with its war industries, and as an essential air base for the prosecution of attacks on the Japanese.[1] But Wavell did not give him any advice as to what he should do if the unimaginable happened and Rangoon fell. It was clearly not something that Wavell had ever envisaged. Nor did he provide an overall objective for the army: was it to defend central Burma indefinitely, or to withdraw carefully and in good order to India or China? This lack of direction was to have profound implications for the future course of the campaign.

Alexander was now faced with two clear choices. He could accept Hutton's assessment and withdraw 17 Indian Division from Pegu, evacuate Rangoon and draw back the Burma Army onto the Irrawaddy. Alternatively, he could obey Wavell's instructions and launch attacks to close the gap that had developed between 1 Burma and 17 Indian Divisions. Mindful of Wavell's orders and yet unaware of the deadly realities of the battle situation west of the Sittang, Alexander chose the latter. Against the frantically proffered advice of Hutton, 'Taffy' Davies and Cowan, he countermanded Hutton's order for the evacuation of Rangoon and ordered attacks to be launched by both divisions into the area between Pegu and Waw.

Predictably, the attacks yet again proved abortive. Neither of the Burma Army's two divisions was in any way able to carry out Alexander's instructions. 1 Burma Division didn't even move. Brigadier Wickham, commander of the newly arrived 63 Indian Brigade, was severely wounded and all three of his battalion commanding officers were killed in an ambush at this time – Japanese soldiers hidden in trees above a road firing down into their open Bren Gun carrier – rendering the newly arrived and untried brigade virtually helpless. When the dire reality of the situation became apparent to him, Alexander had the sense to reverse his orders, risk Wavell's ire and evacuate Rangoon. The only alternative was catastrophe. As Alexander himself was later ruefully to admit, his decision to disregard Hutton's advice on 5 March was made based on instructions that differed markedly from the facts of the situation. To his credit, it took him only 24 hours to recognise that Wavell's ambitions for the retention of Rangoon, even to turn it into a 'second Tobruk', would result in the complete loss of the Burma Army.[2] In the late afternoon of 6 March, therefore, he ordered Rangoon to be evacuated and the remaining demolitions blown. The garrison began its withdrawal towards Prome in the early hours of 7 March. On the same day, Wavell cabled the Chiefs of Staff in London: 'I will do everything possible to maintain a hold on Burma.' He never acknowledged how close he had brought the Burma Army to disaster, commenting in his despatch merely that 'On balance, I am satisfied that we gained by the delay.'[3]

The narrowness of Alexander's escape became apparent on 7 and 8 March when the remnants of the Rangoon Garrison, which included Alexander's Army HQ and the Gloucesters, were halted by a roadblock 12 miles north of the burning city. Sakurai had been ordered to attack Rangoon from the north, advancing on the city to the west of the main road that led to Prome. In order to allow 33 Division an unimpeded advance around the north of Rangoon, the road to Prome was blocked at the village of Taukkyan.[4] Despite repeated but piecemeal attacks throughout 7 March, the block proved impossible to break. Thousands of troops, including the new army commander, and hundreds of vehicles in a nose-to-tail convoy stretching 40 miles, were trapped. By luck alone, they managed to escape. It had never occurred to the Japanese that the British would abandon Rangoon without a fight, and the regimental commander responsible for establishing the block had been instructed not to get embroiled in a battle while the bulk of 33 Division crossed the road to the north. In strict observance of his orders, he lifted the roadblock at first light on 8 March when the crossing was safely complete. The way was thus clear to allow Alexander and the remnants of the Rangoon Garrison to make good their escape.

When Wavell received the message that Alexander had evacuated Rangoon, he was incensed that his clear instructions had been ignored, sending a terse telegram demanding to know whether battle had taken place. When he received this cable, on 10 March, Alexander, even more tersely, replied that he and the remnants of the Burma Army had escaped only by the narrowest of margins.[5] Wavell replied, magnanimously congratulating Alexander on his escape. Alexander's so-called Burma Army following the evacuation of Rangoon comprised about 13,000 effectives, together with perhaps 35,000 men of the Chinese Expeditionary Force, facing Iida's 15 Army, which, once it had been reinforced, totalled at least 50,000 veterans.[6]

The air attacks on 23 and 25 December 1941 precipitated a human catastrophe as the civilian population fled the capital city. After the Japanese invasion, this crisis magnified, the battle for Burma swirling amid a vast migration. It is not possible even today to determine just how many people, mainly poor Indians, died attempting to flee on foot to India. It has been estimated that nearly a million people were on the move in Burma during the first five months of 1942, most of whom were heading north with little more than what they could carry, escaping the advancing Japanese. It's hard to be precise about the numbers, but perhaps as many as half a million or more attempted to walk all the way back to India, with at least 50,000 dying in the attempt, perhaps even twice as many.[7] No one really knows, although the large number of eyewitness accounts talk in harrowing detail of the pitiful bundles of rags expiring, exhausted, along all the tracks leading westwards into India, dying of exhaustion, smallpox, cholera and starvation, although dacoits and general thuggery also took their toll.[8] News of the barbarity with which the Japanese Army treated anyone whom it considered to be its enemy, exemplified by its brutal treatment of civilians in China, had long gone before it, together with the innate fear of Indians for their Burman hosts (anti-Indian riots in the early 1930s and 1938 had killed hundreds), fanning the flames of panic. In mid-February 1942 the government had ordered the compulsory evacuation of Europeans and selected Asians from the country: those who'd worked for the colonial power and would be vulnerable if left behind. If they couldn't get out by sea, air, or upcountry by the now thoroughly disorganized train service (which went as far as Myitkyina, 750 miles north in Kachin territory) or by road transport, they had no choice but to walk. The prospect was a terrible one. The journey from Rangoon to Imphal, in the eastern state of Manipur, was 750 miles, but for much of this route they would be at the mercy of indifferent roads; the vagaries of the weather, including the monsoon;

the effects of disease (malaria was rampant) and lack of food. But even worse was the fact that law and order had broken down in many parts of the country – including much of Rangoon – and the hostility of the Burmese population and marauding companies of dacoits who plagued the countryside during times of disorder proved a dangerous threat to those making their way to safety. For those unable to take the route to the Burmese border at Tamu on the Chindwin, the alternative was to travel north from Mandalay to Myitkyina, and from there attempt to make their way through the Hukawng River Valley, a dangerously malarial stretch of remote country in the extreme north of the country. A few tried to make their way through the equally difficult Chaukan Pass.[9] Some succeeded, but in the monsoon those lost to starvation in the deeply jungled wilderness would have far outstripped those who made it, starving, diseased and exhausted, over the mountains into remote Assam. If hostile Burmese didn't get them, disease, exhaustion or starvation would. 'No one buried them,' recalled 'Taffy' Davies, commenting on the bodies lying alongside the roads and trails into India; 'they were just pushed off the road into the verges of the encroaching forest, or down the steep bank to the lush ravines below. The stench was terrible.'[10]

The American in-country custodian of America's developing relationship with China arrived in Burma in January 1942, already accompanied by the sobriquet 'Vinegar Joe'. Lieutenant General Joseph Stilwell was a Chinese-speaking infantryman who had spent many years of his military service in the country and was thought to know its people and its politics better perhaps than any other American serviceman (although many Chinese disputed this). A gifted linguist, he had travelled extensively and independently before the onset of war, observing the warlords of the Kuomintang coming to power and seeing at first hand the devastation wrought by the Japanese invasion and the consequences of internal revolution.

He was thus ideally placed to serve as General Marshall's representative to Chiang Kai-shek.[11] Stilwell was to serve both as Chiang Kai-shek's Chief of Staff with direct responsibility for training the Chinese Army for war, and for commanding all American forces in what was to become the 'China, Burma and India Theater'. He was expected simultaneously to serve the interests of the United States and the Chinese. It soon became clear to many observers that his primary concern was to protect American interests, rather than Allied – or British – ones.[12] The problem for Stilwell in 1942 was the opaqueness of the command arrangements established when the men of the Chinese Expeditionary Force (CEF) moved into Burma to support the British effort to halt the Japanese invasion. Stilwell certainly believed that the Generalissimo had conferred on him the authority to command this force, although this was not what General Lo Cho-yin and his officers understood to be the arrangement. As Brigadier-General Ho-Yungchi – Chief of Staff of the CEF – was later to write, Stilwell's role in 1942 was not to command the CEF, but 'to assist the Chinese field commander in tactical planning.'[13] This dispute lay at the heart of mutual US and Chinese misconceptions about Stilwell's actual role vis-à-vis field command of Chinese troops, and was to cause endless difficulties as the 1942 campaign progressed.

With the two sides following diametrically divergent strategies – one to ensure the complete destruction of the Japanese armies, and the other to ensure the safety of China – it was not possible for Stilwell to find a way to serve two masters. Both Marshall and Stilwell believed that the Chinese should be forced to commit troops to fight the Japanese in Burma in exchange for US support, but until April 1944 Roosevelt refused to tie aid to any specific military demands, allowing Chiang Kai-shek to do what he willed with the thousands of tons of American supplies pouring into China first through the Burma Road from Rangoon, thence via the airbridge over the Himalayas that American ingenuity and logistical muscle created between airfields in northern Assam, along the higher reaches of the Brahmaputra Valley, and China. It quickly became known as the 'Hump'.[14] It did not help that, with British and American grand strategy from 1942 focused primarily on the defeat of Germany, Stilwell would always be short of necessary supplies and adequate forces.

Stilwell was also thrown into a political and cultural milieu that the United States did not fully understand and for which Stilwell was not prepared. Unlike Churchill or Roosevelt, Chiang Kai-shek did not possess unequivocal power and relied for support on a broad base of warlords. Chiang Kai-shek also sought to retain his authority by means of the principle of divide and rule: if he allowed a degree of confusion to exist among his army and divisional commanders it would ensure that they would never be organized enough to band together to depose him. The 300 Chinese divisions under the 'authority' of Chiang Kai-shek were in fact only nominally so, all belonging to the warlords who owed allegiance, in full or in part, to Chungking. Of this number, Chiang Kai-shek had direct control over 30 divisions, one-tenth of the whole. His warlords supported him as long as he remained successful in generating and protecting their wealth. Their armies constituted a significant part of that wealth and were not to be frittered away in needless offensives that did not contribute to the perpetuation of their own positions and status. The long and protracted war against the Japanese during the past decade had forced them to develop an approach which conserved forces and avoided pitched battles. Large-scale actions and offensives were sought only when the Chinese, not possessing artillery or air support, otherwise enjoyed overwhelming odds over the Japanese. His entire position was threatened, additionally, by a powerful communist movement that was as much a worry to him as the Japanese. The British view was that what Chiang really wanted was 'an army copiously stocked with modern weapons with which he could eventually fight the Communist Chinese.'[15] As Jack Davies, Stilwell's political advisor, was presciently to observe in July 1942, Chiang Kai-shek's two objectives were to ensure, first, the perpetuation of the Kuomintang, and its domestic supremacy, and second, to come to the peace talks at the end of the war as militarily powerful as possible.[16]

Even when supposedly under his authority, therefore, Stilwell's Chinese divisions continued to receive orders directly from Chiang Kai-shek. Lieutenant General Du Yuming, for instance, commander of 5 Army, told Dorman-Smith in March 1942 that Stilwell 'only thinks he is commanding. In fact, he is doing no such thing. You see, we Chinese think that the only way to keep the Americans in the war is to give them a few commands on paper. They will not do much harm as we do the work.'[17]

In March 1942 Wavell decided to do what Hutton had long urged, and bring his disparate fighting forces into a single Corps. I Burma Corps was to comprise what remained of 1 Burma and 17 Indian Divisions, together with the newly arrived 7 Armoured Brigade. To command it, Major General William ('Bill') Slim was called from commanding 10 Indian Division in Persia. Wavell continued to believe that the Japanese offensive could be halted, perhaps even reversed. Even at this stage he harboured some considerable delusions about the scale of the threat posed by the Japanese and about the ability of his disparate and poorly prepared troops to halt the invaders.

Slim was ultimately to imprint himself indelibly on the war in Burma and India in the three and a half years that followed. But there was little to indicate that the future of the war would bring anything other than ignominy for Britain when he took command on 19 March 1942, setting up his HQ in the now derelict Law Courts in Prome, a dusty, straggling river port on the east bank of the Irrawaddy. An Indian Army officer with a successful though unremarkable career, at the outbreak of the Second World War he had been given command of 10 Indian Infantry Brigade, part of 5 Indian Division, and sent to Sudan.[18] He took part in the East African campaign to liberate Ethiopia from the Italians. He was to learn much from this experience that was to influence him in later years, and in these early days came to the attention of his superiors as a man of above average talent. In June 1941 he was promoted to the rank of acting major general and given command of 10 Indian Infantry Division in Iraq during the closing stages of the Anglo-Iraqi War and the opening of the Syria-Lebanon campaign. It was during the second of these campaigns that he demonstrated extraordinary qualities of resourcefulness and ingenuity. By means of an audacious action, Slim helped achieve Wavell's plan to invade Vichy Syria to prevent Hitler from gaining a foothold in the Middle East. Following the successful capture of Deir-ez-Zor, Slim led his division in the four-day invasion of Persia in July 1941. His experience of command was developing rapidly, and in the deftness and calmness of decisions made under the threat of imminent failure, he made an immediate impression on his superiors. He was twice mentioned in despatches during 1941 and received the Distinguished Service Order for his victory at Deir-ez-Zor.

At Prome he found to his delight that several of his key subordinates were old friends. By some 'trick of fate', he recalled, his two divisional commanders were good friends, fellow officers from 1 Battalion, 6 Gurkha Rifles (known in the Indian Army as the Mongol Conspiracy, for reason of the large number of senior officers it produced), and his Chief of Staff had commanded a battalion in Slim's old brigade. Bruce Scott commanded 1 Burma Division, 'Punch' Cowan now commanded 17 Indian Division, and his right-hand man, the Brigadier General Staff, was Brigadier 'Taffy' Davies. Furthermore, Brigadier 'Welcher' Welchman, a gunner with whom he shared the shrapnel from an Italian mortar bomb in Eritrea, was on the staff of 17 Indian Division. Slim immediately poached him from Cowan and made him commander of what little corps artillery he possessed.

The loss of Rangoon removed at a stroke Alexander's ability to sustain his forces for a protracted campaign in central Burma. Hutton had fortuitously stockpiled stores in central Burma during January and February, but these would only support Alexander for another two months. Likewise, the Japanese capture of the airfields in southern Burma rendered Burma useless in Britain's wider prosecution of the war in the Far East. Alexander nevertheless realized that his immediate task was to prepare defences to the north of Rangoon to prevent Iida's inevitable exploitation towards Mandalay given that the Japanese were likely to pour reinforcements into Rangoon. An additional two divisions and two tank regiments in fact were made available by the surrender of Singapore.[19] 5 Air Division, following reinforcement, totalled 420 aircraft. Japanese mastery of Burma's skies in 1942 was complete.

Hutton's original plans to fall back on the Irrawaddy offered a readymade solution for Alexander. When he had first considered how best to continue fighting if Rangoon had to be evacuated, Hutton had suggested leaving Chinese troops to cover the Sittang Valley, assisted by 1 Burma Division, while 17 Indian Division retired on Prome (162 miles north of Rangoon), as a forward defence for the vital oilfields at Yenangyaung. Prome was important for another reason. Much of the large stock of stores shipped out of Rangoon before the fall of the city, and necessary for the continued sustenance of the Burma Army, littered the docks and required back loading upriver to Mandalay.

Alexander decided to create a general defence line running from Tharrawaddy in the west (76 miles north of Rangoon) through to Nyaunglebin on the Sittang in the east. Successful holding of this line would allow contact to be maintained with the Chinese and provide time for India to build up its defences. There was no thought yet of a withdrawal to India, although the task now facing the Burma Army was daunting, especially with Japanese control of Rangoon port.

The geography of central Burma played a considerable part in determining first Hutton's, and then Alexander's, plans. The city of Mandalay dominates the centre of the country, sitting astride the mighty Irrawaddy as it traverses due south from the roof of Burma, before turning south-west to Yenangyaung and then falling south again towards its mouth at Rangoon. The Sittang, which falls due south to the Gulf of Martaban from its source in the Karen Hills just south of Pyinmana, flows parallel to the Irrawaddy but closer to the Thai frontier. These two rivers are separated by an 80-mile-wide range of roadless and thickly forested hills called the Pegu Yomas.

The two principal routes to Mandalay from Rangoon in 1942 were by road and rail through the Sittang Valley and by road along the Irrawaddy, to the west and east of the Pegu Yomas respectively. Alexander's defence of both the Irrawaddy and Sittang Valleys was based on the not unreasonable assumption that the Japanese would use both these arterial routes to make their way to Mandalay. Alexander did not know, however, where Iida's main effort would fall. Consequently, he felt constrained to guard against the eventuality of a Japanese advance northwards on both routes. By doing this, however, he accepted that he was dividing, rather than concentrating, his forces. The plan was simple. Alexander decided to block any Japanese advance by placing the Burma Army in the Irrawaddy Valley and asking Stilwell to place the Fifth Chinese Army roughly parallel in the Sittang. Brigade groups were to be placed in Prome and Allanmyo, which were to be made defended localities and stocked with supplies and ammunition for 21 days. If the Japanese got around these, the garrisons were to remain and fight on. The remainder of Burma Corps were to form mobile groups ready to counterattack Japanese incursions into the defence zone when required.

Hutton, however, opposed these plans, not because of any criticism with the theory behind Alexander's approach, but because he was convinced that they simply did not take account of the ragged state of the Burma Army. Alexander would have been hard pressed to provide counterattack forces that had enough mobility and striking power. Without the benefit of air supply, it would have been impossible to supply the defended localities when they were inevitably cut off by Japanese encirclement. Hutton's concern was that the Japanese would bypass these 'strongpoints' with ease, and then starve them into submission or attack and defeat them in detail once the mobile groups had been pushed back. An additional consideration was the potential use of the Irrawaddy to outflank Alexander on his right (the Japanese left) by moving forces rapidly northwards by water. The extended nature of the defence line and the British reliance on roads meant that the use of the river by the Japanese was not properly considered.

The viability of Alexander's initial plans was also dealt a sharp blow by a decision by Chiang Kai-shek not to allow the Fifth Chinese Army to deploy any farther south than the town of Toungoo. The town provided the key bridge over the Sittang River, taking the Burma Road through the Shan States and up to Lashio and from there to China. If the town were lost it would close the Burma Road and turn the whole of the Allied eastern flank. Not being able to defend forward of the town thus placed a severe restriction on Alexander's freedom of action, as it forced him to balance his forces on the Irrawaddy with this on the Sittang. In order to keep the defending armies on a line roughly level with each other, Alexander had no choice but to withdraw 1 Burma Division from the lower Sittang Valley. On 13 March he gave the orders to withdraw. Scott was to move back through the Chinese and thence to Prome, some elements crossing the Pegu Yomas to the Irrawaddy Valley while the remainder entrained for Taungdwingyi. 17 Indian Division was ordered to move to Okpo, a village some 60 miles south-east of Prome, by 15 March.

Following their fortuitous escape from Rangoon, the garrison and HQ Burma Army had met up with 17 Indian Division north of Taukkyan, withdrawing to the area of Tharrawaddy by 10 March, many troops marching on foot. Thereafter 17 Indian Division reorganized itself as best it could. During this time Scott's division, which was covering the Sittang Valley south of Nyaunglebin, had mounted an offensive south on both sides of the Sittang on 11 March but had achieved indifferent results. The withdrawal to Tharrawaddy was accomplished without a fight, but in the process some 80 miles were sacrificed, and huge quantities of rice stockpiled for the two Chinese armies were lost.

Alexander's decision to defend both the Irrawaddy and the Sittang Valleys bore out to the full Hutton's fears that it would encourage the Japanese to use infiltration against the widely dispersed Allied forces, a tactic which they had by now developed to perfection and which, after the battles in Tenasserim, had become such a bogey to the Burma Army. In such circumstances it was simply not possible to be everywhere at once. The inevitable consequence of Alexander's decision was that wide gaps were created across the Allied line, easily identifiable to the Japanese from both aerial reconnaissance and local Burmese fifth columnists. The opportunity existed for the Japanese to attempt to turn either of the flanks by driving a wedge deep through the 80-mile gap in the Pegu Yomas.

An alternative approach to the defence of the Prome–Toungoo Line would have been to place light forces on the floors of both the Irrawaddy and Sittang Valleys. These could have blocked any Japanese advance, while mobile strike forces hidden in the tangled mass of the Pegu Yomas itself could have launched attacks upon the advancing Japanese columns. However, for such a plan to succeed it would have been necessary for Alexander to have been able to prevent the Japanese at the same time from conducting a wide envelopment up either the Irrawaddy to the west or through the Shan States to seize Mandalay from the east, either of which would have served to cut off the Burma Army from the possibility of escape. Alexander simply did not have a means to block the Irrawaddy and his troops were not trained, equipped or confident enough to operate in this way. Nor, of course, did they have the air support that would have been essential to the success of this strategy. The truth is that such an approach was 'pie in the sky' in 1942, the cruel realities of the situation giving Alexander no choice but to attempt to cover both routes northwards as best he could.

The only other option would have been to give up that part of Burma which lay to the south of Mandalay entirely and adopt instead a defensive posture on the north bank of the Irrawaddy. At the certain risk of losing the Burma Road altogether, this would at least have given the Allies time to recover from the effects of the Sittang disaster. Crucially, it would also have reduced the extreme vulnerability of the RAF and aircraft of the AVG in the airfields in the Irrawaddy Valley and would have drastically shortened the long and rickety line of communication to India. It would also have acted to remove what Slim derided as the 'rather nebulous idea of retaining territory', a policy which inevitably led to the dispersion of forces over wide areas and created 'a defensive attitude of mind'.[20] It would also have served decisively to stop the process of incremental withdrawals, a practice that had been demonstrated during the withdrawal to the Sittang ceded initiative to the enemy, prevented longer term planning and had a deleterious effect on the morale of the men forced into repeated retreats.

Whatever the merits or otherwise of Alexander's strategic plan, Slim was convinced, like Wavell, that offensive action was the only way to take the initiative from the Japanese. He remained hopeful that Iida might become too confident and overextend himself and make his divisions vulnerable to sharp and timely counterattack. If Burma Corps did not attack, Slim reasoned, it would relinquish the initiative, however momentarily and locally, and would therefore always be at the mercy of the Japanese. To wrest the initiative from the Japanese it was necessary, he wrote of his first assessment of the problem, to 'hit him, and hit him hard enough to throw him off balance. Could we do so? I thought so.' He knew that an army that failed to attack would quickly lose its fighting spirit and as rapidly thereafter succumb to despair and defeat. Fully expecting his flank in the Prome–Allanmyo area to be turned by Japanese exploitation of the largely unguarded Pegu Yomas, Slim intended to form a powerful reserve to strike and defeat this attack, using his trump card, 7 Armoured Brigade, when and where the Japanese attack emerged.

Slim gave orders on 22 March for 1 Burma Division to concentrate in the Allanmyo area, while 17 Indian Division held the open country lying to the south of Prome. He needed time to gather the scattered elements of 1 Burma Division to collect together after their withdrawal through Toungoo. He had hoped to have at least ten days at Prome-Allanmyo to recover, re-equip and reposition his corps. In the event, Alexander's defensive plans came to nothing. This was in part because of the virtual elimination of the Allied air forces in Burma in late March 1942 after devastating raids on the remaining British air base at Magwe. It was also due to the successful Japanese offensive against 200 Chinese Division at Toungoo, which removed any hope Slim had of fighting his corps as a single entity, as he was forced into a premature commitment of his already weakened forces.

During the first two weeks of March, Sakurai rested and replenished 33 Division in Rangoon while 55 Division continued to probe northwards along the Sittang Valley against 1 Burma Division. Possession of Rangoon allowed the Japanese to be substantially reinforced. 56 and 18 Japanese Divisions, along with two tank regiments, artillery and supporting troops, made available by the fall of Singapore on 15 February, arrived during March and April. These reinforcements enabled Iida to make plans for an offensive into central Burma. His plan was for 55 Division to advance on the right flank up the Sittang Valley, seizing the airfield at Toungoo before advancing on Meiktila. 33 Division was to advance in parallel up the Irrawaddy Valley to Prome with the aim of occupying the Yenangyaung oilfields by mid-April. Thereafter 56 Division was to move through 55 Division to seize Taunggyi in the Shan Hills by way of Toungoo and Meiktila. Iida was confident that the decisive battle for Mandalay would be over by the middle of May, when the British would be forced to fight with their backs to the Irrawaddy, and that the opening of this door would be followed by the rapid collapse of northern Burma.

The Japanese began to probe forward in strength in both the Irrawaddy and Sittang Valleys on 16 March. Attacks against Toungoo began three days later, just as 1 Burma Division was handing responsibility for the town to the Fifth Chinese Army. Scott managed to extricate himself safely and make his way to Allanmyo. Although 200 Division, one of the best equipped and trained divisions in the Chinese Army, fought hard to retain Toungoo, the town was cut off on 24 March by 55 Division and an assault with considerable air support was launched on 26 March. With the situation looking increasingly desperate, Stilwell ordered 22, 55 and 96 Chinese Divisions to counterattack in support of 200 Division, but the order was not obeyed. Stilwell, in desperation, asked Alexander to take the offensive in the Irrawaddy Valley to relieve the pressure on Toungoo.

The Fifth and Sixth Armies of the Chinese Expeditionary Force played a very significant role in the defence of Burma in 1942, despite the many and varied obstacles associated with their effective deployment. Many Chinese couldn't understand, as the campaign ran its weary course, how Britain could be bettered by the Japanese in battle, such was the persistence of the myth of British military invincibility. General Ho-Yungchi, for instance, was convinced, even after the war, that the British 'failure' in Burma could only be explained by a dastardly ploy by the 'clever British' to preserve its precious manpower by withdrawing to India, while at the same time inviting the Chinese armies into Burma as bait for the Japanese, thereby allowing poor Chinese soldiers to die in the defence of British colonial interests. It never crossed his mind that the supposedly all-powerful British could simply have been bettered in a straight fight by an Asian enemy.[21] These suspicions underlay a whole array of more prosaic issues between their new allies, from language and culture to logistical and command arrangements. When Chiang Kai-shek agreed to create the CEF for service in Burma, he assumed that Britain had the wherewithal to feed and transport it. In truth, it didn't have the resources to do this for its own, tiny, garrison, let alone an additional 40,000 hungry mouths.

Chiang Kai-shek had originally suggested – sensibly – allocating the CEF a specific geography in Burma to defend – Mandalay – recognizing the difficulties that would be encountered were his forces required to integrate fully with British formations. It appears that Britain misinterpreted the request as something akin to a 'land grab', with the result that Chinese intentions were considered suspicious from the outset. Although Chinese and British troops ended up fighting alongside each other, there was never a fully unified command, as General Ho-Yungchi noted:

> The British commanded their own troops, the Chinese theirs. On top of it all, there was an American military mission which did not quite know where it belonged. On the Chinese side, besides General Lo there was General Stilwell, and in addition to both of them there was the Chinese General Staff Delegation. And over them all, there was the Generalissimo who, though far away in Chungking, was nevertheless ceaselessly consulted on field tactical questions to which there would invariably be answers and directives. It was a general misconception of authority that produced in Burma an impotent leadership which was thus forced to refer everything to Chungking.[22]

The problem was a combination of the natural misconceptions and misapprehensions that arise when two bodies of soldiers, entirely ignorant of each other's ways, are forced to fight together without any preparation, training or common language. That so much in fact was achieved is testament to the soldiers' ability to get things done despite multifarious impediments.

The fundamental problem with defending Burma using two separate formations defending their own patches of territory was that the British and Chinese ended up fighting separate campaigns. It was too much to hope that they could have achieved unified command in 1942, given the relentless intensity and brilliance of the Japanese attack, and the many weaknesses of the troops and formations – British, Indian and Chinese – facing them. Fighting a divided campaign, where each Burmese side attempted to protect its own prerogatives, and in which coordination and support between the two was a political rather than merely a military decision, proved to be disastrous for the coordinated defence of Burma. The political pressure by the British to support the Chinese on their eastern flank, and by the Chinese to support the British on their western, created a series of perverse outcomes for the entire Allied defensive line. In addition, the detailed mechanisms for operating together were not established, let alone rehearsed, with the inevitable result that when coordination was required the procedures failed repeatedly. Ho-Yungchi complained that 'the Chinese never knew what their British allies were doing. The Chinese were never told. When the British retreated in their sector, the Chinese would be still holding their lines in blissful ignorance of having been outflanked.'[23] Ho seemed to think that this was another example of British perfidy, but in reality it was simply a result of the chaos of an uncontrolled battlefield, the lack of a single controlling mind in Allied strategy, together with a lack of preparation and training in joint working.

On 28 March Alexander met Chiang Kai-shek at Chungking. The Chinese leader repeated Stilwell's plea for him to do something to relieve the hard-pressed 200 Division at Toungoo. The request placed Alexander in an awkward predicament. He knew that Burma Corps was not yet ready to take offensive action following its withdrawal to Allanmyo–Prome, but he also recognized the strategic necessity to hold Toungoo. At the same time Alexander knew that failing to help the Chinese in their hour of need would allow Chiang Kai-shek an excuse for withholding assistance from Alexander at a time when the British might require it in the future. But how exactly could Burma Corps assist the Chinese?

There seemed to be two options. The first was to launch an attack through the Pegu Yomas against the Japanese at Toungoo. But the state of Slim's forces and their inherent immobility led to this idea being dismissed. The newly trained Indian formations had only recently been mechanized in preparation for deployment to the Middle East, and however hard they tried during the withdrawal, Burma Corps was unable, as Slim described it, to 'shake loose from the tin-can of mechanical transport tied to our tail'. This constraint made the British vulnerable not just to constant air attack but also to outflanking actions by the enemy and repeated punishment at the hands of the roadblock.

The only other option was to mount an offensive sweep south from Prome in the hope of engaging the forward elements of 33 Division, thereby frustrating their plans to advance deep into Burma, perhaps even of forcing them to relax their grip on Toungoo. This in the circumstances was all that Alexander felt he could do. Accordingly, he ordered Slim to mount an immediate offensive.

The situation was compounded by systemic weaknesses in the Chinese Army's ability to respond decisively and as a coherent whole to the developing military situation, an issue which revealed itself to Stilwell for the first time at Toungoo. It was here, too, that the limited extent of his operational authority over the Chinese commanders was exposed to him for the first time. All orders from Chiang Kai-shek were routed through the Commander of the CEF, General Lo Cho-Ying, and reports heading back to Chungking were filtered by General Lin Wei, the Generalissimo's personal representative at Lashio. To complicate matters even further, the Chinese divisional commanders tended to choose what orders to obey, and what to discard. No amount of cajoling by Stilwell could persuade them to commit themselves to do anything they did not want to do. Trying to persuade the army and divisional commanders to concentrate their forces at Toungoo was an exasperating and exhausting experience for a commander used to instant obedience. He found Chiang Kai-shek to be supportive one minute, and cautious the next, his divisional commanders full of excuses for inaction. Stilwell was equally outraged and exhausted by this inexplicable behaviour. He had certainly not expected it and did not realize that Chiang Kai-shek was promising him one thing, while at the same time urging his own commanders not to over-commit themselves. He vented his rage in his diary and contemplated resignation. The entry for 25 March reads, 'Chiang Kai Shek has changed his mind. Three [radio] letters on the 23. 3.00 p.m., 5.00 p.m., and 9.00 p.m. Full of all kinds of warnings, admonition and caution.'

On 26 March he furiously reported that a planned movement by rail had been interrupted: 'Tu is too far back, too lackadaisical, doesn't supervise execution.' Complaints to the newly appointed General Alexander, and to Lieutenant General Tu-Ming, commander of the Fifth Chinese Army, availed little. On 29 March Stilwell remained as frustrated as ever. This was no way to organize a war: 'As usual they are dogging [sic] it. General Liao... is [full] of excuses – how strong the Jap positions are, and how reinforcements are coming to them etc. Two days ago it would have been easy, but now... They'll drag it out and do nothing unless I somehow kick them into it... Hot as hell. We are all dried out and exhausted. I am mentally about shot.'

Alexander's orders to mount an immediate offensive provided Slim with few viable options. From even a superficial evaluation, Slim recognized that there was nothing the offensive could conceivably do to assist the Chinese in Toungoo, and there was virtually no information on Japanese movements in the Irrawaddy Valley with which to form a detailed plan. In the event he decided to launch a thrust southward by 17 Indian Division with the strongest mobile force Cowan could cobble together, with the simple aim of disrupting any Japanese advance. The instructions were unavoidably vague. Cowan dutifully created a 'strike force' based on 7 Hussars and a total of one and a half battalions of infantry hastily brought together from the remnants of four depleted battalions. Commanded by Brigadier Anstice of 7 Armoured Brigade, the force set off on 29 March towards Okpo through the villages of Shwedaung and Paungde.

Unbeknown to either Slim or Cowan, who did not now have the benefit of air reconnaissance, the move towards Paungde on 29 March coincided with a Japanese advance up the Irrawaddy to seize the straggling riverside village of Shwedaung. At a stroke this move cut Anstice off from Prome. Rather than becoming a threat to 33 Division, Cowan's force had been outflanked long before it had the opportunity even to engage the enemy. By evening, after sharp skirmishes around Paungde, news of the Japanese block behind the force reached Anstice. Cowan, recognizing immediately that there was now a very real chance that he would be cut off, promptly ordered Anstice to withdraw to Prome.

In Prome, Cowan was now aware that he was faced by an advancing column up the railway from the south-west and a strong force at Shwedaung which threatened to cut off his force completely. Accordingly, he placed a block on the railway which led to Paungde and ordered a counterattack on Shwedaung from the north to assist Anstice's now retreating troops.

The block at Shwedaung proved to be impossible to break. Anstice's troops threw themselves boldly against it throughout the evening of 29 March in the knowledge that if they could not break through, they would otherwise not make good their escape to Prome. That night the Japanese in Shwedaung were further reinforced from the Irrawaddy. The river was fast flowing and a significant ally to the Japanese. The entrapped British column stretched back down the road to Paungde and was attacked throughout the following day. In desperation Anstice launched further attacks on the block on 30 March. When it became apparent that bludgeoning their way through was unlikely to succeed in rescuing the whole of the trapped force, and that the cost was ever-increasing casualties, units were forced to break off the engagement and escape as best they could across country to Prome.

The Prome offensive was a disaster for Slim's weak corps. It suffered just over 400 killed and missing and many more wounded and lost two 25-pounder field guns and ten tanks, all for no purpose. 17 Indian Division was now severely weakened. The Gloucesters and a company of the West Yorkshire Regiment were down to 100 all ranks; the Cameronians were down to 100 and the Duke of Wellington's Regiment were down to 150. There was no hope of reinforcement. Worse still, morale plummeted. To many of the men there seemed to be no hope of a successful outcome to the campaign, and the feeling of isolation, along with the fact that the future alternatives appeared either starvation in the jungles of northern Burma, or the unpleasant prospect of a POW camp. Hutton had firmly opposed the idea of an offensive at this time, considering it premature and foolhardy and partly therefore asked to be relieved as Alexander's Chief of the

General Staff. In retrospect he was right. Insisting on an offensive with such an ill-defined objective before Burma Corps was in a position to carry it out was a considerable error of judgement. A thousand miles away in Chungking, Alexander was simply too far distant to make a valid assessment of the situation, although the pressure applied by Chiang Kai-shek 'to do something' to assist the Chinese at this critical juncture of the battle for Burma was undoubtedly considerable.

In any case, the Chinese were only two days away from abandoning Toungoo. If action were to have been taken at all, it should have been in direct support of the Chinese at Toungoo, which Burma Corps, on the wrong side of the Pegu Yomas, was incapable of offering.

7

The Battle for Lower Burma

As Anstice's battered force crept back to Prome on 30 March, 200 Division's grip on Toungoo on the other side of the Pegu Yomas was finally loosened. The Japanese 56 Division attacked the town from the east after crossing the key bridge over the Sittang on the road north to Lashio, which unfortunately had not been demolished, following a wide outflanking movement through the Shan States. The Chinese, although having fought well, suffered heavy casualties and lost all their heavy equipment, and were forced to withdraw. Because it served to uncover Alexander's eastern flank and unbalanced the defence line, Slim came to regard the loss of Toungoo as 'a major disaster second only to our defeat at the Sittang bridge.' Stilwell was apoplectic. The defeat could have been avoided if, in his view, the other Chinese generals – he called them 'pusillanimous bastards' – had come to the aid of their fellows. Toungoo had been lost, he considered, by a failure of command. He flew to Chungking on 1 April 1942 to remonstrate with Chiang Kai-shek. From Stilwell's perspective, Chinese commanders never knew whether they were coming or going, or indeed, which order took precedence over the other. There was little certainty in orders, and considerable ambiguity and confusion in instructions. What could he do? he asked himself. 'I can't shoot them, I can't relieve them; and just talking to them does no good. So the upshot of it is that I am the stooge who does the dirty work and gets the rap.' He wasn't blind to the predicament the Chinese commanders found themselves in, however:

> The fact that Tu could treat me with gross discourtesy indicates that he took his cue from the highest quarters. What a gag. I have to tell Chiang Kai Shek with a straight face that his subordinates are not carrying out his orders, when in all

probability they are doing just what he tells them. In justice to all of them, however, it is expecting a great deal to have them turn over a couple of armies in a vital area to a goddamn foreigner that they don't know and in whom they can't have much confidence.[1]

The loss of Toungoo meant that the way was now open for the Japanese to exploit deep into the Shan States, which in turn served to force the British on the Irrawaddy to withdraw to avoid being encircled and trapped from the north-east. Iida needed no encouragement to exploit his success. He immediately trucked 56 Division across the Sittang and headed for Lashio, intending to cut the Burma Road and destroy the Sixth Chinese Army, which was supposed to be covering Alexander's eastern flank in the Southern Shan States.

Slim was having his own difficulties. Prome was not easy to defend and the abortive offensive of 29 and 30 March made it even less so. The town had been bombed from the air on 28 March and large areas were gutted by fire. 17 Indian Division was now very weak, but the state of 1 Burma Division shocked Slim when he first met its units straggling towards the Allanmyo area at the end of March. It had little heavy equipment and artillery and its troops were largely Burmese, many of whom had taken the opportunity to return to their villages. By 3 April Wavell was reporting to London, 'British troops fighting very well but are weak in numbers. Some Indian units shaken and not very reliable. Remaining Burmese units of little fighting value.'[2]

Slim's plan for the defence of Prome involved the weak 63 Indian Brigade holding the town and its straggling southern outskirts, 48 Indian Brigade guarding the road that ran south-east along the railway to Paungde, while 16 Indian Brigade guarded the open left flank of the division at Tamagauk, just to the north of the town, facing onto the Pegu Yomas. Slim admitted that in retrospect he made a mistake in planning his preliminary corps dispositions for the defence of Prome–Allanmyo. 17 Indian Division was initially deployed in the open country forward of the town, but Slim, fearful of the threat to his flanks from the direction of both the Irrawaddy in the west and the Pegu Yomas in the east, withdrew the division into Prome itself. 'I was anxious at this stage to gain time for the corps concentration', he wrote. 'I should have done better to leave 17 Division forward and to concentrate 1 Burma Division about Prome. Apart from all else it was a mistake to begin my command by a withdrawal if it could have been avoided.'

The problem now was that the loss of Toungoo on 30 March had made the retention of Prome impossible, as Burma Corps found itself too far down the

Irrawaddy, threatened by the possibility of the Japanese outflanking it by a wide movement up the Sittang Valley. Accordingly, it was agreed on 1 April, during a fleeting visit to Burma by Wavell, who met with Alexander and Slim at the latter's HQ in Allanmyo, that 17 Indian Division should be withdrawn from Prome immediately and Burma Corps concentrated farther north to defend the Yenangyaung oilfields. In a demonstration of just how fast the Japanese could move, 33 Division pre-empted these plans with a sudden assault on Prome's defences on the night of 1 April, overwhelming a battalion of 63 Indian Brigade. Early the next morning, with the brigade in some disarray and falling back through the town, Cowan feared, correctly as it transpired, that the Japanese were about to establish roadblocks to his rear. He sought Slim's permission to disengage. Slim agreed and the withdrawal of 17 Indian Division began at midday on 2 April, a decision that prevented it from being completely encircled. The division now faced a prolonged trial of discipline and endurance as it withdrew into the notorious 'dry belt' of central Burma. The countryside presented a stark contrast to the jungles of Tenasserim. James Lunt recalled: 'The heat was intense, the road dusty and the march a severe trial to the troops. Water was scarce and it was difficult to prevent the men crowding around the infrequent water holes.'[3] Constant Japanese air attacks added to the difficulties of the withdrawal, although fortunately the exhausted Japanese did not press the pursuit.

Japanese air superiority and his own lack of air support compounded Slim's difficulties. The problem was only slightly exaggerated by Dorman-Smith in a telegram he sent from Maymyo to Leo Amery on 30 March, when he declared that 'at this moment our total air strength is one aged [Tiger] Moth.'[4] Not only did a paucity of aircraft severely restrain Slim's ability to observe forward of his positions and so gain intelligence about Japanese movements, but the Japanese roamed at will across Burma's sky, entirely dominating the few roads during the hours of daylight. Allied casualties from enemy air action were high, with a concomitant depression of morale. 'Enemy air activity continued throughout 3 and 4 April', Alexander reported to Delhi and London on 6 April, 'dive bombing and machine gunning our troops and transport. Casualties estimated as 100 killed and wounded sustained by 63 Brigade, by bombing attack 3 April south of Dayindabo.'[5] Evidence continued of widespread Burmese involvement in support of the Japanese, reporting on British and Chinese movements (by the use of bonfires) and attacking stragglers.

The previous day, Alexander had despatched a short telegram to Wavell pleading for more air support. Its lack, he wrote, 'is adversely affecting morale of troops under my command. Request as matter of urgency that aircraft, particularly fighter aircraft, be made available. The three or four transport aircraft serving this theatre are totally inadequate.'[6] Wavell replied that he wished he could do more, but he simply had no more aircraft to give. He explained to the War Office on 13 April that with only 40 Hurricanes and Mohawks available for the defence of Calcutta and North East India, he did not want to fritter the few precious aircraft he had in pursuance of what he increasingly regarded as a forlorn hope in Burma. Command of the air was undoubtedly one of the critical factors in the Japanese victory in 1942. In addition to attacking at will, the Japanese launched widespread attacks across the country. The largely wooden towns and villages were methodically destroyed in a process that exacerbated the panic in the civil population and removed the last vestiges of civil government and confidence in the viability of government. Their plan was to weaken the morale of the civilian population and the young war-raised battalions of the Indian Army. Considerable effort was placed on propaganda, using radio and leaflets, to complement the terror tactics of aerial bombardment of the civilian centres of Rangoon, Prome and Mandalay. In devastating attacks on the old wooden city of Mandalay on 3 April 1942, thousands were killed and as much as 75 per cent of dwellings were destroyed. This wasn't just a war against armies, but against people and against the idea that the colonial ruler could protect the country from Britain's enemies.

To the troops, the sullen hostility of the Burmese, their active support for the Japanese, the lack of any certain role or destination, the knowledge that there would be no further reinforcements, the almost complete loss of air support, the intense heat and lack of water, the condition of the thousands of desperate refugees who were clogging the roads, the prevalence of malaria and cholera and their complete isolation from news or mail from home, created the potential for widespread hopelessness. Only the willpower and determination of individuals and the discipline and *esprit de corps* of small units held the army together. A small number of unit-less men were making their way to India under their own steam, in places requisitioning illegally and, in some recorded cases, committing theft and even murder. But for the vast bulk of Burma Corps, military discipline held, units fighting and withdrawing in an order that belied the chaos in which the men found themselves. There was an acute lack of essential stores, from ammunition to vehicle spares and maps, and a lack of information led to floods of rumours which themselves exacerbated the decline in morale. A lack of proper medical attention for the wounded, together with the bitter knowledge that the Japanese invariably bayoneted wounded prisoners rather than go to the trouble of looking after them, was also a constant worry. Seemingly pointless offensives, such as the one launched out of Prome at the end of March, did nothing to help.

Following the collapse of the Prome–Toungoo Line, Alexander tried desperately to create a new defence line farther north. Wavell had given him three tasks during his fleeting visit at the beginning of the month. There was as yet no consideration of an acceptance of defeat and a withdrawal to India. His orders were to concentrate Burma Corps to the north of Prome, to continue to take every opportunity for offensive action and to prepare to withdraw to the area south of Magwe–Taungdwingyi. Seeking a second opportunity to halt Iida, Alexander decided to place his forces along a new east–west line running from the Irrawaddy through to Loikaw in the southern Shan States. This would serve to defend the extensive oilfields at Yenangyaung as well as preserve the army's base at Mandalay. The line ran through the towns of Taungdwingyi and Pyinmana, with Taungdwingyi lying midway. Alexander intended that the Chinese would garrison the eastern flank of the Taungdwingyi Line and Burma Corps the western.

The problem was that Burma Corps' frontage amounted to nearly 60 miles, which was considerably more, in Slim's judgement, than he could hope to defend properly. A further problem then emerged. Alexander directed that Slim place forces in Taungdwingyi itself to protect Mandalay to the north and to maintain a firm link with the Fifth Chinese Army on the eastern flank. This instruction, however, limited the depth Slim was able to provide to the whole of his frontage. It also meant that he now had insufficient forces to create the reserve he needed to counter the inevitable Japanese infiltration between his widely dispersed brigade locations. Keeping a firm hold of Taungdwingyi regardless of where the Japanese point of main effort emerged was, Slim considered, a mistake. He feared that if he was forced to fight two separate divisional battles, one based on Taungdwingyi and the other far away at Magwe on the Irrawaddy, his two weak and geographically diverse divisions would be no match for the concentrated might of 33 Division, which could choose where and when to attack. He was convinced that if he were able to fight the forthcoming battle with his two divisions working closely together, he would have a much better chance of challenging Iida and even, as he hoped, of counterattacking him decisively. But to do this he needed the entire 17 Indian Division to be freed from its responsibilities for Taungdwingyi and given over wholly to the task of counterattacking the main Japanese thrust against the oilfields. Alexander was aware of Slim's difficulty but felt constrained by the need to keep on good terms with Chiang Kai-shek, believing that if the British abandoned Taungdwingyi it would enable the Chinese to claim that the British were not serious about defending Burma. Equally, concentrating forces was fine in theory, but ultimately a waste of time if Iida contrived to merely sidestep the British position, intent on moving to a far distant objective.

Unable to concentrate his corps, and with Alexander insistent on the need to defend Taungdwingyi, Slim did the only two things open to him. First, he shortened his line. This required a further withdrawal from Allanmyo to the area just south of Magwe, which was completed by 6 April. The Japanese occupied Allanmyo on the day the troops of 1 Burma Division departed. 'I did not like the idea of another withdrawal', Slim wrote. 'We were fast approaching the dangerous state when our solutions to all problems threatened to be retreat, but I hoped this would be the last.' But at least this withdrawal reduced the extent of his responsibilities to about 40 miles. Burma Corps was complete on the Taungdwingyi Line by 8 April.

Second, Slim asked Alexander to give responsibility for Taungdwingyi to the Fifth Chinese Army. On 6 April Alexander asked Stilwell for help in defending the town. Stilwell agreed to help, and a Chinese regiment was promised for the task. But Slim was to be disappointed. 'We waited expectantly for them' to arrive, he wrote. 'We waited in vain.' Unbeknown to Slim, Chiang Kai-shek had countermanded Stilwell's order and instructed him not to provide the regiment after all. Slim now had no choice but to hold the whole of the Allied right flank himself, including Taungdwingyi and the vital oilfields at Yenangyaung.

Not aware of any sign that might indicate that the Chinese would not do what they had promised, Slim went ahead and issued orders for the defence of the line on 6 April. Water was scarce. 2 Burma Brigade was tasked with holding Minhla on the west bank of the Irrawaddy, and 1 Burma Brigade was given the area of Migyaungye on the east bank. 63 and 16 Indian Brigades held the eastern flank at Taungdwingyi itself. From the remainder, including 13 and 48 Indian Brigades and 7 Armoured Brigade, Slim intended to form a powerful 'strike force' under the command of Bruce Scott, which would counterattack against the flanks of the enemy whenever and wherever the Japanese thrusts developed.

One officer recalled Slim explaining his plan to the assembled officers of 63 Indian Brigade during this realignment of the defence line. 'You've probably been wondering why we have had these everlasting withdrawals,' Slim told them, 'and I sympathise with you. I've loathed them too. The reason, however, is that I must have good open country where the tanks can operate with good effect against the Japs, and this is it. And this is my plan: You, 63 Brigade, are to hold Taungdwingyi, 1 Burma Division is in Magwe, 48 Brigade and the Tanks are in the middle. Now, wherever the Japs attack, the other two will close in, and we'll really knock him this time.'[7]

However, the problems of attempting to hold too much ground with too few troops now became painfully apparent. Scott's brigades were unable to support each other, with wide gaps between the four principal defensive positions. The line was full of holes, ripe for Japanese infiltration. 48 Indian and 7 Armoured Brigades found themselves at the town of Kokkogwa 10 miles to the west of Taungdwingyi with 13 Indian Brigade a further 8 miles to the west. Partly in order to make up some of his deficiencies in battlefield intelligence Slim placed an observation screen, made up of troops from the Burma Frontier Force, a dozen miles to the front of the position, in order to provide information about the direction of the Japanese advance.

For his part, Iida's plan was to seize the oilfields at Yenangyaung before they were destroyed, as they would be vital for subsequent operations in northern Burma. This, and not Mandalay, was to be his main effort. His plan was that 33 Division would advance along the Irrawaddy, exploiting the opportunities the vast river provided for the transport of troops and supplies. Sakurai intended to hold British attention to the area between Magwe and Kokkogwa while inserting a strong river-borne force up the Irrawaddy to seize the oilfields. This would also serve to cut off Slim from the rear. It was a classic Japanese manoeuvre and it very nearly succeeded.

Japanese patrol actions developed against positions held by 1 Burma, 13 and 48 Indian Brigades on 10 April. The following day attacks were launched in strength against 1 Burma and 48 Indian Brigades (with part of 7 Armoured Brigade) at Kokkogwa. Success in either of these attacks would have driven a wedge between 17 Indian and 1 Burma Divisions. But Slim's eastern flank held firm. 48 Indian Brigade succeeded brilliantly in halting the attack against Kokkogwa between 11 and 14 April, a battle which 33 Division regarded as their one defeat of the 1942 campaign.

However, the situation was far less secure on Slim's western flank, where 1 Burma Brigade was fighting a confused battle on the banks of the Irrawaddy to the south of the vulnerable Magwe–Taungdwingyi Road. Considerable infiltration had taken place through the Burma Corps position in the period from 10 April onwards, much of which was by Japanese and Burma Independence Army soldiers disguised either as refugees, Chinese soldiers or members of the Burma Frontier Force. British and Indian troops were caught out regularly by such ruses. They were difficult to counter. During 12 April the threat of a strong

Japanese advance towards the oilfields forced Scott to withdraw 1 Burma Brigade westward in order to reinforce the village of Migyaungye. The enemy, however, seized the village before it could be secured, and the village could not be retaken in a counterattack launched by Scott on 13 April. 'The Striking Force, moving down to counter-attack,' recalled Slim, 'became involved in a series of fights with enemy groups, and exhausted itself by marching and counter-marching to deal with them.'

The truth was that Alexander's positioning of the Taungdwingyi Line was able to do very little to prevent the Japanese from threatening Yenangyaung. Indeed, Alexander's plan served to sacrifice Yenangyaung in favour of securing the link with the Chinese west flank. A key village dominating the east bank of the Irrawaddy was now in Iida's hands, and British counteraction was feeble and confused. Captain Ian Lyall Grant of King George V's Own Bengal Sappers and Miners levelled the blame for this confusion squarely on Scott and Slim, for still believing that 'aggressive action would neutralise the apparent Japanese superiority.'[8] The charge is fair. Scott's division was probably incapable at this stage of mounting more than aggressive patrols against the highly professional 33 Division. The problem for both Scott and Slim at this time was that the alternatives were appallingly stark, and they sought every opportunity to regain the initiative.

Slim consistently held out hope that something could be done to recover the situation using offensive action. By 14 April, however, the whole of Slim's right flank had begun to crumble. By midday on 13 April it was already clear to both Slim and Scott, when they met at Magwe to discuss the deteriorating situation, that Japanese gains threatened to outflank 1 Burma Division entirely. A powerful divisional counterattack against the flank and rear of 33 Division might succeed in removing the threat to Yenangyaung, but Slim could only launch this if Alexander allowed him to relinquish his grip on Taungdwingyi. This Alexander would not permit.

Seventeen years later, when writing *Defeat into Victory*, Slim could hardly restrain his frustration at this lost chance to inflict a grievous blow onto Sakurai's overstretched regiments. During the days preceding the first Japanese attacks on 10 April, it was obvious to him that Iida would make a concerted effort to seize the Yenangyaung oilfields along the course of the Irrawaddy. He remarks candidly that when he could not persuade Alexander to agree to reduce the Taungdwingyi garrison, he ought to have done it himself, with or without the sanction of the army commander.

Both divisions now had no choice but to fight separate battles.

On 13 April Slim duly ordered 1 Burma and 13 Indian Brigades to disengage and withdraw to temporary positions on the line of the Yin Chaung. This almost dry water course, lying 10 miles to the south of Magwe, followed a meandering south-easterly course from the Irrawaddy, some 30 miles south of the Yenangyaung oilfields, to Taungdwingyi. The only source of water north of the Yin Chaung was at the Pin Chaung, just to the north of Yenangyaung. Slim also transferred two battalions from 17 Indian Division to Scott. Slim's units were now becoming dangerously depleted as casualties and sickness ate away at his force, a factor that had a depressive effect on the morale of those remaining. The Cameronians, for example, even after it had been reinforced following the battle for Shwedaung, had fallen to only 215 men. On the same day 48 Indian Brigade and 7 Hussars withdrew from Kokkogwa to Taungdwingyi, flushed with their success against two battalions of 215 Regiment.

Slim realized that he now had no hope of holding the oilfields and on 15 April ordered their destruction. The following day he moved his HQ north to Gwegyo. Disaster now stalked 1 Burma Division. The troops were in a state close to exhaustion, and the heat, lack of water, constant harassment from the air and relentless demoralization of retreat conspired to force Scott to consider resting his troops before continuing the withdrawal to the Pin Chaung. Not realizing how close the Japanese were to cutting him off from his escape route, Scott decided to take the risk.

But it was a near-fatal error. In the early hours of 16 April Sakurai used the opportunity to outflank Scott's division to the east, infiltrating a whole regiment in small groups through Scott's thinly held defences in a race to slam shut the Pin Chaung gate. At the same time, attacks were made on 1 Burma and 13 Indian Brigades' hastily prepared positions on the Yin Chaung. The Yin Chaung proved to be nothing like the obstacle Scott had hoped for, and the retreating 1 Burma Division was too exhausted and had too few resources to cover every part of it. Both brigades were unable to hold the Japanese attack and were pushed back, withdrawing during the remainder of the night to the Kadaung Chaung, which followed the southern outskirts of Yenangyaung. While this attack was underway, Sakurai's outflanking force managed to get a force across the Pin Chaung and cut the road running north out of Yenangyaung to Kyaukpadaung. Another block was quickly placed at the village of Twingon, south of the ford, and a strong force put on the ford itself. Scott's only escape route to the north was now blocked.

Worse was to come. During the oppressively hot day that followed (17 April), Sakurai managed to insert troops into Yenangyaung itself by boats from the Irrawaddy. Not only was Scott now cut off from the north, at the Pin Chaung, and pursued from the rear, but the Japanese were also now in Yenangyaung itself.

The withdrawal of 1 Burma Division into the Yenangyaung pocket over the period 17 and 19 April, and into the trap Sakurai had set for it, was the severest trial yet faced by Slim's troops. It turned out to be not a battle for the oilfields, as these had already been destroyed, but rather a battle for the survival of the entire division. A taste of the agonies to come had been provided by the withdrawal from Prome to Allanmyo over a week earlier, but this was far worse. For much of the route to Yenangyaung, 'the scrub and occasional palm trees ceased and the country was bare and shadeless', recalled Ian Lyall Grant. 'Moreover, it was very broken with small hills and deep nullahs, and marching off the road became impracticable.'[9] There was virtually no fresh water, as the east bank of the Irrawaddy, the only source of water, was now in Japanese hands.

Although having denied Iida the opportunity to exploit the wealth of the oilfields, it was now clear to Slim that with 1 Burma Division on the verge of extinction, Iida was likely to take advantage of Slim's weakening west flank to make a powerful thrust up the Irrawaddy to threaten Mandalay. It was crucial therefore that Scott hold on for as long as he could. Despite his earlier experience with the promise of Chinese assistance for the defence of Taungdwingyi, Slim realized that with no reserve of his own, Scott's only hope of relief lay in assistance from the Chinese. If he could engineer a Chinese attack into the pocket, across the Pin Chaung, combined with a breakout attack by 1 Burma Division, Scott might have a chance of escape. Nothing else looked likely to succeed.

Fortunately, Stilwell was able to comply with Slim's request for urgent assistance and gave him 38 Chinese Division, the Salt Guards.[10] This was commanded by one of Chiang Kai-shek's ablest commanders, Lieutenant General Sun Lijen.[11] Slim rated Sun highly, considering him 'a good tactician, cool in action, very aggressively minded, and, in my dealings with him, completely straightforward.' At midnight on 16 April Sun received an order from General Lo Cho-yin, 'to dispatch his 113th Regiment to Kyaukpadaung, there to be commanded by the British General Slim'. Sun's friend, Dr Ho-Yungchi, recorded that by 3 a.m. he had arrived at Lo's HQ at Pyawbe to discuss the order. Lo explained that the British were in serious trouble 'in the oil town of Yenangyaung and had sent repeated requests for help.' By 6.30 a.m. it was agreed that Sun would personally take command of 113 Regiment, while the two remaining regiments stayed to defend Mandalay. Sun and 1,121 men of 113 Regiment (commanded by Colonel Liu Fang-wu) arrived at Kyaukpadaung on the morning of 17 April. Slim recalled:

> The situation was not encouraging, and I was greatly relieved to hear that 113 Regiment of the Chinese 38 Division was just arriving at Kyaukpadaung. I dashed off in my jeep to meet their commander and give him his orders... this was the first time I had had Chinese troops under me... I got to like all, or almost all, my Chinese very much. They are a likeable people and as soldiers they have in a high degree the fighting man's basic qualities – courage, endurance, cheerfulness, and an eye for country.

Slim, partly as he admits to gain Sun's confidence, placed all his available tanks and artillery under Sun's direct command. Despite the initial anguish of Brigadier Anstice, the arrangement worked remarkably well. But it was not simply good politics: unity of command for all forces involved in the battle required a single commander and a clear, unambiguous chain of command. Slim could conceivably have taken command himself but this may, perversely, have served to prevent Sun's troops from fighting at their best.

Slim's plan was for 38 Chinese Division to attack from the north on the morning of 18 April, while 1 Burma Division, within the pocket, fought its way out. The heat was intense, a thick pall of black smoke lying over the battlefield from the burning oil wells. There was no water. The Chinese attempt did not succeed, Japanese machine guns having full rein over the ford and village at Twingon. The wounded lay untreated, and men were beginning to die from the heat. To make matters worse, Japanese machine gun and artillery fire played constantly over the exposed positions to which Scott's beleaguered and depleted units now clung desperately, although there was a welcome respite from air attack during the day.

Scott sought Slim's permission in the late afternoon of 18 April to break out of the pocket that night across the Pin Chaung. It would be fraught with risk and would result in Scott's abandonment of all his remaining vehicles and heavy weapons. But Slim held out one last hope that he could break the Japanese stranglehold and relieve Scott's division. Using the radio truck belonging to 2 Royal Tank Regiment (2RTR), now his only means of communication with the troops in the pocket, Slim asked Scott to hold on until the following morning, when a further attack over the Pin Chaung towards Twingon by 38 Chinese Division was planned. If this went well, as Slim hoped it would, it would prove decisive in securing the relief of Scott's division. 'I was afraid, too', wrote Slim, 'that if our men came out in driblets as they would in the dark, mixed up with Japanese, the Chinese and indeed our own soldiers, would fail to recognize them and their losses would be heavy.'

Scott and Slim were old and close friends, and a sentimental response would have been for Slim to agree with Scott's desperate request to withdraw. Major Brian Montgomery, the Intelligence Staff Officer in Slim's tiny headquarters (and brother of the future Field Marshal), watched and listened to Slim talking into the microphone in the back of the radio truck, telling Scott to hold on. He recorded 'how gently and courteously he talked to Scott, never relaxing the iron grip of authority but never domineering or dictating.'[12] Trusting therefore to the promise of relief the next morning, Scott agreed to hold on, and 1 Burma Division dug into its tenuous positions on the eastern outskirts of Yenangyaung. The Japanese kept up constant pressure on the perimeter throughout the remainder of the day and during the night that followed.

Slim, and most other British accounts, including the Indian and British Official Histories, record that the promised attack did not take place in the morning of 19 April as planned, finally going in at 3 p.m., when Colonel Liu's 113 Regiment successfully captured the ford and penetrated into Yenangyaung.[13] The suggestion is that the delay to the Chinese attack imperilled further Bruce Scott's weakened division. Slim attempted to soften the criticism by talking up the bravery of the Chinese troops. 'When the Chinese did attack, they went in splendidly', he wrote. 'They were thrilled at the tank and artillery support they were getting and showed real dash. They took Twingon, rescuing some two hundred of our prisoners and wounded. Next day, 20 April, Sun's Chinese 38 Division attacked again and with tanks penetrated into Yenangyaung itself, repulsing a Japanese counterattack. The fighting was severe, and the Chinese acquitted themselves well, inflicting heavy losses, vouched for by our own officers.' Chinese and Japanese accounts dispute this narrative, not in terms of the effectiveness of the attack, but its timing. A range of compelling sources assert that Chinese troops were in Twingon by the early morning of 19 April.[14] Indeed, the US account is very different to the British:

The Chinese (113th Regiment) attacked into Yenangyaung at 0800 on 19 April, expecting to meet the Burma Division there. Instead, they found the Japanese entrenched in five strong points. By 1130 three were taken, but there was no contact with the exhausted Burma Division. That force had managed to hold during the night of the 18–19th, though to the south it was now in contact with elements of the 215 Regiment. An attack toward the ford in the morning made little progress, some of the troops were demoralized. Another attack planned for later in the morning was cancelled for fear it might lead to an inadvertent clash with the Chinese. Unknown to the Burma Division, a renewed Chinese attack by 1500 was making steady progress. To meet it, the Japanese shifted some of their men, leaving a gap. Consequently, when the tanks with the Burma Division were finally ordered to leave the road and look for a way out to the east over the oxcart tracks, at about 1300 they reported an unguarded track, and by using it, a part of the Burma Division with some tanks and vehicles was able to escape to the north. About 1600 under the force of the Chinese attack the Japanese fell back to the south and east, and the rest of the division was withdrawn over the black-top road. For its escape the division paid with most of its motor transport, its 40mm anti-aircraft guns, most of its 3-inch mortars, eight cannon, four tanks, and 20 percent casualties.[15]

What accounts for this disparity? Is it significant, given the description of this delay in British sources? Was Slim wrong? The first thing to observe is that Slim was not at his HQ near the pocket on 19 April, called away to a conference at Pyawbe by Alexander, and so did not observe the attack – and the alleged delay – at first hand. It is likely that the information that the Chinese had delayed their attack was not wrong, but it related to a small, perhaps minor section of the attacking force involved in a 'renewed Chinese attack at 1500'. The main force, as Japanese and Chinese accounts confidently suggest, was in fact in Twingon by about 8 a.m. that morning, and in the confusion and fog of war this information never got back to HQ 1 Burma Corps and was not recorded in the 1 Burma Division War Diary. Meanwhile, the attack the British recorded was an additional one later that day, and not the primary one undertaken first thing that morning. Slim's material is corroborated by too many original accounts on the British side to be suggested as erroneous, but so too are the Chinese and Japanese accounts. It seems probable therefore that both are true.

The result was that the CEF, and General Sun Lijen and Colonel Liu in particular, have never received full approbation for their remarkable success in the battle of Yenangyaung, a victory that saved 1 Burma Division – and 1 Burma Corps – from annihilation at the hands of the Japanese 33 Division, and allowed the remnants to limp home to India the following month. It was achieved at the loss of 204 men killed and 318 wounded, a desperately high casualty rate.

While 33 Division had failed to seize the oilfields intact, they had still inflicted a severe defeat on 1 Burma Division. Slim returned from Pyawbe in the evening in time to watch the survivors of Scott's division come out of the pocket. It was a moving experience. 'The haggard, red-eyed British, Indian and Burmese soldiers who staggered up the bank were a terrible sight,' he recalled, 'but every man I saw was still carrying his rifle. The two brigades of the division had reached Yenangyaung at a strength of not more than one'. Ho-Yungchi nevertheless recorded that the otherwise incomprehensible Britishers (his account is full of wild accusations of anti-Chinese behaviour by Cowan and Alexander) were delighted with their Chinese comrades, calling out such greetings as 'ting hao', 'China wan sui' and 'the Generalissimo wan sui' as they passed, grimy and exhausted, across the Pin Chaung.[16] Feelings of British perfidy and arrogance were sealed by announcement by All-India Radio that the British had successfully extricated themselves from the Yenangyaung pocket, making no mention of their Chinese saviours. Nevertheless, the depth of British–Chinese cooperation was reinforced at the end of the battle, when the Chinese troops clubbed together to provide the 85 men of Major Mark Rudkin's tank squadron of 2RTR with a rupee each as a token of their appreciation for their cooperation during the battle. The 'gesture was very touching, especially as the Chinese were paid next to nothing. So ended the only occasion in history when British troops were directly under Chinese command.'[17]

8

Exodus

At the Pyawbe conference Alexander had sought to reinforce the need to hold a defensive line running through Chauk, Kyaukpadaung, Meiktila and Thazi. Slim, however, was convinced that the effort required to ensure the creation and maintenance of a viable defence line would be wasted without a serious attempt to counterattack the advancing Japanese. With 33 Division investing Yenangyaung, Slim reiterated forcefully the need for a powerful counterattack against Sakurai in the Irrawaddy Valley, and argued that 17 Indian Division should be allowed, with Stilwell's help, to attack westwards. Only a single, concerted offensive against 33 Division, he argued, promised to do anything to halt the Japanese advance. If successful it would allow the British to transfer support to the Chinese in the Sittang Valley. The only alternative to offensive activity of this type was to continue to fight separate actions across the whole of the front, a situation Iida would exploit to his own advantage. Slim was simply repeating his arguments of the previous week, arguments which Alexander had at that time rejected. However, it is unlikely that Slim realized at the time the extent to which Sakurai was being supplied by boat up the Irrawaddy and was thus less vulnerable to counterattack than Slim expected because he did not have an extensive, road-bound logistical 'tail'. Slim acknowledged openly that his hopes for a counter-offensive were ambitious, and often little more than 'a house of cards'. Why, then, did he repeatedly insist on launching attacks? Without clarity regarding the ultimate purpose of the Burma Army, and if his task was to deny the Japanese from seizing central Burma, he had only two choices. The first was to find a place of strategic importance that could be defended by all of Alexander's forces, including the CEF, where troops could be concentrated, and Iida drawn into decisive battle. This, in 1942, was a pipe dream. The only place of truly strategic importance, the acquisition of which was vital to Iida's plan, was Lashio. Any other location that the British might choose to defend, including Mandalay, could simply be bypassed. In any case, the military resources available to create such a defensive bastion – including air power – simply did not exist in 1942. The other option was to attempt to stymie Iida's relentless and multi-faceted advance by means of offensive action.

In the face of these arguments Alexander gave way. He directed that Burma Corps, with Stilwell's help, launch an offensive on 22 April against what was assumed to be the exposed Japanese flank running south along the Irrawaddy from Yenangyaung. There was a sting in the tail, however. Alexander continued to refuse to release 17 Indian Division from Taungdwingyi. This left only Scott's battered division, which now amounted to not much more than a brigade, and which was largely unfit for further action, supplemented by any units Stilwell could provide. Without the support of 17 Indian Division, the impact of any attack was never going to be significant. Stilwell was nevertheless eager to contribute. He agreed that Sun's 38 Chinese Division be placed under Slim's command and he also allocated 200 Division and one regiment of 22 Division. Stilwell planned, at the same time, to counterattack with Fifth Chinese Army south of Pyinmana.

However, between 18 and 20 April disaster struck again. The Japanese proceeded to break through in the east at Loikaw and Pyinmana on Alexander's eastern flank, effectively negating Slim's plans. The Sixth Chinese Army fell apart with such alarming speed that Stilwell had to reinforce it with 200 Division, the same troops who only three weeks before had been forced out of Toungoo and who were now earmarked for Slim's counter-offensive. In desperation, as the Japanese drove through the Chinese Sixth Army in the east in mid-April with little effective opposition, Stilwell took personal command of the remnants of a Chinese division at Taunggyi on 23 and 24 April, and through gallant personal leadership led a counterattack that drove the Japanese back and recaptured the towns of Ho Pon and Loilem, and killed some 500 of the enemy.

With the threat of a wide envelopment deep into the Shan States, Slim's hoped-for offensive against 33 Division now had to be abandoned and his forces rapidly rearranged to meet the requirements of the deteriorating situation. As had been clear from the outset of the withdrawal from Rangoon, the ability of the Japanese to turn either the Sittang or the Irrawaddy fronts would make the other untenable. The security of central and northern Burma depended on both fronts being held together. Now, with the eastern flank apparently shattered, Slim's position on the opposite flank was impossible to sustain. It looked increasingly inevitable that continued fighting was useless, and the only choice confronting Alexander was to withdraw his troops from Burma entirely. Wavell and Alexander could also see the writing was on the wall for the Burma Army. Iida enjoyed every advantage in 1942.

Alexander had received the first written directive from Wavell since 4 March on 18 April, the day before the Pyawbe conference. This gave instructions as to what he was to do if the situation necessitated a wholesale evacuation of Burma. Alexander was instructed to keep in close touch with Stilwell's Fifth and Sixth Chinese Armies, to which were to be attached one of Slim's brigades, to cover the route that led from Kalewa through to Tamu in Manipur and to retain as many options as possible to facilitate future offensive operations into Burma. He was also instructed to maintain the integrity of his fighting troops so that a 'force in being' could eventually be withdrawn for the defence of eastern India.

There were two possible routes back to India. The first, and least practicable, was in the far north, via Mogaung or Myitkyina through the Hukawng Valley to Ledo. While there was a good road and railway link with Myitkyina, the route into Ledo thereafter was by foot only, through the Hukawng Valley. The area was remote, mountainous and interspersed by rivers passable only with considerable difficulty. This was the route chosen by many escaping civilians, and many thousands of those unable to escape by air from Myitkyina had died in its wooded vastness.[1] The second was the cross-country route that led north-west from Shwebo to Kalewa on the Chindwin, through the notoriously malarial Kabaw Valley to Tamu in Assam, and thence to Imphal. The latter was the closest and made the most sense for Burma Corps, were the decision made to withdraw.

On 23 April Alexander gave Slim and Stilwell orders for the further defence of Burma. Even at this stage Alexander was hopeful that Mandalay could be held, and a withdrawal to India unnecessary. He ordered Burma Corps to hold the area west of the Mu River, with 1 Burma Division on both sides of the Chindwin River, a strong element covering the exposed Myittha (also called the Gangaw) Valley which ran northwards to Kalewa. Anstice's 7 Armoured Brigade, together with Sun's 38 Chinese Division, were to hold the area between the Irrawaddy and the Mu River, while 22, 28 and 96 Chinese Divisions were to hold the area south of Mandalay, including the crossings over the Myitnge River. So that there was to be no repeat of the Sittang experience, Alexander ordered that in the event of its defences becoming untenable his forces were to withdraw across the Irrawaddy in the Mandalay area and the Ava Bridge, the only one to span the river, to be destroyed.

Despite Alexander's optimism, however, the situation on his left flank continued to deteriorate. Only two days later he recognized that he now was faced with the evacuation of Burma. Alexander, Slim and Stilwell met again at the small town of Kyaukse, 30 miles south of Mandalay, on 25 April. All were agreed that the events of the past week meant that it was not possible for either the British or the Chinese to retain any significant forces in northern Burma, and the only option left to them was a complete withdrawal to Assam and China.

It was a momentous decision. For the first time during the campaign, a clear objective had been determined. There was no time to be lost. Indeed, the withdrawal north of the Irrawaddy began that night, and was to be complete within a week, after which a general withdrawal to India and China began. The decisive issue during the first stage was speed in getting all elements of the British and Chinese armies safely across the Irrawaddy before Iida had the chance to catch Alexander with his back to the river.

On returning to his HQ at Taungtha, Slim issued his orders for the first phase of the withdrawal, which was to recover Burma Corps to the north side of the Irrawaddy while providing rearguard security for the withdrawal of the scattered and collapsing Fifth Chinese Army. Slim's plan was for 38 Chinese Division to cover Kyaukpadaung, while 1 Burma Division completed reorganizing itself following the escape from Yenangyaung prior to moving on Taungtha. 17 Indian Division was to move immediately from Taungdwingyi to Meiktila to allow 22 and 96 Chinese Divisions to complete their withdrawal northwards from Meiktila.

The Fifth Chinese Army was already reeling from the Japanese offensive and needed protection as it attempted to move northward and safely cross the Irrawaddy. The use of Burma Corps as a secure rearguard for the Chinese paid an immediate dividend over the following days, as the Japanese applied pressure across the front to unbalance Alexander's defence of the Irrawaddy. Slim pays tribute in *Defeat into Victory* to Cowan's division and Anstice's armoured brigade for ensuring the success of this difficult rearguard action. Both formations had recovered much of their previous confidence, in large part due to the skilful handling of the battle by their respective commanders. Following the successful clearance of the Meiktila area, Slim ordered Cowan to withdraw north to the Irrawaddy through the towns of Wundin and then Kyaukse, which was to be held by 48 Indian Brigade.

The all-Gurkha 48 Indian Brigade and 7 Hussars had only just reached Kyaukse during the night of 26 April and were busy preparing a strong defensive position as the remainder of Cowan's division passed through the town on their way north. In the event this gave them the respite of only one day before Major General Mutaguchi Renya's 18 Division, yet unbloodied in Burma but glorying in its capture of Singapore, attacked the town on the evening of 28 April. The attack was launched amid a ferocious thunderstorm, but the defenders were well prepared, and Mutaguchi's confident soldiers were bloodily repulsed. The brigade positions emerged largely unscathed, and a counterattack on the morning of 29 April was successful in removing groups of Japanese from positions to the front of the town. However, the ever-reducing numbers brought about by daily increases in casualties across Burma Corps meant that even the most determined stand was not guaranteed to last for long, and, their task completed, the brigade, now only about 1,700 strong, withdrew from their positions that evening.

On the same day Slim received final instructions from Alexander for the evacuation to India. Alexander ordered Slim to place a 'strong detachment' to cover the Myittha Valley on the vulnerable western flank, and for the remainder of Burma Corps, including Sun's 38 Chinese Division, to withdraw on Kalewa through the rough and incomplete track that traversed the 120 dry and dusty miles from Ye-U on the eastern side of the river.

From his new HQ at Sagaing on the northern side of the Irrawaddy as the great river turns west from Mandalay, Slim issued his own instructions to Burma Corps. The troops of 1 Burma Division were to cross using several hastily prepared ferries at Sameikkon, while the remainder of Burma Corps, together with all vehicles, tanks and guns, were to cross over the Ava Bridge at Mandalay. Once over the Irrawaddy 2 Burma Brigade was to withdraw up the Myittha Valley to protect Slim's vulnerable western flank, while 1 Burma and 13 Indian Brigades withdrew to Kalewa following the course of the Chindwin River, the former by boat and the latter securing the river port of Monywa. This town lay some 50 miles north of the confluence of the Irrawaddy with the Chindwin and commanded all movement along the latter. The remainder of the corps was to hold the northern bank of the Irrawaddy and the road to Monywa against Japanese infiltration across the river for as long as was necessary. Thereafter Burma Corps would converge from its various approach marches on Kalewa, before re-joining for the final move up the malarial Kabaw Valley to Tamu for the relative safety of Manipur.

On the surface the plan sounded simple, but the task facing Alexander and Slim was vast. The Burma Army was exhausted. The physical geography of the region was daunting, and the monsoon approached. The harsh reality, however, was that without enough aircraft to evacuate the army, together with the thousands of pitiful refugees who continued to clog the few dusty tracks that led to safety over the mountains, Alexander and Slim had no choice. Walking to India by the most direct route was the only way to save what remained of the Burma Army. It was march or die, and it had to be completed before the monsoon broke in all its destructive ferocity in mid-May.

Slim's skilful handling of the Irrawaddy crossings and the rearguard actions that protected the crossings from interference by the Japanese averted a repeat of the disastrous Sittang experience. Despite some nervous moments, such as the discovery that the maximum capacity of the two cantilevered roads on the Ava Bridge was a mere 6 tons, while the Stuart tanks of 7 Armoured Brigade weighed some 13 tons each, the crossings were successfully completed and the central spans of the Ava Bridge were blown into the fast-flowing waters of the river at midnight on 30 April. 1 Burma Division, including 500 oxen and 250 bullock carts, successfully crossed the Irrawaddy by ferries at Sameikkon on 28 April. In contrast to the chaos of the pre-Sittang days, the Burma Corps' conduct of the retreat was masterful. Nothing, however, could stop the relentless advance of Iida's victorious legions, all somewhat astonished at the progress they were making, the sometimes-rapturous support they were receiving from the Burmese they encountered and the speed with which the once-vaunted Western empire was collapsing at the point of their bayonets.

As this evacuation was taking place, the Japanese seized Lashio on 29 April, cutting the Burma Road and opening the way to Bhamo and Myitkyina, making it doubly necessary for the whole Burma Army to make its way to India with the greatest of speed.

Despite the successful crossing of the Irrawaddy, disaster continued to stalk Burma Corps. After crossing the river, Scott despatched 2 Burma Brigade from Pakokku on the evening of 28 April on the first part of its journey to the Myittha Valley, which ran due north to Kalewa some 60 miles west of the Chindwin. The security of the extreme western flank of the Burma Army's withdrawal route was vital, as without this protection Slim was concerned that Iida might outflank him by sending a force up the Myittha Valley to seize Kalemyo before Slim could withdraw his troops to the town from the east bank of the Chindwin.

However, worrying about the security of his flank presented another, potentially catastrophic problem in the area between Pakokku on the Irrawaddy, and Monywa on the Chindwin. Slim had planned to protect Monywa from a Japanese incursion up the west bank of the Chindwin. But instead of making for Monywa with best speed after successfully crossing the Irrawaddy on 28 April, Scott allowed the remainder of his exhausted division (1 Burma and 13 Indian

Brigades) to rest on the north bank of the Irrawaddy on 29 and 30 April. The division did not continue its withdrawal to Monywa until late on 30 April. Alexander was content to allow this delay because it gave an opportunity for the stream of wounded and the thousands of refugees cluttering the withdrawal routes to get a head start before the main body of the army withdrew.

But it was the second mistake of this kind – the first being Yenangyaung – by Scott. The departure of 2 Burma Brigade for Pauk on 28 April allowed the road leading from Pakokku to Monywa to remain unprotected throughout the period to 30 April. The route to Monywa along the west bank of the Chindwin was thus wide open for exploitation by the Japanese. The Japanese seized the opportunity they were offered. Following his failure to destroy 1 Burma Division at Yenangyaung, and his subsequent failure to trap Alexander on the south side of the Irrawaddy, Iida had ordered his four divisions on 26 April 'to strike wide and deep in [the] rear of the Allied forces, so as to cut their lines of retreat and thus destroy them in one blow.'[2] 33 Division was to form the left flank of the Japanese advance with the object of preventing Alexander from withdrawing his troops successfully to India, tasked with seizing Monywa and Ye-U. 55 Division was to form the right flank with the objective of advancing on Myitkyina. In the event Sakurai drove his increasingly exhausted 33 Division so hard that it occupied Pakokku on the evening of 28 April, only a few hours after Bourke had left the town. Surprised to see that the town lay undefended and suspecting that the door to Monywa might be wide open, the regimental commander trucked an advance guard up the road to the point where, 45 miles later, the road came to a halt in the jungle opposite the unsuspecting town of Monywa. It was dusk on Thursday 30 April.

The regimental commander's enthusiasm now got the better of him, and that night he attacked Monywa with artillery, mortar and machine gun fire from the west bank of the Chindwin, revealing his presence many hours before he tried to cross the river to Monywa itself. At his HQ some miles to the north of the town on the Monywa–Ye-U Road, Slim first feared that the outbreak of firing indicated that Monywa had already been lost. Alive to the serious threat this would now pose to Shwegyin–Kalewa and the prospect yet again of looming disaster, Slim ordered 1 Burma Division immediately to recapture the town. He also ordered Cowan to divert a battalion of 48 Indian Brigade, as well as the entirety of 63 Indian Brigade, together with a squadron of tanks, to gather at Chaungu, 15 miles south of Monywa, in order to assist Scott. The remainder of 17 Indian Division were instructed to make best speed to Ye-U to prepare for what would now be a rapid evacuation to Shwegyin, the river port on the Chindwin a few miles to the south of Kalewa. Slim then gathered up some 300 stragglers in the vicinity and sent them on to Monywa. Scott now had three brigades assembling, albeit all very weak, with which to attack and recover Monywa the next morning.

Additionally, in order to expedite the withdrawal of the corps to Kalewa once the situation in Monywa had stabilized, Slim advised Major General Tom Winterton, Alexander's Chief of the General Staff, to commandeer all vehicles, dump their loads and personnel and send them on to Shwegyin. Winterton was later to recall, 'it was this action that, above all else, saved the bulk of the Burma Army from being captured. As it was, the Japanese were beaten to Shwegyin, where transhipment across the Chindwin had to take place, by the very shortest of short heads.'[3]

Early on the morning of 1 May the Japanese crossed the river and attacked Monywa, dispersing Scott's HQ and occupying the town. The situation was complicated by the fact that the town was considerably swollen by refugees and 2,000 rear echelon staff awaiting evacuation upriver to Kalewa. 63 Indian Brigade counterattacked from the south in the morning but was unable to penetrate the town. Alexander and Stilwell met at Ye-U on 1 May and, in view of the situation at Monywa, agreed that the withdrawal from the Irrawaddy Line should begin without further delay. Stilwell also agreed that 7 Armoured Brigade, which had been assisting in the withdrawal of the Fifth Chinese Army through the Shwebo area, should be allowed to re-join Burma Corps for the withdrawal to India. Following his failure to eject the Japanese from the town on 1 May, Scott planned to attack Monywa on 2 May with all the forces at his disposal. 63 Indian Brigade and a squadron of 7 Hussars were to attack astride the railway from the south, with 13 Indian Brigade attacking from the east.

The attack, although vigorously pressed, failed a second time to eject the Japanese from the town. As the battle continued during the afternoon an order to withdraw, purporting to come from Alexander himself, led Scott to break off the engagement and move 1 Burma and 63 Indian Brigades north to Alon. But no such order was issued by Alexander or his HQ. It is possible that the message emanated from the Japanese who were now very experienced in monitoring and interfering with Burma Corps signals from British tanks captured at Shwedaung. If the order had been genuine, it would have been given to Scott by Slim in the first instance. Slim, however, knew nothing of it. That night 16 Indian Brigade was sent to secure the crossing at Shwegyin, as control of Monywa now gave the Japanese control of the direct route up the Chindwin to this vital crossing.

In all the options of difficulties facing Slim as he carefully husbanded his diminishing resources back behind the safety of the Chindwin, Sakurai's exploitation of the unguarded gap at Pakokku and the rapid advance on Monywa were not unforeseen. Slim knew from the outset just how vital the security of Monywa was to his plan for the withdrawal of Burma Corps. The retention of the town was important to move considerable quantities of stores, heavy equipment and troops upriver to Kalewa without the necessity of carting them laboriously over the jungle track from Shwebo to Ye-U and thence to Shwegyin–Kalewa. For the same reason it was important that the Japanese were denied control of the town, as otherwise they could use the Chindwin to insert troops to outflank the Burma Army toiling slowly overland to Kalewa. Alexander and Slim both recognized this, as Alexander's original instructions on 25 April to place a brigade on both sides of the Chindwin at Monywa indicate. Slim's instructions on 27 April could not have been clearer. Scott was directed to place a strong brigade group (13 Indian Brigade) on the west bank of the Chindwin at Monywa, and for the remainder of the division, less 2 Burma Brigade, together with a brigade group from 17 Indian Division, to hold the Chindwin – on both banks – as far south as possible.

Likewise, there was no miscalculation in Slim's decision to send more than a 'strong detachment' to guard the Myittha Valley, as Alexander had first wished. The risk that Iida would exploit Slim's western flank to seize Kalemyo by *coup de main* before the Allies could withdraw through the town and up the Kabaw Valley to Tamu demanded that it be guarded well. The fact that this potential risk demanded some form of insurance by Slim, even though in the event Iida's main effort did not fall in this area, was prudent generalship. Similarly, in sending Bourke to guard the Myittha Valley, Slim did not assume any lessening of the importance of Pakokku as guardian of the approach to Monywa. The problem stemmed solely from Scott's failure to hold Pakokku at the same time as he inserted the required protection into Monywa itself. The door left open at Pakokku after Bourke's departure for Pauk, and before Monywa and the west bank of the Chindwin could be properly secured, created the difficulties that now confronted Burma Corps.

Characteristically Slim blamed himself for this failure to keep this door closed, for not delaying the march of 2 Burma Brigade until Monywa had been secured. 'Threats were growing in many directions with competing claims on our slender resources', he wrote. 'Forgetting the speed with which the Japanese might come up the river by boat, I chose to meet the wrong one, and we paid heavily for my mistake.' Scott, as the divisional commander, should have taken adequate steps to ensure the security of the vital road that ran alongside the west bank of the Chindwin to Monywa. It was another example of the mistakes that were forced on the retreating British commanders by the relentless pressure of an enemy able to choose where and when to strike.

On 3 May 1 Burma Division and 7 Armoured Brigade began the withdrawal to Ye-U, the start of the track to the Chindwin. Most of Burma Corps reached Ye-U by 4 May following a 100-mile forced march from Monywa, in desperate conditions, harassed for much of the time from the air. The army was now in a pitiful state, with battalions reduced to scores rather than hundreds of men. There were three immediate threats to the survival of Burma Corps in what was now a race for Kalewa and the safety of India. The first was that Sakurai would manage to cut off Slim's forces on the Ye-U track from Shwegyin and Kalewa, by inserting troops up the Chindwin. This would act to cut the British escape route to India and bring the retreat to an ignominious end. But the second threat was equally pressing. The monsoon was due to break in mid-May and would make the track to Tamu impassable to vehicles and the task of evacuation and resupply of the army immeasurably more difficult. The third problem was that of supply. As soon as the decision to withdraw to India had been taken, great efforts were made to stock the route to Kalewa with the provisions required for the retreating army, and similar action was taken from the Imphal end of the track. This was not easy, and as a precaution the troops were placed on half rations. The task was immensely hampered by the fact that many thousands of desperate refugees, many starving and diseased, were using this track to escape into India. Those who couldn't go any further died, singly or in small groups, along the route.

Slim wasted no time in Ye-U. The withdrawal to Shwegyin and Kalewa got underway even before the evacuation of Monywa had been completed. The urgent task now was to get all his units, including vehicles and heavy equipment, to Shwegyin and then ferried across the Chindwin to Kalewa with the greatest possible speed. With Iida on his heels, any delay would prove finally to be fatal. But the track was atrocious. For the most part it was unmade and difficult for wheeled vehicles and was made passable to vehicles only through strenuous efforts by engineers. Many sections of the route had no water.

Ever mindful of the Japanese penchant for inserting devastating blocks onto withdrawal routes, Slim ordered 17 Indian Division to picket the route to Pyingaing. Likewise, a plea by Alexander to GHQ India brought a series of successful British air attacks on the Chindwin between 3 and 5 May, which considerably delayed the Japanese advance up the river. To reduce pressure on the

Shwegyin–Kalewa crossing Slim ordered 1 Burma Brigade to branch north off the track at Pyingaing and make for Pantha, from where they successfully crossed the Chindwin on 13 May. The remainder of Burma Corps, with the ubiquitous 7 Armoured Brigade providing the rearguard, made direct for Shwegyin, which it reached between 8 and 9 May.

Shwegyin provided a small ferry service up the river to Kalewa, but the weight of thousands of pitiful refugees, together with the assembled units of Burma Corps, was too much for the limited capacity of the ferries, and the embarkation point at Shwegyin, known as the 'basin', became hopelessly clogged with the detritus of a defeated army. Refugees lay dying amid scores of abandoned civilian vehicles and military equipment. Shwegyin became the graveyard not merely for the British colonial project in Burma, but for the Burma Army: it was literally the end of the road for virtually all of Burma Corps' remaining vehicles, tanks, guns and other heavy equipment. What could not be carried to Kalewa had to be destroyed where it stopped. Only one Stuart light tank, the 'Curse of Scotland', made it across the Chindwin and into India.[4]

Just as Slim had feared, and despite a security screen in the jungle to the south, Sakurai managed to insert a battalion rapidly by boat, largely by luck, up the Chindwin. This arrived unnoticed on the hills to the south and east of the 'basin' at Shwegyin, early on 10 May. Slim, having inspected the ferrying arrangements upriver at Kalewa, landed just as the Japanese assault on the basin began. Battle was immediately engaged, but despite this display of Japanese initiative they were unable to penetrate the perimeter of 17 Indian Division's defence during the day, and the last desperate evacuation of stores and personnel continued amid constant fire.

Their presence, nevertheless, severely disrupted the pace and equanimity of the evacuation process. Cowan was forced to divert 48 Indian Brigade to support the defence of Shwegyin, but despite the attempts by the Japanese to break in, the ferries managed to continue shipping out personnel during the day. By 4 p.m., however, Cowan was told that only one more ferry would be made to Shwegyin. With no more reason to hold the position, he ordered the destruction of all remaining vehicles and equipment. As darkness fell and remaining troops prepared to march through the jungle along the east bank of the Chindwin to Kalewa, all remaining tanks and guns fired off their ammunition. By late on 11 May what remained of Burma Corps was safely on the west bank of the Chindwin. 2 Burma Brigade, after an agonizingly slow march for 200 miles through the Myittha Valley, during which movement was only possible at night, reached Kalemyo on 10 May.

Burma Corps now limped slowly into India through Tamu along the recently completed dry weather road to Imphal, having beaten the full force of the monsoon by a few days. The last unit of Burma Corps passed through Tamu on its way to Imphal on 19 May. Although mercifully now not pressed by the Japanese, Slim recalled this final part of Burma Corps' march into India as 'sheer misery'. The Japanese reached Kalewa on 14 May but were too exhausted themselves to follow across the Chindwin. They had achieved what Iida had set out to do and had done so in exemplary fashion. No army could have done more. Virtually all men of the Burma Army were sick with malaria, and while all were exhausted Slim noted proudly that the fighting elements marched into the Imphal plain as soldiers. 'On the last day of that nine-hundred-mile retreat I stood on a bank beside the road and watched the rear-guard march into India. All of them, British, Indian and Gurkha, were gaunt and ragged as scarecrows. Yet, as they trudged behind their surviving officers in groups, pitifully small, they still carried their arms and kept their ranks, they were still recognizable as fighting units. They might look like scarecrows, but they looked like soldiers too.' They had been defeated, he admitted, but not disgraced. 'Taffy' Davies watched Slim take the salute from the ragged remnants of Burma Corps as they marched into India, remarking afterward that 'I thought his eyes had misted a bit.'[5]

The withdrawal had been an incredible feat. Despite the humiliation and bitterness of defeat, Burma Corps had not collapsed or surrendered, and for the most part had held together under the most trying circumstances imaginable. As the Official British Historian asserted, 'the Army in Burma, without once losing its cohesion, had retreated nearly one thousand miles in some three and a half months – the longest retreat ever carried out by a British Army – and for the last seven hundred miles had virtually carried its base with it.'[6] It is possible to talk of the defeat in 1942 as a profound political failure. It was a military defeat for the British, Indian and Burmese troops caught up in the campaign, but after the Sittang Bridge it is notable that the Burma Army had not been destroyed. It had, in fact, withdrawn in reasonably good order, under the command of Alexander and Slim, obeying Wavell's injunction to retain a 'force in being' in eastern India on which to rebuild. Equally, it proved to be an important schooling for British commanders – Slim, Cowan and Scott in particular – in how to deal with the Japanese in battle. Certainly, Slim ended the retreat confident that with the right tools – trained soldiers, air power, effective weapons and equipment – a reconstituted British and Indian army could beat the Japanese at their own game. They were not invincible. But that was for tomorrow.

Trudging back into India, 26-year-old Captain Ian Lyall Grant recalled that during the long march to Imphal from Tamu in the last stages of the retreat, 'General Slim, riding in a jeep, had been much in evidence. He watched his troops intently, asking the name of each unit as it passed and making some encouraging remark. General Alexander did not appear. On the 20th he [Alexander] handed over command of the Burma Army to General Irwin of 4 Indian Corps in Imphal and then left to report to Wavell and return to England.'[7] What became known as the 'First Burma Campaign' marked Slim out as someone who refused to give up when all the facts seemed to indicate that there was no hope for his bedraggled and defeated forces. 'He was not afraid of anything,' recorded Stilwell, 'and he looked it.'[8] His composure made a dramatic and decisive impact on his men. Major 'Mad Mike' Calvert recalled watching Slim during the hot, dusty days of the withdrawal, the corps commander presenting 'an indomitable and unshaken front in the face of these disasters, and his rather ponderous jokes cheered his staff and commanders when they were at their lowest ebb'.[9] When Ian Lyall Grant met him during the second week of April 1942 with only six weeks of the retreat from Burma left to run, he was, despite the otherwise apparent hopelessness of the situation, buoyed up by Slim's calm reassurance that the situation, although bleak, was under control. After listening to Slim brief them, he and his fellows felt for the first time that they 'now had a leader who realised that new methods were required to counter Japanese tactics and was prepared to think them out.'[10] Morale in Burma Corps, despite some bitter blows, remained strong. The retreat had been a hard lesson in the fundamentals of leadership, and the experience reinforced Slim's determination thereafter to ensure that his men were commanded by the best leaders he could gather around him. Punch Cowan wrote to Hutton on 31 May with genuine pleasure at how his rebuilt 17 Indian Division had performed following the Sittang Bridge. 'It has come out as a first class fighting formation with 100 per cent morale, excellent spirit and a knowledge gained by experience that they can put it across the Jap.'[11] This was particularly important given that the Japanese did not encounter the well-trained regulars of the pre-war army, who were in North Africa and the Middle East, but the 'odds and sods' available at the time, thrown, entirely unprepared, into battle against a single-minded, better trained, better prepared and vastly better equipped enemy.[12] It was this fact to which Wavell and others in India hung. Better soldiers, better prepared, would undoubtedly prove themselves the equal of the Japanese if they had the chance, if they had commanders intelligent enough to adapt the way they fought to the new requirements placed on them. It was a small consolation for an otherwise humiliating defeat that many soldiers fought well, dominated the enemy in both ad hoc and set-piece engagements and came out of Burma with their morale intact. Wavell was, belatedly (in 1948), to acknowledge that Burma Corps had, in the circumstances, performed probably better than expected:

> There is no doubt... that although some units and some individuals may have failed, the Army in Burma, as a whole, fought extremely well. For many months they withstood the onslaught of superior numbers, with little reinforcement, no rest, and practically no hope of relief. During most of the time they have suffered heavily from enemy air attack and have received little or no support from our own air forces. They have had no canteens, few amenities and practically all lost their complete kit early in the campaign. The climatic conditions have been very trying. The fall of Singapore has undoubtedly had a depressing effect on morale.[13]

This came later, however. At the time, it was the Indian Army and its 'sepoy generals' who were forced to take the blame for the loss of Burma. Churchill's animosity towards the Indian Army was partly to blame. His description of the retreat in his memoirs, for example, 'is lavish in praise of... Alexander – Churchill's favourite general and a Guardsman – but never mentions Slim, the real architect of the longest fighting withdrawal in British military history.'[14] Churchill was never persuaded of the military ability or war-winning capability of the Indian Army or of its generals. He had entered the war with this attitude, and nothing persuaded him that the Indian Army was anything other than an armed constabulary unable to do much more than undertake limited operations against second-tier enemies, like Japan.

9

Independence Armies

In Burma, the success of the Burma Independence Army in gathering recruits and gaining popular support for Burma's independence took everyone – Burmese, Japanese and British – by surprise. It demonstrated a significant anti-British (and anti-Chinese and anti-Indian) prejudice within the general population for it to secure perhaps as many as 5,000 recruits in the space of a few weeks. It was far too unwieldy, however, for it to be useful for the new occupiers of Burma, and in July the Japanese disbanded it and replaced it with a new, smaller Burma Defence Army, under the command of Aung San. A year later the BDA boasted a strength of 55,000 men.

Additional salt was further rubbed into Britain's wounds in 1942 by the fact that the Japanese were able to persuade large numbers of surrendered Indian personnel to turn their back on their erstwhile employers and take up arms against Britain. Following the urging of the Bengali separatist Rash Behari Bose ('Basu'), long resident in Japan and originator of the Indian National League, Major Fujiwara Iwaichi had originally been tasked with persuading the independence-minded elements of the Indian expatriate community living in Thailand, Malaya and Singapore to support the Japanese in event of war. What he actually managed to achieve, as the Commonwealth forces collapsed in the face of the Japanese onslaught in Malaya and surrendered at Singapore in February 1942, was an entire army sourced from the discombobulated mass of defeated members of the Indian Army, what was in 1944 to be named the Azad Hind Fauj (the Army of Free India) but which was initially called the Indian National Army (INA). The actions of a tiny diaspora of radically minded Indians coalesced serendipitously with British military failure in 1942 and with Japanese political ruthlessness: the INA, for all the genuineness of the nationalistic enthusiasm of some, became the tool of the Japanese. Fujiwara believed that a Japanese invasion would not be supported by prominent Indian nationalists such as Gandhi and Nehru and could even be counter-productive to Japanese plans for the downfall of the Raj. An invasion needed to be covered by a lie. Fujiwara's plan was that if and when the Japanese decided to invade India it would be the INA that should spearhead the advance, demonstrating to the Indian people that Japanese intentions were not aggressive or proprietary but designed merely to eject the British and to create an 'India for the Indians' under the benign watch of the Japanese.

Fujiwara's interest in the issue of Indian independence had begun the previous year, when in October 1941 he was sent to Saigon in command of a team of five officers and two Hindi-speaking interpreters, tasked with developing plans to win over expatriate Indian populations in South East Asia. His message was that the Japanese respected the nationalist aspirations of Asian people, supporting their struggle to free themselves from foreign oppression. The fatal irony that they would replace one form of colonialism with another was lost on most expatriate supporters of Indian independence at the time. It was certainly lost on Fujiwara, who believed passionately in his mission of deliverance, and in Japan's redemptive undertaking. Accompanying Yamashita's 25 Army in the invasion of Malaya in December 1941, Fujiwara instructed the Japanese, where possible, to separate Indian soldiers and officers from their British colleagues and not to treat the Indian officers as enemies. While their white officers had their heads cut off, Indian officers and NCOs were treated as friends. Weeks earlier Major Fujiwara had set up the headquarters of his 'Fujiwara Organization' (*Fujiwara Kikan*, or more commonly F-Kikan) in Alor Star and had begun the first sifting of Indian prisoners. One of the first was Captain Mohan Singh of 1/14 Punjab Regiment. Captured by Japanese troops after wandering in the jungle for several days following the disastrous Jitra battle – when British and Indian troops had been scattered in a matter of hours by fast-moving Japanese all-arms columns – Singh was taken to meet Fujiwara. Persuaded by the Japanese officer's overtures and depressed at the collapse of British arms, Mohan Singh had, by the end of December 1941, agreed to raise an army of volunteers rounded up from other dispirited Indian captives. In the next six weeks this group of men followed the advancing Japanese columns attempting, with some success, to persuade prisoners of war to cease fighting for the British, and to throw in their lot instead with the cause of Indian independence. By the time Singapore had been reached, Mohan Singh, by now thoroughly converted to the cause of creating an independence army, based soundly on Congress principles, had managed to recruit 2,500 of his comrades into the INA.

Then, two days after the British surrender of Singapore, the captive Indian soldiers were separated from their British officers and the troops of Australian and British units (who were marched east in the direction of Changi Prison) and paraded on the Farrer Park sports ground. There they were told by a British officer that as prisoners of war they were duty-bound to consider themselves under the authority of the Imperial Japanese Army. They were spoken to by Fujiwara himself, translations being made first into English and then Hindustani. Telling the vast crowd of subdued Indians of Japan's plans for the Asian Co-Prosperity Sphere, of the Japanese vision of a free India and of their plans to raise an army for the freedom of India, and of the fact that those who volunteered for this army would be treated not as POWs but as friends, Fujiwara then introduced Mohan Singh. Singh spoke briefly though passionately through the loudspeaker, inviting the troops to join the army he was going to build that would, with help from the Japanese, provide independence to India.

These combined messages were received well, and in some cases enthusiastically. Subedar Major Baboo Ram of 1/14 Punjab recalled Mohan Singh saying, 'We are forming an Indian National Army that will fight for free India. Are you prepared to join the Indian National Army?' According to Ram, 'the audience lifted up their arms, threw their turbans in the air, and showed great pleasure.'[1] Two of Singh's fellow officers from 1/14 Punjab, Captain Shah Nawaz and Lieutenant Gurbaksh Singh Dhillon, joined Singh. During 1942 some 40,000 Indian POWs joined the INA, representing 60 per cent of those captured in Malaya and Singapore, and a few recruits were raised from the expatriate Indian populations of Malaya and Singapore. Fifty per cent of the Indian officers and 25 per cent of the Viceroy's commissioned officers joined the INA. As the British struggled north to sanctuary in Manipur in 1942, the message the Japanese preached was that 'all Asians belonged to one family' in which Burma, for example, was to be reserved for the Burmese, and India for the Indians. To Indian soldiers the Japanese argued that only through supporting the Japanese would India receive its long-awaited independence. Their propaganda leaflets trumpeted, 'In India the opportunities to get freedom have arrived and the Indians rush to concentrate and sacrifice themselves with the movement bravely. Now is the time for you to do this work of resistance against your friend. Come and surrender yourself to the Japanese Army. The Japanese Army will safely protect you and will give you the way back to India.'

Over the airwaves from Berlin on Radio Free India came the voice of Subhas Chandra Bose, the exiled militant, charismatic Bengali Congress party leader (and enemy of Gandhi) and ex-mayor of Calcutta, urging Indians everywhere to support the cause of independence, an essential part of which was the removal, willing or otherwise, of the British.

It was hardly surprising that so many Indian soldiers were persuaded to throw their lot in with the victorious Japanese. The victor's propaganda was particularly appealing in the face of the humiliation of the British defeat and the irresistible charge that in poorly equipping and preparing them for the challenge of defending Malaya the British had let them down, sentiments which built on the innate, though latent, nationalism of many Indian officers.[2] 'The result was a defeat so resounding that the confidence of all Indians in their British leadership was badly shaken. The esprit of the army had revolved around a history of glorious victories. World War II was not even a glorious defeat.'[3] In the circumstances of the moment, facing the actual or imminent collapse of the Raj, the Japanese appeal made sense, and in this context it is hard to condemn men for determining that this was the moment to seek to create a new India. Most men who were committed to the idea of an India independent of Britain were sufficiently realistic in recognizing nevertheless that the Raj was the 'devil they knew' and were prepared to allow the natural process of political negotiation about the future governance of India to run its course. Indeed, many men who were emotionally, culturally and intellectually committed to the idea of India were at the same time loyal to the Raj because they believed that at the present point in time the British alone were able to advance India's national interests. The British knew this ambivalence well. A report written for GHQ New Delhi in late 1942 argued:

> We have by our policy towards India, bred a new class of officer who may be loyal to India and perhaps to [the] Congress [Party] but is not necessarily loyal to us. That support has not yet permeated through the rank and file who still retain the old loyalty. The basis of our problem is how to convince the politically minded younger generation that loyalty to India and to Indian interests is identical to loyalty to the Commonwealth...[4]

Prior to 1942 those Indian servicemen who thought about the subject were prepared to support the Raj in opposing what they regarded to be naked Japanese aggression, and those who had strongly nationalistic beliefs were ready to subordinate them for the duration of the conflict until the immediate danger was averted. Although the influence of nationalism in the army prior to 1939 was negligible, those who were nationally minded 'believed that collaboration would win concessions from Britain and eventual independence.'[5] However, for those captured by the Japanese a more immediate decision was required, challenging even the most loyal of servicemen to consider whether joining the INA could bring about a post-Raj settlement. Many were prepared to do so, although theirs was a cautious, pragmatic conversion and perhaps owed much to fear of remaining prisoners of war, with all the deprivations that would entail, for the duration of the war. After all, in 1942 it was clear to many, especially to those who had been involved in the defeats in Malaya, Singapore and Burma, that Britannia's centuries' old hegemony in Asia was over. What if that which the Japanese declared so emphatically was indeed true and the British were a spent force in the region? Was not this the time for all Asians to pull together and to create for themselves a future without the dead hand of the European colonialists? In any case, as Auchinleck acknowledged in 1946, presenting a view by no means widely accepted among British officers in the Indian Army, those soldiers who had been taken prisoner in Malaya and Singapore (but not the officers, whom Auchinleck accused of proving 'false to their trust') had not pledged their troth to Britain, but to India, and their primary loyalty – unlike British soldiers – was not to Britain, but to the officers of their regiment. They had no loyalty 'towards Britain, not as we understand loyalty.'[6] In the vast and rapid expansion of the Indian Army after 1939, when units were full of green and inexperienced recruits, it is unsurprising that Japanese propaganda had such an effect. David Omissi succinctly encapsulates the dichotomy that lay at the heart of the relationship between the Sepoy and the Raj: 'Indian soldiers were not simply the passive victims of colonial manipulation. The sepoys had their own objectives, pursued their own strategies and made their own choices. Like any collaborative structure, the relationship between the sepoy and the Raj could have broken down if either party had grown disenchanted.'[7]

This is precisely what happened in Malaya in 1942. For those Indian nationalists able to take advantage of the Japanese victory by supporting the INA, a great opportunity had arrived: to have the stain and humiliation of defeat removed and to form their own army. Nationalists had long sought first to emasculate the army, as a tool of imperialism. They supported attempts to change its nature, from its perceived mercenary status to something much more nationally representative in character. From the 1920s they sought to gain control of the army, through Indianization. They were not successful, the British conscious that control of the army determined control or otherwise of the empire.

Denied what they most desired – the tools of power, of which an army was a fundamental component – Indian nationalists now had the opportunity to create one of their own.

However, the Japanese, on the whole, when they considered the issue, saw in the INA merely the tools of some useful propaganda although there were a few – the young and idealistic Fujiwara among them – who took the slogan 'Asia for the Asiatics' more seriously than Tokyo itself was prepared to countenance in practice. There were significant factions in Tokyo and across the Imperial Army who considered it a mistake to consort with the INA: practical and unequivocal Japanese commitment to the INA, as opposed to more general support for the cause of Indian independence, was never anything other than lukewarm and self-serving. The demands of the INA leadership were accommodated when they suited the requirements of operational policy and did not prejudice the support required by regular Japanese formations.

For this reason, it didn't take very long for Mohan Singh's and Tokyo's ambitions to come into conflict. Singh's ambitions verged on the hubristic – he had promoted himself Major General, merged all officer ranks into one, removed separate messing arrangements for all ranks and classes, mixing Muslims and Hindus together for the first time – and the Japanese, who wanted subservience, found that they had had enough of his ambitions.[8] In December 1942 he was arrested and placed in custody on an island off Singapore, where he was to remain for the rest of the war. Singh's strongly nationalist, socially idealistic and egalitarian instincts did not fit with Tokyo's utilitarian vision for the INA, which was thereafter limited to a single division of 16,000 men (the other volunteers reverted to POW status). Size and numbers did not matter. What remained key was the propaganda effect of this 'nationalist' army on the men of the Indian Army, ruled as they were by the perfidious British. Why would anyone fight for foreigners, went the argument, when they could fight for India? Many of those who remained determinedly committed to their salt, largely forgotten in the post-1945 pro-INA euphoria that swept India, were executed by the Japanese. Their resistance to Japanese racial propaganda and refusal to bow down to the Japanese-scripted decolonization narrative, was an embarrassment to Japanese polity during the war, and Indian independence sensibilities after it. Likewise, that the men of the Indian Army already considered themselves to be fighting for India, rather than Britain, was not an answer that the INA propagandists, or their Japanese supporters, ever considered. Major Fujiwara was in any case posted to Burma, to serve on the staff of Major General Mutaguchi at Maymyo, on the cool periphery of the delightful Shan States, 4,000 feet up in the hills east of

Mandalay, and a new officer – Colonel Hideo Iwakuro – was given command of the Kikan for a time. Iwakuro had none of Fujiwara's idealism, seeing in the INA a more utilitarian agenda in support of the Imperial Japanese Army.

A new figurehead for a reincarnation of the INA was found, in the figure of Subhas Chandra Bose. He arrived in Japan from Germany in June 1943 after travelling halfway round the world first by German and then by Japanese submarine. Bose saw in his captured compatriots the ideal opportunity to secure the means – his very own army – to help secure his political ambition. His first task was to ensure that the Japanese deployed the INA in battle, for without military action to free India, the propaganda effect of this force would be limited. Indian blood needed to be spilled in order to create the conditions for Bose's revolution. In Nazi Germany, Bose had formed the Free India Legion, a brigade-sized group of Indians (about 4,500 strong) captured by the Germans in North Africa and persuaded to fight for the cause of Indian nationalism against the Allies. An initially sceptical Tōjō was taken aback by the frankness of Bose's question, on first arriving in Tokyo: 'Will Japan send soldiers to India or not?' Tōjō responded positively and in response to Bose's next question, 'Can Japan give unconditional help to the Indian independence movement?' the Japanese Prime Minister quickly replied in the affirmative. The newly formed Azad Hind Fauj now began to prepare for the *Challo Dilli* – the March on Delhi – which Bose confidently asserted would roll back the Raj. When the soldiers in the Indian Army came up against the passionate nationalists in his army, they would, he thought, as had Mohan Singh before him, change sides in such large numbers that the Azad Hind Fauj would lead the victorious Japanese Army all the way to Delhi.[9]

10

The Reason Why

The Japanese were thoroughly prepared for the rapid capture of Rangoon in 1942 and thereafter the offensive to seize central Burma. Much of the ground had been reconnoitred, intelligence gathered, plans made, troops trained and rehearsed. Iida's offensive stratagem was the driving charge (*Kirimomi Sakusen*), designed to establish and maintain a battlefield rhythm that would allow him to retain the initiative, overwhelming both the thinking and the fighting faculties of his enemy and focused on achieving his initial operational objective – Rangoon – above all else. The approach created a point of force designed to enable a breakthrough at the required (and weakest) point in the enemy's defence. The operational hallmarks of this approach were speed, surprise, the fixing and bypassing of enemy defences, and cutting the enemy's lines of communication and supply routes. The overriding principle was to apply constant and overwhelming pressure on the enemy to allow him no opportunity for rest, in effect to always operate faster than the enemy commander could react.[1] As a concept, *Kirimomi Sakusen* fitted perfectly with *dengekisen*, the Japanese transliteration of the German term blitzkrieg. The German experience in Poland and France in 1939 and 1940 fascinated Japanese society in 1940 and 1941, seeming to offer a way out of the imbroglio that was tying the army down in a slow, agonizing meatgrinder in China. In 1942 *dengekisen* appeared to be the answer to overwhelming a Western enemy, particularly one as weak as the British, French and Dutch, who had collapsed like a house of cards in Europe in 1940.[2]

It was the Japanese ability to move off-road, and onto jungle tracks for short periods of time to 'hook' behind British positions and to place roadblocks on their lines of communication, that created an atmosphere of confusion and uncertainty among British, Burmese and Indian troops, poorly trained in 1942 to deal with a fluid battlefield or anything other than a linear defence, and with an enemy that excelled in doing the unexpected. The tracks and paths they would use in Burma had long been reconnoitred during the years of peace by Japanese 'tourists' and salesmen. Early tactical lessons from the fighting in Malaya had already been disseminated to all units. They already knew that the act of infiltrating small groups of men through, around and behind enemy positions unsettled and confused the defenders. They would emerge from the jungle far to the rear of a defensive position to set up a block – sometimes merely a few logs covered by the fire of a handful of men with a machine gun and grenades – on the all-important road upon which the British relied for movement and supplies. The block would cut the rearward line of communication, and those affected would believe themselves cut off. Over time, recalled Slim, 'our troops and commanders began to acquire a road-block mentality which often developed into an inferiority complex.' The Japanese knew of and exploited the opportunities provided by operating at night. They would crawl up to the perimeter at night, call out in the enemy's language or languages, offering threats and inducements to surrender or issuing false commands. They would sometimes attempt to unsettle defenders by so-called 'jitter raids' to give a sense that the Japanese were far stronger than they were, and to persuade the enemy to unnecessarily expend their ammunition and reveal their positions. Moving quickly through thick jungle to appear far behind the 'front line', they would induce panic in rear-echelon and lines-of-communication troops.

In an army deficient in artillery and armour, it was the power, flexibility, energy and versatility of the infantry arm that gave Iida his success in 1942. Additionally, Iida's troops were used to operating together – infantry, armour (where it existed), artillery and air power – to a degree that was unheard of in the British services at the time. Likewise, the planning and the conduct of operations were jointly conceived and executed. Air and land operations were regarded by the joint army–air staff to be inseparable, and the Japanese showed special prowess in air-to-ground coordination, and in bringing down accurate mortar and artillery fire in support of infantry attacks.[3]

Much of the myth that was created as a result of British defeat in 1942, in both Malaya and Burma – that the Japanese were exquisite jungle warriors and that it was the lack of comparable jungle training that stymied the British Empire troops – was not true. Japanese troops were hardly better equipped to deal with the difficulties of jungle warfare than their opponents. The difference lay in their competent leadership, effective training and their aggressive approach to battle. They fought to win. Japanese soldiers had confidence in themselves, their leaders and their training, based on their experience in China and their thorough preparation for the invasion of South East Asia. It was this confidence that allowed them to undertake tasks at which their more conservatively minded enemy baulked. For instance, to force his division away from the roads, Takeuchi had replaced his divisional motor vehicles with mules. The dank, close jungle with its animal and native tracks was the ideal medium through which they could move. It offered a canopy under which they could hide from British planes, and jungle tracks along which they could infiltrate through and around British defensive positions. British commanders assumed that an enemy would have to clear these positions from the front in the traditional military manner before they could proceed, but Iida's men simply bypassed them. The Japanese rarely fought in the jungle but used it extensively to outwit their enemy, to multiply their own strength, and to undermine any natural advantages enjoyed by their opponents.

They had trained thoroughly. Training schools on Hainan Island and Formosa had undertaken research in the tactics required to defeat the British and Americans. The Japanese had rehearsed extensively in heavily forested and jungle terrain, becoming accustomed to moving quickly at night by compass, without relying on roads. Imperial Headquarters in Tokyo had begun planning for military operations in Malaya and Burma at least a year before.[4] Tokyo was supported in these endeavours by Headquarters 5 Army in Saigon, and by the establishment of a small specialist operational investigation unit in Formosa. This was responsible for collecting and analysing all the information necessary to prepare its forces to fight a tropical warfare campaign. Its remit was comprehensive, being tasked with advising on everything from 'the organization of Army corps, equipment, campaign direction, management and treatment of weapons, sanitation, supply, administration of occupied territory, and military strategy, tactics and geography.'[5]

But there is a qualification. The Japanese succeeded in 1941 and 1942 in part because they had the advantage of surprise and savagery over an unprepared and complacent enemy, not only because they possessed better military science. Time would demonstrate that, like other armies, the Japanese would also fail when faced with an organized, prepared and committed foe. The Japanese triumphed because they were able to surprise and overwhelm the European powers in Asia. The ferocity of their soldiers caused panic in 1941. By 1944 this ferocity was seen for what it was: an expedient that allowed Japanese commanders to cover truly gargantuan blunders and hubris, countered when Allied forces became adept at allowing the Japanese to die for their country, in vast numbers. Japan's military endeavours in 1941 and 1942 were empty of much other than the promise of *kamikaze*, *hari-kari* and *bushido* (the Japanese military code).

But these discoveries lay in the future. In 1941 the British – politically and militarily – were woefully unprepared for war against a first-class opponent in Asia. Everything about the Japanese approach to land warfare in 1942 completely outclassed their British, American and Indian opponents, who had existed for decades in a cocoon of self-imposed ignorance about the fighting abilities of this formidable and determined nation. The pre-war head-in-the-sand-and-hope-for-the-best approach to Burma's security, common to both politicians and soldiers alike, who blamed their passivity on a lack of money for defence, of not wanting to frighten the population by making preparations for war and a failure of European armies grown soft under their tropical punkahs* to understand the type of fast and furious warfare that the Japanese would deploy against them, combined with appeasing Tokyo in 1940 by temporarily closing the Burma Road, had the effect of making the Japanese military adventure, when it started in December 1941, all the more spectacular.

Likewise, the amateurish, ink stain expansion of the empire in the 19th century had exceeded Britain's willingness to pay for effective defence following the enormous costs incurred in the Great War. The defeats of 1942 were the consequence of building an empire without the means to protect it.

What is more, Britain had done little or nothing to enrich Burma – materially, culturally, intellectually – such that when the Japanese came, most Burmans were pleased to welcome the invaders. Britain's attempts to persuade Asians to support them in the war against fascism 'were met with derision'.[6] At least the Japanese talked about an Asia for the Asians, a stark contrast to the resounding silence regarding self-government emanating from Government House in Rangoon.[7] There just wasn't enough about British colonial rule to persuade the Burmese of the Irrawaddy delta to support them against the Japanese. British colonialism, in Burma at least, failed to present a coherent or attractive argument to convince the broad expanse of the Burmese population to regard Britain as its best hope for an independent future. Dorman-Smith observed perceptively on taking up the role of Governor General in June 1941, shortly before the Japanese invasion, 'It is definitely disappointing that after all our years of occupation… we have not been able to create that loyalty which is generally associated with our subject nations.'[8] The war against the Japanese didn't become a Burmese war in the same

---

*Ubiquitous among the governing classes in India, a punkah is a large cloth fan on a frame suspended from the ceiling, moved backwards and forwards by pulling on a cord.

way that Indians decided in vast numbers to support India's war against the Axis powers, even as the Japanese trumpeting of co-prosperity soon began to be seen for the hollow propaganda it was. The attitude of the British to their empire was as caretakers, rather than as overlords, a factor that hastened their demise.[9] Even if the Japanese were eventually to be defeated in Burma, Britain no longer had the credibility to rule: independence immediately after the war was the political consequence of British military failure in 1942.

The loss of Burma crashed uncomfortably into the consciousness of Britons, providing further unwanted evidence of the inability of their armed forces to defeat the fascist menace, whether it be in Europe, the Mediterranean, or now, in Asia. In May 1942, for most Britons the war, in its 33rd month, dragged interminably on, with no prospect of any resolution, let alone success, in sight. The widely held view across all strata of society was that the military situation was gradually worsening. For some that decline was considered irreversible. Worrying about the mental health of the Prime Minister, a few weeks before on 4 March, Alexander Cadogan, the Permanent Under-Secretary for Foreign Affairs, had noted in his diary, 'Poor old PM in a sour mood and a bad way.' A month before he had complained, 'Our generals are no use, and do our men fight?'[10] Sir Henry 'Chips' Channon, Member of Parliament for Southend, depressed, recalled in his diary on 30 March, 'We are living in a Gibbonian age – Decline and Fall'.[11] In January the Cabinet received a report from the Ministry of Information in which they were told that the prevailing mood across the country was fatalistic; a lack of British military success was leading to a sense of 'frustration and loss of interest in the war and war news'. The year 1942 was to be one of defeat and pessimism. Life was bleak, and dangerous, for soldier and civilian alike, and the news from the front was rarely anything but gloomy. As the new year dawned, this gloom was compounded by the astounding reports of rapid Japanese gains down the Malayan Peninsula, including the startling news that the battleship *Prince of Wales* and the battle cruiser *Repulse* had been lost to Japanese air attack. To a British population imbued with the myth of their vessels ruling the waves to enforce Pax Britannica, the loss of these capital ships to Japanese pilots widely derided as having such poor eyesight as to be virtually blind, was almost incomprehensible. Perhaps the snide 'Pax Umbrellicus' jibe levelled at London by muscular fascists in Europe was correct after all, a visual metaphor for bumbling ineptness?

Assailed on every side by bad news, Averell Harriman, Roosevelt's special envoy to London, noted to the President that Churchill's confidence had been shattered, 'to such an extent that he has not been able to stand up to this adversity [the relentless news of defeat] with his old vigour'.[12] Churchill's doctor, Charles Wilson (later Lord Moran), recalled that the news of Singapore 'stupefied the Prime Minister'. A month later, Wilson observed, 'something of the old crusading fire had already left him'. Morale, he thought, was much lower than it had been during the Great War.[13] Cadogan agonized to his diary on 10 February: 'News all round frightful. Singapore is going to be a bloody disaster and sinkings – especially of tankers – are climbing up to a murderous figure.' Two days later, his diary reached a new level of despair: 'The blackest day, yet, of the war. Singapore evidently only a drawn-out agony. Burma threatened… We are nothing but failure and inefficiency everywhere and the Japs are murdering our men and raping our women in Hong Kong'.[14]

In a further embarrassment, at the same time as it was running rings around the British on land in Malaya and Burma, the Japanese Navy collided with an Allied fleet in the Java Sea in February and won a convincing victory, which allowed them to launch deeper operations against the Indian Ocean and Ceylon in April. The Japanese appeared utterly triumphant, on land and at sea. Who could stand against them? The limited military successes of 1941, several of which had consequences of strategic significance for the Allies, such as the defence of the Middle East (Iraq, Syria and Persia) against Axis expansion in the region, together with the 242-day defence of the siege of Tobruk, which prevented Rommel from steamrolling his Afrika Korps all the way to the Nile, were now long forgotten in the anxiety of the present moment. Even worse, Tobruk surrendered to Rommel on 21 June 1942, an event which seemed to show all the large sacrifices and small victories of the previous year to have been in vain. What was going on? All the while, the Battle of the Atlantic was raging unabated, threatening Britain's survival, let alone its ability to fight back against its enemies. The German North Sea surface raiders such as the *Tirpitz* threatened to join the massive U-boat campaign in the Atlantic against shipping en route to the British Isles, a shockingly effective offensive that Churchill later described as the only thing that ever really frightened him.

Indeed, with all that it had on its plate in Europe, the Mediterranean and the Atlantic, was it even worthwhile defending Britain's Asian colonies? Most Britons thought not. In a poll in mid-1942, 'only 6% of those asked disapproved of the intention to fight on until Japan was beaten, even if Germany were defeated beforehand.'[15] By late 1942 there had been a sea change in British attitudes to the empire. With Britain itself fighting for freedom, what right had it to rule others? What was good for the goose was increasingly accepted as good for the gander. Even Dorman-Smith, now in exile in Simla, agreed that a concomitant of the 1941 Atlantic Charter, the joint US–British commitment to the restoration after the war of self-government to those deprived of it, was 'the end of the British Empire.'[16]

Colonialism was a sin of the age and the political process for the granting of independence – in India as in Burma – was new, ill-formed and fractious, as much in Britain as it was in India.[17] The argument that loyalty to Britain in the short term was in the best long-term political interests of the country in terms of future independence – if indeed that were the case – simply had not been made by the point the Japanese invaded, despite limited self-government from 1937.

But, it can be argued, the greater sin of the age was the aggressive expansionism of the competing empire of Japan, a nation with a ruling class steeped in militarism and without any compunction to use murderous violence to achieve its aims. Japanese racial exceptionalism left the country in the grip of a moral blindness to the lives of those they would blight in pursuit of national war aims. War, for Japan, was not undertaken to right a wrong, but to perpetuate an evil. Japanese military aggrandizement began in China in 1931 and through to 1945 resulted in perhaps 20 million Chinese dead. The people of South East Asia were not the inheritors of a Greater Co-Prosperity Sphere as crude Japanese propaganda claimed, but its victims. The millions of innocents who died in Malaya, Burma, Thailand, Singapore, the Philippines, modern Indonesia and India – including the Bengal famine – died as the direct or indirect result of Japanese warmongering. Japan's expansionist rhetoric in 1940 and 1941 claimed that the Greater East Asian Co-Prosperity Sphere would free the region from colonialism. In truth, Japan was exclusively concerned with the creation, through the use of war, of its own, competing Asian empire, to secure oil and other resources to allow it to fuel its own relentless military expansion.[18] As a result, even those who first expressed allegiance to Japan were eventually to turn against it. Japan's inability politically to capitalize on its extraordinary military victory in 1941 and 1942 was to consign it to eventual defeat. It had no big ideas beyond the ultimately empty one of militarism in pursuit of a grandiose view of what it meant to be a successful imperial power.

By their victory in Burma in 1942, the Japanese planted the seeds of their eventual defeat. The principal problem was that they had not won their war outright. Instead, by pushing the British out of Burma, they merely introduced a period of hiatus, during which Britain was provided with the time to rebuild, rearm and reconquer. They thought that, humiliated by defeat, America and Britain would simply give up and go away, as the Romanov dynasty had done in the Russo–Japanese War in 1905.[19] As they discovered with the destruction of the Pacific Fleet at Pearl Harbor, the Japanese inability to achieve a decisive victory meant that they were destined to face a battle of decline, in which the mathematics of obliteration only went in one direction. Japan had sown the wind, and would, in due course, reap the whirlwind.

PART TWO

Hiatus, 1943

Prologue

Lieutenant Philip Brownless, 1 Essex Regiment*

Central India, autumn 1943

Then came the great day when we were to draw up our main complement of animals, about 70 mules and 12 ponies. We were dumped at a small railway station. It was all open ground and there was a team of Army Veterinary Surgeons to allocate fairly between the three battalions, the Essex, the Borders and the Duke of Wellington's. Lieut. Jimmy Watt of the Borders was a pal of mine: he and I, with a squad of men, were to march them back nearly 100 miles to our camp, sleeping each of the five nights under the stars. As soon as we arrived at the disembarkation site, I got all our mule lines laid out, with shackles (used to tie mules fore and aft) and nosebags ready. I had also picked up the tip that the mules would be wild, having spent three days in the train, and almost impossible to hold, so I instructed our men to tie them together in threes before they got off the train. As all three pulled in different directions, one muleteer could hold them. Not everybody had learned this trick, so the result was that wild mules were careering all over the place, impossible to catch. When our first handful of mules arrived, they were quickly secured in a straight line and fed. They were familiar with lines like this and cooled down at once, long ears relaxed and tails swishing amiably. When the wild mules careering round saw this line, they said to themselves, 'We've done this before' and came and stood in our lines.

In a highly optimistic mood early on, I decided to practise a river crossing. We marched several miles out from camp to a typical wide sandy Indian river,

---

*Soon after his return from the Arakan front in autumn 1943, Brownless had been told that the whole division was to be handed over to General Wingate and trained to operate behind the Japanese lines. All motor transport was to be taken away and they were to be entirely dependent upon mules for our transport. As told to the author.

300 yards across, made our preparations, i.e. assembling the two assault boats, making floating bundles of our clothes and gear by wrapping them in groundsheets, unsaddling the animals, and assembling at the water's edge. A good-sized detachment of muleteers was posted on the opposite bank ready to catch the mules. The mules waded into the shallow water but no one could get them to move off. We tried all sorts of inducements in vain, and then suddenly, one sturdy little grey animal decided to swim and the whole lot immediately followed. Calamity ensued! Mules are very short sighted and could only dimly see the opposite bank but downstream was a bright yellow sandy outcrop and they all made for this. The muleteers on the other bank, when they realised what was happening, ran through the scrub and jungle as fast as they could, but the mules arrived first and bolted off into the wilds of India. I swam my pony across with my arm across his withers and directing him by holding his head harness, the gear was ferried across and the mule platoon, with one pony, began the march back to camp. Deeply depressed, I wondered how to tell the CO I had lost all his mules and imagined the court martial which awaited me (or, serving under General Wingate, would I be shot out of hand?). An hour and a half later we came in sight of the camp and to my utter astonishment I could see the mules in their lines. When I arrived at the mule lines, the storeman met me and said that the whole lot had arrived at the double and had gone to their places. He had merely gone along the lines, shackling them and patted their noses. Salvation! I kept quiet for a bit but it got out and I was the butt of much merrymaking.

Once back with the brigade, serious training began as we were due shortly to go into Burma. There were marches to toughen up both men and mules, and brigade schemes lasting two or three weeks, with all supplies dropped by air. On one scheme, hearing some planes overhead, we lit a line of signal fires and managed to collar the ration drop of the 'enemy' who were on this occasion the 2nd Black Watch – we were briefly not popular. Bags of grain for the mules fell as 'free drops' – without statichutes – sometimes hazardous. Often the wind took the chutes away from the steep hillside and we could only watch as our stores sailed out of reach. My batman, addressing the sky, was telling everyone what he thought of the wind, the weather and the Japanese when half a dozen shovels, tied together, landed at his feet with a smack which silenced him for a whole minute.

One night march was a miserable failure: the importance of total silence had been impressed upon us by the Second in Command, a slightly jittery man at the best of times. All might have been well if the cooks in camp had not served bacon and beans to the column for supper... The struggle not to laugh as the accompanying farts reverberated through the jungle would have betrayed our presence to the Japanese had this exercise been for real. The need for silence on the march meant that our mules and ponies had to be de-voiced. Mules have keen hearing and if one detected the presence of mules in another column, even a mile away, a deep bray would have evoked an instant response, developing into a 'conversation' and betraying the presence of both columns to the Japanese. A team of veterinary surgeons arrived one morning in our training camp, set up their tables and each mule was led forward by his muleteer. With rope through his shackles to bring his feet together, he was gently 'cast' (capsized) and with a chloroform pad held to his muzzle, he quickly became muzzy and unconscious while the vet made a small nick in his neck to sever his vocal chords. It was skilfully done and a few minutes later the mule got to his feet and was soon back in his place munching happily.

11

Aftermath

In mid-1942, when the withdrawing Burma Army moved up the road from Tamu, the state of Manipur and the upper reaches of Assam now constituted India's war frontier with Japan.[1] The monsoon brought a halt to offensive activity and provided welcome respite to both sides, although that year the rainfall was remarkably heavy and was followed by a malaria epidemic in the Assamese hills that devastated the units struggling to maintain the vast and fragile line of communication to Imphal. Indeed, the rainfall was so heavy, its impact on the fragile road from the Brahmaputra across the Naga Hills into Manipur so dramatic – with road slips washing away the few roads and the malarial casualties so high – that many intelligent and experienced officers observing the situation concluded that it would be impossible for either the British or the Japanese to mount effective military operations between the period May to October. The mountains that lie between Burma and India are some of the wettest in the world. Valleys and low-lying areas flood, heavy cloud descends and giant cumulus clouds gather in violent clusters in the skies. For the troops on the ground, particularly in the hills and mountains, the entire monsoon meant constant wetness, and if in the jungle or heavily forested areas, semi-permanent darkness. Malaria was endemic, with 76,000 episodes treated by medical staff in Assam in 1942, and more cases undiagnosed.[2] Amoebic and bacillary dysentery caused debilitating diarrhoea in many and no one was ever really free of 'the runs'. The disposal of raw sewerage was a serious problem in the Imphal plain where the water table sat only 18 inches below the surface. The concentration of troops and limited hygiene facilities encouraged the spread of scabies and fungal skin infections. Leeches infested the forest and their bites could progress to jungle sores. All these features emphasized, as if it were needed, the huge challenges of deploying an army in this type of terrain, and in this type of weather.[3]

It wasn't just the so-called 'blimps' of contemporary humour and historic imagination who said that it wasn't possible to fight a jungle campaign during the monsoon, but well-meaning and experienced soldiers. In any case, there wasn't much in India's arsenal at the time to defend the country from the Japanese if they had decided to continue their advance across the hills. The so-called 'Assam Division' was headquartered at Jorhat on the Brahmaputra on the western side of the Naga Hills, but most units assigned to it (primarily the two battalions of 1 Indian Infantry Brigade, recently arrived from the North West Frontier) were understrength and poorly trained.[4] The newly raised 1 Battalion, Assam Regiment, was in Digboi in the northern Brahmaputra Valley until redeployed to Manipur in May 1942. Otherwise, the closest fighting units were a thousand miles away by rickety road and rail to the west, in Ranchi (the capital of Bihar), where the recently arrived Lieutenant General Noel Irwin's IV Corps was headquartered. They were there because the resources to support them in Assam simply did not exist. Dimapur ('Manipur Road'), where the road from Imphal via Kohima debouches from the Naga Hills[5] onto the Brahmaputra Valley, and the point at which the line of communication arrived from Calcutta and bifurcated north to Ledo – the strategically vital launch pad for future Hump operations to China – had no encampment facilities or the wherewithal to look after anything other than incidental travellers making their way to Manipur. There were no barracks, depots, equipment parks or fuel bowsers. The place was, before the onset of Japanese hostilities, a dusty administrative hub for the production and export across the empire of Assam tea. The infrastructure to sustain even an infantry battalion, let alone anything larger, had to be built, in Imphal and Dimapur, from scratch. The weakness of this limited part of what was grandly called the Assam Line of Communication, running from Calcutta all the way to Ledo in the northern Brahmaputra and into Manipur ('a complicated system of port, railway, road, river and pipe-line transport'), was the primary reason why it was physically impossible to mount anything other than minor operations out of Manipur into Burma until 1944.[6] When noisy strategists in London or Washington talked glibly of manoeuvring this corps or that division across hundreds of miles to take up this position or undertake that operation, and loudly criticized New Delhi for its inertia, more than anything else they were displaying the enormity of their ignorance about the physical possibilities for warfare in the region. Across the jungle-matted mountains that lay between the Brahmaputra in Assam and the Chindwin in Burma lived a scattered aboriginal population of perhaps 200,000 Kachin, Naga, Kuki and Chin people, with significant population groupings at Imphal and the Naga hill station at Kohima. The Nagas remained notorious headhunters, especially in the more remote areas where this practice proved hard to eradicate.[7] The Imphal plain, originally an ancient lake, was now a flat alluvial basin some 2,500 feet above sea level in the middle of these mountains stretching north to south some 40 miles, by 20 miles east to west. The Naga Hills lay to the north (Kohima sits at 5,000 feet above sea level), the Somra Tracts to the north-west, and the even higher Chin Hills to the south and west. Both location and topography made Imphal difficult to supply.

Ranchi, the nodal point for Eastern Army responsible for the entire land defence of eastern India, was headquarters for two weak corps:

1. IV Corps, based also at Ranchi, comprising:
    a. 70 Division (British)
    b. 23 Indian Division
    c. 50 Indian Tank Brigade,[8] at Poona, near Bombay
2. XV Corps, based at Barrackpore, near Calcutta:
    a. 14 Indian Division
    b. 26 Indian Division

Because of the effects of the rapid expansion of the army, at this time there were only nine rather than the usual 12 infantry brigades in Eastern Army (each division would ordinarily comprise three brigades), which meant that the army was at only 75 per cent of its authorized infantry strength. In 1942, only 70 Division possessed combat experience, having recently arrived from North Africa. Each brigade had an infantry strength of about 2,500 men, which meant that in IV Corps there were 10,000 trained soldiers available to defend north-eastern India from the Japanese, although many of these men were 1,000 miles away from where they were required.[9] Irwin's IV Corps was responsible for the defence of Assam, while XV Corps at Barrackpore, a grim industrial suburb to the north of Calcutta, was responsible for Bengal, facing Burma's Arakan province. As well as being understrength, both corps were under-trained and ill-equipped. The expansion of the army had been conducted at a pace that outstripped the country's – and the empire's – ability to equip it with the necessary warlike stores, from boots to rifles, guns, ammunition of many different types and calibres, vehicles and radios. If combat effectiveness was measured by its ability to defeat the Japanese in a stand-up fight, it had some way to go. Irwin's headquarters IV Corps had itself only just arrived in India from Iraq. It had landed in Basra in February after a long journey around the Cape of Good Hope from Britain, then arrived in Ranchi in April. As to its components, Major General George Symes' 70 British Division had recently arrived from Tobruk, and its victory over Rommel in the breakout battles the previous November, while Major General Reginald Savory's 23 Indian Division, raised in January 1942 at Jhansi in Central India, was in the process of moving to Ranchi when it was ordered to take responsibility for 1 Indian Brigade and the defence of the Manipur frontier. In May 1942 its second brigade (123 Brigade) moved to Dimapur and thence to Imphal, the third brigade (37 Brigade) joining in June, taking a full seven weeks to make the journey by road and rail to Dimapur and thence across the Naga Hills to Imphal. Resources were threadbare at the end of the road from Dimapur. There were no stocks of food or ammunition, the road failed repeatedly in the monsoon rains, and the troops – together with 6,000 Chinese and 40,000 refugees from Burma still under canvas and atap on the Imphal plain – were on barely subsistence rations. The truth was that, along the Chindwin, facing off against the Empire of Japan, a single battalion of Indian troops – 600 men – defended India through the long, wet, malarial monsoon period of 1942. If Iida had wished or had had the energy to drag his 15 Army into India, there would have been little to stop him.[10] When men of the Assam Regiment patrolled into long-deserted Tamu in June 1942, they came across scenes that epitomized the horror that had been inflicted on Burma and its people, as much by British unpreparedness and complacency as by rampant, unheralded Japanese militarism. The fast-decaying skeletons of hundreds of refugees littered the roads, ditches and hamlets of this sparsely populated area in the hills to the west of the Chindwin, the terminus of the road from Imphal. A group of 20 sat huddled together in the deserted telephone exchange, one with his hand resting on the telephone receiver.[11]

But in May, the Japanese were as exhausted as the British, Iida's 15 Army having suffered 30 per cent casualties during the campaign. Nor had they any intention of pursuing their defeated foe into India: winning the whole of Burma was itself an unplanned surprise. Japan now stood on the edge of its suddenly acquired empire unsure of what to do next, but believing that it had achieved all – and more – of its military goals. To the victor the laurels.

In addition to the 25,000 infantry soldiers of Eastern Army, India had two further infantry divisions allocated to the defence of its eastern seaboard in 1942, although they were divisions at this point in time in name only. These were part of General Sir Brodie Haig's Southern Army at Bangalore, the role of which was to protect India's eastern seaboard from Japanese invasion, a threat that only receded in late 1943. 19 Division at Madras (Major General Geoffrey Scoones), had been raised the previous October in Secunderbad, and 20 Division (Major General Douglas Gracey), being raised at that moment in Bangalore, offered when fully trained a further 15,000 fresh infantry troops – making a total of 50,000 – men available for the defence of eastern and north-eastern India.[12]

Following the debacle in Burma, a new general was given the task of guarding India's eastern frontier. This, the newly arrived Noel Irwin, was Wavell's great hope for a new start in India. In the first instance, he was a British officer, an old British-service prejudice against 'sepoy generals' undoubtedly asserting itself in Wavell's mind when considering the options for higher command. Replacing the ageing and retiring General Charles Broad, Irwin took the reins of Eastern Army determined to demonstrate that his brand of leadership, and his approach to war, would deliver success. A remarkably courageous infantry soldier in the Great War (he had been awarded the Military Cross, the Distinguished Service Order with two bars, the Croix de Guerre and was four times mentioned in despatches), he had enjoyed an exemplary military career, though he had been unfortunate of late. It was this recent (1940) reversal in his military fortunes that he wished to redeem. He had successfully commanded every unit in the army from platoon to corps; had commanded 6 Infantry Brigade in the British Expeditionary Force to France in 1940 before taking command of 2 Division[13] during the final stages of the withdrawal to Dunkirk, and had commanded the ill-fated Dakar expedition in September 1940. GHQ India – and Wavell personally – undoubtedly believed that India was receiving a commander of high renown and was grateful for his arrival.

On 11 May 1942 Irwin meet Alexander at Tamu to prepare to take responsibility for the eastern frontier with Japanese-held Burma, defending it against invasion if necessary. He had received reports over previous days of the withdrawing Burma Corps with incredulity, concluding on the basis of what he saw of the bedraggled, ill-disciplined stragglers arriving into Manipur two weeks before the arrival of the marching troops of Burma Corps that he had nothing to learn from this rabble, or from its Indian Army commanders. He convinced himself from what he saw along the Chindwin that at the heart of the defeat was poor soldiering, accompanied by the inadequate 'grip' of units and formations exercised by their commanders. British and Indian soldiers had clearly put on 'a poor show' and had been trounced by a second-rate, Asian enemy. This was not how he had remembered Dunkirk, where 2 Division had returned to England intact and in good order, although without its heavy weapons. He was certain that he could do much better than this. A man with no previous experience of Indian troops (although he was born to a family with long experience of India), nor of any understanding of the course of the campaign in Burma, he spectacularly misjudged the quality and capabilities of Burma Corps, and failed to understand the reasons for the withdrawal. He may well have suffered from a touch of the characteristic anti-Indian Army bias shown by officers of the regular British Army, but whatever the wellsprings of his animosity, he was certain that he had nothing to learn from the beggars who stumbled across the Lockchao Bridge and made their way over the Shenam Saddle in the Imphal plain during these final weeks of Britain's humiliation in Burma.[14] There seemed no capacity in his appreciation of the loss of Burma that there might have been other factors at play other than the pusillanimity of the troops. Perhaps his own bitter experience at Dunkirk two years before, and then at Dakar with the Free French, played some part in his view of this evacuation. Dunkirk and Dakar were not the names of battles or campaigns with which to end a successful military career. When Slim tried to explain the reality of Burma to him, he was rebuffed. Slim, surprised at the rudeness of Irwin's dismissal of his request that assistance be provided for his men, complained. Irwin replied, 'I can't be rude: I'm senior.'[15] In any case, as far as Wavell was concerned, Irwin was the man of the hour, the British commander who had arrived to re-energize Eastern Army and lead it to victory. It was to him that responsibility for both defensive and offensive operations along Indian's eastern frontier fell. A few months later, Wavell wrote a letter to *The Times* on 23 October 1942 explaining the 'Qualities that make a Great General'. Wavell stipulated that the candidate, 'must have handled large forces in a completely independent command in more than one campaign; and must have shown his qualities in adversity as well as in success. Then the considerations should be... his worth as a strategist; his skill as a tactician; his power to deal tactfully with his Government and with allies; his ability to train troops; and his energy and driving power in planning and in battle.'[16] It's not clear whether Irwin ever read this article, but there is no doubt that he believed himself to be the man of whom Wavell spoke.

The return of Lieutenant General Bill Slim from Burma in May 1942 had a silver lining for Wavell, as he reorganized Eastern Army for war. Having promoted Irwin to be its commander, he now had two corps appointments to make. He gave one to Slim, ordering him to Barrackpore to take command of XV Corps. Lieutenant General Geoffrey Scoones, another Gurkha officer like Slim, was promoted from command of 19 Division and given command of IV Corps.[17]

Hollow-eyed and exhausted by the retreat, Slim duly travelled to Calcutta and Comilla to inspect the two divisions of his highly dispersed command. He was horrified by what he saw. Of the two, the best equipped, was Major General Wilfred Lloyd's 14 Indian Division, based at Comilla, 90 miles north-west of Chittagong. Until two months before, it had been at Quetta preparing for service in the Middle East. Lloyd had led his division with some considerable élan in Syria the previous year, but neither he nor any of his commanders or troops had experience of fighting the Japanese.[18] The division was undermanned and under-equipped. In this state it was nonetheless responsible for the defence of the whole of India's south-eastern frontier with Burma, including Arakan. It had been issued with its equipment and transport, but its training for jungle fighting was far from complete. The other, 26 Indian Division, based in Calcutta and commanded by Major General Clive Lomax, was in a far worse state. It was responsible for the internal security and coastal defence of the states of Bengal and Orissa. But it was not, wrote Slim, 'a mobile or battle-worthy division at all, being woefully short of all forms of transport; nor could it, by any stretch of the imagination, be regarded as a trained formation.' Depressed but not beaten, he got to work preparing it for war.

12

Taking Stock

In the immediate aftermath of the defeat in Malaya in February, and that in Burma in May 1942, the British and Indian armies in India took stock. The process of understanding the cause of their defeats by the Japanese and of responding to each of these proved, however, to be disjointed and rudder-less. It was one thing to understand what had gone wrong, entirely another to put in place a system of changes and improvements to rectify the deficiencies identified, in terms of new organization, tactics, weapons or equipment. Nevertheless, India saw a flurry of creativity from mid to late 1942 by officers writing up the lessons and experiences they had taken away from the campaigns in Malaya and Burma.[1] Many wrote reports, memoranda and assessments and recommended new tactical ideas and approaches to training, equipment, unit composition and weapons. In May 1942 Wavell published a report on the analysis of the fighting in Malaya in which he described the primary deficiency to be inadequate training.[2] Likewise, his *Despatch*, written by him in 1942 (but not published until 1948) and containing the reports to him of the fighting by both Hutton and Alexander, provides an intelligent and considered rationale for the failure in Burma. He concluded that failure was caused by:

a. The presence of large numbers of recently joined and very young recruits in the ranks.

b. A number of very recently joined officers who did not know their men and whose knowledge of Hindustani was hardly sufficient to raise their confidence quickly.

c. The effect of units being thrown into battle before they had time to collect themselves.

d. The utterly strange conditions of warfare in the jungle.

e. A distrust, often exaggerated, of units of the Burma Army.

In light of the course of operations in Arakan in 1943, Wavell didn't seem to identify a number of other deficiencies in the training, preparation and equipping of the troops for war against a modern, well-equipped enemy. He failed for instance to mention the lack of automatic platoon weapons, integrated company weapons (such as mortars and medium machine guns) or the intimate support to the infantry by armour or aircraft, or of a decent radio by which battalions could communicate with each other in hilly and forested terrain. Alexander's report, however, did note that 'the lack of aircraft in India, as in Malaya, was one of the causes of failure.' Despite these failings, Alexander had been impressed with the ability of the army and its commanders to respond quickly to reverses on the battlefield. One outstanding example was 17 Indian Division following the Sittang disaster:

> It is a high tribute to the Commanders in this formation that the Division was reformed and re-equipped and with the addition of the 63 Infantry Brigade fought gallantly for another three months before withdrawing into India. The 1 Burma Division suffered constantly from the disintegration of its indigenous units but it in turn reorganised to include battalions brought in from outside, and remained a fighting formation to the end. This clearly illustrates the influence which a few really good Commanders can exercise. Practically every formation in these two Divisions had at one time or another been surrounded by the enemy and had fought its way out. This had a cumulative effect.

Alexander likewise understood the essential point that when threatened by fast-moving infiltration, troops that had been bypassed needed to stand firm, counterattacking hard against the flying columns moving behind and beyond them. To do this required having a means of resupply once units had been surrounded. In due course the solution would be provided by air transport, but this required large numbers of transport aircraft, and few were available at this point in the war. What he suggested was the concept of the box taken from the Western Desert and applied to a jungle environment:[3]

> This campaign was fought by comparatively small forces over a very large area and therefore militarily the offensive, coupled with air superiority and the help of the local population, enabled the Japanese to concentrate superior forces at the decisive point, since the defence had necessarily to be more dispersed. The right method of defence was, I am convinced; to hold defended localities well stocked with reserves of supplies and ammunition; covering approaches and centres of

communication and to have behind these defended localities hard-hitting mobile forces available to counterattack the enemy should he attempt to surround the defence. When this method was tried in the battle south of Prome it was already too late, for by that time supplies were too scarce to be risked in any large quantity in the forward area and the fear of being cut off was already too deeply implanted in the minds of the soldiers.

Likewise, Wavell and Alexander stressed the need for soldiers, units and formations to be thoroughly trained – individually and collectively – in the conditions in which they were to fight. With respect to the jungle, Alexander observed:

> The technique of jungle fighting, as understood by the Japanese, was virtually non-existent in my force. Success in this type of fighting depends largely on the ability of parties to find their way through the jungle and to keep touch with one another. It demands a knowledge of all types of signalling by visual and by sound and also requires a high scale of low powered wireless sets with infantry battalions. It demands also training to eliminate the sense of loneliness which so often saps the morale of those who are not used to it. Quite apart from jungle fighting, however, the infantry were not sufficiently well trained in modern tactics which require above all else the ability to manoeuvre in small parties under the fire of their own weapons.

'Punch' Cowan also submitted a detailed report of the fighting in Burma. He agreed that a significant mismatch existed in the training, preparation for war and leadership between the British and Indian soldiers and the Japanese. The young, poorly trained and unbloodied recruits of the division (most had not fired their rifles in anything other than basic range shoots before and had never seen or heard, let alone come under fire from, automatic weapons) came across 'modern weapons, and especially the automatic one, face to face at close quarters for the first time.' Cowan continued:

> They were meeting the picked, trained, hardy, fanatical Japanese soldier, who had already been blooded in the Chinese struggle. The strangeness of the jungle, novel to most, and the individualistic nature of the fighting in it, had to be overcome and learnt. Practice without weapons had been of the slightest, or none at all, and mastery of them was only obtained day to day as each new experience was met. Under these circumstances, there can be no substitute for the bold, resourceful

and remorseless leadership of the officer... Nothing of tactical theory will avail if common sense and guts are lacking in our future fighting in the East... If the troops are well led, the fight will prosper.[4]

Cowan, and the report's primary author, Brigadier Ronnie Cameron of 48 Brigade, the masters of Kokkogwa and Kyaukse, knew only too well that the competence that came from rigorous training was a vital ingredient of battlefield success, but only a part of it. The other essential part was to have section, platoon, company and battalion leaders who knew their trade, were confident and capable in battle, and who had the trust – the 'earned followership' – of their men. Without the vital ingredient of personal leadership and command competence, the battle would never be won, regardless of the quality of the military tradecraft demonstrated by each individual soldier. Captain Ian Lyall Grant expressed the problem of Burma 1942 as akin to 'entering a team of amateur footballers, who had never seen each other before and were uncertain of the rules of the game and how to play it, into the field against a well-experienced and highly motivated team of professionals.'[5] If that mismatch was not to be remedied it seemed that the whole of India lay at the mercy of Japan's relentless legions.

But the reviews, reports and debriefs were themselves somewhat haphazardly produced – there wasn't a 'Lessons Learned Committee', or some such, for instance in GHQ India, to coordinate or lead this flurry of reflection – which meant that many of the ideas coming from the pens and lips of survivors of these encounters were not collated in an organized fashion, nor did they receive the formal imprimatur of GHQ India Command, and thus the force of the direction of the Commander-in-Chief. The challenge in mid-1942 was not an absence of ideas about the nature of the problem posed by the Japanese, but the lack of a coordinated and systematic means of organizing the variety of lessons and ideas generated. As a result, the reports and reviews of mid-1942 did not immediately influence GHQ India's approach to preparing and equipping its forces for war. A full year was to pass before GHQ India systematized the learning from the First Burma Campaign into a series of endorsed actions and training methodologies.

Some lessons proved more long-lasting than others. Lieutenant Colonel Ian Stewart, the Commanding Officer of 2 Battalion, Argyll and Sutherland Highlanders in Malaya, who had been regarded as something of a crank by some before the war because of his insistence on professionalism in training, preparing his battalion well for the requirements of fighting in heavily jungled terrain, wrote a report that was to form the basis for the first 'Army in India Training

Manual' on jungle warfare.[6] He and two of his regimental officers formed No. 6 Training Team, touring units across India following their escape from Singapore speaking of their experiences.[7] One of them, Captain David Wilson, recalled:

> Initially our job was to visit formations and units describing what had happened in Malaya and Singapore, but later we were to actually stay with them and assist in their training. Our time was spent in GHQ writing our own script... When this was complete we were to be launched forth, rather like the apostles, to spread the gospel. The trouble was there wasn't any gospel to spread except one of defeat and disaster. In some ways it was the blind leading the blind, except that we had been in contact with the Japanese and knew a little about how they worked.[8]

In the absence of any doctrinal structure, or an owner for tactical doctrine in GHQ India (this was seen as a centralization too far, as the regiments and divisional commanders in the rapidly expanding Indian Army considered this to be their prerogative), every part of the army in India ended up doing its own thing. A plethora of approaches and tactical doctrines were developed, all derived from a variety of personal views and experiences, unconstrained by central diktat, authority or direction. It was a period of experimentation, and units and formations were allowed to get on and work out for themselves the best way of fighting and defeating the Japanese.[9] In the rush to discover ways of learning how to live in the jungle no stone was left unturned. For instance, the big-game hunter, 68-year-old Jim Corbett, author the 1935 book *Jungle Stories* and renowned destroyer of scores of man-eating tigers in Garhwal and Kumaon, was dragged uncomplainingly out of retirement to lecture the army on jungle craft. When in 1944 his best-selling *Man-eaters of Kumaon* was published, it was 'translated into Roman Urdu by GHQ India, so that officers could read it out to soldiers.'[10]

This variety of approaches and advice was unhelpful, as it didn't allow the many thousands of well-meaning training staff in units that had no experience of fighting the Japanese any direction, insight or specific knowledge about what tactical situations they could expect in battle, and the best approaches, weapons and drills to use in response. Before long, a wide range of training pamphlets and documents were circulating, some of which offered competing advice about how to deal with specific tactical situations. The first formal, British step in attempting to understand the challenge of fighting in the jungle or heavily forested terrain was published in Britain in August 1942. *Forest, Bush and Jungle Warfare Against a Modern Enemy* (Military Training Pamphlet, MTP 52) captured many of the lessons learned in Malaya and Burma. Its distinctiveness was the recognition in its title that the Japanese were a modern enemy, no longer to be ignorantly dismissed as a 'savage'.[11] The pamphlet recognized for the first time that there was no such thing as a 'front line' in this type of warfare; that aggressive patrolling and ambushes by well-trained troops, carrying plenty of automatic weapons and grenades was the only way to dominate territory and to keep the initiative over the enemy; that local native populations were an ideal source of intelligence and support; and that both aircraft and radio were essential ingredients in successful operations. But it was a British Army pamphlet, not an Indian Army one, and wasn't published in India. Instructions for jungle warfare in India remained the responsibility of MTP (India) 9. Even in areas of tactics, the British and Indian armies remained separate.

The loss of Malaya, Singapore and Burma came at a point when the Indian Army was growing rapidly. Numerical growth placed tremendous pressure on India's training infrastructure. The greatest requirement was for men who understood that training to defeat the Japanese required different approaches – and a different mindset – to that which had previously prevailed when the army was focused on providing reinforcements for the Middle East. Where training proved to be inadequate, it was because trainers failed to understand the frightening new imperatives imposed on warfighting in Asia by the Japanese. Where this was understood, units and formations proved entirely equal to the task that faced them. Fortunately, in the absence of central direction, those given divisional and corps command from 1942 were, with a few notable exceptions, thoroughly competent commanders and trainers. Each of the corps and most of the divisional commanders understood these issues intuitively, and were determined to ensure that, in practice, their formations worked to improve to the point where the men were confident in battle. In other words, they didn't need diktats from on high to find ways to energize their men into preparing for war, even if some of the nuances of fighting the Japanese, or fighting in a heavily wooded, forested or jungle environment, remained unclear. Those formations that developed their own training material and delivered their own military training, both individual and collective – such as 7, 17, 20 and 23 Indian Divisions – whose commanders rose to the challenge of providing training guidance and material in the absence of anything formally imposed from above – were not the cause of the problem. What was needed was that the training undertaken by these divisions was spread among and shared with all other units and formations in the army so that the armies in India (both British and Indian) received a consistent training 'product' to enable it to fight uniformly and to the same high standards. The two corps commanders (4 and 15) – Scoones and Slim – led the way. The divisional commanders needed no prodding, and from the very start of their time in command trained their divisions hard. Frank Messervy (7), 'Punch' Cowan (17), 'Pete' Rees (19), Douglas Gracey (20), Reginald Savory and then Ouvry Roberts (23), Clive Lomax (26), Francis Festing (36) and Bruce Scott (39)[12] were all exceptional leaders and understood that soldiers needed to be thoroughly trained, properly equipped and well led before they could be expected to fight.[13] Slim, Cowan and Scott had all, of course, been blooded in Burma.

For example, within two weeks of his new division being raised on 1 April 1942, Gracey had prepared a comprehensive 'Policy for Training and Operations' derived from the information he had garnered from news reports, official communiqués and men returning from the campaign.[14] It was clear that information was being reported back to India about Japanese soldiers and their tactics. 'Our job is to fight and destroy Japanese forces wherever we meet them', Gracey wrote. 'Nothing… suggests that the Japanese are unbeatable. He is NOT, and has many weak flaws in his fighting and characteristics which good leaders and well-trained troops will exploit to the full.' He drew up a list of eleven 'cardinal principles', demonstrating that he had been paying close attention to the reports from Burma:

1. Outflank, encircle, attack by day and night;
2. If temporarily in a defensive position, always make plans to attack and counterattack;
3. Shoot to kill and never waste a round;
4. Noises and diversions in rear and flanks must be regarded as normal and the immediate action must be to send a small patrol to kill the makers of these at once;
5. Don't allow anyone to get lorry-bound or road bound;
6. Make the jungle your friend by day and night;
7. Be prepared to travel light and fast on foot; to live on little food and drink;
8. Disregard stereotyped out-of-date methods;
9. Be expert in movement in vehicles and on foot in all types of country by day and night;
10. Be cunning and bold and beat the Jap at his own game;
11. Be alert always.

There would be no problem with 20 Indian Division. The only weakness lay with Wilfred Lloyd's 14 Indian Division, thrown in to precipitate battle in Arakan without the necessary period of training and preparation to ready itself for the demanding task it faced. Most divisional commanders got on with it like Gracey. 'Punch' Cowan's' 17 Indian Division produced seven training instructions between June and December 1942, and training exercises were conducted alongside Reginald Savory's 23 Indian Division. Cowan and Savory were friends, and had taught together at the Indian Military Academy between 1932 and 1933.[15] But having individual officers here and there who wanted to do the right thing, and train their men accordingly, was not the same as having a whole army approach to training, developing and promulgating centralized approaches, methodologies and materiel, and ensuring that it was consistently delivered and applied. Major General Harold Briggs of 5 Indian Division issued 'Five Commandments' to his men, on the basis that he only needed half the number given to Moses to defeat the Japanese:

1. Be determined to kill every Jap you meet, then some more Japs.
2. Be determined not to let the Jap frighten you with ruses and induce you to disclose your positions and waste ammunition. Ambush him and do unto him as he would do unto you.
3. Be determined to hold fast when ordered, whatever happens. The Jap will then have to give you the target you want, while our reserves are on the way to help you.
4. Be determined to carry out to the letter every task given to you, whether on patrol, in attack or defence. No half measures. Plan for all eventualities, after anticipating enemy reactions. Plans cannot be too thorough. Be observant and suspicious.
5. Be determined – even fanatical.[16]

13

Arakan Round One

Even before Slim had got his troops over the Irrawaddy, Churchill had sent a memorandum to the Chiefs of Staff stating that he wanted plans framed for 'a counter-offensive on the Eastern front in the summer or autumn.'[1] During the spring and early summer he continued to pressure Wavell for decisive action to reverse the humiliation of defeat, although Churchill's initial dream of recovering Rangoon by the end of 1942 quickly faded as the lack of amphibious shipping, troops and resources required to mount this scale of operation became apparent. Prompted by Churchill's instructions, Wavell minuted the Chief of the General Staff (General Sir Edwin Morris) on 16 April 1942, instructing him 'to begin as soon as possible consideration of an offensive to reoccupy Burma.'[2] The pressure on Wavell to do something, and to do it quickly, was irresistible. Churchill was equally concerned with providing support to Chiang Kai-shek's China, to retain it in the fight, and urged harmonious relations with the prickly Joe Stilwell, ever conscious of American prerogatives against those of a Britain that many Americans believed could not be trusted. But it was one thing understanding American interests in China, another reconciling these with those of Britain, especially in the context of military defeat and an extreme poverty of resources. The war in the Far East was never entirely to remove the undercurrent of suspicion and distrust between Britain and America in respect of Burma. The situation was not helped by an almost continuous run of disappointing military results through to early 1944, and the repeated setting-back of plans for military operations that all crashed on the rocks of the Germany First policy, which took for itself resources that might otherwise have found their way to support the war in Asia. An important, underlying attitude during 1942 and 1943 among many Americans was that despite Churchill and Wavell's warlike rhetoric, the British

MAP 3   The First Arakan Campaign 1942

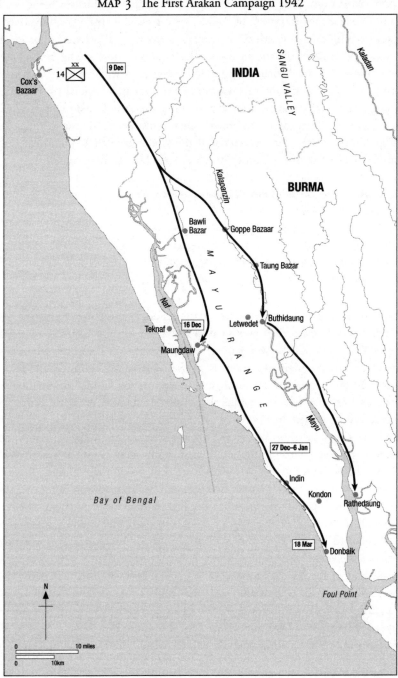

simply didn't want to fight. They had been beaten once and feared being beaten again. The extreme limitations of military resources in the region and the need to rebuild the fighting strength of the Indian Army were dismissed as convenient excuses for British military passivity. The need to build strong relationships between the Allies – Britain, China and America – while understood in the corridors of power in London, was sometimes less well applied by Delhi and Chungking, where personalities and prejudices often combined to interfere with the effective delivery of a combined military strategy to defeat the Japanese. Philip Mason, at the time Secretary of the Chiefs of Staff Committee, India, attended a meeting in 1942 at which Wavell and Stilwell were present:

> Wavell: 'Are you satisfied that this operation is not feasible?'
> Stilwell: 'Yes, I am.'
> Wavell: 'Are you satisfied on purely military grounds?'
> Stilwell: 'Yes, I am.'
> Wavell: 'What will you say to Chiang Kai-shek?'
> Stilwell: 'I shall tell him the bloody British won't fight.'[3]

The first challenge was to overcome, or at least understand, the competing pulls of national strategy as they pertained to India, Burma and China. For Britain, the focus throughout the war was the south, centred on Rangoon, whereas for the Americans it remained the north, as the route to sustaining its interests in China. Britain remained consistent in its support for China, although it was sceptical about the means by which this could be achieved. From the outset, the United States applied an industrial mindset to the problem. If the old Burma Road via Lashio was no more, the answer was simply to build a new one, bulldozing a route through the mountains, from Ledo in upper Assam. While this was being built, a transport airlift would fly equipment and supplies over the mountains to China in an air bridge nicknamed the Hump, returning with Chinese troops for training in India. The British were sceptical about whether a new road was technically feasible, or necessary, given that circumstances would have changed by the time the road was finished. In return, the Americans endlessly speculated that Britain was only interested in Burma to recover its lost empire and to assuage the humiliation of defeat. This was only ever partly true. The key issue for Churchill and the Chiefs of Staff Committee was straightforwardly the military defeat of Japan; less straightforward was the best way of doing so, where and *when*. For London, the most urgent global requirement, agreed with Roosevelt at the Arcadia Conference in December

1941, was the defeat of Germany. This would always receive priority in terms of war materiel and resources: the war against Japan would need to play second fiddle until the primary task was done. By contrast, most American attention naturally found itself on the side of the war against Japan, and a strong competing imperative in the United States focusing first on Asia worried Churchill and the British Combined Chiefs of Staff that effort was being diverted away from Europe. Certainly, this found its way into American concerns that Britain was only ever half-hearted about applying enough men, materiel and effort to the immense task of defeating the Japanese. Insistence from the US to launch a decisive land and seaborne campaign against Burma – Operation *Anakim* – in 1943 to retake Rangoon, reopen the Burma Road and take some of the pressure away from the south-west Pacific, was intense.

Wavell determined to launch an offensive into Burma in 1942, not just to satisfy Churchill but to prove that the loss of Burma was an aberration, and that the Japanese were beatable. He was also convinced that their occupation of Burma had exhausted and stretched the Japanese. Philip Mason recalled Wavell one hot evening in Delhi in June 1942. He 'stood, square and dogged, before the map of Burma, gazing at it, his hands behind him. "Think how stretched they must be!" he said. "This is the moment to hit the Japs if only we could! If I had one division in India fit to fight I'd go for them now!"'[4]

When he gave his instructions to Morris, Wavell's intention was merely to investigate the options for taking offensive action against the Japanese, from which a detailed plan would then be developed. It was clear, he added, 'The prerequisite for any counter-offensive must be the establishment of undisputed air superiority and how to do this should be the first problem.' The Director of Military Operations in GHQ India had already examined the options for launching a counter-offensive against the Japanese in Burma. The most suitable appeared to be combined air, land and naval operations along the Arakanese coast involving the capture of both Akyab and the Ramree Islands, supported by irregular operations against Pyawbe. The idea was attractive to Wavell. But to pull this sort of operation off he needed someone, he told the CIGS in London on 20 March, 'with a mind not wedded to orthodoxy to plan a reconquest of Burma or operations against Japanese lines of communication as they advance towards India.'[5]

The first response of GHQ India Command's Joint Planning Staff to Wavell's instructions of 16 April was Paper No. 15, presented on 11 May 1942. It was a comprehensive assessment of the forces available to undertake offensive operations into Burma, and the strategic purpose of any such activities. Three options were examined. These included an overland offensive from Assam, and overland and seaborne operations along the Arakanese coastline. The paper concluded that a large-scale offensive against Burma proper at the time was out of the question, and that the strategic purpose of action against the Japanese remained unclear and needed to be clarified by London. While the Joint Planning Staff in New Delhi had been working away, the Chiefs of Staff in London, too, had put some thought into the reconquest of Burma. On 9 May 1942 Wavell was told by telegram that the recapture of Rangoon was essential in order to reopen the road to China by which Chiang Kai-shek's forces could continue to be resupplied.[6] The Chiefs of Staff considered that simultaneous operations should be mounted from both Assam (into Upper Burma) and Bengal (into Arakan). Wavell agreed and told London that he and his staff had come to the same conclusion, believing that opportunities existed for operations to secure most of North Burma on the Chindwin and Irrawaddy Valleys north of Mandalay, as well as Arakan. With both London and India thinking on parallel lines, Wavell then instructed his Joint Planning Staff to turn this appreciation into a plan for an offensive scheduled to begin on 1 October 1942.

The Joint Planning Staff accordingly prepared a plan for a three-phase offensive, starting in October 1942, building up gradually to an advance by up to three infantry divisions and two tank brigades against Shwebo and Katha in northern Burma, together with air support, by April 1943. Wavell, however, was disappointed with the scale of these proposals when they were presented to him. He had been expecting something grander, regarding them as unduly pessimistic, piecemeal and lacking in 'offensive spirit'.[7] He amended these plans himself over the following days. Wavell believed that insufficient consideration had been given to the difficulties that the Japanese would be experiencing in Burma, and that with his own air superiority (29 squadrons would be available to him by 1 October 1942) he had the wherewithal to inflict a serious defeat on the Japanese and so raise morale in both India and farther abroad.

The plans that emerged during the first two weeks of June ranged from the practical to the absurd: all would be considered, and most rejected, in turn. The core idea did not change: two simultaneous operations would be mounted, one from Assam and the other into Arakan from Bengal. The primary operation was to be Operation *Ambulance*, an offensive into northern Burma from Assam along the lines of the Joint Planning Staff proposal of 1 June, but now much enhanced and more aggressive. IV Corps would advance across the Chindwin from Imphal with three infantry divisions (17, 23 and 39) and with 70 British Division in reserve. 14 Indian Division would guard Bengal at Chittagong.

Simultaneously a subsidiary offensive would be launched against the Arakan coast, initially named *Probation* but later changed to *Cannibal*. This entailed an amphibious assault against Akyab by the British 2 Division and 29 Independent Brigade, accompanied by an overland advance down the Arakan coastline by 14 Indian Division. To follow up both offensives Wavell planned to provide at least three other divisions (19 and 7 Indian Divisions, together with either 20 Indian Division or 5 British Division).[8] The ambitious and ultimately unconsummated plan to launch an amphibious assault on Rangoon, Operation *Anakim*, was finally scotched by the Chiefs of Staff in London, for want of resources, on 15 April 1943.

Wavell presented his plans for *Ambulance* and *Cannibal* to Churchill in a telegram on 9 June. He described the original Joint Planning Staff plan and the subsequent changes he had made to make them much more powerful and aggressive. At the same time Wavell was careful to explain the geographical and logistical difficulties that would have to be overcome to achieve these goals. He knew only too well Churchill's penchant for disregarding the irritating nuisance of such detail, but he tried, nevertheless:

1. Communications of all kinds from rest of India to Assam and in Assam extremely poor... No possibility yet to begin building up reserve of ammunition or supplies and troops are living from hand to mouth though rains have hardly begun yet. It will take time to improve this situation.
2. Forward of Palel [on the Imphal plain] only means of communication into Burma one incomplete mountain road (on which first rains caused six landslides in ten miles from Palel) and rough hill tracks. Any force operating into Burma will be dependent on animal transport and jeeps.[9]
3. Labour and other personnel of all kinds tend to disappear instantly over wide radius on bombs falling.
4. There are practically speaking no roads in Upper Burma, and maintenance inside Burma will present great difficulties. So will aerodrome construction.
5. Assam climate unhealthy and sick rate already high, though most malarial months still to come.
6. Troops will require much training. Doubtful whether I can use better-trained British divisions owing to maintenance problem... In any case they will require training in bush warfare and animal transport.

7. Though we hope to have local air superiority, both our bomber and fighter aircraft have much shorter range than enemy aircraft, and this in view of large distances involved and paucity of aerodromes will neutralise much of superiority we hope to have and hamper close support of land forces. This is most important consideration of all.[10]

Churchill's response did not surprise Wavell, the Prime Minister's complaint being that these were 'minor operations, very nice and useful nibbling'. They did not constitute the grand strategic gesture he so desired to hit back against the Japanese, such as an attack to seize Rangoon as a first step towards striking against Bangkok.[11] Wavell replied to the Prime Minister two days later, assuring him, 'We can now begin definitely to plan the recapture of Burma, which has been in my mind ever since it became obvious that I was likely to lose it.'[12] On the same day Wavell issued instructions to Lieutenant General Sir Charles Broad, GOC-in-C Eastern Command, to adopt a forward policy in the area around Chittagong as the first step in preparation for Operation Probation/Cannibal/Nibble.[13]

The tyranny of both distance and geography conspired to prevent any meaningful offensive into upper Burma from Imphal, at least until Manipur had been substantially reinforced. This conclusion gradually sunk in at GHQ India during the planning period in the middle of 1942, bringing them to the reality that the only practicable place to mount an operation against the Japanese in 1942 was Arakan. The long Burmese coastline against which lapped the Bay of Bengal was weakly defended and easier to reach than central or northern Burma. The line of communication necessary to support a British advance was, although long and complicated, at least far shorter and less difficult than that necessary to support an offensive mounted from Assam. Akyab Island and Akyab, a bustling trading town of some 45,000 inhabitants, contained an all-weather airfield and a port that accommodated the shipping that plied the peacetime coastal trade between Burma and India. Its possession would offer the British the prospect of being able to mount air attacks against Rangoon – only 330 miles distant – as well as strikes against the long Japanese line of communication into central Burma. Equally, it would serve to prevent the Japanese from using the airfield to launch aerial attacks on the valuable industrial areas around Calcutta. It also offered the possibility of a side door into Burma proper when the time came to attempt the reconquest of the country.

As other options for offensive action gradually lost their lustre or disappeared entirely during 1942, the view that Arakan could provide an ideal location for an offensive against the Japanese in Burma grew. However, although distances were not great, Arakan contained in microcosm some of the worst features of Burma's topography. The Mayu Peninsula stretched like a bony finger down the Arakan coast 90 miles from the coastal port of Maungdaw to Foul Point, which was separated from Akyab Island by the estuary of the Mayu River. Along the centre of the peninsula ran the Mayu Range, a ridge of densely forested and precipitous hills which rose to some 2,000 feet above sea level. On the eastern side of the peninsula the Mayu River, which in its higher reaches above Buthidaung was called the Kalapanzin, flowed down the centre of the Mayu Valley. At Buthidaung the Mayu Valley stretched some 10 miles wide: it was wider still at its mouth as it entered the Bay of Bengal opposite Akyab. The river was itself a formidable obstacle to movement, as for most of its length it was tidal, which meant that even the smallest *chaungs* – stream beds, coursing with water in the monsoon but often otherwise dry – were difficult to cross at high tide. Through a parallel valley farther inland flowed the Kaladan River, which also found its exit at Akyab.

The Mayu Range was crossed by an all-weather road in only one place, between the coastal port of Maungdaw and the river port of Buthidaung, the route between which passed through two tunnels. Possession of this road and the tunnels secured the whole of north Arakan. Apart from this road the Arakanese infrastructure was, in 1942, virtually non-existent. The situation was made doubly worse in the monsoon when fair-weather roads became impassable to vehicles, the standard means of transport became waterborne, and even foot patrols had difficulty moving away from tracks and paths. The single greatest debilitating factor from the British perspective, still heavily dependent on wheeled transport, was the almost complete lack of motorable roads. That the country was highly malarial added to the nightmare. Arakan was to be universally loathed by the troops of the British and Indian Armies. One can only imagine that the Japanese hated it too.

Not unreasonably, Slim, whose geographical responsibilities included the frontier region with Arakan, assumed that should an offensive be mounted to seize Akyab, XV Corps would be given the task. On taking command in June 1942 he ordered his divisional commander – Wilfred Lloyd – to deploy patrols well forward of the main divisional positions, regardless of the monsoon. He wanted Lloyd's troops to gain a feel for Japanese dispositions and to find out their intentions: he also wanted to ensure that 14 Indian Division did not forget that the ultimate purpose of their existence was offensive. Slim then began planning for an advance in Arakan. He assumed from the outset that he would have insufficient shipping and landing craft to mount an all-out amphibious assault on Akyab, which seemed to him to offer far and away the best chance of success. After studying the problem with Lloyd, he decided that the least attractive option would be a straightforward advance down the peninsula. It lacked any sparkle of imagination, would fail to surprise the Japanese and, given the nature of the terrain, would be guaranteed to be slow. This left only two realistic alternatives. The first was a series of 'hop, skip and jump' minor amphibious operations working down the coast in hooks behind the successive Japanese positions, using a flotilla of small coastal vessels – the 'Sundarbans Flotilla' – which Slim had been instrumental in gathering together for the coastal defence of Bengal and Orissa. The second was a long-range penetration expedition to the rear of the Japanese positions in the Kaladan Valley against their line of communication into Arakan. Wavell had recently appointed Brigadier Orde Wingate to train a brigade for long-range 'hit and run' type operations behind enemy lines, and Slim believed that this type of formation would be ideal for an attack on Akyab from a direction the Japanese would least expect.

Slim's final plan involved a combination of all three ideas. 14 Indian Division would exercise frontal pressure against the Japanese in north Arakan, while a series of short amphibious hooks were made to outflank the Japanese positions down to Akyab Island, with Wingate's long-range penetration brigade assisting by hooking in from the Kaladan Valley in the east.

However, in July 1942 Irwin told Slim that he wanted to take personal control – as army commander – of the Arakan offensive, and would swap locations with Slim to facilitate this. He would take direct command of 14 and 26 Divisions, and Slim would be tasked with forming and training the remainder of Eastern Army at Ranchi. It was a strange decision. The truth may have resided in Irwin's ill-concealed antipathy to Slim, although it is more likely that the root of the decision lay elsewhere.[14] With only Dunkirk and Dakar behind him – neither of which was a conspicuous success – Irwin had arrived in India with something to prove. It is possible that he arrived seeking both personal redemption and confirmation as Wavell's man of destiny. It didn't help that he had a combative personality. He trusted no one and involved himself constantly in detail which should have been of no concern to an army commander. He gave little or no latitude to his subordinates to use their initiative and ensured that in every point of detail his orders were carried out without discussion or deviation. When he looked at Slim's plans for the Arakan offensive they were peremptorily dismissed. Slim's imaginative approach using his flotilla of small boats was rejected in favour of the very option which Slim had discarded – an orthodox, direct advance overland. At the same time Wavell decided to use Wingate's brigade elsewhere, and so the option of deep penetration from a wide flank was unavailable to Irwin had he wanted to employ it.

14

Bharat Choro!

The loss of Burma in 1942 was a surprise to everyone, from Tokyo to London and to New Delhi. Suddenly, the British grand narrative of empire, and its control of this narrative, had changed, and in a way that London or Viceroy House in New Delhi had never anticipated. Britain and its empire had been humiliated. Its armed forces in Asia, which included the Indian Army, had been defeated, and, although not decisively – India had not fallen as a result of these defeats – Britain's stature in Asia and in India had been fatally diminished. In an instant Britain, by failing to protect the country from invasion, had lost the moral high ground in the independence conversation, and everyone knew it. Churchill could bluster and attempt to retain the political initiative, but this didn't fool anyone. Defeat in Malaya, Singapore and Burma might not yet have destroyed Britain's empire in Asia, but it had decisively changed the nature of the relationship. In India, the nationalists now held all the political cards and India's response to the threat to the empire was suddenly all important. Would it support Britain in its battle to defeat Japanese militarism, or would it remain disdainfully apart from this sordid squabble between battling empires?

It had begun badly. On 3 September 1939 the Viceroy, Lord Linlithgow, had unilaterally and to the unmitigated fury of the Indian National Congress, told India that it was now at war. In this single 'silly and unnecessary' (though strictly legal) announcement, the Viceroy had revealed his attitude to the elephant in the Indian room.[1] The fact of nationalism, either in terms of popular sentiment or of political action, was not going to go away. To simply ignore it in Linlithgow's typically imperious, 'literally as well as metaphorically stiff-necked'[2] and intellectually hidebound manner – it never crossed his mind that it might be politic to discuss the subject with the Indian National Congress and Muslim League – was foolish.

In 1942 Britain, for its part, appreciated that the situation had changed. Far from being in control, London needed now to negotiate with the various leaders of an independence movement that had dominated Indian political consciousness at least since 1857. In 1942 these men weren't united in anything other than the desire for full and complete independence. Congress Party leaders, such as Gandhi and Nehru (Subhas Chandra Bose had been ejected from Gandhi's 'big tent' in 1939), all broadly wanted a united India to receive full independence from Britain, able to forge its own future in the world as an independent sovereign state. The political leader of India's Muslims, the Muslim League – Muhammad Ali Jinnah – however, as had been announced in the Lahore Declaration of March 1940, wanted the legacy of the Raj to be two states, one for Muslims (Pakistan) and the other for everyone else (India), setting himself against Gandhi – a visceral advocate of a free, *united* India. Pakistan was to be the Muslim League's price for its agreement to play by British rules: they preferred a disunited India if the alternative was one dominated by the Hindu majority.[3] Linlithgow, the archetypical praetorian prefect, the King Emperor's personal envoy, who unwaveringly interpreted his task as protecting the status quo, didn't much mind either way what these noisy *fakirs* thought. He had no interest in organizing the future; what mattered was protecting the present within the correct, legal construct of the past. Due to retire in 1941 and extended in post to mid-1943 at Churchill's request, riding easily at the Prime Minister's anchor, he was perfectly comfortable letting the future take care of itself, admitting that he wasn't 'a bit fussed about the post-war period.'[4]

The Congress-orchestrated civil unrest during August 1942 – the 'Quit India' campaign in which Gandhi urged Indians not to cooperate with the British ('I see no difference between the Fascists or Nazi powers and the Allies') until London provided acceptable terms for independence – proved a sudden and worryingly dangerous impediment to the challenge of creating a united economic, social and military response in India to the threat posed by Japan. This brief but violent *'Bharat Choro!'* – the 'Quit India' – campaign involved two weeks of mob violence, largely in eastern parts of the country. In places disruption to civil society and the war effort was severe. Rioters brought life to a halt in many places, people were killed, railway tracks were torn up, businesses set on fire and visible representations of government – telephone lines, police stations, customs offices, courts and such like, were torched. The statistics of violence were dramatic: 208 police stations, 332 railway stations, 749 government buildings,

945 post offices, 268 railway carriages and 411 separate items of railway sabotage.[5] The danger for Britain was that Congress agitation in general and the Quit India campaign in particular would have a doubly negative effect. By causing civil disturbance across the country, it would divert military effort away from the fight against the Japanese and it might also reduce the number of recruits applying to join the Indian armed forces. The two together would potentially make India ungovernable and unprotected. The colonial authorities took no risks and clamped down hard on civil disorder, regarding it to be a serious threat to India's ability to fight the Japanese. Repression was severe. Those considered agitators within the Indian National Congress were arrested in large numbers, many to remain in confinement until the end of the war. Some 57 infantry battalions, British and Indian, were deployed to disperse rioting; live rounds were fired 369 times, killing and wounding about 3,000 demonstrators. These were harsh measures to restore order. They were not designed to repress nationalist sentiment, if that were possible, but to contain disorder. The army knew all too well that it couldn't dismiss the rioters, acknowledging 'freedom and independence are probably sought after by the troops themselves.'[6]

The Quit India campaign had an unsettling effect on British and Indian soldiers alike, and on some views of the army. For a brief moment, the British authorities worried that it might affect the loyalty of the Indian Army. This, of course, was one of Gandhi's ambitions, but the truth is that the trouble did not have any discernible impact on the army's loyalty or its effectiveness. There was a job to be done, first. Nor did it halt recruiting. Most of the protest was Hindu in origin. Jinnah described it as a Congress plot, which drove a further wedge between Hindu and Muslim opinion in India. In any case, although Hindus considerably outnumbered Muslims in India, 65 per cent of the Indian Army was Muslim and remained unswayed by Congress.

Despite political violence across parts of India later in 1942, the surging emotions of the political backstory to India's slow path to self-rule did not come to dominate the conversation in India about what to do about Japan. There are several reasons for this. First, the sword waving and drum beating of militaristic Japan had horrified most Congress politicians since Japan had first smashed into China in 1931. Congress, after all, stood for the independence of all subject peoples, not just in India but also those in Japanese-held China. Second, the humiliations of early 1942 came at a time when India had already mobilized for war, if at least a war that was to be fought far from its shores. The army at the end of 1942 stood at well over a million men, a dramatic increase over the number on the muster in September 1939. The withdrawal of the Burma Corps across the Chindwin in May 1942 merely changed the nature of the military conversation in India, without calling into question whether this meant the end of the Raj, the removal of its systems and structures of government and authority (which all derived, of course, from London), or that India should cease fighting. Even after these disasters, the recruitment of Hindus into the army increased, confirming Churchill's belief that the Hindu politicians were unrepresentative of the 'real' India, a mask for the 'Hindu priesthood machine'.[7] What continued, of course, was the political dialogue around the nature and extent of independence, although this did not challenge the notion that the Indian Army should continue to defend India from its enemies, even if those enemies had been decided for India by Linlithgow in September 1939 without the consent of India itself.

Between 1939 and late 1941 India perfectly fulfilled its role, in the wider context of British defence strategy, of being an imperial reserve for British military requirements outside India – in North Africa, the Mediterranean and the Near and Middle East. With the Japanese invasion of Malaya in December 1941, however, attention in India switched from the west to the east, not just in terms of its military effort, but also its industrial and economic energy. In 1942 the requirements of fighting the Japanese along the massive distances of the Assamese and the Bengal lines of communication, not to mention the full extent of its eastern seaboard and Ceylon, demanded much more of India than hitherto. The Indian Army was needed not merely to suppress unruly Pathan tribesmen on its North West Frontier, but to defend the country for the first time in recent history from conventional military attack. This had never been planned, let alone envisaged. Suddenly, the role of India as a base for both defensive and (ultimately) offensive operations on its eastern border and its extensive eastern littoral needed to be reconsidered, including India's industrial capacity and its ability to provide for itself what it couldn't secure elsewhere.

During 1942 the pressure of defeat, the existential threat to India as the result of the Japanese onslaught, Tokyo's offer of an Asia for the Asiatics, and the Quit India campaign, alongside the shock of the creation of the INA, forced Britain to consider how its colonial administrations in Asia would need to change to respond to both the short-term exigencies and the long-term implications of war. The problem was not merely the loyalty or otherwise of the Indian Army, but the challenge of ensuring that India remained economically, socially and politically stable at this point of extreme crisis for the empire. This conversation would also need to consider what the empire would look like once the war was over. It seemed axiomatic at the time to most British and Indian political commentators that the world had changed, and future issues of governance needed to take account of the interests of subject peoples. The Atlantic Charter of August 1941 and Roosevelt's announcement of his Four Freedoms and its commitment to political self-determination elevated the demands for independence to a new, moral and international stage. Political opinion in Britain, pressure from the USA, and nationalist agitation within India forced Britain to evaluate India's place in the empire. Was it to be complete independence or a variety of self-government? Likewise, when would it happen, and how? Just days before the fall of Singapore Leo Amery found himself observing, 'It looks as if we were on the verge of very great changes in the relation of Asia to Europe. Indeed, the whole question arises whether in the future empires like our Asiatic empire, based on a very low degree of militarization and interference with the life of the people, can subsist.'[8]

Given the extent of the nationalist movements in the 1930s would India – and *some* Indians – see British reverses as a heaven-sent opportunity to secure their collective political liberty, through a pragmatic alignment with Japan? The 1920s and 1930s had seen an increase in the efforts of the Indian National Congress and the Muslim League to press their competing claims for self-government, which effectively meant independence from Britain. The nationalist movement wasn't united or monolithic, but it was increasingly influential, not merely in India, but in Britain and, importantly for British alliances during the global war, in the United States. Gandhi had, in particular, brought to the nationalist movement an effective way of mobilizing mass civil protests and civil disobedience. With the rise in pro-independence sentiment within India came an increasingly influential (though still small) body of political opinion in Britain, largely linked to the Labour Party, opposed to the continuance of colonialism. In response, Whitehall had passed the Government of India Act in 1935 to allow more representation of local political opinion in India, although without removing any of the levers of executive power. Nevertheless, 1935 was a further milestone in the slow journey of India to some form of independence, even if, at the time, parties and opinion – in London and Delhi – remained bitterly divided as to the form that independence would ultimately take.

To deflect the threat of significant disruption to Britain's ability to wage war against Japan, the new coalition War Cabinet[9] (from 19 February 1942) engineered a piece of diplomatic theatre in which Sir Stafford Cripps – the honest, upright but naïve Cabinet minister and friend of Nehru – was despatched to India in March 1942 on a mission to 'offer' a conversation about dominion status independent of direct control by Britain, as afforded to colonies such as Canada, Australia and New Zealand, once the war was over. He had in his pocket a 'draft' declaration agreeing to the creation of an Indian 'constituent assembly' to draw up a constitution for India, in which each of the provinces would be free to join or make its own arrangements. In a nod to the Muslim League, which had determined that Muslim interests would only be secured by means of an entirely independent Pakistan, Cripps' offer included an opt-out for any province that did not wish to join a united India. It was far from a promise of full independence. Likewise, although it was offered in good faith by Cripps, neither Churchill nor Linlithgow had any intention of negotiating anything more substantial until long after the war. In any case the conversation would be conducted on British terms, with Indians as supplicants in the conversation. Indeed, a cynic might view that the primary purpose of Cripps' so-called 'mission' was to demonstrate to Roosevelt and the American public – now that Pearl Harbor had made Britain and America co-belligerents – that Britain was serious about engaging in the question of India's future, and appeared to be presenting something of substance.

Gandhi and Nehru saw through the subterfuge – they had, after all, been dealing with such slipperiness for a very long time – and rejected Cripps' entreaties. It was full independence for them, or nothing. Unfortunately, this response played into Britain's policy of divide and rule: the Hindu-dominated Congress, which wanted a united independent India, versus the Muslim League, who wanted a disunited India and supported Britain's general 'India Policy' of fighting fascism first. Cannily, Churchill considered 'Hindu-Muslim antagonism as a safeguard for British power.'[10] For London, rejection of the Cripps Mission by the Congress appeared petulant, Britain appearing to the watching Americans at least to be the injured party. It had apparently offered independence to India (which of course was never on the table in a form that would be acceptable to India) only to have had its generosity (at a time of national extremis) thrown back at it. Consequently, when 'an old-style colonial repression' was carried out, the 'Quit India' movement followed in 1942, which Linlithgow, the Viceroy, described as 'the greatest rebellion to arise in India since the Mutiny of 1857'. In response, the United States was content to largely support Britain and condemn Indian nationalists as being unreasonable. Churchill's policy of prevarication had worked. Cripps, spectacularly out-manoeuvred, was the fall guy.

Confounding many expectations, both in Britain as well as nationalist India, India did not collapse into chaos or break under the political strain of the Quit India movement and its repression. Despite considerable disruption in 1942, disturbances were localized, and losses were, in the circumstances, relatively light, although at the expense of full freedom of expression where the freedom so expressed was anti-government. The Indian Army and the Indian Civil Service remained unwavering in their loyalty to the Raj, as did the vast majority of the population. If the Raj truly was weak as some suggested, the politically disaffected populace would have risen en masse against the colonial oppressors and demanded immediate independence. That India did not, given its self-evident political maturity, suggests that, unlike the leaders of the Indian National Congress and the Muslim League, all of whom were incarcerated by the British for the duration of hostilities, most Indians in fact were prepared to accept the Raj's right to prioritize for the time being the military defence of the country and to wait for Britain's offer of independence at the end of the war.

In Britain the colossal expense, the relentless pressure for independence, the waning interest in the British political class in empire – together with the fact that independence had been long promised – removed any desire to stay any longer than the current crisis required, for the majority of British policy makers at least. The fact was that the imperial diehards on both left and right were themselves a declining breed, the coalition government of Churchill and Attlee providing a socialist leavening of the British political establishment that was firmly committed to applying the principles of the Atlantic Charter to all subject races as quickly as was practically possible. Although Churchill refused to accept that the charter applied to India, the logic of Nehru's argument that 'it was absurd for a subject India to fight for the freedom of Poland' would invariably trump the emotional illogicality of Churchill's. Indeed, as Nehru asserted, it was absurd to think that 'the present-day world of empires and colonies and dependencies will survive the holocaust of war.'[11] The tragedy was that Britain – because of bitter political divisions across Westminster – did nothing to prepare a subject India for an independence almost everyone now accepted was inevitable. Attlee prepared a War Cabinet paper on 2 February 1942, decrying Linlithgow's lack of vision for the future, arguing that 'a representative with power to negotiate within wide limits should be sent to India now, either as a special envoy or in replacement of the present Viceroy, and that a Cabinet Committee should be appointed to draw up terms of reference and powers.'[12] Churchill, horrified, ignored any such proposals as akin to opening the door on the dissolution of the empire. The result was that Britain was left with no policy with regard to the future of India, other than 'the negative aim of keeping things quiet on the subcontinent.'[13] That Britain was distracted by war is an excuse. Ignoring those, like Churchill and Linlithgow, who did not want India to achieve full independence at all, the fact that Britain did nothing to define the nature of the independence that was (or wasn't) on offer, or prepare for it in any meaningful way, led directly to the confusions and chaos of 1947.

15

Vinegar Joe's Travails

Of all the oddities and eccentricities who washed up in the Far East during the Second World War – and there were many contenders for the prize – the strangest was 'Vinegar Joe' Stilwell. Remembered among other things for his blasphemies and the virulent Anglophobia exposed in his notorious, posthumously published diary, Stilwell was ultimately undone by the failure of his relationships with Chiang Kai-shek and Lord Louis Mountbatten, who eventually took over as the 'Supremo' in command of the new South East Asia Command in late 1943. He nevertheless made a distinctive impact on the progress of the war in South East Asia between 1942 and 1944, not least in the training, preparation and leadership of the Chinese Army for war, as well as in the staunch defence of American national interest in the face of Chinese corruption and graft. He survived the war in Asia retaining the full confidence of his mentor, General George Marshall, who was never to waver in his judgement that Stilwell was 'exceptionally brilliant', while losing the trust and regard of virtually everyone else.

After little more than a month of campaigning in Burma during 1942, Stilwell concluded that all the command problems he had encountered in the Chinese Army were the fault of Chiang Kai-shek. He would never change this view. By April 1942 he already regarded the Chinese leader to be mentally unstable, two-faced and surrounded by parasitic sycophants. Frustrated that he was being asked to command the Chinese armies in the field against a ferociously competent and disciplined enemy, and yet constantly undermined by the Chinese system of command, Stilwell complained bitterly to whoever would listen. Unfortunately, Stilwell's complaints were countered by effective messaging from

Chungking to the contrary, and by the fact that Stilwell was well known for his misanthropic language and racist attitudes, not least towards the British.

Following the retreat, Stilwell wasted no time in making plans to rebuild his Chinese forces and re-take Burma. To do this he proposed a new Chinese Army of 100,000 men, trained in India, equipped with American supplies and commanded by American divisional and corps commanders. Once training had been completed, which he estimated to take six months, Burma could be attacked simultaneously from the north – down the Hukawng Valley – and east, from Yunnan. The first thing that was needed was a thorough weeding of Chinese commanders. Only the best should be retained, and the remainder dismissed. He continued to fume about those generals that had let him down and argued privately that a number of army and divisional commanders be executed. The lack of training and basic competence in commanding large numbers of troops in the field with primitive communication systems and weak staff procedures was compounded by the fact that Chinese commanders were constrained by a system in which they received no coherent direction from above. Competing instructions could come from a variety of equally valid sources, one often contradicting and overriding the other, and in Stilwell's view the clear responsibility for the mess lay with Chiang Kai-shek.

While the essence of these plans was accepted by both Chiang Kai-shek and Washington (although Stilwell's request for a full American infantry division was turned down), Stilwell was now entering the dangerous waters of Chinese politics, which turned especially treacherous when they touched on relations with outside powers. As he was to discover, things were not always as they seemed. Stilwell's desire was to create an effective, fighting army. It needed clear and unambiguous structures of command, the modernization of administration and supply, and the concentration of scarce American equipment on 30 elite divisions.

Simple as these plans were in concept, they nevertheless foundered repeatedly on the rocks of international politics and the domestic struggles for power in a divided China. Chiang Kai-shek's policy towards the Allies was based largely on his belief that China played a critical role in Asia because it tied down large Japanese forces that would otherwise be directed against the Allies in South East Asia and the Pacific. He used this bargaining chip ruthlessly for his own advantage, going so far as threatening to withdraw from the fight and to strike terms with the Japanese if the Allies did not meet all his demands. Stilwell bore the brunt of Chiang Kai-shek's politicking, finding himself – unwillingly – caught between a demanding and ungrateful China on the one hand and an uncomprehending United States on the other.

In all of this he struggled to hold to a position of benign neutrality, insisting that his task was not to broker deals between Chiang Kai-shek and Roosevelt, but to prosecute the war against the Japanese. Chiang Kai-shek undoubtedly wanted Stilwell to become a mouthpiece for Chinese demands, and saw his purpose to be the key that unlocked American largesse. Stilwell, however, in refusing to kowtow to Chinese demands, and in insisting on remaining concerned merely about military affairs, raised Chiang Kai-shek's ire. Within months of Stilwell's appointment, Chiang Kai-shek was calling for his dismissal.

Stilwell's persistent refusal to give in to Chinese demands showed possession of moral courage. He refused to support Chinese demands for American supplies (which he constantly reminded the Chinese were 'the gift of the hard-working American taxpayer') for their own sake, insisting they were within the context of the military reconstruction of Chiang Kai-shek's armies for the purpose of invading Burma. Stilwell recognized, as did most of Washington by mid-1942, that Chiang Kai-shek was as interested in acquiring American resources to fight off the threat to his hegemony by the Communists, as much as to fight the Japanese. Because he refused to change his position, Stilwell was of no use to Chiang Kai-shek, who worked thereafter to engineer his removal. He was eventually to succeed.

For his part, Stilwell quickly came to despise Chiang Kai-shek with an antipathy that he found hard to disguise, and which ultimately served to undermine his position. To his diary, in letters home and even in public, the Chinese leader was the 'Peanut', 'coolie-class', 'incompetent', and the Chinese government in Chungking the 'Manure Pile'. Given the pungency of Chungking's atmosphere, Stilwell tried hard to avoid the place. His focus was on preparing the Chinese to fight, and his natural orbit that of Ramgarh, halfway between Delhi and Calcutta, where 9,000 of his Chinese troops were being trained and re-equipped.

In late 1942, so as to better coordinate his wide responsibilities, Stilwell created the China–Burma–India (CBI) theatre command. With its main headquarters in Chungking, he established a rear headquarters in New Delhi and attempted to provide structure, purpose and energy into a command that stretched from Karachi in the west to Chungking in the east. Stilwell's drive, energy and personal commitment were responsible more than anything for the success of his training programme and for the reinvigoration of the Chinese Army. It wasn't easy. Stilwell's view was that the supply and maintenance of these forces could only be achieved by the building of a new road to China, this time from Ledo in India across northern Burma. Building this road would necessitate

British–Indian and American–Chinese combat operations to push the Japanese back far enough to provide security for this new line of communication. Henceforth Stilwell's single-minded focus lay on recovering those parts of northern Burma that had been captured by the Japanese in 1942 and were essential to the maintenance of a land supply route to China from Ledo. To achieve the building of this road, Stilwell pressed both the Chinese and the British hard during 1942 and 1943 for concerted operations to drive the Japanese back into Burma. The objective Stilwell had in mind was the capture of the airfield and town of Myitkyina. The town in Allied hands would greatly assist the air route to China, by adding a staging post to China far from the dangerous mountains over which the Hump aircraft had otherwise to fly.

Discussions with Wavell in New Delhi on 18 October 1942 regarding the possibility of operations in Burma the following spring using the newly trained Chinese divisions concluded with agreement to mount an offensive down the Hukawng Valley to capture the vital airfield at Myitkyina. This would take place in conjunction with a British offensive against Arakan and a further Chinese offensive into the Shan States from Yunnan. Chiang Kai-shek eventually agreed to prepare a force of 15 divisions, known as Yoke Force, for the Yunnan offensive.

With these agreements secured, things were looking up for Stilwell. It appeared that both Wavell and Chiang Kai-shek were committed to operations in which the retrained and reorganized Chinese would play a significant part, and the hostility in Chungking towards Stilwell had abated. But by December 1942 the situation had quickly begun to unravel, and Stilwell's plans were assailed on all sides. Chiang Kai-shek had agreed to the creation of Yoke Force only on condition that the Allies mount massive air and amphibious operations in the Bay of Bengal to prevent the Japanese from using Rangoon. Stilwell knew this was impossible (because of a lack of resources), although he promised to make appropriate representations to Washington. Then the War Department in Washington refused to underwrite Stilwell's request for extra supplies to ensure the success of these plans. He responded angrily to Washington that their pusillanimity threatened to undo everything he was trying to do in China and Burma.

At this time also in 1943 the proponents of Major General Claire Chennault's air power strategy began pressing his ideas of an aerial bombing strategy against the Japanese from China as an alternative to a land campaign in Burma, and to voice public criticisms of Stilwell's plans for an advance to Myitkyina. Chennault, commander of the American Volunteer Group before being given command of the US Air Forces in the region, worked hard to persuade Roosevelt with a plan to win the war in six months by launching a bombing campaign from China, with himself in command. His plan – a shortcut to victory if there ever was one – was to provide 147 fighters and bombers on Chinese air bases to fly long-distance missions against the Japanese homeland, in the sure and certain hope that such aerial bombardment would quickly bring Japan to its knees. Chennault's ideas resonated positively in Chungking, as such a strategy would not entail any greater Chinese commitment to the war effort than the provision of air bases, and Stilwell's plans for an expensive land campaign, with the expenditure of blood and treasure that it would entail, could be shelved.

Stilwell rejected the idea of an air-only campaign. He realized precisely what Chennault had failed to learn from experience of air campaigning elsewhere in the war, namely that air forces alone could not retake lost ground. Stilwell was angered as much by Chennault's failure to comprehend this fact as he was by Chennault's disloyalty in proposing alternative plans to Washington, behind his back, but the irony of the situation was not lost on observers who saw Stilwell doing the same thing to Mountbatten the following year. Such plans were, he considered, just the excuse that Wavell and Chiang Kai-shek (although for different reasons) sought to halt offensive operations into Burma. He believed that the British would do anything possible to avoid a commitment to a land offensive into Burma, and saw the difficulties with which he was faced as a vindication of his fears: 'What a break for the Limeys. Just what they wanted. Now they will quit, and the Chinese will quit, and the goddamn Americans can go ahead and fight. Chennault's blatting has put us in a spot, he's talked so much about what he can do that now they're going to let him do it.'[1] To reinforce Stilwell's fear of British perfidy, Wavell, a month after his agreement to support an advance to Myitkyina, suggested that he might not have the air supply resources available to do so after all.

The truth is that there were a series of competing strategies for defeating the Japanese through China. One was Stilwell's, another Chennault's, and another the British idea of using amphibious solutions against Burma's littoral. As is so often the case in these matters, the debate between Stilwell and Chennault was driven down party lines, the army supporting Stilwell and the air force Chennault. The fact that Stilwell had been appointed by the War Department (i.e., the army) under General Marshall and not the Joint Chiefs of Staff did not help his cause, despite Marshall's consistent loyalty to Stilwell.

In theatre, Stilwell found it difficult to confide fully in peers, superiors or subordinates (although he wrote regularly to Marshall), with the result that there was little effective dialogue in the CBI headquarters and the group mental processes that existed in other headquarters, to weigh up and conclude issues of military strategy (and even, on occasions, grand strategy) were non-existent. Stilwell's unhelpful habit was to bottle up his frustrations and only express himself freely to his diary. He was a poor communicator, unable to press his ideas with the dispassionate vigour needed to ensure that his voice was heard in a reasoned and winning manner. The situation was not helped by the fact that Chennault's powerful personality gave considerable impetus to his grandiose, ill-formed plans for the aerial bombardment of Japan from airfields in China, allowing little opportunity for disagreement.

The clamour around Chennault's ideas intensified. The basic problem Stilwell faced was that US military strategy remained undecided. US grand strategy was to support China; the military strategy, however, remained an issue of dispute between the War Department and Chennault's air power supporters. Disregarding the fact that in Europe the impact of aerial bombardment had already been shown to be grossly exaggerated, Marshall and Stilwell were concerned that such a plan would provoke the Japanese to launch strong counter-offensives against Chennault's air bases in China, and without effective land forces these bases would quickly fall.

Chennault's plan, and the support it so rapidly acquired in the persons of Madame Kai-shek and her brother T.V. Soong, Chinese ambassador to the USA, made Chungking's agreement to Stilwell's requirements increasingly difficult. The fact that Stilwell was ultimately to be proved right in 1944 did not help him to fight the argument in 1943. On 2 January 1943 Chiang Kai-shek proposed the Chennault Plan to Roosevelt and added the rider that Yoke Force could only be used from Yunnan in conjunction with a wider Allied attack – by sea and air – in Burma. Without these commitments, insisted the Chinese leader, Stilwell's spring offensive could not be countenanced. The battle with Chennault for strategic dominance raged throughout 1943 and was one that Stilwell, loyally supported by Marshall, lost in the face of Chennault's successful lobbying of Roosevelt and the American press, combined with the vociferous support given to Chennault by Chiang Kai-shek.

Stilwell found himself struggling against the enemy within – Chinese ignorance, selfishness and greed, as he saw it, dangerously combined with American political naïveté – as much as he was fighting the Japanese. In preparation for the meeting of Churchill and Roosevelt at the Trident Conference in May 1943, the strategic dilemmas he faced and the consequences of not keeping a close rein on Chinese demands were summarized by his biographer, David Rooney:

1. President has no idea of Chiang's character, intentions, authority or ability.
2. British and Chinese ready to shift burden on to US.
3. Chiang's air plans will stop formation of effective ground forces.
4. Air activity could cause Japanese to overrun whole of Yunnan.
5. Chiang would make fantastic strategic decisions.
6. Chiang will seek control of US troops.
7. Chiang will get rid of me and have a 'yes' man.
8. Chinese will grab supplies for post war purposes.[2]

In many of these accusations and prophecies, Stilwell was to be proved right. His logic remained compelling to the War Department in Washington, but he failed completely to ensure that his views had the political impact they needed to survive. He was pre-eminently a fighting soldier, unable to deal with the complex nuances of the political environment in which he was forced to operate. Watching him closely in Chungking, British General Carton de Wiart put his finger on the problem, describing Stilwell as having 'strong and definite ideas of what he wanted, but no facility in putting them forward.'[3]

Chennault, by contrast, fought to gain direct access to Roosevelt, bypassing Marshall altogether, and in these overtures he was assisted in Washington by T.V. Soong. Stilwell's wholly admirable though ineffectual approach was to state what he believed, and state it loudly so that all could hear, but his failure was to believe that this was all that was necessary for him to do. The Chinese, seeing their strategies potentially undermined by this unwavering defender of American interests, applied every political pressure they could to undermine his views. In the end, Stilwell lost the argument. Roosevelt had admonished him a year earlier for speaking sternly to Chiang Kai-shek (and he was to do so again at Cairo in November 1943 for calling Chiang Kai-shek 'Peanut' in the President's hearing), and the sharpness of his tongue, whatever the prescience of his observations, served to whittle away what political capital he retained in Chungking, New Delhi, London and Washington.

Under the ill-informed pressure of the aerial strategists, the Trident Conference in May 1943 endorsed increasing the quantity of air resources to China, and agreement was reached in principle later in the year for a strategic bombing offensive to be launched from new bases in eastern China against Japan, once the war in Italy and Europe had been successfully concluded. This outcome encouraged renewed opposition in Chungking for land-based operations in Burma and continued the difficulties that Stilwell faced in preparing Chinese troops for war. As supplies to Chennault burgeoned, roadbuilding from Ledo almost stopped, the training of Yoke Force became half-hearted, and plans for the attack on Burma received renewed criticism from Chungking.

Chiang Kai-shek repeated his demand that any Chinese commitment of ground forces be accompanied by overwhelming Allied amphibious and aerial attacks on Burma. Stilwell was furious that Chiang Kai-shek had the nerve to demand more resources from the Allies while offering little in return. In circumstances like these, Stilwell was at his most eloquent: 'This insect, this stink in the nostrils, superciliously inquires what we will do, who are breaking our backs to help him, supplying everything – troops, equipment, planes, medical, signal, motor services ... training his lousy troops, bucking his bastardly Chief of Staff, and he the Jovian Dictator who starves his troops and who is the world's greatest ignoramus, picks flaws in our preparations, and hems and haws about the Navy, God save us.'

When, finally, Chiang Kai-shek appended his signature on 12 July 1943 to the plan for an offensive down the Hukawng Valley, Stilwell exclaimed with relief as much as fury at the pain he had to go through to win even this concession: 'What corruption, intrigue, obstruction, delay, double crossing, hate, jealousy and skulduggery we have had to wade through. What a cesspool... What bigotry and ignorance and black ingratitude. Holy Christ, I was just about at the end of my rope.'[4]

Chiang Kai-shek did nevertheless provide Stilwell with the full command of the Chinese divisions at Ledo on 19 December 1943. It was a sea-change from the situation only the month before, when Stilwell was facing dismissal. He spent little time trying to understand the reasons for this change of Chinese heart, and from December 1943 dedicated his remaining time in theatre to leading his small army into battle. There is a sense that he realized that he would never achieve any more in Chungking, and that more could be achieved by demonstrating on the ground that Chinese troops, when well trained, properly equipped and efficiently led, could be more than a match for the Japanese.

16

Trying to Crack the Donbaik Nut

Just how difficult, Irwin thought, could capturing Akyab be? He was certain that careful planning, comprehensive logistical preparations and firm leadership would achieve success. The obvious answer was to attack Akyab from the sea, while pushing a force down the coastline from Chittagong. Two brigades – 6 British and 29 Indian – were prepared for the amphibious assault, while Major General Wilfred Lloyd's 14 Indian Division was to undertake the land offensive. Irwin was confident. Opposition was light: Japanese forces in Akyab were estimated at a mere two dispersed infantry battalions from a total force of some 3,600 in Arakan. Lloyd was ordered to build a road behind the leading troops on which the advance could be centred and supplied. Lloyd's primary task, therefore, was to be a methodical advance to Foul Point at the pace of the construction of a road, in support of the main, amphibious, attack. There seemed no reason to rush troops into Arakan, especially if there was no road to supply them. It seemed sensible to allow battle to commence once the line of communication was complete. After all, the decisive element of the plan was the amphibious assault against Akyab.

The campaign got underway on 21 September 1942, with elements of 14 Indian Division moving to secure the coastal port of Maungdaw. The requirement to advance at the pace of the newly built road dictated Lloyd's timetable from the outset. This resulted in the initial slow advance being easily halted by a weak Japanese force in October. The continuing fury of the monsoon, which should have petered out by this time, didn't help. But the first major blow came in November, coinciding with the invasion of North Africa – Operation *Torch* – with the cancellation of the amphibious assault on Akyab. The assault shipping – and fighter cover for the landings – were in the end simply not available because of the demand elsewhere on these scarce resources. A compounding error was the decision to remove the long-range penetration brigade commanded by Brigadier Orde Wingate from the mix. Accordingly, the entire plan was rethought. Wavell ordered Irwin to press on with the land element of the offensive, supported by a scaled-down version of the original amphibious plan in which 6 Brigade would assault Akyab, not directly from the sea but across the Mayu River from the direction of Foul Point.

Irwin now instructed Lloyd to seize Foul Point by 15 January. He was ordered to clear the whole of Arakan, as well as to continue the construction of the road all the way to Foul Point. By now the Japanese had been alerted to British intentions and had begun reinforcing Arakan. For the British, speed was now imperative, a fact that jarred with the requirement to build a road. If the Japanese had time to reinforce their defences in the Mayu Peninsula in general and at Akyab specifically, the success of the venture would be jeopardized. The need for speed meant that Lloyd should have thrust his troops aggressively into Arakan, seeking new and innovative ways of supplying his rapidly expanding line of communication, rather than dissipating his effort to build a road. But, as was the case earlier in the year, Irwin's and Lloyd's knowledge and understanding of Japanese capabilities and techniques, and plans were precisely zero. There seemed, therefore, no reason to change the plans, and the advance continued on its ponderous way unchanged.

From the moment the advance was restarted in December, caution remained the British watchword. Long delays took place and prevented a quick attack on the first objective, Buthidaung. Irwin wanted to guarantee the success of each set piece attack, so he insisted that it should only go ahead once all of Lloyd's division had been deployed into the area. 'I believe it essential to win the first round and without acting as a brake to Lloyd I must satisfy myself that the chances of doing so are adequate', he wrote to Wavell on 14 November.[1] But waiting for Lloyd's division to move up took more time than even he had expected. Three weeks later he rather disingenuously blamed the delay on Lloyd's faulty planning, rather than his own reluctance to initiate an attack without overwhelming superiority. 'I decided to put Lloyd's operation … back a little over a fortnight,' he wrote to Wavell, 'because I was confident that as planned it would go off at "half cock".'[2] It seemed not to occur to him that by acting more quickly, the Japanese would retain the initiative, despite the overwhelming British numerical superiority at the time both on the ground and in the air. Irwin's repeated delays to ensure superiority of numbers meant that the Japanese, time and again, were given the opportunity to reinforce, to outflank and to prepare thoroughly for every British attack. Indeed, it took three wasted months before Lloyd was able to advance astride the Mayu Range in the direction of Foul Point.

These delays gave the Japanese valuable confirmation of British intentions, and they made haste to reinforce substantially their forces in Arakan. General Iida knew that to prevent the British from securing Akyab he needed to stop them from dominating the Mayu Peninsula, and to do this he needed to block their advance along the coast and in the Mayu River Valley. Wasting no time, his troops immediately began the long march into Arakan. In contrast to Lloyd's snail-like pace, the Japanese made rapid progress from central Burma using jungle tracks and paths, arriving long before Lloyd. Positions across the Mayu Range reaching down to the sea at the fishing village of Donbaik were now reinforced. By April 1943 Iida had eight battle-hardened battalions in the Mayu Peninsula. When the first patrols of 6 Brigade reached the outskirts of Donbaik on 6 January 1943 they were repulsed by heavy Japanese fire. Equipped with machine guns, mortars and anti-tank guns, 250 men had dug themselves deep into the edges of the wide *chaungs* – dried-up riverbeds – between the jungle edge and the sea. The *chaungs* had steep sides – up to 9 feet high – and proved to be natural anti-tank obstacles. Mangrove trees covered the entire length of the position. Japanese positions were deeply dug-in and heavily camouflaged. Each trench or bunker provided fire support to at least one neighbour, so that defensive fire was always interlocking. Forward troops were equipped with plentiful automatic weapons; ponderous and predictable British attacks, even when launched by brave, well-trained soldiers, never had a hope of overcoming resolute defenders. A British attack the following morning by an infantry company, preceded by a heavy artillery bombardment, was easily repulsed. The Japanese were able to predict and counter British methods of attack. Artillery bombardments were designed to 'soften' the target before the assaulting infantry left their trenches. The Japanese quickly adapted their defensive procedures to reduce casualties caused by British artillery. The orders were:

1. During the enemy's concentrated shelling, each platoon will leave one sentry in position, and the majority will take shelter in nearby caves.
2. When enemy guns extend their shooting range, everybody will move to the front bunker and await the signal for everyone to begin firing simultaneously.
3. The leader of the machine gun platoon will judge the timing when the enemy approaches close enough to our line, and order his medium machine guns to fire. All rifle platoons will then start firing.[3]

Two further attacks on 8 and 9 January respectively, again supported by mortars and artillery, failed to make an impression on the ever-strengthening Japanese defences. The attack on 8 January involved two companies – one company on the left and another on the right. Despite an early success along the jungle fringe, it made no progress. The right company was held up almost at once by a devastating crossfire of machine guns and mortars, while that on the left managed to penetrate through to the village of Donbaik, even forcing the Japanese to leave behind a prepared meal of rice. But the Japanese counterattacked in strength, pushing back both companies to their start point.[4]

Thus, by 9 January the Japanese, to stop the British from reaching Foul Point, had managed to create a defensive line in the Mayu Peninsula with little more than a company of infantry, and had repelled four British attempts to get through. The Japanese worked tirelessly to create an intricate web of interlocking defences, based on bunkers and killing zones of mortars and machine guns. Over the ensuing weeks the position developed into a network of seven well-dug and skilfully concealed bunkers stretching from the jungle edge down to the beach. Many posts were held for periods of time by only a single soldier with a machine gun and a bag of grenades, who was nevertheless expected to fight on his own initiative and not to expect relief when under pressure or when wounded. The bunkers themselves were difficult to locate in the jungle undergrowth and every new attack was like starting all over again from scratch. Two jungle-clad hills dominated the battlefield and provided the Japanese with concealed locations for mortars, artillery and machine guns. Compared with the relatively large quantities of artillery ammunition enjoyed by the British, the Japanese made up for extremely limited supplies by rapidly switching artillery fire from position to position, to where it was most needed.

By 10 January 1943 Lloyd's division was far from achieving Irwin's objective to secure the Mayu Peninsula by 15 January. Donbaik had become a serious problem, completely halting the British advance. The Japanese position now began to develop a legendary status for the British and Indian troops, reinforcing the 'superman' myth from Malaya and Burma the previous year and convincing them that the bunkers were constructed of some new type of armour-plating or concrete. As late as 26 March 1943 Irwin could write to Wavell, 'Cavendish [Commander of 6 Brigade] has been shelling [the enemy bunkers] at point blank range as well as shooting at them with 0.5 AT rifles, and it appears ... [that they] may contain some form of armoured plate protection rather than the concrete which was previously suggested. No penetration has yet been claimed. We are examining the possibilities of getting Naval depth charges to hurl at these posts.'[5]

In fact, the walls and roofs were made simply of logs, but were up to 5 feet thick and sunk deep in the ground. The product of long experience in China, they were invariably well camouflaged, so that they often could not be seen until the troops stumbled on them. The art of successful bunker clearance, involving the burning of surrounding vegetation prior to direct sniping by tanks, was not perfected until 1944.

In addition to the physical strength of the Donbaik bunkers, Japanese defensive positions were held with a tenacity that took the men of 14 Indian Division by surprise. If the Japanese in the attack were innovative and freewheeling, in defence they were immovable. None of 14 Indian Division's limited training had prepared it for such a determined foe. British tactics assumed that an enemy who was overwhelmed would invariably surrender. This might have been the case elsewhere – in North Africa, Iraq and Syria perhaps – but it was not true of the Japanese. In order to capture a Japanese position every defender had to be killed or incapacitated. Slim was later to remark, 'If five hundred Japanese were ordered to hold a position, we had to kill four hundred and ninety-five before it was ours – and then the last five killed themselves. It was this combination of obedience and ferocity that made the Japanese Army, whatever its condition, so formidable, and which would make any army formidable.'

The wholly unexpected failure to break through at Donbaik and the inability to make any impression at Rathedaung prompted a flurry of meetings between British commanders on 10 January. Wavell and Irwin flew forward to meet with Lloyd. Irwin had already concluded that the problem was obvious: Lloyd was not using a big enough hammer to crack the Donbaik nut, and that if only he employed more force, he would succeed where to date he had not.

Irwin was convinced that with concentration of force and thorough planning, the position would easily be broken. Like many of his generation, brought up in the hard school of the Western Front during the Great War, Irwin thought that only meticulous preparation, careful planning and precise battlefield choreography would bring about success in battle. He also believed implicitly in the power of force, assuming that overwhelming firepower would be sufficient to destroy the enemy's will to fight and thus allow a position to be taken. At no stage does it appear that Irwin considered bypassing Donbaik, striking instead against Akyab and the Japanese lines of communication, cutting off the Japanese from their base. Irwin's concern to prepare thoroughly meant that weeks were required to rehearse the various phases of the plan, and to build up sufficient stocks of ammunition and stores to cater for every eventuality. The lack of surprise this entailed, coupled with a rigid inflexibility in procedures once battle was joined, enabled the Japanese to read and pre-empt every British move with ease. Irwin's caution handed to the Japanese the advantage. Irwin didn't seem to consider evaluating how the Japanese had achieved success when they invaded Burma in January 1942, and apply those lessons to his own situation.

Accordingly, the British spent their time between attacks organizing themselves for the next methodically planned and prepared set-piece attack, rather than keeping up a constant drip of pressure against the Japanese positions and their supply routes by the use of aggressive patrolling and sniping. No degree of planning and organization based on pre-war tactics, which included methodical infantry advances behind closely timed artillery barrages, appeared to be sufficient to win the day against a Japanese defensive position.

Because of the length of time required to organize and prepare for battle, the next attacks against Donbaik did not take place until 18 January. Wavell was critical of Irwin's failure to make faster progress. 'It may be that the urgency of the situation was not fully recognised,' he wrote in his despatch, 'and that troops should have been pushed forward in spite of all difficulties to take advantage of the situation.'[6] But throughout the campaign Lloyd walked in step with Irwin. He was as convinced as Irwin that overwhelming force was bound to prevail. He concluded that if he could concentrate four battalions on a very narrow frontage, supported by all his available artillery, he would finally succeed where all previous attempts had failed. His plan was to hold the left flank among the foothills with a battalion, launch a two-battalion frontal assault on Donbaik, keeping one battalion in reserve ready to exploit the breakthrough. The attack was to be supported by 25-pounder guns and a machine-gun company. However, despite Irwin's optimistic belief that the long preparation time would pay off in a successful breakthrough at Donbaik, this attack once again failed, with heavy loss. Despite the ferocity of the pre-assault artillery bombardment and the fact that the infantry got in among the Japanese positions, they were beaten back at a cost of some 130 casualties. The tried-and-tested British tactics from the previous war of rolling artillery barrages, followed by the infantry advancing onto the enemy positions, simply did not work at Donbaik. The Japanese defensive position was too deep for artillery to have much effect, and in any case the defenders had perfected the art of reinforcing their bunkers once the artillery barrage had lifted, in time to catch the advancing infantry. The night, too, was dominated by the Japanese, who used it to collect their rations and ammunition, gather up the dead and wounded, and repair and reinforce their bunkers, camouflaging them with fresh foliage as well as setting up fake positions to attract enemy shelling and bombing.

Irritated but not deterred by this failure, Irwin pressed Lloyd to mount another attack, now planned for 1 February 1943. Irwin remained confident that persistence would be rewarded, but he failed properly to understand why every attack was being thrown back with heavy loss. Irwin saw the problem of Donbaik in terms of quantity and force, and he was determined to build up the largest possible numbers for another deliberate attack. The brigade that had led the advance thus far was replaced by the fresh, though inexperienced, divisional reserve. Four battalions found themselves preparing for a new assault on Donbaik on 1 February, of which two had no battle experience, one was rapidly tiring and one had been severely weakened in the fighting to date.

To strengthen this attack Lloyd asked Irwin to release a small number of Valentine tanks from 50 Tank Brigade. Irwin agreed to send a troop of eight. When Slim – by now no more than an anxious observer on the sidelines of the Arakan operation – heard of the request, he protested that such a small number of tanks would be wholly insufficient. Using small numbers in penny packets was 'against all my experience in the Middle East and Burma,' he wrote, where the principle was 'The more you use, the less you lose.' 'I argued that a regiment could be deployed and used in depth even on the narrow front chosen for attack.' But Irwin rejected these representations. 'We were overruled,' Slim recalled, 'on the grounds that more than a troop could not be deployed and that the delay in getting in a larger number across the chaungs was more than could be accepted.'

Lloyd's attack on 1 February started badly and mirrored in every respect the dismal pattern of its predecessors. Three tanks soon ended up in ditches. Of the six that started out only two returned, and in the face of fierce Japanese artillery fire the attack petered out. The Valentines at Donbaik were expected to attack the enemy unsupported by infantry or artillery, and in extremely difficult terrain. The infantry able to get close to the Japanese bunkers were unable to force out their obstinate occupants. By the end of 4 February, the local brigade commander admitted failure and called off his offensive. No new way of breaking through the Donbaik position seemed to present itself.

Irwin's self-belief now began to waver. Wavell, nevertheless, had yet to be persuaded that the task was impossible. On 9 February 1943 he met Irwin in Calcutta to discuss the situation. Aerial reconnaissance provided strong indications that the Japanese were reinforcing Arakan. Together with the difficulties already encountered, Irwin and Wavell acknowledged that it would be difficult to clear the whole of the Mayu Peninsula in time to deliver the planned amphibious assault on Akyab before the first rains of the monsoon fell in mid-May. Nevertheless, still trying to drive the campaign from too remote a vantage point, Wavell believed that there was sufficient justification to continue the attempt to secure the Mayu Peninsula and launch an assault on Akyab if the circumstances permitted, and he gave Irwin his old, well-trained and experienced 6 Brigade for the purpose of mounting a fifth major attack on Donbaik. It was considered that if a breakthrough could be achieved at Donbaik, the last possible day for an attack on Akyab would be 15 March.

Irwin was in full agreement with Wavell's assessment, and the offer of 6 Brigade appeared to provide precisely the means – overwhelming force – that would finally enable him to overcome the problem of Donbaik. In order to ensure that sufficient troops were available for the next attack, Irwin also gave Lloyd 71 Indian Infantry Brigade from Major General Clive Lomax's 26 Indian Division. Irwin instructed Lloyd to ensure that the combined 6 and 71 Brigade attack took place on or soon after 25 February.

The danger now was that the Japanese, while holding Irwin's attention at Donbaik, were threatening to outflank him to the east. Lloyd took several days to realize this danger. It was not until 22 February that Lloyd warned Irwin that the last safe moment to attack Donbaik had passed. He recommended that 14 Indian Division should be allowed to withdraw to prepare robust defensive positions between Maungdaw and Buthidaung before the onset of the monsoon in May, to avoid his elongated line of communication down the Mayu Peninsula being cut in half by a Japanese counterattack during the wet season.

Irwin reluctantly agreed. Watching his offensive dreams disappear into the ether, he ordered Lloyd to consolidate the positions he held in the Mayu Peninsula and to hold them until the arrival of the monsoon made a withdrawal inevitable. Lloyd was instructed to prepare reserve positions at Indin and Buthidaung, and Lomax was ordered to prepare to bring his division forward to relieve Lloyd's in late March or early April. Irwin then explained these arrangements by letter to Wavell on 23 February and assumed that Wavell would agree to them. But to Wavell such views were unduly pessimistic and he overruled them. Wavell ordered Irwin to rescind his orders to Lloyd, and to continue with the plan to attack Donbaik with 6 and 71 Indian Brigades. It was a foolish decision, and out of touch with the real situation in Arakan. Lloyd's troops were in no position to mount a successful, 'morale-restoring' attack. Irwin now recognized this truth, and Wavell, who appeared wilfully to ignore the advice of his army commander, should have known it, too. Equally, the tactics advocated by Wavell were precisely those which had failed so dismally in bloody and inconclusive attacks during the previous six weeks. They were clearly seriously flawed. Through his demand for 'more of the same', Wavell served to reinforce failure in Arakan, exacerbate the ever-growing crisis of morale in 14 Indian Division and lead to a growing sense of helplessness among the troops and their commanders. For his part, Irwin meekly acquiesced in these arrangements. He did not have the moral courage to take issue with Wavell, and dutifully ordered Lloyd to plan a sixth attack, to take place on or soon after 15 March 1943. Lloyd's sense of despair must have been palpable. His plan was to send 6 Brigade to attack Donbaik frontally down the coastal plain, 71 Indian Brigade to attack along the Mayu foothills and 47 Indian Brigade along the summit of the Mayu Range. But when Lloyd presented this plan to Irwin, the latter rejected it as being too similar to the last and thus likely to fail. This was only partly true. Brigadier Cavendish of 6 Brigade had come up with the plan, which involved, among other things, a silent night attack without a preliminary artillery bombardment to give away British intentions. Irwin's rejection of this plan condemned Lloyd's troops to failure.

But it was clear that Lloyd had run out of ideas, having already admitted to Irwin that he saw no point in continuing to attack Donbaik now that the capture of Akyab was no longer achievable. During January and February Lloyd had been Irwin's dutiful servant, implementing plans that Irwin had approved and authorized. Now, with failure crowning Lloyd's loyal efforts, Irwin's trust in his junior began to falter. It says much about Irwin's personality that he could not see that the seeds of Lloyd's failure lay in his own exercise of command. To Irwin, the blame for failure at Donbaik lay squarely with Lloyd.

Irwin's solution was to take over the detailed planning for the attack himself. He wrote a long exculpatory letter to Wavell on 9 March:

> I found it necessary to overrule all plans which had been prepared for carrying out the operation on the Donbaik front and to give Lloyd instead, an outlined plan of my own…
>
> In some ways I have been disappointed because Lloyd has not shown that determination of command which I had expected and is more prone to wait for suggestions or requests from his subordinate commanders than to impose his will on them. He is not sufficiently meticulous in examining plans put up by them or in supervising the detailed conduct of their operations – long distances account for this to a considerable extent. I have warned him to this effect.[7]

Writing that he had sat on a hill overlooking the Donbaik position for an hour, Irwin's assumption that no previous commander, be it Lloyd or any of the successive brigade or battalion commanders who had had a go at cracking the Donbaik nut, had done anything similar, seems remarkably arrogant. His failure to appreciate the reasons for the successive failures of past attacks is clear from the explanation of his plan he then gave to Wavell: 'I have gone for a highly concentrated attack on a very limited objective… I have gone for the extreme of concentration (although) threats and distractions east of the [Mayu] River… give rise to considerable anxiety, and may force us to concentrate our attention on defence in that direction.'[8]

Had not highly concentrated attacks been tried, unsuccessfully, before? There seems no explanation for Irwin's failure to concede, even to himself let alone to Wavell, that everything which he now ordered had been tried before, or indeed for his implication that his commanders had been so negligent as to mount attacks in the past without a proper military appreciation of the problem. Yet this is what Irwin believed. Irwin damned Lloyd unequivocally:

> It is a monstrous thought that it should be necessary to undertake in this way the duties which should be properly carried out by the Divisional, Brigade and Battalion commanders, but not only in this instance but also as a result of the day I spent on the Rathedaung front, I am left in no doubt that we are most weakly served by our relatively senior commanders and by the lack of training and, unpleasant as it is to have to say so, the lack of determination of many of our troops…[9]

Against the Japanese in 1942, such tired and unenterprising tactics proved to be as wasteful and hopeless as those on the Western Front in 1916. Irwin's criticism of his subordinate commanders was only partly fair. Soldiers need to believe in what they are doing and be certain that their object is attainable. After innumerable fruitless attempts to get the better of the Japanese in the jungle of Arakan, the officers and men of 14 Indian Division knew that they needed more than 'determination' to break through at Donbaik. Above all they needed new tactics to meet the challenges posed by Japanese tenacity, proper training and equipment allowing them to fight and live in the jungle; they needed more tactical imagination by their leaders so they were not faced, time after time, with the morale-shattering news that the next attack was to be a frontal one against the same Japanese positions that had held off countless 'highly concentrated attacks on limited objectives' before.

By this time, as Wavell was attempting another assault on Donbaik, Japanese intentions were wholly offensive. The plan, as Lloyd surmised, was to hold

Donbaik while mounting a wide encirclement to cut off Irwin's line of communication on the coast at Indin, before driving aggressively north to Maungdaw, where the British advance had begun so tentatively the previous year. The plan worked better than they had dared imagine. On 7 March the Japanese attacked British forces to the east of the Mayu Range. Two weeks later these troops had been forced back to Buthidaung and the Japanese lay poised to cross the Mayu Range to cut off the coast at Indin.

17

Irwin's Blame Game

The rapidly deteriorating situation in Arakan now prompted Irwin to invite his spare corps commander, Slim, to visit Arakan in order to assess the situation facing 14 Indian Division. Reaching Lloyd's headquarters near Maungdaw on Wednesday, 10 March 1943, Slim visited units over the following few days, and was shocked by what he found. He quickly formed the view that Lloyd could not cope with having nine brigades under his command when the norm was three or, at most, four: the situation was clearly preposterous and demanded a corps headquarters between Lloyd and Irwin.[1] He found morale to be appallingly low. On the battlefield nothing the British did seemed to have any effect on the Japanese. Every attack was repulsed; the Japanese moved where the British could not, seemingly without the same requirement for supplies, and at far greater speed. They were determined in attack and immovable in defence, even when faced with overwhelming firepower. Signs of an imminent collapse in morale were widespread. Troops were nervous and jumpy, fire discipline so lax that at night noisy gun battles erupted in the darkness against phantoms. Obvious too was the fact that the tactics repeatedly employed at Donbaik were discredited and wasteful. Every attack had been frontal, and no effort had been made to use the jungle to outflank the Japanese positions or to cut them off from the rear. Even worse, commanders appeared not to have any idea how to solve the problem, and Lloyd's plan for the sixth attack on Donbaik using 6 Brigade entailed more of the same.

Slim was horrified. When challenged, Lloyd assured him that there was no alternative to mounting another direct frontal attack, because he had no ships for a hook down the coast and his patrols had reported repeatedly that the ridge and its jungle were impassable to a flanking force. Wrote Slim:

> He [Lloyd] was confident that with this fresh British brigade, improved covering fire by artillery and aircraft, and the increased knowledge he had gained of the Japanese defences, he would this time succeed. I told him I thought he was making the error that most of us had made in 1942 in considering any jungle impenetrable and that it was worth making a great effort to get a brigade, or at least part of one, along the spine of the ridge.[2]

Slim returned to Calcutta to deliver his report in person to Irwin. At his meeting Slim deduced that Irwin was not too enthusiastic about making yet another attempt at Donbaik, 'but that he was being pushed from Delhi [i.e. Wavell] to undertake it.'[3] His job done, and being assured that no more was required of him, Slim retired from the scene.

Irwin's 'highly concentrated attack on a very limited objective' by 6 British and 71 Indian Brigade was launched against Donbaik on 18 March. He overruled the pleas of Cavendish and his battalion commanders for a silent attack – i.e. one that would have dispensed with the preliminary bombardment to allow the greatest opportunity for surprise. The attack was to be 'loud', like all those that had preceded it. Irwin's plan was predicated upon meticulous planning and faultless timing. At 5.40 a.m. a heavy artillery bombardment would begin in which 140 tons of shells were to be fired onto the *chaung*, and a squadron of RAF Blenheims flying from Dum Dum airfield outside Calcutta was to offload their bombs onto the main bunkers. At 6 a.m. the first of the six battalions – five British and one Indian – would advance methodically against the Japanese positions.

But like its predecessors, the British attack failed. The web-like complexity of the Japanese defences proved too much even for the disciplined soldiers of 6 Brigade to unpick. Unsurprisingly, the notoriously inaccurate Blenheim bombers missed their target, hitting the village of Donbaik instead. The positions at Donbaik quickly came to resemble those of a First World War battlefield. The attack failed to move the Japanese from their positions. The stinking bodies of British and Indian soldiers killed in previous assaults littered the battlefield and did nothing to help the morale of the new attackers. By midday on 19 March the brigade had suffered more than 300 casualties for no appreciable gain. 'Advancing again', wrote Slim, 'straight in the open, over the dead of previous assaults, they got among and even on the tops of the bunkers; but they could not break in.'

Frustrated, Lloyd ordered Cavendish that evening to call off the attack and go onto the defensive.

Irwin, desperate for a successful resolution of the Donbaik problem, was quick to blame others for the failure to break through. In a letter to Wavell on 20 March he complained:

> … my parting words to the Brigade and Divisional commanders was to be sure that there were sufficient waves of troops not only to capture each objective, but to swamp anything which might be encountered en route… Obviously, this was not done. Whereas I feel that we will no doubt find some means of eating up Jap defences by small mouthfuls [sic], of perhaps one strong point at a time, we must continue to search for some means of making the mouthfuls [sic] much larger. I had hoped that the 6 Brigade attack would go some way towards solving this problem. It failed obviously because – although the local commanders think otherwise – there were not enough troops following each other up. It was not, in my mind, the frontages that were wrong, but the depths.[4]

Wavell, too, was bitterly dissatisfied with the result but blamed Irwin, at least in part. Knowing that he had personally planned and supervised the attack, Wavell wrote to his army commander on 22 March:

> I was, as you probably realise, most disappointed at the Donbaik attack. It seemed to me to show a complete lack of imagination, and was neither one thing or another. An attack in real depth with determined soldiers like the 6 Brigade would, I am sure, have accomplished something, though it might have cost us casualties. But to use one battalion at a time, and that usually only deploying one company, seems to me to be poor tactics.

Wavell's exasperation drove him to try to do the job that his various subordinates were patently not able, in his mind, to do themselves, and, mirroring the advice he gave Hutton the year before, a string of suggestions flowed from his pen. These included (yet again) a massive artillery barrage; point-blank fire from 25-pounders; and damming the *chaung* and drowning the defenders.[5] Both Irwin and Wavell clearly refused to accept the more obvious but unpalatable truth that frontal attacks of the kind launched repeatedly at Donbaik could never hope to prevail over an enemy so tenacious in defence as the Japanese, particularly with troops of the sort that were available to Lloyd in 1943.

Following this defeat Irwin met Wavell again at Lloyd's headquarters at Maungdaw on 20 March. The outcome of the meeting was more or less an acceptance of defeat at Donbaik. It was determined that no immediate attempts would be made to capture the Mayu Peninsula and that defensive positions in depth as far back as the Maungdaw–Buthidaung Line should be taken up as early as possible in preparation for the monsoon (i.e. back to the plan of 23 February which had been overruled by Wavell). From Buthidaung, 71 Indian Brigade would conduct offensive operations to harass the enemy rather than to retain ground. But there was to be no precipitate withdrawal, and certainly no move back without Irwin's express permission. Lloyd's divisional headquarters at Maungdaw was to be replaced by Lomax's 26 Indian Division (two brigades of which – 4 and 71 – were already serving with 14 Indian Division) in early April. Nevertheless, and despite continued setbacks at Donbaik, the seriousness of the situation on the left flank of 14 Indian Division did not appear to be appreciated by Wavell, even at this late stage. 'I am quite clear that the best, and in fact the only, way to upset the Japanese and take the initiative from him,' he wrote to Irwin on 22 March, 'would be by getting the whole of the Mayu Peninsula and thereby controlling the river mouths and threatening Akyab.'[6]

All the while the threat to Lloyd's left flank continued. On the night of 24 March 1943 the Japanese crossed the Mayu River and three days later had secured the high point of the track over the Mayu Range. Their plan was to infiltrate a blocking force 10 miles north of Indin to cut the line of communication to Indin and Donbaik. Desperate attempts to eject the Japanese from the top of the Mayu Range over the ensuing days failed. Nothing Lloyd seemed able to do could halt the onward rush of the Japanese: nor did the thick jungle pose such great difficulties to the Japanese as it did to the British. On 29 April, fearing that 47 Indian Brigade would be cut off and destroyed piecemeal, Lloyd ordered them to abandon their positions on the Mayu Range and withdraw to join 6 Brigade on the coastal strip, which was simultaneously ordered to disentangle itself from Donbaik and withdraw north to new defensive positions halfway between Donbaik and Indin.

Despite the fact that these orders were designed to save 47 Indian Brigade from destruction, they ran counter to Irwin's instructions of 20 March that there were to be no further withdrawals. On hearing of Lloyd's order, Irwin promptly sacked him, took direct control of 14 Indian Division himself, rescinded Lloyd's instructions to both 47 and 6 Brigades and called up Lomax to take command. Lloyd's removal was so rapid that he was in New Delhi that same evening, 29 March, Irwin flying forward to Maungdaw from Calcutta and Lloyd leaving on the returning plane. After a brief visit to 4 Indian Brigade on 30 March Irwin sent a message to 47 Indian Brigade: '4 Brigade is on the move, stick it out.'[7] He also reiterated the instruction that neither brigade (47 nor 6) was to withdraw without explicit orders from him.

Staying put and fighting in his current locations presupposed that Lloyd (and now Lomax) would be able to hold the ground he was on. There had been no evidence in the past month that the troops in Arakan were able to do this in the face of determined Japanese pressure. As Lloyd recognized but Wavell did not (and for his part Irwin obeyed Wavell), it would have been far wiser to withdraw, while the opportunity existed, so as to prepare robust defences at Maungdaw–Buthidaung in advance of the Japanese pursuit.

As usual, the Japanese put paid to all of Irwin's over-optimistic and unrealistic plans. By the afternoon of 1 April, he was forced to rescind his instructions not to withdraw. He instructed 47 Indian Brigade to retire, in a deliberate fashion and with all its equipment, to the coast, but because of the time necessary to bring these plans to fruition, not to do so before 10 April. Irwin believed that his key task was to restore order to the battlefield, and that by conducting a staged withdrawal he would retain flank protection to 6 Brigade for as long as possible. Thereafter, Irwin planned to withdraw both 47 and 6 Brigades north along the coast to positions where they could wait out the monsoon. The Japanese were no respecters of Irwin's timetable, however. On 2 April the final positions on the Mayu Range were evacuated, leaving the Japanese with unhindered access to the coastal strip. The door was now ajar, and they made the most of the opportunity presented to them, realizing that this was the moment for boldness.

As if to reinforce the hopeless unreality of his perception of operations, Wavell – resolutely persisting on remaining in cloud cuckoo land – sent instructions to Irwin on 1 April ordering him to regain the initiative and to conduct offensive operations on both sides of the Mayu River, in order to inflict a severe defeat on the enemy. But both Irwin and Wavell were too late. They no longer retained any control over the timetable of battle. The Japanese had set up a block at a bridge north of Indin, threatening Irwin's entire line of communication between India and Donbaik. The forces still on the Mayu Range (47 Indian Brigade) were now cut off, as of course was 6 Brigade farther south at Donbaik. The bold crossing by the Japanese of the Mayu Range, which entailed considerable risk, proved, as had such tactics during the retreat in 1942, to have a profound psychological effect on their enemy. 'Straight over the Mayu Range they came,' wrote Slim, 'following or making single file tracks through the jungle and over the precipitous slopes that we had complacently considered impassable.'

This crisis forced Lomax to ignore Irwin's instructions on the very day they had been issued. Instead he ordered 6 Brigade to launch an immediate counterattack on the Japanese block prior to regaining communications with 47 Indian Brigade and then to withdraw north. At 6 p.m. on 4 April attacks were launched on the block from south and north. They had no effect. Now, in complete disregard of Irwin's extraordinary orders, Lomax ordered Cavendish to withdraw his whole brigade to the Indin area that night. The task was completed successfully. The next morning – 5 April – the sense of overwhelming crisis was palpable. Lomax, however, was imperturbable. He told Cavendish that he had ordered 47 Indian Brigade to withdraw west to the coastal strip at the earliest opportunity and to join 6 Brigade at Indin. That afternoon, attacks by 6 Brigade only partially recovered the high ground overlooking Indin, and the brigade remained cut off except for vehicles that were able to make their way along the beach, bypassing the roadblock, at low tide.

The Japanese noose continued to tighten on Cavendish at Indin. An attack on the night of 5/6 April led to Indin falling the next morning, Cavendish being killed. The loss of Indin destroyed 47 Indian Brigade, forcibly retained on the Mayu Range by Irwin and now cut off, as Lloyd had feared it would be. Unable to break out to the coastal strip as a complete brigade, the commander broke his units into small groups, abandoned his heavy weapons and equipment and ordered his men to make their way back to the coast as best they could. Many managed to do so between 8 and 14 April, but the brigade ceased thereafter to exist as a fighting formation.

The loss of this brigade was the direct result of Irwin's persistent blindness to the needs of his men. In a letter to Wavell on 9 April from his headquarters in Calcutta, far removed from the reality of the situation on the ground, he wrote in anger of one British battalion: 'I believe a great many of them who have come out, have done so without their weapons, and a captured Jap document ... indicates that British troops are surrendering readily.' Irwin fumed characteristically: 'I'll have courts of inquiry all ready for such cases including the loss of equipment when I get the 14 Division troops out.'[8] The truth was, of course, that had Lloyd's original instructions to withdraw been followed, 47 Indian Brigade would not have been lost. Despite his earlier recognition of the security of his left flank, Irwin seemed not to recognize, in late March, the immediacy of the threat of encirclement to Lloyd's brigades on the coastal strip. Irwin's fixation with retaining ground had contributed directly to the brigade's destruction.

The Japanese had achieved all their objectives, and had inflicted a crushing defeat on Irwin, in little over a month. The weeks that followed comprised for the British a fighting withdrawal to monsoon positions north of Maungdaw. In a replay of the previous year, Slim was given the difficult task of commanding the retreat. On the evening of 8 May he gave instructions to Lomax to withdraw from Maungdaw when he felt it necessary. Morale was shot. The command psychiatrist of Eastern Command recorded that at the end of the campaign, 'the whole of the Indian 14 Division was for practical purposes a psychiatric casualty.'[9] A less flattering verdict was that of Mutaguchi, who considered the British to be 'weaker than the Chinese'.[10]

With recrimination looming, Irwin sought to deflect blame for the Arakan debacle. He accused the troops, for 'not yet [being] up to tackling a skilled Jap soldier in country in which he has obviously had much training.'[11] He found, perhaps to his surprise, however, that it was he who had lost the confidence of Wavell, and was sacked. Slim was appointed into the vacancy. Wavell had the unfortunate task of giving the Prime Minister the bad news. Churchill, embarrassed and angry, observed bitterly to General Alan Brooke on 21 May 1943, 'The campaign is one of the most disappointing and indeed discreditable which has occurred in this war. A complete outfit of new commanders must be found. Severe discipline must be imposed upon troops whose morale is "lessened". The whole British Army in India is being brought into disrepute by the thoroughly bad conduct of these operations.' The only compensation, he noted sarcastically, 'was that the relatively small scale of operations kept them from attracting much public notice.'[12]

More than anything else, Irwin and Lloyd's conservatism had allowed the Japanese to dominate the battlefield. Lack of imagination had prevented them from thinking about alternative tactical approaches to fighting the Japanese. The subsequent evaluation by IV Corps identified ten lessons of the fighting. The only positive point made about the British performance was that battlefield administration was extremely good: at no stage did forward troops run out of food or ammunition. It was noted that the Japanese made especial attempts to attack the British line of communication, realizing that this was a weak point in the British organization for battle. It was recognized that the British had insufficient intelligence about Japanese locations, procedures and methods and as a result operated with a blindfold. It was as though the army had simply assumed that it knew how the Japanese would fight, and maintained this arrogant fiction until the Japanese, in battle, had shown it the error of its ways. British and Indian troops lacked confidence in operating in the jungle. There was no organization for the intimate support of ground troops by aircraft. All the failed attacks had been frontal. There remained no anti-malarial prophylactics, with far more casualties from sickness than from battle.[13] What was required was speed of action – both in thinking and doing – as British decision-making had been slow and predictable. Surprise needed to be made a fundamental tenet of every operation. Terrain needed to be used advantageously, especially in cutting off the enemy's rearward lines of communication and ground vital to the enemy (never targeted in 1943). New tactics were required to overcome the formidable Japanese bunker, and commanders needed a readiness to be confident in taking logistical risks and to assert an aggressive domination of the battlefield by patrols, ambushes and sniping. The Japanese seemed to know much more about the terrain than did the British, because of their extensive use of reconnaissance patrols in the gathering of intelligence. Above all, received assumptions about how best to assault a defended position needed to be radically rethought, and the weakness of relying on the land line of communication needed to be overcome. Looking back at these operations from the advantage of 1945, with two years of experience tucked into the collective belt of what soon was to become 14 Army, Gurkha Lieutenant Colonel Jack Masters, then on the staff of 19 Indian Division, was to dismiss the performance of Lloyd and Irwin as similar to that 'of New Orleans, Passchendaele and the blockhead stupidities of the Boer War.'[14] It is hard to disagree with his assessment.

It was to take the leadership of a raft of new commanders to think through and apply these lessons in 1944 and 1945. One of the principal lessons from 1942 and 1943 was that it wasn't just the training of the soldiers and their units and formations that mattered, but the preparation, mental agility and leadership skills of commanders at all levels that was essential to success. These were lacking, in conspicuous cases such as Irwin and Lloyd, in 1942 and 1943. Fortunately for the armies in India, these deficiencies were not universal.

18

'Our New God, Orde Wingate'

The year 1942 saw Orde Wingate burst onto the Burma scene, a place which he has continued to inhabit, despite his death in an air crash in February 1944. Such is the emotional impact he made on military opinion at the time that it has proved hard for contemporaries then, and historians since, to stay out of either of the two Wingate camps: those who are supportive of the man and his methods and those who are not. The only way to assess Wingate's legacy is not by an analysis of his personality, but of his arguments and the overall impact of the operations he espoused and undertook.

As Wavell continued to search for the one man – or men – who would rescue India from military ignominy, he was approached by Wingate, whom he had sent to Burma to organize guerrilla forces earlier in the year. Arriving back in India following the retreat from Burma in May 1942, Wingate had sketched out a plan to mount counterattacks against the Japanese by using infantry columns operating as 'long-range' penetration forces, which would strike deep into the heart of enemy territory, there to create chaos and confusion behind enemy lines. Wingate's ideas weren't new, and in the presentation of them he was merely expressing long-held views in the British Army about the effectiveness of irregular forces, approaches that he had indeed used previously under Wavell's tutelage in Palestine and Abyssinia. Indeed, irregular or guerrilla warfare was an accepted element in the British approach to war – in support of more conventional operations – and it had gained considerable experience in South Africa at the turn of the century and on India's North West Frontier. At the time, all the principal commanders in India recognized the value of operations of the kind Wingate espoused. In particular, Auchinleck, Wavell's successor as C-in-C, had made a name for himself through the sponsorship of long-range raiding in North

Africa. Likewise, while Wingate was preparing his arguments in a paper for Wavell, draft orders were being separately created at GHQ India entitled 'Guerrilla Forces, Eastern Frontier – Plan V', which captured the requirement to create and deploy guerrilla groups to counter any Japanese advances into India; to dominate the ground over vast, scarcely populated distances and to support offensive forays into the enemy's territory. This plan produced 'V Force', consisting in the main of Naga irregulars who undertook a 'watch and ward' function in the tangled mass of jungle-covered hills between the Chin Hills in the south and Kohima in the north.[1] Slim, who had first met Wingate when they had been fighting the Italians in East Africa in 1940, met him again in Burma, commenting that they 'had several lively discussions… on the organisation and practice of guerrilla warfare.' Slim's view of irregular warfare was that it had its place; like Wavell, he was a firm supporter of the concept, as long as it was closely linked to the activities of the main forces, fitted into the overall strategic plan and did not create divisive and expensive private armies. What he opposed was the vast spawning of a plethora of 'special units' designed only for one type of operation, which were wasteful and did not give, militarily, a worthwhile return for the resources in men, materiel and time that they absorbed.

In July 1942 Wavell gave Wingate permission to raise an ad hoc brigade to test these ideas in action in Burma. Slim had originally hoped that the force Wingate was to be given – three and a half battalions formed into 77 Indian Brigade – would be used in conjunction with his proposed XV Corps advance into Arakan.[2] This would have suited Slim perfectly, as it would have provided him with useful flank protection as well as having a valuable disruptive effect on the Japanese supply lines into Arakan. But it was not to be. Operational *Longcloth*, the name of the first brigade-level expedition across the Chindwin in February 1943, was a well-argued plan to send a series of infantry columns deep into the heart of enemy-occupied Burma, sustained by mule transport and air drop, there to disrupt Japanese railways and roads and cause military mayhem deep in the enemy's vitals. The specific target was 18 Division in the region between Indaw and Myitkyina. Columns, each 400 strong, would be self-contained with 3-inch mortars and Vickers machine guns. If they met resistance they would disperse by platoons to reassemble at a pre-arranged rendezvous.

From Wavell's point of view, it also made sense, as 77 Brigade would merely be accompanying a larger, more conventional attack into Burma from Assam, combined with a Sino-American advance (Yoke Force) under Stilwell from Yunnan. Wingate's task would be to disrupt Japanese attacks against these forces by means of sabotage and the disruption of enemy supply lines, precisely what the Japanese had done to great effect against the British in early 1942. In the event, the conventional attack did not take place, and there was now no strategic rationale for a deployment into Burma by Wingate's force. Undaunted, Wingate badgered Wavell to allow him to go anyway. Wavell needed little convincing and, supported firmly by Irwin, agreed to take the risk. Any form of successful offensive action against the Japanese was sought, no matter how small. The expedition was launched from Imphal on 8 February 1943. As an exercise in discovering the art of the possible, Wavell was right to authorize the operation, although it's hard to understand why the brigade wasn't sent to operate behind the Japanese in Arakan, closing off the routes into central Burma via Taungup, for instance, or restricting enemy movement in the Kalapanzin and Kaladan Valleys.

In the event, the brigade, divided into six infantry columns, advanced across the Chindwin from Manipur. The first phase went well, with the Mandalay–Myitkyina railway being demolished at various points. However, thereafter the Chindits – a mispronunciation of the Burmese word 'Chinthe', the stone lions that guard Buddhist temples – found themselves the hunted rather than the hunters once the initial element of surprise had been lost, and all efforts had then to be focused on avoiding large-scale engagements and on preserving the safety of the columns. Large guerrilla groups were relatively easy to locate and attack, and two of the original columns were lost very early on in the operation to enemy action. Columns got into trouble when they left the dense jungle and moved into areas where the Japanese had superior mobility. Despite the courage and endurance demonstrated by the Chindits, the expedition ultimately did little harm to the Japanese and casualties were high. Eight hundred and eighteen of the 3,000 men who set out in February did not return (360 of them became prisoners of the Japanese), and virtually all of the brigade's heavy equipment and weapons were lost. A further 600 men proved subsequently unfit for any further combat duty.

Wingate's proposition had been based on the premise that foot and mule-bound troops could be supplied exclusively by air, the aircraft being called forward by radio when required. Operation *Longcloth* provided valuable experience in this regard, although Slim was right to describe it as 'a costly schooling'. The biggest problem at this stage of the war was that sufficient transport aircraft had to be dedicated to support even minor guerrilla operations, and in 1943 these were in very short supply. Local air superiority was required to protect the supply drops, which could take as long as two or three days to complete for the entire brigade. Relying on air supply for survival alone left no margin for error if for any reason the drop had to be cancelled, and the distance patrols could travel away from the airhead was restricted by the range of the aircraft. Wingate was also to discover that the use of bombers and ground attack aircraft did not compensate for the weakness of his columns in terms of firepower. Ground attack aircraft were not as accurate as artillery and could not provide prolonged assistance to troops engaged on the ground without enormous effort, which was often impossible for a Chindit column several hundred miles from the nearest airfield.

Longcloth did, however, show that even the most impossible terrain was not an obstacle to mobility, a lesson that arguably the Japanese were quick to exploit the following year. Wingate also proved that well-led and well-trained troops were capable of moving through difficult jungle country and operating in the heart of enemy-held territory. Ordinary troops – British conscripts and young, inexperienced Gurkha recruits and survivors of the original Burma Army – were trained to a peak of physical fitness and military training that surprised many. Wingate's emphasis on hard training, his unrelenting pursuit of mental and physical robustness in the drive to prepare his men for war, all augured well for the future of the armies in India in the fight against the Japanese. 'The key change in our fortunes lay in imaginative and thorough training for war,' recalled Lieutenant 'Birdie' Smith. 'To this end, many junior officers were sent on courses run by ex-Chindits. We came back to the [Regimental] centre astonished that our bodies had been capable of surviving such taxing experiences.'[3]

When it was underway, the foray into Burma had been a closely guarded secret. However, General Sir Alan Hartley, deputy Commander-in-Chief India Command, decided that for reasons of morale and propaganda, the story of the expedition – at least in part – should be told. An announcement was made on 21 May 1943 and a subsequent press conference allowed Wingate the opportunity to give an account of the operation and to expound his theories. The message was that the British had bettered the Japanese at their own game, by infiltrating behind their lines, blowing up installations such as bridges and railway lines, and generally causing havoc. There was no mention of the huge losses, or indeed of the failure to achieve anything of any physical permanence. The excited hyperbole of the press response – 'A British Ghost Army' and 'Japanese Bamboozled' – indicates something of the desperation for good news – any news – to come out of India.[4] The apparent success of Wingate's operation spread like wildfire across the army and did untold good to troops desperate to hear that in the face of the Japanese, British and Indian troops weren't entirely useless. Lieutenant 'Birdie' Smith was enthused by this talk of derring-do, describing Wingate as 'our new god', enthusing that the 'news that British and Gurkha soldiers had penetrated behind the Japanese forward positions, cocking a snoot [sic] at the dreaded foe, had a most remarkable effect on our spirits... There were ripples of criticism, yes, but the tonic of aggressive action was like a strong medicine that surged through British and Indian units. We *could* beat the Japs.'[5] On 29 December 1943 Wavell recorded in his diary a visit by Brigadier Bernard Fergusson, who had been his aide-de-camp between 1935 and 1937: 'He says the venture was well worthwhile, and that Wingate's theories are right, though the troops did not do all that Wingate claimed that they did. He said Wingate was, and is, extremely difficult – impossible at times – and he had many rows with him, but he still believes in his ideas.'[6]

It was therefore in the area of moral rather than material effect that Wingate's force between February and May 1943 achieved a considerable victory, not least of all because it instilled a sense of pride and achievement in the otherwise hang-dog British and Indian armies at the time. It served specially to deflect some of the fall-out from the disastrous Arakan experience, which was concluding ignominiously. The contrast with Lloyd's futile battering ram in Arakan could not have been starker. The Arakan operation looked backwards to a set of failed tactics and approaches to war, whereas for all its faults and losses *Longcloth* looked forward, with hope, to the future, where things would be done differently. Despite the casualties incurred, Wavell (without informing Wingate) ordered another brigade – 111 Indian Brigade – to be formed, commanded by the experienced Gurkha Joe Lentaigne. Part of the problem in assessing Operation *Longcloth* is that by early 1944, when Wingate's second expedition – Operation *Thursday* – was launched, many, from Wingate himself through to Winston Churchill, had begun to believe the propaganda that had been pumped out a year before. 'Unfortunately,' concluded the historian Anthony Barker, 'the widely publicised exploits of (the operation)... gave an exaggerated impression of the possibilities of this kind of operation... and Wingate was depicted as a new "man of destiny". More sober judgement on the operation described it as "an engine without a train".'[7] Certainly the consensus in late May 1943 was that raids, no matter how spectacular, could not win wars, unless they were coordinated with wider operations, contributing to a broader operational or strategic objective.

The problem began in the immediate aftermath of *Longcloth*, as Wingate vied with those he considered to be his natural enemies – the uniformed 'blimps' of GHQ India Command (a category which included anyone who offered even the mildest hint of challenge to his prognostications) – to control the narrative of the enterprise. Wingate had immediately sat down and written his own account of the operation, heavily critical of those whom he considered had failed to provide him with full support from the outset. He sent drafts to the Director of Military Operations (Major General Mallaby) and the Chief of the General Staff (General Sir Edwin Morris), both men supportive of, and friendly to, Wingate. They were, however, concerned about Wingate's harsh criticisms of his own officers, soldiers and GHQ India, and suggested delaying the report's publication until those involved in the preparation and conduct of the expedition could comment. Wingate sensed censorship and sent a copy directly to Leo Amery, who passed it on to Churchill. Thus it was that the Prime Minister read an unexpurgated and mildly hysterical report, one that India did not have the opportunity to rebalance, in which GHQ India (and the Indian Army) appeared to be a bigger problem than the Japanese.[8] A wholly unnecessary debate, and political battle, ensued, one that served to distract from the efforts to rebuild the Indian Army in 1943, and an equally needless distraction in 1944 from the efforts to defeat the Japanese invasion of India. The cause of the distraction was unarguably Wingate's sense of self-righteousness and certainty of purpose.

At the heart of the Wingate imbroglio was his aberrant personality. Was he mad? Plenty of friends and enemies believed so, as he self-evidently suffered from a series of severe mental problems, the evidence for which is voluminous.[9] But claiming that he was mad ignores other evidence of his charisma and lucidity. He inspired remarkable loyalty from many of his officers, and most of those who worked with him in 1943 and 1944 would respect him for the quality of his ideas. He wasn't a team player, however. He accepted people and ideas on his own terms. He was dismissive of those whom he considered to be too orthodox, and insufficiently radical in their ideas. He was certainly a thinker, but can be criticized for failing to test these ideas to the degree required before they were adopted as authorized policy or practice. A widely observed attribute of his personality was 'a profound and incurably religious temperament'.[10] Examples of his bible-quoting are legion, one soldier recording that a speech by Wingate prior to deployment was 'barely understandable – mostly about guts and God', another recalling that 'he regarded himself as a cross between God and Cromwell and his conversations were copiously larded with quotations from their recorded utterances.'[11] Perhaps this gives some insight into his attitudes and behaviours. It appears that Wingate's entire life was crippled by the trauma of religious exceptionalism. He had been raised as a hell-fearing member of the Plymouth Brethren. As such he knew himself to be not merely a predestined member of God's elect, but a member of its spiritual aristocracy. He knew from his earliest moments that he and his family were set apart, spiritually unique. Accordingly, he expected ridicule and opposition, precisely because he had come to believe the world hated the elect and opposed its message of singularism. Those who are brought up to consider themselves close to God often have an acute sense of the presence of evil, one biographer suggesting that Wingate felt 'frequently threatened and doomed' and analysed 'all his thoughts lest they be the voice of Satan'.[12] He was brought up to be different and to think differently; consequently, he was utterly indifferent to criticism. He behaved as a man apart, as if everyone was the enemy. The intrinsic belief that it was him against the world 'was one of his less agreeable, more irrational traits.'[13] Indeed, he lived on the basis that people would hate him, assuming that all his interactions with other humans would be hostile, and even 'rejoice[d] in making enemies'.[14]

It might be concluded from the stories of his childhood, adolescence and young manhood, that he revelled in his uniqueness. He would be the prophet calling to a new form of virtue – a new way of doing things – and in prosecuting his prophetic duties he would brook no opposition, but persevere with a determination and singularity of purpose only given to those who truly knew they were called to wield God's righteous sword. His doctor observed that the 'religion of the Old Testament was the basis of his life [and] he believed himself a prophet [thus] he sometimes attained a state of equilibrium – when receptive to the will of God, but otherwise never relaxed.'[15] For those who thought he was mad, he would merely have responded that a prophet was never welcome in his own country.

This brand of exceptionalism did nothing to endear Wingate to the Indian – or British – military establishment, particularly when his brazen method of demanding what he wanted for his operations so outrageously flouted the chain of command. It seemed then, as now, impossible to be indifferent about Wingate. What one saw as enthusiasm was regarded by another as the meddling of a 'scatterbrain allowed power without any responsibility'.[16] His unconventional manner was regarded by many as nothing more than inconsiderate rudeness. Consequently, and without doubt unintentionally, Wingate alienated many people who were actually prepared initially to give him a fair wind: in many others he created bitter opponents.

All this was unknown, of course, to the Prime Minister who, grasping straws in the face of the embarrassment of Arakan, saw in Wingate's report a route to persuading the Americans that Britain was listening to them, or at the very least a stick with which to beat his generals. Excited by the evidence of someone who was not merely able to fight the Japanese, but who was at the same time being held back by the reactionary forces in Delhi, the Prime Minister's prejudices against the Indian Army and India Command were inflamed. On 24 July 1943 Churchill sent an infamous memorandum to General Ismay, which one historian describes as 'a good example of Churchill's capacity for impetuous folly in the field of military direction':[17]

> I consider Wingate should command the Army against Burma. He is a man of genius and audacity, and has rightly been discerned by all eyes as a figure above the ordinary level. There is no doubt that in the welter of inefficiency and lassitude which has characterised our operations on the Indian Front this man, his force and his achievements, stand out, and no mere question of seniority must obstruct the advance of real personalities to their proper stations in war.[18]

In his consideration of and discussion about operations against the Japanese, Wingate exhibited a combative energy that delighted Churchill. In part as a spur to his generals, the Prime Minister invited Wingate to accompany him on the *Queen Mary* to the Quadrant Conference at Quebec in August 1943, along with Mountbatten – soon to take up his role as Supreme Allied Commander, South East Asia Command – and the Chiefs of Staff. Wingate reached London on 4 August and immediately accompanied Churchill to Canada. During the voyage, Wingate won the full attention of Churchill and presented himself as 'the expert – and the only expert present – on fighting in Burma'.[19] No one was available to represent GHQ India, or any alternative viewpoint. His forceful assertions and certainties swept the floor. In part this was Churchill's rationale for taking this admittedly strange character with him to the United States – here was a Brit who knew how to fight the Japanese, and had some ideas about doing what the United States and China wanted: getting back into Burma to take on the Japanese and thereby to reopen the Burma Road. It was also an opportunity for Wingate's own hostility to the India Army – in his view 'the world's largest system of outdoor relief' – to have full rein, and in so doing reinforce Churchill's anti-Indian Army prejudices.

Striking while the iron was hot, Wingate presented to the Chiefs of Staff on 10 August a vast expansion of the long-range penetration (LRP) programme, to the extent of creating two divisions' worth of troops – 20,000 men – with associated air support. They accepted the role and effectiveness of the LRP idea, assuming that Wingate's own understanding of their operational, even strategic, utility had been proved. This was not true, of course, but Auchinleck was given no opportunity to challenge the decision. Then, a week later, Wingate worked his magic on the Combined (i.e. British *and* American) Chiefs of Staff. There is no doubt that he made a deep impression, but did so by presenting a deformed and inaccurate picture of the strategic difficulties facing India Command in the reconquest of Burma. On this occasion Auchinleck was given the opportunity to respond by telegram, but the environment into which he sent his response was a hostile one. Here was the supposedly cautious man of orthodoxy, sacked by Churchill in the desert, surrounded now by a panoply of punkah-wallahs of the same ilk, presenting all sorts of difficulties and hindrances in the way of Churchill's new 'man of destiny'. Auchinleck responded in moderate tones on 19 August. He calmly demolished Wingate's grossest distortions about the ability of the India Army to defeat the Japanese in battle, errors that in fact would be vanquished in the hard fighting in Manipur in only eight months' time. He rejected Wingate's notion that LRP forces could provide significant results against organized forces of all arms, 'for the task of the irregular was not to fight but to evade the enemy and harass him in guerrilla warfare.'[20] He reminded the Chiefs of Staff of the intractable nature of the Assam line of communications, and stated that the requirement for air supply would be far above the 'twelve to twenty C47s' rather naïvely proposed by Wingate. He also suggested that relying on the Yunnan Chinese to advance in support of an LRP operation was strategically unsound. He objected to the idea of breaking up three divisions (including the battle-experienced 70 British Division) to find the troops required, and believed that a separate Special Force HQ was not required. Auchinleck's assessment was not all negative, however. He 'saw considerable value in LRP operations in Burma on a scale and according to administrative and logistical principles which he believed to be practicable.'[21] But Auchinleck's appreciation differed significantly from Wingate's, in that the latter regarded LRP operations in great strength to be all that was necessary to prosecute the war against the Japanese in Burma, whereas the former, with virtually all other senior military commanders in India, including Slim, regarded them as useful adjuncts to the main engagement, which by strategic and practical necessity needed to be elsewhere.

Auchinleck's appreciation arrived at Quebec, where Wingate promptly and publicly refuted its arguments and attacked their author, both verbally with Churchill and in memoranda he sent to the Chiefs of Staff. The mood music was for Wingate, and with the wider strategic-level organizational changes to be pursued, was to give Wingate the opportunity he craved in 1944. For his part, Wingate never realized that he was being used by Churchill as a pawn in a game of transatlantic confidence building. He genuinely believed himself to be the messiah of Britain's problems in Burma, revelling in Churchill's interest. Churchill's intuition was right. The Americans loved this concept of cowboys and

Indians in Burma's wild west, lapping up Wingate's exuberant braggadocio. He had served Churchill's purpose perfectly. Sent back to India as the cat among India Command's and SEAC's pigeons, Wingate was promptly forgotten, leaving Slim, under whose command he was placed, to pick up the pieces. The result was that there now existed two competing plans for the defeat of the Japanese. One was the product of arm-waving and expostulation, the other the hard experience of battle. By June 1944, after the deaths of many of Wingate's men, and of Wingate himself, it was clear which one of these had been built on sand.

19

Re-thinking Training

It so happened that Irwin's otherwise incomprehensible decision in July 1942 to take direct control of operations in Arakan had a silver lining. The most significant impact on training across the whole of Eastern Army was made in the autumn of 1942 by the new commander of XV Corps, Bill Slim, who was instructed by Irwin to prepare the whole of Eastern Army for war, while he conducted operations in Arakan. It was an interesting reversal of roles. It was a fortunate decision for Slim personally, as he emerged untainted from the debacle that followed. It also meant that he could exercise decisive leadership across the rest of Eastern Army in respect of the new training programme he had already instituted in XV Corps. HQ XV Corps exchanged locations with HQ Eastern Army in the last days of August 1942: Slim went to Ranchi and Irwin moved into Barrackpore, Slim taking on responsibility for 70 Division, 50 Tank Brigade (at Poona), corps troops and, for a time, 36 Indian Division.

From the moment he had returned from Burma in May, Slim had been convinced that well-trained, well-led and well-motivated soldiers could beat the Japanese. He knew that the peculiar conditions of 1942 had not allowed any scope for British success. During his time in XV Corps Slim manufactured a set of practical approaches to fighting in Burma. He started with four principles upon which planning for future operations against the Japanese were to be based:

1. The ultimate intention must be an offensive one.
2. The main idea on which the plan was based must be simple.
3. That idea must be held in view throughout and everything else must give way to it.
4. The plan must have an element of surprise.

Slim had given considerable thought during the months following the miserable march up the road from Tamu to the ideas that would form the theoretical platform – the military doctrine – upon which these principles could sit. In the absence of anything else – and the 1935 Field Service Regulations were too imprecise and general to be of any use – he came up with his own. Slim's programme to rebuild the fighting spirit of his troops from the shock of both Burma and Arakan was based on three principles. They dealt with spiritual, intellectual and material factors. 'Spiritual first,' he wrote later in *Defeat into Victory*, 'because only spiritual foundations can stand real strain. Next intellectual, because men are swayed by reason as well as feeling. Material last – important, but last – because the very highest kinds of morale are often met when material conditions are lowest.' By the 'spiritual' principle he meant that there must be a great and noble object, its achievement must be vital, the method of achievement must be active and aggressive, and each man must feel that what he is and what he does matters directly towards the attainment of the object. It was critical, he argued, that all troops, of whatever rank, background and nationality, believed in the cause they were fighting for. It had to be just. 'We fought for the clean, the decent, the free things of life', he wrote. 'We fought only because the powers of evil had attacked these things.' By the 'intellectual' foundation he meant that soldiers had to be convinced that the object could be attained. The principal task was to destroy the notion that the Japanese soldier was invincible. Equally, the soldier had also to know that the organization to which he belonged was an efficient one. He knew that the physical care of a soldier in the field has a direct bearing on his performance in battle: lack of food, water, medical support or contact with home worked to weaken the resolve, over time, of even the stoutest man. By the 'material' foundation Slim meant that each man had to feel that he would get a fair deal from his commanders and from the army generally, that he would, as far as humanly possible, be given the best weapons and equipment for his task and that his living and working conditions would be made as good as they could be.

To achieve these aims, men needed to be trained to enable them to master the art of fighting in the jungle and elsewhere against a skilful, determined and resourceful opponent by day and night. Training – both individual and collective – was core to the discipline all soldiers needed in order to control their fear, and that of their subordinates, in battle; to allow them to think clearly and shoot straight in a crisis, and to inspire them to the fullest physical and mental endeavour. Slim understood that the strength of his army lay not in its equipment or its traditions, but in the training and morale of its soldiers and the personal competence and leadership of its officers. He also recognized that the psychological dimension of battle against the Japanese was formidable. The Japanese were not bogey men, as many in Burma Corps had realized during the retreat, but the myth of their invincibility had swept the Indian Army following the unprecedented disasters of the loss of Malaya, Singapore and Burma. Only men confident in their own military strength could ever hope to better them in battle, and he had seen – at Kokkogwa and Kyaukse – that they could be beaten by straight-firing, well-drilled and confident soldiers unafraid of the ballyhoo of *bushido*.

In Barrackpore he had prepared a summary of the key tactical ideas that had impressed him in Burma which he then promulgated to his corps:

1. The individual soldier must learn, by living, moving and exercising in it, that the jungle is neither impenetrable nor unfriendly. When he has once learned to move and live in it, he can use it for concealment, covered movement, and surprise.

2. Patrolling is the master key to jungle fighting. All units, not only infantry battalions, must learn to patrol in the jungle, boldly, widely, cunningly and offensively.

3. All units must get used to having Japanese parties in their rear, and, when this happens, regard not themselves, but the Japanese, as 'surrounded'.

4. In defence, no attempt should be made to hold long continuous lines. Avenues of approach must be covered and enemy penetration between our posts dealt with at once by mobile local reserves who have completely reconnoitred the country.

5. There should rarely be frontal attacks and never frontal attacks on narrow fronts. Attacks should follow hooks and come in from flank or rear, while pressure holds the enemy in front.

6. Tanks can be used in almost any country except swamp. In close country they must always have infantry with them to defend and reconnoitre for them. They should always be used in the maximum numbers available and capable of being deployed. Whenever possible penny packets must be avoided. 'The more you use, the fewer you lose.'

7. There are no non-combatants in jungle warfare. Every unit and sub-unit, including medical ones, is responsible for its own all-round protection, including patrolling, at all times.

8. If the Japanese are allowed to hold the initiative, they are formidable. When we have it, they are confused and easy to kill. By mobility away from roads, surprise, and offensive action we must regain and keep the initiative.

He noted subsequently that the one feature missing from this list was air transport and aerial resupply, simply because the resources did not exist in 1942 to give the troops any hope that a line of communication in the sky could replace, in the immediate term at least, the one provided by road. Other tactics needed to be developed to overcome the dependence on the road: building up a formidable air transport fleet was one of them.

But despite the work Slim was able to undertake with XV Corps, it took a year following the retreat from Burma for the wider India Command to grip the issue of training. In 1942 schools had been established for specialized arms and services, and infantry regimental centres were expanded to cope with the growth in the numbers of recruits, but for some time it wasn't the quantity of training that was at issue, but its quality and relevance to the war that would need to be fought in the east. It was only in June 1943 when Wavell created the Infantry Committee, under the leadership of Major General Reginald Savory, to examine the causes of combat failure in the Indian Army in the First Burma and First Arakan campaigns, that the first centralized steps were taken to reform the army's approach to individual and collective training. The committee – which sat for two weeks – initiated the first systemic change in the process of training in India Command and was to have as profound an impact on the warfighting capability of British and Indian troops in India Command (and later, SEAC) as the Australian innovations had on its two deployed divisions in New Guinea. Critically, the Infantry Committee took the ideas that Slim had already built into his XV Corps and Eastern Army training programme, and adopted them as policy for the entire army. First, recruit training was immediately focused on preparing men for war, rather than the drills and routines of peacetime soldiering. Battle drills were systematized: the idea was that, when the bullets began to fly, troops would be able to follow a series of rules and respond appropriately to whatever situation they faced, rather than having to make things up as they went along. For the advance to contact, the attack, defence, patrolling and withdrawal in contact, troops were no longer left with the vague 'principles of war' to frame their conduct of operations. Now they had a precise set of instructions as to what to do under certain circumstances. The key task was enabling men to learn how to fight the Japanese on more than equal terms, in difficult terrain and climatic conditions, in the face of the curse of malaria, a long way from home with the minimum of domestic comforts and far fewer support functions of the sophistication that the Eighth Army was able to enjoy in North Africa. Second, it was recognized that the regimental training centre approach wasn't working. By late 1942 the evidence was overwhelming that the previous system, designed to support an army of 190,000, could not cope with the challenge of an army soon to reach a strength of nearly 2 million.[1] Large numbers of new recruits needed consistent battle drills. Equally importantly, the massively inflated number of instructors across India Command, most of whom had only a fleeting acquaintance with the Japanese – or none at all – needed to be given the wherewithal to train their recruits. Simple drills, based firmly on lessons passed down from experience in Malaya, Burma and New Guinea, would enable them to do this. Likewise, the evidence for the need for change from the Arakan debacle was overwhelming, reinforced both by the dramatic results secured by the Australians in New Guinea after they had thoroughly rethought their approach to training, and from the results of Slim's relentless retraining of Eastern Army. What was needed was ruthlessly enforced uniformity in a new way of fighting which placed greater emphasis than ever before on the individual fighting skills and mental fortitude of each soldier. The evidence of regular studies of morale undertaken by GHQ India indicated the effect of better training on the confidence of the troops.[2]

Two training divisions were established – 14 Indian, re-purposed following the debacle in Arakan at Chhindwara, and 39 Indian (previously Major General Bruce Scott's 1 Burma Division) at Saharanpur, near Dehra Dun in Uttar Pradesh, through which all recruits who had completed basic training would then undergo two months of 'battlefield inoculation'.[3] Further, a training headquarters was created specifically to organize the collective training of one infantry division at a time in combined operations and jungle warfare. This training was compulsory for all British and Indian troops proceeding to the battle area, whether they were experienced soldiers or new recruits, and included a significant component of jungle training as well as more traditional military skills such as weapon training, physical fitness and tactical skills. One of the conclusions of the Infantry Committee was that some troops in Arakan were not much better than mobs 'of partially trained village youth'.[4] This changed, and did so dramatically. At the level of section and platoon the emphasis was on battle drills in heavily forested or jungle terrain by day and by night: how to engage the enemy in close terrain with a selection of weapons; how to patrol, lay ambushes, build defensive positions, operate at night, and launch attacks on defended positions. Men were taught to look after themselves rather than expect others – Indian followers for example – to do it for them. They were taught to navigate for themselves, stay dry in wet weather, and make the jungle their home.[5] All of this training was designed to enable soldiers to operate with confidence in the tangled hills of eastern India, far from the logistical certainties of the battlefields for which the Indian Army had traditionally trained. When this training was complete, recruits would move to a Rest and Reinforcement Camp for their allocated divisions – there were 12 in 14 Army for instance – after which they would travel forward to their battalions. While at the Reinforcement Camp they would continue useful preparation for battle.[6] When batches of recruits ('drafts') were ready to be sent forward to their front-line units, they were accompanied by experienced NCOs, to ease the inevitable challenge of joining their new units. British or Indian battalions coming to jungle fighting for the first time had to go through a unit training regime provided by the specialist 116 Brigade (joined by 150 Brigade in 1944), which took units through a range of realistic training simulations with live ammunition, explosives and physically and mentally tough exercises to prepare all ranks for combat.

In addition, a series of specialist schools was established on the model of the Australian Army's Jungle Warfare School at Canungra in Queensland, such as the Tactical School near Poona and two Jungle Warfare schools at Sevoke near Darjeeling and Shimoga in Karnataka, to build on the pre-existing Jungle Warfare Training School near Dehra Dun. The syllabus for each of these schools was refreshed with newly developing tactical doctrine, and the number of places for students massively increased. Importantly, it was agreed that all troops in India – British or Indian – needed to study a centrally endorsed tactical doctrine, together with centrally tested and locally applied tactical training.[7] Finally, a raft of changes included the abolition of 'milking'; improving the quality of infantry recruits, including pay and conditions; and improvements to battlefield cooperation between infantry and other arms – artillery, armour and aircraft. Fixed battle drills for dealing with tactical situations from the individual infantryman up to company level were laid out in comprehensive detail. The aim was to ensure that whatever event soldiers found themselves in, they could immediately adopt a process of activities to allow them to control the situation and defeat the enemy. In this sense, the emphasis on carrying out a set of drills was no different in this army to that of its forebears in the 18th century, for instance, and the requirement to drill against a set of specific instructions had been part and parcel of the Indian Army for most of its life.[8]

Auchinleck, the incoming Commander-in-Chief, pushed through the changes required without ceremony.[9] Indeed, he provided the direction and drive for the changes that were ultimately to transform the armies in India, both British and Indian. He took the leading role in transforming the Indian Army, and in believing in its potential. Unlike Churchill, for whom the Indian Army was an army of putative mutineers, Auchinleck, wrote his biographer, 'was one of them in every fibre of his being' and knew what it could achieve.[10] The radical egalitarianism achieved by the 'new' Indian Army in 1944 and 1945, building on reforms he had overseen while Commander-in-Chief in the early war years, was largely achieved by Auchinleck, as was the mass recruitment from the 'non-martial races'. Likewise, it was Auchinleck's complete embrace of the need for robust jungle training that led to the development of specialist jungle warfare schools, such as that at Comilla, which ran 15-day jungle warfare courses for all ranks, British and Indian, focusing on living and fighting effectively in the jungle.[11] He revamped the training syllabus of Indian recruits so that they were taught, in tandem with the doctrines that Slim had quickly begun to espouse in XV Corps in 1942, the need for all combatants in the jungle to possess exemplary fieldcraft, tactical and weapons skills in a jungle environment. In the second half of 1943 a dramatic transformation could be seen in the quality of Indian recruits and British conscripts.

Why did it take so long to set in place the solution to these problems? Part of the answer is that highly centralized and directed training was simply not the way the Indian Army had ever done things. Before war came to Asia in 1941 there was no suggestion that the existing training arrangements weren't up to it. The processes for providing trained soldiers and units for the Middle East were working well. Training remained the responsibility of individual regiments (for recruits) and formations (for subsequent collective training). Initial training was provided by each infantry regiment, the tenth battalion of each of which was responsible for giving each recruit eight months of training in peacetime, and six months in war.[12] Other training (specialist, sub-unit and unit) largely took place within each regiment or battalion in accordance with each commanding officer's directives. This left considerable room for variation in the quality of training across the army. Likewise, in 1942 there were no formal processes to harvest battlefield experience from those who had direct knowledge of fighting the Japanese. Some of the lessons learned from Malaya and Burma were rushed into a third revision of 'Military Training Pamphlet No. 9' – now 73 pages long – in August 1942, and 45,000 copies were printed for distribution down to the level of junior non-commissioned officer. But as India Command was to discover, pamphlets, even good ones, don't win wars. Nevertheless, MTP 9 provided some immediate ideas for solving the problem of Japanese infiltration, and the idea of the defensive box borrowed from the open spaces of North Africa saw the light of day in this publication. Rather than a linear defence, units of all sizes were instructed to concentrate themselves in all-round defence sited on the enemy's avenues of approach, from there not just to fight defensively, but to 'fight the gaps', denying the enemy the 'mobility, speed, infiltration and encirclement' that were the hallmarks of their approach to war.[13] Then, by aggressive counteraction the Japanese would have their own supply lines cut in turn. Unfortunately, as a slow trickle of instructions and guidance started to come down to units from GHQ India (such as the updated version of MTP 9), there was no mechanism for ensuring that the entire army learned the same lessons, to the same standards.

All the changes instigated in 1943 by Wavell (initially), Auchinleck and Slim came together in the revolutionary fourth edition of MTP in September 1943, with the engaging title of *The Jungle Book*. Eighty thousand copies were produced. The booklet was designed as an attractive and interesting read and was as unlike a boring training manual as anyone had ever seen. Replete with cartoons, drawings and photographs, *The Jungle Book* was specially designed in a format that soldiers wanted to read, because it offered to help them survive in the jungle and 'beat the Jap'. A raft of new training manuals appeared, including the 41-page *Japanese in Battle*, the second edition of which, in 1944, provided a detailed explanation and analysis of Japanese tactical approaches in Arakan. A total of 85,000 copies were printed.

But perhaps the biggest change, in conjunction with the work that individual divisional and corps commanders were undertaking, was the restructuring in the autumn of 1943 of India's organization for war, which led to a total change in the thinking and conversation about training, tactics and the 'professionalisation of fighting the Japanese' in the Indian Army. The new South East Asia Command, with its own Supreme Allied Commander – Mountbatten – would be responsible for the delivery of military strategy, and would be separated from the functions of supply and provision, which would rest with India Command. The latter would provide the former with the infrastructure, tools, materiel and trained manpower to be able to fight, and would have its own Commander-in-Chief. Auchinleck's role in preparing India for war has long been forgotten. He was committed to ensuring that his divisions went into battle only after extensive collective training in simulated combat conditions. Individual training needed to coalesce into platoon and company training; then battalion, brigade and divisional training on a collective basis. In mid-September 1943 he wrote to General Alan Brooke to explain some of the differences his new broom had been able to effect in the three months since his appointment in June:

> The reorganisation of the system of instruction in training centres, and the institution of training divisions, as well as the reorganisation of the instruction as officers' training schools will, I hope, go far to improve the individual efficiency of reinforcements, particularly in jungle warfare, both of junior officers and other ranks.
>
> Collective training is not easy owing to the widely separated location of the tracts suitable for jungle warfare training, and the fact that they are almost invariably highly malarious. Troops have often to be moved long distances by rail and this throws an additional strain on the already overworked transportation system. We are doing our best, however, to compete with this problem and I hope that all divisions will be trained and ready for operations by the end of this year. I can assure you that I shall not allow any formation to go into battle until it is adequately trained.[14]

Auchinleck expressed his conviction that, provided the difficulties imposed by great distances, poor communications and natural obstacles of climate and terrain were appreciated, and plans were laid accordingly on a realistic basis, the troops would not again fail their leaders, and that they would do all that was asked of them. In a sharp note at the end he wrote in longhand: 'I feel too that we have now got good leaders and I do not think they will fail the troops!' The reference to Irwin and Lloyd was barely disguised.

The measures Auchinleck sponsored had an immediate and dramatic effect on the fighting efficiency of Eastern Army.[15] In particular, the work of the training divisions was to have a profound and positive effect on the quality of individual reinforcements, units and formations destined for the battle area because they were first comprehensively inducted into jungle warfare before they made their way to the front. 'Some of the measures introduced', he later observed, 'constituted fundamental changes in our policy and practice in regard to military training as a whole.' In addition to the collective training already described, with 14 and 39 Divisions, the types of training affected included:

1. Officer selection for all candidates, British and Indian, was undertaken using centrally imposed standards using scientific methods;
2. Short staff training courses were laid on at the Staff College, Quetta for officers who would otherwise have not been selected for staff training;

3. Improved officer training courses were introduced at UOTCs and for Armoured Corps training;
4. Fifty officers were sent to Australia and New Guinea to study Australian jungle fighting methods;
5. Regular senior officer briefings were held in Simla in July 1943;
6. Soldier training was lengthened to eleven months, to include two months jungle training;
7. A second jungle warfare school was opened;
8. Schools were established to deal with the engineer issues raised by fighting the Japanese;
9. Combined operations training was enhanced by the expansion of the combined operations Directorate.[16]

By the time Mountbatten arrived in early October, new life was cascading through the veins of what was shortly to become 14 Army.[17] The improvement in morale accompanying the rapidly revitalizing army – better training, equipment, medical preparation and treatment, new uniforms better suited to jungle fighting, equipment and weapons – was obvious to see. It was the self-inflicted disaster in Arakan that finally persuaded Wavell that action needed to be taken. It was Auchinleck who made it happen. It was Slim, as GOC-in-C of 14 Army, who was so successfully to wield the formidable weapon that had been created.

As Slim made clear in *Defeat into Victory* (writing at a time when he was Governor General of Australia), it was the Australians who first broke the spell of the invincibility of the Japanese Army and did much to provide guidance and advice to the Indian Army when it was most in need of help. The Australian Army in New Guinea led the way in the centralized application of training knowledge and expertise, down to the minute detail of how, for example, to live and fight in the jungle, to patrol effectively, to master a firefight in the jungle, attack an enemy bunker, camouflage a platoon harbour, carry out a successful ambush and to stalk an enemy sniper. Systematic, top-down training for war on a doctrinal basis began in the Australian Army as a reaction to the poor showing of ill-prepared Citizen Military Forces (i.e. previously part-time troops, called up for regular service) in New Guinea in 1942. The shock that Yamashita's forces had first given Australian Army regular soldiers in Malaya and Singapore and then the part-timers of the CMF on their first engagement in New Guinea was profound, and the effectiveness of groups of Australians subsequently sent as reinforcements to

New Guinea confirmed the realization that better approaches to battle preparation were urgently required. By the end of 1942 the famous Jungle Warfare School at Canungra in southern Queensland was producing its first recruits, as young officers completed an intensive six-week battle training course to prepare to lead their platoons in combat. Australian efforts dramatically to upskill their soldiers, starting at Milne Bay in August 1942, along the Kokoda Trail by mid-November 1942 and then in wiping out the Japanese diehards at 'Bloody Buna' – Buna–Gona–Sanananda – in January 1943 and at Wau the same month, served as a light in the gloom of British despondency about the failures of British and Indian forces, most latterly in Arakan.[18] In November 1942, Wavell wrote to the Australian Army C-in-C, General Thomas Blamey, whom he had come to know well – indeed to enjoy a robust relationship – in the Middle East, asking for assistance: 'All my best congratulations on the successes in New Guinea. I shall be very interested to hear the story of them, as the country seems to be much the same as many parts of Burma. I should be very grateful if you could send me as much detailed information as possible of the operation and of Japanese tactics and methods.'[19]

Wavell had formed a strong appreciation of the fighting capabilities of the soldiers under Blamey's command in the Australian Imperial Force (AIF) while C-in-C Middle East, and his approach was warmly received. Australian successes were building up at a time when British failures in Arakan were starting to cause embarrassment in New Delhi, although some months were to pass before substantive exchanges could take place between India and Australia. Indeed, Wavell was planning to visit Australia personally at the point at which he relinquished his post, on promotion to Viceroy, in the middle of the year.[20] The first of a series of exchanges between the two armies now began, all with the purpose of learning from Australian experience. Between July and October 1943 two experienced Australian company commanders toured India Command giving lectures on minor tactics from their experience of fighting on the Kokoda Trail and at Buna–Gona–Sanananda. In October a group of 50 British and Indian officers began an attachment to the Australian Army in New Guinea, beginning with completion of the platoon commander's course at Canungra. They then returned to India in February 1944,[21] many having commanded troops in action, to promulgate the lessons and methods they had learned as part of small training teams despatched across the length and breadth of India. Simultaneously, No. 220 Military Mission under Major General John 'Tubby' Lethbridge, who was to become Slim's Chief of Staff in 1944, toured Australia between October and December looking at best practice in terms of fighting organizations, equipment and tactics.[22] After being in Australia for less than a month, Lethbridge reported to London:

> The Australians have seen more fighting against the Japanese than anybody else, and are morally absolutely on top. They are confident, man for man, they can beat the Japanese anywhere, and at any time. Their ideas on training are eminently sound, and they have all facilities for training large numbers. I am convinced that very serious consideration should be given to using existing Australian experiences and facilities for training British instructors for British troops in jungle warfare.[23]

In December 1943, Brigadier John Lloyd,[24] who had successfully commanded the Australian 16 Brigade on the Kokoda Trail and at Buna in 1942 and 1943 prior to becoming chief instructor at the Land Headquarters Tactical School, began a seven-month posting to India Command to provide up-to-date jungle warfare experience and advice to the Director Army Training. Lloyd explained that before being committed to battle Australian troops were taken through 'a period of progressive individual, sub-unit and unit-level jungle training', as well as a period of physical and psychological acclimatization in actual jungle conditions. A new range of specific individual skills and knowledge was required – collectively dubbed 'jungle craft' and 'jungle lore' – for troops to live and move in the jungle with comparative ease. Instruction in anti-malaria/ hygiene discipline also formed an essential part of preparation for jungle fighting, with tropical disease remaining one of the most intractable opponents faced by units operating in New Guinea and the islands of the south-west Pacific. Finally, 'knowledge of Japanese military characteristics and fighting methods was also badly needed to prepare troops before being committed to battle.'[25] The lessons paid off. In the fighting in 1943 the Australians had demonstrated that success could be achieved against the Japanese through high-quality patrolling skills and infantry tactics. The key lesson was that with careful preparation and the right tactics the Japanese could be beaten.[26] Additionally, tactical flexibility became a watchword of Australian operations, an uncanny precursor to Indian Army operations in 1944. Well-trained, confident and courageous infantry remained key to success, as did their integration with artillery and armour. Command flexibility, enabling troops to be moved to where they were most needed, was key in maintaining offensive operations. Flying troops into battle by air, and conducting well-thought-out amphibious landings, were a fundamental component of the Australian military repertoire in 1943.[27] The influence on India Command, by means of the mass of printed pamphlets and memoranda that it produced over the period based on the AIF experience in New Guinea, was profound.[28] In June 1944 Auchinleck attempted to have 600 experienced Australian officers transferred to India Command, not for combat, but for training purposes. He got 168.[29] It was enough. The new doses of experiential DNA Australian experience managed to inject into the armies in India in 1943 and 1944 (both British and Indian) helped transform its bloodstock, and its resulting performance in battle, in 1944 and 1945.

20

Building a Base

In 1942 the sub-continent became a base camp for military operations along its long frontier with Japanese-occupied Burma, running from Chittagong on the Bay of Bengal to Ledo in the far north of the Brahmaputra Valley. The task of creating this base, and of growing it to the extent necessary to sustain an army at the end of a line of communications that ran many hundreds of miles all the way to the Burmese frontier, was principally that of the Commander-in-Chief, a post handed from Wavell to Auchinleck in June 1943. Wavell was promoted to the role of Viceroy, taking the baton from the departing Lord Linlithgow. The task was to build a military infrastructure in otherwise empty Assam and Bengal, comprising new airfields, roads, expanded railways, oil pipelines and storage depots from which Assam and Bengal could be defended, China reinforced from the upper reaches of the Brahmaputra Valley, and the eastern frontier regions thereafter used as the basis for offensive operations to take the war to the Japanese in Burma. In 1942 these challenges were daunting, not least because in order to achieve the creation of a sophisticated infrastructure from scratch, the entire mobilization of Indian industry and India's economy was required. One of the greatest triumphs of the Indian experience of war between 1942 and 1945, despite the mistakes and horrors that led to such terrible events as the Bengal famine in 1943, was that this purpose was largely achieved.

India had proved itself able once before – during the Great War – to deliver a dramatic upscaling and upskilling in its military capabilities to support the imperial demands for trained manpower. It could arguably do so again. But one area where Burma's peripherality to Allied strategy was evidenced in full was its place on the list of destinations for essential warfighting stores, materiel and supply. It was firmly at the bottom, a place it had held since long before the

Second World War. India had always received Britain's cast offs and during the war remained at the bottom of Allied priorities. The Far East came last in terms of priority for modern aircraft, tanks, amphibious shipping, weapons and warlike stores. As a result, it was forced to self-provide – the design and manufacture, often on the battlefield itself[1] – much of the equipment it required to keep fighting, and this created a new industrial base in India to make equipment which before 1939 it imported.

In 1941 India's economy was largely agrarian, with little industrial infrastructure to speak of and a transport infrastructure not designed to respond to the demands placed on it by a modern enemy trying to force its way through its eastern gates. It produced 750,000 tons of steel annually in 1939, for instance, but not of the quality required for munitions, most of which, alongside precision machinery, was produced elsewhere in the world and imported. Its engineering capabilities were unsophisticated, and it had no motor vehicle or aircraft building capability. It didn't make any of its own shipping, nor could it produce anything but simple armaments.[2] Its workforce was poorly educated and unaccustomed to mechanization.

The army's problem was as much logistical as it was about developing successful stratagems for defeating the Japanese in battle. Long before the Japanese could be engaged in successful battle, the seemingly intractable problems posed by logistics in Assam and Bengal needed to be solved. In a lecture he gave in 1946 Slim observed that before 14 Army could even fight, 'with a ration strength of 750,000 – the population of a great city – scattered along a 700 mile front in an area as big as Poland with the poorest of communications and most meagre of resources... we had to feed, clothe, house, and all the time we were doing it, equip, doctor, police, pay and transport by road, ship, rail and air of all those men. All that and jungle too!'[3] He observed that his command stretched from China to the Bay of Bengal, covering 'some of the least suitable campaigning country in the world ... [with] some of the world's worst country, breeding the world's worst diseases, and having for half the year at least the world's worst climate.' A strategy for defeating the Japanese in Burma depended principally on the ability to get sufficient forces into Manipur and North Arakan, and to maintain them there. Both geography and climate conspired to complicate this, as did 14 Army's low priority for stores and the bureaucratic peacetime procedures that still burdened the procurement system.

In north-east Assam and eastern Bengal the transport infrastructure was poor and airfields were few and far between. There was no infrastructure worthy of the name to sustain a growing import-export economy (as opposed to a subsistence one) in peace, let alone war, except for that which had grown up over previous decades to support the Assamese tea industry. Indeed, the mountain vastness of Assam, which stretched over the deep green corrugations between the Brahmaputra Valley and the Chindwin Valley 150 miles farther east, needs to be appreciated when considering the potentiality for the defence of India's eastern frontier. Both 4 (Assam) and XV Corps (Bengal) were painfully isolated from the rest of India. The lack of roads in Bengal forced a dependence upon a rickety system of railways between Calcutta and the northeast frontier. There was only one all-weather airfield in Assam, at Dinjan, in the far north of the Brahmaputra Valley near Chabua. In Manipur, there was no airfield at all. The capital, Imphal, was joined to the Brahmaputra River at Dimapur by a 134-mile road that for much of its length was single track and unmetalled, long stretches in the mountains frequently washed away in landslides during the monsoon. From Dimapur the local railway track – part of the Bengal and Assam railway, running on a 1-metre-gauge track all the way to the north to Ledo and Dibrugarh (the railway bifurcates at Chabua, 779 railway miles from Calcutta) – didn't extend across the Brahmaputra, which was unbridged. Designed for the peacetime jute and tea industries, in 1942 it had a daily capacity across its length of about 600 tons per day. While by strenuous effort the capacity had increased to 2,800 tons per day by October 1943, this was still inadequate to meet all the requirements of IV Corps, Stilwell's NCAC and the Hump airlift.

Stores carried on the broad-gauge railway from Calcutta had to be transhipped to the metre-line gauge at either Santahar or at Milestone 235, before travelling to Gauhati, where they were unloaded again on the western bank of the Brahmaputra and transhipped by ferry across the river. Flood damage during the monsoon regularly inhibited transhipment. The ferry journey from Dibrugarh downstream to Calcutta took a full seven days; the full turnaround, including the upstream travel, took as much as 33 days. Wheeled vehicles had to be transported by rail 235 miles from Calcutta to Siliguri before they could join the road to Assam, which ran on to the Brahmaputra. A fleet of river steamers and barges plied between the ports on the Brahmaputra, but the capacity of the river route had been greatly reduced by the despatch of boats to other theatres of war, and by the behaviour of the river itself: its level fluctuated by as much as 20 feet, and its course changed every monsoon with the result that jetties, roads and rail spurs at river ports were frequently washed away or left high and dry and had to be entirely reconstructed. There was no military infrastructure worthy of the name in either eastern Assam or eastern Bengal; the 'nearest military logistic base was at Benares, on the Ganges, as far from the Assam front as London is from Iceland.'[4] Each bullet, blanket and bucket had to travel over 1,100 miles to the front line, by rail, ferry and truck over probably the Second World War's most tortuous logistics route. The condition of the existing roads was poor. Few were all-weather, and the machinery to improve them did not exist on a scale to make a difference in the short term. To improve the line of communication into Manipur necessitated the construction, much of it by hand using Indian labour, of hundreds of miles of roads, pipelines and airfields. In Arakan, to support the build-up of XV Corps, thousands of bricks had to be baked alongside the road that ran forward of Cox's Bazaar to make it all-weather because of a lack of road-making stone in the region. The resource demands of such a long and difficult line of communication were considerable. For example, 50 per cent of the tonnage which left Chittagong for the forward areas was absorbed by the line of communication personnel and services before the corps areas were reached.[5] It was the transformation of these lines of communication in 1942–44 that made possible the military successes of 1944 and 1945.

One of the reasons for India being unprepared for war on its eastern frontier in 1942 was because its defence policy, formed in London, had never considered the threat of an army on its doorstop. Singapore was the eastern bastion, guaranteeing – it was believed – India's defence. From 1939 the military purpose of India was to reinforce the British effort in North Africa and the Middle East. Its best troops – two brigades' worth – had been shipped to North Africa in 1939, and a further brigade sent to Burma. Most of India's stock of modern weaponry accompanied the troops to Egypt. The 1940 expansion programme envisaged another six divisions being formed, all for imperial reinforcement, one armoured and five infantry divisions, resulting in 120,000 men in training in India by September 1940. It needs also to be remembered that for every man in a combat unit in the Indian Army, up to a further four were required in support, logistics and non-combatant roles. For an infantry division of 15,000 men, for example, a total force of 56,000 was required. The following year, a further five divisions were created, resulting in a strength of 900,000 in the Indian Army by the end of 1941, of whom 300,000 were posted outside India. The expansion was facilitated by new battalions being built up from more experienced men sourced (or 'milked') from other units and formations. The extraordinary expansion of the army left it with very large numbers of new recruits, but men recruited and initially trained and prepared for war in the Middle East rather than Asia, and vastly undertrained, inexperienced and underequipped.[6] They certainly were no match, by any measure, for the Imperial Japanese Army, against which they would find themselves pitted in Malaya and Burma.

Unprecedented numbers of recruits, building on the massive expansion already undertaken in 1941, were brought into the army, trained and equipped for war. Utterly transforming the Indian Army, recruits flooded in from across India, and large numbers of Indian officers were trained, commissioned and deployed into this army. The shape and culture of the Indian Army was already very different to the pre-1939 army, changes being forced through by Auchinleck, Commander-in-Chief of the Indian Army in 1941, and again from 1943 to 1947.[7] Indian officers had traditionally been excluded from posts where they might command British officers. Such racial shibboleths were swept aside in an orgy of innovation that at a stroke transformed the ethos and culture of the army. No longer was status or racial origin to be considered important, only professional competence. Recruiting in large numbers from the non-martial races and recruiting young Indians in large numbers had the effect of re-creating the Indian Army, transforming it from its 1939 character to something entirely different by 1944. Most of the newly recruited Indian Army officers proved equal to the task, although the short time span from when someone was commissioned into the army in 1940 and 1941 to the great battles of 1944 and 1945 meant that few rose beyond field rank (i.e. command of a company). Those Indians who had been commissioned in the 1920s and 1930s were able to command battalions and brigades and did exceptionally well in these roles. As Daniel Marston observes:

> The first Indian officer to command a combat unit was Lieutenant Colonel D.S. Brar, 5 Mahratta Machine Gun Battalion… in late 1943. By the end of the war, several Indian lieutenant colonels as well as three brigadiers commanded infantry, cavalry, and artillery units. Many of these had been decorated for bravery in the field. The most highly decorated Indian Army battalion in the war, the 2/1 Punjab Regiment, included one ICO [Indian Commissioned Officer] who received the Distinguished Service Order (out of five awarded to the battalion) and seven ICOs who received MCs (out of twelve awarded to the battalion).[8]

What also helped change the army was the large number of British ECOs recruited into the Indian Army or seconded to it from British units. They tended to have more liberal views on India than those young Britons who had joined the Indian Army as professional soldiers prior to 1939. By 1943 the political world in Britain and India had changed irrevocably from that which it had been in 1939, and not just because of the Congress Party. British public opinion, as reflected in the attitudes of the thousands of young Britons serving in India and looking forward to returning to their families and civilian life when the fascist beasts in Europe and Asia had been destroyed, did not look upon the colonial project as their own. Indeed, many saw it as anachronistic, views hardened by virtue of the experience of working alongside Indian officers in the same great crusade. These views were codified and then evangelized by official channels. In January 1943 a pamphlet entitled 'British Way and Purpose' issued by P.J. Grigg, the Secretary of State for War (a document presumably never seen by the Prime Minister) and taught in classes by the Royal Army Educational Corps, told soldiers that the empire was on its way out:

> We no longer regard the Colonial Empire as a 'possession', but as a trust or responsibility. 'Imperialism' in the less reputable sense of that term is dead: there is obviously no room for it in the British Commonwealth of equal nations, and it has been superseded by the principle of trusteeship for Colonial peoples... The conception of trusteeship is already passing into the more active one of partnership... Self government is better than good government.[9]

Likewise, the air forces in India grew rapidly. The peacetime air command in India was managed by a mere 30 officers. In June 1942 the Chiefs of Staff authorized the expansion of the Indian Army to 28 divisions (from the base of one deployable division in 1939) and 66 squadrons of aircraft.[10] To meet the Chiefs of Staff's commitment – as well as the demands of the Hump airlift to China – a massive programme of airfield construction was required. In April 1942 the target of 200, later that year rising to 215, airfields was set. This staggering civilian engineering project was to transform India's war economy. Each runway required 40,000 tons of crushed stone and 4,000 tons of cement; petrol, oil and lubricant storage facilities and pipelines; electricity, water and a panoply of support services for both aircraft maintenance and to accommodate the hundreds of men and women needed at each site. By early 1943 five were complete in all respects (multiple, all-weather 1,600-yard strips), and a further 148 were partially completed. India had few aircraft before the war, the inventory totalling seven squadrons of vintage biplanes. The subsequent growth of air power in the region reflected the nature of the war in the Far East – vast distances covered by mountains or jungle or both, supported by few all-weather roads – and the central role played by air power in prosecuting this war and overcoming these encumbrances. In September 1941 there were 11,600 RAF personnel in India and Burma, representing 2 per cent of the RAF's total strength and supporting the deployment, in April 1942, of 426 aircraft. In September 1943 the figure was 80,000 supporting, in November, 2,820 aircraft. In March 1944 there were 3,700 RAF aircraft (i.e., excluding Indian Air Force (IAF) and United States Army Air Force (USAAF) aircraft), which in September 1944 represented 10 per cent of the RAF, together with 18 squadrons of 10th USAAF. In May 1945 there were 122,000 RAF personnel in theatre (13 per cent of the RAF's total strength).[11] The IAF (in 1945 it became the RIAF) grew to 28,500 personnel in 1945, with nine operational squadrons flying fighter reconnaissance, ground attack, light bomber and fighter aircraft (Hurricanes, Spitfires and the less elegant looking, but effective, Vultee Vengeances).[12] Air power sustained the Hump from India to China, supporting 356,000 forward troops of 11 Army Group and the NCAC in the field (including the Chindits); in 1945, 90 per cent of all combat supplies reaching 14 Army in Burma came by air.[13] '615,000 tons were to be lifted by air to the armies in Burma in the course of the campaign – including 315,000 reinforcements flown in and 210,000 casualties flown out.'[14]

When, in January 1943, Operation *Anakim* – the proposed amphibious assault against Rangoon – was planned, the number of divisions India was required to maintain (both British and Indian) increased to 31, along with 100 squadrons, both RAF and IAF. *Anakim* gave strategic purpose to the dramatic growth of India as a base, even though the lack of shipping and amphibious resources led to *Anakim* being shelved entirely mid-year, in exchange for the task of expanding the Assam line of communication, from Calcutta through to Dimapur and Jorhat to support the American airlift to China, and to support the slow build-up of military resources in Imphal. During the year it provided the backdrop to the massive expansion of Indian support capabilities and military infrastructure. Military basing increased from 2.5 million square feet in 1939 to 24 million square feet completed and under construction in January 1943. A massive programme of depot building took place supporting the lines of communication from Calcutta to Assam, and Calcutta to Bengal.

One of the problems with the massive growth of the armed forces in India was the challenge it posed to the Indian economy to keep pace with the demands now made upon it. The ability of India to sustain its forces building up in Assam and Bengal had to be accompanied by the growth of the Indian economy. It had to provide huge numbers of vehicles, rifles, bullets and stores of every kind. What India could not provide had to be sourced from British, Commonwealth or American factories, although this put pressure on shipping resources and scarce dollar currency to purchase goods in the United States. For instance, at the end of 1941, India was producing 8,000 rifles each month, but had a deficit of 78,000 against its requirement. Every other area of weaponry required had a substantial deficiency, such as tanks (27 per cent), 25-pounders (36 per cent) and Bren-guns (19 per cent). In every area of demand, India was found wanting. There simply weren't enough resources to procure and provide fuel for the army, or men who knew how to drive the new vehicles with which the army was being equipped. All had to be trained from scratch. But from where would come the driving instructors, for instance, or the mechanics? These, too, had to be trained, from a very low base of knowledge and experience. During the war, India's ability to provide the materiel to support the armed forces in India never fully matched the massive requirements placed against it. The result was that for many items of military necessity, the fighting units were forced to deliver themselves, with a make-do-and-mend and self-help philosophy that transferred the initiative for getting things done back to the front-line commanders. Nevertheless, both 1942 and 1943 saw a dramatic growth in the production and import of war materiel. The import of military vehicles increased from 7,500 in 1939 to 35,000 in 1942 to 115,000 in 1943, but all imports were constrained by enemy activity in the Mediterranean until 1943, which forced vessels to travel from Europe around the Cape of Good Hope, as well as the global pressure on scarce shipping resources.[15] The requirements for petrol, oil and lubricants increased exponentially, especially with the advent of the Hump airlift from the Brahmaputra Valley. Petroleum products that weren't produced and refined in India (only 5 per cent of the SEAC requirement in 1944) were imported through Bombay, from where they had to be transhipped by rail across India. A 275-mile pipeline was constructed from Bombay by May 1943, but the burden of transmission remained on the increasingly overstretched railway, which formed the primary artery of war as India's base grew. The pressure on the railways demanded many hundreds of new locomotives and thousands of pieces of rolling stock. Some of this pressure was relieved with a drive to increase the effectiveness of coastal shipping, much of which on the eastern coast had shrunk dramatically in 1942 as a result of the Japanese naval threat. In particular, the Calcutta and Chittagong ports were developed in 1943 and 1944 to be able to form the setting off ports for amphibious operations against the Japanese-held littoral in Arakan and Malaya. Wavell asked London in April 1942 for 185 new rail locomotives, a decision Whitehall was unwilling to take, as the only source of such equipment was the USA, and the purchase would consume scarce dollar reserves. Such inhibitions were overturned by the force of global events, however, and by September 1943 a total of 1,200 locomotives had been ordered from firms in the UK, Canada and the USA, 485 of which had been delivered by May 1944.[16]

At the same time as India Command was being pressed to produce large numbers of trained recruits for the eastern frontiers of Assam and Bengal, India itself was groaning under enormous economic pressure. A significant challenge existed for the Indian government in balancing the requirements for the defence of India with those of feeding its population. In 1943 these pressures reached breaking point, and it was within this context that famine occurred in Bengal, leading to the loss over time of perhaps 3 million lives. The 1942 rice crop was poor, dangerously exacerbated by the loss of Burma, which had provided a substantial proportion of pre-war domestic rice consumption (2 million tons per annum, or 15 per cent of consumption) in eastern India. The famine in Bengal was a dark stain on the administration of India, a consequence not so much of ignorance (because famines were common) but of war-induced neglect. The well-proven (though imperfect) Famine Codes that had managed to preserve life in the midst of previous such disasters had been put aside.[17] This was a failure shared by national government, local administration and unregulated private sector greed, as scarce rice was hoarded as a device to force prices to rise. It is reasonable to argue that the real reason why India was fighting – the defence of India and its people – was shamefully neglected by the Indian government. Bengal in 1943 may be explicable as an event, but it was also unconscionable, irreparably damaging Britain's moral right to govern, and a leitmotif, together with the repression of political dissent in 1942, for criticism of colonialism ever since. The fundamental censure of government was that the self-evident organizational skill and centralizing authority that even then was being used to design a system to build effective lines of communication into Assam and Bengal to sustain the fighting armies being built up could also have been directed to preventing famine, regardless of the military challenge presented by the Japanese. It was in this political judgement and the speed of relief that the government was found wanting, although it is also fair to acknowledge the efforts made by London and Delhi to divert grain to India to alleviate the crisis.[18]

In August 1943, at the Quadrant Conference in Quebec, another imperative emerged to reinforce the American insistence on building a replacement overland route to China from India, together with the need for military operations inside Burma to support this strategy. This was the planned arrival in early 1944 of the new US 'very long-range' bomber, designated the B29. One option American planners were examining was the possibility of using bases in China to bomb mainland Japan. This would require further enhancement to the airfield and support infrastructure (such as fuel pipelines) in eastern India over and above the dramatic building programme already underway.

British strategic inclinations were to avoid getting involved in a land campaign to retake Burma from the north, preferring an amphibious strike at Malaya in order to seize Singapore. There was considerable merit in this argument but it had several flaws. The first was that it appeared to be a shortcut to victory, especially to Britain's critics in Chungking and Washington. Avoiding a hard fight with the Japanese in Burma by launching an amphibious attack on Rangoon (Operation *Anakim*) presupposed that the very considerable numbers in the Japanese Burma Area Army – five fighting divisions consisting of 135,000 or more men, together with many more thousands of occupation troops across Burma – would either surrender or not fight tooth-and-nail to drive the Allies back into the sea. The 'indirect' strategy underpinning *Anakim*, a peculiarly Churchillian strategic conception, would in reality never be able to replace the hard fighting necessary to remove the Japanese grasp on Burma, fingernail by bloody fingernail. Second, it also presumed the availability of considerable quantities of amphibious equipment and vessels to conduct a landing, material that would be hard to justify in the context of the Germany First policy. Finally, it ignored the needs of China, which wanted demonstrable proof, by means of boots on the ground, that Britain was committed to the full support of China, and therefore the Burma Road, not merely the recovery of its lost colony by the back door. As the junior partner in the alliance, Britain ultimately needed to agree to a formal strategy for the defeat of the Japanese in Burma, instead of appearing endlessly to prevaricate and offer alternatives that weren't practical or immediate. As it was it took the victorious troops of 14 Army in late 1944 to create strategy in Burma by crossing the Chindwin in pursuit of the Japanese.

The ability of India to create a robust industrial base at speed, build a sophisticated forward logistical infrastructure in Assam and Bengal – with the railway, port and air transport links reaching back deep into India, and across the sub-continent to

Bombay and its port – and grow the size of its armed forces tenfold – defeating the Japanese in 1944 and 1945 in the process, including the reconquest of Burma – are extraordinary though largely forgotten *Indian* achievements. They were brought about by means of a powerful central government pursuing a single, clear plan, repressing dissent where it threatened to disrupt the war effort (seen most notably in its response to the Quit India campaign in 1942) and embolden India's enemies, and supported by an at least acquiescent population; some 8 million Indians found themselves employed in these defence tasks, a million on the airfields alone. The massive construction of barracks, depots, roads, pipelines, airfields and ports across India was accompanied by the dramatic industrialization of the Indian economy after 1942, as India was forced to produce everything it required to sustain both its armed forces and domestic consumption at a time when the global constraints on shipping limited what could be imported to essential war supplies. Food, clothing and arms were manufactured in massive quantities, in many cases for the first time. The defence infrastructure undertaken along India's eastern frontier was not merely an imperial, but an Allied one, as it was from the Brahmaputra Valley in northern Assam that the massive airlift of supplies to Yunnan was initiated and sustained for well over two long years. Without India, without Assam, the Hump, with its 650,000 tons of supplies airlifted into China between 1942 and 1945, would have made the United States China strategy stillborn.

These phenomenal achievements were brought about by Indian political and administrative planning and commitment, together with previously untapped ingenuity, muscle, brains and the loyalty, if only transient, of a great proportion of the population. These efforts along its eastern frontier were not merely defensive, but offensive in origin and concept. They were also entirely unanticipated, given that no enemy attack had ever been envisaged from the east. For this work, India was promised payment from the British exchequer. Britain had agreed to pay India for any costs associated with the provision of men and war materiel outside India. 'In 1940–41 Britain paid £40 million towards Indian defence, and India paid £49 million. A year later, Britain was paying £150 million, and India £71 million. In 1942–43, Britain's bill had soared to £270 million.'[19] Britain, despite its pre-war parsimony, was now putting its money where its mouth was, a recognition of the reality that India, in being the front line against the Japanese, was playing its role in defending the empire from attack. 'In 1939 India owed Britain £356m; by 1945 Britain owed India £1,260m', one-fifth of Britain's Gross National Product.[20]

Consequently, the war created a new type of government in India. From the laissez-faire, hands-off pre-war government which demanded little more than civic obedience and gave little back in exchange, India became a centrist state, involving itself in the affairs of its citizens to a previously unimagined degree. This was in major part because the state, paid by Britain, now needed to buy the resources India had in profusion – people, raw materials and manufactured goods – and to use these to build, manufacture and produce in India on an unprecedented scale. This entailed a degree of organization, down to local-level, civic administration, taxation and public accounting never before seen in the country.

A range of practical initiatives lay at the heart of the rebuilding of Eastern Army in mid to late 1943. These had a measurable impact on morale. News of Wingate's expedition earlier in the year had also provided a significant boost, but this contributed to the process of invigoration sweeping through the army rather than being its cause. But the situation was still far from satisfactory. In almost every area – ammunition, rations, vehicles, radios, medical equipment and stores of every kind – 14 Army was seriously deficient. Stocks of rifle and artillery ammunition, for example, were between 25 and 45 per cent below requirement. Slim's approach to the problem of administration was to develop self-reliance from within rather than to wait for help from outside. His staff in 14 Army were second-to-none, he declared in a lecture to the Press Club in 1946, because 'it realised that it existed to keep the fighting troops supplied and second, because it regarded any difficulty whether of man or nature as a challenge and a challenge to be taken up.'[21]

Welfare provision improved dramatically. The delivery of mail, the introduction of a theatre newspaper, and improvements to rations and accommodation were all key elements in this programme of change. A particular effort was made to ensure that the many thousands of troops in support functions and on the lines of communication, who were not involved in the fighting but who were essential to the maintenance of the combatant units, benefited from these changes and were made to feel part of the army as a whole. All men, however menial the tasks they performed, were vital for victory.

Information and honesty were key ingredients to the approach to the problems faced by 14 Army. Slim was convinced that the army as a whole had to understand the reasons for delays and deficiencies, and collectively develop new and innovative ways of solving them. He talked frankly to his troops at every opportunity, and he encouraged his commanders to do likewise. While there was nothing new in this, Slim gave it renewed priority. 'It was the way we had held the troops together in the worst days of the 1942 retreat', he recalled; 'we remained an army then only because the men saw and knew their commanders.' Information rooms were set up in units to keep the men informed not only of the progress of operations but of other items of interest to them, including the course of the war in Europe and the Pacific. Slim was determined from the outset to explain the difficulties he faced in getting supplies to his troops, giving them the reasons for equipment shortages and keeping them informed about efforts made on their behalf to improve the situation. He knew that whatever he had been promised in the way of increased resources from Britain, 14 Army would remain, for a long time, desperately short. 'In my more gloomy moments', he wrote, 'I even doubted if we should ever climb up the priority list.' He impressed upon his troops the realities of a global war effort – that defeating the Germans had to take first priority but that despite every difficulty he and his commanders would endeavour to obtain everything that the army needed. If this were not possible then they would all have to improvise. Slim commented that 'it is not so much asking men to fight or work with inadequate or obsolete equipment that lowers morale but the belief that those responsible are accepting such a state of affairs. If men realize that everyone above them and behind them is flat out to get the things required for them, they will do wonders, as my men did, with the meagre resources they have instead of sitting down moaning for better.' 'No boats?' asked Slim rhetorically to the Press Club in 1946. 'We'll build 'em! No vegetables, we'll grow 'em! No eggs? Duck farms! No parachutes? We'll use gully!* No road metal? Bake our own bricks and lay 'em! No air strips? Put down bithess!† Malaria, we'll stop it! Medium guns busting? Saw off three feet of the barrel and go on shooting! Their motto, "God helps those who help themselves".'[22]

Two areas of especial interest were pursued with scientific vigour. One was the effort to reduce the impact of malaria on the troops. In 1943, for every combat casualty there were 120 malaria casualties. This had dropped to 1:20 in 1944, and then as low as 1:10 in 1945.[23] In 1944 the armies in India suffered 250,000 casualties from malaria and dysentery[24] and a further 2,400 casualties from scrub typhus, of which 20 per cent were fatal.[25] A range of measures were responsible for this reduction, which combined new treatments for malaria with the relentless application of military discipline at unit and sub-unit level to ensure that soldiers limited their exposure to the mosquitos that spread the disease. The Australian

---

*Woven jute.
†Hessian strips soaked in bitumen, invented by 14 Army's Chief Engineer, Bill Halsted, as a means of hardening road and airstrip surfaces.

experience of the suppressive effect of the drug mepacrine was applied successfully to troops in Arakan. The problem was supply, although by 1945 SEAC's needs were largely being met, consuming 40,000,000 tablets a month. The Medical Advisory Division of the Indian Army had adopted a pest control substance in the USA called DDT which was deployed with spectacular effect – although not until 1945 – against areas in Manipur where malarial larvae grew. In terms of military discipline, Slim's solution for 14 Army was actively to support medical proposals for reorganizing the medical services in the forward area. Men who contracted malaria were no longer sent to hospitals in India, thus reducing the pressure on transport and on the individual who was otherwise forced to undergo an uncomfortable and often hazardous journey to the rear. Forward treatment meant that now a man who contracted the disease would be in a Malaria Forward Treatment Unit within 24 hours and could be back in his unit in weeks rather than months. The application of robust military discipline helped ensure that anti-malarial instructions were obeyed. Commanding officers of units that did not have over 95 per cent of the men test positive for taking their daily dose of mepacrine were sacked.[26] Through these measures the annual malaria rate fell to 13 per cent by 1945. Likewise whole units were de-wormed. As in the campaigns in North Africa and Italy, surgeons operated in 'forward areas, performing major operations within a few hours of a man being wounded',[27] and nurses were sent as far forward as possible. These measures not only saved many lives but also had a dramatic effect on morale.[28]

Another medical advance involved the steps taken to improve military rations. Food, in terms of its quality, quantity and consistency, was a constant nightmare for an army that contained 30 ration scales, as without adequate nutrition infantry soldiers in particular would not have the physical wherewithal, not to mention the morale, to enable them to undertake the demanding tasks associated with combat.[29] Srinath Raghavan points out that the vast expansion of the Indian Army led to a plummeting of the physical standards of recruits, a major reason for which was poor dietary intake. 'Given the widespread scarcity of food across most parts of India – including famine in some – it is hardly surprising that recruits were malnourished and afflicted with nutritional diseases such as anaemia. Special feeding was required to bring them up to the minimum acceptable operational standard. Indeed, the availability of good quality food was a major incentive for joining the army.'[30] But progressive steps needed to be adopted to improve the food provided for the men, as the weight of recruits on entry was often lower than required, and the army needed to provide the additional calories required by men undertaking strenuous work in a demanding physical environment and climate. A pragmatic decision was taken to accept underweight recruits and look to improving weight during the 11 months of training that followed. Early evaluations in 1942 had identified that whatever its calorific intake, the food that soldiers were actually getting was often deficient in vitamins such as A and C, indeed that many 'Indian troops were subsisting on a very narrow margin of nutritional adequacy.'[31] In addition, the target intake of 3,385 calories per day was too low, and following extensive testing was raised to 4,200 calories in early 1944, including at least 100 grams of animal protein daily. Meat was recognized to be by far and away the best means available to ensuring the right level of energy, although the harsh reality of the strained line of communication forward into Burma meant that soldiers received only 23–26 grams a day, far short of the level required. Another challenge was to ingest over 4,000 calories a day. Traditional Indian Army practice was to have two meals a day, one mid-morning and the second in the early evening. In another overturning of precedent, the Indian Army in 1943 introduced a third meal, much to the chagrin of some who thought it an innovation too far: *chai* (hot, milky and sugared tea) and sugared chapattis at 5 a.m. was added to the other two meals held at more traditional hours.

What complicated the science of calories, protein and vitamins was religious and cultural practice. Although soldiers were willing to train, serve, fight and die together in closely bonded military units, they usually drew the line at eating each other's food (although there were exceptions). In forward areas, such as beyond the Chindwin in Burma in 1945, the challenge of meeting every culinary requirement exercised the logistics efforts of the army to their maximum. 'Muslims would not touch pork and ate only halal meat; Hindus often forswore beef and the meat of female animals; Sikhs took only non-halal meat; and certain groups like Jats were strictly vegetarian. Soldiers of all backgrounds regarded even certified meat with considerable suspicion.'[32] The military effort to provide nearly 2 million meals every day across SEAC's fighting front in 1944 and 1945 was prodigious, necessitating a dramatic expansion in the line of communication and supply infrastructure in India, and to the front. Only limited quantities of food could be obtained from local sources, which meant that the bulk of all rations – both fresh and dry – had to come up the already overburdened line of communication from Calcutta. The lack of cold storage created great deficiencies in the procurement of meat, and there were no alternatives to the monotonous diet of bully beef. The same deficiencies occurred in the provision of milk and milk products, and vegetables. Consequently, 14 Army was forced to develop innovative ways of feeding itself. Chinese farmers were flown into the plain to start a duck farm to produce eggs. 'Eventually,' comments Julian Thompson, 'in a reversion to the logistic methods of earlier wars, sheep and goats were kept at Imphal, where there was plenty of rice straw available for feedstuff, and 18,000 acres of vegetables were cultivated.'[33] In fact, by February 1945 there were eight farms on the Imphal plain, each manned by 800 farmers, cultivating 18,000 acres, 'producing 100 per cent of the fresh vegetables for 170,000 troops and 273,000 civilian labourers forward of Dimapur.'[34]

21

'A Blind Man Searching for a Black Cat
in a Dark Room'

Irwin's desperate failure in Arakan between September 1942 and May 1943 demanded the complete reshaping of command responsibilities in South East Asia. Because the region was a melting pot of divergent national interests, it seemed to many observers that a single international commander was required to weld these otherwise competing interests into a unified command structure. Arakan had confirmed to Churchill that India Command as it was then arranged could never hope to defeat the Japanese at the same time as organize itself for war. The conduct of the war against the Japanese needed to be separated from India Command, which was also concerned with the administration of the fighting base in India. It could not do both. Accordingly, at the Trident Conference in Washington in May 1943 a new theatre of operations – South East Asia Command (SEAC) – was agreed. At the Quadrant Conference in August a new Supreme Allied Commander was announced.

The United States was a keen supporter of the appointment of a Supreme Commander, agreeing also that it be commanded by a Briton, which would allow them to claim the more prestigious post – Europe – for themselves. Wavell had lost Churchill's trust entirely and was not considered for the post. Explaining the rationale of the appointment in a letter to Clement Attlee on 22 August 1943, Churchill wrote, 'There is no doubt of the need of a young and vigorous mind in this lethargic and stagnant Indian scene.'[1] Wavell had in any case been 'kicked upstairs' to his new role as Viceroy.

The man chosen to be the Supremo was Vice-Admiral Lord Louis Mountbatten, a cousin of King George V. He was not the first choice. He was initially nominated by Leo Amery, before being first rejected and then accepted by Churchill, but it was a popular appointment except within the Royal Navy, which still believed in promotion on the basis of time served and was suspicious of Mountbatten's talent for self-promotion. Mountbatten skipped many more senior officers to take the appointment. His undoubted vanity and showmanship irritated his more conventional colleagues, and accusations of superficiality proved difficult to shift. Nevertheless, Mountbatten's remarkable ability to make friends among otherwise fractious allies made him stand out as the ideal joint commander, a point recognized by both Roosevelt and Churchill in 1943. Indeed, the notorious American Anglophobe, Admiral King, regarded Mountbatten to be the single most impressive officer at the Quebec Conference in August 1943.[2]

Mountbatten's strengths mattered more to Churchill than his evident weaknesses. The power and resilience of Mountbatten's exuberant personality were going to mean much more in this theatre than experience or technical proficiency. It was vitally important that a Supremo possessed the charisma necessary to attract and retain the loyalties of soldiers, sailors and airmen from a wide set of backgrounds, and to unite them in a common cause. He had to make them believe that what they were setting out to do – the defeat of the Japanese on land, at sea and in the air, and their expulsion from South East Asia – was achievable. He also had to have great reserves of emotional resilience to overcome not just the widespread defeatism he would face at the outset, but the constant setbacks that were certain to follow, not least because Germany First would, until the war in Europe had been won, consign SEAC to the bottom of the waiting list for equipment, men and supplies. Mountbatten's unique personal qualities, his proven leadership ability and his experience of knitting together diverse national and international teams in Combined Operations – Churchill described him to Attlee on 9 August 1943 as 'young, enthusiastic and triphibious' – made him ideally suited for this task.[3] General Alan Brooke finally felt able to support the appointment, but only so long as Mountbatten was accompanied by the 'steadying influence' of a 'carefully selected Chief of Staff' to counterbalance his self-confidence and 'boundless energy and drive'.[4] Churchill's instincts were right: Mountbatten was by far the best choice that could have been made.

The purpose of the Supreme Allied Commander was intended to be political as well as military. His task was to meld together a disparate mass of competing interests – British, American and Chinese – in the pursuit of a single object: the destruction of Japanese military hegemony in Asia. Of critical importance to later events was the fact that Mountbatten was invested by the Joint (British and

American) Chiefs of Staff with *supreme command*. He took up the appointment in October 1943, aged 43. News of the appointment by his newly designated Chief of Staff, Lieutenant General Sir Henry Pownall, was positive, reflecting perhaps the briefing General Alan Brooke had given him about his new master: 'Mountbatten... will certainly have all the necessary drive and initiative to conduct this war. The difficulty will be to restrain him, or rather to direct his energies into really useful directions and away from minor details. He throws out brainwaves daily – some of them very good, too, but not always timely. And he is obviously rather volatile.'[5]

Within two months an affectionate bond had been established between the two men, Pownall noting in his diary:

> The pace is pretty hot for Mountbatten gives neither himself, nor his staff, time for relaxation. His active mind is perpetually at work. Very often his push and drive are used in useful directions. But not always and he is apt to put urgency into matters which are not the least urgent, or subjects which ought to be carefully considered... But for all that, his energy and drive are most admirable features; for so young a man his knowledge is extremely good; his mind receptive; his experience of two years on the C.O.S [Chiefs of Staff] Committee stand him in admirable stead; he has a most attractive personality; and his judgement is good when things are put fairly and squarely to him.[6]

The first task Mountbatten faced was to imprint his authority on a wide range of military commanders of differing services (Army, Navy and Air Force), traditions (British Army, Indian Army, American), nationalities (British, American, Chinese), all of whom were more senior and more experienced than he. There were still no signs of any recovery of British fortunes in South East Asia. General Irwin's initial and unfounded optimism in the autumn of 1942 had swung like a pendulum to a state of contagious pessimism in May 1943 at the end of his Arakan debacle as to whether British and Indian troops could ever defeat the Japanese. He preached this defeatist message to whomever would listen. Indeed, in the two years that followed, resonances of this despair could still be heard in London, Washington and New Delhi.

But others saw the situation very differently. Slim, for one, did not believe the grounds for this pessimism, considering Irwin's reverse in Arakan to be the fault of poor strategy, and of ill-considered plans and assumptions that ignored the need for appropriate training and suitable equipment for those sent to do the fighting. Likewise, Mountbatten, with his endless store of optimism, did not fall prey to these negative emotions and arrived in India to take up his new post convinced that no task was impossible, and no problem insuperable. Most strategic decision-makers in London and Washington viewed the task SEAC faced as so huge as to be impossible. The geographical, topographical and meteorological challenges of fighting in the hinterland between Assam and Burma; the grossly inadequate global prioritization of India for military stores; the global lack of shipping; insufficient engineering resources; the prioritization of American transport aircraft to support the Hump airlift rather than operational support to land forces in Assam; the recent embarrassing failure in Arakan, and the seemingly insurmountable problem of finding individual soldiers capable of matching the Japanese man-for-man: all of these factors persuaded many observers that SEAC's task was impossible. Only once these challenges had been overcome could the newly trained formations of Indian, African and British troops be deployed effectively against the Japanese in Burma. These were incredibly tough tasks to achieve, and the accusations of tardiness against India Command by Churchill and others in 1943 demonstrated perhaps a level of ignorance of the challenges India had to overcome in delivering these outcomes. In the political hurly-burly of late 1943, however, it was difficult for many to believe that dramatic change was possible out of India.

In the international sphere Mountbatten had to create harmonious relationships with Chiang Kai-shek and Stilwell. Within a week of arriving in Delhi Mountbatten flew across the Hump to pay his respects to the Generalissimo in Chungking. The trip was a resounding success and paid testament to the new Supremo's skills as a diplomat. But Stilwell struggled to find a level at which he could relate to his new boss, never ridding himself of his deep suspicion that Mountbatten's easy charm obscured an absence of military talent. On their first meeting in October 1943, Stilwell, in a burst of enthusiasm, had described him as 'a good egg… full of enthusiasm and also of disgust with inertia and conservatism'. But thereafter the relationship between the Supremo and his deputy quickly deteriorated. By January 1944 Stilwell was describing Mountbatten as a mere 'glamour boy' who lacked the killer instinct: 'He doesn't wear well and I begin to wonder if he knows his stuff. Enormous staff, walla-walla [endless talking], but damned little fighting.'[7]

The situation was complicated by the fact that the relationship between Chiang Kai-shek and Stilwell had all but broken down by the time of the creation of SEAC. Stilwell believed that Chiang Kai-shek was abusing American goodwill for his own selfish political purposes, and not for that with which American largesse was proffered in such huge quantities: the destruction of the Japanese.

Stilwell never appeared to appreciate the strategic pressures facing the Chinese leader. In the first place, Chiang Kai-shek was convinced that his greatest threat came from the Japanese to his north, not the south-west, and was reluctant to divide his forces. Second, he was nervous about committing his forces to action in Burma to recover the old Burma Road to Rangoon when he had no guarantee that the Allies would also commit to the same objective. The last thing Chiang Kai-shek wanted was to find himself battling alone against the Japanese in Burma. To Stilwell, however, these difficulties meant little: in his view, Chiang Kai-shek was vague, indecisive, corrupt and untrustworthy.

Despite the impasse that had developed between Chiang Kai-shek and Stilwell, Mountbatten was determined to try to make the relationship work. His trusting and possibly slightly naïve nature made him hope that he would win the loyalty and support of Stilwell, while at the same time persuading Chiang Kai-shek that Stilwell's motives and ambitions were in China's best interests. General Marshall encouraged him to regard his difficult American deputy benevolently. In a letter to Mountbatten on 16 January 1944 he wrote, 'You will find… that he wants merely to get things done without delays and will ignore considerations of his own… so long as drive and imagination are being given to plans, preparations and operations… Impatience with conservatism and slow motion is his weakness – but a damned good one in this emergency.'[8]

Mountbatten's appointment nevertheless masked the fact that overall strategy between the Allies for the prosecution of the war in South East Asia remained undecided and continued to be earnestly debated. From the outset two competing strategic visions existed between the United States and Great Britain. The United States wanted to recapture Burma, or at least the northern part, so as to reopen the Burma Road and continue to resupply China. The British, by contrast, never much enamoured with the role that China could supposedly play in the war, wanted to recover Burma as a steppingstone to the recapture of Singapore, while not denying the need to support China to an extent. London, when it spurred itself to think about the situation in the Far East, preferred an amphibious flanking attack on Malaya or Sumatra, avoiding the entanglement of the Burmese jungles altogether.[9] The prospect of a long and slow jungle campaign to retake Burma from the north was viewed by London with ill-disguised hostility. It would be akin, as Churchill famously described it, to 'going into the water to fight the shark', or as General Alan Brooke reported another of Churchill's sayings, to 'eat the porcupine quill by quill'.[10] Frightened perhaps by the experience of battle in 1942, Churchill (and others) fell prey to the idea that British and Indian soldiers were incapable of defeating their fearsome Asian foe.

Britain was committed, nevertheless, to recovering its old colony, less for reasons – as is often supposed – of prestige, but because London came to believe that the whole of Burma needed to be recovered if the Japanese threat to both China and India was to be removed. It was this basic dichotomy in strategic ambition that was to divide the Allies throughout the war, national emotions on both sides tarnishing their view of their allies. The Americans remained suspicious throughout that they were being played in a subtle game by the British, the end goal of which was the propping up of the British Empire. To many Americans 'SEAC' famously stood for 'Save England's Asian Colonies'. The problem was perhaps less the differences in views about what to do with Burma and China, than with the fact for much of 1943, at least until the Cairo Conference in November 1943, no actual plan was agreed upon. In Cadogan's famous phrase, determining Britain's strategy with regard to the defeat of Japan was akin to a 'blind man searching for a black cat in a dark room'.[11]

London's rather pessimistic view – although never stated as such – was that only technology and technical proficiency would defeat the Japanese, by means of amphibious attacks along the vulnerable littorals in Burma, Malaya and Sumatra, thus avoiding becoming embroiled in long, expensive and unnecessary land campaigns. On the basis of this reasoning, an entanglement in Burma could be avoided altogether. It was partly because of this consideration that Mountbatten was deemed by Churchill, with his amphibious planning experience in Combined Operations – limited though it was to the disaster of Dieppe – to be the ideal candidate for the task of Supremo, and capable of putting into place the wide flanking seaborne movements against the Japanese the Prime Minister hoped would form the basis of the theatre's strategy.

SEAC's core strategic ambiguities were ultimately resolved by both a severe impoverishment of resources and by Japanese offensive action into India in March 1944. Plans for an ambitious amphibious invasion of northern Sumatra, from where an attack on Singapore could be launched across the Malacca Straits, did not survive Mountbatten's first week in theatre. All other plans went the same way, sinking on the rocks of inadequate shipping and amphibious craft. A smaller operation against the Andaman Islands, together with a resurrected amphibious assault against Akyab, did not get beyond outline planning.

The harsh reality of limited resources was eventually to make ambitions for an amphibious strategy redundant, and plans for such operations, at least during 1944, perished. This was despite the insistence by Chiang Kai-shek that the *sine qua non* for Chinese help in the reconquest of Burma was the recovery of British naval control of the Bay of Bengal. This was never practically possible: with the wars in the Pacific and Europe still raging, there were simply not enough ships available to achieve this goal even if it were strategically necessary.

Chiang Kai-shek also demanded that the British make every possible effort to seize Mandalay and Rangoon without delay to facilitate the building of a new road to China. Unless he had assurances to this effect, together with a commitment to deliver at least 10,000 tons of supplies a month over the Hump, he was not prepared to move his forces any farther south than Lashio. Chiang Kai-shek's approach to strategic dialogue was one based on brinkmanship and blackmail, and quickly exhausted the patience of the Allied war leaders at the Cairo Conference in November 1943. The impasse led General Alan Brooke to note wearily but presciently in his diary: 'This may lead to [Chiang Kai-shek] refusing to carry out his part of the Burma campaign. If he does so, it will be no very great loss.'[12] Nothing had prepared Mountbatten for the difficulties and setbacks he would face in trying to get fractious allies to collaborate. Following his return to New Delhi from Cairo in November 1943, he admitted to his diary: 'I must confess that for the first time since I have been out here I was really in a distressed state of mind, all my plans for all operations appear to be going astray.'[13] He was shocked by what he considered to be the dead weight of Indian military bureaucracy that acted to take the energy out of his proposals. Within two weeks of his arrival, he remarked wearily to his diary, 'There is... no doubt that the climate and the antiquated and slow methods used in India have their effect on the keenness of officers after a year or two, and so I have found that the plans made by the India Staff are somewhat pessimistic and unenterprising.'[14]

It was a refrain he was to repeat constantly. Two weeks later he noted that 'the Commanders-in-Chief and the senior staff officers who attended the [planning] meetings subconsciously produced the usual effect of enlarging on all the difficulties of every plan and very rarely enthusing about the merits of any of them.'[1] Even as late as 14 April 1944 he again lamented, 'Why is it that in Delhi there always appears to be a somewhat negative atmosphere whereas at the Front everybody is full of dash and go?'[16]

These pressures did much to eat into Mountbatten's natural optimism. Wavell recorded seeing the naturally ebullient Mountbatten early the following year (1944), 'a bit overworked and depressed... His resources are gradually, or not even gradually, being taken away and he sees little prospect of accomplishing much of what he had planned this winter.'[17]

PART THREE

Resurrection, 1944

Prologue

*Lieutenant John Twells, 1 Gurkha Rifles**

The Chindwin River, December 1943

It was a quiet December day. The winter sunlight of Upper Burma dappled the well-spaced trees, while the brook, which aspired to be a young river, ran chuckling and bubbling along the edge of the clearing where clumps of tall but sapless elephant grass stood dry and unstirring.

The Japanese, ten to a dozen miles away, lay safely upon the far bank of the Chindwin.

Yet for several hours, four Companies of the Divisional Reserve Battalion, from the Madras Regiment, had been deployed in defensive positions within a few hundred yards of the clearing, while overhead droned a standing patrol of Spitfires.

By ten minutes to the hour, two-thirds of the King's Commissioned and Viceroy's commissioned officers and many non-commissioned officers of the brigade were assembled in informal groups, chatting casually, wondering why they had been called together. It was a cool and pleasant day, which made its impression upon the assembly so that they were cheerfully relaxed, uncertain of what was to come, yet anticipating something of interest as if they were about to watch a theatrical performance or a football match.

Thirty seconds before his appointed time came Slim.

He walked into the clearing steadily rather than quickly, a grim-jawed sturdy figure above the middle size, rolling a little from side to side, automatically

---

*This description, revealing Slim's plans to counter a Japanese invasion of India by retreating to the hills and allowing the Japanese to die on the wire around Imphal, is taken verbatim from John Twells' posthumously published memoir, *Unto the Hills* (Kibworth Beauchamp: Matator 2020), pp. 241–246, and quoted with permission.

transferring the weight and the impetus from the ball of one foot to the other in the manner of a hillman working up a slope.

Instinctively Ramsaran Pur, a phlegmatic veteran, sucked in his breath. 'Hamro!' he muttered like a man fulfilled.

With no words of command, the whole gathering stood to attention. The army commander came on into the centre of the clearing like a thick-set yeoman farmer striding across his land. The tight chin strap of his bush hat emphasised the line of the square jaw above the bull neck. Ruddy cheeks glowed, closely shaven jawbone reflected light and the long level gaze fell first on one side of the clearing and then the other, looking men straight in the eye and holding their attention.

He came to the centre of the open space, threw up a quick and easy salute in acknowledgement and gestured to his feet. Someone brought two ammunition boxes and Slim stepped up onto them. He drew the men towards him with a curt clawing motion from the wrists. 'Come round, gentlemen,' he said, 'stand easy.'

He paused a moment, jaw thrust up, looking beyond their heads into the distances beyond the teak. His cheeks shone, almost matching the scarlet of the tabs upon the collar points of his open-necked bush jacket. A neatly pressed and folded green cotton neckerchief covered his throat like a cravat.

He said, '*Main ap ko tin Zaban men holunga.*'* Then, '*Mon topainharu lai tinjana kura mon bunchhu hola.*'†

He tapped the open palm of his left-hand with the short cane he carried and slowly drew it through his hand. 'Gentlemen, I am going to talk to you in three languages. But first I shall speak to you all in English and then I will move about among you and chat and answer questions in Urdu and Gurkhali, particularly from those of you who may not know a great deal of English. I wanted to come and see you because you are the Brigade that is further east than any other in the 14 Army. I also wanted to tell you that this is not "The Forgotten Army". That's rubbish. We are not forgotten. I can tell you that from the top. But you know there is a lot of sense in beating your enemies one at a time. At Staff Colleges they call that defeating the enemy in detail. Well, that's what we're doing.'

He paused, thrusting his jaw round his intent audience. 'You've seen the Army newspaper SEAC. Perhaps not every day but most of you will have seen it often enough to know what is going on in the world. You know that we're going to put our enemies out one by one. The Italians. Well that's settled. Then the

---

* 'I will give you three words.' (Hindi)
† 'I have a lot of work to do.' (Nepali)

Germans. They will be settled next. The Russians in their winter campaign are tearing the guts out of them at the moment although there is a lot of hard fighting ahead. Then the Japanese.'

The powerful voice paused. It was not great oratory but a practical, soldierly tour d'horizon. Blunt, factual and honest. Designed to imprint itself in the mind of his listeners and with facts assembled in such a way that they in turn could present a simple but honest overall account of the situation to the men who served under them.

'Yes, the Japanese will be next.' He paused again for emphasis. 'Even our friends the Americans who are giving us fine support in the air and with supplies have agreed that the war in Europe must be won before Japan is smashed. That is an unselfish decision because it is they who suffered the attack by the Japanese at Pearl Harbor. Now, what does all this mean to us in 14 Army in practical terms? First of all we must be patient. Oh, yes, I know, some of you have been a long time without leave. At least without home leave to Britain. Well you must be patient and take pride in the fact that you are winning a war. A just war. Against evil. If ever men had a just cause you have. And you must take pride in it.'

A ghost of a grin crossed the straight line of his lips. 'I haven't had any home leave either,' he said. 'Not since before the war. I have been without leave longer than anyone else.

'Then remember also that we are free men from all the continents of the world, Europe, Africa, Asia – India and Nepal especially, of course – and, with a New Zealand fighter squadron, even Australasia – come to stop a tyranny in its tracks.

'The Indian Army... over 2 million men, all voluntarily recruited, is the greatest volunteer army the world has ever known. An army in which all races, all castes, all Regiments, all men are equal and have freely volunteered to rid the world of a tyranny. All India can take pride in that and all of us can take pride in our service.

'I told you we were not the "Forgotten Army". We are not. I also told you we are beating one enemy at a time and the Japanese are the third enemy. Well that does mean one thing. We are at the end of a long supply line. Not only here in Burma where everything has to be brought up to you over hundreds of miles of bad road from railhead at Dimapur and over a single line of railway from Calcutta to Dimapur. But our supply line doesn't even start there. India, of course, is making a fine contribution to the war effort and there are also supplies coming in directly by sea and even by air from America, from South Africa and from Australia.

'But here in Burma our principal source of supply is the United Kingdom. The bulk of our armament comes from Britain. And is paid for by Britain. As are the costs of the Indian Army itself.

'Think what this means. Take a Bren gun, for example. It is assembled, let us say, by a lassie in a Glasgow factory. A young woman getting her hands hardened by unfamiliar tools using dangerous machinery, doing her work on rationed food, possibly going short of food so that the troops may have enough, and a young woman doing her work by day in a city where her home may be bombed by night.

'Then that Bren gun was loaded on to an overworked railway system and taken to the docks and shipped out to India round the Cape in a vessel subject to attacks all the way down the Atlantic by German submarines or aircraft and then, perhaps in the Indian Ocean, in danger from Japanese underwater attack. It is unshipped in Bombay and transported across India on that magnificent railway network to Calcutta. After that you know the road.'

He looked round the silent listeners, tapping his left palm again with the point of his stick. 'Gentlemen, do I make myself clear? We are not the "Forgotten Army" but I have to ask you for economies. Never waste a round. Never waste a weapon. Throw nothing away. We must have victory. We shall have victory... but the way to win is through thrift. Through saving men's lives through your efficiency and attention to every trivial detail. And that starts through attention to malaria discipline and saving unnecessary casualties through sickness, and attention to saving our arms, equipment and materiel. Those are in short supply for the reason I have given you. The Germans must be beaten first before we turn the entire strength of the allies on Japan. Waste nothing. Neither time, nor blood, nor men, nor ammunition, nor weapons. All armies tend to be careless. To swagger, to boast and be open-handed.' The cane tapped once more. 'You, this Army, must be thrifty.'

Slim rolled his shoulders and cocked his head to one side. For the first time the low sunlight illuminated the height and width of his massive forehead which now could be seen to dominate the powerful jaw. For an instant the mouth widened and softened. 'You need not spare the Japanese, of course. You should know by now that the Japanese military leadership is foolish. I do not want you to underrate the courage of their troops – but I want you to understand that they are badly led. That won't make your job easier. It simply means that I shall have no excuses for my mistakes.

'But remember. The Jap is not a superman. He is a very good soldier. A very brave soldier. I have talked to you about the need for economy. You should be proud of being able to manage on very little – especially when you realise that the Jap will be managing on less. But the Jap can and will be beaten. Apart from the fact that he has probably bitten off more than he can chew and that his leadership is stupid, he is not superhuman. He is only human. He can be killed. We have proved this. We are killing him. In ever increasing numbers. That is the only way wars can be won. And this war has got to be won. And you are beginning to win it. Now.'

For an instant, coolly, almost casually, Slim looked round the ring of rapt listeners who pressed to within a yard of his ammunition boxes. Then, quickly, he stepped down. There was no time for three cheers. No opportunity for hero worship. The public party was over.

He began to stalk through the crowd and stopped before a Havildar of the Frontier Force Regiment. Instantly they were deep in a private conversation. They spoke of the winter duck flying down from beyond the passes of the Himalayas and of the jheels* near Hoshiapur, which one had known from childhood and over which the other had shot in '34 and '35.

There was a universality about the man. He kept his distance, yet was popular. To one he talked of his home, to another of his Regiment. To a third of the service both had known. A fourth was told what the manual stressed, 'The answer to noise is silence.'

'Don't,' said Slim, 'let your fellows worry when the Jap comes crawling round at night. His jitter parties are meant to upset you and draw your fire and so pinpoint your position and find out your strength.'

'Got too much malaria in your Battalion,' he snapped to a startled Colonel. 'Sleeves down at night. Repellent paste on the skin not being used? Nets? Umm. Seen the figures. Won't do. You've got to get your sick rate down.'

He came up to Ramsaran. 'Lo, zhungi, Subadar Sahib. We've met before.' Ramsaran told him when. 'Yes. All well? Anything you want to know?'

'Yes, Sir. When are we going to get at the Japanese?'

Slim smiled grimly. 'Tell the men,' he said, 'that next year I shall allow the Japanese to come over the Chindwin. It will lengthen their line of communications. I might even ask you to go back to Imphal to defend the high ground and let the Jap die on your wire. Then we'll walk down to Mandalay and throw him out of Burma.'

Ramsaran laughed, 'Isn't all that secret, General Sahib?'

---

*Pool or lake.

'Yes. Between you, me and the men. Perhaps I shall tell the Colonel Sahib…
but we won't tell the Japs until after we've done it.'

Ramsaran threw his head back laughing. Beyond the army commander, who
was 6 Gurkhas, he could see other Gurkha generals, Scoones of the 2nd, who
commanded IV Corps and Gracey of his own Regiment who commanded their
20th Indian Division. For thirty years he had served with them and their
predecessors. And his father and grandfather before him. They had never failed.
Together they had held a sub-continent. They would do it again. Now. They
could not be beaten. This combination of British and Gurkha, and of sense and
strength would prevail. He, Ramsaran Pur knew. And he would see to it.

He laughed again, 'Shahbash, General Sahib, Sarkari Bundobust!' He
chuckled again, 'We shall retreat to the hills and they will die on our wire.'

His shoulders shook in merriment at the simplicity of it all and the thought
of the killing to come.

22

Arakan, Again

By the time the first rains swept in from the Bay of Bengal in late May 1943, making northern Arakan virtually unnavigable except by boat, the Japanese, exhausted by their bold exertions against 26 Indian Division, contented themselves with consolidating their positions along the Maungdaw–Buthidaung Road. Indeed, very little Japanese activity took place during the months that followed. Slim, however, whose XV Corps was responsible for the defence of Bengal, saw the period of impending stalemate in northern Arakan as a priceless opportunity to develop the fighting abilities of his troops. On 14 June 1943 he laid down that the 'policy of formations in contact with the enemy will be aggressive defence' and that 'contact with the enemy will be maintained continuously and the monsoon period will be used for gaining the upper hand of the Japanese in patrol and minor enterprises.' Slim's purpose was to develop confidence in his troops that they could fight and prevail against the Japanese in battle. Battle skills were infinitely better practised for real than artificially in training, and aggressive patrolling allowed the development of the all-important low-level soldiering skills which Slim so urgently sought in his soldiers. Combat skills were and remain the essential core of soldiering. They must be mastered before success can be achieved in battle. To do this, they need to be constantly benchmarked against a country's prospective enemies. The prospect of fighting the Imperial Japanese Army had simply been ignored by Britain and India in the years prior to 1942, with inevitable results. Now, with a background of failure and defeat, the aim of such activity was 'to convince the doubters that our object, the destruction of the Japanese Army in battle, was practicable. We had to a great extent frightened ourselves by our stories of the superman.' Superiority over the

MAP 4 Operation *Ha-Go*

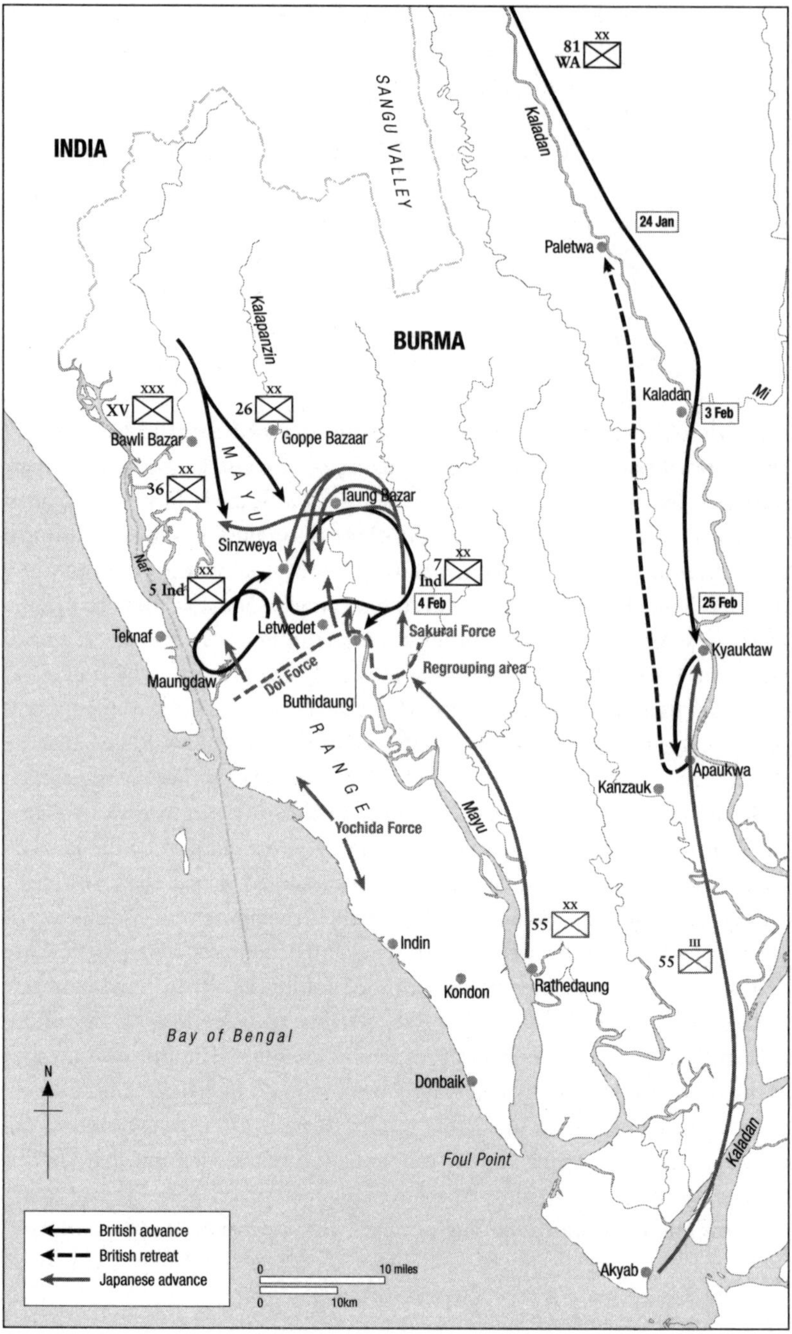

INDIA

BURMA

SANGU VALLEY

Kaladan

81 WA [XX]

24 Jan

Paletwa

Kaladan

3 Feb

Mi

25 Feb

Kyauktaw

Apaukwa

Kanzauk

Kalapanzin

XV [XXX]

Bawli Bazar

26 [XX]

Goppe Bazaar

36 [XX]

M A Y U

Taung Bazar

Sinzweya

7 Ind [XX]

4 Feb

Nar

5 Ind [XX]

Teknaf

Letwedet

Sakurai Force

Doi Force

Maungdaw

Buthidaung

Regrouping area

R A N G E

Mayu

Yochida Force

55 [XX]

55 [III]

Indin

Kondon

Rathedaung

Bay of Bengal

N

Donbaik

Foul Point

Kaladan

Akyab

←	British advance
◄- - -	British retreat
←	Japanese advance

0 ——— 10 miles

0 ——— 10km

Japanese had to be demonstrated publicly, and although Wavell had attempted to do this in Arakan, it had proved premature and ill conceived.

With Irwin gone, his replacement as Eastern Army commander – General Sir George Giffard – instructed Slim to prepare XV Corps for offensive operations at the end of the monsoon in October to prevent the Japanese making the most of their success in Arakan, possibly by threatening Chittagong. Giffard's instructions gave Slim less than three months to prepare and train his troops for war, all of it during the rainy season. Slim would have three divisions for the task. 26 Indian Division would withdraw to Chittagong to form the corps reserve at the end of the monsoon and be replaced by the fresh 5 and 7 Indian Divisions.[1] For the first time since the end of the retreat, responsibility for successful operations against the Japanese from Bengal rested with Slim. Slim's influence over the future conduct of operations in India and Burma was to be profound. Much would change across Eastern Army and India Command over the next few months, including the work prompted by the Infantry Committee and the new broom wielded by Claude Auchinleck, but it was on Slim that the spotlight now shone.

It was the second time that Slim had examined the problem of planning an offensive operation in Arakan. It wasn't a surprise that the two-phased plan he came up with mirrored that which had been so peremptorily dismissed by Irwin. The first phase – Operation *Cudgel* – would entail a land advance by XV Corps against the Tunnels on the Maungdaw–Buthidaung Road, before moving to Indin–Rathedaung. The second – Operation *Bullfrog* – would be an accompanying amphibious assault – by the British 2 Division, against Akyab. The target was to capture Indin by March 1944.

To provide flank protection in the Kaladan Valley, Giffard promised to supply him with Major General Woolner's 81 West African Division when it arrived in India from Ceylon in August 1943.[2] These brigades would maintain a parallel advance down the Kaladan Valley not only to protect the left flank of 5 and 7 Indian Divisions from a wide Japanese envelopment, but also to threaten the Japanese lines of communication into Arakan. Slim proposed that the West Africans be exclusively supplied by air, to remove the prospect of having a vulnerable land-based line of communication deep in the Arakanese hills. For the size of force involved this was a novel innovation in the theatre, but the way had clearly been forged by Wingate's first expedition. Giffard readily agreed, and it became an integral part of the plan Giffard submitted to Auchinleck in September 1943.

The requirement to train 5 and 7 Indian Divisions for an offensive late in 1943 necessitated the full gamut of collective training be conducted during the wettest and most difficult time of the year – the monsoon. This in itself was no easy task. Indeed, there were many in India – not all of them the desk wallahs who so infuriated Wingate – who considered it impossible to train or fight during this time of year. When Mountbatten arrived to take command of SEAC, he directed – to the incredulity of some – that operations were to continue throughout the monsoon. But he received the immediate and unequivocal support of Slim. For two successive monsoons (1942 and 1943) Slim successfully prepared XV Corps for war despite the constant downpour and without much of the wet weather equipment many thought necessary to be able to survive and operate in such conditions. He knew that while large-scale fighting would never be possible in Arakan during the monsoon, small-scale operations and training certainly were. 'I had been told by a lot of people,' Slim told assembled troops of 11 East African Division on 25 January 1945, 'that it was impossible to operate in the monsoon. However, I had done two monsoons myself, and I was sure that really good troops would be able to move and fight even in the appalling conditions of the monsoon.'[3]

Slim's training regime for the May–October 1943 monsoon built upon the principles he had so clearly enunciated in his Training Directive of 1942. Of his two formations, Frank Messervy's 7 Indian Division had by far the greater opportunity for training and preparation. When battle was joined the following January, this disparity showed. Training in 7 Indian Division had begun, and was conducted with seriousness and rigour, from as early as March 1943. 'Every man... was, in fact, rigorously trained to be a fighting man', wrote Henry Maule, Messervy's biographer. 'Only a handful of unarmed Indian followers, traditional to the Indian Army, were allowed to be classified as "non-combatant"... Messervy saw to it that every unit had its own jungle lane or lanes set out with dummy Japs to be attacked with the utmost ferocity... Every man was put through battle inoculation, crawling along a shallow trench or across open paddy while... machine guns fired a few inches above'.[4] Live training with artillery, mortars and medium machine guns was undertaken too – a novel undertaking even for experienced soldiers – and in March 1943 battalions took part in a divisional exercise. The divisional historian recalled:

> Realistic, and at times exciting, these manoeuvres were to prove of immense value. Time and again problems and situations arose which were to be reproduced within the year in real battle. For the first time operations were being carried out on a large scale in forest, and the outstanding lesson was perhaps the ease with which surprise could be achieved. Officers and men learnt to expect the

unexpected and to realize that, given good battle procedure, the worst threat could be held at bay long enough to enable a plan to be made to deal with it and perhaps even to turn the tables by an unexpected counter thrust. Day patrolling, wide encirclement, unexpected encounters on jungle tracks, all combined to build up in everyone's mind a picture of war in a country of forest and few roads, where infantry use the tracks made by elephant and deer, and battle often opens at fifty yards range.[5]

When units of 7 Indian Division deployed to Arakan from June 1943 in preparation for the relief of 26 Indian Division, Messervy placed the greatest stress on determined patrolling against Japanese forward positions. 'Not only would this help build up a picture of what the Japs were doing', explained Maule, 'but it would also give officers and men the confidence so desperately needed in the weird gloom. Thus inoculated they would then take part in ambushes and fighting patrols of platoon or greater strength. Morale gained by training was to be confirmed into even higher morale gained by fighting.'[6] The solution lay in mounting extensive patrol activity against the Japanese to develop the troops' confidence. For the most part these small-scale operations were successful, and by them both 7 and 26 Indian Divisions gained the initiative in northern Arakan during the monsoon. 'By the end of November', wrote Slim, 'our forward troops had gone a long way towards getting that individual feeling of superiority and that first essential in the fighting man – the desire to close with his enemy.' The next step was to escalate these actions, and a series of carefully stage-managed minor offensive operations to drive in the Japanese outposts forward of the Maungdaw–Buthidaung Road were mounted during November and December 1943. These were also very successful. Battalions attacked enemy platoon positions while brigades attacked companies. Slim was the first to admit that this approach was akin to using a hammer to crack a nut, but he was satisfied that the results, not least in terms of the morale of his troops when they saw for the first time the defeat of the once-exultant Japanese, fully vindicated his approach. He knew, as did a growing proportion of his army, that victory against the Japanese was no longer the inconceivable notion it had been only seven months earlier. Although the evidence still remained thin, Slim was confident that the forthcoming year would see the turn of the tide.

5 Indian Division returned to India from Iraq in June 1943, after which it began intensive jungle training, discarding its trucks for mules and preparing to fight a considerably different type of war for which it had trained in the Middle East, and against a vastly different enemy. It deployed to Arakan in November

1943. Under Slim's careful tutelage the division prepared for war. Briggs directed that every member of the division learn by memory his 'Five Commandments'. 'The jungle called for better junior leadership than any other theatre of war', recorded the divisional historian. 'Mental and bodily endurance would be essential. Individual fieldcraft, observation and concealment had to be learned and practised. Japanese characteristics and methods were studied with care; the troops were trained in fire discipline and control to avoid shooting at mere noises; they were taught to treat the jungle as a friend, able to supply them with shelter and food. Aggressive tactics was to be the basis of our tactics.'[7]

The success of Slim's ideas depended entirely upon the ability of the defended bastions to be supplied from the air with everything they required for their defence. This in turn required not just a substantial transport aircraft fleet but local air superiority as well. Throughout 1943 air transport and fighter aircraft grew substantially in number, allowing for the resupply of troops to an extent not possible in 1942.

Once the decision had been taken to support 81 West African Division exclusively by air, Eastern Army built up the aircraft and air supply organization during the 1943 monsoon to supply a division continuously in the jungle for a prolonged period. More importantly perhaps, both Slim and Giffard worked hard during this period to inculcate in the minds of all troops a sense of what Slim described as 'airmindedness'. In time all who served in Burma came to regard the supply of units from the air as no more unusual than resupply by rail or road. Commanders also came to regard the support provided by ground attack aircraft and bombers as indispensable – and as readily used – as they had traditionally regarded the use of mortars and artillery.

Critical to an appreciation of the importance Slim placed on the full utilization of air power was the degree of integration he insisted upon between the land and air forces, first in XV Corps, and then later in 14 Army as a whole. The bitter experience of the retreat confirmed to him the key importance well-integrated air power played in land operations: indeed, he came to believe there was no such a thing as an exclusively 'land' campaign. By 1943 – if not much earlier – he was convinced that all successful operations in modern warfare were in fact 'air-land' operations, in which military forces in both environments had to work seamlessly, at tactical, operational and strategic levels, in pursuit of a common objective. He suffered from none of the debilitating prejudices that had so often stifled the growth of effective communication between services in the past. When he arrived in Barrackpore on 3 June 1942 to command XV Corps, Slim discovered that he had been co-located with the Air Officer Commanding Bengal and Burma, Air

Vice-Marshal Bill Williams. 'He should... by rights, have been with Eastern Army who were responsible for the same areas as he was, not with 15 Corps', Slim recalled. 'However, the arrangement suited us admirably'. The air element assigned to XV Corps was No. 224 Group, RAF, based in Chittagong (No. 221 Group was assigned to IV Corps in Manipur). We 'at once began', Slim comments, 'the close and friendly cooperation that lasted between the corps and the group until the end of the war.' The same pattern repeated itself when Slim was given command of 14 Army in October. 14 Army, Air Marshal John Baldwin's 3 Tactical Air Force and American Brigadier-General Old's Troop Carrier Command 'worked to a considerable extent as a joint headquarters... [growing] into a very close brotherhood, depending on one another, trusting one another, and taking as much pride in each other's triumphs as we did in our own.'

With the appointment and arrival of Mountbatten as the new Supremo, other changes were made in the Far East's fighting structures. General Sir George Giffard was promoted to command the land elements of SEAC, which comprised the British and Indian fighting components in Assam and Bengal, together with a new theatre reserve (X Corps) and the American-led Northern Combat Area Command. In its turn Eastern Army, long since tarnished with defeat, was given a makeover, with a new name, a single task and a new commander. On the recommendation of Auchinleck and Brooke and enthusiastically supported by Mountbatten, Slim took command of the newly renamed 14 Army, an army with the sole function of the security of India and the conduct of land operations against the Japanese east of the Meghna River.

A furious flurry of energy accompanied the appointment, which coincided with the lifting of the rains. The first thing that Slim did was move his HQ to Comilla, which was a short 45-minute flight over the Naga Hills to Imphal. The strongest possible vindication of Slim's approach to war came within a week of his taking command. Mountbatten paid a fleeting visit to the joint 14 Army/3 Tactical Air Force Headquarters in Barrackpore on the afternoon of 22 October 1943 on his way back from visiting Chiang Kai-shek in Chungking, and the two men met for the first time. Slim invited him to address the 80 or so officers of his and Baldwin's joint HQ gathered to meet him. In a profound way the occasion proved to be a meeting of minds and began a relationship that was to be dramatically fruitful over the following 20 months. Many years later Mountbatten recalled that 'something happened that first meeting – somehow we clicked... and we developed a friendship – a lifelong friendship so that although we were never actually next to each other in the Command, because I always had an Army Group Commander in Chief or a Land Force Commander in Chief between Bill Slim and me, we always saw eye to eye.'[8] Although no one knew it at the time, the winning command combination in the war against the Japanese in the Far East had been found.

Frustratingly, however, little of the strategic planning effort expended during 1943 bore any fruit. By December 1943, following the Tehran Conference, only four operations in SEAC were scheduled for 1944, all of which were to be under the command of Slim. Churchill's hopes for an amphibious strategy (Operation *Culverin*) had come to nought, sunk on the rocks of an Allied strategy that placed the defeat of Germany foremost. This demanded all available landing craft and amphibious vessels to be concentrated in Europe for the invasion of France. In the Far East, the strategic priority, pressed on an unwilling British by Roosevelt, was for the continued sustenance of China through the expansion of land and air lines of communication from India. Land operations were to be mounted in Burma merely to allow the construction of the new 'Burma Road' from Ledo to Myitkyina. The first of these was to be an offensive by XV Corps in Arakan – Operation *Cudgel*. Slim intended to include a much-reduced amphibious operation against Akyab at the same time by 36 Division under the title of Operation *Bulldozer*. The second offensive into Burma was to be an advance by Scoones' IV Corps in Imphal to the Chindwin, the third an advance by Stilwell's forces to Myitkyina, and finally, to assist Stilwell, a second, more ambitious long-range penetration operation by Wingate, to be called Operation *Thursday*.

23

Ha-Go

Shortly after Christmas Day, 1943, Colonel Nishiura Susumu of the Military Affairs Section of the Japanese Imperial General Headquarters, Tokyo, found himself standing in front of Prime Minister Tōjō, who was splashing about in his evening bath. The maid had let him into Tōjō's private quarters. Only a clear glass screen separated the two men. 'What's the matter?' enquired Tōjō. 'Sir, we urgently need a decision on the Imphal Operation,' replied a nervous Nishiura. As he completed his wash, and water spilled onto the wooden floor, Tōjō pondered the question and challenged Nishiura about the details of the plan. Had the distance over the mountains been considered, and the attendant issues with supply? Nishiura replied in the affirmative: 'The whole plan has been gone into in great detail.' Tōjō paused to take in this information, and then fired off a series of questions regarding General Mutaguchi, and whether the commander of 15 Army realized exactly what he was taking on. Had he considered air cover given the acute lack of aircraft in the region, and had he given thought to the possibility that the Japanese might be outflanked by a British amphibious landing along the Arakanese coastline? Nishiura, fresh from a three-day-long briefing by Major General Ayabe of Southern Army in Saigon, who had flown back to Tokyo to explain the plan to the Imperial Headquarters, replied, 'He is anxious to go ahead, sir.'[1]

To Nishiura's amazement Tōjō then climbed out of the bath and opened the glass door between them. Stark naked, he questioned the colonel on every aspect of the plan that Ayabe had relayed to the Operations Staff at Imperial Headquarters. Eventually the grilling came to an end and the Prime Minister began rubbing himself down with a towel. It appeared that Tōjō was satisfied, albeit reluctantly. 'Tell Ayabe that they should not be too ambitious,' he concluded, at which point Nishiura made his exit. Tōjō certainly hadn't been overly enthusiastic, but at least he hadn't rejected the idea of a substantial operation from Japanese-held Burma into British-defended India. The idea had in fact surfaced in Tokyo in June 1942 soon after Burma had fallen, and Field Marshal Terauchi's Southern Army HQ in Saigon, under the sponsorship of Colonel Akira Hayashi, conducted detailed planning between July and October 1942. Tōjō had even made positive noises on this subject earlier in the year, although these reflected the requirements of political rhetoric rather than of operational policy. Akira believed that the momentum of the invasion of Burma, which had produced dramatic and unexpected results, should continue into India to exploit Britain's discomfiture more fully. This had led to a plan being drafted in the summer of 1942 for what was then known as Operation *21*, in which a two-division force would be thrust north into the top of the Brahmaputra Valley through the Hukawng Valley, and a further two divisions would follow on the coat-tails of Slim's retreating ragtag army into Imphal. A third force of divisional strength would skirt the coastal waters of the Bay of Bengal to seize Chittagong. The strategy was not to bring India into the wider orbit of the 'Greater East Asia Co-Prosperity Sphere', but to make the most of the propaganda effect of an 'invasion' of India and prevent the British from creating bases on the frontiers of Burma from which they could launch a counter-offensive.

These plans were stillborn, however. The capture of the whole of Burma had not originally been envisaged by Tokyo, and the subsequent occupation of the country stretched Japan's occupation forces to the limit. Two other factors were to put the kibosh on Operation *21*. At the time Major General Mutaguchi Renya, commander of 18 Division (which had played a key role in the capture of Singapore and was now garrisoning north-eastern Burma), was firmly opposed to the plan, believing that the huge natural barrier of rivers, mountains and jungle which separate Burma from India made Imphal impregnable from attack and would likewise prevent a British invasion of Burma. These views were shared by his colleague in 33 Division, Lieutenant General Sakurai Shōzō (who had captured Rangoon). General Iida Shōjirō eventually urged Terauchi to scrap these plans, and Colonel Akira was told to shelve them.

In February 1943 Japanese illusions about the imperviousness of the mountain barrier between Imphal and the Chindwin were rudely shattered by the arrival in their midst of Orde Wingate and his 3,000 Chindits in Operation *Longcloth*. It demonstrated that the hill country along the border with India was not the obstacle to mobility some Japanese commanders considered it to be, and it was to this lesson in particular that Mutaguchi latched. If the British could do this, thought Mutaguchi, so too could the Japanese. The following month, March 1943, aged 55, Mutaguchi was promoted to Lieutenant General and replaced Iida in command of 15 Army. He moved his headquarters to the old British hill station of Maymyo, resplendent with an ordered botanical loveliness, rhododendrons and orchids competing with each other and with a range of other colourful flowers for space in a well-planned oasis of tranquillity and beauty. What the Chindits had demonstrated made Mutaguchi change his mind about the ability of Japanese troops to advance against Imphal and he began entertaining thoughts of reviving Operation *21*. He hated the thought of sitting idly in a backwater in Burma twiddling his thumbs, especially as it was clear that the British were slowly but surely building up their strength in Imphal, and would one day pose a serious threat to Japanese control of Burma. Mutaguchi's initial idea was that he could launch a pre-emptive strike to destroy these bases, before reverting to establishing a more formal defensive position in Assam.

The more he considered his options, however, the more he believed that something far more dramatic could be achieved. The prospect of a full-scale invasion of India beckoned. His evaluation of the British position in north-east India revealed that the three key strategic targets in Assam were Imphal, the mountain town of Kohima and the supply base at Dimapur. If Kohima were captured, Imphal would be cut off from the rest of India by land. In the back of Mutaguchi's mind was the thought that any prospective attack into India should do more than merely capture Imphal. From the outset Mutaguchi believed that with a fair wind Dimapur, rather than Kohima, could and should be secured. He reasoned that capturing this massive depot would be a devastating, possibly terminal, blow to the British ability to defend Imphal, supply Stilwell, and mount an offensive into Burma. With Dimapur captured, Bose and his Indian National Army could pour into Bengal, initiating the long-awaited anti-British uprising.

Since December 1943 the primary task of Scoones' IV Corps was to dominate the hill country east and south of the Imphal plain in order to prepare for an offensive across the Chindwin in the spring of 1944. Scoones had about 30,000 troops in 17, 20 and 23 Indian Divisions in Manipur, together with a tank brigade, the most that the difficult line of communication to Dimapur could sustain. These forces were accordingly placed to prepare for an attack into Burma, not to receive one coming the other way. In the centre, based on Imphal, was Scoones' headquarters and a rapidly growing array of supply dumps, hospitals, workshops and airfields: the entire, complex paraphernalia of an army preparing to advance. The offensive was intended as a limited affair, designed to support both the insertion of a second expedition by Orde Wingate (transported this time by air into central Burma – Operation *Thursday*), as well as an advance towards Myitkyina from Ledo of Stilwell's Chinese and American forces. Consequently 20 Indian Division at Moreh and Tamu was preparing to advance across the Chindwin. To support this, IV Corps had built up extensive supply and administrative bases along the line of communication to Imphal and thence to the growing base at Dimapur. By an enormous human effort the peacetime capacity of the Dimapur to Imphal road of 600 tons per day had, by November 1943, increased to 3,070 tons.[2] A large forward base, sufficient to supply two divisions in an offensive, had been established close to the front at Moreh.

The two Gurkha brigades (48 and 63) of Punch Cowan's experienced and self-confident 17 Indian Division (amounting to about 7,000 soldiers) was located at Tiddim, 165 miles south of Imphal in the Chin Hills, from November 1943. Its task was to dominate the hills and to prevent the Japanese from gaining a foothold in the mountains overlooking the Chindwin River Valley. Tiddim was connected to Imphal by a road which, even after many months of painful upgrading work by Cowan's troops during 1943, remained little more than a mule track for much of its route, and which was to prove a serious problem for the division's maintenance. At the southern end of the Tiddim Road was the famous 'Chocolate Staircase', which rose 3,000 feet over 7 miles on a gradient of 1 in 12. During the wet season men and vehicles trampled it into ankle-deep mud and large chunks were often swept away by mud slides triggered by the monsoon.

The three brigades of Douglas Gracey's well-trained 20 Indian Division (32, 80 and 100 Brigades) arrived in Manipur in November 1943. It was based around Tamu, 60 miles south-east of Imphal on the main track to the Chindwin at Kalewa, and was responsible for the base at Moreh. The journey to Tamu from Imphal followed a metalled road for 25 miles to the key airfield at Palel, on the edge of the Imphal plain, after which it rose steeply to Shenam at the western edge of the 6,000-foot mountains which separate the Imphal plain from the Kabaw Valley. Shenam was the final obstacle the Japanese would have to overcome in any attack on Imphal from the south-east. The position ran between Shenam Saddle and 'Nippon Hill', 3½ miles farther east. From 'Nippon Hill' the road then ran for a further 25 miles to Tamu. From Tamu, the Chindwin lay a further

70 miles to the east along an unmade road. When the monsoon rains fell, landslides would often close the road for up to 24 hours.

Geoffrey Scoones' Third Division – 10,000 men of 23 Indian Division (comprising 1, 37 and 49 Brigades) – had guarded Imphal since the start of the campaign in 1942. Commanded by the 41-year-old Major General Ouvry Roberts, it was in reserve with 254 Tank Brigade, comprising American-built Stuart ('Honey') light tanks of 7 Indian Light Cavalry with the Lee-Grants (also American) of 3 Carabiniers on the Imphal plain.

During late 1943 and early 1944 the tempo of operations for both 17 and 20 Indian Divisions intensified. Both divisions were tasked with continuous, intensive patrolling in order to maintain contact with the Japanese and obtain intelligence of their moves and intentions. While neither side gained a decisive advantage in these operations, they nevertheless raised the confidence of the troops. This period proved also to be an important learning experience for IV Corps, and especially for those units that had no direct experience to date of the Japanese.

Deep in the jungle-clad hills west of the Imphal plain, between Milestone 105 on the Tiddim Road and the Silchar Track, 30 miles to the south, the remarkable English anthropologist Ursula Graham Bower led a widely dispersed group of V Force Nagas in a 'Watch and Ward' scheme that covered over 800 square miles of jungle hills separating the Tiddim Valley from Silchar.[3] These loyal Zemi Naga villagers, equipped initially with only their spears, but later with rifles, Bren guns and grenades, protected the hills from Japanese patrols and warned of any enemy depredations into the hills. A woman of remarkable persistence and strength of character, Bower played a significant role in protecting the vulnerable right rear flank of the Imphal plain, a huge area otherwise entirely devoid of military protection of any sort. The challenges she faced would have stumped most professional soldiers. Nothing else protected the hill country in the vast rectangle of green matted mountains between Kohima and Imphal and the Brahmaputra Valley.

The greatest challenge to achieving Mutaguchi's new-found enthusiasm for an attack into India was not just the terrain his troops would have to conquer in crossing the tangled hill country between the Chindwin and the Manipur plain, but the reluctance of his own side to take the risk of offensive operations at a time when the Japanese empire was at full stretch. By early 1943 the strategic story for Japan had begun to sour. Defeat at the hands of the Americans at Guadalcanal, Midway and New Guinea had not merely halted their advance but in places had turned it. This was hardly the time to take new strategic risks, especially when it remained unclear what benefit these might bring and whether the risks of failure were outweighed by the chance to provide for the forward defence of Burma and perhaps to strike a devastating – even terminal – blow against British India.

At the time of his epiphany, Mutaguchi was virtually alone in Burma to believe in the requirement to invade India. He also believed it to be practicable. With the enthusiasm of the newly converted, Mutaguchi started lobbying his superiors – General Kawabe Masakazu, commander of the Burma Area Army in Rangoon, Field Marshal Terauchi of Southern Army in Saigon, General Sugiyama at Imperial General HQ in Tokyo (who had spent two years in India as an attaché before the war) and even Tōjō himself – to be allowed 'the honour' to launch an offensive into India. When first confronted by Mutaguchi on 1 April 1943 with the request to do this, Kawabe initially dismissed the request, considering it 'grandiose'. However, he did not reject the idea entirely. For Mutaguchi the idea quickly became an obsession. Doubts among the sceptical were quickly squashed, and those in his own headquarters who opposed Mutaguchi's burgeoning plans, including his own newly appointed Chief of Staff, Lieutenant General Obata Nobuyoshi, unceremoniously lost their jobs. Mutaguchi harangued his staff, browbeating any other opponents of his grand vision. In April he told them, 'The overall situation of the war is a stalemate. If there is any possibility of changing this situation, it will be in the Burma theatre. Therefore, we should not be passive. At this time we should take the offensive and force Imphal's surrender. And furthermore, if possible, I would like to lead my force into Assam. From now on, we should stop planning defensively, and think offensively.'

Mutaguchi's bubbling optimism had, within two months, persuaded Kawabe at least to consider the options for an attack into India, and in late June 1943 the army commander oversaw in Rangoon a four-day planning conference. It was attended by representatives from Southern Army in Saigon, as well as the Imperial General Headquarters in Tokyo. Even the Emperor's brother, Prince Takeda, on a tour of the region, appeared, Mutaguchi shamelessly lobbying him to provide royal support for this plan. Impetuous as ever, Mutaguchi and his staff arrived at the conference intending not to discuss the idea in principle, but rather to outline his plan for the operation.

At the beginning the idea of an offensive into Burma had few supporters. The air cover, supplies and troops necessary for such an undertaking did not exist in Burma in 1943, and Kawabe did not want to commit himself to an operation for which he had inadequate resources. Any plan would need therefore to be efficiently and speedily executed. But Mutaguchi had come well prepared, with not just one proposal, but two. His first, presented to the conference on its first day, was to drive an army north through the short but malarial Hukawng Valley, and then, turning left, to fall on Assam from the north after cutting the vital road and air links in the northern Brahmaputra Valley that sustained Stilwell's Chinese forces. The enormous administrative effort of maintaining an army through this trackless and mountainous wilderness not surprisingly found little support, however, and was rejected. That night Mutaguchi prepared his alternative plan. Presented on the second day, this was significantly constrained in scope and entailed less risk, involving the resurrection of the main principles of Operation *21* which had received detailed examination two years before. An army would cross the mighty Chindwin River – 300 feet at its narrowest – then make for, and seize, Imphal. The mountain village of Kohima guarding the route to the Brahmaputra Valley would be blocked, to prevent troops from escaping from the Imphal plain or reinforcements entering.

Mutaguchi's stratagem for winning over the conference – or more accurately to bully it into acquiescence – worked perfectly. By presenting first an impossible plan, followed after its rejection by one that was far more reasonable, and which had been considered before, as well as by ruthless lobbying, Mutaguchi ensured that what he most desired became policy. Kawabe eventually succumbed to Mutaguchi's arm-twisting, authorizing him to begin planning for this offensive and promising to secure permission from Saigon and Tokyo to proceed – on the clear understanding that this was to be an offensive designed to secure the long-term defence of Burma rather than being a 'mad rush into Assam'. Despite this authorization, however, few outside of Mutaguchi's immediate circle were convinced of the soundness of his idea. Kawabe's Chief of Staff, Lieutenant General Naka Eitaro, believed that the plan was too optimistic and insufficiently founded on accepted principles of supply. In any case, he thought he could see through Mutaguchi's rhetoric about 'defending Burma' to recognize that what the 15 Army commander wanted to do was to launch an invasion of India. He wrote in his diary:

The Mutaguchi Plan is full of fond hopes. He counts his chickens before they are hatched. The Mutaguchi Plan goes like this: the Army crosses the Chindwin River and goes over the Arakan Mountains[4] [sic], where there is no road, with as much ammunition and food as it can carry. And when rations run out, food and ammunition are to be gained in Imphal and supplied to the divisions, using as much transportation as necessary gathered there. Such an operation might have been possible in the spring of 1942. But now that the enemy is preparing for a counter-attack [into Burma] this plan is senseless. In any case the Mutaguchi Plan lacks flexibility. At this time, the operation is a means to defend Burma, not to make an all-out attack against India. Mutaguchi doesn't make this kind of acknowledgement.[5]

The greatest fear was that Mutaguchi was attempting to do too much with too little, motivated solely by the prospects of achieving undying military glory at the expense of 15 Army. Most of the staff officers of Terauchi's Southern Army in Saigon hated Mutaguchi. Major General Inada Masazumi, Vice-Chief of Staff at Southern Army, opposed Mutaguchi's plans because he feared that they were merely the instrument for the 15 Army commander's self-aggrandizement. One of Inada's colleagues represented the consensus view of Mutaguchi in Headquarters Southern Army in a comment to a listening journalist: 'Mutaguchi would fling his troops anywhere if he thought it would bring him publicity. How they are supplied he only thinks about afterwards.'[6]

Kawabe was aware of this too, of course, but believed he knew Mutaguchi well enough to allow his headstrong subordinate enough room for manoeuvre without placing his army at too great a risk. Kawabe had been Mutaguchi's immediate superior in China in 1937, when the latter had been at the centre of the machinations which had led to the expansion of the Sino–Japanese War, and he was well aware of his subordinate's penchant for ungovernable enthusiasm. Kawabe was certain that he could control Mutaguchi and keep him within the limits that had been agreed, believing that Mutaguchi's single-mindedness made it more rather than less likely that the operation would succeed. He told the nervous Naka to relax, and to 'have some regard for his [Mutaguchi's] positive way of looking at things.' In his diary entry for 29 June 1943 Kawabe wrote, 'I love that man's enthusiasm. You can't help admiring his almost religious fervour.'[7]

Unknown to Mutaguchi at the time, one other factor persuaded Kawabe to think more positively than he had done initially about the prospect of an attack into India. This was his meeting with the new leader of the Indian National Army, Subhas Chandra Bose, in July 1943. Bose persuaded Kawabe that a Japanese invasion of even a small part of India – suitably propagandized as a 'March on Delhi' designed to free India from the oppression of the British Raj – would spark an unstoppable nationalist bushfire across the whole of India with potentially transformational prospects for both Japan's war aims and the defeat of European colonialism in Asia. Persuaded by Bose's passion, Kawabe told the Indian nationalist that an invasion was indeed being considered, and that when the time came the men of the INA would be allocated a leading role in an

Bushido in action. A Japanese infantry attack on Mandalay, 1942. It was considered dishonourable for Japanese officers to fight with anything other than swords. (Getty Images)

The realities of an imperialist and overtly racist war. An Indian POW, presumably who refused to join the INA, executed by the Japanese, 1942. (IWM)

The failure of the British Empire to protect its people led to the deaths of hundreds of thousands of innocents. The exodus of Indian refugees from Burma, 1942. (Magnum Photos)

Blitzkrieg, Japanese style. It worked in Burma in 1942 against an unprepared opponent. However, IJA tactics and methods did not change when they tried it again in India in 1944, and Japanese troops, weak in artillery and armour, with little air support, were slaughtered. (Getty Images)

Japanese logistics arrangements were novel, but poor. Elephants, mules and bullocks were occasionally useful but in the end were no match for Allied logistical mastery. (Getty Images)

Part of the mythology of defeat in 1942 and 1943 was that the Japanese were fearsome jungle soldiers. This was an exaggeration. Their troops were infantry dominated and were hardy and formidable fighters, but they were also unimaginative and, at the operational level of war, often badly led. (Getty Images)

Arakan, February 1944. C47s dropping supplies to the 7 Division 'Admin Box' at Sinzweya. Large scale aerial resupply transformed Allied fortunes, allowing for new tactics to be implemented and for morale to soar. (IWM)

This photo shows USAAF C47s lined up on Myitkyina airfield after its capture in August 1944. (NARA)

India's vast reservoir of labour enabled the transformation of the country in 1943 and 1944, building the huge infrastructure needed to sustain military operations against the Japanese and in support of beleaguered China. (Getty Images)

Japan's military endeavours were sufficient for it to triumph in 1942. By 1944 and 1945 it had been dramatically outclassed in every area except hubris, where it still reigned supreme. (Getty Images)

Training Chinese soldiers to be in every way superior to their Japanese opponent was one of the primary commitments of Lieutenant General 'Vinegar Joe' Stilwell, who recognised before anyone else that very large numbers of well-trained Chinese soldiers could pose an effective counter to the Japanese. (Getty Images)

Men of the 17 Dogras bayonet training in 1943, as part of the massive rebuilding of the Indian Army. It was the hard training of soldiers like these, combined with good leadership, effective logistics and superior weapons that gave these men the edge over their opponents. (NAM)

The operations of the 81 West African Division behind Japanese lines in the Kaladan Valley in 1944 and 1945 proved to be of considerable strategic impact, as it forced the Japanese to withdraw entirely from Akyab, enabling an unopposed amphibious operation to take place. (NAM)

The road between Palel on the Imphal Plain and Tamu, during the advance to the Chindwin and the rout of Mutaguchi's 15 Army. The road is being maintained by men of the Bombay Sappers and Miners. (NAM)

US medics tend British wounded in the northern railway corridor, 1944. The Chindits supported the American-led capture of Myitkyina in August 1944, after which the British 36 Division pushed south down through the railway corridor towards Mandalay. (NARA)

By mid-1945 three-quarters of the fighting elements of 14 Army were supplied by air. This photo shows supplies being dropped to 81 West African Division in the Kaladan Valley. Some elements of this division were on aerial resupply for 9 months. (NAM)

'The tables turned'. Few Japanese allowed themselves to be taken prisoner. Unusually, this sniper had been captured in the act of firing at British troops near Pegu in May 1945, but was persuaded to surrender. (Getty Images)

Here, Gurkhas swim their mules across the Irrawaddy above Mandalay in January 1945, as part of the 19 Indian Division feint on the eastern bank of the great river. Most of the boats that were used for this crossing had been made on the banks of the Chindwin. Once it was beyond the Chindwin, the bulk of supplies of 14 Army came by air. (Getty Images)

The landscape after the months of fighting at Kohima and Imphal looked similar to what Great War veterans had seen in France. This photo, taken by Colonel H.C.R. Rose, is of a Japanese bunker on Garrison Hill, Kohima, with Kuki Piquet behind. (IWM)

Thundering into battle around Meiktila in 1945, Indian infantry hitch a ride on Sherman tanks. This picture demonstrates just how advanced the Indian Army had become by 1945 and just how qualitatively superior it was to the Japanese in just about every way. (Getty Images)

An Indian infantry 3-inch mortar platoon operating in support of Sherman tanks in central Burma, 1945. (NAM)

Indian infantry advancing through a burning village, Burma, 1945. (NAM)

A USAAF C46 transport plane making its way across the mountains between Upper Assam and Yunnan Province in China, a journey known as the 'Hump'. This was the aerial Burma Road, a substitute for the physical one cut by the Japanese in 1942. (Getty Images)

90 per cent of the 606,000 men and women of 14 Army in 1945 were Indian and African. Here troops wash close to the Irrawaddy, Burma, 1944. (NAM)

14 Army had to build its way through Burma in 1945, to support the advance. Here Indian sappers rebuild a bridge. (NAM)

The SOE played a pivotal role in Allied victory in Burma in 1945. Here an RAF Lysander aircraft flies from an airstrip in the Burmese jungle. (Dr Richard Duckett – Courtesy of Simon Leney, Sergeant Roger Leney's son)

Troops of Punch Cowan's 17 Indian Division advance through Pyawbe, south of Mandalay, in April 1945. (Getty Images)

Men and vehicles of Major General 'Punch' Cowan's 17 Indian Light Division nearing Rangoon, April 1945. The end is near. (NAM)

operation which he fondly hoped would amount to a crusade to free India from the unwelcome yoke of the Raj. This, in any case, was what Tōjō had already told Bose during the latter's time in Tokyo in March 1943, namely that 'the measures we take in relation to Burma are really the first steps in our policy towards India. I would like to stress that our main objective lies there, in India.'[8] Kawabe, however, cautioned Bose that as the Burma/India theatre had the lowest priority of all (the two others being the Pacific and China) any operation into India, when it came, needed to guarantee success for Japan, and would not be undertaken lightly. Two months later Bose met with Field Marshal Terauchi in Saigon. Telling him that the Japanese were preparing plans to invade India, Terauchi sought Bose's support and the military involvement of the INA in the operation. Excited at this prospect, Bose demanded a full operational role for his troops. Somewhat melodramatically, Bose declared to a bemused Terauchi, 'The first drop of blood shed on Indian soil must be that of a soldier of the INA.'[9] Terauchi had, together with Kawabe and Mutaguchi, been considering the Indians merely for guerrilla and propaganda purposes, and Japanese instructors had been training the INA in these skills in the jungles of Malaya during the year.

Whether or not they agreed with Mutaguchi, it was abundantly clear to all Japanese observers that an advance into Imphal could only succeed if the issue of supply was solved. By 1943 the sea resupply route into Rangoon through the Bay of Bengal was already too dangerous because of attacks by Allied submarines, and supplies had to rely on the railway being constructed by forced labour and POWs from Thailand. Mutaguchi was not ignorant of these issues, but he was, nevertheless, prepared to take the sort of risks that had given Japan such dramatic success in Malaya and Singapore. He recalled that in Malaya the British had left behind large quantities of what the latter referred to as *Chāchiru kyūyō* (Churchill rations) in their haste to flee the advancing Japanese. Accordingly, the capture of the British supply dumps at Moreh, at Milestone 109 on the Tiddim Road, and at Imphal were central to Mutaguchi's plan.

Based on both the experience of Malaya and of Iida's advance to Rangoon in 1942, Mutaguchi confidently assumed that his three Japanese (15, 31 and 33) and one INA divisions would take three weeks to fall on the British supply dumps. Accordingly, he ordered that his men be equipped with rations for only 20 days. Without the capture of these supplies, success could not be guaranteed, but it seemed inconceivable to Mutaguchi that a decisive, overwhelming attack against Imphal would not bring with it rapid and substantial rewards. At no time was he concerned that he might not secure these supplies. Despite his optimism, he nevertheless made every effort to build up logistical capacity to support the offensive and did not rely entirely on the prospect of winning his *Chāchiru kyūyō*. He asked Kawabe for 50 road-building companies and, taking a leaf from Wingate's book, 60 mule companies. These, however, were not available in Burma at the time, and despite Mutaguchi taking the unusual step of appealing directly to Tōjō in Tokyo (over the head of both Kawabe in Rangoon and Terauchi in Saigon), he was forced to do without.

In the absence of these resources extreme measures were now called for. Mutaguchi ordered his new Chief of Staff, Kunomura, to undertake studies into the feasibility of taking cattle on the hoof, an idea he borrowed from Genghis Khan, in order to fuel the advance. These experiments were not wholly satisfactory. The cattle's rate of march was very limited, those bred for beef were unused to carrying loads or travelling long distances, and in the precipitous jungle terrain they proved both difficult to corral and susceptible to falling down slopes to their death. Nevertheless, Mutaguchi believed the exercise worth the effort, and some 30,000 were mustered for the long trek to Imphal, along with 12,000 horses and 1,030 elephants.

Despite the range of objections to Mutaguchi's plan, Terauchi's headquarters on 7 August 1943 gave the go-ahead to the Burma Area Army to prepare for the operation, although ultimate sanction needed to come from Tokyo before any troops crossed the frontier. Mutaguchi anticipated being able to launch his offensive in October. As the months went by and the offensive was prepared, those senior officers opposed to the idea found themselves sidelined or posted away. Major General Inada was himself transferred in October 1943, to be replaced by the more acquiescent Ayabe who, in due course, was to take the final plan to Tokyo. However, at the turn of the year permission had not yet been forthcoming, and Terauchi despatched Ayabe to Japan to force the issue with Imperial Headquarters, the visit which culminated in Colonel Nishiura's bath scene with Tōjō. So it was that on 7 January 1944, two weeks later, the Imperial General Headquarters issued Army Directive No: 1776: 'For the defence of Burma, the Commander-in-Chief of the Southern Army shall destroy the enemy on that front at the appropriate time and secure a strategic zone in north-east India in the area of Imphal.'

Aware of Mutaguchi's penchant for liberal interpretation of orders, Tōjō gave Kawabe strict instructions to ensure that 15 Army went no farther than Imphal. The Burma Area Army commander needed no urging, and despite having every confidence that Mutaguchi's plan would succeed, was determined to keep the lid on anything that might deviate from the strict adherence to the instructions Mutaguchi had been given. The strategic rationale for Operation *U-Go*[10] as it was labelled, was therefore merely to extend the Japanese outer defensive perimeter across the Chindwin and into Manipur, and by preventing a British offensive into Burma, to secure Burma. Bose's INA would provide a useful supporting role by raising in a corner of India the flag of free India.

Kawabe gave detailed orders in turn to Mutaguchi on 19 January 1944. The commander of 15 Army was instructed to mount a strong pre-emptive strike against Imphal before the onset of the monsoon in May. To help, a strong diversionary attack was planned for Arakan, to be called Operation *Ha-Go*. This onslaught, launched in classic Japanese fashion (with a bold right hook to surround General Frank Messervy's 7 Indian Division in the hills between Buthidaung and Taung Bazar), was designed to force the British to scuttle back to Chittagong and panic them into committing their reserves, drawing these away from the Imphal plain where the real action was planned. At the same time, aggressive Japanese operations in the Hukawng Valley would also prevent interference by Stilwell's Chinese.

24

Okeydoke

On the morning of 8 February 1944, the headlines of the Japanese-sponsored *Greater Asia* newspaper in Rangoon had trumpeted the end of the British in northern Arakan: 'Nippon Forces Launch Bold Offensive: Second Arakan Debacle Imminent'. If somewhat premature, the newspaper's claim nevertheless caught a measure of Japanese optimism about the prospects for Operation *Ha-Go*. Equally, it touched a raw nerve in British military sensibilities. Slim's long-planned operation to retake Arakan by XV Corps, now commanded by Lieutenant General Philip Christison, had begun a month before. A British offensive in Arakan once the monsoon was over was essential to prevent any Japanese move against Chittagong, and initial operations by Harold Briggs' 5 Indian Division and Frank Messervy's 7 Indian Division in November and December 1943 had produced promising results. Coordinated battalion actions by both divisions resulted in a series of rapid lessons. Slim, Christison and the divisional commanders (5, 7, 26 and 81 West African) were determined to record and learn rapidly from their experience of combat. No reliance was to be placed on past doctrinal templates. If it didn't work, it was ditched. The lessons of the first two months of operations were:

1. The enemy's positions were completely invisible to patrols and Observation Posts from the air.
2. The jungle was so thick that it sometimes took 8 hours to traverse one mile.
3. The best method of gaining contact was by leap-frogging companies from one prominent feature to another. These were preceded by fighting patrols which seized these features if empty and held them

until the arrival of the company. Each patrol was accompanied by an artillery Forward Observer to assist them to do this.

4. At each advance the engineers had to bulldoze a central artery track on each battalion front for maintenance.

5. Once features were found held, battalions or companies were moved behind the enemy holding the feature so as to attack him from the rear and hold off reserves. This often led to heavy fighting but the enemy generally withdrew after a few days.

6. The divisional artillery was available and was brought down when called for by the leading company commander. Brigade and Battalion commanders had the regimental or battery commanders 'in their pockets'. Each infantry company had an attached artillery observer to direct the guns.[1]

The initial success in forcing a measure of withdrawal against the Japanese gave Briggs and Messervy hope that a strong attack against the Tunnels area would do likewise. Operation *Cudgel* comprised an advance to the Japanese-held Maungdaw–Buthidaung Road across the Mayu Hills by 5 and 7 Indian Divisions; a long-range penetration operation against the enemy's right flank deep in the Kaladan Valley – relying on porters and air supply – by 81 West African Division; and an amphibious assault against Akyab by 36 Division (Operation *Bulldozer*). Briggs' 5 and Messervy's 7 Indian Divisions were to capture the defensive line the Japanese had built during the monsoon, a formidable barrier of defensive positions stretching across 16 miles of the Mayu Range, grandly named the Golden Fortress, whose centrepiece was three powerful bastions which the Japanese had worked feverishly to prepare in the months following their capture of the feature. One was in the centre at the Tunnels, another guarded the western approach at Razabil and the third the eastern approach at Letwedet. The defences comprised networks of deep, well-constructed, well-camouflaged bunkers largely impervious to mortar and light artillery fire. The result, concluded the 7 Indian Division historian, when added to 'the fanatical courage of the Japanese soldier, ordered to defend to the last man and last round… has all the ingredients of the impregnable position.'[2] It was Donbaik on steroids.

Cudgel was designed to be a series of pincer movements against the Golden Fortress, with Razabil on the right attacked by 5 Indian Division and Buthidaung on the left by Messervy. Messervy's division would then move on to attack the Letwedet bastion from the rear before both divisions closed in on the central bastion, the Tunnels, from opposite sides. In order to supply 7 Indian Division, a jeep track had been built in late 1943 for 5 miles through dense jungle over the Ngakyedauk Pass, for reasons of its unpronouceability by British troops nicknamed the 'Okeydoke Pass'. Building this road over a precipitous pass with a dizzying 1,000-foot rise and fall in 3 miles was a remarkable engineering achievement. Where the Pass debouched into the valley at Sinzweya, an administration area had been laid out to support the division's advance. But *Cudgel* had a difficult birth. On the right, frontal attacks by Brigadier Dermot ('Daddy') Warren's 161 Brigade (the aptly named Operation *Jericho*) failed to penetrate the Japanese positions guarding the forward slopes of the Razabil fortress. The enemy had constructed these with considerable care. The 4/7 Rajputs attacked one Japanese hilltop position (Point 124) continuously for six days but was unable to penetrate the deeply dug and mutually supporting trench systems, despite remarkable demonstrations of courage by the troops. Despite the recent arrival of tanks, on this occasion 161 Brigade had no armour or medium artillery in support, the attacking troops having to rely solely on hard-pressed mortars for indirect fire. It was not enough to help them make an impression on the defences. Nearly 90 casualties were suffered by the end of the first day of attacks by the Rajputs alone. During the ensuing days the leading Rajput sections reached the barbed wire at the top of the position but were forced back under a deluge of grenades. Captain Anthony Brett-James described the Japanese tactics:

> Each little scrub-covered hilltop had rings of trenches dug round the summit, and each was covered by the fire of at least one machine-gun from another hillock. When a particular hill was attacked by our men, the defenders would fire a red Very light and at once take cover. This was the signal for all other Japanese posts giving covering fire to open up with machine-guns on the post being attacked. The enemy soldiers holding the post would lob showers of grenades over the parapet, when the assaulting troops were only five or ten yards from the crest.[3]

Hopes of better success were raised when in late January 1944 the heavy (28-ton) Lee-Grant tanks of 25 Dragoons, equipped with powerful 75mm guns, together with the 25-pounders of the corps artillery, arrived in conditions of great secrecy. Briggs had wanted to attack the Japanese from the rear, but had to give up these plans as he had no means of supporting troops so deployed by air, and aggressive Japanese patrolling would have severely interfered with these attempts. A second series of frontal attacks by the long-suffering 161 Brigade against the full might of the Razabil fortress and two of its surrounding hill features, known respectively as Tortoise and Scorpion – Operation *Jonathan* – also failed, despite a massive preparatory bombardment by American bombers, which dropped 90 tons of explosives on the position. The infantry advanced under the cover of a creeping artillery barrage, tanks shooting directly into Japanese bunkers exposed from their jungle camouflage by the aerial bombardment. But the Japanese positions proved virtually impregnable to frontal assault. Even 3.7-inch anti-aircraft guns fired at point-blank range made very little impression on the log bunkers. The Japanese defended tenaciously and intelligently. Small groups hidden in the jungle forward of each locality counterattacked the flanks of the attackers. Casualties in 161 Brigade mounted quickly and little of substance was achieved. When direct frontal assault failed, a policy of strangulation and starvation produced better results, and after some weeks of receiving no supplies the Japanese were forced to abandon their positions, slipping away under cover of the wind and teeming rain of the early monsoon.

Unwilling to pursue such an unprofitable objective, at the end of January Christison left part of 5 Indian Division to mask the Razabil fortress while he switched his main effort to the eastern side of the Mayu Range. Perhaps more firepower on a more concentrated front would work this time. Armour, artillery and an additional brigade (9 Indian Brigade)[4] was transferred across the 'Okeydoke' Pass to prepare 7 Indian Division for its attack on Buthidaung and Letwedet. From the outset of the preparation for battle, Messervy determined to learn the lessons Briggs had learned the hard way. Two weeks before Briggs mounted his abortive attacks against Razabil, Messervy had told his brigade and battalion commanders that the only way to attack Japanese positions was by infiltration rather than frontal attack. 'All experience in the Arakan has demonstrated the utter futility of a formal infantry attack supported by artillery concentrations or barrage against Japanese organised jungle positions', he insisted. 'Normally, one appreciates that superior fire power and superior numbers are dominating assets', he continued. 'Here this is NOT so; we shall get into trouble and have unnecessary casualties and set-backs if we fail to realise this clearly... The right answer to capturing Japanese positions and killing Japanese in this type of country and in these tactical circumstances is quite simple. It is infiltration and encirclement for which the country is extraordinarily suitable.'[5]

Messervy began issuing directives for his commanders, in which he carefully developed these ideas, towards the end of 1943. He emphasized the importance of avoiding stereotypical attacks, and to plan in advance using both guile and boldness. 'We want to be much more subtle and tricky', he ordered on

28 October 1943. 'We must be constantly "putting a fast one" on the little yellow blighter – outwit him, out think him, out fight him and lick him.'[6] Two weeks later he argued that although the conventional frontal attack seemed more attractive and straightforward, it was by far the most dangerous against the Japanese and the least likely to succeed in the difficult jungle country of Arakan. The only sure way of surprising and defeating the formidable defences of the Golden Fortress was by mounting brigade-sized infiltration attacks against his flank and rear, even though these would involve movement through difficult and unknown country. Messervy concluded, 'We will undoubtedly have a Neapolitan sandwich of British-Jap-British-Jap, but it will be one made by ourselves, and with the initiative in our hands will soon be transformed to British-Jap-British.'[7]

By early February Messervy's headquarters was located at Laung Chaung, a few miles to the north of Sinzweya. 33 Brigade held the front from the Mayu foothills to the Kalapanzin River, including two hills astride the Maungdaw–Buthidaung Road – Abel to the north and Cain to the south – captured from the Japanese after fierce fighting in mid-January. The King's Own Scottish Borderers had seized Abel, 3/2 Punjabis took a hill close by nicknamed Italy, and 4/1 Gurkha had crossed the Buthidaung Road to occupy Cain. Messervy's plan was for 33 Brigade to cut the Maungdaw–Buthidaung Road south of Letwedet village, then form a corridor to allow 89 Brigade, together with the tanks of 25 Dragoons, to seize Buthidaung. While this was going on, 114 Brigade would move to cut off the east and rear of Buthidaung in order to prevent the withdrawal or reinforcement of the Japanese garrison. With Buthidaung captured, the division could then turn due west, and apply its whole effort to breaking the Letwedet bastion.

As Briggs fruitlessly battered at the gates of Razabil throughout January, it became increasingly obvious to Slim and Christison that the Japanese were planning to launch a counterattack of their own, perhaps even threatening Chittagong. After watching the size of their garrison in Arakan grow during 1943, Slim instructed that if the Japanese did attempt to outflank 7 Indian Division, Christison's corps were to stand firm. Units were to draw themselves into defensive bastions ('pivots of manoeuvre', as he called them, or 'hedgehogs' in Christison's language), fight off any attacks and rely on air drops of supplies to survive. While they fought off any renewed Japanese offensive, the fresh 26 Indian Division – XV Corps' reserve – would smash down from the north, the hammer to the anvil provided by the bastions. Once the first Japanese assaults had been stayed, the 'boxes' would also take the offensive to break up Japanese columns.

By now the plan for an amphibious assault against Akyab had been shelved for want of landing craft, freeing up 36 Division to assist. Detailed preparations had been undertaken to supply the boxes by air, should this be required, building on the few months of experience already garnered of supply dropping to 81 West African Division (now reduced to two brigades after one had been siphoned off for use in Wingate's Special Force), successfully operating against the Japanese supply lines far to the south-east in the Kaladan Valley. 'The complete maintenance for over a division for several days, everything it would require, from pills to projectiles, from bully beef to boots, was laid out, packed for dropping, at the air strips', wrote Slim. 'We were as ready as we could be.'

Messervy had planned to launch his attack on Buthidaung on 7 February 1944. Three days before, however, General Slim, ill with dysentery, was watching a flame-thrower demonstration at his headquarters at Comilla, when he received a message that the Japanese attack had fallen on the rear of the division. Protected by the usual heavy mist which shrouded the Arakanese river valleys in the early morning at this time of year, and by heavy rain that morning, a Japanese force of uncertain strength had emerged unexpectedly from the jungle and rushed Taung Bazar, 6 miles to the rear of Messervy's headquarters. Except for the final part of the Japanese column, containing food, ammunition and a complete medical unit which had been intercepted and destroyed, the force had moved undetected through the division's left flank. No warning had been received, and 89 Brigade, positioned north of Sinzweya, and in its first day of rest from the heavy *Cudgel* battles for three months, was immediately engaged. At 11.30 a.m. Major Michael Lowry, in his company position overlooking the Letwedet *chaung*, was handed an Order of the Day signed by the Supremo, Lord Louis Mountbatten. 'Hold on at all costs', it read. 'Large reinforcements are on their way.'[8] The message he received was that at least 1,000 Japanese were far behind them, in the area of Taung Bazar.

The Japanese plan was that Operation *Ha-Go* was to be a strategic feint to persuade the British that this would be their main offensive effort against India. They hoped that the British would divert large numbers of troops from Assam to reinforce Arakan, leaving Imphal – Mutaguchi's primary target – poorly defended. Planned by General Hanaya Tadashi, the hard-bitten commander of 55 Division and led by Major General Sakurai Tokutaro, his infantry commander, the attack involved in all about 7,500 experienced troops. The first phase was to secretly infiltrate an infantry group (112 Regiment, plus two additional infantry battalions, 2/143 and 1/213, together with 55 Engineer Regiment) under Colonel Tanahashi – the fabled victor of the offensive into Arakan the previous year – through positions held by 114 Brigade at Kwazon, to capture the small Arakanese trading town of Taung Bazar on the Kalapanzin River. Tanahashi was then to wheel south-west to fall on the rear of 7 Indian Division, cutting the Ngakyedauk Pass and capturing the huge British administrative base at Sinzweya, from which he would replenish his stores. The action would simultaneously cut off the British in the forward areas from their escape route north. The second element involved a battalion under Colonel Kubo striking west across the Mayu Range from Taung Bazar to block the road running north from Maungdaw to Bawli Bazar, thereby isolating Briggs' division. Finally, two remaining battalions under Colonel Doi ('Doi Force') were to maintain pressure across the whole of 7 Division's front forward of the Maungdaw–Buthidaung Road. Hanaya's plan was not merely to destroy the British in northern Arakan, but to drive on into India itself. Indeed, he made no secret of his desire to reach Chittagong if he could, despite clear instructions from Kawabe in Rangoon that this offensive was to be merely a feint, supporting the 'March on Delhi' that was to begin several hundred miles to the north-east in Manipur. He had every reason to think that the goal was attainable.

Operation *Ha-Go* was a classic Japanese manoeuvre, characterized by speed and deception. It was typical of Japanese tactical ingenuity that the plan was to infiltrate *through* the enemy's front lines but without engaging them head on, in order to attack them from *behind*, where they were least expected and where lay all their administrative paraphernalia, and to rely on confusion and disorder to break the enemy's spirit. Sakurai had no reason to think that the British wouldn't (as they had always done in the past) be frightened into a panicked defence of their lines of communication, retreating to consolidate their positions and to protect the roads that supplied them. The physical and psychological dislocation caused by Tanahashi's unexpected descent on 7 Indian Division would, it was hoped, force Messervy to retire in confusion back across the Mayu Range, during which the division would be destroyed piecemeal. As they had done in the past, the British would abandon their positions, together with the stocks of ammunition and rations they had been building up for offensive operations, leaving artillery and weapons behind. Sakurai was so certain of this that INA artillerymen, trained to use British 25-pounders and Bofors guns, were brought up to man these abandoned weapons against their erstwhile owners. Speed was of the essence, as the Japanese were so lightly armed that any dilly-dallying would allow the British the opportunity to recover. With 7 Indian Division in full-scale retreat, Tanahashi would turn his attention to isolating and destroying 5 Indian Division, a process which would be made quicker if Briggs attempted to escape northwards in the direction of Chittagong, where he would be blocked by Kubo Force, a battalion of 213 Infantry Regiment. 'As they have previously suffered defeat', Sakurai declared encouragingly in his order of the day on 4 February 1944, 'should a portion of them waver, the whole of them will get confused and victory is certain.' From their experience of 1942 and 1943, the Japanese expected that Christison's corps would be routed in ten days. They had every reason to be confident. The Japanese had never before suffered a serious reverse at the hands of the British. Sakurai's plan was characteristically bold, utilized surprise to the full, and was led by the man who had succeeded so brilliantly against the British in Arakan the year before. Morale was high.

The attack went exactly as Sakurai had intended. The speed and depth of Tanahashi's hook around the extreme left of the British positions on 4 February, through the scattered units of 114 Brigade, came as a complete surprise to the men of Messervy's division, preparing as they were for their own renewed offensive against the Golden Fortress. The early morning mists shrouded the infiltration from sight, but as the day progressed it became clear that a large-scale Japanese infiltration was underway. Alerted, British and Indian troops engaged columns moving around them with machine gun and artillery fire. Tanahashi ignored casualties and tried to avoid direct fights with his enemy, although this wasn't always possible. To his surprise, resistance was unexpectedly stiff. Nevertheless, his troops pushed on, and in the early morning mist of 6 February a force of about 200 – mainly Tanahashi's signallers and support troops – stumbled into Messervy's divisional headquarters on the top of a slope above Laung Chaung. This area was not prepared for all-round defence, and after being overrun survivors – including Messervy – were forced to escape 2 miles south to the divisional administration area, known as the 'Admin Box', at Sinzweya, which Messervy reached in the early afternoon. Over the following days British and Indian troops cut off in small groups across the area made their way back through the jungle to Sinzweya or to the other scattered brigade boxes.

In the 7 Indian Division area – some 7 miles wide by 4 miles deep – order, certainty and purpose lay behind initial confusion. In accordance with their training, units stood resolutely firm, digging themselves into positions of all-round defence when they found themselves to be surrounded, and not withdrawing in panic as both Hanaya and Sakurai had expected. Evidence of new-found confidence, borne of leadership, training and relentless preparation, could be found across the division. Tails were up. At news of the attack on

Messervy's HQ, and fearing that he had lost his divisional commander, Christison ordered that 9 Brigade (from 5 Indian Division) be transferred from the Maungdaw side of the Mayu Hills to make all haste and reinforce the vulnerable depot at Sinzweya. This action brought experienced fighting troops – such as 2 Battalion, West Yorkshire Regiment, 4/8 Gurkha and two squadrons of 25 Dragoons with their newly arrived and powerful Lee-Grant tanks, together with two batteries of 24 Mountain Regiment, two batteries of 6 Heavy Artillery Regiment RA, a troop of 8 Heavy Artillery Regiment, some Bofors AA/AT guns and 3-inch mortars – into the Admin Box. They arrived with hours to spare, but confidence was high. Within days four principal 'boxes' had been formed, which, as the battle for north Arakan developed, became the focus for 7 Indian Division's defence. From these positions the men in the Admin Box (Sinzweya), 89 Brigade (south of Awlanbyin), 33 Brigade (Sinohbyin) and the 114 Brigade Box (Kwazon) fought off their attackers. On 7 February Slim ordered that 7 Indian Division be put on air supply, and because of the high degree of preparation that had taken place, was able to turn it on immediately. Ten days' supplies for 40,000 men had been laid out on airfields in Assam ready for immediate use. 'Air supply for 15 Corps was on', wrote Slim, 'and, as long as needed, never faltered.'

Two days after Colonel Tanahashi's troops fell on Taung Bazar, Doi Force began fierce attacks on 33 Brigade along the original positions on the Maungdaw–Buthidaung Line in an attempt to drive their way north from the area of Letwedet and to link up with their compatriots in the north. But here Japanese expectations were also confounded. Over the next two days of fierce fighting, instead of overrunning 33 Brigade as they confidently expected, Colonel Doi's force succeeded only in capturing a mortar position, the mortars of which were successfully recovered a few days later. Fighting was intense and hand-to-hand, the guns of 136 Field Regiment in 33 Brigade Box firing over open sights at massed Japanese assaults over the first few days. By this stage in the north of the area 89 Brigade had done all it could to lessen the impact of Tanahashi's assault and was ordered, as best it could, to fall back to cover the rear of 33 Brigade, while troops in isolated positions were ordered to make their way into the Admin Box at Sinzweya to bolster the garrison.

The Indian National Army achieved their first success at this time, an event that provided enough propaganda effect to continue to justify their use, in Japanese eyes, for Operation *U-Go* in Assam. On 3 February 1944 Major Misra and Captain Shingo Hattori of the *Hikari Kikan*, together with several INA soldiers, marched into the hills forward of Buthidaung to remonstrate with

Indian troops facing the Golden Fortress. A handful of Indian soldiers at Point 1800 on the track between the Tunnels and Wabyin surrendered and joined the INA, but this defection was an isolated incident, and did nothing to make the Indian Army collapse, contrary to what the INA propagandists encouraged their Japanese masters to believe would happen. Elsewhere, special orders had to be given to prevent mistreatment of INA POWs by Indian soldiers when they were captured.

25

Sinzweya

The Admin Box at Sinzweya was the weak link in 7 Indian Division's defences. When originally laid out it was deemed to be far enough to the rear to avoid the effects of any Japanese counter-offensive. It was not designed for defence, forming a bowl at the foot of the Ngakyedauk Pass about 1,200 yards in length, for the most part devoid of vegetation. It was surrounded on all sides by jungle-clad hills. It was thus remarkably vulnerable to direct observation, fire and encirclement. The Admin Box was critical to the viability of XV Corps' defence, as it provided the door to the Ngakyedauk Pass and contained the vast cache of stores built up to support Messervy's offensive. If captured it could fuel Tanahashi almost indefinitely. To complicate matters, it was manned, initially at least, and until the arrival of 9 Brigade, largely by administrative and logistical personnel. No one knew how the support troops would fight, although the experience of 1942 and 1943 in this regard had not been good. Most of the garrison comprised muleteers, drivers, storekeepers, medical orderlies, artillery gunners separated from their weapons, laundrymen, workshop artificers and surveyors, all now with rifles and Sten guns thrust into their hands, allocated a patch of scrub or jungle and ordered to dig for their lives. Each small unit was ordered to form its own 'box within the box'. They lacked everything a defensive position would normally require, such as barbed wire and anti-personnel mines, and were forced to improvise. Despite these impediments the Admin Box held out against the odds. The first Japanese attack fell on the evening of 6 February and was repulsed by the soldiers of a mule company, crouching in their trenches and breaking up the attacking Japanese with volleys of well-aimed rifle fire. Most attacks in the first week took place during the day; thereafter they were all undertaken at night. The attacks which now fell on the various 'boxes' for the next three weeks followed a remarkably similar pattern. The Japanese attacked the positions with bayonets, grenades and infantry rushes repeatedly, few positions escaping a nightly attack. Each was stopped by the resolution of its defenders, firing point-blank and defending their positions with hand, bayonet and grenade. On the night of 7 February a party of Japanese from Major Matsukihira's 2 Battalion (of 122 Infantry Regiment) managed to break into the bashas of 66 Indian Field Ambulance on the south-eastern slopes of the Admin Box, slaughtering doctors, orderlies and patients, some with deliberate and calculated cruelty. The Admin Box was so small that many heard the sounds of massacre, which lasted the whole night, waiting helplessly for the dawn to be able to retaliate. There were only three survivors: Lieutenant Basu of the Indian Army Medical Corps, a British medical orderly and a private soldier of the King's Own Scottish Borders. All three had feigned death after they had been shot.

By 8 February the extent of the Japanese encirclement had become apparent. The Japanese were in control of the Ngakyedauk Pass and had thus effectively cut off 7 Indian Division from the remainder of XV Corps. Additionally, Kubo Force had managed to reach – and block – the road between Maungdaw and Bawli Bazar. The omens for another Japanese success looked good, and the Japanese media in Tokyo, Singapore and Rangoon made the most of these initial gains, trumpeting headlines such as 'The March on Delhi has Begun!' and 'New British 14th Army Destroyed In One Thrust!' The Japanese were able also to concentrate a significant air effort over Arakan. For the first six days of the offensive, Sakurai was supported by 45 aircraft of 7 Air Brigade, and in the first ten days some 350 sorties were flown, aircraft for the most part supporting Tanahashi's troops by bombing and strafing the British defensive boxes.

However, the Japanese failed to break into and hold any defended position. This was not what they had expected. Day after day the Japanese threw everything they could at these scattered, poorly prepared yet remarkably resilient defensive positions, surrounded and under relentless attack from ground and air. When they did manage to overcome a key position, a rapid counterattack by ad hoc groups of troops with bayonets, supported by the 75mm guns and machine guns of the Lee-Grant tanks, would throw them back. In this way, although there were insufficient troops fully to man each perimeter, the defenders beat off successive attempts to overrun the boxes. All the positions inside the Admin Box were horribly exposed to the enemy. There was no place to hide, and casualties built up steadily. For the defenders of each box, growing increasingly tired with each advancing day, the nights were desperate affairs, the history of the West Yorks admitting that 'Hearts sank with the sun and rose with the dawn'.[1]

But the longer they held out the more clearly a new phenomenon appeared among the British and Indian troops in Arakan: despite the ferocity of the fighting and the daily increase in casualties, the morale of the men began to rise. As each day passed, and the men in the boxes realized that the Japanese were failing to break their defences, confidence that they could win grew palpably. The prospect of victory against a frighteningly savage, alien enemy who only months before had held 'superman' status across the British and Indian armies, was an extraordinarily powerful antidote to depression. 'It was good to see how the attitude had altered from that of 1943', wrote Slim. 'Now confidence and the offensive spirit reigned in everyone.'

Many casualties were evacuated directly from the battlefield by L5 'Sentinel' light aircraft, flown by young American pilots, although it was not possible to do this from within the Admin Box. A makeshift airstrip was constructed in 11 days at the 114 Brigade box at Kwazon, and in the week following 16 February 240 seriously wounded were flown out. The troops of 81 West African Division did even better than this, constructing a light plane strip at Khonwei in the Kaladan Valley between 2 and 9 February 1944 and flying out 156 casualties. The knowledge that they would receive the best care possible if wounded and not left to the tender mercies of the Japanese was of very great importance to the troops and contributed significantly to the raising of morale across the army during 1944.

The fighting in and around 7 Indian Division 'boxes' was relentless. Dug in on key ground – there were never enough troops to defend every single part of each perimeter – the defenders watched warily for signs of Japanese attack. The night made its own noises, for the jungle was rarely quiet, and the men were forced to discriminate between sounds made by the jungle's natural inhabitants, and those of Japanese troops who might be creeping slowly towards them. Fortunately, most massed Japanese attacks were 'loud', as the Japanese would break into wild banshee-type yells and screams as they launched their final assaults. At Sinohbyin on 5 February a crowd of screaming Japanese threw themselves against the well-dug-in 4/15 Punjabs, leaving behind scores of dead but failing to intimidate the Indians, by now hardened to this form of psychological warfare. In the same location the gunners of 136 Field Regiment, used to engaging the enemy at a range of miles, were forced to fight for their lives in their trenches and gun pits, using knives and bayonets.

Within a week of opening their offensive the Japanese began to feel the effect of the huge gamble they had taken. The British stubbornly refused to flee. The decision to enhance mobility by travelling light made the Japanese vulnerable to starvation and disease if they failed to capture British stores. This was the fate that befell both Tanahashi and Kubo. By 12 February the supply situation for both columns had become critical. The act of passing Sakurai's force through 7 Indian Division meant that subsequent resupply to both Tanahashi and Kubo had to run the gauntlet of the aggressive defence adopted by those units not trapped in Sinzweya. This quickly reduced resupply to a trickle. By the second week of the siege 7 Indian Division was killing hundreds of Japanese every day, and it was increasingly apparent that Sakurai's position was hopeless. Lomax's 26 Indian Division (reinforced with 71 and 4 Indian Brigades) had quickly recaptured Taung Bazar and had begun to press down from the north. To the west, troops of 5 Indian Division were fighting through the Ngakyedauk Pass. In the south, the Japanese maintained heavy pressure on 33 Brigade's positions throughout the period, but repeated attacks made no progress and were repulsed with heavy loss.

The Japanese refused to accept failure, however, continuing to throw themselves profitlessly against the British boxes which, after the first supply drops on the evening of 11 February, began to grow in strength and determination. During the 21 days of the main action over 1,600 tons of supplies were dropped from RAF and USAAF aircraft flying round the clock from airfields in Bengal and Assam. Everything required by the troops on the ground, from clothing, fuel, medical supplies, mail, rations, ammunition, rum (and even a beer ration for the wounded), fell out of the sky often from a height of only 200 feet, either free falling or coming down under locally made parachutes cheaply constructed from jute. Only one aircraft was lost during the entire operation. Air supply was a critical feature of the ability of XV Corps to stand firm, and it was air superiority, by newly arrived Spitfires, which cleared the skies for the lumbering transport aircraft who kept the aerial resupply routes open, by day and night, over Arakan.

With the brigade boxes standing firm, it was apparent even to the Japanese that it was they who were now surrounded. By 13 February Slim knew that he would win the battle. As long as the disparate units of 7 Indian Division held firm and did not run, and 5 and 26 Indian Divisions pressed hard from the outside cutting Sakurai's own supply lines, and the West Africans threatened their long-range supply lines in the Kaladan Valley, the enemy position would become increasingly untenable. Disastrously for the Japanese, Hanaya refused to accept this logic, failing to realize that the opportunity for breakthrough diminished with every day that passed without his capture of British stores. No amount of fanatical bravery could make up for the lack of supplies reaching Tanahashi and Kubo Force which, trapped, now grew rapidly weaker. The diary of a wounded Japanese officer dated 13 February 1944, later found on his body, complained, 'Planes are bringing whiskey, beer, butter, cheese, jam, corned beef and eggs in great quantities to the enemy. I am starving.'[2] Instead of withdrawing his troops, Hanaya allowed Sakurai to continue to battle fruitlessly against 7 Indian Division until death, starvation and, in a few instances, despair and surrender overtook them. With every day that passed the mathematics of battle became inescapable: as the Japanese strength rapidly waned so Allied confidence and fighting ability soared. Between 17 and 24 February the final battle was fought. On 16 February 4 Brigade reached the Laung Chaung where Messervy's headquarters had been sited two weeks before. In the southern area, 33 Brigade began going over to the offensive, and in the east 114 Brigade established contact with troops of 71 Brigade. On 24 February the Admin Box was relieved, Major Ferguson Hoey of the Lincolns gaining a posthumous Victoria Cross as he led his company in the attack on Point 315, opening up the path into the Ngakyedauk Pass for the first time in three weeks. A Lee-Grant of 5 Indian Division lumbered into the Admin Box, trundling slowly across the shell-pitted scrub of the Sinzweya bowl to the clump of trees which denoted Messervy's divisional HQ. The expectant onlookers saw the turret opening and out jumped an ebullient Major General Harold Briggs, clutching a bottle of whisky which he thrust into a delighted Messervy's hands. The siege was over.

Immediately, the 500 casualties from Sinzweya were evacuated over the pass, and air supply to 7 Indian Division ceased. The relief of Sinzweya signified the end of the Japanese offensive. Weak and starving, the few survivors of what had begun as a bold and promising enterprise struggled through the jungle to the relative safety of their 'Golden Fortress'. For the British it was hard to believe that the siege was all over. Although they looked like ragged, bearded scarecrows, Captain Wilson Stephens testified that their happiness was unbounded in the knowledge 'that we had had a front seat in the first defeat of the Japanese Army in recorded history'. Australians fighting in New Guinea would forgive this overstatement, but there is no doubting the huge relief in the army in India that after so long the hitherto invincible Japanese had been worsted.

A significant opportunity to destabilize the Japanese was squandered in February and March 1944, however. Slim had long harboured a desire to strike at the Japanese flank in the Kaladan through long-range penetration operations supported by air. Major General Woolner had initially been instructed to take the two brigades of 81 West African Division into the heart of the Kaladan Valley, there to become a thorn in the Japanese side, and being supported entirely by air. Slim's view of the West Africans' role was offensive, expecting the West Africans to move 'down the Kaladan Valley well to the east [where they] would provide a flank guard and would... be in its turn a threat to the Japanese flank and their west to east communications.' But Christison demurred, ordering the West Africans to stay put. He didn't want to risk having two divisions caught by the Japanese offensive and in need of aerial resupply, so the West Africans played little role in the battle. There is a strong argument, however, that if they had continued to advance to the southern end of the Kaladan Valley along the Japanese western flank, seizing Myohaung with its airfield into which more heavily armed troops could have been flown, the West Africans would have trapped the Japanese in Arakan completely. The Japanese recognized this threat as soon as it became apparent and began reinforcing the area. Unfortunately, Christison then changed his mind, gave Woolner hopelessly contrary orders, and the opportunity, despite the success of the West Africans' guerrilla-like penetration deep into Japanese territory, petered out into strategic insignificance.[3]

British and Indian casualties totalled 2,000, of whom 500 were killed. It was the first major Japanese defeat in Burma and as such represented a turning point in British fortunes. It gave an enormous boost to the morale of the army as a whole and provided absolutely the right counter to the bitter defeats of the previous year. For the first time the Japanese had been significantly bettered in battle by opponents they had come to despise. Slim's defensive concept provided the framework for the success of 7 Indian Division and the thwarting of Japanese plans, and the merciless training regime he had begun to impose on XV Corps 18 months before gave it the substance. Mountbatten's willingness and ability to provide the aircraft necessary for the air dropping operation, the respective leadership of Messervy, Briggs, Lomax and their brigade and battalion commanders, together with the renewed fighting spirit and efficiency of the troops, were also crucial determinants of victory.

Aerial resupply was a crucial enabler of victory, but it was not solely responsible for the success of 7 Indian Division in first halting, and then routing, the Japanese. The air supply of 7 Indian Division began only after Sakurai's assault had been stayed and his ambitions denied, by which time the Japanese were well on the way to defeat. The first airdrop on the Admin Box took place on 11 February. The new policy of standing firm and fighting back – the staunchness and aggressiveness of XV Corps, especially 89, 33 and 9 Brigades – was responsible for Sakurai's defeat. As long as the units of 7 Indian Division held firm, and 5 and 26 Indian Divisions pressed on from the outside, cutting Sakurai's own line of communication, thus inhibiting their own resupply, the Japanese position was untenable. The air supply operation was a remarkable feat, but proved to be more important in enabling XV Corps quickly to resume the offensive when the time came than in bringing about the Japanese defeat in the first place. 'Above all', concluded the XV Corps history of the battle, 'the great possibility of really bold manoeuvre in offensive planning was beginning to be apparent.'[4]

Hanaya's attack had failed. He had not reached Chittagong, and in fact had made it no farther north than Taung Bazar. Halted in the straggling jungle hills at the eastern exit of the Ngakyedauk Pass, his troops had been beaten off by the dispersed and unprepared troops of 7 Indian Division, all of whom had surprised the enemy by their determination to stand and fight. Certainly, in Japanese experience, this was a new and surprising phenomenon. They had been unable to break into the scattered but defiant brigade boxes as a result, even when enjoying a substantial local superiority in both ground troops and aircraft. Paradoxically, however, the Japanese feint in Arakan was a dramatic success. Hanaya had achieved precisely what Mutaguchi and Kawabe had desired, namely for Slim to speed scarce fighting resources to Arakan, leaving Manipur – the point of Japanese main attack – dangerously exposed. It now waited to be seen whether the Japanese could profit by their success.

With the Japanese offensive in ruins, no impediment now remained to the smashing by the triumphant British of the Golden Fortress. When XV Corps resumed their offensive on 5 March 1944, British tactics had changed dramatically. To the east of the Mayu Range, Messervy's aggressive pursuit of the remnants of Sakurai Force led to the seizure of Buthidaung on 11 March. To the west of the range Briggs tried again to reduce the Razabil fortress, which was achieved by copying Tanahashi's tactics. The men of his division infiltrated through and between the Japanese positions to seize and hold dominating features to the rear, cutting Japanese supply lines and allowing for their methodical destruction. To the west of the range, Briggs tried again to reduce the Razabil fortress. His approach was now markedly different than before, and was characterized by both stealth and guile. 'The plan was… to close a tight ring around the fortress by surprise, to bring 161 Brigade in from the foothills to the south, and to sever the enemy's lines of communication', recorded the divisional historian. 'The success of a scheme designed to bypass the fortress and appear on dominating features, so isolating it from the rear, depended on accurate preliminary reconnaissance both of the route and final positions. Officers of 161 Brigade spent several days behind the Japanese lines, making these reconnaissances. And their daring and careful observation was amply repaid when the operation began.'[5] The operation was a resounding success. After two months of frontal attacks the Japanese were entirely surprised by the skilled night insertion of the brigade behind their position, and Razabil fell in fighting between 9 and 12 March 1944. The secret to success in Arakan had ironically been taught to the British and Indian armies by the Japanese themselves. By early 1944 they were assiduous – if slow learning – students.

New tactics accompanied Briggs' successful new approach to the problem of reducing Japanese defences. Firepower was employed selectively and intelligently, rather than as a battering ram. Short, rapid, surprise artillery concentrations to help the infantry onto their objectives were employed in place of the lengthy bombardments which had consistently failed to make any real impact on Japanese positions in the past. Bunkers were exposed from the surrounding jungle by light artillery, then demolished with direct sniping from tanks. Cannon fire from ground attack aircraft proved to be of the greatest value, especially on enemy reverse slope positions. While the infantry were closing in, dummy attacks were made to keep the defenders' heads down during the few vital minutes required to allow attackers into enemy trenches. Tanks were also used to get behind Japanese positions to snipe against the reverse slope bunkers so they could be neutralized and destroyed.

Using these methods, the Western Tunnel was seized by 36 Division on 27 March, and the Eastern Tunnel was taken after fierce fighting on 6 April. The final Japanese position was Point 551, the loss of which had prevented Slim's chances of retaining the Maungdaw–Buthidaung Road exactly a year before. 'It was under attack throughout April, during which 26 Indian Division delivered three separate assaults on it. Its capture on 3 May, at the fourth attempt,' he recalled, 'was the toughest fighting of the whole Tunnels battle.'

At the time the successes of XV Corps – first in stopping *Ha-Go* and then in capturing the Golden Fortress – were trumpeted by HQ SEAC and India Command as great victories. Were they? The accusation sometimes made against Slim was that he used a sledgehammer to crack a nut, and that such preponderance of strength made a British victory inevitable.[6] In total numbers of troops, measured across the campaign as a whole, this was true. Nevertheless, pure statistics disguise the real picture on the battlefield. The critical point is that a year before, Irwin had possessed overwhelming superiority over the Japanese in Arakan, and had yet been comprehensively beaten. Now, in early 1944, at the decisive point – the eastern exit of the Ngakyedauk Pass – where the Japanese concentrated their forces to achieve overwhelming superiority in early February 1944, the Japanese were beaten by the dispersed and unprepared troops of 7 Indian Division, many of them administrative units, all of whom were nevertheless determined to stand their ground and fight. The Japanese were unable to break into the scattered but defiant brigade positions even when they enjoyed a substantial local superiority in both ground troops and aircraft. Where and when it was needed, XV Corps did not enjoy a superiority of numbers over the enemy: the reverse in fact was the case. But these troops were imbued with a fighting spirit unseen in the campaign so far. It was this fighting spirit in support troops – men who never expected to be in the front line of the battle – which so emphatically emphasized the change which had come over the Indian Army since the dark days of May 1943. There is no doubt that 7 Indian Division's victory was genuine and well deserved. On the left flank, 81 West African Division did extremely well to penetrate deep into the Japanese rear in the Kaladan Valley, and only excessive caution by Christison prevented it from achieving a victory out of all proportion to their meagre resources and dramatically reducing the pressure on the troops in north Arakan.

14 Army needed a victory, and *Cudgel* provided it. 'I hoped that the Arakan campaign would be the first step towards building up a tradition of success,' Slim argued later, 'and I did not intend to take more risks than I had to at this early stage. Later we would take on twice or thrice our number in Japanese divisions – but not yet. At this time all my plans were based on ensuring a superiority in numbers and force at the decisive points.' If not a battle on the scale of many others during the Second World War, it was a turning point as significant as the defeat of the Afrika Korps at El Alamein. The enemy had been turned away from the gate of India and had been resoundingly defeated. 'For the first time,' he asserted, 'a British [and Indian, and African] force had met, held and decisively defeated a major Japanese attack, and followed this up by driving the enemy out of the strongest possible natural positions that they had been preparing for months and were determined to hold at all costs.'

The Japanese had, nevertheless, thwarted the plan to advance to Rathedaung and had removed the possibility of an amphibious assault on Akyab by 36 Division. They had also forced Slim and Giffard respectively to concentrate army and army group reserves to Arakan, leaving Manipur dangerously weak. However, these were insignificant achievements compared with the far-reaching success of XV Corps in smashing *Ha-Go*, capturing the Golden Fortress and inflicting massive and irreplaceable casualties on the Japanese. The victory provided an enormous tonic for British morale. Equally important, 'the fact that Messervy's men had taken fifty Jap prisoners, something previously unheard of in Burma, proved this point emphatically.'[7] 'It was a victory', Slim insisted, 'about which there could be no argument, and its effect, not only on the troops engaged but on the whole Fourteenth Army, was immense. The legend of

Japanese invincibility in the jungle, so long fostered by so many who should have known better, was smashed.' With the long struggle for the Imphal plain yet to come, it was a victory that could not have come at a more opportune time. The ghosts of late 1942 and early 1943 had finally been laid to rest. Hard and realistic training had created soldiers – British, African and Indian – able to cope with the many demands of the jungle battlefield, and against a ruthless and tenacious enemy. Firm bases, air supply, and the movement of reserves to counter the otherwise debilitating effects of infiltration and encirclement proved outstandingly successful tactics and gave the troops of 14 Army a new confidence in their leaders, training and their approach to fighting the Japanese. While the generals still had much to learn, Slim had undoubtedly designed a pattern for victory, and XV Corps had given British, Indian and African troops their first success against the Japanese in the war. At long last, Cavendish and many others of the ill-fated Arakan operation a year before had been avenged. It was the perfect foundation upon which 14 Army as a whole could build as the threat to Manipur drew nigh.

26

The March on Delhi

But the focus on Arakan had done exactly what the Japanese had intended: draw resources away from the point of the primary attack, on Manipur.[1] On 17 January 1944 Churchill confided to General Ismay, his Chief of Staff, his belief that the threat of a Japanese invasion of India had passed.[2] The picture from Comilla, however, was far different. Along the Chindwin, as January proceeded through February into early March, it was clear that a massive Japanese offensive into Assam, instead of being merely the strong raid that some had originally expected, was imminent. Long-range reconnaissance patrols by 20 Indian Division over the Chindwin and far to the south in the Kabaw Valley demonstrated unequivocally that a Japanese offensive was in the offing. Along the Chindwin and in the mountain barrier that lay between this mighty river and the Imphal plain, the scattered outposts of V Force forward of both Kohima and Imphal reported by radio on growing evidence of Japanese activity on both sides of the river. Even further into Burma, a secret organization (Z Force), comprised of small parties of Britons and Anglo-Burmese, including former employees of British firms in the teak trade, was reporting directly to Slim's 14 Army HQ in Comilla, describing the large-scale movements of Japanese troops towards the frontier with India. Likewise, Burman and Karen agents of Force 136 (Special Operations Executive, or SOE) under the command of Major Edgar Peacock – a group known as P Force – sourced intelligence from Japanese-occupied villages. By early March elements of all three Japanese divisions and supporting units of 15 Army – 15, 31 and 33, ultimately comprising 115,000 men – appeared on the Chindwin's eastern bank. Likewise secret signals intelligence ('Ultra') garnered by careful listening to Japanese radio traffic by the Delhi outstation of Bletchley Park – the Wireless Experimental Centre (WEC) which controlled 88 radio sets in India and a code-breaking team of about 200 personnel – also pointed unerringly towards this certainty. Slim was one of two men in his headquarters with access to the extremely sensitive and 'invaluable' WEC intelligence, which included 'operational and movement orders, strength returns and locations… and a complete order of battle of the Japanese force.'[3]

In a letter home, written on 28 January 1945, Lieutenant John Twells of 1 Gurkha Rifles told his parents, 'As early as 8 December 1943 we were able to tell the men that the Japanese would cross the Chindwin at Homalin about the middle of March and roughly two divisions strong.'[4] By the end of January a glut of various sources, much of it coming through the Eastern Wireless Signal Centre at Barrackpore, a sub-station of the WEC (and known for cover purposes as Intelligence School 'C'), had made it clear to Slim that his forces in Manipur faced attack by the whole of 15 Army. Ultra signals intelligence sent through the Special Liaison Unit at Comilla, a small team created to ensure that intelligence could be acted upon immediately by transmitting it directly to commanders on the spot, allowed him even to put a date on the start of the offensive: 15 March 1944.[5] It was also clear that the Japanese attack would be conducted in great strength with at least the three divisions his forward reconnaissance had identified, as well as a division of the INA, together with a regiment of tanks. What they did not know in any detail were Mutaguchi's precise intentions. The potential area for the offensive was greater than any other in the Second World War outside of Europe's eastern front – about 16,000 square miles. Slim calculated that the Japanese would attempt to isolate and destroy his three frontline divisions in Manipur, and cut the Imphal road at Kohima to prevent reinforcements from reaching Imphal, before striking against the strategic base at Dimapur. While destroying the offensive capability building up in Manipur, Slim was certain that the real task of an offensive would be to wring the neck of the Allied chicken at Dimapur. In the two years since the withdrawal from Burma, Dimapur had become the logistical linchpin in Allied operations against the Japanese in Burma and in support of China. As Mutaguchi had concluded, its capture would suffocate any future offensive aspirations against Burma. It would halt the Hump airlift to China. It might also serve as the first stage in a deeper penetration of India, with political ramifications for the Raj that were not worth thinking about.

That the Japanese were contemplating an offensive against India in early 1944 was a surprise to Allied planners, who had given it no thought. Japan had reached the apogee of its power. By early 1944 the tide had turned decisively in the Pacific, the American-led island-hopping advance reaching steadily but surely towards Japan itself, the Japanese fighting back with desperation, and for every inch of every remote, jungle-covered Pacific island they occupied. The struggle on the landmass of Asia was a strategic sideshow – although a necessary fight – in the context of a global conflict: at this time the British and American high commands were occupied with Europe and the Pacific. The British and Americans were preparing for D-Day. The Soviets were advancing in Ukraine. There was a stalemate in Italy along the Gustav Line. The Americans were preparing to land in the Philippines. Germany and Japan were both in retreat, but not defeated. In this global context, India and Burma were strategically peripheral, even inconsequential. Yet in this month, at a time when on every other front the Japanese were on the strategic defensive, Japan launched a vast, audacious offensive deep into India in an attack designed to destroy for ever Britain's ability to challenge Japan's control of Burma.

Knowledge of Japanese intentions posed an immediate challenge to Slim: how to reverse the disposition of his forces and reinforce Assam, while not at the same time losing the fight in Arakan? This would take time, especially as the only means of doing so was either by sea or road to Chittagong. The lack of a land link covering the 400 miles between Arakan and Manipur meant that troops had to be laboriously transported by road and rail back through Chittagong and thence into Manipur through Dimapur. With the relief of the Admin Box, Slim wasted no time in ordering Briggs' 5 Indian Division to make its way to Imphal during the period between 13 March and 14 April and for Messervy's 7 Indian Division to be withdrawn from Arakan and placed in army reserve.

The next difficulty lay in determining how best to defeat the impending Japanese offensive. This was not a simple proposition. Where would Mutaguchi focus his attack? He would certainly confront 17 Indian Division at Tiddim, and 20 Indian Division at Moreh, guarding the approaches from the Chindwin. He would also send at least a regiment (equivalent to a British or Indian brigade) to Dimapur. The most sensible course for Slim was to withdraw 17 Indian Division *before* the enemy offensive fell, placing it in the hills guarding the southern approaches to Imphal town at Bishenpur. Meanwhile, 20 Indian Division would be kept forward at Moreh for as long as possible, keeping the battle away from the Imphal plain, absorbing and wearing down the rush of the enemy attack as it surged across the Chindwin. The corps reserve, 23 Indian Division, would be able to counterattack individual infiltration behind and beyond the forward disposition of his troops as it occurred. The Japanese units thus deployed against Imphal from the south and south-east would be forced to advance through difficult and hostile territory, extending their lines of communication, while the British would be able to concentrate theirs.

Slim's big picture was that, instead of keeping his forces forward and investing in a strong defensive barrier along the Chindwin to the south-east and south, he would instead withdraw his troops judiciously – out-of-contact with the enemy for 17 Indian Division, but in-contact for 20 Indian Division – finally concentrating them on the hilly outskirts of the Imphal plain itself. The Japanese would be encouraged to advance deep into Manipur, following behind the apparently scared and demoralized enemy. Far from being defeated, however, the two Indian Divisions would then occupy positions around the periphery of the Imphal plain where, supported by 23 Indian Division, they would hold fast against the Japanese attack. Key points, including Imphal town itself and the six airfields on the plain, would be transformed into defensive bastions capable of defending themselves unaided for at least ten days.[6] Allowing them to advance directly onto Imphal would stretch the Japanese supply lines through more than 100 miles of jungle-clad hills from the Chindwin.

By contrast, IV Corps would, by withdrawing, enjoy vastly reduced lines of communication and benefit from concentration. Slim's primary concern was to ensure that he had overwhelming force at the point of main effort. As 'much as our troops had improved in training and morale', he wrote, 'I did not want the first big clashes to be on equal terms, division for division. I wanted superior strength at the decisive point for the opening of the struggle'. By pulling IV Corps back towards Imphal, Slim's intention was to grasp the initiative, not relinquish it, but doing so would deliberately send a different message to the Japanese. Pulling back his forces from their forward positions to the Imphal plain would be precisely what Mutaguchi expected, and would reinforce Japanese expectations of an early and easy victory. The Japanese assumed that the British would have no stomach for a fight and would crumble quickly under pressure. Slim's hope, however, was that once concentrated, with a clear superiority in armour, artillery and air power, IV Corps would be able to create a defensive area far too strong for Mutaguchi to break. 'I was tired of fighting the Japanese when they had a good line of communications behind them and I had an execrable one', Slim reasoned in 1944. 'This time I would reverse the procedure.'

It would then be possible for the British to take advantage of their growing strength in aircraft, armour and artillery while simultaneously exploiting the enemy's weaknesses in logistics and resupply, problems that would be compounded by the onset of the monsoon at the end of April. However, in attempting such a plan, Slim risked undermining the still delicate morale of his army. Not only were withdrawals difficult to manage but failure would have a deleterious effect on the morale of his troops, which he and his commanders had built up so painstakingly after the disasters of 1942 and 1943. A withdrawal would also have a correspondingly negative effect politically on friends and allies. He knew well from his own experience that there was no guarantee that 17 and 20 Divisions would be able successfully to withdraw at the required moment, particularly if the withdrawal was conducted in contact with the enemy. Slim's plan, to lock the enemy into a close battle in which superior British firepower would combine with Japanese blind tenacity – and hugely overextended supply lines – to utterly destroy Mutaguchi's 15 Army, was a stratagem that not everyone fully understood or accepted. In particular, it entailed an acceptance of a significant Japanese advance into Assam. While Slim believed (and Mountbatten accepted) that this would be the Japanese undoing, there were many who believed that such a defensive strategy was wrong, and that Slim needed to be much more offensive. Mountbatten's American deputy Chief of Staff, Al Wedemeyer, was one such. While in Washington in June 1944, he spread the entirely false story – based not on malicious intent but on misinformation – that the British did not have their heart in taking the war to the Japanese in Burma, and were quietly waiting for 'the monsoon so they can de-emphasize operations'.[7] It is clear that Wedemeyer had not grasped the essence of the strategy Slim was advocating. A premature offensive into Burma would remove the opportunity he sought to catch the Japanese at their weakest. It would be far better, he reasoned, to allow the Japanese to beat themselves head-on against IV Corps in Assam, until they had no energy either to continue fighting or to retire. Mountbatten, fortunately, was persuaded by Slim's argument, and supported him to the hilt.

But there was no guarantee either that the defences of the Imphal plain would be sufficient to defeat every attempt by the enemy to break in, or that he could reinforce IV Corps quickly when required. Replying to a letter from Mountbatten on 5 March, Slim wrote, 'I think we are in for something… serious on 4 Corps front, where our dispositions are not quite so favourable for meeting it. I hope, however, that the 3rd Indian Division* will have a very great effect on the Jap's plans, but I am very anxious to reinforce that front if I possibly can.'[8] If the Imphal defences were strong enough and if Slim could maintain a steady flow of reinforcements and supplies into Imphal by some means, the Japanese would merely exhaust their strength in ultimately fruitless attempts to overwhelm the defenders. These were big 'ifs'. To be successful, Slim's plan would require careful planning, a finely honed assessment of his troops' capabilities and the ability to

---

*The cover name for Operation *Thursday*, Wingate's 'Special Force', the second Chindit operation. See Chapter 34.

MAP 5 Operation *U-Go*

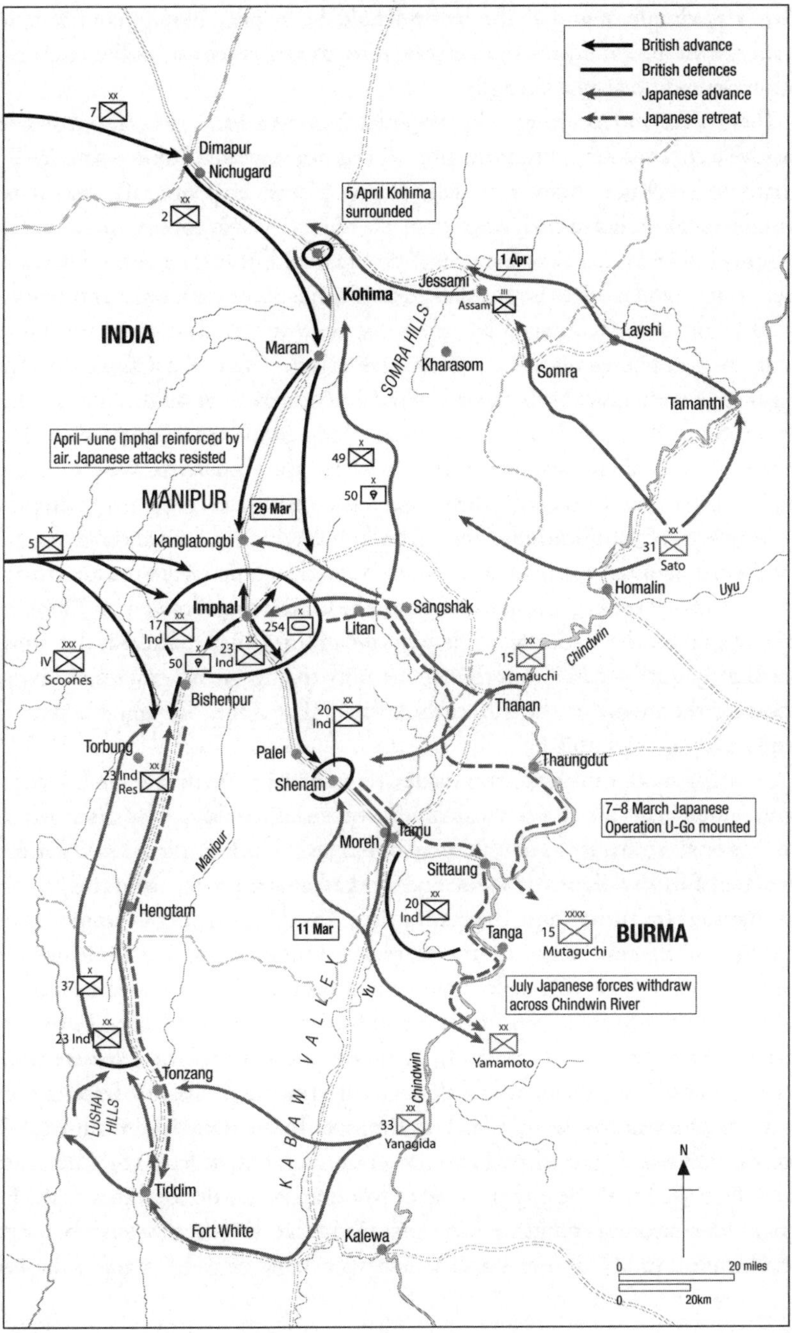

	British advance
	British defences
	Japanese advance
	Japanese retreat

7

Dimapur
Nichugard

2

5 April Kohima
surrounded

INDIA

1 Apr

Jessami

Kohima

Assam

Layshi

Maram

SOMRA HILLS

Kharasom

Somra

Tamanthi

April–June Imphal reinforced by
air. Japanese attacks resisted

49

MANIPUR

29 Mar

50

Kanglatongbi

5

31
Sato

Homalin

Uyu

Imphal

254

Sangshak

Litan

17
Ind

23
Ind

15
Yamauchi

Chindwin

IV
Scoones

50

Bishenpur

20
Ind

Thanan

Torbung

Palel

Thaungdut

23 Ind
Res

Shenam

7–8 March Japanese
Operation U-Go mounted

Manipur

Moreh

Tamu

Sittaung

Hengtam

11 Mar

20
Ind

Tanga

15
Mutaguchi

BURMA

37

Yu

July Japanese forces withdraw
across Chindwin River

23 Ind

Yamamoto

Tonzang

Chindwin

LUSHAI
HILLS

33
Yanagida

N

Tiddim

K A B A W   V A L L E Y

Fort White

Kalewa

0   20 miles

0   20km

317

juggle limited resources between competing priorities at a moment's notice. What was certain was that the battle would be a long, bloody confrontation where the victor would require perseverance, as well as considerable reserves of both moral and material strength.

There were indeed some who opposed Slim's plans. It was altogether too sensitive a concept for many at the time. 'I was not surprised,' Slim wrote, 'to find it hard to convince many, especially highly placed civil officials, that it was possible to fight defensively and even to retreat, yet keep the initiative.' By withdrawing he lay open to the charge that he had lost his nerve and lacked the courage to stand and fight the Japanese. Rather than suffer the indignity of retreat, Slim was encouraged by some not to withdraw but to anticipate the enemy by launching his own pre-emptive attack across the Chindwin. Such suggestions were quickly dismissed. 'Had I accepted their advice,' he recalled, 'the enemy could easily have concentrated, along good communications, a force greatly in excess of any we could maintain east of the Chindwin. We should have fought superior numbers with the dangerous crossing of a great river behind us and with our communications running back through a hundred and twenty miles of the worst country imaginable.' 'I noted,' remarked Slim rather caustically, 'that the further back these generals came from, the keener they were on my "flinging" divisions across the Chindwin.' 'It was not ground that mattered,' he argued consistently during 1944, 'but the opportunity to engage, on ground of his own choosing, the might of the Fifteenth Army.' 'That done,' he argued, 'territory could easily be reoccupied.'

So far, so good. But the British made a series of misjudgements about Japanese plans. Mutaguchi, for all his personal idiosyncrasies, could not be described as a conventional strategist, and he developed an offensive plan that correctly calculated British defensive moves, and worked around them. Mutaguchi's plan was daring, inventive and aggressive. He intended to seize Imphal by a combination of guile and extreme physical endurance, seeking to achieve the same advantages that *Kirimomi Sakusen* had brought Japanese commanders in their previous encounters with British and Indian troops in Malaya, Burma and Burmese Arakan. Not unreasonably, Scoones assumed that the Japanese would attack along the two major routes that led into the plain, the first leading north from Tiddim and the second leading through Tamu from the south-east. He thought that a regiment (three battalions, or no more than 3,000 or 4,000 men) would be tasked with closing the road at Kohima. So, he decided that at the first sign of the Japanese offensive Cowan's 17 Indian Division would withdraw unmolested from Tiddim to Imphal, leaving a single brigade to guard the back door at Bishenpur. The second brigade would join 23 Indian Division and 254 Tank Brigade to form a powerful reserve inside the Imphal plain itself, able rapidly to counterattack any ingress as it occurred. In the south-east Gracey's 20 Indian Division would withdraw to hold positions between Moreh and the Shenam Pass, against which it was expected that the greatest weight of the Japanese offensive would fall, as it provided the fastest route into the plain. The vast swathes of jungle-covered hills that rise protectively from the basin floor to encompass the plain in every direction appeared themselves to deny any invader easy access to Imphal. As he did not have the troops available to guard every stretch of his enormous front, Scoones considered that it was better to place the major part of his forces on these routes while reserving sufficient forces on hand to counterattack Japanese breakthroughs wherever they appeared. This was a better alternative, he decided, than attempting to defend every part of a huge sector and thus being weak everywhere, leaving only a limited reserve available to deal with crises as and when they arose. Accordingly, huge stretches of territory, much of it apparently impenetrable jungle or impossible hill country, were deprived of real defences. As a result, the 80 miles or so of rugged country between Litan and Kohima through the Naga village of Ukhrul came to be defended by only a few weak battalions.

Mutaguchi knew that Scoones would attempt to hold Tiddim and Tamu in strength and decided, therefore, to appear to attack through these areas, while in fact reserving his most dangerous attack for a direction that the British would never expect. His plan entailed four simultaneous thrusts deep into Manipur. In the first place, in the south, the two regiments of Lieutenant General Yanagida Motozo's 33 Division were to strike against Tiddim and cut the recently extended dirt track that led up the Manipur River Valley north to Imphal. While the main part of 17 Indian Division was to be attacked, 214 Regiment would cut the road behind them at Tongzang, and a further regiment (215) would bypass the road to the west and cut it at Milestone 100, cutting off the division from its escape route north. Yanagida would take his victorious division north, along the Tiddim Road and into the now unprotected underbelly of the Imphal plain. For Mutaguchi this victory would be sweet: Cowan had fought the Japanese to a standstill in the mountainous terrain forward of Tiddim in the months since May 1943 and had proved himself a serious irritant to the Japanese plan of dominating the Chin Hills.

The date set for the start of this advance was in fact 7 March, not the 15th as the British had learned from their signals intelligence. Mutaguchi's hope was that this early threat would force the British to send reserves down the Tiddim Road from Imphal on their southern flank, thus denuding their defences elsewhere on the Imphal plain. The second move, a week later, entailed a strong force of tanks, artillery and infantry from 33 Division (reinforced by two battalions of 15 Division), under the command of Major General Yamamoto (33 Division's infantry commander),[9] which was to strike against 20 Indian Division, spread out along the border with Burma in the southern Kabaw Valley. The centre of gravity of Gracey's division was formed by the villages of Witok and Tamu, the latter of which boasted a forward fighter strip. This attack was to be launched on the night of 15 March. Its immediate objective was the Shenam Saddle, the high point in the mountains south-east of the Imphal plain through which the road from Palel rose and threaded its way down towards Tamu, and from where, at its highest point, Imphal itself could be observed.

These moves would conform to British expectations and, in so doing, Mutaguchi correctly assumed that Scoones would then commit his reserves to his Tiddim and south-eastern sectors. But cunningly, just as Scoones struggled to address the problems in the very two areas where he had always expected an attack to fall, Mutaguchi planned to launch his two most powerful attacks in the east and north. This would take the British by surprise, and at a time when their reserve had been allocated elsewhere. Farther north along the Chindwin, Lieutenant General Yamauchi Masafumi was to take his 15 Division by raft and pontoon and advance across the mountains of the Somra Tracts to attack Imphal from *the north*. The division's line of advance was to take it through the village of Humine on the Burmese border and then along tracks and paths to Sangshak, before heading due west, crossing the road to Kohima and falling on Imphal from the north. Still farther north, and directed against the mountaintop town of Kohima, the entire three regiments of Lieutenant General Sato's 31 Division – about 20,000 fighting men – would cross the Chindwin between Homalin and Tamanthi, heading north-west. In the southern prong of this advance, 138 Regiment would make for Ukhrul, cutting the Imphal–Kohima Road at Maram in the middle; 58 Regiment would make for Somra and then Jessami before moving the final 30 miles west to Kohima; and in the far north, 124 Regiment would cover the northern flank in the Naga Hills. This triple pincer was calculated to cut Imphal from its external sources of supply and place intolerable demands on Scoones. Mutaguchi hoped that in facing multiple threats on all but the western side of the compass, Scoones would be unable to cope with the desperate and disparate calls for his limited reserves to fill the inevitable gaps that the Japanese attack would force in his defences. To be successful, Mutaguchi needed to ensure that his troops captured Imphal before the monsoon rains fell and transformed the jungle tracks his men would use into impassable quagmires. He also needed to do it quickly, as the supplies he could promise his three divisional commanders were meagre indeed. The date Mutaguchi set himself for victory at Imphal was 10 April. This would give him plenty of time to achieve victory before the Emperor's birthday on 29 April.

But Imphal and Kohima were not in themselves his ultimate objective. The trap he laid for Slim and Scoones was to make them believe that the main attack was to be placed against Imphal, whereas in fact Mutaguchi's strategic eye lay on Kohima as a route through to Dimapur. If he could capture Dimapur then Imphal would rapidly wither on the vine. Capturing Dimapur would cut off the railway to Stilwell's base at Ledo in the north, threatening the continuance of American supplies to the Chinese and American forces that faced off Japanese-held Burma from the north. It would irreparably harm the huge air base operations in northern Assam that served as the eastern end of Hump operations. It was a bold plan that relied on the acceptance of a considerable logistical risk, the absolute commitment by his three divisional commanders and of the need, above all else, for speed. Mutaguchi's proclamation to his troops on 18 February 1944 announced:

> The army has now reached the stage of invincibility and the day when the Rising Sun shall proclaim our victory in India is not far off. This operation will engage the attention of the whole world and is eagerly awaited by 100,000,000 of our countrymen.[10] By its very decisive nature, its success will have a profound effect upon the course of the war and may even lead to its conclusion...
>
> When we strike we must be absolutely ready, reaching our objectives with the speed of wildfire... we must sweep aside the paltry opposition we encounter and add lustre to the army's tradition of achieving a victory of annihilation.[11]

Not to be outdone, Bose, on the same day, encouraged the men of the INA on to 'Liberty or Death!', urging them while so doing to have the slogan *Chalo Delhi* ('Onward to Delhi') on their lips. On 7 March 1944 Tokyo Radio announced to the world that 'The March on Delhi has begun. Our victorious troops will be in Imphal by 27 March.'

27

Cock-up on the Tiddim Road

The geography of the great battle that raged across Manipur and the Naga Hills between March and August 1944 is not easy to follow.[1] The way Slim explained it was to use the analogy of spokes on a wheel. With Imphal as the hub, a spoke ran north to Kohima, one followed the line of the Iril River Valley, another the track north-east to Ukhrul and yet another along the road south-east to Tamu. The fifth spoke was the Tiddim road, and the sixth followed the track running west from Bishenpur to Silchar in Assam.

It was on the fifth spoke, the road from Tiddim to Imphal, that Slim's plans nearly came unstuck at the outset of the battle. That they didn't was due to the fighting abilities of 17 Indian Division, the rapidity of the response by Scoones and Roberts when they realized the extent of the threat to the division's withdrawal route from Tiddim, the ready availability of aerial resupply for the withdrawing division and the command failures of General Yanagida.[2] For Scoones, although the plan was to withdraw Cowan's division into Imphal, the question was when? He had been told by Slim (by means of ULTRA intercepts, although Scoones was never told the source) that Mutaguchi's main offensive would begin on 15 March. There wasn't any point in withdrawing Cowan much earlier than this, as the division was carrying out the important function of keeping the Japanese at bay in the Chin Hills. The problem was that this intelligence was only half of the story. In fact, Mutaguchi's plan was to launch 33 Division a week earlier, crossing the Manipur River on 7 March, and cutting the road to Tiddim in a number of places with the precise object of preventing an orderly withdrawal. On 7 March Colonel Sakuma's 214 Regiment began to cross the hills from Yazagyo on the Chindwin to cut the road where it crossed the Manipur River at Tongzang. The following day, the three battalions of Colonel Sasahara's 215 Regiment crossed the Manipur River 12 miles below Tiddim and began

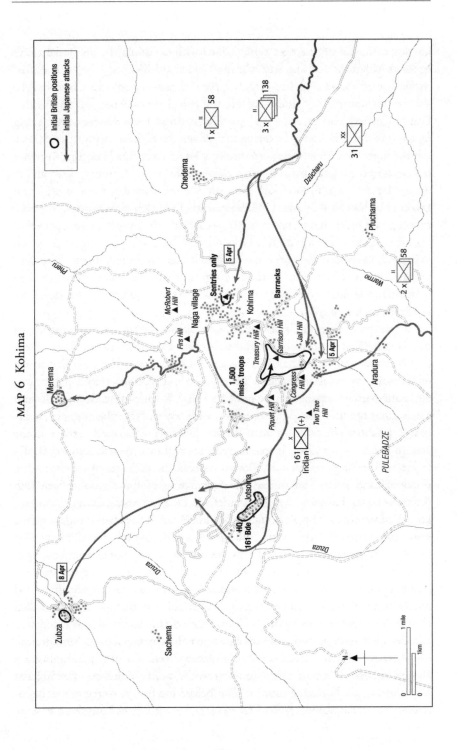

MAP 6 Kohima

Initial British positions
Initial Japanese attacks

moving upstream on the west bank, tasked with capturing the divisional stores depot at Milestone 109 and with placing a block at Milestone 100 – moves that would cut off Cowan's division from Imphal. Yanagida hoped that he might be able to cut the road to Tiddim before the British knew what was happening. Punch Cowan's patrols, however, quickly reported back the fact that strong Japanese forces appeared to be trying to outflank the division's forward positions. On the night of 8 March, Japanese probing attacks were made on British patrol positions in the hills above Tongzang, positioned there by Cowan to keep an eye on any Japanese attempt to block the road. On the same day, from information garnered by his patrols, Cowan told Scoones that an offensive was imminent and, expecting an order to return north, began carefully to prepare the withdrawal of his two brigades. This was no easy task, as many of his troops occupied positions in the hills to the east. Engineers demolished bridges over the Manipur River and prepared the destruction of parts of the precipitous mountain road they had spent many months labouring to construct. Stores, equipment and casualties were sent back to Imphal.

While it was increasingly obvious to Cowan that the Japanese opening moves had begun, Scoones discounted the possibility that this was the start of the decisive move against Imphal. This was a serious mistake, as it denied Cowan the opportunity to securely withdraw his division out of contact with the enemy. Not anticipating a Japanese move until 15 March at the earliest, Scoones did not believe that the time was right to order a withdrawal. Nevertheless, as each day passed a picture was built up by 17 Indian Division of Japanese activity to the west of the Manipur River. Increasingly concerned that his warnings to HQ IV Corps were falling on deaf ears, Cowan ordered the backloading of extraneous personnel and stores and started the preparation of the divisional area into defensive boxes. He knew that the Japanese 33 Division would attempt to cut off his line of withdrawal by blocking the Tiddim Road. It was their standard tactic. Thus surrounded, his units would fall prey to a slow defeat in detail. He needed no convincing that he had to make all speed back to the Imphal plain before his division was cut off completely. On 13 March, worried that he had not yet received orders from Scoones to withdraw, Cowan decided to act alone and ordered the full withdrawal of his division. At 8.40 p.m. that day, Scoones called Cowan by telephone and gave the long-awaited and undeniably late order to withdraw his division. Scoones then informed Slim by signal of the situation.[3]

Many subsequent accounts unfairly blame Cowan for not reacting quickly enough to Scoones' instructions.[4] In retrospect, Cowan should have been ordered to withdraw north, out of contact, long before the first Japanese moves began against him. That Scoones waited far too long very nearly endangered the entire battle, because it sucked in the corps reserve at the very beginning of the Japanese offensive, allowing Scoones no forces to counter any further surprise he might encounter elsewhere on the spokes of the Imphal wheel. It was one of several significant mistakes made by both Slim and Scoones in the early stages of the battle.

Scoones worked quickly to undo the harm he had created. He ordered the corps machine-gun battalion (9 Jats) to make all haste down the Tiddim Road from Imphal to Milestone 122, a bottleneck on the road where, just short of Tongzang, it crossed the Manipur River over a Bailey bridge. At the same time Major General Ouvry Roberts (the commander of 23 Indian Division) ordered Brigadier Vivian Collingridge's all-Gurkha 37 Brigade to deploy to assist Cowan, clearly suggesting that he thought Scoones was acting too slowly.[5] A day later, Scoones ordered 49 Brigade to the Tiddim Road as well. These two brigades, however, constituted the whole of Scoones' infantry reserve, and their deployment to the Tiddim Road meant that there was little left available for other emergencies. If 17 Indian Division and the two brigades sent to help their recovery got bogged down on the Tiddim Road, the whole plan for the defence of Manipur would collapse. With 17 Indian Division about to be embroiled in a fight for its life, and with a major part of this reserve assisting Cowan, Scoones' cupboard was suddenly bare. There was an urgent need for reinforcements to be moved into Imphal to replace those of 23 Indian Division now moving to positions on the Tiddim Road. How was this to be done? 5 Indian Division was not scheduled to arrive in Imphal from Arakan until mid-April, which would be far too late to alleviate the current crisis.

From the outset Cowan's withdrawal was a model of discipline and cool planning, despite the lateness of the withdrawal and the fact that the division would now be forced to fight its way out of the trap Mutaguchi had set for it. Surplus equipment was carefully destroyed, and on 13 March, as 63 Brigade began to march the 20 miles from Tiddim to Tongzang, 48 Brigade guarded the rear, setting extensive booby-traps to catch Japanese troops who might attempt to follow. Instructions had been given that the troops were to carry with them only a day's rations: transport aircraft from Air Commodore Vincent's No. 221 Group RAF would provide for all their needs by parachute as they withdrew.

The battle for the Tiddim Road lasted two weeks, the first actions against British warning posts guarding the hilltop approaches from the Chindwin on 10 March. In Rangoon the newspaper *Greater Asia* declared that 'the vanguard of the Indian National Army in close collaboration with a Nippon unit' (214 Regiment) had captured Tongzang. This was a reference to an incident six weeks before, on 29 January 1944, when an INA company had attacked the positions held by 7/10 Baluch in the hills east of Tiddim. They received a hostile reception from the Indian jawans (soldiers), who were contemptuous of those who had deserted the Indian Army. Compared with the ferocity of a Japanese assault, the INA attack was 'half-hearted. Our chaps jeered at them. We've come here to fight proper soldiers [they called out], not a lot of yellow deserters like you.'[6] The true intent of some INA soldiers was demonstrated occasionally. On 16 March at Milestone 125, a party of Gurkha 'Jifs'* surrendered to men of 1/7 Gurkha. It transpired that they had been captured in Burma in 1942 and this was their old battalion. The men had used their membership of the INA as a means of escape, never having had any inclination to fight with the Japanese, and sought to return to their regiment at the first available opportunity.

Japanese columns now seeped through the peaks and valleys to overlook Tongzang by 14 March. But, despite trying hard, they were not able to overcome any of the tiny, self-contained British positions. But the men of 17 Division could not defend everywhere, and on the night of 13 March troops of the Japanese 214 Regiment slipped into the valley and took possession of the Tuitum Saddle, an important piece of scrub-covered ground directly overlooking the road. By now the first troops of 63 Brigade – 1/10 Gurkha – had arrived at Tongzang along the road from the south and were immediately pressed into assaults to eject the Japanese from Tuitum. It was the first Japanese experience of a 14 Army all-arms assault, with infantry working closely with artillery (25-pounders and 3.7-inch mountain howitzers), coordinated with Hurricane strikes. To Japanese surprise they were swiftly expelled from their briefly held position.

By the time of this attack, 17 Indian Division was well on its way along the road from Tiddim, leaving the Japanese with no idea that they had gone. Yanagida had expected the British to stand and fight for these positions. It was only as Cowan's men moved into Tongzang 20 miles north that the Japanese attempted cautiously to probe the now vacated Tiddim defences. The extensive array of mines and booby-traps left severely delayed their plans. Several armoured vehicles were destroyed by mines on the roads around Tiddim, and it was not until 23 March that five tanks and two field artillery pieces managed to make their way into the village. During 18 March Cowan moved his two brigades through Tongzang in carefully choreographed leapfrog moves, with his vanguard, rear and flanks constantly protected against attack, ensuring that the support troops and vehicles were safely shepherded to safety.

---

*The formal British term for members of the INA: 'Japanese Indian Forces'.

On the road farther north, however, at Milestones 110 (Sakawng) and 100 (Singgel), Colonel Sasahara's 215 Regiment, moving fast along the west bank of the Manipur River, had secured positions along the road as early as 12 March, two days before 17 Indian Division had even begun its withdrawal from Tiddim. Scoones' action in despatching 37 Brigade, a squadron of Stuart light tanks from 7 Light Cavalry and the 36 Vickers medium machine guns of 9 Jats from Imphal came just in time and meant that the Japanese were now caught in a sandwich between Cowan pressing up from the south and Collingridge pressing down from the north.

On 18 March, Major Sueki's 3/215 captured the supply depot at Milestone 109, but not before some 2,700 non-combatants and several hundred soldiers, many from 9 Jats, had been spirited through the hills northward to safety. In the battle to secure the depot the Japanese lost 40 killed and 70 wounded, the accompanying INA company also losing heavily. To his surprise, Sueki found that he was now in possession of a vast supply of stores and 1,000 vehicles, although most had been immobilized. The pace of the battle was such that he had no time to enjoy his spoils. The RAF was paying him frequent visits and, a mile or two to the south, 48 Brigade, the vanguard of 17 Indian Division, was pressing against him hard.

To the north Collingridge now concentrated his forces in two boxes near Milestones 98 and 93. The positions secured at great cost forward of Milestone 100 were evacuated after three days of continuous fighting. Casualties were mounting after fierce hand-to-hand fighting, and food, water and ammunition were exhausted. Late on the evening of 17 March, the defenders slipped out of their position and reformed at the box at Milestone 98. The withdrawal coincided with the arrival of part of the fresh 49 Brigade at Milestone 82, which released the whole of 37 Brigade to clear the road between Milestones 82 and 98. For three days, Vengeance dive-bombers struck against the Japanese positions at Milestones 100 and 99. These efforts demonstrated to Japanese discomfiture an entirely new and surprising degree of competence from their foe. Infantry attacks were accompanied by the Stuart light tanks of 7 Cavalry simultaneous with the assault, rather than by the previously unsuccessful 'softening up' by artillery, mortars and fighter-ground attack. This was an unpleasant experience for the Japanese, who increasingly found themselves resorting to futile banzai charges in order to overcome the embarrassment of local reverses. On the morning of 22 March, at Fir Tree Hill at Milestone 99, an assault by a company of 3/19 Gurkha accompanied by tanks methodically destroyed all the Japanese trenches. Crawling up the slope, as each set of bunker positions was reached, the tanks lowered their guns to the lowest possible elevation and pumped their 37mm high-explosive rounds into the aperture. Slow progress was made, although the Japanese fought hard for every inch of ground, and a Japanese suicide bomber managed to throw himself onto a tank. The battle raged all day. The next morning, just as they were preparing to counterattack, a Hurribomber* strike broke up the Japanese assault party, and a 20mm round tore through Lieutenant Colonel Masakiro Irie, the dynamic commander of 1/215, killing him instantly. The following morning, 24 March, attacking from the south, two companies of 3/10 Gurkha managed to penetrate but not entirely secure the Japanese position.

The British continued to be supplied by air, an urgent request for 750 gallons of water, mortar bombs, ammunition and barbed wire being dropped accurately on the defensive box at Milestone 98 on 23 March. The Japanese had no such support. The ability of the USAAF and the RAF to supply their necessities from the air gave tremendous hope to the British, Indian and Gurkha troops of 17 Indian Division, and was a tangible sign of the resources that lay behind 14 Army.

While 37 Indian Brigade fought bitter battles to break through the blocks in the north, Cowan replenished his force at Tongzang. With great skill, C47s flew at low level down the valley over the next few days, dropping food and ammunition to the troops and the defensive positions built around the Tuitum Saddle. A major attack developed against positions held by two battalions on the night of 24 March, in which Japanese tanks attempted to bypass the position. Mines placed on the road destroyed all four tanks, however, and machine guns, firing on fixed lines in the dark to cover the minefield, killed the crews.

The vanguard of the division, Brigadier Ronnie Cameron's 48 Brigade, now began to infiltrate into the hills south of Milestone 109 from 20 March, sandwiching Sueki's force between them and the troops and tanks of 37 Brigade just to the north of Milestone 98. Seeking to outflank Sueki's defences, Cameron successfully attacked each Japanese position in turn in a series of fierce engagements across the hilltops, in which Gurkhas and British infantry demonstrated determined courage in the assault – together with well-coordinated artillery and air strikes – and the Japanese showed once more their penchant for fighting to the death. These battles proved the last gasps of Sueki's exhausted battalion. With no ammunition remaining, having had no food for several days, and after suffering very heavy casualties, Sueki on the early morning of 26 March was forced to vacate his positions overlooking the supply depot at

---

*A Hurribomber was a Hurricane fighter first converted for use in the ground-attack role in 1942, equipped with four 20mm cannon and two underwing 250lb (130kg) bombs.

Milestone 109. Virtually surrounded, he admitted that he could not have resisted another attack.

The message to Lieutenant General Yanagida's HQ on the night of 25 March from Colonel Sasahara suggested that the entire 3/215 had been destroyed, which meant that at least half of his force advancing on Imphal had not managed to progress any farther up the Tiddim Road than Milestone 109. This, of course, was an exaggeration, but Yanagida, who had never been convinced by Mutaguchi's plan, panicked. His private fears about the risks he was being asked to undertake flooded to the surface, and he sent a signal to Mutaguchi in which he expressed his disquiet about the operation. The original does not exist, but eyewitness reports suggest the following signal:

> The combat situation of 214 Regiment is not developing satisfactorily and discouraging reports are coming in from 215 Regiment. The capture of Imphal within three weeks is now impossible. The wet weather and lack of supplies will only lead to disaster. The strategic importance of Imphal has in any case been exaggerated. Accordingly, the 33 Division is unable to comply with the orders of 15 Army. I suggest that you give alternative orders so that some failure does not occur elsewhere.[7]

This extraordinary act of insubordination, in which Yanagida suggested that Operation *U-Go* be terminated, came as a thunderbolt to Mutaguchi, who furiously demanded that Yanagida comply with his instructions. The commander of 33 Division was in no mood to compromise, however, and refused to be bullied. Yanagida proceeded to advance on Imphal in a slow and deliberate fashion, eschewing the taking of risk and the opportunity for dash, allowing Cowan and Scoones to deal with the threat from Tiddim in an equally controlled and methodical manner. Unfortunately for Yanagida, his own headquarters was divided against him. Some supported their divisional commander, while others supported the chief staff officer, Colonel Tanaka Tetsujiro.

Tanaka had a poor opinion of Yanagida and regarded his superior's reaction to the fighting at Tongzang to be tantamount to moral failure. The two engaged in bitter argument that verged on insubordination by Tanaka, but Yanagida was too weak to discipline or dismiss him. Mutaguchi, enraged at what he regarded to be Yanagida's defeatism, began now to deliver instructions directly to Tanaka – a man of his own ilk – and to ignore Yanagida altogether. This disintegration of the senior command relationships augured badly for the mutual trust and confidence that are indispensable to the exercise of high command and which were essential to the achievement of Mutaguchi's plans.

Yanagida's extraordinary 'go slow' prompted Mutaguchi to send one of his trusted staff officers, Major Fujiwara Iwaichi – the same man who had originally commanded the F-Kikan in Malaya – to Tiddim to remonstrate with Yanagida and to order 33 Division to make all haste for Imphal, where the great prize of capturing the capital of Manipur awaited. Yet Yanagida ignored these instructions and continued to advance at a snail's pace, determined above all to preserve the integrity of his force. His caution was a boon to the British, allowing Cowan to withdraw in good order to the relative safety of the Imphal plain, and for Slim to reinforce Imphal.

With the road now open through to Milestone 105, Cowan ordered the demolition of the Manipur Bridge, farther south at Milestone 126, and the withdrawing convoys of his division pressed up to the recaptured supply depot at Milestone 109. Hurricanes flew low and dropped sandbags full of rotor arms for the disabled trucks, allowing many to be driven out. Most of the troops marched out of the broken Japanese trap, reaching the forward positions of 37 Brigade at Milestone 82 on 30 March, both 37 and 49 Brigades coming under Major General Cowan's direct command for the first time. The Japanese were known to have constructed a final block on the road in the vicinity of Milestone 72. This comprised the bulk of 2/213 battalion, which had descended on this part of the Tiddim Road after marching directly across the hills from the Chindwin in the east over the Mombi track. The men of 48 Brigade did not know it at the time, but this was the battalion that had decisively bettered the British at Rathedaung in Arakan the previous year. On this occasion, however, the Japanese proved no match for the determined troops of Cameron's brigade. After severe fighting, the road was cleared and the long convoys of ambulances and support vehicles began to flow directly into Imphal. Then, in a carefully managed leapfrog manoeuvre, Cowan guided his division to safety south of Imphal over the period between 2 and 4 April, with one brigade holding the rearguard, while the others (the division now temporarily comprised 37, 48, 49 and 63 Brigades) moved methodically from each position towards the safety of the Imphal outskirts.

By 5 April, with no further casualties, Cowan's entire division had arrived safely on the outskirts of Imphal, and 37 and 49 Brigades were able to re-join 23 Indian Division. Scoones now had his reserve again, and 17 Indian Division's 1,200 wounded were flown out to India. During these three weeks, Cowan's 16,000 troops, 2,500 vehicles and 3,500 mules had travelled slowly northwards, fighting their way through four major Japanese roadblocks, while elements of 37 and 49 Brigades, together with the Vickers medium machine guns of 9 Jats and a squadron of Indian light tanks of 7 Cavalry, had fought southwards from Imphal. The British had found themselves interspersed along the road with the Japanese, who attempted constantly to encircle and cut off the retreating British columns. 'The situation on the Tiddim road was now for a time as it had once been on the Arakan coast,' explained Slim, 'a Neapolitan ice of layers of our troops alternating with Japanese... But in both training and morale our men were much better fitted to deal with such a confused and harassing business than they had been in 1943.' Air support, both in terms of air supply in the closing days of the withdrawal, and of ground attack throughout it by No. 221 Group RAF, proved to be of considerable value to 17 Indian Division. 'Had our fighters not maintained continuous cover and given quick support at call,' Slim acknowledged, 'the withdrawal, if it could have been carried out at all, would have been a much grimmer and more protracted affair, with serious consequences to the main battle around Imphal.'

Despite the confusion evident at the start of the battle brought about by Scoones' strange unwillingness to order an early withdrawal, and the casualties suffered by the division, Cowan's fighting withdrawal from Tiddim, under constant pressure from the Japanese, was highly successful. Substantial delay had been imposed upon 33 Division, and the heavy casualties it suffered (probably 2,000) severely reduced its ability thereafter to break through to Imphal. Certainly, the morale of its commander was seriously compromised. Astonished at the unexpected ferocity of the resistance by the confident 17 Indian Division, as Cowan carefully and methodically shepherded his division back to Imphal, Yanagida did not throw his troops into the aggressive and unrestrained headlong charge that Mutaguchi demanded. Apoplectic with fury at Yanagida's persistent refusal to recognize the need for haste, Mutaguchi finally made his way by air to Yanagida's headquarters north of Tiddim on 22 April. The resulting confrontation with Yanagida left Mutaguchi physically shaking with rage. Yanagida's explanation to Mutaguchi's angry demand as to why his division was not yet in Imphal, namely that he was not strong enough to break through Cowan's defences, was instantly dismissed. Instructing Tanaka to ignore his divisional commander, as from henceforth orders would come to him instead, Yanagida was thereafter forced to look on helplessly as Mutaguchi commanded his division from afar. His agony lasted a month, until a replacement commander was found.

28

The Chindwin

Moreh and Tamu sit to the east and south-east of Manipur, where the jungle-clad mountains drop steeply first into the wide Kabaw Valley (through which flows the Yu River) before rising slightly and then falling again to meet the wide, muddy Chindwin. It was here that Gracey's three brigades watched and patrolled in the days that followed news of the Japanese attacks on the Tiddim Road. Two battalions of 100 Indian Brigade were deployed forward in the Kabaw Valley, dispersed on the tracks and high grounds that centred on the village of Witok, while a third battalion guarded the track over the steep Kuki-occupied hills to Mombi, which provided access to the Imphal plain. Farther forward, and closer to the Chindwin, lay the three battalions of 32 Brigade, while 80 Brigade, based in Sibong, was responsible for defending the road from Moreh to Tamu along the main track that led from the Chindwin into Imphal over the Shenam Saddle. The division was supported by the 25-pounders of 9 Field Regiment and the 5.5-inch medium guns of 8 Medium Regiment. Sixteen Lee-Grant tanks of 3 Carabiniers operated in troops of three tanks each to strengthen the dispersed infantry positions dotted across the network of tracks, hamlets, padi fields and clumps of trees that characterized the country on either side of the Yu River.

Scoones' initial plan to deny the Japanese access to the Imphal plain was to create three brigade-sized defensive positions in depth along the road between Moreh in the east, leading back to the rear brigade box on the Shenam Heights, the point at which the road dropped dramatically into the plain. Scoones concluded, in an appreciation of the operational situation on 29 February, that, in the event of an overwhelming Japanese offensive, his worst-case option would not be to fight 'forward', i.e., in the central Kabaw Valley where 20 Indian

Division was currently situated, but instead to concentrate the division 'around Moreh, the site of his divisional administrative base, and to fight a delaying action back to Shenam after covering the withdrawal of other units on the road. Shenam will be held to the last.' This way, Scoones argued logically and in accordance with Slim's overall strategic intent, the 'disadvantages of [a] long L of C [Line of Communication] will then fall on the Japanese'.[1] On receipt of the code word 'Wellington', the division would withdraw into these three 'boxes', the first in the foothills of the mountains in the area of Moreh (100 Brigade), the second around the crucial Lokchao Bridge at Sibong 15 miles behind on the road to Imphal (80 Brigade), and a third providing a backstop on the Shenam Heights (32 Brigade). It is apparent, given subsequent developments, that while Scoones informed Gracey fully about these immediate plans, he did not divulge to him his plans for the 'doomsday scenario' (i.e., the entire withdrawal of 20 Indian Division to the Shenam Heights). Perhaps he did not believe that it would ever lead to this. In any case, Gracey judged that, concentrated and with the prospects of many months' supplies to hand, his well-trained and highly motivated division could fight in its three boxes every bit as well as Messervy's 7 Indian had done at Sinzweya in February, if not better. The tangled, knotty jungle hills, riven with deep rocky gorges, were considered impassable to large numbers of invaders and were deemed, therefore, to strengthen the power of the defenders. The failure of Gracey to understand fully Scoones' plan for the battle, and, conversely, for Scoones not to articulate it clearly to Gracey, was one of the strange command failures to befall IV Corps at the start of the battle. Scoones didn't clearly communicate his plans with Cowan at Tiddim; nor did he do so with Gracey at Moreh.

From 9 March, the back loading began from the forward area to Imphal of the engineers, logisticians and non-combatants. The rapidly developing intelligence picture suggested that the Japanese blow against the belly of 20 Division in the Kabaw Valley would begin on 10 March, which happened to be, in Japan, National Army Day. But the only action that day was a surprise encounter by troops of 14/13 Frontier Force Rifles with a patrol of Bren-gun carriers, containing men of Colonel Kiani's 2 (Gandhi) Regiment of the INA. It was the first sign that INA units were in Mutaguchi's order of battle for the ensuing offensive. Three days later the first signs of Major General Yamamoto's striking force – four infantry battalions[2] – became evident as they crossed the Chindwin at Kalewa 40 miles to the south. There was nothing subtle about the Japanese approach. It was as if they wanted to be heard, perhaps to scare the defenders into a precipitate withdrawal. When the first attacks were made against

Witok, they came in as charges by large groups of infantrymen behind officers waving swords, proving easy prey to rifle, machine gun and artillery fire.

Undeterred by failure during the days that followed, the Japanese attempted to penetrate the stubborn Indian defences across a wide front, seeking those decisive points at which a successful infiltration could be transformed into an expanding torrent, and the irresistible force of the offensive overwhelm the enemy all the way across the hills into Imphal. But small groups of British tanks co-located with infantry in prepared positions during 15 March, pre-arranged artillery barrages on road junctions and potential forming-up points, together with carefully sited ambushes, all exacted their toll on the men of Yamamoto's force attempting to find a way through to Tamu.

While these fruitless assaults were underway, V Force and patrols of 1 Battalion, The Assam Regiment, and the Assam Rifles provided evidence of large-scale crossings of the Chindwin farther north on 14 March.[3] Mutaguchi's northern columns were now on the march, Yamauchi's 15 Division crossing at Thaungdut and Sittaung and Sato's 31 Division farther north at Homalin, Kawya and Tamanthi. At least 45,000 fighting troops, accompanied by many thousands of porters, made their way into the jungle-covered hills along the carefully reconnoitred paths towards Sangshak and Kohima.

It was now clear that a considerable Japanese operation was in play, as both 15 and 31 Divisions made multiple crossings of the Chindwin along a very wide frontage. It was time, Scoones decided, to withdraw 20 Indian Division into its three prepared defensive boxes. As they withdrew, most units fought intense actions with the advancing Japanese, including the first tank-on-tank battle between British and Japanese armour near Witok on 20 March. For the loss of one Lee-Grant, five Japanese Type-95s were left burning, with one captured intact. It was driven back to Imphal. Japanese infantry assaults on 20 Division's defensive positions during this withdrawal period were often reckless, displaying the attitude that the Japanese expected their advance into Assam to be a re-run of February 1942. But now the defenders – well coordinated with tanks and artillery – exacted a fearful toll on the cocksure Japanese. Japanese tactical carelessness cost them many unnecessary lives during these early skirmishes, as they attempted to use speed to overcome the British defences. An ambush by 3/8 Gurkha Rifles some miles down the track from Tamu caught a long column of Japanese soldiers marching to the front in threes, who were cut down in large numbers by the concentrated fire of the battalion's Bren guns, which had been brought together for the purpose. After the successful action at one of the boxes, codenamed 'Charing Cross', 32 Brigade was pulled back into Moreh the following morning, allowing 100 Brigade to withdraw farther back to Shenam. 20 Indian Division was thus ready in its prepared positions, the men confident that they could take on whatever the Japanese were to throw at them.

In the days that followed, the Japanese fought increasingly desperately to squeeze Moreh dry. Attacks took place by day and night, the Japanese employing infiltration raids by infantry and armour as well as 'jitter' raids by INA soldiers designed to reveal their positions. Nevertheless 32 Brigade withstood these attacks, and a feeling of superiority developed, although the Japanese had considerable artillery support (including huge 155mm guns) against Moreh, employing it very accurately.

The operations to withdraw 20 Indian Division to its three brigade boxes went largely according to plan. But the orderliness of Gracey's withdrawal to the Tamu Road positions hid a fundamental problem for Scoones, who had assumed that a Japanese offensive would require the use of roads, principally those that led to Imphal from both Tamu and Tiddim. By concentrating his defensive effort around these routes, he risked leaving open significant gaps in IV Corps' defences in areas of steep hills and deep jungle, gaps that were ruthlessly exploited by Mutaguchi. In the south-east, the Japanese Army commander placed Yamamoto and his armour on the Tamu front in an attempt to punch through 20 Indian Division and use the road to gain access to Imphal. This front was also the focus of an operational deception that succeeded completely in reinforcing Scoones' perceptions of Japanese intentions. To the north of the Imphal–Tamu Road, through horrendous terrain regarded by Scoones as impassable to large bodies of troops, Mutaguchi was going to thrust a strong column of 15 Division, to attack Imphal from the north.

Unlike Scoones, Mutaguchi had done his homework and knew that this terrain was far from impassable. His spies had told him that the British were close to completing the construction of a jeep track through the hills between Humine and Imphal. It seems that no one in Scoones' headquarters ever considered this track to be a potential invasion route. Mutaguchi had a contrary view, informed by a series of very effective long-range patrols that for at least six months had been scouring the hills for tracks, measuring bridges and fords and identifying ways in which a division, together with its supporting arms and services, could make its way across the hills to Imphal and Kohima. Mutaguchi's plan was to cut the Imphal–Kohima Road 15 miles north of the vast British supply depot at Kanglatongbi, and then to drive down on the Imphal plain along the route Kamjong, Sangshak and Litan, the latter of which was the site of the HQ of 23 Indian Division. Mutaguchi hoped that the British, distracted by the battles for the Tamu Road, would not even notice his feint to the north. He was right. What Mutaguchi had not counted on, however, was that Yamauchi's force would be seriously weakened before the offensive began, by British air raids on 15 Division's concentration areas. Yamauchi was further hampered by the slowness in getting his third regiment (67 Regiment) to the Chindwin in time for the start of the offensive, because of British bombing of the railway lines up through Burma from Thailand. He was forced to begin his crossing on 15 March with only 51 and 60 Regiments – totalling perhaps 20,000 troops – themselves both sorely depleted by attacks from the air.

To compound British failings, the territory through which this track ran (centring on Ukhrul), had only the lightest of garrisons and no real defences. Until 16 March it was home to 49 Brigade, despatched to the Tiddim Road. The brigade had considered itself to be in a rear area, and, extraordinarily, no dug-in and wired defensive positions had been prepared. It was one of the most serious planning failures of the campaign. The entire north-eastern spoke of Slim's Imphal wheel lay undefended. The gap left by the brigade's departure had been filled in part by the arrival of the first of the two battalions of the newly raised and part-trained 50 Indian Parachute Brigade (comprising the Gurkha 152 Battalion and the Indian 153 Battalion), whose young and professional commander, 31-year-old Brigadier M.R.J. ('Tim') Hope-Thomson, had persuaded the powers-that-be in New Delhi to allow him to complete the training of his brigade in territory close to the enemy. The area north-east of Imphal was regarded as suitable merely for support troops and training. At the start of March, the brigade HQ and one battalion had arrived in Imphal and began the leisurely process of shaking itself out in the safety of the hills north-east of the town. To the brigade was added 4/5 Mahrattas under Lieutenant Colonel Trim, left behind when 49 Brigade was sent down to the Tiddim Road. To Scoones and his HQ, the area to which Hope-Thomson and his men were sent represented the lowest of all combat priorities. Sent into the jungle almost to fend for themselves, it was not expected that they would have to fight, let alone be on the receiving end of an entire Japanese divisional attack. They had little equipment, no barbed wire, and little or no experience or knowledge of the territory. No one considered it worthwhile to keep them briefed on the developing situation. To all intents and purposes, 50 Indian Parachute Brigade was an irrelevant appendage, attached to Roberts' 23 Indian Division for administrative purposes but otherwise left to its own devices.

Before long, information began to reach Imphal that Japanese troops were advancing in force on Ukhrul and Sangshak. Inexplicably, however, this information appeared not to ring any warning bells in HQ IV Corps, which was preoccupied with the developing threat in the Tamu area where the main Japanese thrust was confidently predicted. It was, perhaps understandably, unwilling to consider information that appeared to tell a story different to its own preconceived notion that an attack would only develop from well south of Imphal. On the night of 16 March, the single battalion of 50 Parachute Brigade took over responsibility for the Ukhrul area from 49 Brigade, which was hastily departing for the Tiddim Road. They had no idea that an entire Japanese division of 20,000 men was crossing the Chindwin in strength opposite Homalin. On 19 March, large columns of Japanese infantry were reported advancing through the hills. No one had expected them to be where they were. But the first shock came to the Japanese 3/58 battalion (Major Shimanoe), part of Sato's 31 Division – troops whose objective was Kohima, and not Imphal – who were bloodily rebuffed by the determined opposition of the young Gurkha soldiers at an unprepared position forward of Sheldon's Corner. The 170 Gurkha recruits refused to allow the 900 men of 3/58 to roll over them and inflicted 160 casualties on the advancing Japanese. In the swirling confusion of the next 36 hours, Hope-Thomson and his staff kept their heads, attempting to concentrate what remained of the dispersed companies of 152 Battalion and 4/5 Mahrattas back to a common position at the village of Sangshak, which dominated the tracks south-west to Imphal. It was at this now-deserted Naga village that Hope-Thomson, on 21 March, decided to group his brigade for its last stand, his staff desperately attempting to alert HQ IV Corps in Imphal to the enormity of what was happening to the north-east. No one seemed to be listening. Urgent pleas for rations and, above all, for barbed wire, fell on deaf ears as the Japanese columns infiltrated quickly around and through the British positions, heading in the direction of Litan. The Japanese now began days of repeated assaults on the position in a battle of intense bravery and sacrifice for both sides. Hope-Thompson's men could only dig shallow trenches, which provided no protection from Japanese artillery.[4] Like all Naga villages, Sangshak was perched on the hill and had no water: anything the men required had to be brought up from the valley floor, through the rapidly tightening Japanese encirclement.[5]

Major General Miyazaki decided that he needed to eliminate the defenders of Sangshak, probably because they posed a threat to his long lines of supply and communication to Kohima, despite the fact that he knew Sangshak to lie not in his, but in 15 Division's area of responsibility. Accordingly, he despatched both the Second Battalion (2/58, commanded by Major Nogoya) as well as 3/58 to Sangshak where they arrived late on 22 March. Hoping to overwhelm the defenders, the Japanese attacked immediately, throwing infantry forward into the assault without undertaking a detailed reconnaissance of the enemy position, or waiting for the arrival of supporting artillery. It was a serious error. The 400 waiting Gurkhas of 153 Battalion could not believe the sight before them as, facing north-west across the valley to West Hill in the failing light of early evening, a swarming mass of enemy rushed to overwhelm what they had imagined to be weak and puny defences. Wave after wave of enemy were cut down as they ran down the slopes of the hill, into the precision fire of 153's Lee-Enfields and the chattering Vickers firing above and behind them. In addition to the four mountain guns, Hope-Thomson's brigade was also blessed with 3-inch mortars. In fact, 8 Company of 2/58 lost 90 men from a total of 120, including Captain Ban, its company commander, in the space of 15 minutes. They learned their lesson, however, and the defenders of Sangshak never again faced such ripe targets. Instead, as the days drew out, they were subjected to increasingly frantic Japanese efforts to break into Hope-Thomson's position. Although the weight of Japanese attacks tended to be on the north and west of the perimeter facing 152 and 153 Battalions, as the days went by increasingly strong probes were made against the Mahrattas on the eastern edge.

Hope-Thomson's men found themselves alone and faced by heavy odds. Fortunately, however, and at long last, Imphal had now awoken to the enormity of the threat on its north-eastern perimeter, Roberts signalling to Hope-Thomson on 24 March, five days after the first appearance of the Japanese, 'Well done indeed. You are meeting the main Jap northern thrust. Of greatest importance you hold your position. Will give you maximum air support.'[6] Gallant attempts to drop precious water to the beleaguered troops, as well as ammunition for the mortars and mountains guns, largely failed, as much as three-quarters of these valuable cargoes frustratingly floating down to the Japanese. Unfortunately, with no barbed wire, no water and rapidly diminishing reserves of ammunition, the long-term prognosis for the hugely outnumbered 50 Indian Parachute Brigade was never in doubt if Miyazaki decided to delay his advance to Kohima in order to crush the defenders. The final day came on Saturday 26 March. With the sun beating down mercilessly on the parched defenders, the Japanese closed in from all sides, with bullet, bayonet and grenade, desperate to break the hold that the defenders had placed on 31 Division's advance. In a day of fierce attack and counterattack across the Sangshak Plateau, the brigade lost more men than in the fighting so far. That night HQ IV Corps recognized the inevitable and ordered the survivors to break out and make their way as best they could – over the hills crawling with Japanese – to Imphal. The immovable wounded, some

150 men, had to be left behind, and the remaining 300 wounded had to walk out with the rest.

While 50 Parachute Brigade was virtually destroyed in the four days of the Sangshak battle (152 Gurkha Battalion lost 350 men – 80 per cent of its strength – and 153 Indian Battalion lost 35 per cent), considerable benefit fell to IV Corps by their sacrifice. The battle cost Miyazaki probably 1,000 casualties and his advance was held up for a week, causing serious delay to Sato's plans. From both 2/58 and 3/58, Miyazaki had lost six of his eight company commanders, as well as most of the platoon commanders. Miyazaki's speculative attack on Sangshak drew him into an unnecessary battle of attrition that delayed the journey of his column to Kohima and proved in time to be a serious setback to Mutaguchi's hopes of capturing all of his objectives within three weeks. It was a common problem among Japanese commanders, who repeatedly sought battle for the glory of it. It would have been far better to have left Hope-Thompson's brigade where it was and hurried on to their objective. The parachute brigade could then have been dealt with later. Too often, however, Japanese commanders failed to understand the nature of military strategy, and to differentiate between the strategic task and the tactics required for its achievement. Something – *bushido* perhaps – acted as a magnet to the egos of some Japanese commanders, dragging them into unnecessary fights to sate their need for blood and glory. The British and Indian armies by 1944 were often able to achieve success by understanding this death-cult imperative, and giving the Japanese the opportunity they desired to die for their country. It was the first sign on this front that Mutaguchi's plan was failing: the British at first seemed intent on flight, but here was stubborn – even fanatical – resistance, and it took the Japanese by surprise. The battle also gave Slim and Scoones valuable breathing space to reorganize and reinforce the Imphal positions, although it seems clear that a significant intelligence coup at Sangshak was not exploited by the British. A map taken from the dead body of a Japanese captain describing Sato's entire strategy in the north and his plans to surround Kohima and to make for Dimapur, was copied and smuggled out of encirclement to HQ IV Corps in Imphal. Unfortunately, it disappeared and was never seen again. Slim received no benefit from this extraordinary stroke of intelligence.

The bitter struggle at Sangshak led Scoones belatedly to an awareness of the danger posed to Imphal from the north-east. On 25 March, his Chief of Staff sent an urgent signal to Gracey warning him that he might have to relinquish one of his brigades in order to bolster the weak sector to the north, through which, if 50 Indian Parachute Brigade gave way at Sangshak, the whole approach to

Imphal lay open. This would mean that Gracey would have to withdraw farther back towards Shenam, and relinquish the defence of the foothills around Moreh. Gracey was taken unawares by the proposition and did not receive it warmly. His division had successfully completed a difficult withdrawal to its new positions between Moreh and Shenam, and he did not view kindly the prospect of another, particularly one that appeared to be the result of poor forward planning. He complained bitterly to Scoones by letter on 26 March:

> This division has fought magnificently so far, and all the troops have been fully aware of the necessity of withdrawing to their present position, with the Army Commander's assurance that behind them is a pile-up of reserves rapidly being reinforced to deal with the situation behind them. Our morale is sky high, as we have beaten the enemy and given him a real bloody nose everywhere. Everyone is prepared to hang on where they are now like grim death. It is their Verdun. It will be most shattering to morale if they are now asked to assist in the Imphal plain and they will feel that someone has let them down.[7]

Gracey was particularly reluctant to abandon Moreh, but the Sangshak battle left Scoones with little choice, as 20 Indian Division was now in danger of being outflanked by the Japanese 15 Division's assault on Imphal from the north-east. If Yamauchi were successful in penetrating the Imphal plain, the whole defence of Imphal would unravel and Gracey's defences at Shenam would become irrelevant. Scoones undoubtedly made the right decision. If he is to be criticized, it is for failing to keep Gracey informed about the overall situation from the outset. Gracey had no option but to withdraw farther west towards Shenam. After destroying virtually everything that remained, 32 Brigade withdrew from Moreh, with the Japanese at their heels, at the end of the month. 80 and 100 Brigades occupied positions between Shenam and Tengnoupal, about 9 miles from Palel, while 32 Brigade was withdrawn into corps reserve. 20 Indian Division now held a 25-mile front from Tengnoupal through Shenam to Shuganu, 15 miles south-west of Palel. Gracey's new plan was to defend a number of fortified boxes on the high ground on Shenam Ridge and keep the road to Shenam and thence Palel open, rather than to hold the whole of his 25-mile front in its entirety. Intensive patrolling was to cover the gaps.

Slim's fears for the security of Imphal were magnified suddenly by Cowan's unexpected withdrawal from Tiddim in contact with the enemy on 13 March, and the loss to Scoones over the following days of the major part of his corps reserve. With 17 Indian Division potentially no longer available to defend Imphal, Scoones' reserve already engaged on the Tiddim Road and Gracey's division about to be fully occupied in the Kabaw Valley, Slim knew that the only way he could prevent Imphal from being overwhelmed was by the rapid and substantial reinforcement of IV Corps. Had Mutaguchi been successful, it would undoubtedly have resulted in one of the most serious reverses of British arms in the war. That Slim was conscious of the need to reinforce Imphal is demonstrated by the orders he had already given to fly in Briggs' 5 Indian Division from Arakan when the situation on that front had stabilized. He had also approached Giffard for extra reinforcements to protect the base area at Dimapur from any long-range Japanese penetration through the Naga Hills, and for additional troops. Giffard, however, regarded Slim's request as impossible because no transport was available. When, on 10 March 1944, Mountbatten visited Slim's headquarters at Comilla and discovered that Giffard had not acted on Slim's demand to move troops urgently to Imphal, he was furious.

The only way that troops could be delivered to the threatened areas in Assam in days rather than weeks and months was by air. Slim, however, had no transport aircraft at all, although in SEAC considerable numbers of American aircraft were of course ploughing their way every day to China over the Hump. By September 1943, the USA had provided 15 squadrons (amounting to 230 C47 and C46 aircraft) for the airlift, flying from airfields in north-east Assam, as part of Air Marshal John Baldwin's 3 Tactical Air Force. These aircraft were the solution to Slim's sudden predicament. On the morning of 14 March – when the Japanese were falling on Witok – Slim and Baldwin met Mountbatten at Comilla airport, explained the grave and unexpected situation facing IV Corps, and asked that some of these aircraft be diverted to reinforce Imphal. 'If we lost the Imphal–Kohima battle,' Slim reasoned, 'the Hump route would be closed. It seemed obvious therefore that it would be madness not to divert some of the China airlift to the vital needs of the Fourteenth Army.'

Realizing the critical nature of the sudden emergency, Mountbatten immediately and on his own initiative agreed to do what Slim had requested. He had, in fact, no authority to do anything of the kind, responsibility for tasking these aircraft sitting very firmly with the US Chiefs of Staff in Washington. Indeed, he had previously been instructed by Roosevelt not to divert these aircraft to any other use. But with no time to lose, he decided to use the aircraft first and ask permission later. On the same day, Mountbatten instructed Giffard to waste no time in reinforcing 14 Army with elements of the army group reserve when Slim requested them – Lieutenant General Montagu Stopford's XXXIII Corps, the major part of which was the well-equipped and experienced British 2 Division,[8] then in training on the other side of India near Bombay. This formidable division (4, 5 and 6 Brigades,[9] comprising nine infantry battalions, a machine-gun battalion, reconnaissance regiment, three field regiments of artillery (25-pounders), an anti-aircraft/anti-tank regiment and masses of supporting services) was home to a roll call of battalions from some of Britain's most famous county regiments: the Queen's Own Cameron Highlanders, Durham Light Infantry, Worcestershire Regiment, Royal Scots, Royal Norfolk Regiment, Lancashire Fusiliers, Dorsetshire Regiment, Royal Welch Fusiliers and the Royal Berkshire Regiment.

That evening Slim quantified his requirement for aircraft, sending Mountbatten a request for no fewer than 260 C47 sorties to get each of the three brigades (9, 123 and 161) of Briggs's 5 Indian Division to Imphal in time to prevent a possible disaster. When, on the next day – 15 March – Slim discovered during a visit to Imphal that Scoones had been forced to send Collingridge's 49 Brigade to the Tiddim Road in addition to 37 Brigade, the seriousness of the situation was reinforced. Slim therefore sent another message to Mountbatten asking urgently for 25–30 aircraft to be made available in two days' time, to be retained until 20 April. Mountbatten immediately agreed. Slim then proceeded on 17 March to give orders for the air move of the whole of 5 Indian Division. A day later, from Dohazari airfield near Chittagong, the battalions of 123 Brigade began the fly-in. Flying two sorties a day, the division was flown into Imphal and Dimapur in the period through to 29 March.

Mountbatten's courage in unilaterally taking aircraft from the Hump to meet the needs of the battle when he had no authority to do so was a critical factor in the successful defence of Manipur. Washington could do little but retrospectively agree Mountbatten's fait accompli on 17 April, authorizing the diversion as a temporary measure to overcome the crisis of the moment. Retaining these aircraft to maintain the airlift into Imphal in order to sustain IV Corps, in addition to the fly-in of 5 and then 7 Indian Division (which was flown to Assam, to support the Kohima front) as rapid reinforcements, was an altogether different problem. On 23 March, Slim wrote to Giffard stressing the need to increase the air supply to 14 Army in the event of Imphal being cut off. With land routes cut, an air bridge was the only way in which IV Corps could be supplied. Slim warned Giffard that if the aircraft supporting IV Corps were withdrawn, he could not be responsible for the consequences. Mountbatten needed no second urging, appealing immediately to Washington for another 70 aircraft to supply IV Corps while it lay besieged. This was no easy thing for the Chiefs of Staff to agree, as there was intense pressure on the limited number of transport aircraft across all theatres of war at the time. But Mountbatten refused to budge. Churchill signalled Mountbatten, giving his support, 'Chiefs of Staff and I are backing you to the full, I have telegraphed the President [that] in my view nothing matters but the battle – be sure you win.' Mountbatten won the argument, and the return of the aircraft was deferred until 15 June.

Even before Slim had come to him on 14 March with his urgent request for air transport, Mountbatten had been exercised by the need to increase the flow of reinforcements to Imphal. Privately he believed that Giffard was not doing enough to ensure that Slim had the resources he required to fight the forthcoming battle. On 5 March, Slim had asked Giffard for a division to defend Dimapur and to provide rapid reinforcement for Kohima and Imphal should it be required. The obvious solution was to send forward the bulk of Stopford's XXXIII Corps from India to relieve an experienced Indian Division in Arakan, and to transfer that division to the Naga Hills. Giffard was concerned, however, that moving an additional division from India would place intolerable burden on the Assam railway. A compromise was reached. Slim was given the two battalions of 50 Indian Parachute Brigade, and Giffard promised him 2 Division should it become necessary. Slim admitted later that this 'was by no means what I asked for', although he recognized Giffard's concerns about exacerbating the already significant supply problem on the Assam line of communication and on the Imphal plain.

Shortly afterwards, Giffard agreed also to give Slim 23 Brigade, commanded by Brigadier Lancelot Perowne, part of the now-dismantled 70 Division allocated to support Wingate's Operation *Thursday*. 'He agreed to rail it to Jorhat,' Slim recalled, 'where I could place it as a mobile force to cover the railway to Ledo, and, if necessary, use it against the flank of an attack on Dimapur.' On 18 March, Slim decided to ask Giffard for the army group reserve – XXXIII Corps – to be sent to Dimapur, at the same time confirming his request for 2 Division to go to Chittagong to replace 5 Indian Division, which was even then beginning to fly into the Imphal plain. Giffard accepted Slim's request for 23 Brigade and decided that, once the airlift of 5 Indian Division was complete, 7 Indian Division would then also be airlifted to Manipur from Arakan. He didn't authorize the immediate movement of 2 Division, however, perhaps because he remained concerned about the pressure the transfer of the division would place on India's creaking railway infrastructure. It was a serious mistake. On 27 March, when the commander of the British 2 Division, Major General John Grover, received a signal from Slim asking that he take his division post-haste to Arakan, to relieve one of the two Indian Divisions (5 and 7) beginning preparations to move themselves to the Imphal battlefield, it came as a surprise. But with remarkable alacrity Grover entrained his division and rushed it east. It was only when the entire division was entrained, sitting outside Calcutta on 31 March, that their destination was changed. Instead of Arakan, their terminus was now Dimapur.

The initial plan was for 2 Division to protect Dimapur, while 161 Brigade did what was necessary to defend Kohima. But two days later, as 2 Division began to arrive into Dimapur from the Brahmaputra ferry in dribs and drabs, the panic surrounding the threat to the Brahmaputra Valley had, if anything, increased, and the first two battalions of 5 Brigade were moved into the foothills of the Naga Hills to block the road to Kohima. The brigade was warned to prepare for a minimum seven-day battle. In the early days following their arrival, confusion was widespread. Were they to protect Dimapur from attack? If so, how? Or were they to push into the hills to engage with the Japanese who were expected to debouch into the valley at any moment? As the days unfolded and Sato built up his strength at Kohima, the situation became somewhat clearer: the immediate threat was to Kohima, not to Dimapur.

The 25 aircraft secured by Mountbatten to support IV Corps in Imphal (i.e., those additional to the ones used from 18 March to execute the fly-in of 5 Indian Division from Arakan) were unable to begin their airlift into Manipur until mid-April. When the airlift began, it put pressure on supplies at Imphal. It would take time to build up combat supplies on the plain given that the immediate priority was to fly in troops. Scoones cut the ration scale by a third and began flying out 43,000 non-combatants and 13,000 casualties to India by means of returning aircraft. Baldwin's 3 Tactical Air Force began Operation *Stamina* on 18 April, but it took some time to build up to the daily deliveries required – 540 tons – into Imphal. By contrast, as Slim had predicted, the Japanese supply situation became increasingly precarious. In his assessments of possible British reactions to Operation *U-Go*, Mutaguchi could have had no inkling of the dramatic power air transport would give to his enemy to move troops around the battlefield. Certainly he could not have expected the rapid transfer of two whole divisions from Arakan to Imphal and Kohima – and the arrival of a third by train, crossing the entire sub-continent in less than a week – to meet the threat posed by the sudden onset of his offensive.

29

Thermopylae in the Naga Hills

Travelling from Dimapur at the foot of the Naga Hills, the final stretch of the road into Kohima climbs steeply up the western edge of the Kohima Ridge, curving tightly across a deep, 2-mile-wide valley separating the Pulebadze Ridge that dominates the right (southern) side and Naga Hill on the northern, atop of which lies the old Naga (sometimes also called Kohima village). Possession of Naga Hill and the ridge that runs due west to Merema (i.e., parallel to the road from Dimapur on the northern side of the valley) allows observation of the northern edge of Kohima Ridge (comprising 'Summerhouse' or Garrison Hill – all terms used interchangeably then as now), and the High Spur or Indian General Hospital (IGH) Spur, as well as a considerable portion of the road that snakes back in the direction of Jotsoma and Zubza. On the ridge itself, after passing the IGH on the right-hand side, the road bends around the ridge and bifurcates at a junction known as the Traffic Control Point (TCP), filtering the road left and up the hill to Naga Village (through what is now Kohima town), while the main road continues around the eastern side of the ridge and on to Imphal. The slopes leading up to the ridge from the valley floor at this point are savagely abrupt and covered in thick jungle. On the northern side of the Kohima Ridge, across a thin saddle connecting the two, Naga Village sits atop a vast rounded hill, as broad and as wide again as Kohima Ridge, and standing much higher. From the top of Naga Village, one can look directly across the valley well over a mile to the Deputy Commissioner's bungalow on Garrison Hill.

The Kohima Ridge is an enormous physical barrier, especially so to an army intent on moving farther west towards Dimapur; consequently, its defence and retention are critical if this route is to be barred to an invader. In 1944, the thickly forested Kohima Ridge was home to the scattered support depots and stores necessary to sustain a small peacetime garrison swollen since 1942 by the pressures of war in Burma and the town's location on the road between Dimapur and Imphal. Considerable quantities of stores, workshops, transport companies, a bakery, hospital and a rest camp dotted the hills. Kohima was also the headquarters of 3 Assam Rifles and of the Shere Regiment of the Royal Nepalese Army. Charles Pawsey MC, the Deputy Commissioner for Nagaland since 1935, veteran of the Western Front and one of the few honorary civilian members of V Force, lived in a bungalow on the northernmost slopes, the driveway to his house winding down the hill to touch the main Imphal–Dimapur Road at the TCP. A short walk above the bungalow was a tennis court, which had been built for the Deputy Commissioner's relaxation, the scene of some of the savage fighting to.[1]

On the remainder of the ridge was 53 Indian General Hospital on the north-western slopes overlooking the road from Dimapur, a Field Supply Depot, and the Detail Issue Stores (DIS). Overlooking the entire ridge from the south-eastern end was a distinctive pimple known as Jail Hill, named after the local prison that lay at its base. The highest point of the ridge was Kuki Picquet. Dominating all these features from a greater distance are the 9,000-foot-high mountains of the Japfü Range on the southern side of the valley, projecting their shadow over the whole of the Kohima area. These hills run parallel to the valley which rises into Kohima from Dimapur. As one approaches from Dimapur, the first point of high ground is Jotsoma, 2 miles from Kohima and enjoying a clear view of the ridge. Leaving the road and heading up the hillside to the right, a stiff three-hour climb carries one to the top of Mount Pulebadze (7,522 feet). Behind Pulebadze, a track crosses the saddle over to the top of Aradura, and spurs flow down northwards into the eastern side of Kohima. In the foothills of these spurs sit, among others, the deeply forested Congress Hill and General Purpose Transport (GPT) Ridge, all of which offer sight of, and dominate, Kohima Ridge from the south. If an enemy could control the whole of Kohima Ridge, it would be in command of the route into Dimapur, the gatehouse to India. If the Japanese could simultaneously occupy Naga Village, the ridge could be observed from two sides. There was virtually no part of the ridge that was not dominated in some way by another feature or could not be fired at or observed from elsewhere. It could easily be surrounded (although the western slope was extremely steep), and without water could not hold out for long. In fact, it was, in conventional terms, indefensible. Because of this no real thought had been given to its protection.

It was at Kohima that the British came close to losing the battle for India.[2] In 1944 the importance of Kohima – obvious to all who had visited the ridge and seen its dominating position on the single mountainous road between Manipur and the Brahmaputra Valley – was not appreciated by those responsible for the defence of India. The mountain town lay 120 miles beyond the Chindwin, across formidably mountainous terrain far beyond where anyone expected the Japanese might be able to reach in strength. If they did advance into the Naga Hills, the British assumed that the most the Japanese could infiltrate was a regiment (i.e., three battalions of infantry, the equivalent of a British brigade). The ridge guards the only route between Dimapur and Imphal: if Kohima fell, Imphal would be without access to succour or supplies. In any case, Slim believed that the real prize, were the Japanese to penetrate this far, was Dimapur and its vast depots and rail link to the north. What would the Japanese gain by securing Kohima if they failed to seize the British supplies in Dimapur? It made no sense to Slim for the Japanese to attack Kohima without also pressing on to threaten Dimapur. The need to defend Kohima was less urgent in this analysis than defending Dimapur.

Giffard, Slim and Scoones met together in Imphal on 20 March to consider the impending crisis. As yet, they did not know the true scale of the imminent threat to Kohima. Slim claims that he had realized within a week of the start of the offensive (i.e., by 22 March) that the situation at Kohima was likely to be more dangerous than he had anticipated. It seems clear, however, that even by early April he had still not realized that the bulk of Sato's 31 Division was pushing on to the town. If he had known this, he would undoubtedly have defended the ridge robustly to prevent its capture. Even without this knowledge, the situation was grave. Cowan's 17 Indian Division and the major part of Roberts' 23 Indian Division were fully engaged on the Tiddim Road, Gracey's 20 Indian Division was withdrawing in contact with the enemy to Moreh, and Hope-Thomson's unprepared and weakened 50 Parachute Brigade had suddenly and unexpectedly been confronted by large numbers of enemy in the Ukhrul area the day before. In addition, enemy forces were known to be at least moving on Kohima, and it was assumed that the Japanese were likewise closing in on Silchar to the south-west.

Certain that Scoones now had enough on his plate with the defence of Imphal, Slim gave temporary responsibility for the defence of Dimapur and Kohima to Major General Ranking, commander of 202 Line of Communication Area. Ranking was to transfer responsibility to Stopford when the latter arrived with XXXIII Corps in early April. When fully constituted, the corps was to comprise 5 and 7 Indian Divisions and the British 2 Division. On 22 March, Slim ordered a scratch garrison under the experienced and capable Colonel Hugh

Richards to move forward to Kohima to act as a forward defence for Dimapur. Richards was a fighting soldier with a fine reputation who had recently been released from the Chindits because Wingate believed anyone over 40 to be too old for his Special Force (i.e. Chindit) operations (Richards was 50 and Wingate was 40). On the same day, Slim briefed Stopford at Comilla. When, exactly a week later, 'Daddy' Warren's experienced 161 Brigade also arrived from Arakan, Slim sent it directly to Kohima to assist in the defence of the ridge.[3] Slim told Warren that he expected the Japanese to arrive at Kohima by 3 April and to reach Dimapur by 10 April, by which time only one Brigade of 2 Division would have arrived to support the defence of this strategically vital base area.

Stopford's plan was to concentrate his corps as it arrived at Jorhat, 65 miles north-east of Dimapur, ready to launch a counterstroke against Dimapur if, in the meantime, the base had been occupied or was under attack. One brigade of 2 Division would be despatched as soon as it arrived to hold the Nichugard Pass, 8 miles south-east of Kohima on the road to Dimapur. Finally, Perowne's 23 Brigade would be diverted to the defence of Kohima. Expected to arrive on 12 April, it would be used to strike north of Kohima and to the east of it to disrupt and cut the Japanese line of communication back to the Chindwin.

On 29 March, the Japanese 31 Division cut the Imphal–Kohima Road at Milestone 72. The race to feed units into Dimapur before the arrival of the Japanese was now one of dramatic urgency. Giffard's slowness in bringing XXXIII Corps forward to the Brahmaputra Valley now threatened to have dangerous repercussions for Slim. 'Even when these moves were in hand my anxiety was hardly lessened,' he recalled. 'They would take time – and time was short. It was a race between the Japanese onrush and the arrival of our reinforcements.' Characteristically, Slim accepted responsibility for mistakes that were not of his making. 'As I struggled hard to redress my errors and to speed by rail and air these reinforcements I knew that all depended on the steadfastness of the troops already meeting the first impetus of the attack. If they could hold until help arrived, all would be well; if not, we were near disaster.'

With Stopford's troops still several days away, following their diversion from Chittagong, the question of how to defend Kohima and Dimapur became critical. There was no simple solution, as the sum total of experienced combat troops available before Grover's 2 Division arrived was Warren's 161 Brigade (1/1 Punjab, 4/7 Rajputs and 4 Royal West Kents). On 29 March, Slim met to discuss the issue, first in Imphal with Scoones and Stopford and then, later in the day, after a short flight from Imphal, with Ranking at Dimapur. Stopford, as incoming corps commander, was concerned that if 161 Brigade was surrounded and isolated at Kohima before Grover's division arrived, there would be nothing with which to defend Dimapur. Slim agreed that this was a serious risk but argued that a well-defended Kohima would certainly force Sato to deal with it prior to proceeding to Dimapur, thus giving valuable breathing space to Stopford to move the remainder of 2 Division into position. A compromise of sorts was reached, but, as with most compromises, some clarity as to the main intention was lost.

Following these two meetings, Slim issued his orders to Ranking in writing. Ranking was to prepare Dimapur for defence and hold it when attacked; to reinforce Kohima and hold it to the last; and to prepare for the reception of the reinforcements from XXXIII Corps. Ranking interpreted in these orders no instruction to evacuate 161 Brigade from Kohima. Indeed, Warren's troops, on Slim's orders, were arriving that very day after having flown directly into Dimapur from Arakan and driving into the hills to Kohima. In a matter of hours, the entire brigade had been safely deposited in Dimapur before making its way to Garrison Hill. Meanwhile, Stopford concentrated on moving his Corps HQ to Jorhat, where it was established on 3 April. That night, the day before Ranking formally transferred command, Stopford made what proved to be a serious error. Still firmly of the belief that the Japanese objective was Dimapur, and in response to erroneous intelligence that Japanese units were at that very moment in the process of out-flanking Kohima, Stopford ordered Ranking to withdraw 161 Brigade from Kohima immediately. All involved in the defence of Kohima – Warren, Colonel Hugh Richards, and the civilian Deputy Commissioner, Charles Pawsey – were aghast at, and protested against – the decision. When told that the Japanese were out-flanking Kohima to the north, Pawsey scoffed, retorting that if true, 'my Nagas would have told me'.

Despite Ranking's protest, that evening the two battalions had fallen back several miles along the road to Nichugard, leaving in Kohima a weak garrison comprising two companies of the Nepalese Shere Regiment and about 500 men of the Assam Regiment and the Assam Rifles, together with odds and sods recovering in the hospital and manning the depots. Ranking, sure that Stopford was making a mistake, went over the head of his new superior officer and called Slim directly by telephone at Comilla to petition him to leave Warren at Kohima. Slim, perhaps unwilling to overrule Stopford, and in any case as convinced as Stopford that Dimapur was the Japanese objective, confirmed Stopford's original order. The compromise reached on 30 March had not led to a clear understanding of whether, with the limited troops available, it was better to defend Kohima or Dimapur. Warren's 161 Brigade, which had been in the process of organizing the desperately needed defence of the ridge, left Kohima virtually undefended only one day before Japanese attacks began. Had Warren's men been allowed to remain where they were, the trauma of the siege that ultimately followed would have been much reduced and the stranglehold which Sato was able to maintain on the vital road to Imphal for two long months would have been significantly weaker. Stopford had made the initial mistake; Slim compounded the problem by not immediately rescinding it. He firmly believed that Dimapur, not Kohima, was the ultimate Japanese target. The truth was that *both* needed to be defended and that because Kohima would receive the first attacks, its immediate defence had to take priority. At the same time, effort needed to be made to prevent Sato from fixing Kohima while he advanced with his main force on Dimapur.

In *Defeat into Victory*, Slim inexplicably blamed Ranking rather than Stopford for this error. 'In taking this action', he wrote, 'Ranking was, I think, influenced understandably by the stress I had laid on his primary task – the defence of the Dimapur base. The reports [of a Japanese envelopment of Kohima] proved untrue, and the withdrawal of the brigade was an unfortunate mistake. Had it remained south of Kohima, Warren would almost certainly have at least delayed the Japanese advance on Kohima for several days. That would have put a very different aspect on the battle which followed.' Quite. But the decision to withdraw 161 Brigade was made first by Stopford, and then endorsed by Slim himself on 3 April, not by Ranking, who opposed it vigorously. Geoffrey Evans suggests that the problem lay in the imprecision in the wording of Slim's instructions to Ranking on 30 March.[4] But this was only a manifestation of the real problem, which was to deem the defence of Kohima of limited consequence relative to that of Dimapur. When reality dawned, and Slim realized that 31 Division's objective was the weakly defended Kohima Ridge and not Dimapur as he had expected, he admitted that the shock was considerable. 'I have spent some uncomfortable hours at the beginnings of battles', he wrote, 'but few more anxious than those of the Kohima battle.'

During this week of embarrassing confusions, Sato was rapidly and skilfully pushing his columns through the mountainous terrain from the Chindwin. The only British defences in the Naga Hills comprised V Force watching posts in the mountaintop villages, a company of the Assam Regiment at Jessami (60 miles east of Kohima) and another at Kharasom (18 miles south of Jessami), several days' march forward of Kohima. The Japanese attacked Kharasom on 27 March and Jessami on 28 March. For five days these young and inexperienced soldiers under Colonel William 'Bruno' Brown at Jessami and Captain John

Young at Kharasom fought like veterans, astounding the Japanese of Colonel Torikai's 138 Regiment by the ferocity – and determination – of their response, even when they knew themselves to be surrounded by an overwhelming enemy force. Brown managed to evacuate Jessami on 1 April, but Young died at his post.[5] He had been instructed to fight to the last round, and the last man. He obeyed this idiotic instruction, after first ordering his surviving soldiers back through the jungle tracks to Kohima. Colonel Hugh Richards records that seeing 'Bruno' Brown with 260 of his men of the Assam Regiment marching into Kohima on 3 April 'was one of the finest sights of the battle'.[6] Richards worked feverishly to prepare Kohima for attack after the instruction to send 161 Brigade to Dimapur. All troops in the hill station – including cooks, drivers, pioneers and those found in the local reinforcement camp awaiting their new postings – were allocated to composite companies and provided with areas for defence. Fifteen days' rations and all available ammunition were shared out across the troops defending Garrison Hill, the single remaining defensive box, Richards having decided to reduce them from four so as to concentrate his forces.

On 3 April Naga scouts sent by Charles Pawsey informed Richards that the Japanese were massing at Mao Songsong, 20 miles on the road to Imphal. On the night of 4 April, Japanese troops from 1/58 Battalion attacked the southern edge of Kohima at GPT Ridge after a march of some 160 miles in 20 days over terrain which both Scoones and Slim had considered impassable to large bodies of troops. The battalion had been badly delayed by the bloody battle at Sangshak. It was a remarkable feat of physical endurance. In its execution Ranking and Warren's worst fears were realized, the Japanese arriving, albeit in small numbers, only hours after Warren had withdrawn his brigade from Kohima. Troops of 2/58 and 3/58 quickly fed through the hills and valleys leading into Kohima from the east. They were surprised to find that they were not expected.

When the message got back to Stopford in Dimapur, the folly of the previous instructions that Warren's brigade withdraw from Kohima were suddenly apparent. In desperation, 161 Brigade immediately began to retrace its steps. By the following morning – 5 April 1944 – the leading battalion of the brigade (446 men of 4 Battalion Royal West Kents, commanded by Lieutenant Colonel John 'Texas Dan' Laverty) had managed to re-join the Kohima garrison on the ridge that stretched from the DIS to the IGH as Sato launched further attacks on the ill-prepared defenders, the remainder of the brigade unable to get in before the Japanese tentacles enclosed the garrison. Fortunately, Sato's initial attacks were weak and disparate, as he was unable fully to concentrate his forces for several days. No serious attack on the frantically digging garrison took place that day, although the initial Japanese tactics of rushing the British positions was undertaken at high cost. A company of 4/7 Rajput managed to squeeze into the perimeter to swell the ranks of the defenders.

Unable to get the remainder of his brigade back into the confined space provided by the Kohima Ridge, Warren decided to position his two remaining battalions (1/1 Punjab and 4/7 Rajput, together with the eight remaining guns of his mountain artillery, from 24 Indian Mountain Regiment) 2 miles to the rear on Jotsoma Ridge, one of the Pulebadze spurs, where Kohima could easily be observed and where the mountain guns could be sited to fire in support of the Kohima defenders. This was an immense stroke of luck, as it meant that when the battle began these guns were outside the perimeter, and hence the danger area, and were able to bring down accurate and unimpeded fire in support of the defenders. Ammunition resupply was relatively easy from Dimapur, with vehicles able to drive up the road to the gun positions at Jotsoma. These guns proved to be decisive instruments in the defence of Kohima. On one target alone the regiment fired some 3,500 rounds in five hours. On average the Indian mountain guns fired 400 rounds each day during the siege.

On the ridge itself the puny garrison now consisted of some 2,500 men of whom 1,000 were non-combatants unable to make their escape along the road to Zubza and Nichugard before the Japanese net closed in on Kohima.[7] Japanese pressure on the perimeter increased on the morning of 6 April: repeated attacks by Colonel Fukunaga's 58 Regiment on Jail Hill and GPT Ridge (to its rear left) overwhelmed the defenders, causing 200 killed and wounded. Heavy artillery and mortar fire quickly denuded trees of their foliage, snapping branches and scattering jagged splinters to accompany the whine and hiss of exploding shrapnel. By 11 a.m. the surviving defenders were forced off Jail Hill. Since this dominated the southern edge of, and overlooked, the ridge defences, the disappearing tree cover became a problem for the defenders, who became visible to the Japanese and consequently could only move at night. Even then it wasn't safe, as repeated night attacks and infiltration patrols, not to mention artillery and mortar fire as well as machine guns firing on fixed lines, were to demonstrate.

The Kohima Ridge was now cut off. Its defenders squeezed inside the perimeter and were soon surrounded by up to 15,000 eager Japanese. That night, when the sun was replaced by a resplendent shining moon, a company of Japanese came down the steep slopes of Jail Hill, crossed the road and climbed up DIS Hill to a cacophony of war cries and blaring bugles. The attack was frontal, entirely without subtlety. So began the first of two weeks of Japanese attacks by day and night on the ever-decreasing perimeter on Garrison Hill, a struggle noted for its savage, hand-to-hand, fury. Within days, hundreds of bodies lay littered across the position, attracting clouds of slow-moving bluebottles feasting on the carpet of corpses covering the ground. Attempts were made to remove bodies where it was possible, but snipers and the sheer number meant that it was not possible to dispose of them all. As the days went by, the effects of artillery bombardment dispersed some of the remains, with the result that the DIS became an unpleasant place to defend at best, and injurious to health at worst. At the outset of the siege, Lieutenant Colonel Young, Commanding Officer of 75 Field Ambulance, had organized centralized medical facilities for the wounded (rather than in the previously separate regimental aid posts) on the reverse slopes of Garrison Hill. Trenches were dug for the wounded, and a pit was dug with a tarpaulin for cover which acted as an operating theatre.

MAP 7   The Imphal battlefield's 'hubs and spokes'

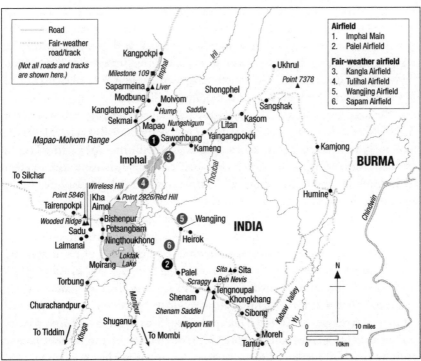

For the defenders, the days began to assume a monotony of intermittent terror and constant discomfort. The men knew that they were cut off from help, but they also knew that they had so far managed to withstand the swamping attacks of Sato's men. When not faced by the threat of direct attack, they crouched in their trenches, alive to the danger of the intermittent machine-gun fire that played over their heads both from Jail Hill and GPT Ridge, and from the sporadic mortar fire that would drop from the sky with no warning, directed from the slopes of Pulebadze. Each night without fail the Japanese launched both real and 'jitter' attacks against the perimeter. Indian soldiers in particular were urged to join their comrades in the liberation of India from the iniquities of colonial rule. When attacks weren't being launched, snipers, artillery and machine guns kept the defenders busy by day.

During 8 April, Warren's base at Jotsoma was cut off by troops of 138 Regiment who had crossed the deep Zubza Nullah from the area of Merema to the north, with the aim of cutting the road to Kohima. Sato had now managed to concentrate the bulk of his division against Kohima, and the pressure exerted by his troops was sustained and inexorable. The result was that, over the ensuing 12 days, the British positions along the Kohima Ridge would reduce to a single hill. For over two weeks fierce fighting raged, the shrinking battlefield a ghastly combination of exhausted men, mud, corpses and trees denuded of their leaves by constant shellfire. But even as 31 Division dug its claws into Kohima, Mutaguchi reminded Sato on 8 April that the real objective, the one that would make the strategic difference for Operation *U-Go*, was Dimapur. Sato obeyed, if somewhat reluctantly, sending a battalion of 138 Regiment along the track that led from Merema to Bokajan. However, Sato's reply to Mutaguchi's order was copied to the Burma Area Army HQ in Rangoon. Kawabe, who had anticipated such a move by his army commander, lost no time in countermanding the instructions. Sato's battalion, five hours into its march on Dimapur, was recalled.

This was the moment that the Japanese lost the battle for India. In such small things are the fates of armies decided. A Japanese battalion falling on a chaotic and ill-defended Dimapur (numerous reports speak of panic stalking its dusty streets) would have had the potential to entirely unravel Allied plans for defensive operations in Manipur, and to severely disrupt if not entirely curtail the Hump airlift to China, all without the necessity for a protracted and bloody struggle for Kohima. He could have feasted off the *Chāchiru kyūyō* at Dimapur for many months, but Sato was bereft of the same strategic intuition that had fuelled Mutaguchi's insight. What might have happened if

Sato had turned a Nelsonian blind eye to Kawabe's order, or if he had delayed its official receipt for another 24 hours? Sato was apparently happy to obey Kawabe and withdraw to Kohima partly because his deep-seated animosity to Mutaguchi led him to assume the army commander's demands to march on Dimapur were motivated solely by visions of military glory. Sato's hatred of Mutaguchi blinded him to the strategic possibilities offered by continuing his offensive through to Dimapur, and lost for the Japanese a crucial opportunity for victory in 1944. Slim was astonished when he realized that Dimapur was safe. The failure to secure Dimapur while the British were reeling in confusion at the speed and scale of Mutaguchi's 'March on Delhi' was one of the great missed opportunities of the war: it led directly to the failure of the Kohima thrust and contributed to the collapse of Operation *U-Go*. It was the consequence of Sato's lack of strategic imagination, framed by Kawabe's rejection of what he regarded as an attempt by Mutaguchi to secure for himself undying glory. What he – and Sato for that matter – failed entirely to see was that Mutaguchi was right. The capture of Dimapur might have been the decisive strategic movement of the campaign leading to a dramatic worsting of the British reminiscent of the capture of Malaya, Singapore and Burma in 1942.

When he heard that Sato had turned back, Mutaguchi was furious at what he regarded as Kawabe's timidity. 'The worst crime of a soldier is irresolution,' he exploded. 'Kawabe... [did] not let me advance on Dimapur, even when the national fate depended on it.'[8] While this is patently unfair – Kawabe provided Mutaguchi with all the support he needed to get Operation *U-Go* off the ground – it is true that Kawabe refused to endorse Mutaguchi's vision for the capture of Dimapur. What Kawabe lacked was not courage as Mutaguchi suggested, but strategic vision. The capture of Dimapur was not, as he surmised, a product of Mutaguchi's fierce egotism but, in actuality, a profound realization that it was the key to British vulnerabilities in eastern India. There is no evidence that Kawabe ever recognized this truth for what it was. It is impossible to conceive of an effective British riposte to a move against Dimapur. Its capture would certainly have denied Slim the opportunity to launch his own offensive into Burma in 1944 or 1945. As Slim saw clearly, Sato's lack of strategic sense in understanding the wider context and broader possibilities of Operation *U-Go* in favour of the strict interpretation of his orders removed the chance for decisive success in 1944. Slim clearly knew nothing of the hatred that Sato harboured for Mutaguchi, nor indeed of the deep-rooted failings of the Japanese command system that allowed such self-destructive antagonisms to flourish so openly. The truth is that Sato could have taken Dimapur had he wished. Mutaguchi, for his part, was still far back in Maymyo, entirely ill placed to manage his subordinates and to control the battle.

There was little to celebrate among the defenders of the Kohima Ridge on Easter Sunday, 9 April 1944. They had no knowledge that Sato's application of Mutaguchi's plan was strategically flawed and doomed to eventual failure. Indeed, issues of higher strategy and leadership interested them not one jot, as they fought for their lives amid the mud, blood and fly-blown, blackening corpses. The numbers of wounded lying in shallow trenches around the IGH Spur were daily increasing, the crowded area offering little protection from either the elements or incoming artillery, men being wounded for the second and sometimes third time. As the days passed, the Advanced Dressing Station became a veritable hell, men lying and dying in their blood and excrement, over 600 wounded crowded into a tiny area by 20 April.

To cap it all, the monsoon rains had come early, and heavy driving rain on 10 April, together with the effects of battle and of sleep deprivation, pushed men to the edge of exhaustion. Tea was rationed to half a mug per man per day. Fortunately, the rain made up somewhat for the acute lack of water within the perimeter, men lying back in their weapon pits and trenches to allow the rain to fall directly into parched, open mouths. For the defenders, the new enemy inside the perimeter was exhaustion, the tidal waves of fatigue that rushed in without warning to swamp men's consciousness in oblivion. But surrendering to this meant certain death. By catching precious doses of sleep, measured in minutes rather than hours, men seemed just about able to go on. Their waking hours were filled with preparing grenades, reinforcing and repairing damaged trenches, completing ablutions in the disgusting conditions and making sure that weapons were clean so they didn't malfunction when most needed. The whole position now smelt of faeces and the putrid, sickly sweet odour of bodily decay from the many hundreds of corpses and body parts that lay mingled on the ground amid the shattered remains of the once luxuriant forest. By now, however, most men were inured to the awful smell that hung over Kohima Ridge like a thick blanket: it was something that was encountered with horror only by those at the end of the siege who entered for the first time. The new fear was that a moment of inattention could lead to the Japanese seizing their chance to leap into one's trench, especially at night when the darkness was replete with dancing shadows that were, at one moment, Japanese soldiers and, the next, figments of one's fearsome dreams.

By 13 April – labelled by the defenders the 'Black Thirteenth' – heavy Japanese artillery fire killed many in the ADS, including two irreplaceable doctors, adding to the misery of that bloody place. Priceless equipment and medicines were also destroyed. Of the 446 men of the 'Dirty Half Hundred' who had moved back into Kohima on 5 April, 150 were now dead or wounded. The thought on everyone's minds was 'when, if ever, is all this going to stop? Are we ever going to be relieved?' Officers attempted to maintain morale, as did Charles Pawsey (he had refused to leave for the relative safety of Jotsoma), who defied the snipers each day to walk around his diminishing fiefdom, pausing to say comforting words to the bearded, black-eyed scarecrows in their trenches.

Attempts were also made to drop supplies during the siege to the defenders from the ubiquitous C47, although, given the tiny, postage-stamp size of the dropping area, most of these failed, with precious food, water and ammunition floating down into the eager hands of the hungry Japanese. On 13 April three entire planeloads, including 3-inch mortar ammunition, were dropped on the enemy (which the Japanese promptly used in captured British mortars against their erstwhile owners), the men on Kohima Ridge watching miserably as the swaying parachutes floated down over the valley to the east.

The garrison was now crammed into an area extending not much more than 350 by 350 yards, running from just above the traffic control point on the ridge to a point just above the tennis court.

For the first time, RAF attacks by Hurribomber with bombs and cannon fire gave the defenders much encouragement, as did Major Callistan of the Assam Regiment, who mounted a successful assault across the tennis court to destroy a Japanese machine-gun crew. Sepoy Wellington Massar was severely wounded in the attack, standing up and spraying the Japanese positions at close quarters with his Bren gun. But by now the dirty, scruffy, exhausted defenders could see elements of the relieving force advancing up the valley to the west, through the trees below the road, and the first shells of 2 Division began to fall thickly on the Japanese positions. By the morning of 15 April, the Royal West Kents on Summerhouse Hill could see, through the damp grey mist, the distinctive turbans of the men of 1/1 Punjab on Picquet Hill, which lay between the ridge and Jotsoma, the final piece of ground that needed securing before the road itself could be opened up. Later that day, the men of a company of the Punjabs made contact with the defenders, bringing with them Lee-Grant tanks which were able to make their way along the road to the side of the IGH Spur, although they remained in full view of the enemy across in Kohima village on Naga Hill, attracting long-range rifle and machine-gun fire. Relief was now only a matter of time.

This was not to be the sort of relief, however, occasioned by the defeat of the enemy. Rather, it was a relief-in-place, where troops from 2 Division and the remainder of 161 Brigade moved in under Japanese sniper and artillery fire to take over the positions eagerly given up by their erstwhile defenders. The Japanese pressed the Kohima Ridge vigorously, even frantically, knowing that this was their final opportunity to seize it before fresh British troops arrived, but, on 19 April, the day before the first of the relieving troops made their way onto the position, Hurribombers strafed the Japanese positions, C47s dropped ammunition, water and food accurately on the ridge and the newly arrived 25-pounders of 2 Division pounded away relentlessly, firing down in the eastern valley at Zubza. The relief took place in the nick of time. On 17 April, the garrison didn't know whether it could carry on, but the men also knew that they couldn't give up. On 20 April, the first of the relieving battalions had arrived. As Japanese bullets and shells continued to fall, the weary veterans of the siege – wounded and unwounded – made their way down the gulleys adjacent to the IGH Spur, strewn with Japanese corpses, to waiting trucks guarded by the Lee-Grants.

Of the 446 Royal West Kents who had made their way onto Kohima Ridge on the morning of 5 April, only 168 remained unharmed. Two hundred and seventy-eight had been killed or wounded during the 16 days of siege in a stand which, although neither they nor the Japanese knew it at the time, would prove to be the turning point in each side's respective fortunes in the war. The two companies of the Assam Regiment had suffered 36 casualties. For the British and Indians on Garrison Hill, it was also a story of extraordinary fortitude in the face of overwhelming odds. For the Japanese, driven on in desperation to overcome the last resistance before the Brahmaputra was reached, it was an epic of dogged perseverance, a determination to overcome or to die in the attempt. At Kohima the Royal West Kents, the Assam Regiment, Assam Rifles and the 'odds and sods' of the Kohima garrison were the inadvertent sacrificial lambs for the defence of India. Without their extraordinary stand – likened without any charge of hyperbole by many contemporary observers and later commentators to that of the Spartans at Thermopylae – Kohima would undoubtedly have fallen, allowing the Japanese to flood, if they so desired, into the Brahmaputra Valley through the unguarded Naga Hills.

Slim admits that, as a consequence of three near-disasters – the late withdrawal of 17 Indian Division from Tiddim; the discovery of the unexpected thrust at

Imphal by Yamauchi via the north-east; and the cock-up at Kohima which led to its defences being dangerously exposed – the first week of April was 'an anxious one. Thanks to my mistakes the battle had not started well; at any time crisis might have slipped into disaster – and still might.' Even though the Japanese were doing what he expected them to do, this knowledge was cold comfort, as they clearly retained the tactical advantage on three different sectors of the front during this time. Indeed, to Mutaguchi everything appeared to be going his way. By early April, 15 Army had successfully pushed IV Corps onto its heels, and had cut all land links to the rest of India. It seemed only a matter of time before Scoones would be starved into submission, unless of course the demoralized British and Indian troops capitulated first. However, by the second week of April, Slim had cause to relax somewhat. The successful concentration of IV Corps on the Imphal plain by 4 April, the rapid insertion of 5 Indian Division and the arrival of XXXIII Corps by the end of the first week of April meant that the immediate danger was over. Despite the poor start to the battle in the Tiddim, Ukhrul and Kohima, IV Corps had not been defeated, and the makeshift defences at Sangshak, Kohima, Tamu and the fighting withdrawal up the Tiddim Road had inflicted grievous and irreplaceable casualties on the enemy. Slim's cautious optimism at the beginning of April grew stronger as the month progressed. By mid-April his command of the situation had been unequivocally reasserted. He acknowledged that the reason for this was the bravery and commitment of his troops – British and Indian. 'Happily for the result of the battle – and for me – I was, like other generals before me, to be saved from the consequences of my mistakes by the resourcefulness of my subordinate commanders and the stubborn valour of my troops.'

Nevertheless, the stabilization of the front heralded merely the end of the beginning of British difficulties. While the immediate crisis was over, Stopford now had to prevent Sato from capturing Kohima and Dimapur; Scoones to prevent Yamauchi from penetrating Imphal from the north; Yamamoto from penetrating Gracey's defences at Shenam; and Yanagida from breaking through at Bishenpur in the south. Slim also had to ensure that IV Corps, cut off in the Imphal plain, was resupplied. While the first signs of panic and chaos were now behind them, a long hard fight lay ahead for the British if they were to guarantee victory.

30

The Spokes of the Wheel

Scoones' original plan for the physical protection of the Imphal plain was to create two complementary layers of defence. The outer layer comprised a defensive ring where his Indian infantry divisions, supported by armour, artillery and ground attack aircraft defended against potential Japanese entry at the four major points of danger – in the north, north-east, south-east and south. With the attacks on Sangshak, the arrival of 5 Indian Division by air from Arakan and the withdrawal of 20 Indian Division from Moreh, in practical terms this meant the concentration of his forces was:

- on the road northwards to Kohima, which the Japanese had cut in late March following the battle of Sangshak;
- on the Iril River Valley which ran parallel to the Kohima Road, both of which were separated by the Mapao-Molvom plateau (both areas the responsibility of 5 Indian Division);
- on the track to Ukhrul running to the north-east (23 Indian Division);
- on the hills of Shenam in the south-east across which ran the main road between Palel and Tamu (20 Indian Division);
- and at Bishenpur on the road to Tiddim in the south (17 Indian Division).

Within this outer ring he constructed a number of self-contained, self-defending 'boxes' on the Arakan model, designed to protect strategic facilities such as the airfields and stores depots as well as providing a local focus for defence against the threat of Japanese infiltration. Most of the troops in these boxes were support and administrative personnel, including some 6,000 RAF ground troops, supporting the expanding resupply and reinforcement requirements of Operation *Stamina*. Troops withdrew into the boxes at night (even aircraft from some of the airstrips were pushed as close to the defended positions as possible), and with the exception of known patrols, all other activity was regarded as hostile. The boxes also contained the heavy guns of the field artillery, although the 25-pounders serving the fighting divisions were located close to the troops they served, dug into positions in the padi fields or hidden among re-entrants in the hills.

Briggs' 5 Indian Division arrived in the midst of a confusing and fast-moving battlefield. The Japanese were advancing in force from what seemed to be every side, attempting to seize the high ground overlooking the plain as a precursor to pouring into it. The battle did not involve massed brigades and divisions fighting in carefully choreographed coherence on a perhaps traditional linear model with an identifiable 'front' and 'rear' but was instead a confused and disparate section and platoon – sometimes company level – struggle fought at many different points of the compass in the jungle-matted hills and valleys encircling the Imphal plain, and the swampy terrain around Bishenpur. None of the land battles were directly interconnected, the struggles for the north and north-east (Sangshak, Nunshigum, Mapao and Ukhrul), the south-east (Tamu to Shenam) and the south (Tiddim to Bishenpur) being conducted largely independently by both attacker and defender.

THE NORTHERN SPOKE

With the cutting by Yamauchi's 15 Division of the road between Imphal and Kohima on 30 March, Imphal was cut off from its lifeline to the north through Kohima. The siege had begun, and until the road was open again the only way in and out was by air. Erroneously imagining the British everywhere to be in panicked flight, Yamauchi urged his regiments to exploit this opportunity (*'senki'*), attacking without hesitation, pushing forward where they could, independently and on their own initiative, taking advantage of the fact that no defender could possibly hold every hilltop, every jungle track, moraine and re-entrant that led onto the plain. Unfortunately for Yamauchi, the dangerous distraction of Sangshak proved to be his undoing. Unable to resist such a ripe fruit ready for plucking, Yamauchi's men missed the opportunity to create significant discombobulation to Slim and Scoones by capturing Imphal Main airfield. They were to come close – the heights of Nunshigum Hill overlooking the runways – but not close enough.

On the news that the Japanese had reached Kanglatongbi and were now bearing down from the north, Scoones rushed 63 Brigade (just back from 17 Indian Division's withdrawal from Tiddim and hoping in vain for a rest) forward to Sengmai, 10 miles north of Imphal on the Kohima road, to plug the gap. The two brigades of Briggs' newly flown-in 5 Indian Division were also rushed north as soon as their planes touched down on the vast airfield of Imphal Main. Everywhere over the next two weeks the three battalions of 123 Brigade, based in the foothills at Kameng, where the Ukhrul Road debouched into the Imphal plain, prevented Japanese attempts to break into the plain. British artillery, Lee-Grant tanks and Hurribombers worked effectively with Indian infantry to smash every attack as it developed.

Meanwhile Yamauchi was making every effort to infiltrate through the mass of jungle-covered hills that swept in a wide crescent across the northern part of the Imphal plain, seeping troops southward through the hills despite repeated reverses. It was not physically possible for Briggs to defend every point of entry on the northern front, so the solution was extensive patrolling to identify and disrupt Japanese routes through the hills. Even the Japanese occupation of the Nunshigum feature, towering dramatically over Imphal town and the airstrip of Imphal Main, was removed by inching Lee-Grant tanks up its steep slopes on 13 April and destroying the hasty Japanese positions trench by trench.

Realizing that Yamauchi would now struggle to penetrate Briggs' defences without reinforcement, Mutaguchi instructed Sato – farther north at Kohima – to send a regiment south to assist 15 Division. This would have been unnecessary if 15 Division hadn't been distracted at Sangshak. If there is one message Japanese commanders repeatedly ignored in 1944 it was to focus exclusively on the strategic objective, without being distracted by the lure of unnecessary battle along the way. Mutaguchi's instructions also coincided with orders Slim gave to Scoones on 10 April to turn Briggs's troops on to the offensive, the key task being the opening of the Kohima road. Scoones' plan was for 5 Indian Division to advance north on either side of the road to Kohima beyond Kanglatongbi and for Roberts' 23 Indian Division to push 15 Division back in the direction of Litan and Ukhrul, through the range of hills now infested by Yamauchi's men. Defeated at Nunshigum, they were far from being beaten, however, although exhaustion and sickness were rapidly taking their toll. Elsewhere, Scoones planned to continue to hold the Bishenpur front with Cowan's 17 Indian Division (now re-joined by 63 Brigade) and to launch a limited counterattack against 33 Division's line of communication on the Tiddim road. Gracey's 20 Indian Division would continue to absorb Yamamoto's punches against the Shenam defences, high in the cloud-covered hills east of the plain. These were clear, practical and aggressive plans. The farther back from the immediate battlefield one went, however, the less confident men were about the ultimate outcome of the battle. On the evening of 14 April, Wavell had dinner with Mountbatten in New Delhi, having met his Chief of Staff, Lieutenant General Sir Henry Pownall in the morning. Both were pessimistic, Wavell noting in his diary, about the state of the Assam battle, 'Mountbatten thinks that at best it will take them 5 or 6 weeks to clear the Japanese out.'[1]

THE IRIL VALLEY SPOKE

In the wild, tempestuous country in an arc running north-west, north and north-east of Nunshigum between the road to Kohima and the Iril River Valley lies a vast inverted triangle of jungle-matted hills (the southern point of which touched Imphal) stretching from the village of Mapao in the south, distinguished amid the dark jungle foliage by its white-painted American Baptist Mission church, 3½ miles north as the crow flies to Molvom. These few miles became a Japanese defensive arena par excellence, the individual peaks and ridges – nicknamed Hump, Twin Peaks, Foston, Penhill and Buttertubs – occupying 5 Indian Division expensively for the next six weeks as they struggled in the teeming monsoon to push their way north and to remove, through battle, the tentacles Yamauchi's troops had wrapped around this rugged terrain.

At least, with 5 and 23 Indian Divisions going on the offensive, the direct threat to Imphal from the north appeared to have reduced, although Slim and Scoones, during April and May, were not complacent. The Japanese were still fighting desperately, refusing to consider any prospect but victory. However, it seemed clear to Slim that Mutaguchi was now playing into his hands. By over-extending himself on three separate fronts, each of Mutaguchi's three divisions was now doing what he had expected, namely fighting tenaciously to hold positions they had secured regardless of their strategic value, unwilling to relinquish ground because of their fear of losing 'face' by withdrawing from the high-water mark of their advance. Mutaguchi, of course, gave repeated sanction to the urge to continue onwards, whatever the cost.

The Shenam Saddle Spoke

In the south-east during early April, Yamamoto's three battalion columns, together with mountain artillery and light tanks, pushed aggressively against the new positions hurriedly occupied by two of Gracey's brigades, following the withdrawal from Tamu and Moreh. This initiated a bloody, ten-week-long struggle for the vital Shenam position. The long 5,000-foot-high Shenam Ridge in fact comprised a range of jungled peaks jutting high into the clouds through which ran the road[2] between Palel and Tamu. Both sides gave names to these hills, variously Brigade Hill, Recce, Sita, Gibraltar, Malta, Scraggy (Ito),[3] Lynch, Crete East (Ikkenya), Crete West (Kawamichi), Cyprus and Nippon (Maejima). Whoever controlled these peaks controlled the road that led over the Shenam position into Imphal.

The monsoon rains that had arrived in late March 1944 brought not only huge volumes of rain but thick mists in the plain, low clouds on the hills and cold nights. At night the temperature often fell below freezing and was achingly miserable. Hunched sodden, in the bottom of a slit trench for day after day and cold night after night with no means of keeping dry, short of drinking water and without warm food or drink while fighting the most formidable foe imaginable, tested the men's mental and physical stamina to the limit. Occasionally during the day the sun would burst through the rain-sodden purple clouds to bring some momentary comfort. With the difficulties posed by the climate came a stark reminder to any troops who had not yet experienced the toughness of their adversary of just how extraordinarily fit and physically hardy the Japanese were, how committed they were to achieving their objectives, how apparently unconcerned they were with respect to human comforts and how determined they were to do what the Emperor (through their officers) demanded, or die in the attempt. Repeated fanatical and suicidal attacks were made against the British, Indian and Gurkha defenders, and counterattacks had to face the toughest defensive positions imaginable, prepared by men whom Slim was to describe as 'warrior ants'. As the days went by, the battlefield became one large charnel house, littered with bodies in various states of decomposition, as it was rarely easy to recover and bury the dead.

When the Japanese turned to the defensive in mid-April in the north and the south-east, jungle-topped hills became bare from the shell fire, and the monsoon turned positions, often only yards apart, into a muddy morass of indescribable horror and ugliness. Once dug in, the Japanese had to be grenaded out, one by one, bunker by bunker. Otherwise they were immovable. On rare occasions bunkers were destroyed by shellfire or by a direct hit from a Hurribomber strike, although the only real guarantee of success, as had been discovered in Arakan, was direct sniping by tanks. Failure to ensure that each bunker was completely clear, or that every stiffening corpse was indeed dead, meant that the next attack often came from within one's own perimeter, from positions that were assumed to be clear and bodies thought to be lifeless.

The fighting for the hills along the ridge did not diminish in intensity until the Japanese offensive eventually collapsed in late July. Desperate hand-to-hand combat night and day characterized the struggle for each patch of high ground. A characteristic of the fighting in the early stage in the campaign was that of the mass, suicidal attack, the Japanese military code (*bushido*) insisting that the moral power of the offensive would overcome any material superiority enjoyed by the enemy. Japanese experience against weak-willed opponents in 1942 had persuaded them of the correctness of this approach to warfare, but it had taught them some false lessons. As time was to show on the Shenam heights and elsewhere around the Imphal plain, it was an entirely inappropriate tactic in the face of well-trained and well-equipped opponents determined to resist the psychological and physical impact of a massed banzai attack. As an example of these tactics, at 3 a.m. on 14 April, a few miles to the north of the Tamu Road on a hill nicknamed 'Sita', 213 Regiment launched a mass assault on the waiting men of 3/1 Gurkha. The Gurkhas had prepared their position well, with liberal quantities of barbed wire and anti-personnel mines, Bren guns covering all the obvious approaches and boxes of primed grenades lying in each trench. In the ensuing fight the Japanese lost an irreplaceable 500 casualties. It was a shocking loss of life for any army determined to preserve its most precious resource, its manpower. But even at this stage Japanese commanders persisted in the belief that the British would be swept away by the force of Japanese samurai willpower alone, as had been the case (they thought) in Malaya, Singapore and Burma two years before, and these costly mass attacks continued. The exercise of command by the Japanese was profoundly flawed, and, in the face of an enemy better able to care for its wounded, with a more humane attitude to the lives of its men and an immeasurably superior logistics system, the end result of Mutaguchi's stratagem should have been clearly observed in the early stages of the fighting, and his tactics adjusted accordingly. It wasn't and they weren't. The struggle in the darkness of Sita Hill cost 3/1 Gurkha 50 casualties in return. Japanese arrogance and inflexibility could be shocking to those who were forced to observe the lack of subtlety in their techniques. On a memorable occasion on the evening of 17 April, the Japanese launched what they considered to be such a devastating artillery bombardment on Crete that no one could have survived. As the bombardment lifted, the waiting and largely untouched 20 Indian Brigade were astonished to see the Japanese marching along the road towards their position in columns of threes, a ripe and unexpected target that was quickly and efficiently engaged by machine guns and artillery.

The belief that theirs was a war of liberation continued to motivate the men of the INA. Moving with his battalion across the Chindwin to reinforce Yamamoto in mid-April, Major Takemura saw men of the INA's 2 Gandhi Regiment on the road from Tamu marching to the chant 'Jai Hind! Chalo Delhi!'* The headquarters of 1 INA Division, together with 2 (Gandhi) and 3 (Azad) Regiments, the men still dressed in the British khaki uniforms they had worn when first captured (the Indian Army had long since converted to wearing jungle green) had made their way to Rangoon from Malaya. In March, Colonel Mohammed Zaman Kiani, the divisional commander, had rushed north to meet Mutaguchi at Maymyo to plead for a role in what he fancied would be the beginning of the end of British India. Mutaguchi, his optimism as yet unchecked, hastened Kiani on to Tamu, there to join Yamamoto's northern thrust over the Shenam Saddle, from where it would emerge like a flood onto the Imphal plain at Palel, sweeping the detritus of the British empire before it. But, to Kiani's disappointment, Yamamoto made no offer to put the Indians in the vanguard of the offensive, placing them instead to guard the Mombi track, which crossed the hills from Witok in the Chindwin Valley into the Imphal plain to the south of Palel. The hype surrounding the INA's despatch to the front, however, left the troops with the expectation that they would not need their heavy weapons and equipment. These – machine guns, mortars and even grenades – were left on the Chindwin at Kalewa, and the troops climbed into the hills from the Chindwin Valley with what they wore, together with a blanket, their personal weapon and fifty rounds of ammunition. By 28 April they were established 10 miles west of Witok, from where their first foray into the plain was to be launched.

This was to be an attack on the British airfield at Palel designed to coincide with an advance by Yamamoto from the east on 1 May. In the event the Indian attacking force, 300 men under the command of Major Pritam Singh, took two exhausting night marches to reach their start point, and launched their attack on the night of 2 May, without a Japanese supporting offensive. For months the INA had been awash with the self-delusional propaganda that when confronted by their kith and kin the Indian troops of the Indian Army would refuse to fire,

---

*'India for ever! On to Delhi!'

and joyfully join in the revolution. The welcoming volleys of the waiting Gurkhas, counterattacks by a company of 9/12 Frontier Force Regiment and a strike by RAF Hurricanes coordinated with an artillery bombardment, reduced the attacking force by a third and decisively demonstrated the true nature of the response the INA was to face by fellow Indians in the Indian Army. Unsurprisingly, the realization of this fact had a dramatic impact on INA morale which, combined with repeated Japanese failure to supply the division with either food or ammunition and with the ravages of disease – especially malaria – precipitated a series of crises in INA ranks. Many men deserted, while others shot themselves through the foot or hand in an attempt to escape the battlefield. Of the 3,000 men of 2 (Gandhi) Regiment who marched into the hills at the end of March only 1,000 remained by 15 June, and then only 750 two weeks later.[4]

THE BISHENPUR (TIDDIM ROAD) SPOKE

Meanwhile, in the south on the Tiddim Road, Gracey's third brigade (32 Brigade) was sent by Scoones on 13 April to block the advance of Yanagida's columns towards Imphal, while Cowan's two exhausted brigades refitted (although 63 Brigade was thrown temporarily into the gap on the Kohima Road north of Imphal). Mackenzie's brigade relieved 49 Brigade, which re-joined 23 Indian Division on the Ukhrul Road. Mackenzie's chosen position was 17 miles behind the original 49 Brigade defences at Milestone 33, because he judged that these could be easily bypassed, and the mountains to the west of Bishenpur offered a far more substantial obstacle to Japanese plans. He was right, although withdrawing enabled the Japanese to move 18 miles closer to Imphal. Arguably, this simply made the Japanese supply arrangements even more difficult. With Cowan's and Scoones' permission, Mackenzie placed his three battalions on defended locations on either side of the Silchar Track, as it entered the deep valley west of Bishenpur. It was here that the desperate struggle to defend the southern approaches to Imphal took place.

On the night of 15 April, a Japanese patrol destroyed the suspension bridge on the Silchar Track, west of Bishenpur, removing the final land link between IV Corps and Assam. On the same night the first of a flood of assaults fell against the rudimentary positions on Wooded Hill. The Japanese managed to seize the village of Ningthoukhong on 22 April. This village lay on the Tiddim road bordering the low-lying area between the road and the Logtak Lake, and as such presented a serious threat to Mackenzie's left flank. An immediate counterattack by two companies of 9/14 Punjab supported by C Squadron, 150 Regiment RAC, failed to eject the new occupants on 22 April, and suffered a severe repulse, a Lee-Grant being struck by a mortar bomb and burnt out, the Punjabis suffering 85 casualties. Each village in this low-lying area was surrounded by a thick earth 'bund', designed to keep out floodwaters but ideal also for use as a defensive bulwark against attack, even that by tanks. A further attack on 25 April by men of 1/4 Gurkha suffered similar ignominy: the long approach over the padi fields (800 yards) allowed a hidden 47mm anti-tank gun to pick off the approaching Lee-Grants one by one, the accompanying troops being unable to locate or destroy the gun. By the time the attack was called off, two Lee-Grants lay burning in the padi and six were damaged, withdrawing whence they came. The accompanying artillery Forward Observation Officer and his precious radio was in one of the destroyed tanks, with the result that artillery could not come to their rescue. In any case artillery ammunition was in desperately short supply by this time. Every round, once the link to Dimapur was closed on 28 March, had to be flown in by air. In a further attempt three days later 1/4 Gurkha gained a lodgement in the village, and further tank attacks took place the following day, a Lee-Grant finally clambering over the bund. The anti-tank fire was too intense, however, and the attack was called off, the Japanese exploiting their success by seeping through to the nearby village of Potsangbam (nicknamed 'Pots and Pans' by British soldiers) and securing the village on 29 April.

THE UKHRUL SPOKE

In the north-east, the offensive by Ouvry Roberts' 23 Division (1 and 37 Brigades) to open the Ukhrul Road as far as Kasom following the victory at Nunshigum succeeded by 20 April in ejecting 15 Division from the area. With the road open, 1 Brigade then continued its pursuit and harassment of Yamauchi's HQ. By early May, Roberts had driven 15 Division 20 miles east to Litan, scattering its units through the remote jungle vastness and persuading Scoones that no further serious offensive could be expected from this direction. He was right, and although no further threat to Imphal emanated from Ukhrul the Japanese caught in these mountains continued to fight with the life-or-death desperation of a cornered animal. The Japanese stubbornly refused to relinquish their hold on the hills. Yamauchi's offensive capability had been severely blunted in the first few weeks of fighting, partly because of his excessive optimism about the ability of his tired troops to defeat the British and their Indian lackeys. Yamauchi's strength now lay in his ability to defend terrain that was key to Scoones' ability to open up the Kohima Road. These efforts were undermined by the fact that, in common with Yanagida and Sato, his relationship with Mutaguchi was deteriorating. The three Japanese divisional commanders had only ever given the venture lukewarm support.

From the beginning the idea for the offensive had been Mutaguchi's: he had given it life and now was its most passionate protagonist. None of his subordinates shared this degree of commitment, a fact that was made worse because Mutaguchi enjoyed extremely poor relations with his three divisional commanders. In fact, Sato and Mutaguchi loathed each other. Sato had long been a political enemy of the army commander, and this underlying belligerence made him a difficult, if not impossible, subordinate. For his part Yamauchi, something of an intellectual, hated the army commander for his lack of intellectual sophistication, considering him to be a 'blockhead' and 'unfit to be in command of an army'.[5] Yanagida likewise had an equally poor opinion of the army commander, considering him to be a womanizing bore and a bully. He had little confidence in the plan for Operation *U-Go* and was overheard on one occasion to lament, 'What's going to become of us with a moron like Mutaguchi as our Commander-in-Chief?' The loathing was reciprocated. Mutaguchi once described Yanagida as 'a gutless bastard' and had little time either for him or Yamauchi, believing both to be too soft and Western in outlook (both having served abroad as military attachés), and even referring to them sarcastically as 'my American generals'.[6] There was a further problem with Yamauchi. He was slowly dying of tuberculosis. Mutaguchi removed him on 10 June and he died in Maymyo on 6 August.

THE IRIL VALLEY SPOKE

Meanwhile Briggs' 5 Indian Division, reinforced by Crowther's 89 Brigade, flown in from Arakan on 7 May, began moving gradually against the enemy up the Iril Valley from Nunshigum on to the heavily defended Mapao Ridge. It was here that the three battalions of Brigadier Joe Salomons' 9 Brigade battled bloodily for six weeks to expel the tenacious Japanese from the positions into which they had dug themselves, determined not to be moved. The most stubbornly defended position on 'Hump' resisted seven separate assaults by 3/14 Punjab during May. Farther to the east, up the Iril River Valley, British troops had attempted to push hard against the Japanese, who turned every hilltop over a wide area into fortified positions. It proved virtually impossible to eject them from these positions, despite repeated and gallant attacks by infantry, supported by tanks and Hurribombers. Infantry battalions were rapidly worn down by repeated attacks on immovable Japanese positions, delivering little more than an alarming number of casualties. A strategy evolved in coming weeks, therefore, to isolate the main Japanese positions by means of heavy patrolling, denying the defenders food, water and ammunition by aggressive attacks on the Japanese supply routes through the jungle, and preventing them from foraging for food. With 123 Brigade now switched to support 89 Brigade on the Kohima Road between Sengmai and Kanglatongbi, 9 Brigade began its task of denying the jungle-covered terrain to the enemy in order to contain and starve their opponents rather than launching unnecessary and costly assaults against his defended positions.

It was a strategy that was to bring decisive if not rapid results. On the left flank of the division's advance the Japanese were slowly inched back along the road. They had constructed three roadblocks at Sengmai, supported by defensive positions in the adjacent hills. A whole battalion was secretly infiltrated through the Japanese front lines on 15 May to form a block to their rear. The main attacks by the brigade on the surrounding heights made little headway, but the block worked superbly, and the Japanese launched furious, though unavailing, assaults to remove it. Briggs was able to reinforce the block, and by 20 May the enemy were forced to give up the struggle and evacuate their forward positions while 123 Brigade applied pressure along the road. By 21 May, the vast dump at Kanglatongbi that had fallen into Japanese hands on 3 April was recovered.

The Shenam Saddle Spoke

The Japanese placed unrelenting pressure on the Shenam Ridge during May. British and Japanese positions snaked through the hills, devoid of vegetation after many weeks of shelling. Only yards apart in places, the ground lay littered with the decomposing corpses of British, Indian and Japanese alike. The smell of putrefaction was often overwhelming, although the monsoon rains did much to wash away the most noxious smells, and the heat aided decomposition. What was unbearable were the clouds of heavy bluebottles feasting on the rotting bodies and then attempting to lunch off the men's bully beef and biscuits, and drink the sweat running from men's lean frames. The Japanese, desperate to break through the hills to reach the promised land beyond, launched repeated assaults on the British positions. Some hilltops changed ownership several times as the battle raged across the mountains.

The British and Indian units mastered attacking when supported by Hurribombers. Usually, the Japanese withdrew into the jungle during the air attack and then reappeared in time to receive the infantry assault as the men clambered onto the position. It was not long before the men of IV Corps learned to counter these tactics by their own ploy: they would agree with the RAF a number of 'attack' sorties into the enemy position, with a 'false' sortie at the end during which the infantry rushed the final position. The Japanese would then re-emerge or reappear, to find enemy troops already on the location. This tactic was also employed very successfully by 5 Indian Division as it progressed slowly northwards up the Kohima road.

The intensity of the fighting was exemplified by an attack on a hill along the road nicknamed 'Crete West'. Desperate to capture it, the Japanese launched an overwhelming attack at 4 a.m. on 9 May, supported by a heavy artillery bombardment. The regimental historian of the Devonshire Regiment records the relentless waves of Japanese infantry, the officers leading from the front wielding their swords (it being dishonourable to fight with anything else), being beaten back each time by men of D Company, 1 Devons.[7] Ammunition was now extremely low – the Japanese had virtually surrounded the hill and resupply was impossible in daylight. Early the following morning, 3/1 Gurkha attempted to retake Crete West, relying in their final assault only on their curved fighting knives – kukris – but the Japanese refused to budge. Later that day, the survivors of D Company, together with their wounded, managed to slip back through the Japanese cordon to the relative safety of Scraggy. That night continuous waves of Japanese infantry fell against the well-dug forward defences on Scraggy, held by 3/1 Gurkha, troops clambering over their dead comrades on the perimeter barbed wire in their desperation to capture the position. Sheer weight of numbers threatened to overwhelm the Gurkhas, so the Commanding Officer called down the divisional artillery on his own position. Fortunately, the well-drilled Gurkhas recognized the signal for such an event and crouched low in their slit trenches as the thunder of 24 guns firing repeated salvoes fell among them, shredding the leading Japanese assault troops in a ground-shaking paroxysm of smoke and fire.

In the morning it was estimated that 800 Japanese corpses lay across the shell-shattered hillside. Gracey's casualties paled into insignificance compared with the extraordinary numbers of experienced fighting men being lost by the Japanese every day to these reckless assaults. Japanese battlefield ferocity had nothing to do with the crude racial stereotypes of Allied propaganda, which presented Japanese soldiers as mindless, bestial savages. Rather, the ferocity of the individual Japanese soldier represented the epitome of the soldier's art: an extraordinary ability to fight on in the most hostile climatic and geographic conditions imaginable, and to continue fighting when most other armies would have given up. Where this ferocity failed was when it was allied to a poverty of generalship that allowed some of the most brilliant soldiers of the entire war to be sacrificed on an altar of hubris that had little equal.

In the course of ten days of fighting the Devons lost nearly 200 killed and wounded. With the change of tactics by Briggs' division in the north and no let-up of pressure on the Shenam Ridge, Scoones decided to replace Gracey's two exhausted brigades with 23 Indian Division, released from the Ukhrul advance, the exchange taking place between 13 and 16 May.

THE BISHENPUR (TIDDIM ROAD) SPOKE

During the first two weeks of May, the exhausting attritional struggle between Yanagida and Mackenzie continued unabated for the positions on the high ground dominating the Silchar Track west of Bishenpur, as well as for the village of Potsangbam. By this time 3/8 Gurkha had been defending the area of Wireless Hill for nearly two weeks, resisting all attempts by the Japanese to eject them, when Cowan decided to replace them with the rested 1/4 Gurkha. The route between Bishenpur and the hills guarding the Silchar Track, however, was now a labyrinth of Japanese positions, and on 27 April an attack on a Japanese block outside the village of Toulang resulted in 29 casualties. The Japanese came out that night on three occasions to try to beat down the temporary defensive position the Gurkhas had thrown up preparatory to another attack the following day, but failed to put off Lieutenant Colonel Oldham's Gurkhas from their purpose. Joined on 28 April by three Lee-Grants, the Gurkhas managed to destroy the block on 29 April, but at the heavy cost of 56 casualties. Without being able to relieve 3/8 Gurkha on Wireless Hill, 1/4 Gurkha had, in the meantime, suffered 85 casualties. It was going to be a long and difficult business to wrest this critical reinforcement route from the Japanese, and to prevent them from returning once the position had been cleared. The way that Cowan sought to achieve this was by reverting to the tactics of the North West Frontier, where picquets were established at regular intervals along the cleared route.

On 30 April, 1/4 Gurkha duly set off on its approach march towards Wireless Hill, joined from the west by a company of the Northamptonshire Regiment from Point 5486 converging on the same objective. Each part of the route needed to be cleared of small pockets of determined Japanese. The position was finally taken, by seven Gurkhas supported by tanks of 3 Carabiniers. Twenty-eight Japanese dead were found on the position. But by now it was apparent that the full-time task of 1/4 Gurkha would be to keep the Silchar Track open by defending their line of picquets stretching into the hills from Bishenpur: 3/8 Gurkha would have to stay where they were, unrelieved, although with hopefully less pressure on them now that 1/4 Gurkha had joined the fray.[8]

This type of intensive fighting was expensive in blood, subsequent attacks by Oldham's battalion resulting in 48 casualties. In a matter of days the fighting had cost 1/4 Gurkha 212 dead, wounded and missing. Despite the huge losses being inflicted on the Japanese, Cowan's precious infantry strength was being whittled away by this type of fighting. It clearly couldn't go on for ever, and a decisive offensive was required to clear the weakening 33 Division from Bishenpur. Potsangbam remained in enemy hands, defended by a ring of powerful anti-tank guns and defying every attempt to broach the defences until 9/14 Punjab managed to capture four of these guns, one of them a new 47mm, on 6 May. But the Japanese held on to the bulk of the village still. At first light on the following day, the Punjabis, together with the Lee-Grants of Major Teddy Pettit's A Squadron, 3 Carabiniers and a troop of Stuart light tanks, closed in on the village following an attack by American Liberator bombers dropping 1,000-pound bombs and dive-bombing by Vengeances. A small breach was made in the bund, but fierce resistance followed.

Yanagida's inability (or unwillingness, in Mutaguchi's view) to break into Imphal from the south resulted in his Chief of Staff, Colonel Tanaka, taking effective command of 33 Division in early May while awaiting the arrival of a permanent replacement. Yanagida's sidelining took place at a critical time for operations on the Tiddim Road, as Cowan turned his troops onto the offensive in order to try to break the Japanese grip on the road. Cowan's plan took time to prepare, and it was not until mid-May that this counter-offensive got underway. The two battalions of Brigadier Cameron's 48 Brigade, then in IV Corps reserve, following its magnificent effort in the fighting withdrawal from Tiddim, were secretly inserted, after an 11-day march, on the road near Torbung far to the rear of the forward Japanese troops in the region of Bishenpur, and Milestone 32, after approaching unseen and unsuspected from the east, across the southern edge of Logtak Lake. The intention was that once this anvil had been formed, Burton's 63 Brigade would then smash through Ninthoukhong and Potsangbam from the north, destroying Yanagida's battalions caught between. Unknown to him, Cowan's offensive in fact coincided with a major effort by Mutaguchi to achieve a successful breakthrough at Bishenpur, using all of 15 Army's artillery and all of its tanks, transferred from the Shenam sector and laboriously moved up the road from Tiddim, reinforced by four additional infantry battalions. Mutaguchi's instinct was right – he had to find the one weak spot where he could effect a breakthrough – but was it now too late?

The Japanese response to the discovery of Cameron's block at Torbung on the morning of 17 May was hornet-like. The men of 48 Brigade had not reckoned with having to fight tanks, but fortuitously they had brought with them a handful of the awkward, short-range, spring-loaded PIAT (Projector Infantry Anti-Tank) weapons. The Japanese, surprised, swarmed around the block furiously from both north and south, but in an action that was to lead to his being awarded the Military Medal, Rifleman Ganju Lama crept forward with a PIAT and managed to destroy two Type-95s, forcing a further two to withdraw. The Gurkhas meanwhile attempted with what few resources they had to prepare a defensive position ready to receive further attack. Cameron's block held, supported by air attacks by Hurribombers and with supplies dropped by C47s flying at tree-top height down the valley.

However, Burton's 63 Brigade was unable to break through from the north, although not for want of trying. The brigade fought furiously for possession of the villages and the hills that lay to the east of Potsangbam, capturing the Japanese-held Kha Aimol and Three Pimple Hill and drawing off Japanese pressure from the Silchar Road. At this time – 19 May – the Japanese 33 Division made a further attempt to break through 17 Indian Division's defences, by inserting a block (400 men of 2/214 Battalion) on the road at Maram, north of Bishenpur, and perilously close (although they did not know it) to Cowan's HQ. Red Hill (Point 2926) nearby was also captured. The 500 men of 1/214 Battalion meanwhile attempted to attack Bishenpur from the north-east. The desperate battles during late May to eject the Japanese from these positions – the closest they had come to Imphal – meant that Cameron was forced to remove his block on 24 May and fight his way back in stages to the British positions at Bishenpur. This he did, holding on the first night, 25 May, a position at Moirang, 8 miles to the north. The retreating brigade was given no respite by the Japanese who attacked repeatedly, by day and night, with both infantry and tanks. Giving the Japanese-defended localities at Ninthoukhong a wide berth, the brigade arrived, with its wounded, at Potsangbam on 30 May, where ambulances – most of which were manned by the volunteers of the American Field Service – recovered the wounded back to Imphal. The operation had been expensive in terms of manpower, and Cowan failed to achieve his objective in shattering Yanagida's division.

He had, however, arguably disrupted Mutaguchi's plans for a final, decisive offensive into Imphal. In the process of the fighting against Cameron's brigade the Japanese lost over 1,150 men, a large number of vehicles and six tanks, while 48 Brigade lost 421 men. The butcher's bill for 33 Division was horrendous, and yet they fought on. By the end of April, Colonel Sakuma of 214 Regiment had only 1,000 fit men remaining from the 4,000 available at the start of the month. Likewise, Colonel Sasahara's 215 Regiment had only 400 men available from a starting strength of nearly 5,000. A month later the situation looked even more desperate. In the fighting for Maram and Red Hill, which ended on 30 May, 214 Regiment had been decimated: 1/214 Battalion was reduced to 37 men, and 2/214 Battalion had entirely ceased to exist. British and Indian casualties, however, had access to a luxury that the Japanese could not afford: rapid evacuation to 41 Indian General Hospital in Imphal and, if necessary, transport by air out of the plain. British medical care was incomparably better than anything the Japanese could offer.

By now Japanese command relationships had broken down irreparably, a consequence of Mutaguchi's repeated insistence to advance whatever the cost. The men were also starving, 17 Division having destroyed rice stocks in the villages around Bishenpur at the start of the fighting. Yet Mutaguchi had refused to listen to Yanagida's explanation in April that the task was too difficult for the resources he had to hand, that the British had placed a wall of steel around the approaches to Bishenpur that he had inadequate strength to break. The fact that Japanese tactics had proved to be entirely inadequate against the determined professionalism of 14 Army – far better supplied, equipped and trained than Yanagida had ever anticipated – was entirely lost on Mutaguchi. It was left to the weary samurai of his rapidly depleting army to make this reality clear on the soggy battlefields around Mapao, Shenam and Bishenpur as they struggled, and failed, to get any closer to the tantalizing prize of Imphal.

31

Forty-Seven Days of Battle: Kohima

Grover's 2 Division was not assembled in its entirety at Dimapur until 11 April. It was now charged with breaking Sato's fierce grip on Kohima Ridge and defeating the Japanese in what clearly was the principal battle in the Assam Hills. If anything, the movement of the division into the hills was slow. It was only on Friday 14 April that the high ground above Zubza was captured: it was to become home to the division's forward administrative area and the base for its 48 25-pounders. Zubza sits at the base of the valley that falls westward from the high point of the Kohima Ridge, standing high and dominant in the distance. Japanese opposition in this area was light, but 2 Division's approach was cautious – an issue of concern for HQ 14 Army – and it took another three days before the road was opened up all the way to Warren's HQ and the gun lines at Jotsoma, sitting a mere 2 miles from the cloud of smoke that denoted the besieged Kohima Ridge. Brigadier Victor Hawkins' 5 Brigade joined hands for the first time on 16 April with Warren's 161 Brigade, offering hope of imminent relief to the defenders of the parachute-garlanded Garrison Hill 2 miles farther on.

With the relief of the original garrison on Kohima Ridge, Grover now formulated a plan for the recapture of the entire Kohima area and the destruction of 31 Division, which held positions in a horseshoe shape, each side of which faced the British advance and the right (northern) side of which rested on the Merema Ridge. His idea was that, while holding Zubza and Periphema to the rear, Brigadier John Shapland's 6 Brigade would attack the Japanese in the centre and gradually push them back on the southern and south-western flanks of the Kohima Ridge. At the same time, he planned two simultaneous flanking movements, one to the left (north) by 5 Brigade and one to the right (south) by

Brigadier Willie Goschen's 4 Brigade. To the north he planned to roll up the long arm that Sato had thrown out along the valley side that ran from Naga Village along the ridge to Merema. To his right he planned something even more dramatic, coming at the Japanese far behind the mountain range that towers over Kohima's southern flank.

It was immediately clear to Grover, when he first saw the terrain at Zubza, looking up the valley to the dramatic ridge 'stopping the bottle' on the distant horizon (the phrase, describing the Kohima Ridge, was Montagu Stopford's), that the situation he faced entailed fighting many simultaneous, small-scale, infantry-dominated battles across a wide area. The heavily jungled Naga Hills swallowed large numbers of soldiers without trace, and single sections deeply dug into carefully camouflaged bunkers could hold off companies for days; platoons could resist battalions, and company positions were well-nigh impregnable without many days and nights of direct and coordinated attack from the ground, by artillery and from the air, as well as by the deliberate starvation of the defenders through encirclement. The struggle for Kohima, which was now to consume his division for the next 47 days, was not a single set-piece engagement, but a desperate close-quarter infantry and artillery battle against tough and determined Japanese soldiers. Sato's division, when it moved from the attack to defence, dug itself deep into many hundreds of small but interlocking defensive positions hidden in the jungle undergrowth across the entire Kohima area. The rain belted down in buckets for long stretches of both day and night, turning roads and tracks into quagmires, filling trenches and bringing with it weeks of wet discomfort. The only saving grace of the monsoon was the low rain-laden clouds that clung to the hillsides like damp blankets and gave a modicum of protection, for periods of time, from the omnipresent Japanese sniper.

On the left flank of 2 Division Brigadier, Hawkins despatched the first element of his brigade to cut the Kohima–Merema–Bokajan Road on the evening of 18 April. In the following days, the remainder of 5 Brigade made the journey across the valley, in single file and cutting across the front of the Japanese positions on Kohima Ridge. Not a man was lost. From a dead Japanese despatch rider were discovered orders to 1/138 Battalion to make its way to the south of Kohima and from there to assist Yamauchi's struggling 15 Division in the capture of Imphal, an order precipitated by the failure to secure Nunshigum. These orders had been received from Mutaguchi three days before. With the increasing pressure being placed on him by the arrival of 2 Division, however, Sato saw no way of acceding to this demand, regarding it as evidence of

Mutaguchi's ignorance of conditions on the Kohima battlefield. Although he assembled three battalions on the Aradura Spur in preparation for a move south, he made no other move to obey Mutaguchi's order, as it would, in his judgement, have dangerously reduced his own ability to secure a decisive advantage at Kohima. It was an act of disobedience, but also of ignorance. Mutaguchi's single desire now that Sato (and Kawabe) had failed to see the importance of Dimpur, was to break into Imphal. Nothing else mattered. Sato's task was to block Kohima, not to fight to the death. He should have seen his task as being the single-minded pursuit of the army's objective: capturing Imphal. Expending the life of his valiant division in the jungle-matted hills at Kohima did not now assist in the achievement of this goal.

Relations between the two men, never good, were now disintegrating. Believing he had been promised that at least 250 tons of supplies would arrive by 8 April, Sato testily demanded food and ammunition. In fact, very few supplies ever reached 31 Division from Burma, the men having to survive on what they had brought with them, what they could beg or steal from Naga villages, or what *Chāchiru kyūyō* they could capture from British stockpiles. Sato's fury at the lack of promised supplies was fuelled by his belief that 31 Division was being let down by Mutaguchi's abject failure to break into Imphal. In response to Mutaguchi's demand that he send troops to assist in the Imphal battle, on 20 April Sato sent the first of a number of increasingly tetchy signals to the army commander: 'We captured Kohima in three weeks as promised. How about Imphal?' Mutaguchi replied: 'Probable date for capture of Imphal April 29 [the Emperor's birthday].' Sato plainly did not believe him. Mutaguchi's physical and mental remoteness from the battlefield (he was still in Maymyo), combined with a fatal unwillingness by his staff to give him unpalatable news, meant that he never properly understood the true situation at Kohima. On 30 April Sato signalled again: '31 Division at the limit of its endurance. When are you going to destroy Imphal?'[1] He received no reply.

With no knowledge of Sato's developing difficulties, by 27 April the entirety of Hawkins' 5 Brigade was safely ensconced on the Merema ridge, threatening the right flank of Sato's horseshoe. Meanwhile, in the centre the long struggle for the Kohima Ridge showed no let-up after the relief of the besieged garrison following 20 April. Sato now recognized that it would be better to go onto the defensive, forcing the British to attack, rather than continuing to waste increasingly scarce men on the British position that had now held out for nearly three weeks, and which, despite its fragility, showed no signs of falling.

The bitter battles on Kohima Ridge continued inconclusively for the following two weeks. Increasingly desperate attacks on the extreme northern edge of the ridge – around the tennis court – took place in late April to open up the road that led left from the TCP, to allow access for a troop of Lee-Grant tanks to lumber up the back (i.e., western) end of Naga Hill in order to provide armoured support for 5 Brigade as it advanced slowly along the left flank from Merema. On Garrison Hill, two battalions of 2 Division fought to defend their waterlogged trenches from repeated Japanese assaults and the regular exchanges of grenades across the few yards that separated both sides.

The plan to get tanks onto the back of Naga Hill by driving through the Japanese positions overlooking the TCP finally succeeded on 27 April, the Lee-Grants trundling along the track, wary of mines, but taking the Japanese entirely by surprise at this stroke of legerdemain. Peppered on all sides futilely by rifle and machine-gun bullets, they joined 5 Brigade on Naga Hill. In the fighting for control of the tennis court no means of overcoming Japanese bunkers could be discovered using infantry alone, and attempts were made to bulldoze a path up to the remains of the Deputy Commissioner's bungalow to allow a tank to move farther up the hill onto the tennis court and engage the bunkers directly with its 75mm gun.

While Hawkins' 5 Brigade was moving into the left flank and Shapland's 6 Brigade was battling away on the parachute-shrouded Kohima Ridge, on the right flank, 4 Brigade had been ordered to carry out a daring flank march to the south of Kohima to cut the Imphal Road below the Aradura Spur, beginning on the night of 25 April. This was a distance of 7 miles on the map, three or four times that on the ground, and it was estimated that it would take four days. It was a journey that very few had ever before undertaken. There were no paths. The terrain is the most intimidating and hostile of the entire region, comprising deep, almost vertical, jungle-covered gullies falling between the rear of Mount Pulebadze and the face of Mount Japfü, underneath a thick canopy of jungle. Few Nagas had ever before ventured into its jungled gloom.

On day three, after covering 4 miles on the map, the brigade lay deep in the valley between Pulebadze and Mount Japfü – a miserable, wet and gloomy world hidden under the jungle canopy, lit only by the glowing phosphorescence of rotting vegetation – when a message arrived from Stopford. Instead of attempting to carry on to the Aradura Spur on the extreme east of the Kohima area, the brigade was ordered to climb left over the Pulebadze Ridge and come down on the Kohima side to fall against the Japanese positions on the GPT Ridge, which were proving a serious hindrance to the troops of 6 Brigade attempting to overcome the defiant Japanese defenders on Kohima Ridge. The brigade accordingly turned left, climbing up and over the Pulebadze Ridge that night and beginning the slow descent through the jungle down onto the Kohima side. A prominent pimple above the GPT Ridge, known as Oaks Hill, sitting at 6,000 feet, was occupied by the Norfolks and 143 Company on 1 May, the presence of British troops 1,500 feet above their positions becoming known to the Japanese for the first time.

The heavy jungle on the slopes of Mount Pulebadze meant it was almost impossible to tell where one was, however, and judging where the Japanese position might be on GPT Ridge could not be considered an exact science. 4 Brigade had to make its uncertain journey down the slopes, feeling its way, in torrential rain, alert for the Japanese. One of its battalions – the Royal Scots – stopped and occupied Oaks Hill, the brigade artillery back in Jotsoma on standby to pound any Japanese positions the Norfolks, who were pressing on down the ridge, encountered. The Japanese, alert now to the dangerous presence of enemy troops above them, moved up against Oaks Hill and fought hard to expel the Royal Scots during that first night, without success. The morning that followed a night of screaming, fear-inducing attacks found the jungle undergrowth littered with Japanese bodies. It was usual practice for the Japanese to take away their dead and wounded, but on this occasion there were too few Japanese survivors for the task.

On 4 May the Norfolks found themselves in a position to assault the topmost slopes of GPT Ridge, led by their dynamic CO, Lieutenant Colonel Robert Scott. Despite the fighting the previous night at Oaks Hill above them, the Norfolks achieved almost complete surprise during their aggressive and fast-moving attack. But they managed to seize only the topmost bunkers. They had secured the upper part of GPT Ridge while, simultaneously, Indian troops of 161 Indian Brigade captured the area south-east of Two Tree Hill, offering the possibility of linking Jotsoma with 4 Brigade on the forward slopes of Pulebadze for the first time. But the Japanese bunker complex on GPT was much more substantial than the British had expected, with dozens of small, carefully sited bunkers littering the entire area with interlocking arcs of fire, while the entire position was also covered by Japanese machine guns farther to the east on the high ground on Aradura Spur.[2] No sooner would one be discovered and attacked than another would open up against the attackers from somewhere else. Until the entirety of GPT was cleared, Goschen's brigade could not enjoy the short-cut through to Jotsoma via Two Tree Hill, the road to Imphal remained in

Japanese hands, and their machine guns continued to spray fire on 6 Brigade's exposed right flank.

Attempting to work through Japanese positions across Kohima as a whole proved to be a slow, bloody grind. Close cooperation between infantry and tanks on Garrison Hill was necessary to make even slow progress, each bunker having to be destroyed while fire from supporting Japanese positions was suppressed. On the left, in the sprawling Naga Village that lay atop the large hill on which the settlement was spread, a dozen surrounding hills needed to be captured to remove enemy positions. All of these operations absorbed troops like a sponge. Some were bypassed so as to concentrate on the main Japanese position and Sato's HQ in Naga Village. Meanwhile, the newly arriving units of 7 Indian Division, flown into Dimapur from Arakan between 5 and 9 April, reinforced the centre, on Garrison Hill and Jail Hill. Attacks from the heights of Pulebadze on GPT Ridge resulted in the successful seizure of the Japanese positions, but at high cost. With Garrison Hill cleared, repeated attacks on Jail Hill through the first week of May were unable to break the Japanese stranglehold on this large feature.

Sunday 7 May 1944 was described as the 'Black 7th' by those who were there, as no prospect of a breakthrough against the Japanese appeared in sight. After 34 days of relentless fighting, the Japanese still held all the key ground, together with all of that – and more – they had seized since 4 April. Allied morale was edging lower, as the men struggled to contemplate how the intransigent Japanese might be moved from their bunkers. The Japanese feat of arms at Kohima was a miracle of defensive tenacity rarely matched in the annals of war. Despite their lack of supplies, Sato's troops dug themselves in with skill and imagination, ensuring that each bunker was mutually supported. Sato's defensive technique, while it was not going to enable him to break through Kohima by dint of offensive action, was designed to do the next best thing: to draw the enemy onto defences of great complexity and depth and to break them there, both physically and morally. In so doing, his troops had to withstand the sort of conditions few other soldiers in history could have survived. They did so, and very nearly succeeded in persuading Stopford that battering through Kohima was an impossible task. Between 4 and 7 May, for instance, the 38 3.7-inch mountain guns dug in around Jotsoma fired over 3,000 rounds, the 48 25-pounders supporting the division fired over 7,000 rounds and the big 5.5-inch guns of the medium artillery fired more than 1,500 shells at the Japanese positions, not to mention the almost continuous salvoes from the massed 3-inch mortars of the infantry battalions and the constant strafing and bombing by Hurricanes and Vengeance dive-bombers from the sky. In spite of this almost endless torrent of fire and steel, Sato's troops continued to fight back doggedly and skilfully, boasting little more than their courage and resolve as, with virtually no air support, only a few artillery pieces and anti-tank guns, they repeatedly kept even the most determined attacks by the troops of 14 Army at bay. Their strength of mind and willingness to fight to the death demonstrated the highest physical and moral courage and gained the grudging admiration of their enemies. There was no thought among those who fought them that the Japanese were mindless savages, but rather, horrified admiration for their skill, tenacity and fortitude.

There was a belief in some higher quarters – in particular by those whose only experience of the terrain came from reading a map in the comfort of a headquarters tent in the rear – that 2 Division's offensive lacked pace. While there was an element of truth in this criticism during the first week of 2 Division's assembly in Dimapur and its first hesitant and cautious movement into the hills, it was not true thereafter. These accusations, to the hard-pressed men on the ground, were preposterous. It was impossible for commanders and staff officers in the rear who could not see the ground to understand how a small piece of jungle-topped hillside could absorb the best part of a brigade; how a small group of well-sited bunkers could hold up an advance until every single one – together with every single occupant – had been systematically destroyed; how only medium artillery (the 5.5-inch medium gun) could penetrate the roof of a Japanese trench; how only direct and short-range sniping by Lee-Grant tanks was guaranteed to defeat a Japanese bunker; how the desperate terrain, incessant rain and humidity led even the fittest men quickly to tire, and what an extraordinarily determined opponent they faced. With few exceptions, the Japanese only gave in when they were dead. Every conscious man who could lift a weapon fought until he collapsed. There was another insinuation, too, never written down but whispered by veterans long after the event. This was that Indian soldiers were more robust than their British counterparts. This was one of the reasons why 2 Division hadn't been asked for earlier, and were only invited to the party in extremis. The fighting at Kohima belies this accusation, however. There is no evidence that by 1944 and 1945 where units failed in battle, through exhaustion for instance, British units fared any worse than Indian. In the final analysis, training, small-group leadership and the quality of the support that units received – regular hot food, for instance, the quality and immediacy of the care available for their wounded, regular mail and news from home for British troops – were critical in sustaining morale and enabling the fight to be taken to the enemy over long periods of time in extreme climatic and topographical conditions.

Attacking perseverance with cunning rather than a bludgeon proved to be the key that unlocked Kohima. In the weeks that followed Black Sunday, 5 Brigade on the left flank, 6 Brigade on Garrison Hill, the newly arrived 33 Indian Brigade (7 Indian Division) on the southernmost slopes of the Kohima Ridge, and 4 Brigade on the right below Pulebadze, ate away slowly at the Japanese defences. Nowhere were sudden gains made, but by gradual perseverance and the application of focused firepower the Japanese were destroyed, bunker by bunker, trench by trench. Rarely did the Japanese run, or retreat, remaining to die where they fought. The fighting was so close, so intense, that bullets were no respecter of rank. 2 Division lost four brigadiers in the Kohima battle, two killed and two wounded.

British progress, though slow, remained sure, even though, to the troops on the ground, it seemed as if this battle would go on for ever. 4 Brigade cleared GPT Ridge on 11 May, by which time further costly attacks by 6 British and 33 Indian Brigades had finally forced the Japanese to relinquish their hold on the remaining Japanese positions on Jail Hill, although parts of Garrison Hill, including the tennis court, remained in Japanese hands. The tide was slowly – and painfully – beginning to turn. On the days that followed, the positions seized on 11 and 12 May were carefully consolidated, the remaining Japanese being exterminated one by one, sniper by sniper and gun by gun. No one could ever assume that a position was fully cleared until every body, every trench, every clump of undergrowth or pile of rubbish had been painstakingly checked over, as sometimes, days after a position had been 'captured', an apparent corpse in his foxhole might pop up and fire off his last remaining rounds or throw a grenade at an unsuspecting soldier. The Field Service Depot (known as FSD) was cleared on 12 May, discovering that the Japanese had honey-combed the hill with tunnels, creating an elaborate underground fortress that included a battalion headquarters, repair shop, ammunition storage dump and hospital. Fortunately, the monsoon rain reduced visibility dramatically, bringing with it cloud that worked as effectively as smoke as an obscurant, acting dramatically to reduce the volume of sniper fire which, until the last, remained a pestilential curse across the battlefield. Those Japanese bunkers on the western edge of the ridge that remained out of reach of the British artillery could now be engaged directly and at point-blank range by the Lee-Grants, trundling up the road dividing DIS and Jail Hill. Tanks and infantry finally captured the tennis court on 14 May. The capture of the southern end of the Kohima Ridge a full 37 days after the first arrival of Sato's men enabled the Lee-Grants to trundle their way around the road and to use their guns against the remaining bunkers on the lower slopes of both Pimple Hill and GPT Ridge. Then, on 15 May, patrols from 5 Brigade moved down from Naga Hill, secured Treasury Hill and met up with the victors of Kohima Ridge on the Imphal Road.

The capture of the Kohima Ridge was a remarkable triumph for the men of 2 British and 7 Indian Divisions, following those who had held on so grimly at the start of the siege. But across the rest of the Kohima area lay a string of other Japanese positions, all of which remained to be eliminated: there was never any expectation that they might surrender, and they needed to be cleared by hand, inch by bloody inch. Two principal redoubts remained: Point 5120 on Naga Hill and the Aradura Spur to the east, the last remaining barrier on the road to Imphal. It wasn't until 4 June, in the grim monsoon rains, that the final objective was taken. The Japanese fought to their last breath. For the British and Indians, artillery ammunition was now desperately short. Tanks had to be hauled up the steep hills by bulldozers. But Slim didn't have the time for a protracted reverse siege of Kohima. He needed the road to Imphal open as quickly as possible, and major pockets of enemy resistance were left to wither on the vine. Lieutenant General Montagu Stopford now reorganized his forces in an attempt to maintain the greatest possible pressure on the Japanese. On 23 May, Messervy's 7 Indian Division[3] took responsibility for what had been 5 Brigade's area of operations on the left flank. This switch allowed Grover to concentrate the remainder of his tired division for an attack on the Japanese positions on Aradura Spur. Both sets of attacks, first on Japanese defences around Point 5120 on the left of the battlefield, and then on Aradura Spur by Grover's 2 Division on the right, turned out to be miserable failures. On Naga Hill, heavy attacks by Hurribombers were made from the air during 24 and 25 May, but the Japanese remained firmly entrenched and resolutely immovable. The proud 4/15 Punjab suffered a bloody reverse in these assaults, losing 18 officers and 443 casualties for not a single yard of ground in return. No combination of attacks from the air, artillery strikes, tanks, flame-throwers, infantry or mortars could shift what one soldier described with some awe as 'this incredible Japanese infantry'. Nothing seemed to be working, the troops were tiring, and their morale – as a result of repeated failure to break the most stubborn defences imaginable – was plummeting. It was clear that if success were not achieved soon, morale might reach the point of no return.

The Japanese were, however, at this time beginning to recognize the limits of their own endurance. On 23 May, Sato, in an exhortation almost unimaginable in a British army (although it had been given to Captain John

Young at Kharasom), had ordered his men, 'You will fight to the death. When you are killed you will fight on with your spirit.'[4] But by now Sato realized that he was not going to be able to force the British from Kohima, or even hold on indefinitely to what little he had gained. On 25 May he sent a signal to Mutaguchi which veiled an appeal to allow him to withdraw what remained of his division, on the premise that it had run out of rations, and the effect of the heavy monsoon rains required it 'to move to a point where he could receive supplies by 1 June at the latest'. Reading between the lines, Mutaguchi replied bluntly three days later, 'It is very difficult to understand why your division should evacuate under the pretext of difficult supply, forgetting its brilliant services. Maintain the present condition for ten days. Within that time I shall take Imphal and reward you for your services. A resolute will makes the Gods give way.'[5]

Sato's final defence of Kohima was based on holding the two remaining bastions, one on Aradura Spur on the extreme left of his position, and the other on Hunter's Hill on his extreme right. His last chance was that the British would exhaust and demoralize themselves in repeated attacks on positions that they had not demonstrated any propensity thus far to penetrate, let alone overcome. But the British could not simply ignore Sato's bastions, nor could they be bypassed if the road to Imphal was to be reached and used to bring relief to the beleaguered IV Corps. Accordingly, Grover ordered simultaneous assaults on both to take place on 27 and 28 May. The 6 Brigade attack on 28 May failed miserably. The weather was poor, the terrain atrocious and the morale of the exhausted 2 Division as low as it had been since its arrival. The obstinate Japanese just did not know when they were beaten, and British soldiers begrudged having to lay down their lives merely to teach them this lesson. Further attacks up the steep jungled banks of Aradura Spur were thrown back. It is no exaggeration to say that the failure of 2 Division to secure the Aradura Spur was perhaps the lowest point of the long battle for Kohima. Yet again the Japanese had demonstrated their immovability, defying the odds despite their increasing weakness. The British troops were wet, exhausted and some units reduced to skeleton numbers, while, in at least one battalion, morale had reached the point at which the commanding officer was sacked. The tide began to change on the left flank of the battlefield when a night infiltration by 4/1 Gurkha took the Japanese entirely by surprise. By 1 June it was clear that the Japanese were pulling back.

Sato's sense of alienation from HQ 15 Army had not diminished during May. He was in no doubt that it was Mutaguchi's abject failure to send supplies through the mountains that had forced him to undertake the kind of passive defence in which his division was now engaged, preventing him from continuing offensive operations. On 27 May, Sato signalled Major General Tazoe, commander of 5 Air Division, 'Since leaving the Chindwin, we have not received one bullet from you, nor a grain of rice. We are still under attack by the enemy. Please send us food by plane.'[6] Tazoe was personally sensitive to Sato's plight but perhaps acute embarrassment led to him not sending a response. Waiting in vain for any positive communication from Tamu, where Mutaguchi had finally taken his headquarters, four days later Sato reported that the position was hopeless, and that he reserved the right to act on his own initiative and withdraw when he felt that it was necessary to do so, so as to save what remained of his battered division from inevitable destruction. In fact, later that day he signalled Mutaguchi, 'We have fought for two months with the utmost courage, and have reached the limits of human fortitude. Our swords are broken and our arrows spent. Shedding bitter tears, I now leave Kohima.'[7]

Mutaguchi ordered Sato to stay where he was. Sato ignored him and on receipt of Mutaguchi's threat to court-martial him, replied defiantly, 'Do as you please. I will bring you down with me.' The angry exchange continued, with Sato the following day sending a final message to Mutaguchi in which he declared, 'The tactical ability of the Fifteenth Army staff lies below that of cadets.' Sato then ordered his staff to close down the radio sets. The die was cast. Mutaguchi or no, he now began a fighting withdrawal with the remnants of his division. In an attempt to save face and to show that the withdrawal from Kohima was planned and under control, Mutaguchi published an Order of the Day: 'Withholding my tears and painful as it is, I shall for the time being withdraw my troops from Kohima. It is my resolve to reassemble the whole army and with one great push capture Imphal… ON THIS ONE BATTLE RESTS THE FATE OF THE EMPIRE… Everyone must unswervingly serve the THRONE and reach the ultimate goal so that the Son of Heaven [i.e., the Emperor] and the Nation may be forever guarded.'[8]

But rhetoric could not hide the bitter reality of Sato's defeat at Kohima. Sato's withdrawal demonstrated this truth, but it was a fact that Sato was sure that neither Mutaguchi nor any of his gilded staff officers back in the safe areas truly understood. Only those who had fought at Kohima could appreciate the intensity of the fighting, the desperate nature of the bloody, hand-to-hand struggle in some of the most inhospitable campaigning country on earth, in the full unrelenting fury of the monsoon, a struggle that for the Japanese, with the seemingly inexhaustible resources available to the enemy, had by now only one obvious outcome: withdrawal, or death.

Ignorant of Sato's dilemma, but harried by Stopford's (and Slim's) urgent demands to make progress towards Imphal, Grover thrust troops from the newly captured Naga Hill south-east across the valley that runs east of the Kohima Ridge to seize a series of prominent ridges – Dyer Hill, Pimple and Big Tree Hill – to outflank Miyazaki's rearguard from 124 Regiment on Aradura Spur and to bring 2 Division's embarrassment to an end. Now, the Aradura Spur was itself cut off and Sato, recognizing the inevitable, began to withdraw south on 4 June.

The battle for Kohima could now be said to be over, although the road stretching down to besieged Imphal needed to be peeled open. The most desperate and bloody struggle in the entire war on the south Asian land mass had ended. The siege and battle had lasted 64 days, had seen some of the most obdurate fighting of the war and cost the British around 4,000 men and the Japanese over 7,000. On 6 June news swept the division of the landings in Normandy. The tide seemed to be turning, everywhere.

The move to cut off the Japanese on Aradura Spur worked, although it then took, to some at least, an unconscionable period of time for XXXIII Corps to organize itself to pursue the Japanese with vigour in the direction of Imphal. Ten full days were to pass before, on 17 June, an armoured column began to make its way south, past untidy piles of blackened, bloating corpses littering the roads and tracks south, to brush aside the feeble opposition Miyazaki was able to establish at various ambush positions on the road. This long delay, evidence of the disorganized state of both 2 and 7 Divisions, which reinforced perceptions that 2 Division had not pressed its opportunities with proper vigour earlier in the battle, was to cost Grover his job. Slim and Giffard regarded 2 Division's move into the hills to have been unnecessarily tardy and placed pressure on Stopford – who in turn demanded pace from Grover – not just because of the need to relieve Imphal before the full weight of the monsoon reduced the airlift of supplies through Operation *Stamina* to a trickle, but because they knew that if 2 Division slowed it would lose the initiative and be ground down by Sato's brilliant defensive meat grinder. The first elements had arrived in Dimapur on 1 April and were complete by 11 April, while the garrison on the Kohima Ridge were first engaged by the Japanese with real intensity on 5 April. Yet the vanguard of one of Britain's proudest and best-trained and equipped infantry divisions only reached Warren's headquarters at Jotsoma on 16 April, with the relief of the exhausted survivors only being brought about on 20 April. As with much British military experience in countless wars, success – or rather, the avoidance of defeat – was achieved by the merest whisker. With the defenders of Kohima fighting for their lives in the mud and gore of the Garrison Hill, the measured arrival of 2 Division smacked to many in 14 Army as over-caution. The three brigades of 2 Division embodied the entire majesty and mythology of the old professional British Army, descendants of the 'Old Contemptibles' who had stood up so resolutely to the Hun in 1914. It had been one of the five divisions of the British Expeditionary Force sent to France at the outset of war and in its ranks resounded all the history and glory of Britain's ancient country regiments. The Japanese had never before had to fight warriors such as these.* Some argued that if Iida had had to fight 2 Division in February 1942, Burma would never have fallen. Much was naturally expected of Grover's men. The assumption was that it would storm up to Kohima in a blaze of regimental glory to relieve the siege the moment it crossed the Brahmaputra. It didn't. It appeared reluctant, cautious and stolid. To Indian Army onlookers, it was apparent that a good Indian Division, like the 5th or 7th that had recently dealt the Japanese sharp blows in Arakan, fighting with grit and boldness, was as superior as these much vaunted yeomen of Britain. Some of the shine was rubbed from 2 Division's reputation as a result. However, these same critics – Slim being one of them – failed to acknowledge that the disorganized state of Dimapur was the responsibility of Ranking's 202 Line of Communication Command – part of 14 Army – and not that of the bewildered 2 Division at all, and had forgotten that the division, when first entrained, was despatched initially to Chittagong, diverting to Dimapur only at the last minute. It is perhaps reasonable to argue that this measured advance ensured that 2 Division did not overreach itself, and arrived on the battlefield in a fit state to engage a powerful, well-led and aggressive enemy. Equally, in the days before the armoured column left for Imphal on 17 June, the Poor Bloody Infantry of Grover's division had been battling to remove Miyazaki's stubborn rearguard at Viswema and all points before. Whatever the truth, Grover was punished for the perception of failing to move with the alacrity his masters demanded.

Comparatively rapid progress was achieved down from the hills on the Imphal Road between 17 and 22 June. The route was a defensive paradise on which an army any stronger than Sato's ragged, starving and emaciated troops could conceivably have held up the British advance indefinitely. Sato's rearguard fought determinedly. Often a few men with an artillery piece, grenades and a machine gun would take up positions on the high ground above tracks, ambushing the

---

*Of course, 6 Brigade had been engaged at Donbaik the previous year.

British advance guards before melting away to repeat the performance a few miles farther back or, as was often the case, remaining obstinately in their positions until they were killed. Few were free from disease and fatigue, but surrender played no part in these men's vocabulary: they fought on until overtaken by a British bullet or bayonet or, more often, by starvation and exhaustion. But 31 Division had literally fought itself to death. Exhausted men lay in pits unable to defend themselves, suicide squads with anti-tank mines tottered towards the advancing Lee-Grants and Stuarts to be mown down by accompanying infantry, or obliterated by shellfire. The advancing troops could now see the end in sight: the Japanese blocks at Maram and then Viswema were swept aside with a fraction of the time and effort that had been expended to overcome the Japanese defences at Kohima. All of a sudden the war, or at least the long struggle to defeat the thrust against Kohima, appeared to be nearing its end.

32

Seventy-Six Days of Siege: Imphal

By the middle of May, with the Japanese now on the defensive and with IV Corps pushing aggressively against the Japanese in the north, south-east and south, Slim's worst anxieties about the prospect of Imphal falling to Mutaguchi were over. The Japanese were everywhere showing signs of faltering, despite fighting tenaciously to hold ground they had seized, and attempting still to break through at Bishenpur in the south and on the Shenam Ridge to the south-east. Consequently, Slim's priorities changed: his primary concern was now no longer the relief of Imphal but to seek a means of ensuring that Mutaguchi could not escape the close battle to which he was committed. This meant the prospect of a battle of attrition, but one in which the Allies enjoyed the overwhelming advantage in the air and on land. Slim's objective now became the utter destruction of 15 Army. Better to destroy it in Assam, he reasoned, than allow the Japanese to stream back across the Chindwin only to have to fight and defeat them again at some later stage in Burma and on ground of their own choosing. He could see that by extending his forces deeply and boldly into Manipur on multiple lines of attack, Mutaguchi was playing directly into his hands. By early May, the Japanese had suffered fearsome casualties across each part of the front, losing irreplaceable experienced fighting men, while all the time 14 Army was strengthening daily, in experience, reinforcements and supplies. With the monsoon in full flood, the physical strength of Japanese troops began to break down.

Following the dramatic reinforcement by 5 Indian Division, Imphal was defended sufficiently strongly for Slim to be confident that Scoones had the resources to deal with any eventuality. The only urgency was to ensure that IV Corps did not run out of supplies. The airlift would improve that situation in part, but the monsoon meant that the flying programme was severely disrupted. Accordingly, in early May, Slim determined that Scoones would have to reopen the road to Kohima by the third week of June to prevent the possibility of the 118,000 men and 1,000 animals still in the pocket running critically short of essential supplies. Despite Slim's confidence, more nervous voices could still be heard in the corridors of power urging the need to 'relieve Imphal'. On 1 June, Wavell wrote in his diary, 'I don't feel altogether happy about the Assam and North Burma [i.e., Chindit] operations. There is not much progress being made anywhere, especially in the vital task of reopening the Kohima–Imphal road. Meanwhile the supply by air to Imphal and to the 3rd Division columns [Operation *Thursday*] in North Burma is causing anxiety.'[1] Likewise, five days later General Alan Brooke in London could still talk in his diary of a potential disaster at Imphal, and at this time also Lieutenant General Henry Pownall – Mountbatten's Chief of Staff in HQ SEAC in Kandy – was reportedly unable to sleep because of worry about the fate of the surrounded IV Corps. Indeed, pressure was placed on Mountbatten from London to make the opening of the Kohima Road and thus the relief of Imphal his priority. However, Giffard refused to be hustled. 'Neither General Giffard nor I was as anxious as they appeared about Imphal's power to hold out,' wrote Slim; 'we knew that IV Corps would shortly take the offensive.' To his credit, Mountbatten, thus persuaded, backed his subordinates to the hilt, and directed that the road be opened by mid-July. 'I was grateful to him for not being stampeded by more nervous people into setting too early a date,' Slim recalled. 'I intended that the road should be open well before mid-July, but I was now more interested in destroying Japanese divisions than in "relieving" Imphal.'

During the land battles for the Imphal plain, air power provided the essential lubricant in Scoones' defensive machinery, a crucial ingredient in eventual British success. The role played by fighters in securing air superiority was critical in preventing Japanese attacks on the lumbering transports that provided daily supply runs into the Imphal airfields over the endless green hills rolling like ocean waves between Assam and Manipur. British air activity over the entire battlefield was intense and comprised defensive sorties to protect the airlift and the airfields, offensive ground attack sorties in support of the fighting troops, reconnaissance flights and offensive air sorties designed to hunt down and destroy the 220 Japanese aircraft flying against Manipur and Assam from Burma. In fact, the numbers of British sorties declined as the battle progressed, in part because of the decreasing number of missions launched by the Japanese as a result of their own rapidly dwindling numbers. The massive air operation in support of Operation *Stamina* across the period of the siege was a remarkable success. By 30 June, the operation had flown in 19,000 reinforcements, 14,317,000 pounds of rations, 1,303 tons of grain for animals, 835,000 gallons of fuel and lubricants, 12,000 bags of mail and 43,475,760 cigarettes, an average of 250 tons of supplies being delivered each of the 76 days of the siege. At its height in the second half of April, the airlift employed 404 aircraft from 15 squadrons. As each month went by, the contributions by the Royal Air Force and Indian Air Force were demonstrated starkly by the mathematics of war: in April 1944 there were at least 7,372 separate sorties by Spitfires, Hurricanes, Hurribombers and Vultee Vengeances. During the month 24 aircraft were lost, eight were damaged and 30 men killed. In May, 5,873 sorties were flown with 22 aircraft lost; in June, 3,938 sorties were flown. Thus, in the three months between April and June, 17,183 sorties were conducted by fighter and dive-bomber aircraft alone: the total number of air sorties, including transport flights, directly in support of Imphal and Kohima exceeded 30,000.

The Japanese air force remained aggressive and persistent throughout the long months of the siege, flying formations of aircraft against targets when they could get away with it, and darting single or pairs of aircraft through the cloud or at tree-top height to avoid the British warning radar to strike at the airfields on the plain. But resupply by air for Mutaguchi's forward troops was only ever a distant dream. The greatest deficiency of Major General Tazoe's 5 Air Division was in transport and bomber aircraft. Nor could he replace those aircraft he lost: Tazoe's limited aircraft numbers could mount a mere 1,750 sorties over the battlefields during this time, and by the end of July only 49 aircraft remained in the Japanese inventory. Japanese air power was a diminishing asset in 1944. Although able to concentrate aircraft for short periods of time over the battlefield (and for occasional aggressive sorties against the Hump airlift), overwhelming air superiority was enjoyed by the British in the skies above Manipur and the Naga Hills. The disparity between British and Japanese air strength grew more marked every day. In the period between 10 and 31 March 1944, 5 Air Division could only put up an average of 41 fighters a day. One of Tokyo's worst miscalculations in 1944 was failing to anticipate the combined strength of Allied air forces. Both Kawabe and Mutaguchi saw the invasion of India as an exercise in ground warfare, and in their assessments (if, indeed, they ever made them) of Allied air power they failed grievously to appreciate this war-winning capability enjoyed by their enemy, the dramatic development of the Allied inventory since 1942, and their own dramatic weakness.

To the north of Imphal during June, Briggs' primary focus was to open the road to Kohima while at the same time reducing the freedom of movement for Japanese troops in the mountain vastness skirted in the south by Wakan, Mapao and Runaway Hill. It was here that the hard-won lessons of Arakan were employed to full effect. Companies were launched against single features, with a single platoon advancing, a second platoon providing a firm base for the company headquarters, and the third platoon serving to exploit the position or deal with any flank attack. Long and heavy artillery concentrations were discarded for short, rapid, surprise attacks to help infantry onto the objective. The experience of Arakan had taught Briggs that whenever a position was seized which the enemy considered vital to his defence, they always reacted with continuous and unimaginative counterattacks. It was for these almost suicidal attacks that artillery concentrations were prepared. During operations at Imphal, attacks were made by battalions seizing vital positions (such as high ground and track junctions) behind the enemy, after which the enemy were forced to withdraw. 'It worked every time,' Briggs told a 1945 audience.[2] These tactics were different to those employed by the Japanese against the British in 1942 and 1943, he insisted. Then, Japanese tactics were designed to demoralize the British by cutting the line of communication, forcing the unit's retirement and by doing so relinquishing its heavy equipment. British tactics in 1944 were to force him into the open and kill him with little loss to oneself. The essential requirement was to be able to keep the infiltrating force sustained, identify the most vital feature to the enemy and ensure that artillery was well within range.

In the full ferocity of the monsoon, Salomons' 9 Brigade joined Evans' 123 Brigade in unstitching each part of the Japanese defensive tapestry as it stretched mile after agonizing mile along the road, as every curve and culvert was overlooked by Japanese-held hillocks, each of which had to be prised, painfully, from their grasp. Brigadier Crowther's 89 Brigade took over responsibility for the hilly terrain to the east. The battle for the road consisted of many small actions repeated, seemingly endlessly, often at section, platoon or sometimes company level. A hill, defile or bridge would be isolated and attacked in the traditional way by artillery if available (given the grave shortages in ammunition by this time), by battalion 3-inch mortars, by Hurribombers or Vengeances, possibly a Lee-Grant or Stuart tank firing its main armament from the road, but principally by infantry closing on the enemy bunkers with bayonet and grenade. Enemy blocks sometimes comprised infantry armed with mines and a heavy anti-tank gun, but most contained a few determined men armed with little more than bullets, bayonets and courage. British and Indian battalions were, by mid-June, now advancing beyond their supply lines, and often received urgent stores by air. Sometimes it was necessary for the sappers to construct tracks up and around hillsides to bring up tanks against Japanese positions, winches being used on occasions to inch tanks up the heavily wooded hillsides. Each day was a grind of hard physical exertion under heavy packs (and on half rations) up and down impossible hillsides awash from the torrential rain.

At the end of each day, the brigade staff would collate their casualty numbers, battalions then having to rebalance platoons and companies to take into account their losses in preparation for the next day of fighting. Every day it was the same story: nine killed and 28 wounded here; 23 killed and 42 injured there. On days where large-scale attacks were mounted, the casualty figures easily doubled these. On every occasion the only Japanese captured were those so severely wounded that they were unable of their own volition to take their own lives. All the while the monsoon deluge continued. It was impossible for the troops in the hills or on the road far below to stay dry. The fungal infection called prickly heat affected many; movement was agony for men so afflicted. Streams that had trickled and gurgled in the dry season now angrily smashed their way through every obstacle before them in raging brown torrents that drowned men and mules and swept away bridges and vehicles. The grey, dripping wet misery of the terrain was reflected in the overcast darkness of the sky which only spasmodically opened to allow through the reluctant rays of a half-forgotten sun.

Along the road, tanks inched while infantry outflanked, but at a high cost in killed and wounded. At times it appeared that 5 Division was not making any progress, and tactics being perfected in Arakan were copied in order to inject pace into the advance northwards. Wide hooks through the jungle allowed units to emerge on the road behind the Japanese blocks, and occupying high ground on Japanese lines of communication, isolating their mountaintop positions from resupply, forced them to choose between starvation or withdrawal. The one constant was the tremendous resistance put up by every Japanese position the division encountered. The weather, terrain and tenacious defence by the Japanese in their many positions in the hills overlooking the road made Briggs' advance a prolonged and bloody affair. By mid-June, after two months of fighting, the forward troops of 9 Indian Brigade had only reached a point 16 miles north of Imphal. In fierce fighting to clear the hills around a hill named 'Liver' between 19 and 21 June, for instance, Lieutenant Colonel Gerty's incomparably brave 3/9 Jats had lost 33 men killed and 111 wounded in the fighting. However, on the morning of 22 June, the battalion found that Liver had been abandoned. The Japanese had had enough: the tactics of isolation, heavy bombardment from artillery and air, and repeated assaults with bayonet and grenade had eroded their will to continue fighting. This was a new phenomenon on the Imphal battlefield but mirrored the collapse farther north at Kohima at the start of the month – a sign that what had once been a seemingly unbreakable martial confidence was now considerably more fragile and, in parts, collapsing. Later that day, men of 1/17 Dogras met troops of 2 Division at Milestone 109 on the Kohima Road. The road was open; the first major stitch in Mutaguchi's plan to seize Imphal had been undone.

Along the Shenam Ridge Yamamoto's force was now unable to maintain consistent pressure on the defenders on their muddy, bomb-cratered defences, with the result that the fighting came now in intensive spurts. Between 20 and 24 May desperate struggles developed along the ridge between Gibraltar and Malta, held by Brigadier Philip Marindin's strengthened 37 Brigade, with the Japanese securing a toehold on the former and cutting off the latter. Simultaneously, Brigadier Robert King's 1 Brigade struggled to eject the Japanese from positions they had secured on a series of features dominated by one that 1 Seaforth Highlanders dubbed 'Ben Nevis', which threatened to open up a potential means of outflanking Shenam in the north. On Gibraltar fierce counterattacks with grenade and kukri finally succeeded with the Japanese streaming away down Gibraltar, having suffered at least 150 dead; the Japanese were also driven from Ben Nevis. These actions so exhausted the Japanese that Yamamoto was forced to build up his strength before his next major offensive on the Shenam Ridge, against Scraggy, was launched on 9 June. The period between these major actions was taken up with intensive patrolling by both sides, a difficult task given the precipitous nature of the terrain and the torrential rain that made living in these conditions a debilitating nightmare. The Japanese, poorly supplied, suffered terribly.

Late on 9 June, the Japanese launched a last-ditch attempt to push the small force from 3/3 Gurkha Rifles holding Scraggy. The attack was preceded by a massive artillery bombardment, considered by some to have been the most intensive of the entire campaign. As the Gurkhas watched, swarms of desperate Japanese clambered through the mud up the now naked hillside. It was clear to the defenders, crouching in their slit trenches in the pouring monsoon rain, that this was a last 'do or die' attempt to capture the ridge. Despite inflicting severe losses on the assaulting Japanese infantry, the survivors were pushed back from part of the hill. Ouvry Roberts, recognizing the desperation of the Japanese, decided not to attempt to retake Scraggy, as it would only lead to many more casualties, concluding that the Japanese would be too tired to advance beyond the territory they had gained. He was right. Exhausted by their exertions and depleted sorely by the losses inflicted on them, the Japanese had not the energy to make any further progress towards Imphal. The fighting along this stretch of mountains took on the attritional characteristics of the fighting elsewhere: furious Japanese assaults on British positions, followed by even more furious defence of these positions against British counterattack.

On the track to Ukhrul similarly difficult terrain confronted Gracey's 20 Indian Division, following its switch from the Shenam fighting, as it sought to clear the Japanese from the territory they had captured after the struggle for Sangshak at the end of March. Here, the fighting mirrored that of 5 Division to the north: a multitude of small, though ferocious, engagements that caused daily casualties and forced progress to be undertaken as a snail's pace. Likewise, in the south, the struggle for Bishenpur did not lessen in its violent intensity as June arrived. Indeed, of the five Victoria Crosses awarded during the battle, four were won on this front. Angered by Yanagida's inability to break through, Mutaguchi accused him of timidity and at the end of May replaced him with Lieutenant General Tanaka Nobuo[3] who was rushed from Thailand to take over the job. Japanese command relationships, weak from the outset of the campaign, were now unravelling fast. Tanaka could not bring himself to believe that the task of capturing Imphal was as difficult as Yanagida had made out. 'The officers and men were more exhausted than I had expected,' he recalled when he first met them, 'but their haggard faces did not make me pessimistic about the prospect of battle.'[4] In any case, unwilling to accept publicly the possibility of failure (even though he confided to his diary that he fully expected his division to be wiped out, his men having fought for over a hundred days with little food), and stamping his own robust authority on a division which he feared had grown too pessimistic about the chances of success, Tanaka promulgated a Special Order on 2 June ordering his men to fight on until they were overtaken by either victory or annihilation.

The coming battle is the turning point. It will denote the success or failure of the Greater East Asia War. You men have got to be fully in the picture as to what the present position is; regarding death as something lighter than a feather, you must tackle the task of capturing Imphal. For that reason it must be expected that the division will be almost annihilated. I have confidence in your firm courage and devotion and believe you will do your duty, but should any delinquencies occur you have got to understand that I shall take the necessary action… in order to keep the honour of his unit bright, a commander may have to use his sword as a weapon of punishment, exceedingly shameful though it is to have to shed the blood of one's own soldiers on the battlefield. Fresh troops with unused rifles have now arrived and the time is at hand – the arrow is about to leave the bow. The infantry group is in high spirits: afire with valour and dominated by one thought and one thought only – the duty laid upon them to annihilate the enemy. On this battle rests the fate of the Empire. All officers and men fight courageously![5]

This rhetoric pleased Mutaguchi, who added some encouraging words of his own to the exhausted, hungry and malaria-ridden troops desperately struggling to stay alive in the rain-sodden quagmires of Shenam, Kohima and Bishenpur:

The struggle has developed into a fight between the material strength of the enemy and our spiritual strength. Continue in the task till all your ammunition is expended. If your hands are broken fight with your feet. If your hands and feet are broken use your teeth. If there is no breath left in your body, fight with your spirit. Lack of weapons is no excuse for defeat… There must be no room for historians of the future to say we left something undone which we ought to have done.[6]

Such determination against all odds deeply impressed Slim. 'Whatever one may think of the military wisdom of thus pursuing a hopeless object,' he commented, 'there can be no question of the supreme courage and hardihood of the Japanese soldiers who made the attempts. I know of no army that could have equalled them.' This stubbornness, however, as Slim had calculated, and as events were beginning at last to show right across the Manipur front, was also to prove their downfall. During June Tanaka repeatedly threw his weakened units forward against the hills overlooking Bishenpur and into Ningthoukhong, over which both sides struggled at fearsome cost. Once again it was the courage and stamina of the individual soldier, on both sides, which allowed the fighting to continue in spite of every impediment nature could throw at them. An attempt to seize the British-held part of Ningthoukhong on the night of 7 June by tanks and infantry failed only by virtue of the extraordinary bravery of Sergeant Hanson Turner of the West Yorkshires, who won a posthumous Victoria Cross, repelling the men of Lieutenant Araki's company of 1/67 Battalion as they attacked with tanks and automatic weapons. By heroic determination to hold the position come what may, despite most of his platoon being casualties, Turner repeatedly ran back from his forward trench when under heavy attack, to replenish himself with hand grenades from his platoon stocks. He was killed returning to his trench for the sixth time. The struggle for the village continued until 12 June, Rifleman Ganju Lama of 2/5 Gurkha repeating his performance at Torbung by destroying two Japanese tanks with a PIAT anti-tank discharger despite being severely wounded in the legs. He was awarded the Victoria Cross for his valour. This desperate fighting was reinforcing the Japanese reputation for foolhardy bravery, but it was not bringing them the strategic success that Mutaguchi demanded, and Tanaka so desired. Instead, with no reinforcements, 33 Division was rapidly reaching a point at which it would no longer exist. Following the attacks on Ningthoukhong 1/67 Battalion had no officers left, and only 38 men alive. By 30 June, 33 Division had lost 12,000 men, 70 per cent of its strength.

The physical condition of the troops of IV Corps was now a serious cause for concern. The half rations on which men were subsisting were wholly insufficient to keep them fighting fit and well nourished in the appalling conditions of the monsoon, where the cold and wet sapped the morale of even the most motivated men. Casualties mounted inexorably. In but one example, the three months of fighting for the Silchar Track cost the Northamptonshire Regiment 76 per cent of their starting strength in terms of killed, wounded or missing. Four hundred and fifty began the battle in April but only 107 marched back to Imphal in July. But every one of these men was sick, lice-ridden and hungry. They were also desperately tired and there seemed no end in sight.

33

Down the Hukawng Valley to Myitkyina

The entirety of Upper Burma north of Mandalay was the focus of intense military and political campaigning in 1944, paralleling the great battles in Manipur and Assam. It was here that Stilwell began his march from Ledo through the Hukawng Valley towards Myitkyina[1] with the aim of capturing its airfield. The capture of all the territory north of this key Kachin town would open a northern front against the Japanese, 'blood' the troops of Stilwell's Chinese divisions, link India with China through the road from Ledo, provide a critical staging post in the Hump airlift to Yunnan and, because it sat astride the Irrawaddy, provide a river line of communication into central Burma.

The road from Ledo – the 'new' Burma Road – was the focus of operations. The physical fact of its building was largely an American success story.[2] Taking responsibility for its construction on 10 December 1943, the appropriately named Colonel Lewis Pick of the United States Army Corps of Engineers completed the first 100 miles, to the remote Naga village of Shingbwiyang, where many refugees from the 1942 exodus had ended their tragic journeys, two days after Christmas. Shingbwiyang was in Burma. Reaching the village was the first fruit of a promise by Stilwell, echoing that more famous commitment by MacArthur in the Philippines, to return. Accompanying road construction was the American-trained and supplied Chinese 22 and 38 Divisions.[3] Stilwell, commanding these troops, was in his element. This was where he was happiest, and most successful, a different and much better place for him than the corridors of power in Kandy, where HQ SEAC was established in mid-1944.[4] Tactically, his approach mirrored that developed elsewhere by Slim: fix the enemy by determined resistance and firepower, outflank him and attack those enemy positions that were vital to his ability to continue fighting, such as supply dumps, railways and airfields, all the while relying on supply by air. Stilwell's physical presence in the front line with two of his divisions made a significant difference to the troops' performance. The Chinese divisions – retrained under his watchful eye at Ramgarh in India – were now demonstrating what Stilwell had always claimed they would: success on the battlefield against an enemy that had achieved almost superman status in the eyes of the soldiers.

Sun's forward battalions at the head of the Hukawng Valley made gradual but important progress against the Japanese outposts, and a series of small victories against the otherwise invincible Japanese put new heart into the Chinese soldiery. Stilwell was pleased with their performance. By the end of the month his troops had penetrated the length of the Hukawng Valley and pushed the Japanese out of the Taro plain. Morale among the fighting troops was high, now that they had defeated the Japanese in battle, and by March 1944 the Japanese had largely withdrawn to the area of Mogaung and Myitkyina. It was a remarkable performance, and due much to Stilwell's forceful personal leadership. Slim was impressed with this achievement, observing that 'No one else I know could have made his Chinese do what they did.' Stilwell had told Mountbatten that he would capture Myitkyina by the onset of the monsoon rains in May. Could he do so? Mountbatten wasn't sure.

The fortunes of Joe Stilwell and Orde Wingate collided in early 1944. The relationship between the two men was to prove short and inharmonious. The conference between Churchill and Roosevelt at Quebec in August 1943 following the supposed success of Operation *Longcloth* had given Wingate a force of 23,000 men in 23 infantry battalions – the bayonet strength of two infantry divisions – together with a vast American-supplied air armada, to mount another operation into Burma in 1944. The Air Commando he was offered comprised 12 C47s, 36 Mustang Fighters, 100 L1 and L5 light planes and 150 WACO gliders. The propaganda following *Longcloth*, together with Churchill's flattery and support, had led Wingate to believe that he had come up with a winning military strategy to defeat the Japanese. Operation *Thursday* – the name given to the second Chindit expedition – was wished on SEAC by an anxious Churchill, desperate to hold on to anything that might persuade the Americans that he was serious about his commitment to Allied war aims in the Far East. He wasn't, remaining reluctant to consider a land offensive to retake Burma. But he needed to show willing in Burma, so that the Americans would continue to show willing in the Mediterranean. This meant doing what he could to counter the Japanese threat from Burma to keep the Americans sweet, knowing the extent of the hold of 'China' on the American strategic imagination. The key thing for Churchill was keeping the alliance together: fighting the Germans (and Italians) first. Burma was always peripheral in his strategic consciousness. To this extent, Operation *Thursday* was an important component of *grand* strategy; a commitment by Britain, sealed in the blood and sweat of its soldiers, to undertake offensive ground operations in Burma as a demonstration of its commitment to the need to rebuild a road to China. It was in the tension between grand and military strategy in which Operation *Thursday* must be understood.

The plans agreed at Quebec were to undertake vigorous and aggressive land and air operations at the end of the 1943 monsoon for the purpose of reopening land communications with China by means of a road from Ledo via Myitkyina. Wingate's force was an integral part of a coordinated offensive designed to eject the Japanese from the region between the Chindwin and the Irrawaddy. While Stilwell's Chinese troops drove down the Hukawng Valley against the Japanese 18 Division to Myitkyina from the north, the Chindits would march and fly into the 'railway corridor' between Mandalay and Myitkyina to strike against the Japanese line of communication that it was presumed ran south to Indaw and thence to Mandalay. Wingate's force was thus specifically intended to assist Stilwell. This was the military strategy that reflected the grand strategic design, namely to provide 'support to Stilwell'. Simultaneously, IV Corps would cross the Chindwin from Manipur to the area Kalewa–Kalemyo and thence to Ye-U, and the Chinese – Yoke Force – would advance from Yunnan. 18 Division would be crushed in this mighty pincer. It was an elegant plan, the perfect staff college solution to the question of eliminating the Japanese presence in the region. If it worked it would push the Japanese away from the Chinese border, remove the threat to the new Ledo Road from India to China, provide the Allies with the airfield at Myitkyina, push the Japanese down to Mandalay and free up the vast area between the Chindwin and the Irrawaddy for a follow-up Allied advance into central Burma. Unfortunately, the plans were short-lived. Chiang Kai-shek insisted that an advance from Yunnan ('Yoke') be predicated on a seaborne assault against Burma. When all available amphibious resources were diverted to Europe in preparation for Normandy, he refused to put his forces at risk by advancing into Burma when Britain quite clearly wasn't prepared or able to do likewise. If the operation were to go ahead, it would have to be based solely on the Chindits providing support for Stilwell's slow advance down the Hukawng Valley.

The first problem was to find the six brigades that Wingate had been promised. This was by no means easy in an India Command with limited British troops and Wingate's antipathy towards Indian troops. Brigadier Joe Lentaigne's 111 Brigade had already begun training and joined Calvert's original 77 Brigade as the basis for what was to be called, for cover purposes, 3 Indian Division. The vastly experienced 70 Division, recently arrived from its success against Rommel during the long siege of Tobruk, was broken into three Brigades (14, 16 and 23) – each of four battalions – with the divisional combat support elements (Royal Artillery and Reconnaissance Regiment, for example) converting to infantry. Meanwhile three battalions (3 West African Brigade) were sucked from 81 West African Division, reducing the latter to two brigades.

Brigades were organized into a brigade headquarters column some 250 strong and eight columns each some 400 strong. The column had a reconnaissance platoon of Burma Rifles (Chin, Kachin, Karen or Burma Gurkhas), a demolition platoon of sappers (Garhwalis in the case of 77 and 111 Brigades, otherwise British), a support platoon of two medium machine guns (Vickers), two 3-inch mortars, and two companies each of three platoons. Platoons had radios with which to communicate with column headquarters, and the latter had an RAF set to communicate with the air base and No. 22 sets for use to the Main Brigade Headquarters and Rear Brigade Headquarters at Imphal, where Force Headquarters was initially based until the threat of *U-Go*, when it was withdrawn to Sylhet in north-eastern Bengal. Each brigade had its separate air base, these being divided between Agartala and Sylhet.

The process of developing a coherent plan for Operation *Thursday* became a running debate between Wingate and Slim. All the evidence suggests a series of stimulating and creative engagements between the two men as Wingate crafted the plans for the operation authorized by Quebec. Wingate was to observe that 'the only man to understand him' was Slim. It is clear that the debate from Slim's perspective hinged on how best to fulfil the grand strategic commitment by Britain to place British troops in the heart of Burma 'in support of Stilwell', with an operational plan that was as fully aligned as it could be with nascent British plans for an advance by IV Corps into Burma. Insofar as it is possible to determine Wingate's mind, it appears that his primary goal was to demonstrate that his powerful LRP formation could undo the Japanese militarily in Burma, and prove to be the way in which the country was reconquered. Ill with typhoid for much of the final quarter of 1943, Wingate outlined his first set of ideas to his brigade commanders on 23 December. Special Force would operate in two waves, each of which would be in action for a period of two months before being relieved. The first wave of three brigades (77, 16 and 111) would march into Upper Burma in February and March 1944, with one brigade being flown into Yunnan in China, approaching Burma from the east. In the second phase, 14, 23 and

3 West African Brigades would relieve the original brigades. The aim was to dominate an area of 40-mile radius around the town of Indaw, from where the railway went north to Myitkyina, and roads led west to the Chindwin. The second wave would hand over to two airborne divisions (which existed only in Wingate's imagination), who would fly into the airfield at Indaw and hold the area during the monsoon between June and October 1944. Indaw was to be the locus of subsequent advances by the British (from Imphal), the Americans (from the Hukawng Valley) and the Chinese (from Yunnan). This expansive plan didn't survive contact with 14 Army, however. The resources for an advance by IV Corps from Imphal simply did not exist.

Slim didn't have the opportunity to outline his operational concept to Wingate for 'Special Force' until 4 January 1944. In line with the plan to assist Stilwell, the task given to the Chindits was to dominate the railway corridor north from Mandalay, cutting the Japanese line of communication to Myitkyina, thus taking pressure off Stilwell as he advanced on the town from the north. This, however, was disappointingly small beer for Wingate. Although he conformed to his orders, he harboured grander plans, made clear in two letters to Mountbatten on 10 and 11 February. In his view, the days of the big conventional armies were over. Instead, LRP forces of the type he was preparing to take into Burma could win the war. He, presumably, would lead this army. There is no recorded response in the archives to these two missives. One presumes that they were placed in Mountbatten's pending tray: there is no evidence that they were shown to Slim at the time. Wingate had become fixated on the idea that his Chindit force alone would bring about the defeat of the Japanese in Burma, going so far as to doubt whether conventional forces even had a role in a future campaign. His letter to Mountbatten argued that Slim's 14 Army could never hope to be in a position to fight over the mountains bordering the Chindwin and that only the Chindits had the training and wherewithal to take the war to the Japanese in Burma. Further, Wingate believed that long-range penetration formations like the Chindits 'would supersede conventional formations with such impedimenta as tanks, artillery and motorised transport.'[5] He argued that the seizure of a town in central Burma by long-range penetration forces should be the first of a series of stepping-stones that could take the Allies directly to Bangkok, Saigon and thence up the coast of China. When the Chindits had seized one stepping-stone, they could then be supported by conventional forces following up behind. This reflected Wingate's pessimism about what could ever be achieved by conventional operations against the Japanese.

By mid-January it was found impossible to cross the Chindwin anywhere between Homalin and Kalewa, as the Japanese were in force all along the east bank. The plans finalized by Slim and Wingate at Ranchi on 19 January were adjusted so that one unlucky brigade (Fergusson's 16 Brigade) had to walk in from Ledo to its stronghold at Aberdeen, 27 miles north-west of Indaw, via

MAP 8 Operation *Thursday*

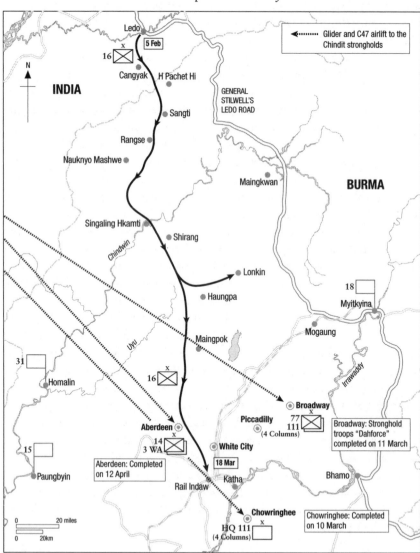

Lonkin at the headwaters of the Meza River. This journey alone measured 360 miles. The other two brigades – Brigadier Michael Calvert's 77 and Brigadier Joe Lentaigne's 111 – following agreement with Lieutenant Philip Cochran, commander of 1 Air Commando Group, were to be flown in by C47 and gliders to 'strongholds' in the Indaw area. The fly-in strongholds were given the code names 'Broadway' and 'Piccadilly'. Broadway – 35 miles east-northeast of Indaw and Piccadilly, 40 miles north-east – were in the Kyaukke Valley. Calvert's brigade was to fly in on 5 March 1944, and Lentaigne's brigade would fly to Broadway and to Chowringhee, 35 miles east of Indaw, on 6 March 1944.

The idea of the stronghold was a new concept, a significant change to the mobile guerrilla concept deployed the year before on Operation *Longcloth*.[6] The idea was that each column would have a secure base deep in enemy territory, which would help sustain offensive operations against enemy targets. The secret would be locating them in areas inaccessible to enemy wheels, artillery and tanks. Each would be strongly protected, with a garrison battalion together with field and anti-aircraft artillery (the lack of which proved to be a severe deficiency during Operation *Longcloth*), while another battalion would provide 'floating' protection. Each was to contain an air strip capable of receiving C47 transports, and they were intended by Wingate to be self-contained, provide their own clean water, and grow rice, chickens and eggs. The remaining battalions would conduct offensive operations using the base as an anchor.

Slim's role was to manage Wingate; he had no ultimate control over the decision to undertake *Thursday*. His underlying suspicion was that Operation *Thursday*, even if it were to achieve the strategic objective set for it, had the wrong operational underpinnings. Slim's view was that while long-range penetration operations might have strategic merit, they did so only when supporting activities by conventional forces, and had little value in and of themselves. Raids, no matter how spectacular, could not win wars. The problem with Wingate's plan, as far as Slim could observe, was that the moment the force ceased behaving as guerrillas it would be a magnet for unwanted enemy attention. The stronghold concept at a stroke changed *Thursday* from a guerrilla operation of the kind that characterized the intent behind Operation *Longcloth*, to a more conventional force requiring conventional troops and weapons. Wingate's insertion would play directly to the enemy's strengths, rather than his weaknesses, because it meant placing his forces precisely where the Japanese were strongest and where his own line of communication would be by air and thus extremely tenuous. By placing his force in the heart of the enemy's own territory, where the advantage of communication and supply lay firmly with the Japanese, Slim knew that Wingate could never hope to achieve the decisive advantage he sought. His aircraft-supplied troops, light in artillery and bereft of armour, would exhaust themselves quickly, particularly if they were used for conventional rather than guerrilla purposes. It would be far better, Slim reasoned, to force the Japanese into this situation of vulnerability instead.

For the time being, however, the debate needed to stop, and Wingate knuckle down against 18 Division.

Shortly before the operation to lift 77 Brigade was due to begin on 5 March, an aerial photograph of Piccadilly showed that the landing site was obstructed with logs. The photograph was immediately shown to Wingate and Slim. Wingate concluded that the Japanese had ambushed Piccadilly, that the whole operation had been compromised and should therefore be called off. Slim disagreed, however, as did Michael Calvert, commander of 77 Brigade. Slim was certain that not all of the landing sites could have been compromised. He knew that Stilwell needed the help Special Force was to bring, and that 16 Brigade, already on its insertion march, could not simply be abandoned. He knew also that morale among Special Force – now at fever pitch – would not recover if the operation were cancelled. Accordingly, he made the decision to continue the operation, Piccadilly was abandoned, and the troops switched to Broadway instead.[7]

Of the 61 gliders that set off for Broadway that night, only 35 landed at their destination. Nevertheless, some 400 men landed during the night, together with enough mechanical equipment to enable an airstrip capable of taking C47s to be constructed. On the following three nights, 272 aircraft sorties landed at Broadway, completing the fly-in of the whole 77 Brigade. There was no interference from the Japanese during the operation. Within a week, both 77 and 111 Brigades, totalling 9,000 men, 1,350 animals and 250 tons of stores, an anti-aircraft and a 25-pounder gun battery, were landed by 650 C47 and glider sorties into the heart of Burma. Together with 16 Brigade, Wingate had 12,000 men well placed, as he put it, 'in the enemy's guts'. There was very little interference from the Japanese air force, which had been reduced by this time to approximately 90 aircraft in the whole of northern Burma. Surprise low-level air attacks were made on a number of enemy airfields, which further reduced the Japanese ability to counter Allied activity both in the air and on the ground over the period of the fly-in. By 15 March, a block was established at Henu, known as White City after the parachutes that littered the site. Throughout the remainder of the month, and in April, Special Force mounted attacks throughout the area, cutting the railway to Myitkyina, and dominating a 30-mile-long corridor astride the railway.

The landings took the Japanese by surprise. The first news of the enemy encroachment reached 15 Army HQ on 9 March, but it took some time for the size and significance of the invasion to sink in. Nevertheless, once this had been appreciated, a force of rear echelon and support personnel – which within four weeks was of divisional size – was formed to counter the landings. After the deployment had begun, Wingate began to press for Special Force to support 14 Army directly by attacking Mutaguchi's rear. He proposed as much in a paper on 13 March 1944. Wingate told Calvert: 'We have got to help 14th Army. We are all, including Stilwell, under 14th Army command, and in spite of my complaints at times, they have been very helpful on the whole, even if they did doubt the practicability of this operation. Now they are converted.'[8]

Slim accepted Wingate's argument that Brigadier Brodie's 14 Brigade could offer some usefulness in attacking for a time the lines of communication to 31 and 15 Divisions. His instructions on 20 March to redeploy 14 Brigade in support of 14 Army, after supporting Fergusson's 16 Brigade attack on Indaw, was manna from heaven for Wingate.[9] So, instead of keeping 14 and 3 West African Brigades as replacements for the first phase, they were flown in to a new stronghold, Aberdeen, 40 miles west of the railway, beginning on 22 March. While this was a change from Wingate's original instructions to support Stilwell, Slim believed that the threat to Imphal was such that he was justified in temporarily re-deploying one of Wingate's brigades to meet the new threat.[10] For his part, Wingate believed that re-deploying his force to assist 14 Army would help prove his principal theory, namely that LRP action alone would degrade 15 Army's lines of communication to the extent that it would be the decisive factor in bringing about the defeat of the enemy. When this had been proved, as he was sure it would be, Wingate believed that Special Force would be substantially reinforced and perhaps even given the lead in defeating 15 Army. The flaw in this logic was that 15 Army took such logistic risks that they planned to be virtually self-sufficient until they had captured British stocks in Manipur, and thus were remarkably resilient to attacks on their long supply chain. Indeed the Railway Corridor itself proved to be much less of an active Japanese line of communication than Wingate had assumed, as the Irrawaddy to the east provided a good alternative. Action to interdict the Japanese line of communication in the early weeks of an offensive therefore only had a marginal impact on Japanese intentions. The force gathered by the Japanese to counter Wingate's operation was hastily cobbled together rear-echelon troops – albeit of divisional strength – and did not constitute a substantive diversion of troops from Operation *U-Go*. Mutaguchi purported not to be worried about Operation *Thursday*. His view was that the more troops Wingate poured into Burma the better, as the key battleground would not be there, but at Imphal. A captured Japanese officer recorded that

Wingate's operation was an irritant to the fortunes of Operation *U-Go* although it didn't change Japanese plans:

> The Chindits interfered with the Imphal Operations from the very start and forced 15th Army to divert one battalion each of the 15th and 33rd Divisions, to deal with them. Also diverted was the main force of the 53rd Division which was to be the general reserve for the Burma Area Army and was, if there had been no such emergency as the descent of the Chindits, to have reinforced the 15th Army at Imphal. The 5th Air Division was obliged to use up half its strength against the Chindits when its full strength should have been employed to support the 15th Army.[11]

A secondary problem was the question of who or what would replace Special Force once its two months in the field had expired. With the deployment of 14 and 3 West African Brigades to the area of operations, the planned end date for the entire operation was now mid- to late May 1944, not the six months that Wingate had first projected.

With the onset of Operation *U-Go*, Stilwell had worried about the defence of the railway between Jorhat and Ledo and told Slim that he planned to divert one of his two Chinese divisions to the Brahmaputra Valley to guarantee the security of this critical line of communication to Ledo. The imminent threat to Kohima and Dimapur gave Slim a similar problem. It was for this reason that on 8 March 1944 he asked Giffard for one of Wingate's brigades for the defence of the vast, remote swathe of the Naga Hills which lie to the north and east of Kohima. This would interrupt Japanese efforts to resupply their forward troops should they launch an offensive against Kohima and Dimapur, and restrict their opportunity to use the mountains to break through into the Brahmaputra Valley, while presenting a tangible demonstration to the Naga people of Britain's intent to expel the invader. It would also solve Stilwell's problem of securing the Brahmaputra Valley and mean that he wouldn't have to divert one of his precious divisions away from offensive tasks in the Hukawng Valley. Slim authorized the despatch of 23 Brigade in early April, where it was moved by road, rail, river steamer, and narrow-gauge railway to Bokajan, 10 miles beyond Dimapur in the Brahmaputra Valley, from where it could make its ascent eastwards into the Naga Hills. The diversion of the brigade, under the command of the tall, gaunt, monocled Brigadier Lancelot Perowne, to help defend Kohima, was inspired by Slim's grasp of what the Japanese would need to do to sustain their operations over incredibly difficult terrain 160 miles from their sources of supply east of the

Chindwin. The RAF would fly interdiction missions against the Chindwin by day and night to harry the Japanese supply boats, convoys, tracks, bridges, rest camps and depots, but this would do little but jab pinpricks into the Japanese operation from the air. What was needed was a complementary force on the ground, which would maximize the effectiveness of air power by giving the RAF eyes on the jungle floor, denied to them by the thick green canopy, and which could occupy ground, something that air power alone could not do. Such operations were ideally suited to the troops of 23 Brigade, who had been brought by dint of hard training to an unmatched level of physical toughness and battlefield preparation.

Other problems began to undermine Wingate's original plans. One was the exhaustion of the 4,000 men and 500 mules of Fergusson's 16 Brigade, who were forced to march 360 miles from Ledo to the Indaw area. The brigade left Ledo on 5 February, but because of difficult terrain it was already ten days behind schedule by 28 March. They were unable to carry with them the heavy weapons and ammunition required to survive a large-scale contact with the Japanese. To compound their exhaustion, Slim was worried that Wingate underestimated Japanese tenacity in battle and believed that Special Force would find the opposition stiffer than expected. Additionally, Wingate now found himself using his brigades in a conventional role, for which they were not suited or trained. For instance, 77 Brigade was ordered to build Broadway into 'a small fortress in open country astride the railway' and to hold it indefinitely.[12] This contravened Wingate's original argument that strongholds were to be bases for rest and supply, protected by 'floater' columns, and sited in country 'so inaccessible that only lightly equipped enemy infantry can penetrate to it... We can transport our defensive stores there by air: the enemy cannot.' Likewise, Calvert's stronghold on the railway at White City made it vulnerable to Japanese armour and artillery. The practical outworking of Operation *Thursday*, perhaps because of the speed with which the plans had been constructed, ignored the fundamental dichotomy between the security principle that lay at the heart of Operation *Longcloth* – mobility – and the physical fact of the strongholds on Operation *Thursday*. Strongholds sound good in theory, but they would nevertheless act as the honey pot to the Japanese wasp. If the latter's sting was powerful enough, the stronghold concept would transform the Chindits into conventional forces stuck far behind enemy lines, requiring conventional weapons and force structures to enable them to respond, and to survive.

Then, the architect of the entire Chindit idea and its unwavering progenitor was killed in an air crash in the hills west of Imphal on 24 March. Perhaps with an eye to the biographer, Mountbatten wrote to his wife, Edwina, on 2 April

1944, 'I cannot tell you how much I am going to miss Wingate. Not only had we become personal friends but he was such a fire-eater, and it was such a help to me having a man with a burning desire to fight. He was a pain in the neck to the generals over him, but I loved his wild enthusiasm and it will be very difficult for me to try and inculcate it from above.'[13]

The nature of the operation changed immediately. 'Without his presence to animate it', wrote Slim, 'Special Force would no longer be the same to others or to itself. He had created, inspired, defended it and given it confidence; it was the offspring of his vivid imagination and ruthless energy. It had no other parent.' Slim's wording of this eulogy is interesting. It reflects the assertion by one of his biographers that the Chindit ideal died with Wingate. Sykes argues that this was because they no longer enjoyed 'Wingate's inventive mind to devise a role for them in new circumstances', indicating perhaps that the Chindit role actually had little to justify it outside of Wingate's personal advocacy.[14] The truth seems more prosaic. Wingate had unwittingly deployed his so-called guerrilla forces into the heart of enemy territory but had given them a conventional concept – the stronghold – against which their operations were to revolve. He was then killed before the inevitable contradiction in these ideas was revealed.

The challenge of resolving these fell to his successor, Brigadier Joe Lentaigne. He flew to Jorhat from Aberdeen in a C64 Norseman for a conference with Slim, Stilwell, Mountbatten, John Baldwin (3 Tactical Air Force), Haydon Boatner (Stilwell's deputy) and Stopford, on 3 April. With Operation *U-Go*, unanticipated of course by Wingate, the situation had suddenly become complicated across every area of the front. In Manipur IV Corps was fighting for its life, and the Japanese were thought to be days away from arriving in the hills above Dimapur. Stilwell's advance in the Hukawng Valley was held up at Maingkwang. Lentaigne explained the situation with Special Force and was surprised by Slim's comment that he had never before heard of the two-month limit on operations. Lentaigne's summary of the situation was:

- Without 23 Brigade, he no longer had a reserve;
- 3 West African Brigade had been broken up to provide garrison protection for Aberdeen and Broadway;
- At Aberdeen:
  - 16 Brigade was worn out with its long march and unsuccessful attempt to capture Indaw;
  - 14 Brigade and the third West African battalion were being flown in very slowly (they did not complete their fly in till 12 April due to the competing airlift to Imphal);

- Aberdeen (14 Brigade) was in no way a stronghold, connected as it was by two 10-mile jeepable tracks to main roads. It would struggle to survive a serious attack;
- The airstrip was not all-weather and would become unusable when the monsoon came in May or June. Thereafter, he would have no opportunity for evacuation or reinforcement by C47 or even light plane.
- At White City:
  - The stronghold was a pinpoint target roughly 300 yards square, accessible by road and rail;
  - 77 Brigade was holding the block at White City by its eyelids and was very tired.
- At Broadway:
  - A Japanese battalion had attacked Broadway and been badly mauled and driven off for the time being;
  - 111 Brigade (2½ battalions) was moving against Japanese communications westward to the Chindwin as ordered by Slim;
  - The same problem pertained to the fair-weather airstrip as Aberdeen.[15]

Slim told Lentaigne that there were no airborne troops to take over from Special Force as Wingate had originally planned (one wonders whether he also explained that these troops had never existed); that Lentaigne should plan for a distinct shortage of C47s for continuing supply operations to Special Force because of the emergency at Imphal, and, because of the advent of Mutaguchi's offensive, there could be no time limit for Chindit operations. He was instructed to come up with a new deployment plan for Special Force which encapsulated these realities, but in which 14 and 111 Brigades would focus on 15 Army's lines of communication on the Chindwin.

Lentaigne proposed that he redeploy his brigades northward more directly to assist Stilwell's efforts in the battle for Mogaung and Myitkyina. His plan was to create another block 50 miles north of White City, near the railway in the Hopin area, to be called Blackpool, after which the exhausted 16 Brigade was to be evacuated by air and the remaining strongholds abandoned. His aim was to concentrate his remaining units (77, 111, 14 and 3 West African Brigades) to attack Mogaung from the south, while Stilwell's forces attacked from the north. Slim agreed to all these plans, as did Stilwell, after some persuasion. Stilwell believed that Special Force could do more harm in and around Indaw than moving north, but when he realized the difficulties involved for the Chindits remaining in that area for too long (and into the monsoon) he agreed to Lentaigne's plan.

On 9 April a meeting between Mountbatten, Slim, and Lentaigne confirmed that Special Force would be firmly committed to assisting Stilwell. Slim was later to consider that his decision on 9 April was a mistake. 'Imphal was the decisive battle', he wrote; 'it was there only that vital injury could be inflicted on the Japanese Army, and I should have concentrated all available forces to that end. I fear I fell into the error of so many Japanese, and persisted in a plan which should have been changed.' He was constrained by the grand strategic direction SEAC had been given by Churchill and Roosevelt, although by this stage enough water had passed under the bridge – not to mention the change in strategic circumstances with the onset of Operation *U-Go* – to amend these plans. As a result, concludes the historian Raymond Callahan, Operation *Thursday*, despite 'an epic of courage and endurance, became irrelevant to the decisive battles taking place around Imphal and Kohima.'[16]

During April Mike Calvert's 77 Brigade enjoyed considerable success astride the railway at White City, despite its accessibility to Japanese artillery and armour. The Japanese, desperate to reopen the line of communication to 18 Division, launched ferocious attacks on the position during the month, with infantry, artillery and light tanks. This wasn't what the men had prepared for, nor indeed was it what the Chindit concept had envisaged. It is a testament to the battle readiness of the troops that they were able to resist all these efforts to destroy them. But it became clear that the strongholds were now acting as magnets for Japanese fury, no longer able to act in the manner Wingate had originally envisaged, as secure and secret bases from which guerrilla action could be undertaken. In May, therefore, 77 Brigade moved north to establish Blackpool, on the railway 30 miles from Mogaung, being joined on 7 May by Lentaigne's 111 Brigade. Special Force came under Stilwell's operational control from 17 May. As was now painfully obvious, the lightly armed Chindits were no longer operating in the way that the concept had been sold, evidenced by 16 Brigade's fruitless attack on Indaw and the increasingly bitter battles for the strongholds. The theories of guerrilla warfare and LRP activity that had been developed before Operation *Thursday* were forced through circumstance to be adapted to the battlefield realities that were faced once Special Force had deployed. Above all, it was an error to keep the exhausted troops in the field for too long, continuing to deploy them in a conventional role in the battle for Mogaung for which they were not suited or equipped.

Fergusson's exhausted 16 Brigade, which had marched all the way from Ledo before being ordered to launch a fruitless attack against Rail Indaw, without the aid of artillery, was flown back to India. By this stage Special Force was down to about 6,000 men. Blackpool itself became the focus of constant Japanese attack, this too being abandoned at the end of the month. Bad weather, a lack of air transport, and difficult country all combined to slow down the move north of the remainder of Special Force. When it was realized that Blackpool could not be held, an area around Indawgyi Lake was secured to evacuate the wounded, and Sunderland flying boats were despatched from Colombo in Ceylon to recover the wounded back to the Brahmaputra.

Lentaigne now supported Stilwell by harassing the Japanese in the Railway Corridor with 14 Brigade and 3 West African Brigade, while Calvert advanced on Mogaung, which was reached on 2 June. By now, 77 Brigade comprised 2,000 very tired men of three British and one Gurkha battalions. The energetic Calvert established an Air Dropping Zone on the reverse side of the hills overlooking Mogaung together with a light aircraft strip. For the next three weeks his men inched forward into Mogaung in the face of terrific resistance. Two 4.2-inch mortars and 12 Vickers machine guns and their crews were dropped in to help the fight. On 22 June most of the town was captured, except a small area round the railway station and bridge over the river. A combined attack with Chinese troops on 23 June failed but Mogaung finally fell on 26 June. The only prisoners were the occupants of 18 Division's brothel (of mainly Korean sex-slaves, euphemistically known by the Japanese as 'comfort women'), together with the brothel keeper who had declined to commit *hari-kari* with his issued grenade. The Gurkhas gained two Victoria Crosses during this attack, but casualties were high. Only 800 men of Calvert's brigade ended the battle for Mogaung alive and unwounded.[17]

Stilwell's newly formed Northern Combat Area Command, which combined his two Chinese Divisions with the all-American three-battalion 'Galahad Force' (nicknamed Merrill's Marauders for publicity purposes, and modelled on Wingate's 77 Brigade) and Kachin guerrillas made steady progress against the Japanese, crowning their achievements with the capture of Myitkyina airfield on 17 May 1944.[18] Unfortunately for Stilwell, the brilliant capture of the airfield was overshadowed during the following three months by a series of disastrous mistakes that prevented the capture of the town itself. It didn't fall until August. The greatest error was his failure to provide sufficient fresh and suitably trained and equipped reinforcements to ensure that remaining Japanese resistance was crushed. It was these three months of hard fighting for Mogaung and Myitkyina that made Stilwell's name odious with survivors of the Chindits. Surprisingly perhaps for his reputation as 'a typical, old-fashioned Indian fighter',[19] Stilwell had never before had experience of commanding troops in combat, and it was this factor above all else that allowed him to ignore the rule that soldiers need regular respite from the trauma and strain of battle, a failure that pushed his men to the edge of mutiny. In addition to the remaining Chindit columns, Stilwell's eight American battalions (including three exhausted Galahad battalions and two engineer battalions) were forced to fight without relief from March through to August 1944. Stilwell's neglect of these exhausted and poorly equipped troops – used by him to launch conventional operations against well-defended Japanese positions for which they were not suited or equipped – and his constant and unjustified complaints about the fighting skills of the British troops under his command, caused considerable and justifiable resentment against Stilwell and some of his staff, who appeared to want to outdo their boss in their Anglophobia. The weakness of his troops in terms of heavy weaponry, their reliance on air-dropped supplies and their gradual wasting without relief made them an ever-reducing asset. One of the two Chindit columns began with 1,300 men but was reduced to 25 by July 1944, and Stilwell himself recorded in May that one of his Galahad battalions at Myitkyina had been reduced to 12 men.

Myitkyina finally fell on 3 August after a siege lasting 78 days, and allowed for the first time in the war the land route to be built from Ledo through to Yunnan, relieving pressure on the Hump. Still falsely believing either that the British did not want him to succeed, or that they believed that he could not, he wrote triumphantly in his diary in capital letters: 'WILL THIS BURN UP THE LIMEYS.' The bitter irony was that it was the fierce Chindit attacks at Mogaung, resulting in the capture of the town on 26 June, that ruined Japanese plans to counterattack the airfield. Stilwell clearly didn't regard 'his' Chindits as Limeys. Major General Festing's 36 Division (now a British designated division) was then flown into Myitkyina and from there travelled by jeep train to Mogaung, taking over the front and beginning its clearance of the Railway Corridor south towards Indaw. Special Force was then evacuated.

Stilwell's success came as a surprise to those in New Delhi and Kandy, who had long written off the Chinese as a source of offensive success against the Japanese, but it was a welcome one at that, and his feat was widely recognized for the magnificent display of planning and leadership that it was. Mountbatten was delighted, writing to his daughter Patricia on 19 May, 'Isn't the news of the capture of Myitkyina airfield great? It is one of my most interesting fronts, commanded by my deputy General Stilwell.' Churchill himself praised Stilwell's achievement and congratulated him personally. But it was a bittersweet moment for the survivors of the Chindits. The author of their great effort was dead. Much of what he had preached had been ditched when the harsh reality of operations had presented itself. Worse, little tangible benefit had been brought to Slim's great fight against Mutaguchi in the hills of Manipur and Assam as a result of their sacrifice. Indeed, the requirements to support the five Chindit brigades on the far-off Irrawaddy served to divide the air resources available to support the remainder of 14 Army, and arguably made their task far more difficult than it needed to be. The Chindit operation brought the Japanese 53 Division north and into the fight for the first time, and although the Chindits fought well, the expenditure of this tremendous effort in an operation misaligned with the task of defeating Mutaguchi in India, meant that the disproportionate effort given to Operation *Thursday* was, on reflection, an error. Too large to serve as a guerrilla force, and ill equipped to serve as an airborne force of the kind that was to make its mark in Europe, it's difficult not to avoid the conclusion that the Chindits' precious resources were deployed on a political distraction that served no military good. Auchinleck laid out judgement on Operation *Thursday* in his despatch:

I considered that the timings and area of employment of LRP Groups are governed by the activities of the main forces. Without exploitation by the main forces concerned, operations by LRP Groups are unjustifiably costly against a first-class enemy and achieve no strategic object. These groups are not capable of achieving decisive results against organised forces of all arms. Their role is not to fight, but to evade the enemy and by guerrilla tactics to harass him. I emphasised that unless the main forces can take advantage of the situations created by these Groups, the latter's efforts are wasted.[20]

Perhaps the only political upside of *Thursday* was to cajole an unwilling Chiang Kai-shek to deploy General Wei-Lei-Huang's four divisions across the Salween River against the Japanese 56 Division on 10/11 May. But this was little return on the effort made to build and deploy Special Force. Lentaigne, in 1946, concluded:

Without our help, I am certain Stilwell would never have got the line Mogaung-Myitkyina much before October and that would have delayed the southward push by 36 Division by at least three months. This respite might have allowed the Jap to hold up 19 Division at Kyaukmyaung very much longer... We picked up over 5,000 Jap dead to the loss of just under 1,000 of our own killed. There is no record of how many more Jap died of wounds, sickness and starvation.

This, however, is no answer to Auchinleck's challenge, which was to question the strategic purpose of *Thursday*, and to evaluate its result. What was the strategic purpose of *Thursday*? It was, as Lentaigne himself noted it was:

- to eat the core out of the Jap apple by dominating the Indaw area till the monsoon when the second wave would be relieved by airborne troops;
- to shame and even help the ringside seat holders [i.e., those in China] to come forward and join us;
- to create the springboard for the southward drive after the monsoon.[21]

At best Operation *Thursday* kept a cobbled-together Japanese force of divisional strength busy along the Railway Corridor between mid-March and late May. After this, a tired rump of Chindits secured – in magnificent fighting – the ejection of the Japanese from Mogaung in June. The operation, in the end, entailed only a single phase rather than the two that Wingate had planned, as all troops were committed in the first phase, and there were no airborne troops available to sit out the monsoon in the defended strongholds, even were the concept to have been proved. On this score, the strongholds had done precisely what Wingate had tried to design them not to do – namely, to draw attention to themselves as the bases from which the offensive columns were operated. Their presence invariably drew enemy attention, and as Dien Ben Phu was subsequently to demonstrate in a different war, would become the story. As Lentaigne observed, strongholds 'are not suited to hold blocks and defensive positions unless they concentrate in large numbers and are given supporting arms. A Brigade block is virtually a pinpoint target. To my mind it is only justifiable if it is also the lump of cheese in the trap with three or four cats in the shape of other Brigades sitting round ready to save the cheese by pouncing on the mouse as it comes to get it.'[22] Fortunately, Lentaigne withdrew the Chindits from the southern strongholds to Blackpool, and Jack Masters withdrew the remnants from Blackpool, before their inevitable subjugation by vastly superior enemy forces. The Railway Corridor appeared, on a map, to be an area of strategic interest to the Japanese. In reality, it wasn't. What might have happened, thought Lentaigne, if this magnificent force had operated in closer conjunction with IV and XXXIII Corps fighting in Assam and Manipur? Quite. On reflection it is hard not to conclude that the entire Chindit endeavour in 1944 provided an unsatisfactory return for such a considerable investment in military talent, resources and lives. Operation *Thursday* was the product not of strategic necessity but of the determined promotion of one man. With Wingate's death, the idea evaporated and the whole exercise, despite the enormous commitment and sacrifice of the men involved, became a strategic sideshow.

Love him or hate him, Wingate nevertheless possessed a magnetic personality that attracted fanatical loyalty. He was able to inspire and motivate men to a degree beyond the abilities of the vast majority of combat commanders. While his strategic convictions – namely that forces positioned deep behind enemy lines, gathered into self-sustaining 'strongholds' and supplied by air, could themselves defeat the Japanese – were proved wrong in the crucible of hard battle, Wingate's crusading zeal, his ability to inspire and his irrepressible self-belief counted for much in the dark, depressing days of failure and defeat in 1943 and the days of uncertainty in early 1944. Certainly, many of his tactical ideas, built on standard British doctrine, were sound. These included the need for hard training, the use of aerial resupply to support marauding guerrilla-type bands operating far behind enemy lines, and the power of air-to-ground attack. But as is often the case with unconventional thinkers, he sometimes took his ideas to illogical extremes. His strategic failure was to assume that the Japanese could never be defeated by conventional means alone, believing that the British and Indian Armies could not rebuild themselves to a state that they could defeat the Japanese in a stand-up fight. It was in the area of military effect that Wingate failed. He believed that he had found the holy grail of success in Burma, urging the idea that long-range penetration should be the exclusive means of defeating the Japanese. In this sense – propounding a theory that sat on the very edge of conventionality – Wingate was a 'maverick' or 'misfit' in the same mould as T.E. Lawrence (who incidentally was a distant cousin). He had proved to himself and others, he thought, what could be achieved by irregular warfare, and believed that the future would be dominated by the death of the heavily lumbering armies of the past, being picked apart by small groups of highly motivated, mobile and well-armed guerrillas. In pursuing this line, to the exclusion of all else, Wingate's obsession with LRPs made him in effect a single-issue lobbyist. His belief in his own cause was at the expense of proper balance in his consideration of strategic problems, a failing that became increasingly pronounced as 1943 ran its course and into 1944.

While Slim throughout saw the possibilities that Wingate's ideas could offer the campaign against the Japanese as a whole, he recognized that they were only a part of a bigger, more comprehensive solution. He intuitively knew in 1942 what he was going to have to prove in 1944 and 1945 – namely that long-range penetration operations, even when mounted on a considerable scale, could never constitute the sum total of all that was required to defeat the Japanese in Burma.

Indeed, by the time Wingate was flying his division into central Burma, the troops of Christison's XV Corps were already demonstrating, in Arakan, the falsity of Wingate's assumptions. By the end of May 1944, the remainder of Slim's 14 Army had confirmed that XV Corps' victory was not an aberration, and the Japanese were on the run. In the final analysis, Wingate's expensive operation played but a small part in the Japanese discomfiture.

34

The Road of Bones

In Manipur the Japanese were by now close to exhaustion. By early June 1944 Operation *U-Go* was near collapse, the fighting during the following six weeks merely prolonging the death agonies of the once-proud, all-conquering 15 Army. Slim knew most of this by means of the signals intelligence he was fed by MI6's Special Liaison Unit in Comilla. He had been impressed with the quality of this intelligence, noting in particular the desperate Japanese supply situation and their almost complete lack of air cover.[1] 'Evidence was now coming in to me daily of the extent of the Japanese defeat, of their losses in tanks, guns, equipment, and vehicles, and of the disorganisation of their higher command', he wrote. At the time he wrote this – 1956 – he couldn't acknowledge the source of this intelligence because ULTRA was to remain secret until revealed in Frederick Winterbotham's memoirs in 1974.[2] On 22 June, Mutaguchi signalled Kawabe for permission to retreat back into Burma. The British had by this time broken through the final blocks on the road between Kohima and Imphal: what remained of Mutaguchi's army was now in desperate straits, starving and demoralized, no match for the growing strength of 14 Army building up in Imphal and flooding through from Dimapur on the now open Kohima Road. Kawabe, seeking higher permission, passed on Mutaguchi's request to Terauchi in Saigon, and it was not until 8 July that Mutaguchi at last received permission to retire. Even then Mutaguchi attempted to control the fighting withdrawal of what remained of his divisions. It was only on 20 July, formalizing what was already happening to his shattered army, that Mutaguchi ordered a general retreat across the Chindwin.

At the same time, Slim ordered Stopford and Scoones to pursue Mutaguchi with vigour, aiming to turn 15 Army's defeat into a rout. But conditions conspired against a rapid British counter-offensive. Many of Scoones' troops had fought continuously in appalling conditions for eight months. Disease and malnutrition had weakened many and exhaustion was widespread. The extreme ruggedness of the terrain made progress difficult and slow. Slim's counter-offensive nevertheless got underway. While 7 Indian Division pressed the Japanese 31 Division through the Naga Hills from the north-west, 80 Brigade of Gracey's 20 Indian Division[3] moved north towards Ukhrul during June to cut the line of communication and withdrawal routes for both 15 and 31 Divisions. The Japanese still held the positions they had secured for themselves in the mountains and proved stubbornly resistant to British attempts to remove them.[4]

As 80 Brigade wound its way deeper into the tangled Naga Hills, the wild country forced them onto resupply by air. Rain continued to fall relentlessly as the heavily laden troops sweated up hills and across valleys, exhausting the fittest. Most of the activity in June revolved around small-scale patrol actions against support troops of 15 Division who were protecting their line of communication back to the Chindwin. Emulating the resourcefulness of their enemy, the column used elephants on occasions to take their wounded to the rear. Towards the end of June, the brigade, spread widely and thinly like a net across a vast swathe of hilly country, began to encounter large numbers of Japanese troops retreating east as the remnants of 31 Division flooded back from the north-west, and 15 Division withdrew from the Kohima Road to the west. At the start of the withdrawal from Kohima, Japanese units attempted to march back in an orderly and disciplined manner, but by July signs of complete collapse became increasingly evident. The war correspondent Shizuo Maruyama, withdrawing with Sato from Kohima, wrote angrily, 'We had no ammunition, no clothes, no food, no guns... the men were barefoot and ragged, and threw away everything except canes to help them walk. Their eyes blazed in their lean bodies... all they had to keep them going was grass and water... At Kohima we were starved and then crushed.'[5]

British tactics concentrated on ambushing roads, tracks and river crossings, although deliberate attacks on Japanese-held villages dominating the road to Ukhrul were undertaken when necessary. Although not seeking battle, whenever so engaged the Japanese fought back with undiminished ferocity, furiously counterattacking whenever and wherever they were attacked with the desperation of men who knew they were using up their last reserves of life to escape the clutches of the enemy and the unforgivable trauma of capture. For the men of both 15 and 31 Divisions, starvation, exhaustion and the savage monsoon rains daily exacted their toll, many hundreds dying on the endless, cloud-covered mountains. The Japanese began to call the trail of rotting bodies the 'bleached bones road'. The absurdly optimistic risks taken at the outset of the campaign, which provided support for an offensive lasting only 20 days, now began to demand their deadly payment. The pursuing British troops came across countless putrefying bodies, skeletons and abandoned weapons and material littering the jungle paths that led back through the hills to the Chindwin. Disease, starvation and despair were accompanied in places by cannibalism. Yet, despite their predicament, still they fought. Japanese trucks and mule trains flowed back towards the Chindwin in considerable numbers, so much so that it was often impossible for the scattered British units in the hills to counter them all. Moving east along the Ukhrul Road, 100 Brigade joined forces with 80 Brigade in early July near Litan. From early July, small numbers of enemy soldiers began to be taken prisoner, most of them too weak to resist capture. Outside the frantic, stabbing, chaotic frenzy of close combat, and for all their hatred of the unnatural barbarity often demonstrated by the Japanese, many British troops came to feel sorry for the ragged specimens of humanity they now came across, helped perhaps by the rarity factor of these occasions.

The advance from Kohima by 7 Indian Division began on 23 June, led by the 1,760-strong 33 Brigade. Starting from a point 15 miles south of Kohima, the brigade's task was to march overland to Ukhrul, to converge on this sprawling mountain village with 80 and 100 Brigades who were advancing from the south. The march was hugely demanding, both mentally and physically. Crossing swollen torrents with heavily laden men and mules was a task in itself, without the challenges posed by the terrain. Mules fell off tracks into steep ravines, the tracks acting as riverbeds for the ever-flowing rainwater seeking to make its way downhill. Progress was painfully slow, but there were few face-to-face encounters with the Japanese. What the men did come across, however, were large numbers of dead bodies, some hit by strikes from aircraft and some dead of exhaustion or starvation, or both. Ukhrul was captured on 8 July against only light resistance, and the brigade struggled on in the wake of the Japanese retreat towards the Chindwin River. By now the British troops were tired, and many were sick. The mules were also in a poor state, disease was rife, and all men were afflicted to some degree with diarrhoea. It was clear that something had to break soon – the Japanese or the ability of 33 Brigade to continue campaigning.

This advance was accompanied, far to the east, by part of Brigadier Perowne's 23 Brigade marching deep into the Somra Tracts in an attempt to cut off the Japanese retreat to the Chindwin. It proved to be one of the most physically demanding challenges of the entire campaign.[6] But by mid-July it was clear that British victory, in the triangle of hills between Jessami, Somra and Ukhrul, was unequivocal and Perowne's columns were withdrawn back to Imphal and Kohima, for their journey to a rehabilitation centre and hospitals in Dimapur.

Likewise, 33 Brigade was ordered to give up its chase on 16 July, the evidence of profound Japanese defeat all around it, and its own troops weakening in the challenging conditions, causing Stopford to recognize that there was now little value in continuing the pursuit: the Japanese were a broken reed, and dying in vast numbers of their own accord, without the intervention of British or Indian troops.

While these events were taking place in the hills around Ukhrul, on the Shenam front in mid-July Roberts' 23 Indian Division was ordered to drive Yamamoto's remnants to Tamu, 49 Brigade cutting off the Japanese line of communication with a flanking march through the hills to the north, while the two remaining brigades attacked the Tengnoupal defences. The men were exhausted after months of fighting, and the monsoon rains still belted down with inconvenient consistency, but for five days the 49 Brigade column weaved its way slowly through the hills before arriving at Sibong, 2,000 feet above the bridge on the Lokchao River. It was heavily defended by the Japanese, with dug-in tanks and copious quantities of barbed wire hidden in the long grass. A fierce struggle developed for Battle Hill, a prominent feature overlooking the road, but without artillery, even the most resolute attack had little chance of prising the Japanese from their positions. Instead, the weak 4 Mahrattas (now numbering fewer than 200 men) moved out from Sibong before first light next day, 26 July, in an attempt to create a road block a few miles north of Tamu. Their arrival stirred up a hornets' nest, the Japanese rushing against the improvised block with angry fury from both directions. The block could not be held, and the survivors withdrew that night. But simultaneously, in the east along the Tengnoupal position, the remainder of 23 Division had thrown itself against the rapidly weakening defenders, and at long last the flood gates broke, the Japanese abandoning the position and pouring east over jungle tracks in disorder to escape the British advance. Artillery came up with the advancing division, and 6 Mahrattas occupied Battle Hill on 31 July with little opposition.

23 Indian Division pushed Yamamoto's limping columns into Tamu, before they were replaced by the rested 2 Division, the fresh 11 East African Division, preparing for the push down the Kabaw Valley, following thereafter. Meanwhile, south of Bishenpur, Cowan's division pushed hard against the shattered remnants of Tanaka's division, which fought back from strongpoints and defended villages with undiminished tenacity. When its own withdrawal was reluctantly ordered it did so carefully and deliberately, mining roads, blowing up bridges and delaying

the advance of 5 Indian Division (who had taken responsibility for the pursuit) along the Tiddim Road through the use of stay-behind parties who ambushed the road and only pulled back when their own position became imperilled. This was a task in which the combat engineers rebuilt the road, often under fire, and made it fit for travel for the Lee-Grants, Stuarts and heavy trucks which followed behind the vanguard troops, while the ubiquitous infantry out-flanked Japanese positions through the hills and protected the men on the road below. When the weather allowed, Hurribombers swooped in to attack these stay-behind positions with cannon fire and 250-pound bombs. Briggs's pace was equally slow, this being less a pursuit than a methodical clearance, but, with the exhaustion of the troops, the narrowness of the front (it being limited to the width of the road and its immediate hinterland) and the challenges of the terrain, malaria and the monsoon rain, this was all that could be managed. It was on 12 November that the division marched, finally, into Kalemyo, meeting up with 11 East African Division, which had completed its clearance of the Kabaw Valley.

This advance proved to be the final chapter in the ignominious destruction of 15 Army. During July its entire command structure had disintegrated, men and units being left to fend for themselves in the life-and-death struggle to evade the clutches of the advancing 14 Army. Even though the pursuit continued until the end of the year, the battle for India could be said to be over by the last day of July 1944. The extraordinary commitment of Mutaguchi's benighted troops in battering away at Imphal until they lacked even the energy to retreat was remarkable, but ultimately pointless. The power of *bushido* could not make up for the reality that the 'Japanese commanders had bungled at the start [and had] quarrelled at the end'.[7] The staggering disunity of command displayed across the whole of 15 Army repaid poorly the commitment, often to the death, of those who had blindly to carry out the incoherent orders of their masters. So perished Mutaguchi's army and, with it, Japanese dreams of victory in India. Casualties are difficult to calculate. Best estimates suggest that of the 115,000 men in Mutaguchi's army – Japanese and INA (65,000 fighting men plus 50,000 support and line-of-communication troops) – 68,000 became casualties. Broken down, this number comprised 30,000 killed, 23,000 wounded and 15,000 'lost' (i.e., killed, wounded or taken prisoner). This represents a casualty rate of an unprecedented 60 per cent.[8] Only 600 allowed themselves to be taken prisoner, most of them too sick even to take their own lives. Some 17,000 pack animals perished during the operation and not a single piece of heavy weaponry made it back to Burma. The battle had provided the largest, most prolonged and most intense engagement with a Japanese army yet seen in the war. 'It is the most important defeat the Japs have ever suffered in their military career,' wrote Mountbatten exultantly to his wife on 22 June 1944, 'because the numbers involved are so much greater than any Pacific Island operation.'[9]

The extent of the disaster that befell 15 Army is captured by a comment by Kase Toshikazu, a member of the wartime Japanese Foreign Office, who lamented, 'Most of this force perished in battle or later of starvation. The disaster at Imphal was perhaps the worst of its kind yet chronicled in the annals of war.'[10] The latter might better have included the caveat 'Japanese' to avoid charges of hyperbole, but his comment captures something of the enormity of the human disaster that overwhelmed 15 Army. When considered with the defeat of 28 Army in Arakan, 14 Army's substantial – even extraordinary achievement – can be seen. Not only had it destroyed five divisions and inflicted some 90,000 casualties on the enemy, something that would have been considered inconceivable only five months before, but in so doing it had severely degraded the fighting power of the Burma Area Army. The Indian, Gurkha, African and British troops of this remarkably homogeneous organization had also decisively removed any remaining notions of Japanese superiority on the battlefield. The cost? 14 Army suffered 24,000 casualties in Arakan, Kohima and Imphal, many of whom recovered under exemplary medical care, the product of the transformation of health services since 1942.[11]

The battles for Imphal and Kohima were a triumph for Bill Slim, at the time a relatively unknown lieutenant general fighting on the very edge of an empire that – had he but known it – was about to collapse of its own accord. The plan for battle had been his, as were its assumptions, risks and mistakes. Given his bitter experience of the Japanese in 1942 and 1943, he believed that he knew what he had to do to defeat Mutaguchi and had accordingly developed a plan of battle to turn that theory into reality, building on the rigorous training programme he introduced in 1943. The plan was unconventional and, with the resources in hand, unproved. But it was successful. Withdrawing IV Corps onto the Imphal plain, transferring first 5 and then 7 Indian Division by air to the Manipur and Kohima battlefields and thereafter relying on air supply to maintain the besieged IV Corps, were all phenomenal risks and yet undoubtedly shifted the balance of the battle in his favour. His self-belief allowed him to deflect the fears of those less certain than himself, especially those few who misinterpreted his risk-taking at the start of Operation *U-Go* as recklessness.

In particular, his recognition of the power of air supply and battlefield air support proved the lifeblood of his defence in Arakan, Kohima and Imphal. He listened to his doctors and instigated the anti-malarial measures that dramatically reduced the non-combat casualties in his army. And by firmness of conviction and strength of character, he was able to bind to his cause the most important senior commander in the theatre, Mountbatten. It was this relationship that was to prove to be the key relationship of the war in the Far East. It was indisputably Slim's concept of battle, and Slim's plan for the destruction of 15 Army, that Mountbatten adopted as his own and represented to Churchill and Roosevelt, revealing a dramatic contrast to the broken relationship the hapless Mutaguchi enjoyed with Kawabe.

Likewise, although the troops of 15 Army – Indian, British and East and West African alike – might still claim that they were the 'Forgotten Army', by 1944 there was no doubt about the strength and depth of the hard-won esprit de corps that now lay at the heart of the army; a sense of moral power that was sealed in the heat of battle and the realization of victory. They had taken on the most fearsome enemy the British and Indian Armies had ever encountered, and had conquered. Slim had stared disaster in its face during those first desperate weeks of the Imphal–Kohima battle, and by his calm and careful handling of the various crises as they arrived brought about their successful resolution. Crucially, he had earned and retained the respect and confidence of his corps and divisional commanders. He had made mistakes, but was the first to admit them, concentrating his effort on solving problems rather than apportioning blame. By the end of these battles General Slim had become 'Uncle Bill', a soubriquet soon in universal currency in 14 Army, and which was to remain with him for the rest of his days.

Slim, of course, was helped in the achievement of his victory by the mistakes of his enemy. Mutaguchi's poor relationship with Sato had the greatest strategic impact of all on his plans for a successful offensive. Sato's failure to strike against Dimapur cost the Japanese the chance of seizing this jewel in the British strategic crown: its loss would have been a catastrophic blow to the British, leading inevitably to the collapse of Imphal. But his biggest failure had been to adequately supply Sato's division. Mutaguchi believed that the advance into India would be rapid and decisive and that captured British supplies would remove the need to bring large quantities of stores across the Chindwin to supply his army, especially if Sato were able to reach Dimapur. Mutaguchi was also convinced that Sato's troops could forage sufficient supplies from the native villages through which they passed, and never believed the reports that subsequently filtered back that 31 Division was starving. However, Sato's hatred of Mutaguchi meant that he was never seriously going to act on his superior's strategic vision (by advancing on Dimapur) in contravention to Kawabe's direct orders. In the circumstances, it is difficult not to accept that Sato's ultimate disobedience of Mutaguchi's orders, and his decision to withdraw from Kohima, was the correct thing to do, even though Mutaguchi knew that 31 Division had been within a whisker of capturing Dimapur – an act that would have dealt a devastating blow to the British and at the same time refuelled his army.

Mutaguchi's failure was compounded by other factors. While an advance into India in 1944 was a distinctly different prospect from 1942, in Mutaguchi's eagerness to launch an offensive he failed to appreciate the nature of the changes that had taken place in British warfighting capabilities during the period, and indeed to understand the extent of his own weaknesses. Japanese commanders drank deeply from the cup of their own hubris in 1944. The problem in 1944 was that he was prepared to secure victory on the assumption that nothing had changed in British training, techniques and capabilities since 1942. Mutaguchi's excessive optimism and high hopes made his failure in Assam more likely and put at risk a sound strategic idea. In the first place, Japanese knowledge of what the new 14 Army was building up in terms of capability and strength unseen beyond the Chindwin was negligible, although a number of audacious long-range patrols had been carried out, deep into Manipur during 1943. The dramatic improvements to the quality of the British forces in India could have been surmised, but were not. Lieutenant General Naka, Burma Area Army's Chief of Staff, told 15 Division, for instance, that it would not need any anti-tank weapons because the British did not have any tanks. They would find in fact that Scoones of IV Corps had two regiments of heavy tanks at Imphal, and many successful British counterattacks in the coming weeks were framed around the effective use of armour. Because of Mutaguchi's airy assumptions, Operation *U-Go* was launched weak in weapons and firepower, especially in 15 and 31 Divisions. The force was stripped of its medium artillery and replaced with lightweight mountain guns which, while easier to transport across the hills, were nevertheless hopelessly inadequate compared with the weight of firepower able to be put down by the British.

Indeed, there was an almost criminal lack of intelligence in the Japanese Burma Area Army about the transformation overtaking India in its preparation for war. The disastrous British showing in Arakan in May 1943, which ended when Mutaguchi was pressing the merits of an Imphal offensive on his superiors, served merely to reinforce existing prejudices that the British would, yet again, run for the rear in the face of Japanese offensive action and decisiveness. On past experience of his enemy (at Singapore), the odds, Mutaguchi believed, were clearly in his favour. But these odds were changing, the first evidence of which was the defeat of Major General Sakurai Tokutaro's bold offensive in Arakan in February 1944. That the British had stood and fought, refusing to be panicked into a hasty withdrawal, was a new phenomenon in Japanese experience, but Mutaguchi took no notice of it. As it transpired, Operation *Ha-Go* began too early, as it took Mutaguchi longer than expected to muster all his troops on the Chindwin ready for the advance against Imphal. This allowed a dangerous hiatus to elapse between the end of the Arakan operations in February 1944 and the launch of Operation *U-Go* in March, a delay that allowed Slim quickly to move 5 and 7 Indian Divisions directly to the threatened areas by air. Instead, he took comfort from the fact that Slim had been forced to divert his reserves away from Imphal, where his own attack was now about to fall, to Arakan. Mutaguchi consistently overestimated his chances of success. He airily dismissed the repeated concerns of Sato and Major General Tazoe, Kawabe's air commander, for instance, and ordered, ten days after the initial advance had begun, that the entire complement of 15 Army's enslaved 'comfort women' be despatched to Imphal, so as not to waste any time before his men could be rewarded for their arduous endeavours, once Imphal had been reached.

Mutaguchi's swift onslaught against Imphal might have worked were he facing a less resolute enemy. In 1944, however, his stratagem failed because he was unable to concentrate his forces. Mutaguchi's rationale for at least five widely dispersed and separate attacking columns made much sense in the context of an enemy that was expected to run away on first contact, frightened by the prospect of engagements on multiple fronts. When the British, however, failed to be frightened into flight, and instead remained to fight, dispersal became a devastating weakness, as the Japanese were denied the opportunity to concentrate their forces at a single point, and by sheer weight of numbers and firepower to overwhelm the defenders. Mutaguchi desperately tried to reorganize his troops where he could, especially by transferring 14 Tank Regiment to Bishenpur in mid-May, but this was too little (it now had 40 serviceable tanks remaining from an initial 66), too late. The British, by contrast, could quickly move units around the plain to support vulnerable locations when required.

Mutaguchi also made the mistake of not being forward with his divisional commanders from the very beginning, to drive, influence and make sure that his plan was followed, only moving his HQ forward from Maymyo in May. To the end he remained in obstinate denial of the crisis facing his army, talking still of breaking through into the Imphal plain despite the battering his three divisions were each receiving, despite the huge casualties he had sustained, and despite the collapse of the rickety line of communication over the Chindwin. The onset of the early monsoon in April added to the misery of his starving troops. Mutaguchi's new headquarters location in Tamu did not materially improve his understanding of what was happening on each of his three fronts. As the news from each division got progressively worse, the staff of HQ 15 Army increasingly resisted passing bad news to their commander for fear of the rage that would ensue. Even when the truth was stated plainly to him (such as by Sato, for instance, or Yanagida), his own pride prevented him from accepting the truth for what it was. Considerations of 'face' meant that it was not only Mutaguchi who was embarrassed publicly to admit defeat. Prime Minister Tōjō himself had already had the opportunity to call back Mutaguchi's army on 15 May but, according to Major Iwaichi Fujiwara, he 'bottled' the decision. General Hata, Tōjō's Deputy Chief-of-Staff, had visited Saigon and Rangoon between 28 April and 1 May and concluded that it would be better to suspend operations in India. Tōjō, when informed of this news on 15 May, agreed privately with Hata but strangely refused publicly to countenance the prospect of failure and refused to call back Mutaguchi's army. Equally, the demands of *bushido* prevented Mutaguchi from publicly admitting that his offensive had been halted and was on the verge of defeat, although on 6 June 1944 he met with Kawabe and tried to tell him that he believed his army should withdraw. Mutaguchi found it impossible to talk plainly about the need to retreat, and hoped that some kind of extra-sensory perception by Kawabe would enable his superior to understand the crisis he faced. He couldn't, of course, and Kawabe remained unaware of Mutaguchi's desperate desire to call off the offensive. Instead, Kawabe offered him more troops, and for a further month Mutaguchi and his three divisions struggled on against the enemy, the climate, the terrain, and each other. So the Japanese army fought on, destroying itself in the process because the senior generals concerned could not bring themselves to communicate openly on the subject.

Kawabe later argued that he was also motivated by the need to give every opportunity to Subhas Chandra Bose to succeed in fomenting rebellion across India. This is a tortuous excuse. By early June it was plainly evident to all that no such nationalistic conflagration was either possible or probable and that the quality of the contribution made by the INA was insufficient to rouse rebellion among their erstwhile comrades who chose to continue fighting for the Raj. The statistics speak for themselves. Of the 6,000 men in the two deployed regiments of the INA Division in March 1944, about 400 were killed in battle, 1,500 died of disease, 800 surrendered and 714 deserted or were captured before July.

It was clear that Mutaguchi's greatest failure was the over-optimism that led to the extraordinary logistical risks he was prepared to take. One of the many lessons that Orde Wingate had learned from the first expedition into Japanese-held Burma in early 1943 was that he needed air transport to ensure that his troops were supplied and casualties evacuated. Mutaguchi believed that Wingate had demonstrated that the mountain range could be broached by an invading force, but he failed to understand the lesson that Wingate had learned about logistics, namely that without supplies his force would rapidly wither on the vine. This lesson was only to become apparent to the Japanese in the logistically induced disaster of Operation *U-Go*. The startling fanaticism of *bushido* provided all that the Japanese needed in terms of spiritual strength but was wholly insufficient to deliver what 15 Army required materially, serving only to add an uncertain glory to the final sacrifice of thousands of Japanese soldiers as the campaign's last breath was slowly strangled from them.

In his excitement Mutaguchi entirely neglected to consider the possibility of failure. The consequences of not capturing Imphal, once he had committed himself to an offensive, were dire. At worst, it would create a vortex that would act to suck the British back into Burma. At best, it would extend Japan's defensive barrier on the frontier with British India to breaking point. But Mutaguchi did not fill his mind with such baleful thoughts, believing that he could not fail. Not preparing for this possibility, however, was a serious mistake. While Allied strategy was to avoid entanglements in Burma, both Slim and Stilwell were convinced that the re-occupation of Burma (rather than merely its bypassing, as Churchill urged) was possible. Until the invasion of France had taken place in June 1944 and released large quantities of landing craft for use in Asian waters, the only way in which the country would be taken from the Japanese was overland from India or China. In Slim's mind, this opportunity would be greatly enhanced if the Japanese advanced in force into Manipur, as a Japanese defeat would open the door to the re-occupation of Burma. Both Mutaguchi and Slim knew this, but Mutaguchi was content to ignore it as a risk that he was certain would remain unfulfilled. He was wrong.

Mutaguchi, soon to be replaced by General Katamura, was not the only senior fatality of Operation *U-Go*. Two others were Giffard and Stilwell. Slim's victory in Assam and Manipur in 1944 was achieved only by virtue of Mountbatten's decisive leadership, usurping the role that should have been played by the somewhat lethargic Giffard. The affair reinforced Mountbatten's fear that Giffard was out of his depth. The army commander had exhibited none of the imagination or energy required to meet the demands posed by fighting the Japanese. Even though Slim had asked for aircraft, Giffard had not considered the requirement important enough to discuss with Mountbatten. Giffard's performance in this incident drove a further nail into the coffin of his relationship with the Supremo. He had never been in tune with Mountbatten, from the outset appearing difficult and curmudgeonly.[12] Giffard lasted until October 1944, when Mountbatten felt constrained to remove him. 'The trouble is we all like him,' wrote Mountbatten. 'He is, however, non-aggressive, a non-co-operator, and unwilling to recognise me as the one responsible for the Burma campaign.'[13] As the Supremo, Mountbatten had to ensure the loyalty and support of his service commanders. Giffard did not fit this mould, and Mountbatten was forced, correctly, to remove him.

The war between Mountbatten and Stilwell was won by the Supremo.[14] Against resistance at Cairo in 1943 and in spite of the debilitating culture of negativity and pessimism in New Delhi and Chungking, Mountbatten had an uphill struggle to ensure that worthwhile operations were mounted against the Japanese in 1944 and 1945. Left to its own devices, SEAC could easily have withered on the vine of Allied strategy. Mountbatten, however, did not give up entirely on the possibility of an amphibious operation against the Japanese-held south-east Asian littorals later in 1944 or early 1945. In February 1944 he despatched his deputy, General Al Wedemeyer, to London and Washington to win the argument for a maritime strategy, if not immediately, then at some stage in the future, in preference to thrashing around fruitlessly in a land campaign in Burma.[15] However, the mission was not successful. Churchill retained his enthusiasm for such an operation, but unknown to Mountbatten his own deputy was simultaneously and assiduously belittling these ideas in Washington and urging an all-out British and Chinese offensive into northern Burma.

Stilwell believed fervently that plans for amphibious operations would put at risk America's support to the Chinese and would thus ultimately be against the United States' national interest. It is possible to see in Stilwell's opposition to SEAC that the American regarded Mountbatten's ideas as somehow treacherous. When he discovered what Stilwell had been doing, a furious Mountbatten demanded Stilwell's dismissal. Although the relationship was patched up, it was only a matter of time before Stilwell's inability to understand the range of strategic imperatives impinging on SEAC, and thus his failure to contribute to the debate inside SEAC about how strategy should develop, led to his ultimate dismissal in October 1944.

Stilwell had done his work in undermining Mountbatten well. Alarmed by Stilwell's scaremongering, the Americans viewed Mountbatten's support for amphibious operations with some concern, as it appeared to them that the whole effort to sustain Chiang Kai-shek was to be abandoned. They believed that by urging amphibious operations against the Japanese, Mountbatten was at the same time proposing a scaling down in the support provided to the Chinese. As Stilwell saw things, this would be tantamount to treachery: the perfidious British getting their colonies back at the expense of American national interests in relation to China.

It was because of these fears that, on 25 February 1944, Roosevelt sent a telegram to Churchill 'urging an all-out drive in Burma', reminding the British leader of the pledges given during the Quadrant Conference at Quebec. He indicated that, having kept their promises, the Americans were now holding the British to theirs. In other words, Mountbatten was not 'let off the hook' by Chiang Kai-shek's refusal to cooperate and must continue to support China despite the obstacles.

It was a reminder for Mountbatten that the United States was the senior partner in the Allied coalition, particularly in Asia. He had little choice but to accept the lead from American strategy and forgo a substantial measure of independence in the decisions made concerning Burma and China. Field Marshal Sir John Dill, head of the British Staff Mission in Washington, was obliged to remind the British planners in this regard that they could not hope to have it all their own way as far as Burma was concerned lest the Americans retaliated by ignoring British interests elsewhere. The result was that Mountbatten had no choice but to ignore his hopes of a maritime strategy and to consider options for the reconquest of Burma by land forces in 1944 and 1945.

Mountbatten was thus thwarted by the implications of American strategy, which emphasized the maintenance of the route to China, and by the practical realities of Allied strategy worldwide, which meant that he had limited resources and no naval support available to him for expansive maritime and amphibious operations until well after the invasion of Normandy in 1944. Where he could make improvements to the British–American relationship, nevertheless, was in shaking up the command arrangements in South East Asia Command. The excuse he used was to emphasize the impossibly broad expanse of Stilwell's responsibilities, commenting that 'only the Trinity could carry out his duties which require him to be in Delhi, Chungking and the Ledo Front simultaneously'.[16]

Before the year was out, Mountbatten had achieved this aim. Mountbatten asked London to gain assurances from the Americans that he was indeed the Supreme Allied Commander, that all forces in the theatre came under SEAC command, and that all communication from London or Washington was to go through him, not his American deputy. In Mountbatten's view the easiest solution would be to dissolve the CBI theatre altogether, a measure eventually approved by the Allied Chiefs on Stilwell's dismissal in October 1944. Stilwell's extensive empire was immediately sub-divided among three American generals, while General Wheeler assumed responsibilities as Mountbatten's deputy. Mountbatten also used this opportunity of unprecedented Anglo-American harmony to create an integrated land force headquarters, commanded until mid-1945 by Lieutenant General Oliver Leese. For the first time, 11 Army Group's replacement, Allied Land Forces South East Asia (ALFSEA), included previously disparate British, American (14 Army, NCAC,[17] XV Corps and the extensive Line of Communication Command) and Chinese forces. Fortunately for inter-Allied cooperation, Wheeler's attitude to the strategic partnership was very different to Stilwell's: he was determined to make it work. He was also able fully to comprehend Mountbatten's considerations with regard to the strategic issues facing campaigning in Burma in a way that seemed to elude Stilwell.

Laurels are awarded to the victor. On 15 December 1944, Wavell knighted Slim at Imphal on behalf of King George VI, alongside his three corps commanders, Christison, Stopford and Scoones. Together they had not only defeated the invasion of India, but had inflicted upon the Japanese the greatest defeat in their country's history. In so doing 14 Army had also completely changed the strategic landscape in South East Asia Command as, at last, the possibility of an Allied offensive into Burma presented itself. The battle for India was over, and that for the re-conquest of Burma about to begin.

PART FOUR

Redemption, 1945

Prologue

Lieutenant Colonel Hugh Pettigrew, 2/14 Punjab Regiment

GSO1, 17 Indian Division, Meiktila, February/March 1945[*]

The fact was that our own 17 (Black Cat) Div. was not very popular with a lot of people, for two reasons I think. The first was plain straightforward jealousy. It was a fine division with a tremendous war record. In the 1942 withdrawal from Rangoon right up to the Chindwin at Kalewa, and then again in its fighting withdrawal from Tiddim and the Chin Hills and the battle of Imphal in 1944. It had killed more Japs and won more VCs than any other division. And now here it was chosen to spearhead the 1945 offensive to re-capture Burma and Rangoon...

At last the great day arrived. The Division started to cross the Irrawaddy on February 18th and everyone was across by the 21st. The thrust for Meiktila was on, the Japs still did not know that we had left Ranchi, and it was weeks and weeks at least before they knew they were up against their old enemies – the 'Black Cats'. You see now I am very proud of my old Division.

The Japs' resistance was as fanatical as ever and reports came back of their riflemen roping themselves up trees to leave both hands free, and officers leaping on to our tanks with nothing but swords in their hands. But the speed and force of our advance had taken them by surprise and they were no match for our Sherman tanks and well-trained, experienced and determined infantry. We swept on...

The only road to Meiktila was through a place called Taungtha and we expected it to be strongly held, especially as the wide sandy crossing of the

---

[*]A GSO1 is the chief staff officer in a division (the 'General Staff Officer Grade 1'). Adapted from Hugh Pettigrew, *It Seemed Very Ordinary* (Privately published, 2017) and quoted with permission.

Sinthewa Chaung had to be negotiated first, so we put in both brigades, 48 Brigade under Osborn Hedley from the southwest and 63 Brigade under Guy Burton from the south. In the event the position was much lighter than we had expected, and the town fell to us during the day. From Taungtha the road to Meiktila bent to the right (eastwards) in an acute angle and late in the afternoon Punch Cowan decided to harbour the whole division near a village called Mingan. Mingan was beyond Taungtha and we would then be poised ready to move straight towards Meiktila the next day. Div. HQ had been following behind 63 Brigade and he then made the surprising decision to move us straight across country to Mingan. One side of a triangle, instead of two, and avoiding the congestion of Taungtha. It was a good idea but my objection, and I had unwisely started to object in a small way by then, was that it was too late in the day. There were not enough hours of daylight left.

Anyway off we went with [Lieutenant Colonel Peter] Oliver's Defence Battalion [9/12 Frontier Force Rifles] in the lead and HQ following. I am not a hunting man but that is what it felt like, wild and exhilarating and I enjoyed every minute of it. The fields themselves, dry hard and reasonably level, were no trouble at all but at each small bund (mud bank) that separated them the majority of the vehicles, especially the jeeps, became momentarily airborne. The heavier lorries, like the wireless vehicles, just crushed them flat. Cactus hedges were no obstacle whatsoever. I was standing up in my jeep, which was one of the customs Punch had introduced to foster divisional pride (and which infuriated some of the other divisions), except at some of the larger 'jumps'. Looking in all directions it was an incredible sight with vehicles of every size, shape and purpose jolting and leaping on a broad front across the Burma countryside. I don't remember how far it was or how long it took, five or six miles perhaps, until two things stopped us. Trees and snipers. We had run into the enemy and the Defence Battalion was already on foot and advancing through the wood to dislodge them. The remainder of us harboured temporarily in a small dip, which gave us some cover, though not many bullets were coming our way. It was not too long a hold up but the sun had set by then and daylight was shortening. We could no longer go straight on and after perhaps half an hour I collected the brigade liaison officers, and a few others, and with a small escort we moved off in jeeps. I wanted to harbour for the night where we were but the General over-ruled me. Just before I left I heard that Oliver had been killed, shot by a Jap tree sniper.

We then had to drive towards Taungtha before we could turn right and out along the Meiktila road to Mingan. As we neared Mingan I honestly think that for a few minutes we were leading the whole Division. It was nearly dusk with thick trees close to the road on both sides in places and it all felt very eerie. I had no time for a proper reconnaissance and finally had to indicate vague brigade group and divisional HQ areas each side of the road. It was already dark as our last vehicles struggled into what was a very rough approximation of my harbour lay out. But without it there would have been chaos. As it was the Japs could have been very close indeed...

It was a quiet night, any Japs around probably in more of a muddle than we were and not proper fighting units anyway. Soon after daylight the next morning the 25th February we were on the move again, 48 Brigade staying behind to collect a supply drop, and on the 26th we were all concentrated in the Mahlaing area. The Tank Brigade was a little further on and with the Thabutkin airstrip in our possession Meiktila was only a dozen or so miles away. Everything had gone extremely well and Punch Cowan and his two infantry brigade commanders (all 'Abbottabad' Gurkhas) had shown how well they knew Burma and the Japanese. The troops had been magnificent...

The brief plan was for a more or less all round attack, 63 Brigade from the west, 255 Tank Brigade from the east, and 48 Brigade from the north. 99 Brigade (just flown in) was in reserve with the Sikh Light Infantry protecting our Div. HQ area about a mile and a half from the town. It took the first three days of March to capture Meiktila and a couple more days to mop up and kill the few Japs still hiding in drains and so on. Very few of the two thousand odd defending the town got away. Their resistance had been as fierce and fanatical as ever, with no surrender and no quarter asked for, but the Sherman tanks of Probyn's Horse and Sam Browne's Cavalry and our efficient, determined infantry (British, Indian, and Gurkha) were too good for them...

On March 5th Div. HQ was able to move into the town and the main airstrip was back in action again. We had captured Meiktila in less than two weeks from crossing the Irrawaddy...

The Sikh Light Infantry under [Lieutenant Colonel William] Barlow-Wheeler was our Defence Battalion then. It was a new battalion with no battle experience and longing to prove itself. The famous old Sikh Regiments were made up of Malwa and Manja Sikhs, warriors and farmers, as were all the Sikh companies in other regiments, like my own 2/14th. The Sikh Light Infantry however was composed of lower grades (the Sikhs' own distinction and not mine) like Mahzbis and Ramdhasias, and were now out to prove their worth. Punch and I had discussed it and agreed that their first battle must be a winner, not a pushover but a fairly certain success to keep their morale as high as it so clearly was. And the day came when a small Jap force was reported seen along the Thazi road to the east, and we sent off a company of the Sikhs. They were terrific and came back in great heart, having carved the Japs to pieces. They shot them up then went straight at them with the bayonet, forgetting in their excitement it seemed that they had machine guns in support. The tragic side of it was that they had far too many, unnecessary, casualties themselves including their British company commander who was killed. They had proved themselves right enough…

35

What To Do About Burma?

The battles in Arakan in February, and at Imphal and Kohima through to July decisively shattered the myth of Japanese invincibility that had for over two years crippled the Allied cause. They also set the seal on the efforts to rebuild the fighting power of 14 Army. Nevertheless, despite the stunning victory that it gave them, the Chiefs of Staff in both London and Washington remained ignorant for some months not just of the scale of the Japanese defeat but also of its implications for the conduct of the war in the Far East. The door to Burma was now wide open, though few outside of SEAC saw this beckoning opportunity. In London, General Alan Brooke was still fearful in June of a disaster in Assam. Even if the Allies were eventually successful at Imphal and Kohima, he could see no virtue in launching a land offensive into Burma: recapturing the country was still key in British strategic conceptions of strategy, but the operational answer to the conundrum of what to do with Burma always, in London at least, came back to an amphibious solution. Consequently, because both battle and victory had taken them by surprise, the Allies were slow to decide how to exploit the new strategic realties offered to them by Mutaguchi's defeat.

It was during these months that Slim and his headquarters staff agitated with 11 Army Group and Mountbatten for permission to follow up Mutaguchi's defeat with a pursuit across the Chindwin. Slim became convinced that the only sure way of defeating the Japanese in Burma was by land, and that he would have to do it with the resources at hand. He realized that he now had the opportunity not just to expel the remaining elements of 15 Army from India, but also to pursue the Japanese back into the heart of Burma. Indeed, were he to do this, he was convinced that bigger prizes were possible, perhaps even the seizure of Rangoon itself. The taste of victory in both Assam and Arakan had injected into 14 Army a newfound confidence based on the irrefutable evidence that the Japanese could be beaten. By mid-1944 Slim was convinced that an aggressive policy of pursuit into Burma to exploit these victories was not just desirable but necessary.

However, few of his superiors saw Slim's vision as clearly as he did. Giffard certainly didn't. During May 1944 Mountbatten badgered the Combined Chiefs of Staff for a decision as to what to do next, and when they did provide orders on 3 June 1944, the issue of an overland advance into Burma was fudged. As far as Washington and London were concerned, the imperative remained the continued maintenance of China in support of Pacific operations. The Hump still took priority. There were to be no extra resources for an amphibious assault on Burma's seaward flank. Mountbatten was nevertheless ordered 'to press advantages against the enemy by exerting maximum effort ground and air particularly during the current monsoon season'. These orders didn't tell him to invade Burma, but they did give him carte blanche to pursue his enemy. Accordingly, on 9 June 1944 Mountbatten ordered Giffard to exploit to the Chindwin between the villages of Yuwa in the south and Tamanthi in the north after the monsoon. Slim, however, wanted more. On 2 July he met Mountbatten and persuaded him that were 14 Army to mount an offensive it could do so with no more resources than those that would anyway be allocated to the defence of India. Furthermore, he believed that an offensive could begin as early as 1 November, once the rains had lifted and the pursuit of Mutaguchi's stragglers could be turned into an offensive into Upper and central Burma. But while Mountbatten was personally persuaded that a successful offensive could be mounted, at least to Shwebo or even Mandalay, Giffard was more cautious, sharing neither Mountbatten nor Slim's optimism, arguing that it would not be possible – reflecting Wingate's arguments – to mount a predominantly land-based offensive across the Chindwin, nor indeed to do this during the monsoon. Giffard saw the victory at Imphal–Kohima more as a relief – that 14 Army had not been defeated – rather than as an indication of the inherent frailties the operation had demonstrated in Japanese warfighting which could therefore be exploited to Allied advantage. Mountbatten, who had already determined to remove him, ignored Giffard's advice.

Keen to engage London on the possibility of recapturing Burma, on 23 July 1944 Mountbatten submitted two plans for approval. One had been requested by London, and the other had not. The first, Operation *Capital*, was drawn up by HQ 14 Army and reflected both Mountbatten's and Slim's views of the potential for following up the retreating 15 Army into Upper Burma, there to engage the Japanese armies in the region of Mandalay, linking up with Stilwell's

NCAC coming down from the north. The second, Operation *Dracula*, requested by an amphibious-obsessed London, entailed a seaborne assault on Rangoon in early 1945 followed by an advance north to Mandalay to meet up with the Allied forces moving south. London's reaction to Operation *Capital* was one of hesitation. Unaware of the spectacular success of the campaign in Manipur and Assam, few were willing to commit to the prospect of waging an offensive in a country which held so many bitter memories and which would self-evidently consume vast quantities of scarce resources. Unsurprisingly, the Chiefs of Staff were taken by Operation *Dracula*, as it meant not having to wage an expensive land campaign from the north, although it demanded additional forces to those already available, specifically naval forces, a further two divisions and a parachute brigade, as well as large numbers of transport aircraft and gliders. They concluded that, while Slim's forces must on all accounts remain on the offensive, 14 Army was to limit itself to holding operations until such time as Operation *Dracula* could be launched at Rangoon.[1] The Americans preferred Operation *Capital*, as it offered the greatest opportunity for opening up northern Burma, but were prepared to consider *Dracula* if the situation in Europe allowed the transfer of the required amphibious resources.

Despite this preference for *Dracula*, Slim believed that he could mount a successful offensive into Upper Burma with the resources he had to hand. It would be unfortunate if the Chiefs of Staff's uninformed pessimism (in his view) halted operations in Burma in favour of the supposedly easier option to land forces directly on Rangoon's doorstep from the sea. Slim knew that a strategic re-prioritization to allow an amphibious assault on the south-eastern seaboard of Burma on the *Dracula* model, especially at a time when Allied eyes were firmly fixed on Europe, was highly unlikely. Despite its obvious disadvantages (mounting a two-corps offensive over nearly 1,000 miles of impossible terrain and across two of the world's largest rivers), Slim was convinced that the only certain way of defeating the Japanese in Burma was by land, and that 14 Army, its tail up following the victories in Arakan, Kohima and Imphal, had the best chance to achieve something that London and Delhi were not even contemplating. Furthermore, Slim believed firmly that if he didn't make the running in preparing a plan to defeat the Japanese in Burma, no one would, and a great opportunity decisively to defeat the whole of the Japanese war machine in Burma would thus be squandered. The difficulty in the aftermath of Imphal lay in bringing this vision to fruition, in the face of the animosity in London and Washington to such proposals and the instructions he had already received merely to pursue 15 Army to the Chindwin. Yet Slim's clear vision throughout 1944 was undoubtedly not just to destroy Mutaguchi's army, but to launch an offensive into Burma that would succeed in driving the Japanese into the sea.[2] It is difficult not to conclude that Slim succeeded in weaving his own strategic ambitions into the limited orders he received from Giffard and that as the months went by he allowed the momentum of successful 14 Army operations to apply their own post-facto legitimacy to plans that were his own rather than those of his superiors. It seems clear that Mountbatten and Giffard, as well as the Chiefs of Staff, accepted Slim's successive faits accomplis not just because they worked, but because they themselves had nothing to offer as alternatives.

By 1944 few Burmese would claim that the Co-Prosperity Sphere had been a success. Most had recognized that independence granted in mid-1943 was a sham, and the bitter experience of occupation had left every kind of nationalist looking forward to their ejection. But nor did they want the automatic reinstatement of British colonialism. Some Burmese politicians actively sought Britain's help to rid themselves of the Japanese, including Thakin Thein Pe Myint, who walked into India in 1942 to seek British help. 'We hated the English', he later wrote, but 'disliked and mistrusted the Japanese.'[3] As planning gathered speed in 1944 for the reconquest of Burma, interest in SEAC in the prospect of help from nationalist quarters grew. The question in Simla (whence the Burma government had decamped in 1942), never fully resolved, was whether arming nationalist Burmans – many of whom, like Thein Pe, were committed Marxists – would backfire against the British, prejudicing its ability to re-establish itself as the colonial power once the war was over, as its new nationalist allies reverted to becoming its peacetime, anti-colonial, enemies. In the end, the need for intelligence about the political situation in Burma trumped all other concerns. During 1945, the Burma government-in-exile wrangled repeatedly with SOE (Force 136), which had been given responsibility for securing political and military intelligence in Burma and for undertaking armed guerrilla activity against the Japanese. The Burma government's Civil Affairs Service (Burma) remained suspicious that Force 136 was playing fast and loose with the future of (British) Burma, by prioritizing winning the war over achieving a British-led post-war settlement. There may indeed have been an element of truth in this; the younger breed of British officers, such as Major Tom Carew, Thein Pe's 'handler' in Burma in 1945, had none of the imperial prejudices of his forebears and no interest in reviving the pre-war colonial status quo once the war was won.[4]

For Mountbatten, the key advantage of engaging men like Thein Pe was to win over the newly formed underground Anti-Fascist Organization in Burma, made up of a broad church of men in the Burma National Army and the Japanese-led government, who wished to play a role in defeating the Japanese and in shaping the future of their country as an independent state. Mountbatten overrode the government-in-exile's objections, appointing Force 136 to work with Thein Pe and other known nationalists and communists on the primary task of defeating the Japanese. For his part, Slim insisted that the primary goal of Force 136 was intelligence gathering rather than the arming of rebel groups or the sponsorship of guerrilla activity, although an exception was made for the Karens, traditionally Christian and supportive of the British. Likewise, in the north of the country, Kachins had been working alongside the British and Americans since 1942 and Kachin irregulars had been included in Stilwell's order of battle.

By September 1944 Mountbatten managed to secure from the Octagon Conference, meeting in Quebec, an extension of the earlier mandate. On 16 September he was given authority to capture all of Burma 'at the earliest date', provided that operations to achieve this did not prejudice the security of the air supply route to China, the grand strategic imperative to supply China reasserting itself. Both *Capital* and *Dracula* were approved – *Capital* to start immediately and *Dracula* to take place, hopefully, before the onset of the next monsoon in Burma in May 1945. One of the advantages of *Capital* was the chance to threaten the lines of supply of the Japanese forces facing Stilwell and the NCAC, the original purpose of Operation *Thursday*. Mountbatten's two operations, following authorization at Quebec, were therefore:

1. To initiate *Capital*, by capturing Kalewa and Kalemyo on the Chindwin. 14 Army was to cross the Chindwin and clear the enemy from the Shwebo plain across to the Irrawaddy, while NCAC forces (including the British 36 Division) were to advance south from Myitkyina to Lashio, deep in the Shan Hills. 14 Army was to advance to liberate the whole of Upper Burma to the area of Mandalay, joining up with the NCAC at Maymyo.
2. To undertake a land offensive in Arakan (Operation *Romulus*) and the capture of Akyab (Operation *Talon*). This would provide the much-needed airfield at Akyab, and release two divisions otherwise tied up in Arakan for subsequent operations in Central and Southern Burma.

Giffard had long before (on 24 July), ordered Slim to initiate planning for Operation *Capital* on the basis that, should it be sanctioned, the offensive could be put into effect in December. On the very day he received these orders, Slim was able to tell Giffard that these plans were already underway: indeed, an advance could start on 15 November, utilizing air transport to resupply forward units. To enable him to concentrate solely on this task, Giffard relieved Slim of responsibility for both Arakan (Christison's XV Corps now reported directly to Giffard at 11 Army Group) and the vast line of communication into Assam and Manipur for which he had been, until then, responsible. Only a month later, however, it was clear that the war in Europe would not end quickly enough to release troops and amphibious equipment for *Dracula* to take place in May 1945, and it was postponed until after the monsoon, in late 1945.

Slim knew that the huge logistical nightmare associated with relying on land-based lines of communication could in large part be overcome by the use of air supply, a factor that had played a significant part in smashing both *U-Go* and *Ha-Go* during the previous six months. He knew also that the Japanese had received a defeat the like of which would make it difficult for them to recover quickly. If he could engineer a second defeat for the Japanese in Upper Burma, it would seriously weaken the Japanese defensive potential in Lower Burma, greatly enabling the success of an overland thrust at Rangoon from the north. He found himself faced with his second great chance and he was determined to seize it. The first task was to get to the Chindwin and seize crossings over the river. 2 Division took Tamu on 4 August, the town lying in ruins and stinking of the sweet, rotting smell of defeat. Thousands of bodies – the place had been a major Japanese base with at least one field hospital (and Mutaguchi's HQ for a time) – lay decomposing in the open. During the advance, the scale of the Japanese defeat was apparent to all. The detritus of a fleeing army was strewn across the jungle hills, bodies and equipment littering the escape routes east. Tamu provided Slim with access to the Chindwin via the road laid out in 1887 by British troops to Sittaung and Kalemyo, as well as the Kabaw Valley. With its precious airfield, Tamu offered the Allies the air dominance that was essential to 14 Army's advance.

With Tamu taken, Slim reorganized his army, ready for the push to the Chindwin. 17 and 23 Indian Divisions (together with HQ IV Corps) were sent back to India for rest. 3 Commando Brigade, which had been responsible during the siege of Imphal for guarding the Silchar Track, returned to Arakan to support planned operations against Akyab by XV Corps; and 2, 7 and 20 Indian Divisions were sent to be rested in the Imphal plain. 11 East African Division (21, 25 and 26 Brigades), which had just moved into Imphal, came forward to relieve 23 Indian Division.[5] On 6 August 1944 – his 53rd birthday – Slim ordered Stopford, who with his XXXIII Corps now had responsibility for all operations east of the Manipur River, to direct his pursuit to Kalewa and Sittaung on the Chindwin via both Tamu and Tiddim. 5 Indian Division advanced down the Tiddim Road, while 11 East African Division led the advance from Tamu towards both Sittaung and Kalemyo on the river, where both divisions were to converge. They methodically pushed their way against last-ditch opposition to the Chindwin. The process was slow and difficult because of continuing Japanese resistance, the appalling monsoon weather and difficult terrain. Men, mules and elephants struggled down jungle tracks after the retreating Japanese, crossing swollen rivers and rebuilding collapsed tracks and roads. The division was sustained exclusively by air. The over-stretched air forces pushed through minimal visibility to deliver their precious loads by parachute and free drop to the troops below them.

The East Africans occupied Sittaung on 4 September, and by 10 September the Chindwin was crossed and a small bridgehead secured. Four weeks later a second crossing was established, again by the East Africans, at Mawlaik. 5 Indian Division's task on the Tiddim front against the still-dangerous remnants of 33 Division was made immeasurably easier by the activities of the semi-irregular Lushai Brigade. This British-officered force of Indian soldiers and Chin levies proved to be very successful in harassing the flanks of the retreating Japanese. Slim regarded the brigade's exploits to be the epitome of successful long-range guerrilla operations, with a significant strategic effect in terms of its contribution to deciding the shape of the battle-scape that Slim was trying to design. 'As an example of effective Long-Range Penetration through "impossible" country its operation had never been surpassed', he wrote in a summary of the campaign published in Australia in 1950.[6] After a hard slog down the road, 5 Indian Division, now under the command of Major General 'Daddy' Warren, following his promotion from command of 161 Brigade at Kohima, occupied Tiddim on 17 October.[7] The Japanese fought hard to stop the advance at the 8,800-foot Kennedy Peak, but they were unsuccessful in bloody fighting in atrocious weather. On 13 November, 5 Indian and 11 East African Divisions joined hands, the Africans having progressively removed Japanese opposition in the Kabaw Valley, at Kalemyo. The fighting had been torturous. The monsoon remained in full spate. Japanese rearguards fought to the death, holding up the advance with snipers, mines and ambushes, and requiring a slow, methodical clearance. Malaria remained a killer. Despite these impediments the East African division seized Kalewa on 2 December, proving Giffard's earlier pessimism to have been ill-placed, despite the immense difficulties posed by climate and terrain. 'I had asked for the impossible', Slim remarked, 'and got it.' By 10 December, in an extraordinary logistical and engineering achievement, sappers erected the largest Bailey bridge then in existence – 1,154 feet long – across the river. The Chindwin, the first great obstacle to 14 Army entering Burma, had been bridged.

For the offensive into Burma, Slim's army (XV Corps in Arakan now temporarily reporting directly to General Sir Oliver Leese, Giffard's replacement) comprised six infantry divisions, two tank brigades and three independent infantry brigades – a combat force of close to 90,000 men. However, logistical realities meant that Slim would only be able to deploy two offensive corps for Operation *Capital*, comprising four infantry divisions (three Indian and one British), two tank brigades and two independent infantry brigades – a force of close to 60,000 men, or only 65 per cent of what he had available. The army reserve of two divisions (one Indian and one East African) and two infantry brigades (one of which, the Lushai Brigade, was not intended for operations outside of its own territory) would remain on the Chindwin. These were:

- IV Corps: Lieutenant General Frank Messervy (effective from 8 December 1944)
  - ○ 7 Indian Division (Major General Geoffrey Evans)
  - ○ 17 Indian Division (Major General Punch Cowan)
  - ○ 19 Indian Division (Major General Pete 'Chota' Rees)
  - ○ 255 Tank Brigade (Brigadier Claude Pert), equipped with Sherman tanks
- XXXIII Corps: Lieutenant General Sir Montagu Stopford
  - ○ 2 British Division (Major General Graham Nicholson, who had replaced John Grover)
  - ○ 20 Indian Division (Major General Douglas Gracey)
  - ○ 268 Indian Infantry Brigade (Brigadier Godfrey Dyer)
  - ○ 254 Tank Brigade (Brigadier Reginald Scoones, the brother of Geoffrey), equipped with M3 Stuart and Lee-Grant tanks
- Army Reserve (remaining on the Chindwin)
  - ○ 5 Indian Division (Major General 'Daddy' Warren)
  - ○ 11 East African Division (Major General Charles Fowkes until Jan 1945; Major General Bob Mansergh Jan/Feb 1945 and then Major General William Dimoline Feb–May 1945)
  - ○ 28 East African Brigade (Brigadier Bob Mansergh until Feb 1945)
  - ○ Lushai Brigade (Brigadier P.C. Marindin)

The vast distances involved in moving even 65 per cent of his army beyond the Chindwin to the Shwebo plain meant that Operation *Capital* was clearly going to be a war of logistics for Slim as much as it would be a battlefield confrontation with General Heitarō Kimura's (General Kawabe's replacement) army. He was faced with fighting a numerically superior enemy at the end of a line of communication that would only grow in length and complexity with every mile he advanced. The vast distances involved were the principal brake on Allied operations. All troops and equipment had either to come over the Naga Hills from Dimapur and thence to Tamu and Kalewa, or by air into Imphal or, when it had been captured, Tamu. As airfields were captured during the offensive they could be pressed into service. The problem with aerial resupply was that an attack on the Japanese on the other side of the Irrawaddy (Mandalay or Meiktila) would outstrip the economical flying range (250 miles) of transport aircraft based at Imphal. Slim would have to win the land battle along the Irrawaddy in order to capture the airfields necessary for the resupply and continued progress of 14 Army towards Rangoon, although the small fleet of homemade boats on the Chindwin would help immensely with ferrying stores, vehicles and troops.

To match the new style of fighting Slim expected once the Chindwin and Irrawaddy had been crossed, Slim appointed Frank Messervy and Montagu Stopford as his two corps commanders. The two men would, he knew, thrive under his type of leadership. Stopford had driven XXXIII Corps through the Kohima battles to the Chindwin. In planning the offensive, Slim was concerned to tell Messervy and Stopford *what* to do, while allowing them virtually complete freedom to decide *how* they carried out his instructions. Choosing one's subordinates well and then delegating responsibility to them was a strong characteristic of Slim's leadership.[8] In Burma this approach to command made especial sense, for two reasons. First, the obvious geographical difficulties in the theatre made regular communication difficult. More importantly, he believed that his commanders could best achieve his requirements without him breathing down their necks while they were conducting operations. 'My corps and divisions were called upon to act with at least as much freedom as armies and corps in other theatres' he recalled. 'Commanders at all levels had to act more on their own; they were given greater latitude to work out their own plans to achieve what they knew was the Army Commander's intention. In time they developed to a marked degree a flexibility of mind and a firmness of decision that enabled them to act swiftly to take advantage of sudden information or changing circumstances without reference to their superiors. They were encouraged, as Stopford put it 'to shoot a goal when the referee wasn't looking.' 'This acting without orders, in anticipation of orders, or without waiting for approval, yet always within the overall intention, must become second nature in any form of warfare where formations do not fight closely *en cadre*' Slim later wrote, 'and must go down to the smallest units. It requires in the higher command a corresponding flexibility of mind, confidence in its subordinates, and the power to make its intentions clear right through the force.' The battles of Arakan, Imphal and Kohima in 1944 had reinforced a lesson that had been learned the hard way in Burma in 1942 and 1943. It wasn't merely the training and preparation of the soldiers that was necessary for success in combat, but the command abilities of its leaders. Lloyd and Irwin had failed dismally in the cauldron of fire they had faced in 1943. The 1944 battles allowed Slim to choose those he would take with him into the next phase of the campaign. Many were his friends and Gurkha comrades. All had been tried in battle and had not been found wanting.

Slim's plan for Operation *Capital* necessitated the retraining and restructuring of his army. Once over the Irrawaddy, the army would have to fight in a very different style to that which had won it victories in Arakan, Imphal and Kohima. After two long years of jungle fighting, the wide prairie-like plains of central Burma beckoned, where fast-moving armoured thrusts, large-scale artillery 'stonks' and attacks on broad fronts by brigades and divisions would replace the intense but relatively slow bayonet, rifle and grenade struggles by sections, platoons and companies in the half-gloom of the wet jungle that had characterized the fighting in Arakan and the hills of eastern India. Speed, the massed use of armour, bold flanking movements and the close cooperation of tanks, infantry, artillery and aircraft would define operations in this new environment. Messervy suggested, among other things, that one brigade of 17 Indian Division be mechanized and another made air transportable to exploit the new terrain. Slim agreed and converted 5 Indian Division to the new organization as well. Messervy's idea proved critical both to the seizure of Meiktila the following February and in the epic dash to Rangoon that followed. Likewise, the armoured brigades were re-equipped with medium tanks (Shermans in one and Lee-Grants in the other) and an infantry battalion, carried in armoured vehicles, added to each. To each armoured squadron was added a troop of flame-throwers. There weren't enough British self-propelled artillery pieces available for Burma, so Auchinleck had gratefully accepted the offer of surplus American 105mm 'Priests'. Despite the different calibre of the ammunition this entailed, the logistical nuisance of having another calibre of artillery ammunition to haul to the front was offset by the tactical flexibility motorized artillery was able to offer Messervy in the forthcoming battles. During September and October

1944, considerable retraining took place in 14 Army to prepare for this new style of warfighting.

Giffard's replacement, Lieutenant General Sir Oliver Leese, newly arrived from command of 8 Army in Italy, took up his post in November 1944. Officially based in Kandy, he nevertheless placed his forward HQ at Sim's old Corps HQ at Barrackpore, where it was collocated with HQ Eastern Air Command, commanded by the American General George Stratemeyer. Giffard's removal enabled Mountbatten to rationalize all land command in theatre into one post. This new organization, Allied Land Forces South East Asia (ALFSEA) comprised 20 combat divisions, in 14 Army, XV Corps, the Northern Combat Area Command (which included 36 British Division), together with the Line of Communication Command and Ceylon Army Command. The widespread reorganization at the time included abolishing the Troop Carrier Command and creating a single, joint army/air supply organization – Combat Cargo Task Force – at Comilla, with two separate components. The army ran the Combined Army Air Transport Organisation, which organized the entirety of 14 Army and XV Corps' aerial logistic requirements, and the RAF ran the Combat Cargo Task Force, which ensured that sufficient aircraft were available to meet the demands of the army. This was substantial. In the period between December 1944 and May 1945, an average of 60,000 tons of supplies were being delivered by airlift each month, and in March a record of 78,250 tons, together with 27,000 military passengers: a peak day saw 4,000 tons being airlifted for troops in Arakan and central Burma.[9] The previous HQ, 3 Tactical Air Force was disbanded, and 221 and 224 Groups were placed directly under Eastern Air Command, reflecting a more streamlined and joint operation that removed, as far as was possible, the distinctions between army and air force when meeting the needs of the fighting formations on the ground.

From the outset Leese had an unhappy relationship with Slim. Leese wanted to exercise command, as was his right; Slim, however, knew what he wanted to achieve, and how to do so. As the author of Operation *Capital*, he didn't want to be told what to do, and in this respect proved to be a difficult subordinate. Leese, for his part, arrived with a critical attitude, perhaps with echoes of the 1942 and 1943 failures still in his ear. He expected to have to remedy tactical deficiencies in his commanders, and 'grip' operations to ensure success as 14 Army launched itself into Upper and central Burma, and as XV Corps tried for the third time to make headway in Arakan. On first impressions he considered that Slim was 'sound in his tactics', but Leese didn't consider the victory at Imphal and Kohima to be on a par with those achieved in North Africa and Italy.[10] He was sceptical about Slim's all-round military prowess and the experience of his senior commanders. In a letter to Brooke on 15 December 1944, he suggested that there was 'a good deal of ignorance in Senior Officers [in 14 Army] about the employment of modern arms and equipment. It is for this reason that I am so anxious to get officers with experience in Europe. Otherwise when we come to fight on the beaches and in the plains by Mandalay we may get into unnecessary tangles.' This underestimation of the ability of 14 Army, at a time when it was already successfully pushing hard out of the Chindwin bridgeheads, was surprising, given what 14 Army was soon to achieve, and suggests that Leese failed to understand the full capability of 14 Army, its commander and its soldiers.

During the pursuit to the Chindwin, Slim had been exercised about how he could engage and defeat General Kawabe's replacement – General Heitarō Kimura – in open battle once the Chindwin had been breached. Kimura was a highly regarded commander who had been Vice-Minister of War in Tokyo and between 1943 and 1944 a member of the Supreme War Council. But he was entirely unknown to British commanders. Intelligence had shown that the Japanese had built up substantial stocks of war materiel on the Shwebo plain, giving a strong indication that Kimura wished to fight his defensive battle for Mandalay to the north of the great river. This suited Slim. The vast Shwebo plain was the ideal terrain for the battle he sought – a battle of manoeuvre in which his artillery, armour (including the newly arrived Sherman tanks) and air support would have devastating effect on the Japanese, 'where tanks would operate in quantities instead of by twos or threes, where guns must be capable of fire and movement, where infantry must manoeuvre fast and far.' Slim believed that Kimura would want to prevent the Allies from dominating the vast space on the western side of the Irrawaddy, even though it would mean that the Japanese would be forced to fight with their backs to the Irrawaddy, in country suited to the type of warfare that did not favour them: a fast-moving series of armour-dominated engagements where the Allied armour, aircraft and artillery would relatively easily discomfit the infantry-dominated Japanese forces. Slim assumed that the typical Japanese fear of withdrawal would mean that Kimura – a commander he did not know, but whom he assumed would be similar to all other Japanese generals of his acquaintance – would not withdraw behind the Irrawaddy.

The Shwebo plain was 400 miles from the nearest railhead, with a single-track earthen road for 250 miles of it that was impassable in the monsoon. Slim's two corps were outnumbered by Kimura's forces which, chastened but far from beaten, amounted to five and a half divisions, an independent mixed brigade, a tank regiment, nearly 40,000 line of communication troops, two INA divisions and troops of General Aung San's Burma Defence Army. Honda's 33 Army[11] was based on Bhamo opposing the Chinese, and 15 Army, commanded after 30 August by General Katamura,[12] defended the Irrawaddy. 'These were not the odds I should have liked,' Slim commented. 'A year ago I would not have looked at the proposal.' But 14 Army's advantage in the air, in armour, in greater mobility in the open, and the spirit of his troops gave him the confidence to press ahead despite what otherwise would have appeared to be unacceptable odds.

Slim's assessment was that the battered remnants of 15 Army would hold a defensive line in the formidable jungle-clad mountains of the Zibyu Taungdam Range. This range of hills lay about 25 miles to the east of the Chindwin and ran parallel to it for a distance of 120 miles. Slim's plan was to punch through them with Messervy's IV Corps on the left and General Stopford's XXXIII Corps on the right, both corps converging on the area of Ye-U-Shwebo. The plan was for IV Corps to break out of the Sittaung bridgehead and, following an easterly course, force its way through the mountains, seize Pinlebu and thereafter change direction to capture Shwebo from the north. Stopford's XXXIII Corps, meanwhile, would advance from Kalewa on a broad front, following the general south-easterly route of the Chindwin towards Ye-U and Monywa.

Wasting no time, 14 Army crossed the Chindwin as soon as it was reached. Slim urged Messervy to advance as quickly as possible and to take risks that would months ago have been unthinkable, in order to maintain the momentum of the advance. The IV Corps advance was led by Major General Peter Rees's 19 Indian Division.[13] Moving out of Sittaung on 4 December, the division headed for Pinlebu, 60 miles to the east. Rees, driving his units on, made rapid progress through the Zibyu Taungdam Hills. The diminutive and popular Welshman, Rees[14] epitomized the type of divisional commander that Slim had spent so long cultivating in 14 Army. Soon after Rees's troops had captured Mandalay Hill in March 1945, Slim visited the town as it was still being cleared of Japanese.

Through all this noise and the clatter of men clearing a battlefield, came a strange sound – singing. I followed it. There was General Rees, his uniform sweat-soaked and dirty, his distinguishing red scarf rumpled around his neck, his bush hat at a jaunty angle, his arm beating time, surrounded by a group of Assamese soldiers whom he was vigorously leading in the singing of Welsh missionary hymns. The fact that he sang in Welsh and they in Khasi only added to the harmony. I looked on admiringly. My generals had character. Their men knew them and they knew their men.

Less than two weeks after the advance had begun, Rees had joined his division up with Major General Francis Festing's 36 Division at Rail Indaw, 90 miles east of Sittaung, part of the NCAC's successful drive south from Lashio against 33 Army.[15] Throughout, Japanese resistance was far less intense than had been expected. Nevertheless, Rees's advance was an extraordinary effort given the appalling nature of the terrain. Roads had to be hacked out of the virgin jungle by troops using what tools they could carry. Farther south, a brigade of 20 Indian Division led the XXXIII Corps advance, crossing the Chindwin north of Kalewa at Mawlaik, while 11 East African Division fought hard to extend the bridgehead at Kalewa. On 18 December, the remainder of 20 Indian Division followed through the bridgehead. During December, leading formations of 14 Army advanced eastwards from their bridgeheads across the Chindwin. In the face of fierce opposition, 2 Division captured Kaduma and on 31 December seized the Kabo Weir on the Mu River, preventing the Japanese from destroying this key part of the Shwebo plain irrigation system. XXXIII Corps now had a firm footing in the centre of the Shwebo plain.

36

A Change of Plan

Within days of the start of IV Corps' advance, however, Slim accepted that his initial plan to trap Kimura on the Shwebo plain in front of the Irrawaddy would not work. The weakness of the opposition facing 19 Indian Division forced him to recognize that Kimura had withdrawn the bulk of his forces east of the Irrawaddy, with the obvious intention of fighting behind, rather than in front of, the river. If this were to happen, 14 Army would be stretched out from Tamu and vulnerable to counterattack just when it was attempting to cross one of the most formidable river barriers imaginable. Slim's original expectation that Kimura would be content to meet 14 Army on terms distinctly disadvantageous to himself was, perhaps, unduly optimistic. In any case, Kimura's withdrawal behind the Irrawaddy dashed this expectation resoundingly. But fighting Kimura on the eastern and southern side of the Irrawaddy, after having first crossed the river, was never countenanced. It would mean dealing with Kimura's concentrated forces just at the point where he was most vulnerable. Slim believed that while the *strategy* for winning back Burma was frontal, and resolutely into the teeth of the entire Burma Area Army, the *operational* design for doing so must not be.

Slim immediately sought, instead, a means not only of crossing his five divisions and three tank brigades without mishap or significant interference over the Irrawaddy but also of creating the decisive advantage he required to bring the Japanese to battle on his own terms. He wanted to fight where he was strongest and where Kimura was weakest. He needed something more cunning and subtle than that offered by the simple though casualty-laden battering-ram of attrition. Seeking an alternative strategy, where he could engage Kimura in decisive battle while retaining the advantages of firepower and surprise, Slim's eyes turned to the towns of Meiktila and Thazi, lying approximately 70 miles south of Mandalay.

These towns were the key nodal points on Kimura's line of communication supporting both 33 and 15 Army. They were in every sense the beating heart of the Burma Area Army. The towns represented ground that was vital to the enemy defence, a concept 14 Army had first learned painfully in Arakan. The railway and main road from Rangoon ran through Meiktila before bending north on their way to Mandalay, and the town formed a natural location for supply and ammunition dumps, airfields and hospitals. If Slim could cut off both Honda's and Katamura's corps from this vital logistical centre, the Japanese ability to resist XXXIII Corps' inexorable pressure in the north around Mandalay would be fatally weakened. Slim recognized that without Meiktila Kimura could not hope to sustain a prolonged battle for Mandalay. Indeed, it might even prove to be the decisive act in the destruction of the whole of Kimura's army.

Within days Slim and his staff had come up with a plan, which was dubbed Operation *Extended Capital*. The idea was to make Kimura believe that nothing had changed, that 14 Army's advance remained focused on Mandalay, with XXXIII and IV Corps crossing the Irrawaddy north-west of the city. The essence of Slim's new plan, however, was that while XXXIII Corps would continue to cross the Irrawaddy to the north of Mandalay as originally planned, the reconfigured IV Corps (Geoffrey Evans' 7 and 'Punch' Cowan's 17 Indian Division, newly returned from rest, together with 28 East African Brigade, 255 Tank Brigade and the Lushai Brigade) would instead cross the Irrawaddy in great secrecy far to the south in the area of Pakokku before striking hard with armour, motorized artillery and infantry at Meiktila. The northern advance by XXXIII Corps (strengthened by 19 Indian Division and 268 Tank Brigade) would be a deception to hide the decisive strike by IV Corps to the south. If Slim could attract the greatest possible number of enemy divisions towards the northern crossing points (where, after all, Kimura expected him to strike), he could minimize opposition to the real focus of his attack in the south. This would provide Slim with, as he put it, 'not only the major battle I desired, but the chance to repeat our old hammer and anvil tactics: XXXIII Corps the hammer from the north against the anvil of IV Corps at Meiktila – and the Japanese between.' Had the aircraft been available, Slim would have employed parachute forces to capture Meiktila, to hold the airfield for his air transportable divisions to land in the heart of the enemy.

Slim explained his revised plan to Messervy and Stopford on 18 December and on 19 December issued his plan. On 17 December he had sent a summary of his intentions to Leese, and on 20 December he sent a full copy of the plan to HQ ALFSEA. On 26 December Slim moved his formations in accordance with his new plan, 268 Brigade and 19 Indian Division transferring from IV to XXXIII Corps. The speed at which Slim made these changes left little time for wide consultation. He regarded his change of plan to be within the wider remit he had been given, and thus decided to inform Leese of what he intended rather than seeking his permission. Messervy and Stopford quickly translated Slim's revised plan into action, and XXXIII Corps' advance continued unabated during this period. The leading troops of 2 Division, together with the Lee-Grant and Stuart tanks of 254 Tank Brigade, passed through Pyingaing (known to the troops as 'Pink Gin') on 23 December. Japanese rearguards attempted to hold up the advance through ambushes and mining. Ye-U and its airfield were captured on 2 January 1945, and by 5 January the division had established a firm bridgehead over the Mu River. 2 British and 19 Indian Divisions now began a race for Shwebo, with the Japanese 15 Division streaming before it in full retreat to the Irrawaddy. Shwebo was captured on 9 January jointly by units of both divisions. Rees's 19 Indian Division had reached the Shwebo area by 5 January, established bridgeheads over the Irrawaddy at Thabeikkyin and Kyaukyaung, and began to advance southward on the east bank of the river towards Mandalay.

Slim's plan was bold. Surprise and secrecy were essential. But the advance depended entirely on Slim's ability to supply his armoured spearheads as they penetrated deep into Japanese-held territory. The administrative effort to supply two corps well forward of their supply bases in inhospitable terrain was formidable. XXXIII Corps had to push rapidly forward in the north, while IV Corps, with its armour, moved in secret down 330 miles of rough dirt track from Tamu to the area of Pakokku before conducting an opposed crossing of one of the world's mightiest rivers. 'We were, in fact, defying some of the principles of war in undertaking the reconquest of Burma from the north to the south – as the strategic situation compelled us to do – instead of in the reverse direction', wrote Leese in May 1945. 'Thus our main line of communication ran at right-angles to the enemy, while we were operating in reverse to, and against the trend of the main river and road arteries of the country. The distances were very great, existing communications were poor, and both climate and terrain were unfavourable.'[1]

The physical restraint of operating in difficult terrain long distances from railheads meant that Slim was able to sustain over the Chindwin no more than four and two-thirds divisions and two tank brigades. However, the decisive advantage the Allies enjoyed in the air meant that he could rely on air transport to maintain his forward units, as long as the requisite numbers of aircraft remained available. With the vast experience of the battle of the Admin Box at Sinzweya Pocket, of Operation *Thursday* and of Operation *Stamina*, the air supply organization supporting 14 Army had become the model of its kind. But having sufficient aircraft available remained a constant headache. Slim's plans were dealt a devastating blow on the morning of 10 December 1944 when he awoke at Imphal to the sound of mass aircraft activity at the nearby airfield. He quickly discovered that 75 of his precious USAAF C47s were being diverted to meet a developing crisis in China. The Japanese Ichi-Go offensive specifically directed against 14 USAAF's air bases in China (about which Stilwell had repeatedly warned), was proceeding well and threatening to reach Kunming. If this happened, the entire Hump operation would be unseated. The Chiefs of Staff ordered two of the Chinese divisions to return to China, together with three combat cargo squadrons, each of 25 aircraft. Slim immediately told Mountbatten that without these aircraft the success of Operation *Capital* could not be guaranteed. Mountbatten fought hard to have the aircraft returned, and on 21 January two of the three squadrons Slim had lost (i.e. 50 aircraft) were returned to him. By this time, anyway, Slim's troops were well across the Irrawaddy, and the prospect of the road from Ledo opening up and consigning the Hump to history was quickly beckoning. Nevertheless, it was estimated that Slim needed 140 transport aircraft permanently allocated to 14 Army to keep his troops on the move. By cajoling the Joint Chiefs of Staff in London, Mountbatten managed to secure a further 30 aircraft destined to support the newly created British Pacific Fleet, and 25 C47s diverted from the Mediterranean theatre. Slim ended up with 145 aircraft, albeit three weeks later than he had hoped, but in time to deal what he hoped would be a decisive blow against Meiktila and Mandalay.

But while air transport answered some of Slim's most pressing needs, the enormous land-based line of communication also required substantial work to ensure that 14 Army could operate far ahead of its bases in Assam. It was 506 miles from the 14 Army depot at Dimapur to Mandalay, the line of communication running through Imphal, Tamu, Kalewa, Shwebo and Mandalay. Road building and upgrading was essential, but limited resources restricted what could be done. This constant crisis of resources, however, had a positive effect on the men of 14 Army. It forced them to become self-reliant and innovative. 'With us', Slim recalled, 'necessity was the mother of invention. We lacked so much in equipment and supplies that, if we were not to give up offensive operations altogether, we had either to manage without or improvise for ourselves… my soldiers forced the opposed crossing of great rivers using inadequate equipment, stretched brittle communication links to fantastic lengths, marched over the most heart breaking country on reduced rations, fought disease with discipline to beat it.' Slim's chief engineer, Bill Hasted, felled forests alongside the Chindwin at Kalewa to make barges able to take 10 tons each, in order to make best use of the Chindwin as a supply artery. Three of these tied together could carry a Sherman tank. An extraordinary 541 were built. Outboard engines were flown in, boat wrecks were repaired, and even sunken vessels on the riverbed were recovered, repaired and pressed into service. These and other measures were so successful that whereas in November 1943 an average of 2,800 tons a day was moved forward, by September 1944 this had increased to 6,500 tons and by March 1945 nearly 9,000 tons a day. To protect this now vital river line of communication two homemade (but leaky) 12-knot armed patrol vessels were built on the banks of the Chindwin at Kalewa, which Slim unofficially commissioned HMS *Una* (after his daughter) and HMS *Pamela* (Mountbatten's daughter). By March 1945 these vessels were protecting an inland water transport system carrying up to 700 tons of men and materiel a day on both the Chindwin and Irrawaddy rivers. It was a remarkable logistical achievement.

IV Corps began its secret march south down the Myittha/Gangaw Valley on 19 January and, despite the difficulties of the terrain, moved quickly. Slim had given Messervy 15 February as the last acceptable date for crossing the Irrawaddy. Elaborate deception measures were adopted to ensure that Messervy's move through the jungle to Pakokku remained concealed from the Japanese, and to reinforce in Kimura's mind the certain belief that IV Corps remained with XXXIII Corps on the Shwebo plain, preparing to cross the river above Mandalay. While the real IV Corps had to keep radio silence during its move southwards, a dummy corps headquarters was established in Tamu, using the same radio frequencies, through which all communications from 19 Indian Division to XXXIII Corps had to pass. Despite the inconvenience this caused for commanders, this complicated deception was spectacularly successful. The signals intelligence capability that had served Slim so well at Imphal and Kohima accompanied 14 Army on the advance into Burma, a 300-strong Special Wireless Group being attached to Slim's headquarters, and travelling with it, from Comilla, to Monywa and then Meiktila. Each of IV and XXXIII Corps (and XV Corps in Arakan) had an attached Special Wireless Company, all for the purpose of immediately decoding enemy battlefield communications.

The Japanese did not believe that a large-scale advance through the Gangaw Valley was possible and never seriously considered this. In order to help reinforce these perceptions, Messervy, when his advance reached the town of Gangaw, arranged with Slim for the town's defences to be overwhelmingly attacked on 10 January by the Strategic Air Force, with follow-up occupation by the

Lushai Brigade, rather than using his divisions for the purpose. Using the latter would have demonstrated to the Japanese that Slim's division was on the march far from where it was expected. Unobserved and unhindered, Messervy's forward units reached Pauk, 40 miles from Pakokku, in late January. Kimura, while aware of some activity on his southern flank, regarded this to be nothing more than demonstrations by minor forces designed to draw him south, and he was not to be tempted into doing something so foolish. All the while he continued to reinforce the Irrawaddy in the Mandalay area, bringing in all available forces from across Burma, so that by February he had a force equivalent to eight Japanese and one and a third INA divisions. He was confident that these would be more than sufficient to defeat the expected five divisions of 14 Army in what he was now calling the decisive 'Battle of the Irrawaddy Shore'. His failure to appreciate the overall subtlety of Slim's approach, the dynamism and mobility of his army, together with the extraordinary power and flexibility afforded to Slim by virtue of air superiority and air transport, proved to be the major strands in his undoing.

In Burma, one man above all others could see the writing on the wall for Kimura. The Allies received news on 1 January 1945 that Aung San and the Burma National Army (BNA) would be prepared to switch sides. An SOE operation – codenamed 'Nation' – was launched to liaise with the BNA and the leadership of another group, the Anti Fascist Organization (AFO) and so facilitate this delicate transfer of loyalties. The first parachute drop of agents was to Toungoo on 27 January and comprised an all-Burma force under Thein Pe Myint. It reported that the BNA – or significant parts of it – was ready to turn, but that the AFO needed arming. A team lead by Major Tom Carew, which parachuted into Burma on 20 March, reported that action by the BNA would begin in a week. That members of the original Thirty Comrades – who had received pre-war Japanese military training to prepare Burma for its liberation and had participated in the Japanese invasion in 1942 – had turned their backs on their erstwhile political sponsors in favour of the returning colonial power, says much about the nature and quality of Japanese imperialism in the years since 1942, and of the desire of many young Burmans to be free of imperialism of every description.

37

Third Time Lucky in Arakan

The onset of the monsoon in May 1944 had coincided with the successful conclusion of the campaign in the Mayu Range. With the demise of *Ha-Go* and the onset of *U-Go* in Manipur, offensive operations by the Allies in Arakan were paused until the onset of the dry season in October. The threat to Chittagong had receded and the Japanese were now stretched impossibly. For Mountbatten, there was no strategic imperative to take any more ground in Arakan during the wet season other than making life as difficult as possible for the Japanese. Lieutenant General Sir Philip Christison's XV Corps held its position during one of the wettest monsoons on record, while Sakurai's weakened 28 Army adjusted itself to focus on defending Akyab and preparing for the inevitable Allied advance when the dry season returned. By the end of the fighting in Manipur in August 1944, and with Slim's plans for pursuit into Upper Burma, the strategic significance of Arakan reasserted itself. It provided a stepping stone by sea and air to Rangoon, and by land via the An Pass and Taungup into central Burma. By now XV Corps had been largely reconstituted, with the departure of 5 and 7 Indian Divisions for the battlefields of Imphal and Kohima. It now comprised 25 and 26 Indian and 81 and 82 West African Divisions, together with 3 Commando Brigade, 22 East African Brigade and 50 Tank Brigade, equipped with Sherman tanks. While Mandalay was the primary focus of the Allied advance into Burma, there to face the concentrated might of Kimura's Burma Area Army, the need to secure Arakan remained a critical component of SEAC strategy. It would prevent the Japanese 28 Army in Arakan from providing support to Kimura's defence of central Burma, and possession of the airfields at Akyab and at Kyaukpyu on Ramree Island would bring Rangoon into economical flying range of Allied transport aircraft. Akyab also offered a side door into central Burma to support land operations against Rangoon when the advance began from Meiktila and Mandalay, once those battles had been successfully concluded. By then 14 Army would have long outrun its logistic support from Imphal and Tamu, and aerial resupply from Akyab would help fill that void. More importantly perhaps for Allied strategy was the opportunity the capture of Ramree and Cheduba offered for the amphibious attack on Rangoon – Operation *Dracula* – which was assumed by most in London and Washington to be the only way to capture the capital before the beginning of the next monsoon season in May 1945.

The arguments for mounting the assault in Arakan were presented by Mountbatten to the Chiefs of Staff against the opposition of his American deputy, Wedemeyer, who worried that the operation would divert resources from China. The unwritten suggestion was the old political canard that had long divided British and American interests in the region – that Britain was attempting to avoid hard fighting in Burma by means of an amphibious strategy that bypassed Burma altogether. But Mountbatten persisted. He argued that operations to defeat Sakurai in Arakan were designed to do precisely what Slim was in the process of doing in Upper and central Burma – namely, to push out the Japanese and so open up the new Burma Road. Defeating the Japanese in Burma was the best way of ensuring China remained supplied and engaged in the fight. Even doubling or tripling the resources available to China (instead of devoting them to *Capital* and *Dracula*) would do nothing to defeat Kimura, and until he was defeated the Japanese would retain control of central Burma. The irony was that it was 14 Army – supported by XV Corps in Arakan – that was now in the process of spectacularly achieving what the Americans had long demanded of the British in Burma, although Wedemeyer's US-tinted political spectacles meant that he still couldn't quite see it.

In the event XV Corps' advance down the coastline when it began in December 1944 – Operation *Romulus* – went far better than planned, Sakurai pulling back before the pressure, despite fierce local resistance. 82 West African Division had already reoccupied Buthidaung, allowing Major General George Wood's 25 Indian Division to advance with 74 Brigade along the coast supplied by sea. A second Brigade – 53 – advanced on the eastern side of the Mayu Range, also supported by a river line of communication on the Mayu and Kalapanzin Rivers. The focus for both brigades was 'fighting forward', rather than looking back to the road behind them. The advancing battalions coordinated their march with integrated armour, artillery and fighter ground attack, bypassing stiff resistance and allowing centres of resistance to be dealt with by troops following

MAP 9 Advance in Arakan 1945

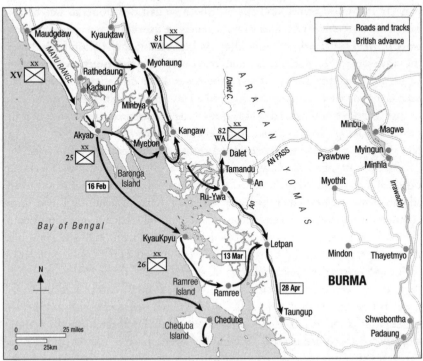

up behind. The confidence of the army had been transformed. Despite the fury of the opposition they encountered, the troops of XV Corps now had an answer to every tactical problem they faced. In the language of the time, their tails were up. Their focus on the strategic imperative – the capture of Akyab – meant that they had no reason to be distracted by opposition they deemed to be strategically insignificant. They ignored repeated Japanese attempts at encirclement and infiltration, driving forward to their objective and shrugging off attempts by the Japanese to divert them from this course.

A new and dramatic dimension to *Romulus* was the flanking march down the remote and roadless Kaladan Valley by Major General Frederick Loftus-Tottenham's 81 West African Division,[1] an opportunity that Christison had missed the year before but was determined to fully exploit now. The Kaladan River drains into the sea at Akyab. The West Africans, advancing down the roadless valley, were supplied by air for nine months, operating behind what would conventionally be described as 'the front line'. Combat operations in the

Kaladan Valley, though significant, were less important to Christison than the pressure this move placed on Sakurai, who now had two fronts to watch. This exercise in long-range penetration was an effective use of the concept, but like the work of the Lushai Brigade in holding the right flank of the Chin Hills during the advance to the Chindwin, and in contrast to the much better-known Operation *Thursday*, is little known. There was no fanfare about its work at the time. No war correspondents accompanied its long march into Japanese-held territory, and few visitors arrived to acknowledge the extraordinary work of these volunteer soldiers from Nigeria, the Gold Coast (the Gambia) and Sierra Leone, few of whom had been soldiers before the divisions had been raised in 1943.[2]

On the coast, Foul Point was reached on Boxing Day two weeks earlier than expected, and preparations were made for the assault on Akyab. This was a task allocated to 3 Commando Brigade, the two Royal Marine and two army commandos (about 500 men each), recently arrived from Europe, which were itching for a fight.[3] In the air, No. 224 Group, and at sea, Force W and a powerful naval bombardment group (Task Force 61, comprising HMS *Queen Elizabeth* – which hadn't fired its 15-inch guns in anger since Gallipoli in 1915 – *Newcastle*, *Nigeria* and *Kenya*, HMAS *Napier*, *Nepal*, *Norman*, and two other fleet destroyers, the escort carrier HMS *Ameer*, and 20 other vessels) prepared to support the first amphibious landings in theatre. In the event Sakurai evacuated the town and it was taken without firing a shot. Sakurai had been forced to use two of the three battalions guarding the town to counter the advance to his rear right flank by the West Africans, who had captured the key ferry at Kyawktaw on Christmas Day. Realizing that he could no longer defend Akyab with the forces at his disposal, he withdrew them to defend the route into Burma proper through the hill tracks via Taungup, 130 miles south. The strategic effect of the Kaladan Valley operation, in terms of the influence it had on achieving Christison's overall strategic objective in Arakan – the capture of Akyab – was enormous. By forcing Sakurai to withdraw from Akyab, a battle that would have consumed considerable time, scarce material and lives, it was 81 West African Division that won the battle for Akyab. It was a classic example of the power of manoeuvre – rather than the bludgeoning tactics deployed by Irwin in 1943 – that forced the issue for Sakurai, obliging him to conform to Mountbatten's plan.

The initiative now lay with Christison. In order to stop Sakurai from withdrawing in good order into central Burma, Christison needed to capture the town of Kangaw. This would also prevent Sakurai from counterattacking the planned offensive by 81 West African Division against Myohaung, the ancient capital of Arakan that lay at the mouth of the Kaladan River. Christison used his amphibious capability to cut the coast road. 3 Commando Brigade, whose amphibious assault against Myebon through a maze of outlying mangrove swamps on 12 January was coordinated with close air support and a naval bombardment, succeeded in forming a bridgehead, through which the all-Indian 51 Infantry Brigade of 25 Indian Division was inserted from the sea.[4] This brigade was commanded by the Sandhurst-trained Lieutenant Colonel Kodendera Subayya ('Timmy') Thimayya.

The Japanese, reacting strongly against this threat to their rear, struck back in a series of savage counterattacks, but failed to dislodge the beachhead. Following the commandos came artillery and a troop of Sherman tanks of 19 Lancers. To clear the Japanese from the Myebon Peninsula required their removal from the village of Kangaw, overlooked by a point denoted on Allied maps as Hill 170, where the roads in the area came together. It was to prove to be one of the most vicious battles of the entire war. After a week of fighting, Japanese attempts to push the intruders back into the sea failed, and the commandos fought to capture Kangaw Village and occupy Hill 170 on 29 January. The Japanese then did what they did best, throwing repeated and suicidal waves of assaults against the entrenched defenders. The Japanese attacks were mounted with considerable skill, accompanied by significant artillery bombardment and supporting machine-gun fire. The terrible hand-to-hand struggles that took place typified the horror of this war, with a significant resonance of Kohima, but it was an unequal struggle for the Japanese. By 3 February it was all over, Japanese bodies in places stacked in piles on top of each other on the slopes of Hill 170. It was estimated that 2,500 died in this last-ditch attempt to delay the inevitable. Allied casualties – some 500 – were also high. Two Victoria Crosses were awarded in this single battle, 'Timmy' Thimayya receiving both the DSO and a Mention in Despatches.

51 Indian Infantry Brigade at Kangaw epitomized the 'new' Indian Army and offered a dramatic contrast to the fighting quality of the units that had faced off the Japanese in Arakan two years before.[5] 3 Commando Brigade was astonished at the fighting proficiency of the Indian troops alongside whom they fought. Their commander, Brigadier Campbell Hardy, who had 8/19 Hyderabad under command for a short period during the battle, presented the battalion with a green beret, the only item they had readily to hand, with a typed message on a card: 'We cannot buy anything here but we would like you to accept this as a token of our great admiration for the bravery and achievement of your battalion.' Success at Kangaw was crowned by the capture of Myohaung by the West Africans. Caught between two pincers, the remnants of the

Japanese 54 Division broke and began to stream across the mountains to the east, through An and Taungup.

The primary military task remaining in Arakan after these victories was to capture Ramree and Cheduba Islands, completed at the end of February 1945. The 15-inch guns of HMS *Queen Elizabeth* covered the successful landing by 26 Indian Division. It was an unequal task, 980 of the Japanese garrison of 1,000 dying before the island fell. At no time did Sakurai appear to realize the strategic significance of these airfields to Allied plans, dissipating what combat effort he had in suicidal missions seemingly disconnected to each other. Japanese generals were good at this. Japanese soldiers were brilliant at dying uselessly for no operational or strategic purpose, a task they were called upon to do with increasing regularity in 1945. Japanese commanders, on the whole, thought little of their soldiers outside of their corporate commitment to sacrifice, evidenced by Tanaka's and Mutaguchi's respective demands of their starving soldiers on the outskirts of Imphal to 'consider death lighter than a feather'. With few exceptions, Japanese generalship had by 1944 and 1945 deteriorated into a means for preserving martial honour in the face of defeat, leading inevitably to the unnecessary deaths of soldiers forced to fight on against impossible odds. The strength of the Japanese Army lay in the willingness of its soldiers to fight to the death regardless of – and in spite of – the quality of its generals. Slim was to observe that this combination of obedience and ferocity 'would make any army formidable. It would make a European army invincible.' But this ferocity could never make up for deficient generalship. Slim saw the results of a Japanese tenacity that was not aligned with flexibility or balance in the execution of command judgements, and it was in this, ultimately, in Slim's view, that the 'Japanese failed'.

For the Allies, Rangoon was now in reach of bombers, as was central Burma, in time to help sustain the advance southwards of 14 Army. More importantly, an advanced base for Operation *Dracula* had been secured. Hard fighting characterized the short campaign between December 1944 and February 1945, but the overwhelming weight of operational ability, tactical skill, manpower and materiel provided a stark difference to the First Arakan campaign two years – and seemingly many years – before.

38

Meiktila and Mandalay

In central Burma the advantage was now Slim's: only six weeks after he had changed his plan, 14 Army was on the shores of the Irrawaddy on a 200-mile front with IV Corps about to cross the river in the area of Pakokku. The advance of 14 Army had been so rapid that Mountbatten reported to London on 23 February 1945 that *Dracula* was no longer required: Slim appeared likely to seize Rangoon before the onset of the monsoon in May. With XXXIII Corps placing growing pressure on the Japanese in the area of Mandalay, the timing of the main crossings became increasingly crucial. Too soon and Kimura would recognize the threat to his southern flank and deploy his reserves to counter it; too late and the pressure on XXXIII Corps might be sufficient to halt its advance on Mandalay.

In early February Stopford made successive and determined efforts from the north to capture Mandalay, reinforcing the impression that this was Slim's point of main effort. Katamura threw 15, 53 and elements of both 31 and 33 Divisions into the attack at the 19 Indian Division bridgehead at Thabeikkyin. Kimura, agreeing with Katamura's assessment that this was the likely location of 14 Army's principal attack, gave Katamura additional artillery and some of his remaining tanks. However, it was to no avail: as the bridgehead strengthened, the Japanese were slowly pushed back despite heavy Japanese artillery attacks. No. 221 Group RAF provided continuous and effective close air support to 19 Indian Division as it built itself up on the eastern bank of the Irrawaddy.

Meanwhile, Gracey's 20 Indian Division approached Monywa and took the town after hard fighting in mid-January. On 8 February Slim moved his and Vincent's joint headquarters to the town that he had vacated in May 1942. Other troops from 20 Indian Division arrived at Allagappa and began to cross the Irrawaddy on the night of 12 February. The Japanese were slow to oppose this incursion, but when they did it was with desperate fury, waves of attacks taking place during the ensuing fortnight against the two bridgeheads, many during daylight. Gracey had chosen to cross at a point that marked the divisional boundary between the Japanese 31 and 33 Divisions, but Kimura reacted strongly when he realized that a second – unexpected – bridgehead was in progress. Again, Allied air power played a decisive role in defeating these counterattacks, the Hurribombers of No. 221 Group destroying the tanks of Kimura's sole armoured regiment in Burma. In losing air superiority, Kimura's remaining mechanized forces became easy targets for Allied aircraft soaring at will over the Mandalay skies.

Despite the second bridgehead at Allagappa, as far as Kimura was concerned the Allied advance into Upper Burma was progressing as he had anticipated. An advance into the Shwebo plain preparatory to an assault across the Irrawaddy, west and north of Mandalay, was the natural course for an enemy

MAP 10 The Assault on Meiktila

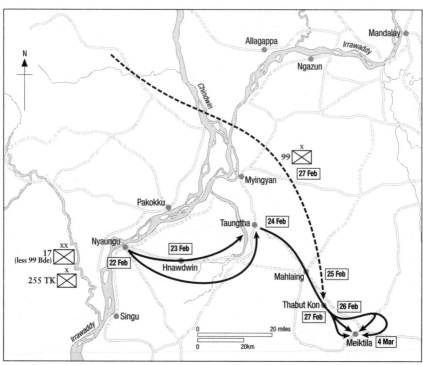

attack on Mandalay. He knew that the American-led NCAC forces were advancing from Myitkyina; a convergence of these with 14 Army prior to an attack on Mandalay from the north was what he was expecting. His decision not to risk engaging 14 Army on the Shwebo plain coincided with orders from Tokyo to consider the land route to China to be of secondary importance to the need to protect southern Burma and Rangoon. It was a simple step to deduce that Mandalay needed reinforcement, to prevent the Allies from infiltrating into central Burma. Accordingly, he restructured the Burma Area Army to enable him to fight the decisive battle for Burma on the Irrawaddy Shore. First, he withdrew 18 Division, a regiment from 2 Division and a regiment from 49 Division – in all the equivalent of close on two divisions – from his Northern Front to reinforce the Central Front, the defence of which centred on Mandalay. He next withdrew the remnants of 54 Division from Arakan and positioned it on the Irrawaddy at Yenangyaung. This would serve to resist any movement on the Allied right flank. Finally, 49 Division was moved up from the Bassein Peninsula in the far south-west of the country, and a further regiment of 2 Division, en route to Indochina, was ordered to return. From Yenangyaung in the south to Mandalay in the north, Kimura was confident that his nine divisions (which included an INA division) sitting behind the Irrawaddy would be sufficient to smash any attempt by 14 Army to cross and win a decisive victory for Mandalay.

The real focus of Slim's offensive, of course, entirely unbeknown to Kimura, lay far to the south. With Kimura distracted by XXXIII Corps' operations in the north, final preparations were being made, in conditions of strict secrecy, for the rapier thrust to seize Meiktila. If Kimura gained any inkling of this threat to his rear area, all would be undone. The first crossings by Geoffrey Evans's 7 Indian Division began at Nyaungu on the night of 13 February, although it took four days to establish a bridgehead, 6,000 yards wide by 4,000 yards deep. Feverish activity then followed to feed the assault formations across the river by boat and barge – Sherman tanks in their scores floating across on homemade pontoons – and to prepare them for the breakout. Messervy's plan for the dash to Meiktila had six phases:

1. The exploitation east from the Nyaungu bridgehead by the two mechanized brigades of 17 Indian Division and 255 Indian Tank Brigade.
2. The concentration of these forces at Mahlaing.
3. The capture of the airstrip at Thabutkon to fly in 99 Brigade.

4. The isolation of Meiktila.
5. The capture of Meiktila.
6. The capture of Thazi.

Messervy's plan was that two brigades (63 and 48) of 17 Indian Division, together with the Sherman tanks of 255 Tank Brigade, would cross the river to seize Meiktila. He needed to capture the town as quickly as possible without worrying about securing the road behind him. The road would subsequently be cleared by 7 Indian Division once the security of the Irrawaddy bridgehead was firm. Cowan's plan was to use his armour to punch through the Japanese lines to seize an airfield at Thabutkon, 12 miles east of Meiktila. He would then fly in 17 Indian Division's third (air transportable) brigade – 99 Brigade – while Taungtha and Mahlaing were either captured or screened by his other two brigades. The whole division with the armour would then continue on to assault Meiktila.

Elaborate deception measures were adopted to cover the Nyaungu crossings. 28 East African Brigade pretended to parry south to recover the Chauk and Yenangyaung oil fields, dummy parachute drops were made east of Chauk to reinforce this picture, and 17 Indian Division applied heavy pressure on Pakokku to make out that crossings were also intended there. These deception schemes were undoubtedly successful and acted to hide, until it was too late, the reality of Slim's strategy. A captured Japanese intelligence officer later explained that they did not believe that there was more than one division in the area, and that it was directed down the west bank towards Yenangyaung.

This was a period of acute anxiety for Slim. The administrative risks he had taken now looked alarming. All but one (5 Indian Division) of his seven divisions and five tank and independent brigades (the Lushai Brigade) was engaged; as the tempo increased, so too did 14 Army's expenditure of petrol and ammunition, increasing the strain on the already stretched line of communication. 'Throughout the battle', he recorded, 'we were never without acute anxiety on the supply and transport side… time and time again, and just in time, the bare essentials for their operations reached those who so critically needed them. Very rarely had any formation more than its basic needs.' His problems were compounded by the fact that on 23 February Chiang Kai-shek suddenly demanded the redeployment to China of all US and Chinese forces in the NCAC, and that US transport squadrons should fly them out. If Kimura withdrew the forces that he had facing the NCAC and threw them into the battle about Mandalay instead, at a time when Slim faced the loss of more of his precious aircraft, the challenge to 14 Army would have been severe. But the threat was lifted in part by the US Chiefs of Staff agreeing, after representation from Mountbatten and the British Chiefs of Staff, to 'leave the bulk of their transport squadrons in Burma until either we had taken Rangoon or until 1 June, whichever was the earlier'. The prospect of recovering Rangoon by means of a land offensive – and thus the reopening of the old Burma Road – was slowly asserting itself in people's strategic consciousness.

Meanwhile, the decisive struggle for Meiktila was underway. Cowan advanced out of Nyaungu on 21 February. Despite having to cover difficult ground for tanks – the countryside was riven with deep, sandy gullies that required careful preparation to traverse – 17 Division and 255 Tank Brigade quickly captured Taungtha, the rear area for 33 Division. 17 Division then captured Kahlaing on 25 February, and on 26 February the airstrip at Thabutkon followed, exactly as planned. On news of its capture, 99 Brigade, waiting expectantly for this moment at Palel on the Imphal plain, boarded its planes to fly in directly to the airfield, landing under small arms fire. Meanwhile, on 24 February, to reinforce Kimura's focus on Mandalay, 2 Division crossed the Irrawaddy opposite the village of Ngazun, about 10 miles east of 20 Division's bridgehead at Myinmu. On 27 February, the vanguard of IV Corps had encircled Meiktila and was preparing to advance on the town from all directions. The Japanese commander of the Meiktila area, Major General Kasuya, had some 12,000 troops as well as 1,500 miscellaneous base troops and hospital patients at his disposal for the defence of the town, and every man able to carry a weapon, wounded or otherwise, was pressed into service. Capturing Meiktila would not be easy. Strong positions were dug-in covering a series of lakes to the west of the town. Routes into the town from the west and south were funnelled by the lakes, and easily covered by Japanese artillery fire. The Japanese, masters of the defence, rapidly turned buildings in the town into bunkers and strongpoints. Cowan decided to close the routes into the town and attack directly from the north and east.

On the morning of 28 February, he began to tighten the noose around the town. While 63 Brigade brushed aside light opposition to move up closer to the town's western defences and placed a block with armour on the Chauk Road, 48 Brigade attacked from the north-east. Meanwhile, 255 Tank Brigade, with two infantry battalions and a self-propelled 105mm M7 'Priest' battery of 18 Field Regiment Royal Artillery under command, attacked east of Meiktila. Cowan's armour, deployed in wide flanking aggressive actions, caught the Japanese defenders in the open and inflicted on them heavy casualties. The divisional artillery was concentrated, to enable it to fire missions in support of all points of the compass, and cab ranks of fighter-ground attack were established to do likewise from the air. With the jungle now behind them, 17 Indian Division's tanks, mechanized artillery and mechanized infantry found the flat lands beyond the Irrawaddy well suited to the tactics of encircling and cutting off Japanese positions. The Japanese had no answer to either 14 Army's use of armour or to the effectiveness of the all-arms tactics in which it was employed. The attack penetrated well, but resistance was fierce and fanatical. Yet again, Japanese soldiers fought to the death, losing 5,000 dead and suffering 5,000 wounded in the battle for the town. Remarkably, 75 per cent of all Japanese defenders of Meiktila became casualties. Only 47 were taken prisoner, most of them in one of the captured hospitals, men unable to fight or kill themselves. By the end of the first day of the battle, Indian troops had penetrated well into the town. During 2 and 3 March, 63, 48 and 255 Tank Brigades closed in, squeezing and destroying the Japanese defenders between them. By 6 p.m. on 3 March Meiktila fell. During 4 and 5 March, even the most fanatical resistance was brushed aside as surrounding villages were cleared and the main airfield secured.

Kimura was shocked, as Slim knew he would be, by the sudden and unexpected loss of Meiktila. The rapier thrust against his vulnerable rear, striking across the Irrawaddy far to the south, many miles from where his attention had been fixed by Slim's deception plan, was a profound surprise. He at once sought to crush 17 Indian Division and recapture the town. Kimura ordered Honda immediately to turn south, and for three weeks from mid-March the Japanese mounted a series of ferocious counterattacks with six brigades, artillery and tanks against 17 Indian Division and 255 Tank Brigade. Isolated in Meiktila – 7 Indian Division had yet to clear the route from the Irrawaddy – Cowan's policy was one of 'aggressive defence'. Combined arms groups of infantry, mechanized artillery and armour, supported from the air by attack aircraft, were sent out every day to hunt, ambush and destroy approaching Japanese columns in a radius of 20 miles of the town. The pressure on Meiktila built up, however. Soon the land line of communication back to Nyaungu was cut, and the Japanese threw everything they had at seizing the airfield. Aerial resupply was key to sustaining Messervy's troops in processes perfected the previous year in Arakan, Kohima and Imphal. The situation was sufficiently disconcerting for Slim to decide to commit his last remaining reserve, 5 Indian Division, one brigade of which (9 Brigade) arrived onto one of the Meiktila airfields, under enemy fire, on 17 March. This was a huge risk for Slim. But he knew that if he did not secure victory in this battle he would have to concede the campaign. His gamble paid off. By 29 March the Japanese had been beaten back, losing their guns and significant casualties in the process. The river port of Myingyan on the Chindwin was captured after a fierce fight by 7 Indian Division, reinforced by one of the mechanized brigades from 5 Indian Division (Slim had moved its second armoured brigade north to support the advance of 19 Indian Division on Mandalay), and its rapid commissioning as a working port substantially reduced the pressure on Messervy's land line of communication. Before long it was receiving 200 tons of desperately needed supplies every day. A few days later Taungtha was recaptured.

Slim's relief at the securing of the Meiktila battlefield was palpable, and he gave thanks where it was due. He was in no doubt that Cowan's success first in seizing Meiktila, then in holding the town against increasingly frantic Japanese counterattacks, secured the success of Operation *Extended Capital*. The battle was, he reflected, 'a magnificent feat of arms... [which] sealed the fate of the Japanese in Burma.' This was no overstatement. IV Corps' thrust against Meiktila was Slim's decisive stroke, on which the success of his entire strategy rested, and for which he had subordinated everything else. Now, the huge risks he had taken had come good. The Japanese also were in no doubt about the significance of Slim's victory, Kimura admitting that it was 'the masterpiece of Allied strategy' in the battle for Burma. The historian Louis Allen regarded it as 'Slim's greatest triumph', a feat that allowed him to place 'his hand firmly on the jugular of the Japanese' and that put 'the final reconquest of Burma within Slim's grasp'.[1]

Slim now needed to attack Kimura hard in order to prevent him from turning against the IV Corps anvil forming around Meiktila. When this anvil was firm Slim intended to allow XXXIII Corps – the hammer – to fall on Kimura hard from the north. The first part of this hammer – 19 Indian Division (62, 64 and 98 Brigades) – broke out of its bridgehead 40 miles north of Mandalay on 26 February. By 4 March the division was in tankable country 20 miles north of Mandalay. The Japanese – 15 and 33 Divisions – had no answer to the pace of Rees's advance, nor to the attacks launched at them from the air. Aircraft – Beaufighter and Mosquito light bombers, together with the ubiquitous Hurribomber – coordinated their attacks with 19 Division's artillery, causing considerable damage to Japanese positions, while 19 Division and its mechanized reinforcements from 5 Division smashed through and around Japanese defences. The following day the Magyi Chaung, the last major physical obstacle in front of Mandalay, was breached, and by 7 March the northern outskirts of Mandalay were reached. Kimura's dilemma was now palpable. He faced a decisive advance against his northern defences by 19 Indian Division; two full divisions were crossing the Irrawaddy west of the city at two separate points, threatening to encircle Mandalay, and his critical administrative nerve centre at Meiktila was under heavy attack. Where should he reinforce? All were vital to him, but his choices were now impossible: reinforcing one vital area would entail reducing his strength at another.

The two strongpoints in Mandalay – Mandalay Hill and Fort Dufferin – were vigorously defended and required considerable effort to overcome. Allied troops entered the city on 9 March but fierce fighting for the strongpoints meant that it wasn't captured until 20 March. True to form, the Japanese defenders fought to the last. Direct fire artillery by 5.5-inch howitzers and 2,000-pound bombs dropped by Mitchell bombers were required to gain access to Fort Dufferin. On top of Mandalay Hill, the discovery that the Japanese had dug themselves into a warren of bunkers was solved by rolling lighted barrels of fuel into the tunnels. While Mandalay was being vested, 62 Brigade struck secretly eastward at Maymyo where they fell upon the town, taking the garrison completely by surprise.

The second part of the XXXIII Corps advance – 20 Indian and 2 Divisions – 40 and 25 miles west of Mandalay respectively, broke out of their bridgeheads in early March, touching each other on 2 March. The Japanese were everywhere pushed back, losing heavily in men and artillery. Slim deduced that Kimura would attempt to hold a line running south-west from Kyaukse to Chauk, with 15 Army holding the right, 33 Army the centre, and 28 Army the left. He knew that despite Japanese efforts to stiffen the line it would still be weak. Accordingly, he aimed to concentrate at weak points in the line and strike decisively at the Japanese command and communication network so as to remove the last vestiges of control Japanese commanders had over the course of the battle. Supported strongly by No. 221 Group RAF, Gracey's 20 Indian Division led the charge. 32 and 80 Brigades sliced through the Japanese opposition to converge on Kyaukse, while 100 Brigade carried out a wide encircling movement to seize Wundin, on the main railway 60 miles south of Mandalay on 21 March, although stubborn resistance prevented Kyaukse from falling until the end of the month. Throughout, Slim's aim was to keep the pressure on Kimura at every point of the compass. His planning cycle remained well ahead of Kimura's. 'No sooner was a plan made to meet a given situation than, due to a fresh move by Slim, it was out-of-date before it could be executed, and a new one had to be hurriedly prepared with a conglomeration of widely scattered units and formations', observed Geoffrey Evans, reflecting from his position of intimate knowledge as GOC 7 Indian Division. 'Because of the kaleidoscopic changes in the situation, breakdowns in communication and the fact that Burma Area Army Headquarters was often out of touch with reality, many of the attacks to restore the position were uncoordinated.'[2]

The Japanese 15 and 31 Divisions now retreated in disarray, breaking into little groups of fugitives seeking refuge in the Shan Hills to the east. Meanwhile, 2 Division progressed methodically into Mandalay from the south-west, cutting the Ava–Mandalay Road on 21 March and joining hands with 19 Indian Division. All around them, the men of 14 Army saw a still-defiant though crumbling enemy. Pockets of desperate men continued to fight until destroyed in their bunkers and foxholes, burnt out by flame-throwers or destroyed by tanks and artillery in preference to sacrificing the precious lives of the infantry in assaults that did not justify loss of Indian or British lives. By the end of the month, the battle of the Irrawaddy Shore had been won, the desperate remnants of the three divisions facing XXXIII Corps hurrying to escape through the hills to the east. Most Japanese divisions had lost between 30 and 50 per cent of their strength in casualties, with 14 Army's battle casualties numbering 10,500. South of the city, at Meiktila, large swathes of the town and countryside lay in smoking ruins amid the dust and heat of high summer. Slim's great gamble had paid off. He now needed to see whether he could capitalize on this victory by seizing Rangoon 390 miles to the south – still an immense task – before the monsoon rains arrived again in all their fury.

39

Extract Digit!

SEAC now faced its final, and arguably greatest, challenge: to capture Rangoon before the monsoon rains in May made such a proposition by land impossible. The rapid advance by 14 Army into Upper Burma since the previous December had led Mountbatten to suggest to London in February that Operation *Dracula* would no longer be required, given the progress of Slim's operations on the Irrawaddy and Christison's in Arakan. In March, however, Slim was not so sure. Kimura had been defeated on the Irrawaddy, but capturing a well-defended Rangoon would be an immense and complex operation. Rangoon was over 390 miles farther on from Mandalay, where the logistics stretch was already being felt by troops in the vanguard of the fighting. Food, fuel and ammunition were all rationed; every bullet, artillery shell, gallon of petrol and tin of bully beef had either to be brought along the tortuous line of communication – a single road – from Dimapur, 500 miles distant to Imphal, or flown from the airfields in Assam and Tripura directly to the battle area. A further push by even half of his army – such as the mechanized IV Corps – would add intolerable pressure on his logistics system, which was already running at maximum capacity. Some pressure on the delivery of fuel had been alleviated by the completion of a pipeline from Dimapur to Imphal and work to push it farther on to Tamu – in its own right a remarkable civil engineering achievement – which reduced the requirement to carry fuel forward in 44 gallon drums in the holds of the precious transport aircraft, which in the days of ubiquitous smoking was a safety nightmare. If the fragile resupply structure failed before IV Corps had even reached Rangoon, Slim's plan to smash Japanese resistance across the whole of Burma would also fail. If the Japanese were intent on defending Rangoon with anything like the intelligence and tenacity that had marked their defensive operations elsewhere in the campaign, Slim did not want his tactical choices determined by lack of fuel, food or ammunition. Failure at the gates of Rangoon for 'want of a nail' was not something he could contemplate. With *Dracula* now off, SEAC planning staff were busy working on another amphibious option, to land a newly constructed XXXIV Corps (23 Indian Division, 81 West African Division and 3 Commando Brigade) on the coast of Thailand in preparation for an overland advance on Singapore. But when Slim voiced his concerns about Rangoon to Mountbatten, the Supremo immediately saw their sense and on 2 April turned planning for *Dracula* back on. In an indication of just how quickly SEAC could operate by 1945, the date for the planned divisional-sized airborne and amphibious assault on Rangoon was set for four weeks hence, 5 May 1945.

If the strategic challenge was the capture of Rangoon before the monsoon broke by means of a two-pronged attack, one from the land and the other by sea and air (i.e. parachute), Slim's operational challenge was to divide his army between a component that could get there in a month, defeating a formidable enemy on the way, and a component that could defeat the still-dangerous remnants of Kimura's army that had been pushed into the eastern hills. The defeat of the Japanese on the Irrawaddy did not mean for one moment that they were now without fight. Far from it. They could still put up a savage resistance at multiple points across southern and eastern Burma that held the possibility of a grinding campaign akin to the desperately bloody battles that characterized the fighting across the Pacific. Slim had originally envisaged both of his corps advancing on Rangoon in a reversal of Iida's 1942 offensive, one corps using the Irrawaddy and the other moving down the general route of the Meiktila–Rangoon railway. A double advance would, Slim considered, provide Kimura with the same option of difficulties that he had been faced with at Mandalay, and which had challenged Slim back in 1942. But the impossibility of sustaining two separate corps with the limited logistical resources at his disposal meant that he only had enough for a single corps advance on Rangoon, through Toungoo and Pegu. In any case, Slim needed speed, to cut off 28 Army in the south, preventing it from reinforcing Rangoon or retreating across the Sittang. The plan on which he determined was for Messervy's corps at Meiktila to strike for Rangoon, punching south while avoiding direct fights, bypassing significant pockets of enemy resistance, all the while being resupplied by air. Meanwhile, XXXIII Corps would methodically clear the Japanese from the Yenangyaung oilfields, before pushing down the Irrawaddy to Prome. To allow IV Corps to sustain its southward advance, a further restructuring of the aerial resupply arrangements to 14 Army were put in place. The whole of IV Corps was placed on aerial resupply, together

MAP 11 The Advance to Rangoon

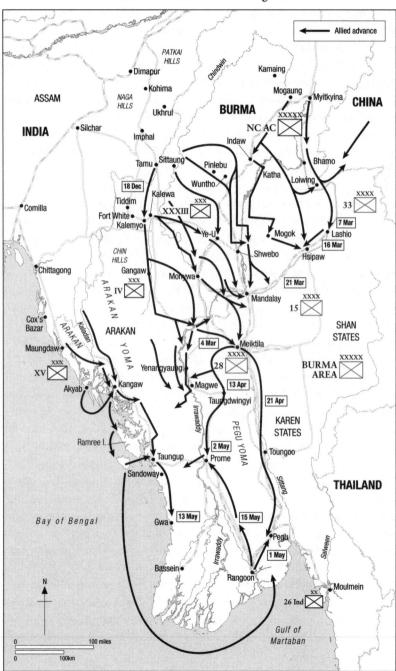

with one division of XXXIII Corps. The remainder of XXXIII Corps was to rely on rail, river and road transport, maximizing use of the considerable river flotilla that had been built at Kalewa the previous December and which was now operating out of the Irrawaddy River port Myingyan. Christison's success in securing Akyab and Ramee greatly facilitated the advance to Rangoon because of the access to Arakanese airfields.

A significant new feature of the fighting in Burma in 1945 was the work of irregular forces inside Burma in support of 14 Army offensive operations. After the retreat to India in 1942, little immediate effort had been made to retain contact with those of the hill tribes in the north and east of the country – the Kachins, Shans and Karens respectively – who would be interested in continuing resistance to the Japanese during the occupation and might be willing to support more conventional operations if and when a reconquest of Burma became possible. In 1942, Karen members of the Burma Rifles had been sent home with their weapons and urged to await the return of the British. Unable to make his own escape, one officer – Major Hugh Seagrim – remained with the Karens, although because of his lack of a radio, contact wasn't made with him by India Command until October 1943. When an SOE team finally reached him, he reported that the Karens were awaiting their liberation and would be prepared to help fight for it. The Japanese, however, had got wind of Seagrim's presence and in a ruthless campaign against the Karens forced him to surrender. He was executed in Rangoon in September 1944.[1]

Nevertheless, the potential of a Karenni-based resistance raised the possibility, long argued by old Burma hands, of a British armed and trained fifth column operating behind Japanese lines for the purpose of gathering battlefield intelligence and undertaking limited guerrilla action of the type that had developed in occupied Europe. Slim had long complained about the poor quality of the battlefield intelligence (as opposed to the signals intelligence, about which he was well provided) that he and his corps commanders received. He was concerned, among other things, about knowing 'what was on the other side of the hill', the product of information provided – where it existed – by effective combat (ground and air) reconnaissance. There was no shortage of organizations attempting to assist in this task – at least 12 – but their coordination was poor and most reported to SEAC or parts of India Command, rather than to 14 Army.[2] Slim dismissed most of these as 'private armies' which offered no real help to the task of defeating the enemy on the battlefield. One of the groups, part of Force 136 (i.e. Special Operations Executive, or SOE), which had operated in front of 20 Indian Division along the Chindwin between 1943 and early 1944 under

Major Edgar Peacock (and thus known as 'P Force'), did sterling work with local Burmese and Karen agents reporting on Japanese activity facing IV Corps. Persuaded that similar groups working among the Karens in Burma's eastern hills – an area known as the Karenni States – could achieve significant support for a land offensive in Burma, Slim (to whom Mountbatten transferred responsibility for Force 136 in late 1944 for this purpose) authorized an operation to the Karens. Its task was not merely to undertake intelligence missions watching the road and railways between Mandalay and Rangoon, but to determine whether they would fight. If the Karens were prepared to do so, SOE would be responsible for training and organizing them as armed groups able to deliver battlefield intelligence directly in support of the advancing 14 Army. The resulting operation – *Character* – was so spectacularly successful that it far outweighed what had been achieved by Operation *Thursday* the previous year in terms of its impact on the course of military operations in pursuit of the strategy to defeat the Japanese in the whole of Burma.

It has been strangely forgotten, or ignored, by most historians ever since, drowned out perhaps by the noise made by the drama and heroism of Operation *Thursday*. Over the course of Operation *Extended Capital* some 2,000 British, Indian and Burmese officers and soldiers, along with 1,430 tons of supplies, were dropped into Burma for the purposes of providing intelligence about the Japanese that would be useful for the fighting formations of 14 Army, as well as undertaking limited guerrilla operations. As historian Richard Duckett has observed, this found SOE operating not merely as intelligence gatherers in the traditional sense, but as Special Forces with a defined military mission as part of conventional operations linked directly to a strategic outcome.[3] For Operation *Character* specifically, about 110 British officers and NCOs and over 100 men of all Burmese ethnicities, dominated interestingly by Burmans (which now also included three-man Jedburgh Teams)[4] mobilized as many as 12,000 Karens over an area of 7,000 square miles to the anti-Japanese cause.[5] Some 3,000 weapons were dropped into the Karenni States. Operating in five distinct groups ('Walrus', 'Ferret', 'Otter', Walrus' and 'Hyena'),[6] the Karen irregulars, trained and led by Force 136, waited for the moment when 14 Army instructed them to attack.

The earlier Force 136 operation to the AFO and BNA – *Nation* – had reaped its reward, with several thousand AFO guerrillas by the end of April operating under Jedburgh teams near Toungoo, the Sittang and Irrawaddy Valley and delta, preparing to assist Operation *Dracula*. As many as 800 Japanese had been killed. General Aung San had, in a remarkable piece of theatre, paraded his army before

General Kimura on the Padang in Rangoon on 27 March, before marching them away 'to engage with the British'. What none of the Japanese knew by this was that by this Aung San meant that he was about to turn his army of 7,000 over to the British, and fight against their erstwhile colleagues.

Despite his failure at Mandalay and Meiktila, Kimura was far from defeated. Although his attempt to defend Southern Burma by holding Slim at bay along the Irrawaddy had been a miserable failure, his divisions were still capable of fighting to a coherent plan and fighting savagely for every inch of ground. The whole of 14 Army knew that the Japanese, even when other armies would consider themselves to be beaten, would fight ferociously until death. The experience of the previous year, with 5 Indian Division advancing down the Tiddim Road and 11 East African pushing slowly down the Kabaw Valley, testified to their tenacious determination to trade every inch of territory as expensively as they could. But strangely, in a mirror of the failed British efforts to stem the victorious Japanese advance through Burma in 1942 – by building largely fictitious defensive 'lines' on a map – Kimura now attempted the same, ordering his troops to reform on a line from Yenangyaung on the Irrawaddy through to Pyawbe, south of Meiktila, in the east. Sakurai's 28 Army and its two divisions, together with remnants of the INA, would hold the Irrawaddy at Yenangyaung (and hence access to Burma from Arakan), while Honda's 33 Army and its three divisions would hold the eastern pivot of this line at Pyawbe, an otherwise insignificant village that nevertheless straddled the road and railway south to Toungoo. What was left of Katamura's mangled 15 Army would be reconstituted as Kimura's reserve.

Between 30 March and 10 April 1945, Pyawbe saw the first battle of 14 Army's drive to Rangoon, and it proved as decisive in 1945 as the Japanese attack on Prome had been in 1942. Otherwise strong Japanese defensive positions around the town with limited capability for counterattack meant that the Japanese were sitting targets for Allied tanks, artillery and air power. Messervy's plan was simple: to bypass the defended points that lay before Pyawbe, allowing them to be dealt with by subsequent attack from the air, and surround Pyawbe from all points of the compass by 17 Indian Division before squeezing it like a lemon with his tanks and artillery. With nowhere to go, and with no effective counterattack potential, the Japanese were exterminated bunker by bunker by the Shermans of 255 Tank Brigade, now slick with the experience of battle gained at Meiktila. Infantry, armour and aircraft cleared Honda's primary blocking point before Toungoo with coordinated precision. This single battle, which killed over 1,000 Japanese, entirely removed Honda's ability to prevent IV Corps from exploiting the road to Toungoo.

Messervy grasped the opportunity, leapfrogging 5 Indian Division (the vanguard of the advance comprising an armoured regiment and armoured reconnaissance group from 255 Tank Brigade) southwards, capturing Shwemyo on 16 April, Pyinmana on 19 April and Lewe on 21 April. Toungoo was the immediate target, attractive because it boasted three airfields, from where No. 224 Group could provide air support to Operation *Dracula*. Messervy drove his armour on, reaching Toungoo, much to the surprise of the Japanese, the following day. After three days of fighting, supported by heavy attack from the air by B24 Liberators, the town and its airfields fell to Messervy. On the very day of its capture, 100 C47s and C46 commando transports landed the air transportable elements of 17 Indian Division to join their armoured comrades. They now took the lead from 5 Indian Division, accompanied by 255 Tank Brigade, for whom rations in their supporting vehicles had been substituted for petrol, pressing on via Pegu to Rangoon. The bold attack in depth that IV Corps' advance represented, the tip of 14 Army's spear, was remarkable. Armour, infantry and tracked artillery worked in combined teams with intimate support provided in the air by continuous fighter-ground attack patrols linked by radio to the leading tanks. Each stage of the attack was undertaken to confuse Kimura; to act before he could respond to the previous threat, resulting in the Burma Area Army remaining in a state of command confusion for much of 1945. The single operational objective – to get to Rangoon before the rains fell – was prioritized before all else. Aerial resupply was a strategic function of SEAC, organized by Mountbatten in a single Air and Ground Supply Committee in March 1945 that prioritized air transport strictly in accordance with strategic priorities across the whole theatre. An additional strategic consideration needs to be recalled. Slim recognized that if the Japanese were able to hold Toungoo, and thus prevent 14 Army making its way beyond this point, Kimura would not need to evacuate Rangoon. If Rangoon were defended, Operation *Dracula* would be opposed, with serious consequences in terms of casualties. Defeating the Japanese at Toungoo would, it was hoped, force Kimura to evacuate Rangoon beyond the Sittang to avoid being caught in a 14 Army/Operation *Dracula* pincer.

The contribution of Operation *Character* to the advance by IV Corps to Toungoo and beyond was battle winning. By April 1945, the Karen irregulars harried the 50,000 Japanese in the hills, directing air strikes, providing close reconnaissance of targets for No. 224 Group's aircraft. Their attacks, beginning in early April, were coordinated by HQ 14 Army to coincide with the advances of elements of IV Corps, and were focused on preventing the Japanese 18 Division from reaching and reinforcing Toungoo before the arrival of 5 Indian Division. To get to Toungoo, 18 Division had to pass through areas of jungle hills to the north-east and east entirely dominated by Force 136. By means of repeated ambushes, the Japanese were fought every step of the way. Large amounts of detailed target information were radioed through for use in attacks by the air force.[7] The official historian of SOE observed:

> ... in the week before the fall of Rangoon (2nd May 1945) almost all their long-range fighter-bombers were employed on Force 136 targets, and that so many high-grade reports came in that it was impossible to act on them all. There were many notable successes, the principal being an attack on the railway station at Pyu which coincided with the arrival of a troop train and caused over 1,000 casualties. No. 221 Group RAF was so impressed with Force 136's later intelligence that they proposed that when operations began in Malaya at least one squadron should stand by to carry out immediate strikes when a mobile target was reported – something that had not been done in Burma.[8]

Roadblocks, ambushes and demolitions held up the Japanese 18 Division's cross-country advance to Toungoo in the area of Mawchi, 50 miles east of Toungoo. In his immediate report on operations, Slim described the operational effect of the Karen irregulars:

> Our own levies led by their British officers were a most valuable asset and had a real influence on operations. They were tactically controlled by wireless from Army Headquarters, told when to rise, the objectives they should attack, and given specific tasks. They could not and were not expected to stand up to the Japanese in pitched battles but they could and did in places harry them unmercifully. Their greatest achievement was the delaying of the 15th Japanese Division on the Loikaw–Mawchi area, thus enabling IV Corps to reach Toungoo first, but they have rendered almost equally valuable services. They had an excellent jitter effect on the Japanese, who were compelled to lock up troops to guard against attacks on the lines of communication.[9]

The work of Force 136, in particular in operations such as Operation *Character*, delivered exactly the sort of support Slim demanded of Special Forces, which was to assist the work of the main, or conventional forces, by gathering close target reconnaissance and mounting attacks on enemy rear echelons, lines of communications and other such 'soft' targets by means of ambushes and hit-and-run raids. Without the operations of these SOE-led Karen guerrillas in blocking the Japanese 56 Division's attempts to defend Toungoo and 18 Division's efforts to reinforce it, 14 Army would almost certainly have been stopped in its tracks. If this had happened, it is reasonable to surmise that Kimura would not have felt the need to evacuate Rangoon, with all the attendant difficulties for Operation *Dracula* of having to assault a defended capital just as the monsoon struck. The estimate of Japanese killed by Operation *Character* was 11,874, far more than those killed by the soldiers of IV and XXXIII Corps over the same period of time. As the historian of SOE Richard Duckett rightly asserts, Operation *Character* achieved dramatic operational effect at 'a low cost in terms of men and equipment' by helping 'to protect the flank of Slim's XIV Army as it advanced into southern Burma... [By] raising the local population and operating in difficult terrain, the *Character* teams assisted regular forces by inflicting significant casualties upon the Japanese, as well as psychological damage.'[10]

With Toungoo secured, XXXIII Corps pressed hard down the Irrawaddy, breaking the western end of Kimura's defence line. With Kimura distracted by Toungoo, Evans' 7 Indian Division struck at Yenangyaung on 22 April, before driving hard down the road to Prome. Simultaneously, Gracey's 20 Indian Division took Taungdwingyi in a surprise attack, thwarting any escape by the remnants of Sakurai's 28 Army over the Pegu Yomas, thus preventing their involvement in the battle for Toungoo. On 2 May Prome fell.

It was the loss of Toungoo that persuaded Kimura that he could not hold Rangoon. He needed to get the bulk of his army onto the eastern side of Pegu to offer it any hope of fighting a battle for Sittang and Tenasserim. Accordingly, he rushed up troops of divisional strength to defend Toungoo just as 17 Indian Division and the Shermans of 255 Tank Brigade arrived. On 29 April Cowan's division reached the town and cut it off from the Sittang, two brigades crossing the river despite Japanese bridge demolitions and strong resistance. Cowan's arrival in the town coincided with that of the monsoon rains. The Japanese defence collapsed, and Cowan's triumphant division now turned right and made its way towards Rangoon.

With 17 Indian Division making slow progress through the rain and mud from the north-east, Operation *Dracula* was launched from Akyab and Ramree Island on 2 May, with Major General Chambers' 26 Indian Division landing in two assault waves onto both sides of the Rangoon River, and Gurkha paratroops of 50 Indian Parachute Brigade jumping on Elephant Point and squashing the resistance provided by the small garrison. It was a measure of the technical and logistical power of the Allies that this assault was organized and launched in less than a month. If ever there was a statement of overwhelming superiority, this was it. Six convoys delivered the troops, covered in the air by No. 224 Group, four escort aircraft carriers, eight squadrons of the Strategic Air Force and four squadrons of the US No. 12 Bombardment Group. At sea the convoy was protected by two battleships, a further two escort aircraft carriers, three cruisers and six destroyers. The Japanese had no answer to this overwhelming display of military power at sea, in the air or on land. Nevertheless, the amphibious assault proved precarious, as the arrival of the invasion convoys coincided with the arrival of a cyclone from the Bay of Bengal, only superlative seamanship enabling the operation to take place as planned. As the operation got underway, aerial reconnaissance of Rangoon Gaol showed that POWs had written 'Extract Digit' on the roof of one of the building's wings, suggesting that the Japanese had left the city, a fact that was confirmed shortly thereafter when an RAF aircraft landed at Mingaladon and the pilot hitch-hiked into the city. The first rain-sodden troops of 26 Indian Division entered the hastily vacated city the following day, contacting troops of XXXIII Corps and IV Corps on the roads to Prome and Pegu respectively on 6 May. *Dracula* had proved to be an essential part of the strategy for recovering Burma. 14 Army could not have secured Rangoon, and recovered its port functionality by means of a land advance from Mandalay and Meiktila, by XXXIII and IV Corps alone.

Rangoon was quickly transformed into the focal point for the next phase of anticipated SEAC operations against Japan, Operations *Zippers* and *Mailfist*, the invasion of Malaya and Singapore, planned for September. But the capture of Rangoon did not mean that the whole of Burma was now in Allied hands. Kimura's troops still held significant pockets in the east and south-east, with at least two groups of troops, amounting to perhaps 15,000 men of Sakurai's 28 Army in the Irrawaddy Valley and the hills of the Pegu Yomas bypassed in 14 Army's rush south, together with 6,000 men in the Shan Hills to the east of Meiktila. Kimura's plan was to concentrate what forces he had on the Sittang and the Salween Valley – about 25,000 men of Honda's 33 Army – together with another 25,000 in the area of Moulmein. He was hopeful that the newly arrived monsoon would be his friend and allow most of the troops isolated north of Toungoo to move through the hills to safety in Thailand.

But operations between early June and 6 August, in what became known as the Battle of the Breakout, demonstrated the complete mastery by the Allies of the battlefield, and led to the destruction of large numbers of Japanese soldiers attempting to move to safety across the Sittang. In a sign that Japanese morale had reached rock bottom, an unprecedented 740 soldiers surrendered in the four weeks up until 4 August, during which time at least 6,270 had been killed. Ironically, the atomic bombs dropped on Hiroshima and Nagasaki that led to the Japanese surrender on 15 August did more than anything to preserve the unnecessary slaughter of Japanese lives in the Far East. Even under more enlightened commanders, such as Kimura, Japanese generalship still depended, when things weren't going well, on the lemming-like sacrifice of its soldiers to shore up poor decisions by its commanders. By the end of the campaign, the Imperial Japanese Army had lost 185,149 dead in Burma, the Allies a fraction of that – in what was otherwise a nasty, brutal war, a mere, by contrast, 14,326 dead. The Japanese Empire had demonstrated that it was good at killing: it allowed more of its own troops to die for their country than it managed to kill of its enemy. They were particularly good at killing prisoners of war and the civilians of the countries they so egregiously absorbed into their ill-gotten empire.

40

The Empire Strikes Back

If the Japanese believed that their attack on British possessions in South East Asia would lead to the replacement of one empire by another (theirs), they were to be disappointed. Japan believed that the loss of their Asian colonies would send the Europeans scurrying back to Europe with their tails between their legs. Britain's empire would collapse on itself. But contrary to expectation and despite the humiliation of defeat in Malaya, Singapore, Borneo and Burma – a trauma that resulted in over 100,000 British, Indian and Australian servicemen going into captivity – the Japanese invasion of South East Asia in 1941 did not end or bring about the collapse of the British Empire. Instead, the attempt by Japan to expand its own empire by means of war in 1942 seemed to do the opposite, at least temporarily. Young Indians flocked in large numbers to the service of the Raj, even at a time of growing nationalist clamour at home. Between 1939 and 1945 India's armed forces recruited 2,581,726 (of whom 2,065,554 were serving at the point the war ended).[1] The Indian Air Force, which had begun the war with 285 officers and men, was now the Royal Indian Air Force, with nine squadrons of aircraft and 29,201 officers and men.[2] The Quit India campaign in 1942 and a rising tide of independence activism did nothing to undermine the efforts of the Indian government, and in so doing its dependence on the willingness of Indians to fight, to build and deploy an army able to defeat the Japanese. Only when its army had been victorious was it passed to India (and the new Pakistan) – in 1947 – when the British Raj came to an end. The crisis of 1942 strengthened the empire temporarily at its point of greatest peril, and allowed it to strike back decisively in 1944 and 1945. Thereafter, Britain relinquished its control of India not because it had been defeated, but precisely because it had been victorious.

The Japanese invasion of South East Asia in 1941 and 1942 did not result in the military defeat of the British Empire but instead forced a change of ownership. British India did not collapse like the Roman or Ottoman empires in the ashes of hubris but was transferred to its new owners as a going concern. In any case, Britain was exhausted and its enthusiasm for empire had evaporated. At the same time, the Japanese failed to hold on to the empire it had shakily created by means of war. Japan gloried in its military victory, but its army did nothing in the months and years that followed to move beyond the infantry-base upon which it had been achieved, and did nothing to enhance the lives and wellbeing of the countries it occupied. Meanwhile, Britain (and America) transformed their military potential after initial defeat in 1942.[3] When India gained its independence in 1947 and Burma in 1948, it was on the foundation of the defeat in Asia of Japanese militarism. That India became a democracy, and remains so, can in part be attributed to the role it played in defeating Japan in 1945. It is deeply ironic that post-1947 Indian history has entirely drowned out the importance of the Indian armed forces in achieving India's security, in favour of a narrative that exalts the nonviolence offered by many in Congress and exalts the role of the INA, which in fact was fighting for the enemy.

In 1941, Japan was fighting to expand its empire, using war as the means by which it grabbed what it desired. Its empire was one of repression, oppression and slavery.[4] The number of innocents across Asia who lost their lives as a consequence of this war demonstrates the animosity of the Japanese regime to any interest other than its own. The British Empire in the Far East constituted Hong Kong, Malaya, Singapore, parts of Borneo, as well as Burma, India, Ceylon and Malaya. Its Commonwealth included, in the region, Australia and New Zealand. Britain was fighting to defend its empire from wanton aggression, and to defend its peoples, the primary responsibility of any civil power. Although it arguably did this insensitively – even badly in places, as the Bengal famine attests – Britain wasn't fighting to expand or extend its empire. There is no moral equivalence between Britain defending its empire and Japan trying to expand its, merely because they were both empires. Nor too did Japan liberate Asia. 'Asians won their freedom by fighting and dying in the resistance to Japanese imperialism', asserts the Japanese writer Saburo Ienaga. 'To call Japan's disgraceful and bloody rampage a crusade for liberation is to stand truth and history on their heads.'[5]

At the time that Japan struck at Malaya in 1941, the major part of the British Empire in Asia was nearing its natural end. Indeed, it was to do so in India in 1947, Burma in 1948, and in Malaya, Singapore and Borneo in the 1960s. A feature of British imperialism was the slow but gradual dialogue with India about the terms of its eventual independence. Britain anticipated that a united India, always a key British goal, would move from being a colony into a favoured and cooperative partner within a wider Commonwealth. The political aim of imperialism in the 20th century was, from Whitehall's perspective, to manage the transition to independence, an imperative that led to a gradualism that infuriated some nationalists. The independence movement was built on a desire by some nationalists to hasten the date of separation from Britain, and the establishment of an India on their terms. This is important to understand. Most Indians wanted independence, and most could be described as 'nationalists' of one degree or another; it is a post-1947 simplification that bundles all pre-war nationalists into the same Congress-voting bundle. A minority of nationalists objected to the Viceroy taking India unilaterally to war in 1939 (although it was a foolish thing to do, politically), and a minority of nationalists objected to fighting Japanese fascism in 1942. Instead, most nationalists were prepared to allow independence measures to take their natural path, and to develop in an orderly fashion, when the enemies to King and Empire – including those to India's own security – had been defeated. There seems no other explanation for the ability of the colonial authorities to oversee the quite incredible expansion of the Indian Army, with a sea-change in its remarkable professionalism, such that it was able to turn the tables on the Japanese in Assam and Burma in 1944 and 1945. That the future for India was one of independence and political freedom on a democratic model inherited from Britain, is one of the reasons why so many young Indians of their own volition joined the Indian Armed Forces during the war. Indeed, it is reasonable to assert that they weren't fighting to defend the past, and certainly not to maintain the old political status quo, but to defend and protect a future for a new India, and for many Muslims, a new Pakistan.

The Indian Army that the war helped to create between 1942 and 1945 emerged at the end of the war as a different entity to that at the beginning of the war in 1939. It possessed a life that in 1945 reflected not the *British* Raj that had gone before, but a new, *Indian,* Raj. The Burma campaign served to crystallize a new Indian Army, representative of an emerging Indian nationhood perhaps, one that united its multitudinous races, communities and regions for the first time into a homogenous whole, able to stand up against the threat of fascism lapping dangerously against its borders. This new-found homogeneity did not completely survive the Hindu–Muslim split that led to Partition in 1947 – the forces of communal exceptionalism proving too strong even for the concept of a new, united India – but in 1944 and 1945 the dramatic coming together that enabled the great military successes in Manipur and Burma, an effort to work collectively to deal with the crisis of the hour, represented the truth that India was capable of uniting to fight this threat to its existence. If any good can ever come out of war, the Japanese invasion of Asia in 1941 had the perverse effect of uniting a previously divided, colonial enterprise in a new, national, endeavour. This new imperative was the product, ironically perhaps, not of fear of or reaction against, British colonial wickedness, but fear of and opposition to Japanese evil.

It can be said therefore that the Japanese threat and the moves to counter it led to the creation of 14 Army in 1943. Men in this army found themselves feeling a new *izzat*, not to their community of origin but, for the first time perhaps, to a new sense of India. 14 Army became an expression of this new purpose, one outcome of which was an acceleration of the journey towards independence. It was a democratic movement, too. As the Indian journalist D.F. Karaka observed in 1944, Indian soldiers had come overwhelmingly to believe that, despite 'its faults the democratic idea of living is the only one worthwhile and that, properly developed, it is the only way of life that will bring peace and greatness and dignity to the civilized world.'[6] And, because 14 Army under General 'Uncle Bill' Slim – an overwhelmingly Indian enterprise – was also a 'commonwealth' (rather, arguably, than an 'imperial') one, most Britons of goodwill who saw and recognized the transition taking place in India did not merely give it their blessing but encouraged and supported its birth. The dominant narrative in Britain since the war is that the Burma campaign was a 'long war' fought by a 'forgotten' British army. Mountbatten had complained of this only a few short months into his time in command. John Masters wrote memorably that in 1945 the men of 4 Army 'were still forgotten in terms of the whole war – I don't know whether we were still lower, or on the general priority list, than the Caribbean, but we certainly weren't very far up it.'[7] It is more accurate to regard the Burma campaign as one in which Japanese militarism was defeated after 1943 by a resurrected army that was largely Indian and African, but which had very significant contributions from Americans (nearly 280,000 of whom served in the 1.3 million men and women of SEAC in 1945), British and Chinese soldiers, many serving in the American-led NCAC. Indeed, many more Americans served in SEAC than did Britons. Britain did not fight the Second World War in Asia on its own, even before the arrival of the United States in 1941: instead, the fightback against first Nazi and then Japanese tyranny was always a remarkable multi-national effort.

As far as Burma was concerned, 1942 saw the effective end of the British Empire in the country, simply because when the reconquest took place three years later, Burma was of such peripheral interest globally to Britain (and India) that the thought of continuing as colonial overlords was entirely unpalatable, except to those few colonial civil servants in exile in Simla whose heads remained firmly in the sand of 1941. This process of change over such a short period of time casts an interesting light on the nature of the British colonial enterprise in India and Burma: it staggered along only as long as the people administering it felt that it conferred advantage on Britain to do so, and for those subject to its indignities to accept them. There was no deep cultural or emotional mindset to continue in the role of colonial overlord in a way that there most certainly existed, for instance, in both France and the Netherlands in 1945 and 1946 – nations that had something to prove following their respective humiliations at the hands of Germany. It was to take more war to eject these two European powers from their Asian colonies in Indochina and the Dutch East Indies.

In this respect, it seems appropriate to suggest that the story of the Burma campaign is also, in part, a story of the birth of an independent India, and the role played by the Indian Army in the advent of a new nation. There were several midwives to Indian independence. One of the founding myths of modern India is that Subhas Chandra Bose's adopted baby (he wasn't there at its birth, in Singapore in 1942, because at the time he was a guest of Hitler in Nazi Germany) – the Indian National Army, subsequently the Azad Hind Fauj – played a distinctive role in energizing India to seize its birthright. If this is true, it is even more true that the much larger and demonstrably more successful Indian Army, comprising a major part of 11 Army Group and then ALFSEA, should also. share some of the founding glory of 1947, for it was in the transformative victories of 1944 and 1945, in which the INA along with its Japanese master was decisively crushed, that the essence of a new India, united and purposeful, was conceived. Equally, if the nonviolence of Gandhi's pacifism played a constituent role in creating the new India (as the national narrative tells us), then so too did the opposite of his *Satyagraha*, namely the extreme violence meted out by the fighting forces of 11 Army Group[8] and Indian Air Force (and the nascent Indian Navy) against the forces of Japan in Assam and Burma in 1944 and 1945. India did not emerge from one wellspring, whatever the national myths might say, but rather from multiple sources that converged on 1947 as a direct consequence of war. Indeed, the argument has been well made by Srinath Raghavan among others that the Indian Armed forces as a whole during the war played a significant role in creating the new India that stepped out into the challenge of Independence (and Partition) in 1947.[9]

The tiny 'mercenary' army that began the war in 1939 was designed for constabulary support to the Raj and support to British military interests abroad. It served primarily British interests. It was based on a small selection of martial races – dominated by north Indian Muslims and Sikhs; a cliché common at the time was that the Punjab was the 'sword arm of India'.[10] By 1945 it had become a truly national army, serving an emerging nation increasingly conscious of and confident in its own destiny, and fighting for its own defence and prerogatives, not for those of a rapidly declining and soon-to-be history British Empire. Nearly half of the 8,578 officers in ALFSEA were now Indian, in a dramatic change since 1939, fundamentally altering 'the character of the Indian Army officer corps'.[11] It was the recruitment of many thousands of young, educated, politically well-informed young Indians as officers in the army that enabled the rapid expansion of the Indian Army to take place, despite nationalist opposition.[12] The martial races dragon, that hoary old legend of the imperial past – the argument that many Indians, mainly southerners and easterners, were too effeminate to be warriors – was decisively slain as the army was swamped by recruits from peoples whom the British had not before recruited into the fighting ranks of their army. The Burma campaign, the front line of Britain's war with Japan, thus saw the transformation of an army, from 'a quintessential imperial creation'[13] to one of the foundation stones of a modern, democratic state. The Indian journalist D.F. Karaka saw this at first hand when visiting Indian formations in the field in Arakan in 1944, observing that the 'Indianness' of the war was changing India in very tangible ways. 'Our men' were 'doing a first-class job in the shape of eliminating a powerful enemy', he recorded. 'This India which is out there on the airstrips of Burma and Arakan is on the march – a disciplined India of that newer generation which is growing up from a conglomeration of communities into a nation.'[14]

The success of the command triumvirate of Mountbatten, Auchinleck and Slim is a distinctive feature of the Burma campaign, in comparison to the stark failures of Japanese command. In the late summer of 1943, the stars aligned with respect to the Allied command arrangements in the Far East. These three men, more than any others, were responsible for transforming Allied fortunes in the Far East and creating and then delivering a plan to win. It was Auchinleck who mobilized India for war and provided Slim with the trained manpower to fight the enemy. Auchinleck took responsibility as C-in-C India in June 1943, while Mountbatten arrived in August to take responsibility for delivering Allied military strategy against the Japanese. In terms of fighting, it wasn't Mountbatten's army group commander (Giffard, and then Leese) who made the greatest impact on the SEAC stage, but Slim, the subordinate commander of 14 Army.

Mountbatten's contribution to victory has been underestimated by those unwilling to look beyond his gilded persona. His role in achieving victory was fundamental to the successful course of the war in the Far East, and in this respect his appointment to the role was inspired. Behind the flannel was a serious mind. He had no trouble grasping the realities of this war. He knew that operational campaigning needed to reflect the strategic imperatives negotiated at the level of the Combined Chiefs of Staff, that his theatre would always be low on the priority list, that he needed imaginative and proactive subordinates, that all needed to 'make do and mend'. He knew that the trained manpower required to defeat the Japanese primarily came from the Indian Army, and he trusted Auchinleck to deliver the number of troops required, at the requisite standard of training and battlefield preparation. He knew that intelligent operational planning, combined with the decisive leadership of 14 Army, was required to achieve success in battle, and he trusted Slim to deliver this success. In particular, he knew the decisive role that would be played in the fighting of logistics, transport and administration, after seeing the elongated lines of communication from India into Assam and Manipur and beyond at first hand. In this environment, he understood why aerial resupply was critical to victory, and took considerable political risks to ensure that aircraft were prioritized to achieve battlefield dominance on each occasion it was required. He was an effective multinational theatre commander, welding the many divergent interests and prerogatives of his staff into the single goal of bringing about the defeat of the Japanese. At the grand strategic level, he understood the need for a combined, multinational headquarters, and indeed enjoyed the frisson of this environment. Importantly also, Mountbatten had an acute political sense. He understood instinctively, as did Eisenhower in Europe, that his was a political and unifying role, a task he fulfilled to perfection. On his appointment, Roosevelt said to him, 'I rely on you to support our policy in S.E. Asia as loyally as Eisenhower supports yours in Europe.' Mountbatten 'decided to be a good American'.[15] As Supreme Allied Commander, criticisms of self-publicity are churlish and wide of the mark, given the extraordinary efforts he made to improve morale, to publish and popularize the exploits of all nations serving in SEAC. At the governmental level, he played the role of representing his theatre of war, and pushing its interests, while simultaneously recognizing that from the strategic point of view, Allied leaders would only be interested in the Far East and Pacific once Germany had been defeated.

In the task of raising morale, Mountbatten succeeded brilliantly, and success for the Allies lay in this area more than in any other. It is also the area for which Mountbatten is best remembered. He deliberately and shamelessly deployed the machinery and principles of public relations to spread the message among the troops that they had not been forgotten by London, and that they were now led by a competent, dynamic and energetic commander, a friend of the Prime Minister and cousin of the King-Emperor no less. A wide range of devices for motivating the troops under his command were developed: the introduction of a theatre newspaper and the *Phoenix* weekly picture magazine were opposed by traditionalists who believed them an unnecessary extravagance, Radio SEAC beamed from Ceylon, while mobile bath units, postal and leave arrangements and, an old Mountbatten favourite, cinemas, did much to improve the lives of soldiers far from home.

The device for which he was best known was his own programme of visits and stump speeches to the troops. Mountbatten had long grasped the vital need for soldiers, sailors and airmen to have confidence in their leaders, not least of all because he was commanding predominantly civilian forces. The men and women of SEAC, of all nationalities, had volunteered or had been conscripted for the duration of the war. They were not regular professionals but rather 'civilians in arms: intelligent, literate, fundamentally unmilitary and longing to get home'.[16] Securing the confidence of such people was only possible if commanders were visible to their men, even if this meant that they became, like Montgomery, larger than life and upset the conventions of an earlier age. For some this natural affinity with their men came naturally, and from the very start Mountbatten set out to see and be seen by the men and women of his command. Others had done and were doing the same, but Mountbatten made it an art form. He knew from first-hand experience of battle the critical importance of being seen by his men. Visits to units were well planned, their apparent spontaneity masking careful preparation. He learned by heart a range of stock phrases in the diverse languages of his command – Urdu, Gurkhali, Burmese, Ceylonese and Hausa. The impact on the troops was remarkable and came as a rebuke to the stuffy naysayers who despised what they regarded incorrectly to be an exercise in self-promotion. Here was someone at the highest level of authority in the theatre of war who was interested in the welfare of the troops and in keeping them informed about the progress of the war and of strategic decisions that would end up having a direct impact on their own destinies. Soldiers who were taken into the confidence of their commanders became far more motivated than those who were kept in the dark and were expected to do as they were told.

The alternative to having an inspirational leader in command of SEAC in late 1943 through to 1945 would have been a continuation of the impoverishment of leadership that had so marked out 1942 and 1943. The impact on morale of such calculated activity was dramatic. Within eight months of Mountbatten's arrival his forces had not only defeated the Japanese in momentous battles in northern Arakan, Imphal and Kohima between March and June 1944, but were pursuing their defeated remnants back to the Chindwin. The adjutant general, General Sir Ronald Adam, on a visit from London, attested at this time to the very high morale of the army. 'In fact', he told Mountbatten, 'I have not seen higher morale anywhere.'[17] The personal leadership of Mountbatten – represented as much by visibility as anything else – was a significant factor in the recovery of morale across the theatre during that period.

The third member of the winning Allied triumvirate was Slim. From the point in May 1942 when he was the only corps commander in India with experience of fighting the Japanese, to mid-1943 when he was appointed to command Eastern Army, the thinking necessary to transform the armies in India from defeat to victory came from his fertile brain. Likewise, the power to persuade soldiers of many nations – but especially those of India – that they could overcome the Japanese in battle, was the product of his calm and inspired leadership. As a general he proved himself in 1942 to be a master of the fighting withdrawal. In 1942 he had created the intellectual and practical framework for the rebuilding of the armies in India, and in 1943 he was promoted to command the army that had responsibility for defeating the Japanese. In 1944 he demonstrated mastery of the defensive battle, in early 1945 the offensive battle, and in April the pursuit. The calculated risks he took at Imphal/Kohima and at Meiktila discomforted Mutaguchi and Kimura respectively and led directly to Japanese defeat in both battles. The capture of Rangoon set the seal on a brilliantly fought campaign that brought about the defeat of the Japanese in Burma. It was a campaign that the strategists had never planned in the first place, and its overwhelming success, like that at Imphal/Kohima the year before, came as something of a surprise to those in both London and Washington who continued to underestimate 14 Army and its commander. Slim's unhesitating switch of plan to *Extended Capital* in mid-December 1944, his acceptance of the administrative and tactical risks that this entailed, and his command of every nuance of the 1945 offensive as it unfolded showed him to be, as his biographer Ronald Lewin concluded, 'a complete general'.[18] Slim would not have achieved his success in 1945 without, among other things, the understanding and support of Mountbatten and the superb cooperation of the Allied air forces in theatre. Likewise, Sultan's advance from Lashio, in which Festing's 36 Division distinguished itself, kept Honda occupied in the north at a time when Stopford was attempting to cross about Mandalay. Commanders at every level, imbued with a knowledge of their superiority over the Japanese, kept their men and their materiel going despite the difficulties of distance, terrain, climate and exhaustion. Ultimately, however, none of these would have even been called into play had not Slim refused to be put off from his grand design to launch aggressive offensive operations against the Japanese in Burma in 1945. When it happened, 14 Army's advance in strength into Burma came about not by virtue of Allied policy, but because of Slim's single-minded determination to pursue the Japanese to their destruction and to exploit the opportunity for so doing that he himself had created at Imphal/Kohima. The invasion of Burma took place according to his plan and his purposes. When he was ennobled, Mountbatten took the title 'Earl Mountbatten of Burma'. For all his greatness, he stole the title from Slim, to whom it more correctly belonged.

The war in Burma has been dismissed by some commentators as a strategic sideshow, in the sense that winning or losing the campaign in Burma was not decisive in ending the war.[19] The dismissal of the Far East as a war theatre of grand strategic consequence began with the 'Germany First' policy agreed at the Arcadia Conference at the end of 1941. Thereafter it was to prove the orphan child of Allied strategy, the product of initial humiliation, never fully to recover or obtain a pre-eminent status in the affairs of Allied planning or indeed in the minds of historians. Churchill gave it but a cursory reference in his highly influential history of the Second World War, conferring on the war the 'forgotten' status the soldiers grumbled about during the fighting. In *Closing the Ring*, Churchill gave the 1944 campaign less than a page. The 'sepoy general' (the phrase was originally Napoleon's, about Wellington) who had commanded the army that secured remarkable military victories in 1944 and 1945 – Bill Slim – wasn't even mentioned. Nor was the name of his army. Why? The Churchill government had been deeply apprehensive about the political consequences of defeat in 1944. The fact that they did not trumpet the victory was also partly political. The less said about anything connected with India, given Roosevelt's public hostility to the British Empire, the better. It's also hard to avoid the conclusion that the real reason the war was ignored by Churchill was that it was fought by 'colonial' (Indian and African) troops, who by 1945 made up 90 per cent of 14 Army.[20]

Indeed most historians, then as now, argue that the Burma campaign was peripheral to the effort by the Allies to defeat Japan.[21] That job was most effectively done by the United States Navy and Marine Corps and the B29, especially the one called Enola Gay, and a remarkable, epoch-defining and history-changing explosive device nicknamed 'Fat Man'. Some use numbers of overall casualties to poo-poo the significance of the fighting, as after all 'only thirty thousand British servicemen died in the war against Japan, as compared to two hundred and thirty-five thousand in the war against Germany... first and always the real enemy.'[22] The growth of 'The Forgotten Army' legend was thus not only caused by the fact that Burma was seen as a strategic backwater but was also a deliberate act of censorship by the British, followed up by the remarkable absence subsequently of any mention of the campaign in Churchill's war memoirs.

The war in the Far East did contribute significantly to the defeat of Japan.

First, Burma unexpectedly became, in 1942, the locus for the defence of India. The campaign retained China in the fight and allowed Allied (and American) strategic imperatives regarding China to be fulfilled, as well as allowing India's vast potential of human and material resources to be used for the Allied war effort. Burma was the one place where the Allies could provide support to the Chinese government, and for that reason alone it was essential that the country was recovered from Japanese control after it was lost in 1942. Until that could be achieved, India became the launchpad for aerial operations over the airlift route between the upper reaches of Assam and Yunnan province in China – the Hump – which between 1942 and 1945 airlifted 650,000 tons to China, the equivalent of 260,000 separate C47 sorties, or nearly 240 aircraft flying every single day for three years. By 1945 the airlift comprised 640 aircraft and 34,000 military personnel, the largest such endeavour in human history. It was in Burma where British and American offensive intentions could be demonstrated to a sceptical China, which was holding down a very substantial part of the entire Imperial Japanese Army and wanted a tangible commitment of Allied effort in Burma in exchange for its continuing sacrifice. By 1944 Burma had, in Japanese planning, taken on the role of the defensive left flank for the rich rice, rubber and oil resources of Malaya, Indochina and the Dutch East Indies. If Burma were lost, the entirety of the Japanese left flank would be opened up, ripe for Allied counterstrike into the heart of Japan's ill-named Co-Prosperity Sphere. Between 1942 and 1945 Burma was home to the Japanese Burma Area Army – at least 308,582 strong at its height – which was a demonstrable threat to India, as indeed it proved in the 'March on Delhi', Operations Ha-Go and U-Go in 1944.

Second, a predominantly Indian Army stopped and turned back the Japanese invasion of India in 1944 and recovered Burma from the hands of the invader in 1945. It is true that Tokyo did not seriously plan a full-scale invasion of India, designed to topple the Raj. It was, nevertheless, a glint in Mutaguchi's eye, and if Operation *U-Go* had been more than competently managed, a very serious threat existed to the security and stability of the whole of Bengal, Assam and Manipur. India was a very significant element in the Allied war effort as a whole. India was the empire's greatest reservoir of military manpower, providing 2.5 million men across several theatres of the war effort. It also became a significant supplier of war materiel, in the process of which the Indian economy was fundamentally changed, ending the war as a large creditor of the British Exchequer. A successful Japanese invasion, even if only into the Brahmaputra Valley, would have had far-reaching consequences both militarily and politically.

Third, the Burma campaign contributed significantly to the destruction of Japanese military power across the whole of Asia and the Pacific. It was in Assam and Burma in 1944 and 1945 that the Japanese suffered their greatest losses in the Second World War, together with a succession of humiliating defeats, losing by their own admission a total of 185,149 *killed*, nearly 13 times British/Indian losses, in the period between March 1944 and May 1945.[23] This destruction subsequently allowed the Allies to manage the narrative of defeat among the Japanese. Demonstrating that their armies had been militarily defeated *in the field* removed any post hoc arguments that Japan had fallen merely as a result of the A-bomb. Defeating the Imperial Japanese Army so decisively was important for removing any residual sense in Japanese minds of the power of militarism.

Fourth, it proved the military effectiveness of the transformation that had taken place among the armies in India after 1943, especially in the Indian Army. Before 1942 the Indian Army was designated an imperial reserve, designed for deployment in support of the British elsewhere in the world. It suddenly became the main means by which India was to be defended. This was a role for which it had not been trained, equipped or prepared. Britain was entirely unable to undertake this task itself, against a first-class enemy. The extraordinary story of the period 1942–45 was that of India transforming itself to take responsibility for its own defence. It did so spectacularly and established itself unequivocally as the guardian of its future. This transformation, built on the basis of thorough training for war, created a new, powerful national army able to serve a new nation on the verge of independence. This new army was distinct from the old, pre-1939 Indian Army, which had existed merely to serve British – rather than Indian

– interests. As the historian Daniel Marston observes, this army, as an institution of state, 'had a profound impact on the development of the independent states of the Indian subcontinent, particularly India and Pakistan'.[24]

Finally, the Burma campaign provided the opportunity for the Indian Army to play a decisive role in defeating the forces of militarism, building a strong historic narrative in the corporate memory of the new nations that would emerge from Partition in 1947. That India and Pakistan seem to have forgotten these 1944 and 1945 victories does not invalidate or deny this historical reality. It is one that, perhaps, a new generation, less encumbered by the commitment of their parents and grandparents to the founding myths of the post-colonial enterprise, can embrace.

In terms of statistics, the Burma campaign was the longest campaign fought by Allied armies in the Second World War, and in 1945 provided the largest army group ever assembled by the British Commonwealth and its friends. In April 1945 the number of Allied service personnel in South East Asia Command (i.e., excluding India Command) totalled 1,304,126, including nearly 300,000 Americans. Of this number the British Commonwealth provided 954,985, of whom 606,149 were in 'Operational Land Forces' – soldiers in the fighting brigades, divisions and corps (4, 15, 33 and the Northern Combat Area Command). Of this total (606,149) 87 per cent were Indian, 3 per cent African and 10 per cent British.

What happened to the competing empires that clashed together in war in 1941? For some colonies in Asia, the transition from colonial to independent status was to take some time and occasion much more bloodshed as the colonial power resisted the inevitable. But this was not so for the British Empire in Asia. While independence for Malaya was delayed by the outworkings of a communist insurgency, in 1947 the Indians inherited the British-Indian Empire, and in 1948 Britain handed Burma to the Burmese. One of the logical underpinnings of British imperialism in India was that of eventual self-government, the ultimate expression of which was independence. The process and timeline by which independence was achieved can and has been criticized, but the nature of the transition of power from a colonial ruler to a democratic entity was notable. India is today the world's largest democracy. Independence in 1947 did not see a rejection of British models of governance, but rather a transference of the ownership of that governance, such that the underpinnings of democracy – among other things a free press, separation of the legislature and executive, an independent judiciary and the principle of personal liberty under the law – were handed over as British domestic legacies and preserved, as in many other post-imperial countries, by the newly independent India.

The pattern of history has tended to be for empires to come to their natural end, some more speedily and bloodily than others, by means of internal chaos or civil war, or by external overthrow, and to collapse in decay and hubris, such as that of the Mughal Empire in India during the early 19th century. From these ruins have emerged, over time, new nations that have forged their own, distinct identities, separate to those of their colonized past. But this type of transfer was not the Indian experience, which in 1947 inherited a country Indians already, arguably, owned. This ownership was vouchsafed in part because the victories that had been won against the totalitarian Empire of Japan had been largely Indian victories, fought by Indians in Indian units and formations in a largely Indian 14 Army. The INA, by contrast, was an artificial Japanese device for placing a pro-independence narrative in the mouths of those, principally at Singapore in 1942, who found themselves humiliated by surrender, and let down by the government in which they had vested their allegiance. It is always worth remembering that many of those Indians taken prisoner at Singapore who rejected the offer to join the INA were executed by firing squad. The photographs of Sikh POWs shot and bayonetted in Singapore – discovered at the Japanese surrender in 1945 – demonstrate powerfully the absence of any moral equivalence between the hegemony of the Raj and that of the Empire of Japan. By contrast, the real victims of imperial rule in 1942 were Indians executed, imprisoned and starved across Asia at the hands of the Empire of Japan, the over 50,000 Indians who are believed to have perished on the escape to India in 1942, and the 200,000 Burmese who died as a result of Japanese occupation between 1942 and 1945.

The INA was always a declining asset for Japan and used ultimately only as a propaganda tool associated with the ill-fated March on Delhi in 1944, legs given to the voice provided by Subhas Chandra Bose. There was never any truth in the INA's central message – that the British Empire had been defeated by Japan, and that the only means of Britain's overthrow in India was military defeat at the hands of Asia's new rulers. The evidence of history is that Indians clearly wanted to achieve independence for India, but not at the expense of another form of fascist tutelage under the banner of the Greater East Asian Co-Prosperity Sphere. Indians didn't flock to join the INA, or to set up mirrors of the INA within India to fight the Raj, for the simple reason that the Raj was not considered to be the enemy. From late 1941 onwards, if not long before, fascist Japan was overwhelmingly regarded in India to be the greatest enemy. The argument for independence within India and Great Britain was reinforced, rather than invalidated, by the determination of Indians to defend their homeland.

For the other empires in this story, the end is straightforward, and well known. The Empire of Japan came crashing around its ears with the atomic bombs in August 1945. A creation of the Meiji Restoration in 1868, its modernization was sullied by the blood of those it oppressed, especially in Manchuria and China after 1931 and 1937 respectively – some 20 million Chinese dying during the Sino–Japanese War, in addition to nearly 4 million massacred directly by the Japanese military.[25] As for the American empire, that story continues. Suffice it to say, it was America, the land of the free, which helped fund by its blood and treasure between 1941 and 1945, the destruction of militaristic ambitions in Asia, by Japan at least.

What did the Burma campaign, as it ran to its end in 1945, mean at this time to both Britain and India? For one it meant the end, and the other a beginning. The Gurkha officer, Lieutenant Colonel John Masters, on the staff of Rees's 19 Indian Division, captured the emotion as well as the essence of the matter for old India hands in *The Road Past Mandalay*, describing the moment he watched men of the division flood out of Mandalay for the advance on Toungoo in March 1945. A man whose family had lived in India for generations, he saw immediately what the crowd of tanks and lorried infantry meant:

Now, as the tanks burst away down the road to Rangoon and the torrent of guns and radios and trucks and machine-guns swirled and rode past in one direction, south, past the bloated Japanese corpses, past the ruins of the empire the Japanese had tried to build here, it took possession of the empire *we* had built, and in its towering, writhing dust clouds India traced the shape of her own future. Twenty races, a dozen religions, a score of languages passed in those trucks and tanks. When my great-great-grandfather first went to India there had been as many nations; now there was one – India; and he and I and a few thousand others, over two and a half centuries, sometimes with intent, sometimes unwittingly, sometimes in miraculous sympathy, sometimes in brutal folly, had made it...

The Nehrus and the Gandhis and the Cripps talked in the high chambers of London and Delhi; and certainly someone had to. But India stood at last independent, proud, and incredibly generous to us, on these final battlefields in the Burmese plain. It was all summed up in the voice of an Indian colonel of artillery. The Indian Army had not been allowed to possess any field artillery from the time of the mutiny (1857) until just before the Second World War. Now the

Indian, bending close to an English colonel over a map, straightened and said with a smile, 'O.K., George. Thanks. I've got it. We'll take over all tasks at 1800. What about a beer?'[26]

For all the rights and wrongs of imperialism, British rule in India was all but over, its swansong marked as much by the tanks and trucked infantry crowding the still dusty tracks that led to Rangoon as by deliberation in London and Delhi, in which all the nations of the new India, forged in war, with a newfound confidence borne of victory in battle, were closely joined. 'O.K. George,' said the Indian Army to the British in India, 'Thanks. I've got it. India's ours now. We'll take over all tasks soon. What about a beer?' In that moment all those with eyes to see could perceive that responsibility for India was being transferred from its old imperial masters to its own people, for a future they had played a leading role in creating.

Masters would have been bemused at the suggestion 2.5 million Indian men and women joined the armed forces between 1939 and 1945 as the result of a 'propaganda offensive' by the British government which 'secured the partial allegiance or at least acquiescence of part of the population'.[27] He would also have looked askance at the suggestion that these men joined solely because they were hungry, and needed employment.[28] Nor could the recruitment of such large numbers to the Indian Army have been caused by subconscious coercion, or any of a number of reasons sometimes provided (such as that men were simply escaping poverty; that loyalty was bought by means of increased pay; that advertising campaigns were propaganda and that many young men had long been indoctrinated into the idea that 'family and personal honour depended on a military career'),[29] as it doesn't explain why the men thus recruited were prepared to die for this compulsion, and why Indian soldiers were to win 22 of the 34 Victoria and George Crosses awarded during the Burma campaign. Instead, Masters would have concluded that, instead, most Indians who joined the armed forces in such extraordinary numbers did so because they had rationally weighed up the options and assessed the nature of the sacrifice they were willing to make for the sake of the government of India, regardless of its political construct and their own lack of political representation. In this sense, their decision was made on the basis of a conception of India much larger than purely politics. Young men in many countries and in many ages have gone to war often in spite of the political party in power, for other, more deep-seated reasons. The threat to their conception of what India was and *could be* therefore far outweighed the rights and wrongs in their minds of colonialism, if the issue or argument ever surfaced at all for the majority of young men intellectually unencumbered with the rarefied concerns of national governance in 1942. It is rational therefore to suggest that reality trumped ideology in the face of the imminent and existential danger to the Indian state.

The truth appears to be that most Indians accepted that the Raj was, rightly or wrongly – or for the time being – the legally constituted government of India. Like all governments everywhere, it had supporters and opponents. Few who opposed the government on nationalistic or self-governance grounds questioned its legitimacy, as that would have invalidated their own claim to be its successor in due course. Likewise, the Indian Army was *India's* army, not Britain's. As the historian Professor Roger Beaumont observes, 'it is most interesting to weigh the charges that the Raj built its army in India as an oppressive instrument against what one sees in how lovingly and energetically the Indians have retained the model.'[30] The evidence suggests instead that the theory of 'prosaic oppression' and its common language of 'unconscious bias and systemic structures of power' is a fabricated political construct – much like Procrustes' mythical bed – that does not relate to what we know through the historical record of everyday human experience in colonial India – especially in wartime – the facts being squeezed to fit within a fixed and unbending political model. It was true that India did not have political independence, but in every other sense the freedom to make social, economic and political choices within this overall environment cannot be said to have been constrained by such oppression that human agency was so deviously manipulated to suit ruling British interests. Young Indian men and young Britons both joined the Indian Army for the same purpose in times of peace: for adventure, employment, the lure of military glory, the age-old attraction of the sword, and for altruistic motives perhaps, such as protecting one's loved ones or fighting evil. Soldiering has always been an attractive activity for young men, in peace as in war, and India before and during the Second World War was no different. In so doing both countries came subtly but inextricably together in a web of complex relationships that lasted for more than three centuries, in a multitude of tangible and intangible ways. Indians were no more victims of their polity than were Britons, both of whom were, of course, victims of the fascist militarism that dragged the world into a second great slaughter in that century of world war.

In Burma the Japanese lost a staggering 185,149 dead, a third of the over 500,000 servicemen sent to fight in the country between 1941 and 1945 (in 1945 there were 316,700 Japanese troops in Burma). The casualty count needs to be expanded beyond the combatants, however, to include the 1,000,000 (probable) Burmese dead; the 3,000,000 (probable) Indian dead from war-made disasters such as the Bengal Famine and the 20,000,000 million dead across China in the years following 1937. The statistics speak for themselves. For all its undoubted flaws, the cause of these deaths was not the British Empire. The cause of death, destruction and human misery on a truly gigantic and previously unimagined scale, setting back human civilization by at least two or three generations and probably more, and staining human history indelibly with the blood of its millions of victims, was Japanese militarism. One of the significant counters to this militarism was the all-volunteer Indian Army, which reached the apogee of its potency in 1944 and 1945. The journalist D.F. Karaka perfectly captured the transformation that was to take place in the Indian armed forces during the Second World War, when he observed, visiting an Indian Air Force Vengeance squadron in Arakan in February 1944:

> There was a spirit of camaraderie among them and they had an unbelievable respect for their comrades and even greater love for the service to which they belonged. If they were proud that they belonged to an Air Force, they were even prouder that it was an Indian Air Force. This was not an Air Force of mercenaries. It was an Air Force of Indians conscious of their country, their heritage and all the things that go to make up this land of ours.[31]

By defeating the Japanese invasion of India in 1944, and destroying them in Burma in 1945, this army demonstrated not merely India's military prowess, but its political and civic maturity, a counter to the (British) lie that India was incapable of self-government, and the (Indian) lie that the Indian Army was a mere tool of the Raj. In a very real sense, Britain's failure to defend its empire in 1942 was assuaged by India's ability to win it back, not for Britain, but for India, in 1945.

By means of a mixture of poor planning, strategic myopia, not a little incompetence and in the face of unprecedented assault, Britain lost its Burma colony to Japan in 1942. This was a failure of a generation in Britain and its empire immersed in an idealistic cocoon of pacific hopefulness following the slaughter of the Great War, something which created an attitude of political timidity in the face of totalitarian posturing in the years before 1939. India, partly through the medium of a resurgent Indian Army and partly by the transformation of its economy, won it back in 1945. Burma was overwhelmingly an Indian war and an Indian victory.

Appendix 1

The Indian and Gurkha Infantry Regiments of the Indian Army

In 1939 the 20 infantry regiments of the Indian Army were:

1st Punjab Regiment
2nd Punjab Regiment
3rd Madras Regiment
4th Bombay Grenadiers
5th The Mahratta Light Infantry
6th Rajputana Rifles
7th Rajput Regiment
8th Punjab Regiment
9th Jat Regiment
10th Baluch Regiment
11th Sikh Regiment
12th Frontier Force Regiment
13th Frontier Force Rifles
14th Punjab Regiment
15th Punjab Regiment
16th Punjab Regiment
17th Dogra Regiment

18th Royal Garwhal Rifles
19th The Hyderabad Regiment/Kumaon Regiment
20th Burma Rifles

The following were raised during the war:

The Indian Parachute Regiment
The Bihar Regiment
The Assam Regiment
The Sikh Light Infantry
The Mahar Regiment
1st Afridi Battalion
The Ajmer Regiment
The Chamar Regiment
1st Lingyat Battalion
1st Coorg Battalion

Each regiment contained a number of battalions, which increased dramatically as the Indian Army expanded in 1940. The various battalions of each regiment were shown in abbreviated form. For example, the Fifth Battalion of 1 Punjab Regiment was 5/1 Punjab; the Second Battalion of 6 Rajputana Rifles as 2/6 Rajputana Rifles, and so on.

The eleven Gurkha Regiments were:

1st King George V's Own Gurkha Rifles (The Malaun Regiment)
2nd King Edward VII's Own Gurkha Rifles (The Sirmoor Rifles)
3rd Queen Alexandra's Own Gurkha Rifles
4th Prince of Wales's Own Gurkha Rifles
5th Royal Gurkha Rifles (Frontier Force)
6th Gurkha Rifles
7th Gurkha Rifles
8th Gurkha Rifles
9th Gurkha Rifles
10th Gurkha Rifles
11th Gurkha Rifles

Appendix 2

Indian Army Structure and Numbers – 9 September 1943[1]

There were about 2,000,000 men in the Indian Army, of whom:

- 1,250,000 were combatants (the others being non-combatants, which in the British armed forces would be civilians and contractors delivering services that in India required men to be enlisted, but untrained). Of these 'combatants':
  - 429,000 were in training establishments;
  - 817,000 were combatant soldiers, of whom:
    - 200,000 were overseas, in Middle East and Paiforce (Iran);
    - 617,000 were on Indian soil, of whom:
      - 70,000 were on the NWF;
      - 129,000 were allotted to the security of internal lines of communication;
      - 8,000 were being raised and not yet allocated to units or formations.

- This left 413,000 combatants able to fight the Japanese. This equalled ten fighting divisions, together with all the ancillary and administrative units required to maintain them. For every infantry division of 18,347 men, a further 26,300 men were required to support them in the field, a ratio of nearly two support troops to every combatant.
- In India there were, in fact:
  - nine infantry divisions;
  - two tank brigades;
  - LRP ('Chindit') and parachute troops;
  - armoured, mechanized and other units not allocated to fighting formations.
- Of these nine divisions:
  - six were allocated to 14 Army (i.e. 6 x 41,300 = 247,000);
  - one armoured division in GHQ reserve;
  - two infantry divisions in GHQ reserve.

Appendix 3

Definitive Numbers for Indian Army in SEAC[2]

STRENGTH OF FORCES IN SEAC
STRENGTH BY SERVICES

LAND FORCES	**April 1945**
OPERATIONAL LAND STRENGTH	
British and Indian troops	561,512
African troops	37,137
US Forces	12,097
British–Chinese	7,500
Chinese	72,725
French (in Ceylon)	1,000
Total	**691,971**
LINES OF COMMUNICATION STRENGTHS	
Assam	
British and Indian troops	117,795
African troops	1,210
US Forces	33,170
West of Brahmaputra	
US Forces	132,526
Ledo Road L. of C.	
US Forces	33,678

Total		318,379
Total, Land Forces		**1,010,350**
Total Air Forces		**175,976**
Total Naval Forces		**117,800**
Grand Total, all Forces		**1,304,126**

Total operational land forces SEAC in 1945, by nation

British Commonwealth – 606,149, of which:

British Chin	7,500	1.2%
African	37,137	6.1%
Indian	498,034[3]	82.16%
British Service	63,478	10.5%

Appendix 4

Estimated Loss of Japanese Soldiers in Operation *U-Go*

FORMATION	PRE-CAMPAIGN STRENGTH	POST-CAMPAIGN STRENGTH	CASUALTIES
15 Division	20,000	4,000	16,000
31 Division	20,000	7,000	13,000
33 Division	25,000	4,000	21,000
Rear Units	50,000	35,000	15,000
Total	115,000	50,000	65,000

Bibliography

All sources used in my research have been referenced in the body of the text. Rather than producing an additional peacock display of bibliographical righteousness, I have listed below a small number of additional books that I have enjoyed reading and consider that others, who are looking for further reading on the subject, might too. Readers wishing to delve more deeply into the subject are encouraged to visit the Burma Campaign Memorial Library, the brainchild of the late Gordon Graham MC and Bar, at the School of African and Oriental Studies, 10 Thornhaugh Street, Bloomsbury, London WC1H 0XG.

Callahan, Raymond, *Triumph at Imphal-Kohima: How the Indian Army Finally Stopped the Japanese Juggernaut* (Lawrence, Kansas: University of Kansas Press, 2017)

Callahan, Raymond and Marston, Daniel, *The 1945 Burma Campaign and the Transformation of the British Indian Army* (Lawrence, Kansas: University of Kansas Press, 2021)

Cross, John, *Jungle Warfare: Experiences and Encounters* (London: Arms and Armour Press, 1989)

Fort, Adrian, *Archibald Wavell: The Life and Times of an Imperial Servant* (London: Jonathan Cape, 2009)

Holland, James, *Burma '44: The Battle That Turned Britain's War in the East* (London: Bantam Press, 2016)

Latimer, Jon, *Burma: The Forgotten War* (London: John Murray, 2005)

Matthews, Roderick, *Peace, Poverty and Betrayal: A New History of British India* (London: Hurst, 2021)

McLynn, Frank, *The Burma Campaign* (London: Bodley Head, 2010)

Myint-U, Thant, *The Making of Modern Burma* (Cambridge: Cambridge University Press, 2001)

Pike, Francis, *Hirohito's War: The Pacific War, 1941–1945* (London: Bloomsbury, 2015)

Probert, Henry, *The Forgotten Air Force* (London: Brassey's, 1995)

Thompson, Julian, *The War in Burma, 1942–45: A Vital Contribution to Victory in the Far East* (London: Sidgwick & Jackson, 2002)

Venning, Annabel, *To War with the Walkers: One Family's Extraordinary Story of Survival in the Second World War* (London: Hodder and Stoughton, 2019)

Warren, Alan, *Burma 1942* (London: Continuum, 2011)

Woods, Philip, *Reporting the Retreat: War Correspondents in Burma* (London: Hurst, 2016)

Notes

BA: Broadlands Archives, University of Southampton
SP: Slim Papers, Churchill Archives Centre, Cambridge
JRL: Auchinleck Papers, John Rylands Library, Manchester
IWM: Imperial War Museum, London
LHA: Liddell Hart Archives, King's College, University of London
TNA: The National Archives, Kew, London

AUTHOR'S NOTE

1 For the 1,035 books on the subject published in English to 2001, see Gordon
   Graham, *The Burma Campaign Memorial Library: Descriptive Catalogue and
   Bibliography* (London: School of Oriental and African Studies, 2001). A steady
   stream of material has found its way into print in the 20 years hence, although not
   on the sub-continent where the events explained in this book are largely forgotten,
   or consigned to the category of 'colonial history'. The library now has over 1,200
   published works. Gordon Graham's account of his experiences are in *The Trees Are
   All Young on Garrison Hill* (Marlow: Kohima Educational Trust, 2006).
2 Summaries of Japanese operations in Burma can be found in the series of
   'Japanese Monographs' organized and published by the HQ United States Army,
   Japan, between 1945 and 1952. These are indispensable summaries of Japanese
   operations in Burma between 1942 and 1945 and were fully revised between
   1955 and 1960. The relevant monographs for Burma are 57, 58, 59a, 59b, 61,
   62, 64, 130, 131, 132, 133, 134 and 148 and have been extensively employed in
   the preparation of this book.

INTRODUCTION

1 Although 'old', J. F. Cady's *A History of Modern Burma* (London: Cornell
   University Press, 1958), remains indispensable to the modern scholar.
2 The Burmans of the Irrawaddy Delta, still the dominant racial grouping in
   modern Myanmar, are the 'Bamar' people, comprising some two-thirds of
   Myanmar's population.

3   Lin Y, *Vigil of a Nation* (London: Heinemann, 1946), p. 637.

4   The background to Japanese expansionism and the question of European and US culpability in the path to war are outside the scope of this book. An excellent starting point in understanding the inevitable nuances at play is Alan Macfarlane, *Secrets of the Modern World: Yukichi Fukuzawa* (London: Nimble Books, 2001).

5   I am grateful to Jeff Pettigrew for this observation.

6   It was always, even in East Indian Company times, known as the Indian Army, and formally so after the Kitchener Reforms of the 1890s.

7   36 Division was initially designated an Indian Division, despite containing exclusively British brigades, until it converted to British status in August 1944 just before it was flown in to Myitkyina to serve under General Stilwell's Northern Combat Area Command (NCAC).

8   There were 14,000 officers seconded from the British Army. Figures for each year are in Bisheshwar Prasad (ed.), *Official History of the Indian Armed Forces in the Second World War, Expansion of the Armed Forces and Defence Organisation 1939–45* (New Delhi: Government of India, 1956), pp. 400–406.

9   'The British ruled India, but never by themselves.' David Omissi, *The Sepoy and the Raj: The Indian Army, 1860–1940* (Basingstoke: Macmillan, 1994), p. 153.

10 Ibid., p. 232.

11 This racial exceptionalism was entirely repudiated by the Indian Army. See Stephen Cohen, *The Indian Army: Its Contribution to the Development of a Nation* (Berkeley: University of California Press, 1971), p. 133. Barney White-Spunner and Yasmin Khan describe the dilemmas of partition even-handedly. Barney White-Spunner, *Partition: The Story of Indian Independence and the Creation of Pakistan in 1947* (London: Simon & Schuster, 2017) and Yasmin Khan, *The Great Partition: The Making of India and Pakistan* (New Haven: Yale University Press, 2017).

12 I am grateful to Professor Nigel Biggar for this observation.

13 A.J.F. Doulton, *The Fighting Cock: Being the History of the 23rd Indian Division 1942–1947* (Aldershot: Gale and Polden, 1950), p. 2.

14 F.W. Perry, *The Commonwealth Armies: Manpower and Organisation in Two World Wars* (Manchester: Manchester University Press, 1988), pp. 97–98.

15 Omissi, op. cit., p. 190.

16 Byron Farwell, *Armies of the Raj* (New York: W.W. Norton, 1989), p. 312.

17 Harry Walker's 'Letters to Annie and Flo', 15 July 1944, Walker family archive, by permission of Professor Katherine Venables.

18 Quoted in David Smurthwaite, 'The Sinews of War' in David Smurthwaite (ed.), *The Forgotten War* (London: National Army Museum, 1992), p. 17.

19 Cohen, op. cit., p. 131.

20 Few Indian battalions followed the British practice of having a separate machine-gun platoon, instead determining that they were best deployed across each of the 12 platoons in the battalion. Ian Sumner, *The Indian Army 1914–1947* (Oxford: Osprey Publishing, 2001), p. 49.

21 Alan Jeffreys, *Approach to Battle: Training the Indian Army during the Second World War* (Solihull: Helion, 2017), pp. 35–37.

22 Of this total 65,000 were non-combatants. There were 82 Indian and 37 British battalions in India in 1939. Four battalions were outside India, two in Hong Kong and two in Singapore. In terms of Indian officers in the Indian Army in 1939 there are widespread discrepancies in the numbers cited in various records. Jeffreys uses the figures of 1,912 British and 344 Indian officers. The relevant files in the British Library are OIOC L/WS/1/924 Annexure A (for 1939) and L/WS/1/707 – Telegram from India Command to the War Office, 1 May 1945. However, using documents in the Ministry of Defence in New Delhi, Prasad (*Expansion of the Armed Forces*, p. 102) says 3,031 British and 697 Indian officers in 1939, growing to 18,752 and 13,947 respectively in 1945. Marston quotes 577 Indian officers in 1939 (*Phoenix from the Ashes: The Indian Army in the Burma Campaign* (Westport, CT: Praeger, 2003), p. 47). The difference between the 344, 697 and 577 *may* relate to that between combat arm officers, and officers in support arms such as medical services.

23 Kaushik Roy, 'Expansion and Deployment of the Indian Army during World War II: 1939–45' in *Journal of the Society for Army Historical Research*, vol. 88, no. 355 (2010), p. 256.

24 Philip Mason, *A Matter of Honour: An Account of the Indian Army, Its Officers and Men* (London: Jonathan Cape, 1974), pp. 449–470.

25 Tarak Barkawi, *Soldiers of Empire. Indian and British Armies in World War II* (Cambridge: Cambridge University Press, 2017), p. 52.

26 Lawrence James, *Churchill and Empire* (London: Weidenfeld & Nicholson, 2014), p. 236.

27 For an explanation of the Indian Army see Rob Johnson, 'Making a Virtue out of Necessity: The Indian Army 1746–1945' in Rob Johnson (ed.), *The British Indian Army, Virtue and Necessity* (Newcastle upon Tyne; Cambridge: Scholars Publishing, 2014), pp. xvii; 1–14.

28 Barkawi, op. cit., p. 2.

29 Perry, op. cit., p. 99; Omissi, op. cit., pp. 178–191.

30 Omissi, op. cit., pp. 154–155.

31 Perry, op. cit., p. 115.

32 Prasad, *Reconquest of Burma* Vol. 1, pp. xxv–xxvi. Major General Stanley Woodburn Kirby's complaints about Prasad's evident bias is in Jeffrey Grey, *A Commonwealth of Histories* (London: Sir Robert Menzies Centre for Australian Studies, 1998), p. 14.

33 Nick Lloyd, *The Amritsar Massacre: The Untold Story of One Fateful Day* (London: Taurus, 2011).

34 Beaumont, op. cit., p. 197; Omissi, op. cit.; Yasmin Khan, *The Raj at War* (London: The Bodley Head, 2015), pp. 20–29.

35 Cited in Christopher Bayly and Tim Harper, *Forgotten Armies: The Fall of British Asia 1941–45* (London: Allen Lane, 2004), p. 74.

36 See, for example, Thein Pe Myint, 'Wartime Traveler' in Robert H. Taylor, *Marxism and Resistance in Burma 1942–1945* (Athens, Ohio: Ohio University Press, 1984), p. 228.

37 Srinath Raghavan, *India's War: The Making of Modern South Asia, 1939–1945* (London: Allen Lane, 2016), pp. 76–78.

38 The Naga people in 1944 largely remained loyal to the Raj, as did the Kukis in the Cachar Hills south-west of Kohima unlike the Kukis in the Somra Tracts and Angousham Hills, many of whom favoured the Japanese. American missionaries had been instrumental in converting large numbers of Nagas to a robust Christianity, beginning as early as the 1830s. See Robert Lyman, *Japan's Last Bid for Victory* (Barnsley: Praetorian, 2011). Two accounts which deal well with the impact of the war on the people of the Naga Hills are Khrientuo Ltu, *World War Two in Northeast India: A Study of Imphal and Kohima Battles* (Norway: Barkweaver, 2019) and Charles Chasie and Harry Fecitt, *The Road to Kohima* (Oxford: Kohima Educational Trust, 2020).

39 Raymond Callahan, *Churchill: Retreat from Empire* (Tunbridge Wells: D.J. Costello, 1984), p. 28.

40 Bayly and Harper, op. cit., pp. 72–76.

41 Omissi, op. cit., p. 242.

42 (Anonymous) Indian soldier in Burma, 1945. TNA/WO/208/804A (Indian traitors and fifth columnists trained by the Japanese: general survey of various organizations employed by the Japanese for espionage, sabotage and propaganda); 208/819, Appendix D, 35C (Japanese use of the Indian National Army and other organizations in the propaganda offensive against India).

43 Gowher Rizvi, *Linlithgow and India: A Study of British Policy and the Political Impasse in India, 1936–1943* (London: Royal Historical Society, 1979), p. 135.

44 Arthur Herman, *Gandhi and Churchill* (London: Arrow Books, 2009), p. 446.

45 See, for example, D.K. Palit, *Major General A.A. Rudra: His Services in Three Armies and Two World Wars* (Delhi: Reliance Publishing House, 1997), p. 252.

46 Major General S. Woodburn Kirby The War Against Japan, Volume. 1, The Loss of Singapore, (London: HMSO, 1957) p. 473. The commonly cited 130,000 casualties, with an additional 8,700 killed, is overstated by 21,000. Of this number 67,340 were Indian prisoners of war and 8,700 were battle casualties, against a total of 9,824 Japanese casualties.

47 See Perry, op. cit., pp. 102, 117; William Arthur, *The Martial Episteme: Re-Thinking Theories of Martial Race and the Modernisation of the British Indian Army in the Second World War* in Johnson, op. cit.; Prasad, *Expansion of the Armed Forces and Defence Organisation 1939–45*, Appendix 1.

48 John Connell, *Auchinleck: A Critical Biography* (London: Cassell, 1959), p. 765. The recruitment numbers cited are in OIOC L/WS/1/126 WS 1680.

49 Omissi, op. cit., p. 235.

50 D.F. Karaka, *With the Fourteenth Army* (London: Dorothy Crisp, 1945), p. 19.

51 Barkawi, op. cit., pp. 82–119.
52 Walter Reid, *Keeping the Jewel in the Crown: The British Betrayal of India* (Edinburgh: Birlinn, 2016), p. 158.
53 See B.M. Bhatia, *Famines in India: Study in Some Aspects of the Economic History of India with Special Reference to Food Problems, 1860–1947* (Delhi: Asia Publishing House, 1967), Part 1.
54 Barkawi, op. cit., p. 50.

CHAPTER 1

1   Leland Stowe, *They Shall Not Sleep* (New York: Alfred Knopf, 1944).
2   T.H. White, *The Hump* (*LIFE* Magazine, 11 September 1944).
3   Prasad (ed.), *Official History of the Indian Armed Forces in the Second World War 1939–45 Campaigns in the Eastern Theatre: The Retreat from Burma* (Calcutta: Orient Longmans, 1959), pp. 418–425.
4   John Connell, *Wavell: Supreme Commander* (London: Collins, 1969), p. 55.
5   Alfred Draper, *Dawns like Thunder: The Retreat from Burma* (London: Leo Copper, 1987), p. 10. A balanced discussion of Dorman-Smith's behaviour is in Philip Woods, *Reporting the Retreat: War Correspondents in Burma* (London: Hurst, 2016), and Alfred Wragg interviewed Dorman-Smith following the retreat. Wragg, *A Million Died* (London: Nicholson and Watson, 1943).
6   E.D. Smith, *Battle for Burma* (London: Batsford, 1979), p. 9.
7   Eve Curie, *Journey among Warriors* (London: William Heinemann, 1943), p. 323.
8   Quoted in Draper, op. cit., p. 3. See also Prasad (ed.), *The Retreat from Burma*, op. cit., p. 33.
9   TNA/CAB 79/8. 'Far East Tactical Appreciation and Report of Singapore Defence Conference', 1 January 1941.
10 Chuck Baisden, *Flying Tiger to Air Commando* (Atglen, Pennsylvania: Schiffer Publishing, Ltd, 2004).
11 TNA/Mss Eur E215/28, Dorman-Smith Papers.
12 O.D. Gallagher, *Retreat in the East* (Sydney: George G Harrap, 1943).
13 *Burma During the Japanese Occupation* (Simla: Government of India Press, 1944), p. 81.
14 617,521, according to the census of 1931. Hugh Tinker, 'A Forgotten Long March: The Indian Exodus from Burma, 1942' in *Journal of Southeast Asian Studies*, 6(1), 1–15 (March 1975).
15 The attack on Pearl Harbor fell on the same day, but as it was across the International Date Line, the date was 7 December.
16 Peter Mauch, 'Asia-Pacific, The Failure of Diplomacy 1931–1941' in Richard Bosworth and Joseph Maiolo (eds.), *The Cambridge History of the Second World War*, Vol. II (Cambridge: Cambridge University Press, 2015).
17 Guerrazzi, Amedeo Osti, 'Cultures of Total Annihilation? The German, Italian, and Japanese Armies During the Second World War' in M. Alonso, A. Kramer,

J. Rodrigo (eds.), *Fascist Warfare, 1922–1945: Aggression, Occupation, Annihilation* (Cham, Switzerland: Palgrave Macmillan, 2019), p. 128.

18   Raymond Callahan, *Burma 1942–1945* (Newark: University of Delaware Press, 1978), pp. 14–15.

19   See John Dower, *War Without Mercy: Race and Power in the Pacific War* (London: Faber and Faber, 1986).

20   Yuki Tanaka, *Hidden Horrors: Japanese War Crimes in World War II* (Oxford: Westview, 1996); Iris Chang, *The Rape of Nanking: The Forgotten Holocaust of World War II* (London: Penguin, 1996) and Lord Russell, *The Knights of Bushido* (London: Cassell, 1958).

21   Helen Foster Snow, *Inside Red China* (New York: Doubleday, 1939), pp. 316–317. Snow wrote as 'Nym Wales'.

22   Jay Taylor, 'China's Long War with Japan' in John Ferris and Evan Mawdsley (eds.), *The Cambridge History of the Second World War*, Vol. I (Cambridge: Cambridge University Press, 2015), p. 59.

23   In 1941 specifically military intelligence was gathered by others, such as Captain Shigeharu Asaeda, an accomplice of the sinister Masanobu Tsuji. John Toland, *Rising Sun: The Decline and Fall of the Japanese Empire 1936–1945* (Barnsley: Pen & Sword, 2005), p. 158.

24   Stephen C. Mercado, *The Shadow Warriors of Nakano: A History of the Imperial Japanese Army's Elite Intelligence School* (Washington: Potomac Books, 2003).

CHAPTER 2

1   Callahan, *Burma 1942–1945*, op. cit., p. 25.

2   A.P. Wavell, *Despatch by the Commander-in-Chief India on Operations in Burma from 15 December 1941 to 20 May 1942* (London: HMSO, 5 March 1948), p. 1667.

3   TNA/WO/106/2620.

4   Ian Beckett, 'Wavell' in John Keegan (ed.), *Churchill's Generals* (London: Weidenfeld and Nicholson, 1991), p. 80.

5   LHA, Brooke-Popham Papers, Wavell to Brooke-Popham, 13 November 1943.

6   For Wavell's mea culpa see LHA/Hutton/3/7 and Wavell, 'Despatch', *The London Gazette*, 5 March 1948, p. 1670.

7   J.D. Lunt, '*A Hell of a Licking': The Retreat from Burma 1941–2* (London: Collins, 1986), p. 69.

8   Connell, *Wavell*, op. cit., pp. 60–61.

9   A.P. Wavell, *Despatch by the Supreme Commander of the ABDA Area to the Combined Chiefs of Staff on the Operations in the South-West Pacific*, 15 January to 25 February 1942 (London: HMSO, 1948), p. 11.

10   Daniel Todman, *Britain's War: A New World, 1942–1947* (London: Allen Lane, 2020), p. 45.

11 Louis Allen, *Burma: The Longest War 1941–45* (London: J.M. Dent, 1984), p. 13.

12 Evocative accounts by men in these units include, inter alia, Terence Dillon, *Rangoon to Kohima* (Gloucestershire Regiment: n.d.); R.E.S. and D.A. Tanner, *Burma, 1942* (Stroud: Helion, 2009); and Gerald Fitzpatrick, *No Mandalay, No Maymyo* (Lewes: The Book Guild Ltd, 2001).

13 Lunt, op. cit., p. 54.

14 A.P. Wavell, *Despatch 15 December 1941 to 20 May 1942*, op. cit., p. 1695.

15 John Randle, *Battle Tales from Burma* (Barnsley: Pen and Sword, 2004), p. 1.

16 Alan Jeffreys, 'Training the Indian Army 1939–1945' in Alan Jeffreys and Patrick Rose (eds.), *The Indian Army, 1939–47 Experience and Development* (London: Routledge, 2017), p. 75.

17 'Military Training Pamphlet No. 9 (India): Notes on forest warfare', (Delhi, 1940) cited in Tim Moreman, *Jungle, Japanese and the Australian Army: Learning the Lessons of New Guinea* (Unpublished symposium paper, Australian War Museum, 2000).

18 Ibid., p. 2.

19 Jonathan Fenby, *Chiang Kai-Shek: China's Generalissimo and the Nation He Lost* (New York: Carroll & Graf Publishers, 2004), p. 368.

20 Quoted in Rana Mitter, *China's War with Japan 1937–1945: The Struggle for Survival* (London: Allen Lane, 2013), p. 243.

21 Ibid., p. 367.

22 It wasn't just the British armed forces that were unprepared. The United States Army 'had fewer than two hundred thousand active-duty soldiers before… 1939. The US Army of 1939 was also utterly ill equipped… Rarely in the history of civilization had so mammoth an economy and so large a population fielded so small a military.' Victor Davis Hanson, *The Second World Wars* (New York: Basic Books, 2017), p. 215.

23 At least nine of Chiang Kai-shek's divisions had been trained by a German training team up to 1938 under General von Falkenhausen.

24 H. Knatchbull-Hugessen, *Diplomat in Peace and War* (London: John Murray, 1949), p. 126. It could also be argued that it was in Britain's interest that China remain divided and weak, as it thereby presented less of a threat to British hegemony in Asia (especially to Burma and India) that might have otherwise been the case.

25 Dennys was killed in an air crash en route to Chunking on 14 March 1942.

26 Woodburn Kirby, *The War Against Japan*, Vol. II (London: HMSO, 1958), p. 16.

27 Hsi-sheng Ch'I, 'The Military Dimension, 1942–45' in James Hsiung and Steven Levine, *China's Bitter Victory: The War With Japan 1937–1945* (London: M.E. Sharpe, 1992), pp. 158–159. Chiang Kai-shek referred to them as 'the cream of Chinese troops'.

28 See Ho-Yungchi, op. cit., pp. 89–90, 130–32; and Chiang Kai-shek, *China's Destiny* (New York, 1947).

29 The size of a Chinese 'division' was around 8,000 men. At full strength, however, each boasted rarely more than 3,000 rifles, 200 light machine guns and 30–40 medium machine guns. Transport comprised one or two staff cars, half a dozen

trucks and a couple hundred ponies. The power of a Chinese battalion was about the same as that of a British company. The Fifth (55, 49 and 93 Divisions) and Sixth (96, 22 and 200 Divisions) Armies comprised therefore in total about 42,000 men, of whom 30,000 were fighting soldiers, and the remainder coolie labourers.

30   C.F. Romanus and R. Sunderland, *United States Army in World War II, China-Burma-India Theater, Stilwell's Command Problems* (Washington: Department of the Army, 1956), p. 56.

31   Quoted in Thorne, op. cit., p. 161.

32   Winston Churchill, *The Second World War, Vol. IV: The Hinge of Fate* (London: Cassell, 1951), p. 120.

33   Mitter, op. cit., p. 249.

34   TNA/CAB 65/25, 2 February 1942.

CHAPTER 3

1   LHA/Hutton/2/11.

2   B. Prasad (ed.), *The Retreat from Burma*, op. cit., pp. 82–83.

3   Hutton, 'Despatch', *The London Gazette*, 5 March 1948, p. 1685.

4   Ibid., p. 1673.

5   Commanded by Brigadier Noel Hugh-Jones.

6   John Smyth, *Leadership in War 1939–1945: The Generals in Victory and Defeat* (London: David and Charles, 1974), p. 156.

7   The military designation of the DC3 civilian airliner was the C47, although in British service they were called 'Dakotas'.

8   Ibid., pp. 161–162.

9   Major General D.K. McLeod, the GOC in 1939, wrote to India Command to the effect that he did 'not regard the land threat very seriously [from Thailand] – air attack by Japan from Siamese aerodromes is the danger.' B. Prasad (ed.), *The Retreat from Burma*, op. cit., p. 31.

10   A Japanese 'army' (two or three divisions) was roughly the same size as a British corps.

11   Joyce Lebra, *Japanese-Trained Armies in Southeast Asia* (New York: Columbia University Press, 1977), p. 45.

12   Masanobu Tsuji, *Japan's Greatest Victory, Britain's Worst Defeat* (New York: Sarpedon Press, 1993). This was first published in Tokyo in 1952 as *Shonan: The Hinge of Fate*, a play on the title of Winston Churchill's own history of this period of the war. Tsuji was one of the most enigmatic characters of the war. A legendary and feared figure in the Japanese Army since the beginning of the China 'incident' in 1932, he was a military fanatic, war criminal and, on one occasion at least, a cannibal. See Allen, op. cit., pp. 381–382 and Ian Ward, *The Killer They Called a God* (Singapore: Media Masters, 1992), pp. 255–256.

CHAPTER 4

1   John Hedley, *Jungle Fighter* (Brighton: Tom Donovan, 1996), p. 6.
2   Allen, op. cit., p. 27.
3   Tim Carew, *The Longest Retreat: The Burma Campaign 1942* (London: Hamish Hamilton, 1969), pp. 67–69.
4   George Forty, *Japanese Army Handbook 1939–1945* (Stroud: Sutton Publishing, 1999), p. 126.
5   Prasad (ed.), *The Retreat from Burma*, op. cit., p. 105. See Hedley, op. cit., p. 11.
6   Ibid., p. 105.
7   Wavell, 'Despatch', *The London Gazette*, 5 March 1948, p. 1671.
8   Quoted in Connell, *Wavell*, op. cit., p. 122.
9   Tatsuro Izumiya, *The Minami Organ* (Rangoon: Rangoon University Press, 1985).
10 John Cady, *A History of Modern Burma* (London: Cornell University Press, 1958), pp. 440–441.
11 Fujiwara Iwaichi, *F: Kikan: Japanese Army Intelligence Operations in Southeast Asia during World War II*, trans. Akashi Yoji (Hong Kong: Heinemann Asia, 1983).
12 Ba Maw was jailed in 1941 for sedition when challenging Britain to describe how supporting Britain against the Axis would bring about the very self-determination it was supposed to be fighting for. See John Toland, op. cit., p. 448. Ba Maw tells his story ('Wartime Traveller') in Robert Taylor, *Marxism and Resistance in Burma 1942–1945* (Athens: Ohio University Press, 1984), pp. 99–303.
13 Thant Myint-U, *The River of Lost Footsteps: Histories of Burma* (New York: Farrar, Straus and Giroux, 2006), p. 232.
14 Ibid., p. 233.
15 Quoted in Joyce Lebra, *Japanese-Trained Armies in Southeast Asia* (New York: Columbia University Press, 1977), p. 44.
16 Cady, op. cit., pp. 432–436.
17 Smyth, *Leadership in War*, op. cit., p. 155.
18 Connell, *Wavell*, op. cit., p. 117.
19 Major General Sir John Kennedy, *The Business of War* (London: Hutchinson, 1957), p. 197.
20 Kirby, Vol. II, op. cit., p. 33.
21 Curie, op. cit., p. 321.
22 Perry, op. cit., pp. 104–105.
23 Cowan had only weeks before been the Director of Military Training in New Delhi. One of his last pronouncements in that post was that 17 Division was unfit to fight a first-class opponent. See Callahan, *Burma 1942–45*, op. cit., pp. 35–36.
24 John Smyth, *Before the Dawn* (London: Cassell, 1957), p. 167.
25 Curie, op. cit., p. 321.
26 LHA/Hutton/2/13, p. 60.
27 Prasad (ed.), *The Retreat from Burma*, op. cit., p. 137.
28 Kirby, Vol II op. cit., p. 46.

29 Curie, op. cit., p. 323.

30 LHA/Hutton/2/13.

31 TNA/WO/106/2681/174.

32 Smyth, *Leadership in War*, op. cit., p. 164.

33 Quoted in Prasad (ed.), *The Retreat from Burma*, op. cit., p. 145.

34 LHA/Hutton/3/1/1.

35 LHA/Hutton/3/6, p. 7. This comment was later incorporated in Wavell's 1948 'Despatch'.

36 The DMO was Major General John Kennedy. TNA/WO/106/2681/151B. See Kennedy, op. cit.

37 Quoted in Connell, *Wavell*, op. cit., pp. 180–181.

38 Quoted in Prasad (ed.), *The Retreat from Burma*, op. cit., p. 149.

39 Ibid., p. 153.

40 Smyth, *Leadership in War*, op. cit., p. 166.

41 Smyth mentions none of this in his 1974 *apologia*, commenting merely that the 'withdrawal on the 20th and 21st reflected the greatest credit on the brigade and battalion commanders... The brigade leapfrogged back through one another and by the morning of the 20th were clear of the Japanese division which had been opposing us on the Bilin'. Ibid., p. 168. The full story is told in Ian Lyall Grant and Kazuo Tamayama's *Burma 1942: The Japanese Invasion* (Chichester: The Zampi Press, 1999).

42 Roy Hudson, 'Disaster at the Sittang Bridge – Burma 1942' in *The Royal Engineers Journal*, Vol. 106, No. 1 (April 1992), pp. 26–33.

43 TNA/WO/106/2681/163.

44 TNA/WO/106/2681/165.

CHAPTER 5

1   Hutton had also gone through an alarming experience that must have shaken him greatly. On a flight to Lashio on 2 February to confer with Chiang Kai-shek, Hutton crashed in his Lysander into the jungle and his pilot was killed. Neither Wavell, Smyth nor Hutton were at their physical best during this campaign.

2   Lunt, op. cit., p. 155.

3   Smyth, *Leadership in War*, op. cit., p. 171.

4   Lunt, op. cit., p. 135.

5   Hedley, op. cit., p. 15.

6   TNA/WO/106/2681/188.

7   TNA/WO/106/2681/180.

8   TNA/WO/106/2681/201.

9   Major General H.L. Davies, 'A Background to the First Burma Campaign 1941–2' in *The Army Quarterly* (1956), p. 221.

10 TNA/WO/106/2681/171c.

11 TNA/WO/106/2681/172.

12   Connell, *Wavell*, op. cit., p. 181.

13   Churchill, op. cit., p. 146.

14   TNA/WO/106/2681/182b.

15   LHA/Hutton/2/13.

16   TNA/WO/106/2681/189. Hartley apologized to Hutton in a signal dated 26 February. See LHA/Hutton/2/13.

17   Later, when Hartley had read a draft of Hutton's despatch, he wrote a personal letter to Hutton thanking him for laying out the reality of Burma's military situation with such clarity, as these difficulties were not obvious to those remote from Burma at the time. LHA/Hutton.

18   Brigadier J.H. Anstice, 7 Queen's Own Hussars (QOH) and 2 Royal Tank Regiment (2RTR).

19   Davies, op. cit., p. 222.

20   LHA, Personal Record, Papers of Lieutenant General Sir Thomas Hutton.

21   Ian Beckett, 'Wavell' in Keegan (ed.), *Churchill's Generals*, (London: Weidenfeld and Nicholson, 1991), p. 83.

22   TNA/WO 106/2681/211.

23   LHA/Hutton/2/13, p. 64.

24   Maurice Collis, *Last and First in Burma* (London: Faber and Faber, 1948), p. 105. Battersby was a member of the Indian Police. He remained in India after 1942 and joined SOE. See Richard Duckett, *The Special Operations Executive in Burma: Jungle Warfare and Intelligence Gathering in World War II* (London: I.B. Taurus, 2018).

CHAPTER 6

1   Kirby, Vol II., , op. cit., p. 86.

2   Compton Mackenzie, *Eastern Epic Vol. 1: Defence* (London: Chatto and Windus, 1951), p. 456.

3   Wavell, *Despatch 15 December 1941 to 20 May 1942*, op. cit., p. 1672.

4   The modern location of the Commonwealth War Graves Cemetery.

5   TNA/WO/106/2681/229. Alexander's draft reply, which was terser still, was never sent.

6   Initially two divisions with 35,000 men, the arrival of 18 and 56 Divisions added a further 15,000 men to Iida's army. Jack Belden, *Retreat with Stilwell* (London: Cassell and Co, 1943), pp. 157–158.

7   Tinker, op cit., pp. 1–15. 'Before the fall of Rangoon, 70,000 Indians were evacuated by sea to India. In April and May 1942, 4,801 Indians were flown out of north Burma by air. Otherwise, the whole exodus took place overland, either via Arakan to Chittagong or via the Chindwin valley to Manipur, or – for the last stragglers – via the northern passes to Ledo and other termini in north Assam. The trek by land was undertaken by at least 400,000 refugees; the figure might have been 450,000, or more.'

8   See, for example, W.G Burchett, *Trek Back from Burma* (Allahabad: Kitabistan Publishers, n.d); Douglas Lackersteen, *Diamonds in the Dust: Tales of the*

Evacuation of Burma (Allahabad: Kitabistan Publishers, 1944); Felicity Goodall, *Exodus Burma* (Stroud: The History Press, 2011); Stephen Brookes, *Through the Jungle of Death* (New York: John Wiley and Sons, 2000).

9 See Andrew Martin, *Flight by Elephant: The Untold Story of World War II's Most Daring Jungle Rescue* (London: Fourth Estate, 2013).

10 Davies, op. cit., p. 225.

11 General George C Marshall was Chief of Staff of the United States Army.

12 David Rooney, *Stilwell: The Patriot* (London: Chatham Publishing, 2005).

13 Brigadier General Ho-Yungchi, *The Big Circle* (New York: The Exposition Press, 1948), p. 4.

14 John Plating, *The Hump: America's Strategy for Keeping China in World War II* (College Station, Texas: Texas A&M University Press, 2011).

15 IWM/P149/Brigadier L.F. Field.

16 John Paton Davies, *China Hand: An Autobiography* (Philadelphia: University of Pennsylvania Press, 2012).

17 Romanus and Sunderland, op. cit., p. 120.

18 Robert Lyman, *Slim, Master of War* (London: Constable, 2004); Robert Lyman, *Slim* (Oxford: Osprey Publishing, 2011); Ronald Lewin, *Slim: The Standardbearer* (London: Leo Cooper, 1976); Geoffrey Evans, *Slim as Military Commander* (London: B.T. Batsford, 1969).

19 A Japanese regiment was the same size as a British and Indian brigade.

20 Slim, *Defeat into Victory* (London: Cassell, 1956), pp. 535–536. Unless otherwise noted, all subsequent references to Slim are taken from *Defeat into Victory*.

21 Ho-Yungchi, op. cit., pp. 7–10.

22 Ibid., p. 6.

23 Ibid., p. 11.

CHAPTER 7

1 Theodore White (ed.), *The Stilwell Papers* (New York: William Morrow and Company, 1948), p. 75.

2 TNA/File 283A WO/106/2682.

3 Lunt, op. cit., p. 206.

4 TNA/File 276A WO/106/2682.

5 TNA/File 293A WO/106/2682.

6 TNA/File 293 WO/106/2682.

7 Hedley, op. cit., p. 26.

8 Grant and Tamayama, op. cit., p. 244.

9 Ibid., p. 249.

10 Ho-Yungchi, op. cit., p. 3.

11 Pronounced '*Soon Lee-Run*'.

12 Quoted in Lewin, op. cit., p. 93.

13 Prasad (ed.), *The Retreat from Burma*, op. cit., p. 296.

14 Dr Peter Chung Chieh conducted extensive interviews of Chinese soldiers for his book (in Mandarin) on Sun Lijen: *Biography of General Sun Li-jen* (Mongolia: University Press of Inner Mongolia, 2000). Interviewees included Colonel Liu, the Regimental Commander, together with his deputy, Lieutenant Colonel Hu Dehua. All insisted that they had reached Twingon first thing on the morning of 19 April. See Dr Chieh, 'Remember the Chinese Expeditionary Force Soldiers', a paper presented to a symposium to commemorate the 70th anniversary of the end of the Sino–Japanese War (Taipei: National Defense University, 23 July 2015).

15 Romanus and Sunderland, op. cit., p. 126.

16 Ho-Yungchi, op. cit., p. 17.

17 Bryan Perrett, *Tank Tracks in Burma* (London: Robert Hale, 1978), p. 66.

CHAPTER 8

1 The horror of this journey is told, inter alia, by Stephen Brookes, *Through the Jungle of Death* (New York: John Wiley and Sons, 2000).

2 Kirby, Vol. II, op. cit., p. 199.

3 Quoted in Lunt, op. cit., p. 242.

4 This tank made the return crossing with the victorious Fourteenth Army in late 1944, two and a half years later, its turret stripped off, serving as the command vehicle for the Indian Army's 7 Light Cavalry.

5 CAC, File 3/9 Slim Papers.

6 Kirby, Vol. II, op. cit., p. 210.

7 Grant and Tamayama, op. cit., p. 319.

8 The Stilwell Papers.

9 Calvert, *Slim*, op. cit., p. 31.

10 Grant and Tamayama, op. cit., p. 233.

11 LHA, Cowan to Hutton, 31 May 1942, Hutton mss, 3/2.

12 Raymond Callahan, 'Were the Sepoy Generals Any Good?' in Kaushik Roy (ed.), *War and Society in Colonial India* (New Delhi: Oxford University Press, 2006), p. 315.

13 Alexander's Despatch, *The London Gazette*, 5 March 1948.

14 These failures were replicated throughout his memoirs. See Callahan, 'Did Winston Matter?', op. cit., pp. 66–67 and Cat Wilson, *Churchill on the Far East in the Second World War* (Basingstoke: Palgrave Macmillan, 2014).

CHAPTER 9

1 Peter Ward Fay, *The Forgotten Army: India's Armed Struggle for Independence 1942–1945* (University of Michigan Press, 1995), p. 84.

2 Any discussion of political matters in the pre-war professional Indian Army, like that of the British Army then and now, was an absolute no-no, especially in terms

of articulating a nationalist voice. Cohen, op. cit., pp. 132–137. However, Mohan Singh was to claim after the war that a significant percentage of Indian Commissioned Officers were closet nationalists, secretly cheering on every Axis victory, op. cit., p. 149.

3   Cohen, op. cit., p. 149.

4   Fay, op cit., p. 415.

5   James, op. cit., p. 236. Nehru, for instance, had in 1929 urged the army to remain loyal to the British until independence had been achieved. These convictions, however, found themselves challenged by men captured in Malaya and Singapore, as the case of Colonel P.K. Sahgal demonstrated. Cohen, op. cit., p. 153.

6   Quoted in Farwell, op. cit., p. 337.

7   Omissi, op. cit., p. 236. It's a point made eloquently also by Roger Beaumont, op. cit., pp. 196–198.

8   'Men began to mix freely and started eating together… It was perhaps for the first time in our known history of thousands of years that we became true Indians and rose over and above the fetters of castism and communalism.' General Mohan Singh, quoted in Cohen, op. cit., p. 150.

9   Joyce Lebra, *Jungle Alliance: Japan and the Indian National Army* (Singapore: Asia Pacific Press, 1971); K.K. Ghosh, *The Indian National Army: The Second Front of the Indian Freedom Movement* (Meerut: Meenakshi Prakashan, 1969).

CHAPTER 10

1   The similarities with Wehrmacht operational doctrine in Poland and France in 1939 and 1940 are striking. It seems probable that these were lessons brought back from a six-month tour of Europe, escorted by the Wehrmacht, undertaken by Yamashita and others in 1941. Yamashita's report on his return recommended dramatic improvements to the Japanese Army to develop the capabilities he had seen demonstrated by the Wehrmacht in France.

2   Daniel Hedinger, *Fascist Warfare and the Axis Alliance: From Blitzkrieg to Total War* in M. Alonso, A. Kramer, J. Rodrigo (eds.), *Fascist Warfare, 1922–1945: Aggression, Occupation, Annihilation* (Cham, Switzerland: Palgrave Macmillan, 2019), p. 128.

3   Hutton's comments on this aptitude are at TNA/WO/106/2681/164. See also Lunt, op. cit., p. 202.

4   Work on the plan began in August 1940, according to Professor Kyoichi Tachikawa, *General Yamashita and His Style of Leadership* in Bond (ed.), *British and Japanese Military Leadership in the Far Eastern War, 1941–1945* (London: Frank Cass, 2004), p. 76.

5   Tsuji, op. cit., p. 3.

6   Ashley Jackson, 'The British Empire 1939–1945' in Bosworth and Maiolo (eds.), Vol. II, op. cit., p. 573.

7 But not necessarily *real* independence. Tōjō told the *Japanese Diet* following the fall of Singapore, 'The objective in the Great East Asia War is founded on the exalted ideals of the founding of the empire and it will enable all the nations and peoples of Greater East Asia to enjoy life and to establish a new order of coexistence and co-prosperity on the basis of justice with Japan as the nucleus.' John Toland, op. cit., pp. 277, 447, 455–456. Japan granted Burma independence on 1 August 1943.

8 Dorman-Smith to Leo Amery, 8 March 1942, Dorman-Smith Papers, British Library, E215/1.

9 Roger Beaumont, *Sword of the Raj: The British Army in India, 1747–1947* (New York: The Bobbs-Merrill Company, 1977), p. 194.

10 David Dilks (ed.), *The Diaries of Sir Alexander Cadogan 1938–1945* (London: Cassell, 1971).

11 *'Chips': The Diaries of Sir Henry Channon* (London: Weidenfeld & Nicolson, 1967).

12 Martin Gilbert, *Road to Victory, Winston S. Churchill 1941–1945* (London: Heinemann, 1986), p. 72.

13 Charles Wilson (Lord Moran), *Churchill at War 1940–45* (London: Constable, 1966), p. 27.

14 Dilks, op. cit., p. 433.

15 Papers of Stanley Hornbeck, Hoover Institute, quoted in Christopher Thorne, *Allies of a Kind: The United States, Britain and the War Against Japan 1941–1945* (London: Hamish Hamilton, 1978), p. 155.

16 The evidence for this change in attitude is considerable. See Thorne, op. cit., pp. 209–223.

17 Piers Brendon, *The Decline and Fall of the British Empire 1781–1997* (London: Jonathan Cape, 2008), pp. 432–433.

18 Paul Kratoska and Ken'Ichi Goto, 'Japanese Occupation of Southeast Asia, 1941–45' in Bosworth and Maiolo (eds.), Vol. II, op. cit., pp. 533–534.

19 H.P. Willmott, *Empires in the Balance: Japanese and Allied Pacific Strategies to April 1942* (Annapolis: Naval Institute Press, 1982), p. 436.

CHAPTER 11

1 The road had been converted from a mule track by the indentured labour of thousands of workers diverted from the Indian Tea Association in May 1942. See Iris Macfarlane and Alan Macfarlane, *The Empire of Tea* (New York: The Overlook Press, 2004), pp. 216–219.

2 F.A.E. Crew, *The Army Medical Services: Campaigns*, Vol. V (History of the Second World War; United Kingdom Medical series) (London: HMSO, 1956), p. 617.

3 Annual rainfall reaches 470 inches in the Khasi Hills in what was western Assam (now Meghalaya), with 200 in Arakan during the monsoon, compared with that in Britain of 30–33 inches. Rainfall of 15 inches in 24 hours has been recorded.

4   1 Battalion, Patiala Infantry (the first of two battalions of the state forces of the Maharaja of Patiala); 1 Battalion Assam Regiment; 1 Battalion, Seaforth Highlanders and 17/14 Punjab.

5   Today, Kohima is the capital town of Nagaland, which became a state in independent India in 1963.

6   *Vice Admiral The Earl Mountbatten of Burma Report to the Combined Chiefs of Staff by the Supreme Allied Commander South-East Asia 1943–1945* (London: HMSP, 1951), p. 12.

7   Robert Lyman, *Among the Headhunters* (Boston: Da Capo, 2016).

8   Comprising 146 Regiment, Royal Armoured Corps (9 Duke of Wellington's Regiment); 19 Squadron, KGVO Lancers; 45 Cavalry Regiment; 2/4 Bombay Grenadiers. In 1942 146 RAC was equipped with Valentines, the remainder with armoured cars and trucks.

9   In IV Corps, 37 Brigade comprised 3/5, 3/3 and 3/10 Gurkha Rifles. At the time 123 Brigade comprised 1/15 Punjab Regiment, 8/10 Baluch Regiment and 10 Battalion, Lancashire Fusiliers.

10   Appendix 15 of Vol. II of the *British Official History* calculated the strength of Burma Corps on 21 April 1942 to be 13,700 British, 37,000 Indian and 12,300 Burmese. Most of the Burmese were discharged to their homes once Assam had been reached, giving a troop state in May of c. 50,000.

11   Willmott, op. cit., p. 434.

12   Both 19 and 20 Indian Divisions had three brigades, so each had an infantry strength of c. 7,500 men.

13   Wavell had also commanded 2 Division, between 1935 and 1937.

14   See Raymond Callahan, 'Did Winston Matter?', op. cit., p. 63.

15   Ronald Lewin, *Slim: The Standard Bearer* (London: Leo Cooper, 1976), p. 105.

16   Wavell, *The Good Soldier*, op. cit., p. 33.

17   The new GOC of 19 Division, appointed in October 1942, was Major General 'Pete' Rees.

18   Lloyd had commanded 16 Indian Infantry Brigade in General Richard O'Connor's Western Desert Force in their victories against the Italians in late 1940 and early 1941 and went on to play a distinguished role in the Syrian campaign in June and July 1941. Bernard Fergusson described him as a 'fire-eater' and Major General Sir Edward Spears described him as 'first-class'. See Bernard Fergusson, *Wavell, Portrait of a Soldier* (London: Collins, 1961), p. 57, and Edward Spears, *Fulfilment of a Mission: The Spears Mission to Syria and Lebanon, 1941–1944* (London: Leo Cooper, 1977), p. 110.

CHAPTER 12

1   Jeffreys, *Approach to Battle*, op. cit., pp. 130–154.

2   TNA/WO 32/11750.

3   The 'box' concept had a limited lifespan in North Africa, as experience demonstrated that they became magnets for superior and concentrated enemy air, artillery and anti-

tank firepower. In the 'close' (i.e. heavily jungled or forested) terrain of eastern India and Burma, however, the air-supplied box was to prove the perfect solution to the problem of infiltration.

4   TNA/WO 203/5716.
5   Grant and Tamayama, op. cit., p. 339.
6   Stephen Bull, *World War II Jungle Warfare Tactics* (Oxford: Osprey Publishing, 2007), p. 10.
7   Alan Jeffreys, *The British Army in the Far East, 1941–45* (Oxford: Osprey Publishing, 2005), p. 12.
8   David Wilson, *The Sum of Things* (Staplehurst: Spellmount, 2001), p. 84.
9   Oriental and India Office Collections, British Library, L/WS/1/1371, Report of the Infantry Committee, 1–14 June 1943.
10 Alan Jeffreys, 'The Officer Corps and the Training of the Indian Army' in Kaushik Roy (ed.), *The Indian Army in the Two World Wars* (Leiden: Brill, 2012), p. 298.
11 Bull, op. cit., p. 22.
12 The re-purposed 1 Burma Division.
13 LHA, Messervy and Gracey Papers.
14 LHA, Gracey Papers 1/4.
15 Marston, op. cit., p. 83.
16 Anthony Brett-James, *Ball of Fire: The Fifth Indian Division in the Second World War* (Aldershot: Gale and Polden, 1951), p. 252.

CHAPTER 13

1   TNA/PREM/PREM 3. 143/9; 142/6. Churchill to Wavell 12 June and 6 July 1942 and to COS 4 and 8 April 1942.
2   Connell, *Wavell*, op. cit., p. 236.
3   Mason, op. cit., p. 225.
4   Ibid., pp. 493–494.
5   Wavell to GIGS, quoted in Bisheshwar Prasad (ed.), *The Reconquest of Burma, Vol. 1* (Calcutta: Orient Longmans, 1958), p. 13. We know in retrospect that Wavell had in mind to use Brigadier Orde Wingate, whom he had known in East Africa, in some guerrilla-type capacity in Burma.
6   Telegram from Chiefs of Staff to Wavell on 9 May 1942. This was followed up by a more detailed appreciation on 16 May 1942 (Chiefs of Staff Committee paper No. 42, S.5) cited in Prasad, *Vol. 1*, op. cit., p. 20.
7   Wavell's textual comments dated 4 June 1942, quoted in Prasad, *Vol. 1*, op. cit., p. 20.
8   5 Division spent three months in India from August 1942 following the invasion of Madagascar before being lost to India Command by being diverted to the Middle East.
9   At this stage the lack of transport aircraft made thought of transport by air a mere pipe dream.
10 Connell, *Wavell*, op. cit., pp. 237–238.

11   Telegram to Wavell from Churchill (using the Air Ministry teleprinter for security) dated 12 June 1942 cited in Prasad, *Vol. 1*, op. cit., p. 21. As late as 30 September the Chief of the Imperial Staff, General Alan Brooke, could confide to his diary, when discussing Wavell's plans to attack Akyab in 1942: 'I don't like the idea of Akyab as an isolated operation without the full-scale operation for Rangoon, Moulmein, etc, for which we are not yet strong enough.' Danchev and Todman (eds.), *War Diaries 1939–1945: Field Marshal Lord Alanbrooke* (London: Weidenfeld and Nicholson, 2001), p. 325.

12   Connell, *Wavell*, op. cit., p. 239.

13   Prasad, *Vol. 1*, op. cit., p. 22.

14   See Robert Lyman, *Slim, Master of War*, op. cit., pp. 74–75; Duncan Anderson, 'Slim' in Keegan (ed.), *Churchill's Generals*, op. cit., p. 305.

CHAPTER 14

1   Reid, op. cit., p. 131.

2   Brendon, op. cit., p. 395.

3   James, op. cit., p. 236.

4   Gowher Rizvi, *Linlithgow and India: A Study of British Policy and the Political Impasse in India, 1936–1943* (London: Royal Historical Society, 1979), p. 130.

5   Raghavan, op. cit., p. 272.

6   Oriental and India Office Collections, British Library, L/WS/1/1337 31 August 1942, quoted in Johnson, op. cit., pp. 11–12. See also Jonathan Fennell, *Fighting the People's War: The British and Commonwealth Armies and the Second World War* (Cambridge; Cambridge University Press), pp. 328–329; Callahan, 'Did Winston Matter?', op. cit., p. 64.

7   Callahan, *Churchill*, op. cit., pp. 116, 208.

8   Letter to Smuts, 12 February 1942, quoted in Thorne, op. cit., p. 157.

9   The Labour Party's Clement Attlee became Deputy Prime Minister and Secretary of State for Dominion Affairs, a role that significantly strengthened the Labour Party's influence on Britain's imperial policy.

10   Callahan, *Churchill*, op. cit., p. 116.

11   Jawaharlal Nehru, *Unity of India, Collected Writings, 1937–1940* (London: Lindsay Drummond, 1942), p. 36, quoted in Brendon, op. cit., pp. 395–396.

12   Reid., op. cit., p. 153.

13   Callahan, *Churchill*, op. cit., p. 208. Churchill's attitude to India is described pp. 27–28, 34–35, 38–39, 185–188.

CHAPTER 15

1   Theodore White (ed.), *The Stilwell Papers* op. cit., p. 183.

2   David Rooney *Stilwell* (London: Pan Books, 1973), p. 80.

3   Adrian Carton de Wiart, *Happy Odyssey* (London: Jonathan Cape, 1950), p. 240.

4   White (ed.), *The Stilwell Papers* op. cit., p. 212.

CHAPTER 16

1   LHA, Irwin to Wavell, 14 November 1942, Irwin Papers.
2   Ibid., 8 December 1942.
3   Quoted in Tamayama and Nunneley, *Tales by Japanese Soldiers of the Burma Campaign 1942–45* (London: Cassell, 2000), pp. 124–125.
4   Sir Frank Fox, *The Royal Inniskilling Fusiliers in the Second World War* (Aldershot: Gale and Polden Ltd, 1951), p. 48.
5   LHA, Wavell to Irwin, 26 March 1943, Irwin Papers.
6   Wavell's 'Despatch', *The London Gazette* op. cit., p. 2512.
7   LHA, Irwin to Wavell, 9 March 1943, Irwin Papers.
8   LHA, Irwin to Wavell, 9 March 1943, Irwin Papers.
9   Ibid.

CHAPTER 17

1   Since the beginning of the campaign Lloyd's original 14 Indian Division had been inflated to include 4, 23, 36 and 71 Indian Brigades and 6 British Brigade.
2   Ibid.
3   Ibid., p. 154.
4   LHA, Irwin to Wavell, 20 March 1943, Irwin Papers.
5   LHA, Wavell to Irwin, 22 March 1943, Irwin Papers.
6   Ibid.
7   Kirby, Vol. II, op. cit., p. 341.
8   LHA, Irwin to Wavell, 9 April 1943, Irwin Papers.
9   Quoted in Ronald Lewin, *The Chief: Field Marshal Lord Wavell, Commander-in-Chief and Viceroy, 1939–1947* (London: Hutchinson, 1980), p. 211. Official British casualties were 5,057: 916 killed, 2,889 wounded and 1,252 missing.
10 Allen, op. cit., p. 96.
11 LHA, Irwin to General Hartley, 8 May 1943, Irwin Papers.
12 LHA, Churchill to Brooke, 21 May 1943, Alanbrooke Correspondence.
13 'Jungle Jinks' (A typed history of the Burma Campaign prepared by HQ 12 Army in 1945, a copy of which is in the author's possession), Part 1, p. 5.
14 John Masters, *The Road Past Mandalay* (London: Michael Joseph, 1961), p. 128.

CHAPTER 18

1   A guerrilla group made up from British officers and loyal villagers, V Force operated to the west of the Chindwin. In 1943 another group was created – Z Force – for the purpose of gathering field intelligence to the east of the Chindwin in support of 14 Army in Manipur.
2   13 Battalion, The King's Regiment; 3/2 Gurkha Rifles; 142 Commando Company (made up in the main of Calvert's Bush Warfare School in Maymyo) and 2 Burma Rifles.

3   Smith, op. cit., p. 10.
4   David Rooney, *Wingate and the Chindits: Redressing the Balance* (London: Cassell, 1994), pp. 100–101.
5   Smith, op. cit., p. 10.
6   Quoted in Penderel Moon (ed.), *Wavell: The Viceroy's Journal* (London: Oxford University Press, 1973), p. 43. Bernard Fergusson wrote the bestselling *Beyond the Chindwin* in 1945 and although respectful of Wingate's forceful personality and achievements nevertheless concluded that 'the truth was simply not in him', supporting the conclusions of the Official History in the 1950s. See Leonard Mosley, *The Story of Wingate: Gideon Goes to War* (London: Arthur Barker, 1955), p. 223; Trevor Royle, *Orde Wingate: Irregular Soldier* (London: Weidenfeld and Nicholson, 1995), p. 152 and Derek Tulloch *Wingate in Peace and War* (London: The History Book Club, 1972), p. 255.
7   A.J. Barker, *The March on Delhi* (London: Faber and Faber, 1963), p. 62.
8   British Library, IOR/L/MIL/17/5/4270.
9   Peter Mead, *Orde Wingate and the Historians* (Braunton: Merlin Books Ltd., 1987), p. 171; Rooney, *Wingate*, op. cit., p. 217; Christopher Sykes, *Orde Wingate* (London; Collins, 1959), pp. 334–335; Royle, *Orde Wingate*, op. cit., p. 218.
10 Tulloch, op. cit., pp. 16–17.
11 Quoted in Brigadier W.E. Underhill, *The Royal Leicestershire Regiment 17th Foot* (Aldershot: Gale and Polden, 1957), p. 193 and Michael Hickey, *The Unforgettable Army* (Tunbridge Wells: Spellmount Ltd., 1992), p. 85.
12 Leonard Mosley, *The Story of Wingate: Gideon Goes to War* (London: Arthur Barker, 1955), pp. 159, 168.
13 Connell, *Auchinleck*, op. cit., p. 744.
14 Rooney, *Wingate*, op. cit., p. 13.
15 Mosley, op. cit., pp. 167–168.
16 Kirby, Vol. II., op. cit., p. 404.
17 Thorne, op. cit., p. 298.
18 Churchill to Ismay, 24 July 1943, NA PREM 3 143/8.
19 Connell, *Auchinleck*, op. cit., p. 741.
20 Ibid., p. 745.
21 Connell, *Auchinleck*, op. cit., pp. 737–748.

CHAPTER 19

1   See Appendix 4. By the end of 1942 recruitment since September 1939 had reached the astonishing number of 1,348,000, with an authorized strength by the end of 1942 of 1,226,000.
2   Oriental and India Office Collections, British Library, L/WS/1/939. GHQ India, 'Report on the Morale of the Army in India, Nov. 1942–Jan. 1943; Feb.–Apr. 1943; May–July 1943'.

3   British infantry reinforcements were trained elsewhere, by 52 Brigade at Budni in Bhopal State.

4   Tim Moreman, *The Jungle, the Japanese and the British Commonwealth Armies at War* (London: Frank Cass, 2005), pp. 80–81.

5   Followers were non-combatant personal and public servants of a battalion or regiment, such as a cooks, saddlers, laundrymen, mess waiters and sweepers, who traditionally accompanied the Indian Army to war.

6   Jeffreys, 'Training the Indian Army', op. cit., p. 84.

7   Marston, op. cit., p. 96.

8   Johnson, op. cit.

9   Despatch by Field Marshal Sir Claude Auchinleck, (The London Gazette, 27 April 1948), 'Operations in the Indo-Burma Theatre based on India from 21 June 1943 to 15 November 1943), pp. 2651 and 2666.

10 Connell, *Auchinleck*, op. cit., p. 765.

11 Jeffreys, *Approach to Battle*, op. cit., pp. 163–168.

12 Jeffreys, 'Training the Indian Army', op. cit., p. 70.

13 Jeffreys, *The British Army in the Far East*, op. cit., p. 14.

14 JRL, Auchinleck to General Alan Brooke 18 September 1943, File 1037, Auchinleck Papers, John Rylands Library, Manchester.

15 JRL, Auchinleck to Brooke, 18 September 1943, File 1037, Auchinleck Papers.

16 Auchinleck, Despatch, op. cit., para. 2666.

17 BA/File C11. Mountbatten took responsibility from Auchinleck for combat operations on 16 November 1944, Auchinleck having fulfilled the role since late June.

18 Moreman, *The Jungle*, op. cit., pp. 10–14.

19 Ibid., p. 10.

20 Despatch on operations in the India Command January 1st to 20th June 1943 (Field Marshal Viscount Wavell) (New Delhi, 1944), p. 11.

21 Except for one, who was killed in New Guinea.

22 Military Mission to India and the Pacific. Memorandum by the Chief of the Imperial General Staff, 7th June 1943, PRO WO 193/836.

23 TNA/WO 106/5031, Lethbridge to Evetts, 31 Oct. 1943.

24 Brigadier John Edward Lloyd, CBE, DSO, MC & Bar, had served with the Indian Army for four years in the 1920s after service with the Australian Army in the Great War.

25 Moreman, *The Jungle*, op. cit., p. 6.

26 TNA/WO 203/2669A. Report by General Sir Claude J.E. Auchinleck, Commander-in-Chief in India covering the period 16th November 1943–31st May 1944.

27 The Australians deployed five divisions in New Guinea between March 1943 and April 1944, losing 1,200 dead but killing about 35,000 Japanese. Peter Dean, *MacArthur's Coalition* (Lincoln, Nebraska: University of Kansas Press, 2018).

28 Moreman, *The Jungle*, op. cit., p. 12.

29 Perry, op. cit., p. 111.

CHAPTER 20

1   As but one example, in late 1944 and early 1945 14 Army built 541 10-ton wooden barges on the banks of the Chindwin at Kalewa, to facilitate the crossings by IV Corps of the Irrawaddy in February 1945.

2   B. Prasad, (ed.), *Indian War Economy (Supply, Industry & Finance), Official History Of The Indian Armed Forces In The Second World War 1939–45* (Delhi: Combined Inter-Services Historical Section, 1962), (pp. 3–5; 9; 34; 130–131; 139–144; 146–147; 241–252; 255.

3   CAC, File 3/2, Slim Papers.

4   See Map No. 2 Assam – Lines of Communication. Gordon Dunlop, *Military Economics, Culture and Logistics in the Burma Campaign* (London: Pickering & Chatto, 2009), p. 37.

5   Julian Thompson, *The Lifeblood of War: Logistics in Armed Conflict* (London: Brasseys, 1991), pp. 90–91.

6   Kirby, Vol. II, op. cit., pp. 47–48.

7   During the interregnum between 1941 and 1943 he was C-in-C Middle East, followed by a period on half-pay, unemployed.

8   Marston, *A Force Transformed*. See Marston, *Phoenix from the Ashes: The Indian Army in the Burma Campaign*, (Westport, Ct; Praeger, 2003), 47–50; 218–220; 222–233.

9   *British Way and Purpose* (The Directorate of Army Education), 1944.

10 This target was largely a guess and was progressively scaled back in the following two years.

11 Ashley Jackson, *The British Empire and the Second World War* (London: Hambledon Continuum, 2006), p. 366.

12 The first Spitfires, which could outperform the Mitsubishi A6M 'Zero' fighter, arrived in SEAC in late 1943. K.S. Nair, *The Forgotten Few: The Indian Air Force in World War II* (Noida, Utter Pradesh: Harper Collins, 2019).

13 Mountbatten of Burma, Admiral the Earl, *Report to the Combined Chiefs of Staff, 1943–1945* (HMSO, London, 1951). 11 Army Group became Allied Land Forces South East Asia in November 1944.

14 Mountbatten's Report, op. cit., p. 15.

15 Dunlop, op. cit., p. 61.

16 Ibid., p. 64.

17 See Roderick Matthews, *Flaws in the Jewel: Challenging the Myths of British India* (Harper Collins India, 2010). The Raj was acutely concerned about the loss of life during times of famine. During the 1873 famine in Bengal and Bihar, for example, only 23 lives were lost, but at a cost of £6 million. This was because of the lessons learned in the Orissa famine of 1866, when dilatory action caused high mortality. In the 20 years that followed the institution of the provincial Famine Codes in 1876, there was no loss of life.

18   Lawrence James, *Raj: The Making and Unmaking of British India* (London: Little
      Brown, 1997), pp. 578–581. The analysis by Janam Mukherjee, *Hungry Bengal:
      War, Famine and the End of Empire* (London: Hurst, 2015) is compelling.
19   Jackson, op. cit., p. 356.
20   Reid, op. cit., p. 142.
21   CAC, File 3/2, Slim Papers.
22   CAC, File 3/2, Slim Papers.
23   Mountbatten's Report, pp. 246–251.
24   Thompson, op. cit., p. 87.
25   TNA/CAB 106/106 Letter 1. Leese to Brooke, 15 December 1944.
26   Slim sacked three commanding officers in 1943. Slim, *Defeat into Victory*, op. cit.,
      p. 180.
27   Lieutenant General Sir Philip Christison, *Autobiography* (Imperial War Museum),
      p. 123.
28   I am grateful to Professor Katherine Venables for these and other observations on
      medical services in Burma.
29   Barkawi, op. cit., pp. 67–77.
30   Raghavan, op. cit., p. 385.
31   Ibid., p. 387.
32   Ibid., p. 389.
33   Julian Thompson, *The Lifeblood of War: Logistics in Armed Conflict* (London:
      Brasseys, 1991), p. 90.
34   Gordon Dunlop, op. cit., p. 95.

CHAPTER 21

1   Gilbert, op. cit., p. 470.
2   Quoted in Philip Ziegler, *Mountbatten* (London: Collins, 1985), p. 221.
3   Ibid., p. 467.
4   Arthur Bryant, *Turn of the Tide* (London: Collins, 1957), p. 693.
5   Brian Bond (ed.), *Chief of Staff: The Diaries of Lieutenant-General Sir Henry
     Pownall, Vol. Two, 1940–1944* (London: Leo Cooper, 1974), p. 108.
6   Ibid., p. 118.
7   White, op. cit., p. 231.
8   Romanus and Sunderland, op. cit., p. 29.
9   During 1943, on the back of repeated humiliations, operational failures and
     seemingly intractable complexities, Whitehall struggled to maintain a serious focus
     on the issues facing the Far East. See Thorne, op. cit., p. 290.
10   See Churchill, *The Hinge of Fate*, op. cit., p. 702; Gilbert, op. cit., p. 884; and
     Danchev and Todman, op. cit., p. 394.
11   Thorne, op. cit., p. 294.
12   Bryant, op. cit., p. 109.

13   Philip Ziegler (ed.), *Personal Diary of Admiral The Lord Louis Mountbatten 1943–1946* (London: Collins, 1988), p. 37.

14   Ibid., p. 22.

15   Ibid., p. 25.

16   Ibid., p. 96.

17   Moon (ed.), *The Viceroy's Journal*, op. cit., pp. 46–47.

CHAPTER 22

1   Commanded by Major Generals Harold Briggs and Frank Messervy, respectively.

2   Giffard, who had spent most of his military career in Africa, placed considerable store by these troops. He told Messervy when the latter was Director, Armoured Fighting Vehicles in GHQ India that 'the real decisive factor is not going to be tanks. It is going to be the new West African Division'. See H.R. Maule, *Spearhead General: The Epic Story of General Sir Frank Messervy and his Men at Eritrea, North Africa and Burma* (London: Odhams Press, 1961), p. 213.

3   CAC, File 3/2, Slim Papers.

4   Maule, op. cit., p. 219.

5   M.R. Roberts, *Golden Arrow: The Story of the 7th Indian Division in the Second World War 1939–1945* (Aldershot: Gale and Polden, 1952), p. 12.

6   Maule, op. cit., p. 225.

7   Brett-James, op. cit., p. 252.

8   CAC, File 3/9, Slim Papers. See also Mountbatten to Lewin, 6 May 1975, BA/ File K19B.

CHAPTER 23

1   For Japanese sources see Swinson, *Four Samurai* (London: Hutchinson, 1968); Anthony J. Barker, *The March on Delhi* (London: Faber and Faber, 1963); Brian Bond (ed.), *Fallen Stars, Eleven Studies of Twentieth Century Military Disasters* (London: Brasseys, 1991); Brian Bond (ed.), *British and Japanese Military Leadership in the Far Eastern War, 1941–1945* (London: Cass, 2004); Edward Drea, *In the Service of the Emperor: Essays on the Imperial Japanese Army* (London: University of Nebraska Press, 1998); Meirion and Susie Harries, *Soldiers of the Sun: The Rise and Fall of the Imperial Japanese Army* (London: William Heinemann, 1991); Lieutenant General Fujiwara Iwaichi, *Burma: The Japanese Verdict* (Purnell's History of the Second World War, 1966).

2   By June 1944 it had increased to 4,690 tons per day, and by March 1945, after herculean efforts to improve its capacity, it was carrying 8,630 tons per day.

3   Ursula Graham Bower, *Naga Path* (London: John Murray, 1952); Vicky Thomas, *The Naga Queen Ursula Graham Bower and her Jungle Warriors 1939–45* (Stroud: The History Press, 2012).

4 The Japanese consistently though erroneously referred to the mountains between Imphal and the Chindwin as the 'Arakan' range.

5 Quoted in Kenichi Arakawa *Japanese War Leadership in the Burma Theatre: The Imphal Operation* in Brian Bond and Kyoichi Tachikawa (eds.) British and Japanese Military Leadership in the Far Eastern War, 1941–1945 (London: Frank Cass, 2004), p. 111.

6 Quoted in Swinson, *Four Samurai*, op. cit., p. 123.

7 Mutaguchi was to claim after the war that he advocated 'the invasion of India' in order to boost Japanese morale at a time when Japan was suffering repeated defeats in the Pacific.

8 Quoted in Allen, op. cit., p. 155.

9 Joyce Lebra, *The Indian National Army and Japan*, (Singapore, ISEAS Publishing, 2008) p. 123.

10 'U Go' means 'C', hence the offensive into Manipur and Assam was Operation *C*, while the feint into Arakan that preceded it was Operation *Ha-Go*, or Operation *Z*.

CHAPTER 24

1 'Jungle Jinks', op. cit., Part 1.

2 Roberts, op. cit., p. 39.

3 Brett-James, op. cit., p. 261.

4 Commanded by the newly arrived Brigadier Geoffrey Evans.

5 LHA/File 5/3, Messervy Papers. 7 Indian Division Commander's Operational Notes No. 8, 3 January 1944.

6 LHA/File 5/3 Messervy Papers. 7 Indian Division Commander's Operational Notes No. 2, 28 October 1943.

7 LHA/File 5/5 Messervy Papers. 7 Indian Division Commander's Operational Notes No. 5, 15 November 1943.

8 Michael Lowry, *Fighting Through to Kohima: A Memoir of War in India and Burma* (Barnsley: Leo Cooper, 2003), p. 123.

CHAPTER 25

1 E.W.C. Sandes, *From Pyramid to Pagoda: The Story of the West Yorkshire Regiment (The Prince of Wales' Own) In the War 1943–45 and afterwards* (Hastings, Sussex: F.J. Parsons Ltd, 1951).

2 Roberts, op. cit., p. 59.

3 See John Hamilton, *War Bush: 81 (West African) Division in Burma 1943–1945* (Norwich: Michael Russell, 2001); *Jungle Commando: The Story of the West African Expeditionary Force's First Campaign in Burma* (1944); *Arakan Assignment: The Story of the 82nd West African Division* (n.d) and *Kaladan Return: The Second Campaign of the 81st West African Division* (n.d).

4   'Jungle Jinks', op. cit., Part 1.
5   Brett-James, op. cit., p. 294.
6   Calvert, *Slim*, op. cit., p. 83.
7   Maule, op. cit., p. 314.

CHAPTER 26

1   See Hemant Katoch, *Imphal 1944* (Botley: Oxford, 2018) and Geoffrey Evans
    and Anthony Brett-James, *Imphal: A Flower on Lofty Heights* (London:
    Macmillan, 1962).
2   Winston Churchill, *The Second World War, Volume 5 Closing the Ring*, (London:
    Cassell, 1952), pp. 576–567.
3   Frederick Winterbotham, *The Ultra Secret* (London: Weidenfeld & Nicholson, 1974),
    pp. 169–170. See also Alan Stripp, *Code Breaker in the Far East* (Oxford: Oxford
    University Press), 1995; Ronald Lewin, *The Other Ultra* (London: Hutchison, 1982)
    and Michael Smith, *The Emperor's Codes* (London: Transworld, 2000).
4   Letter in the possession of Chris Twells.
5   A second SLU was based in Kandy, providing the same intelligence to
    Mountbatten. The SLUs were run by the secret intelligence service, MI6.
6   The main strip was Imphal Main, a handful of miles north of Imphal town,
    overlooked by the extraordinary Nunshigum Hill, a sharp-pointed ridge jutting
    spectacularly 4,000 feet above the valley floor and providing a clear view over
    Imphal town below. Tulihal (the site of today's airport) was just to the south and
    Kangla sat on the town's eastern outskirts. Sapam and Palel lay in the south-east,
    where the Shenam Hills debouched onto the plain, and Wangjing was halfway
    between these two and Imphal. Only Imphal Main, Palel and Tulihal, however,
    were all-weather, the latter being covered with 'bithess', a product made from
    soaking strips of hessian in bitumen and laying them across the dirt strip, a
    process also used extensively on many of the otherwise fair-weather tracks in the
    region to improve mobility during the monsoon season.
7   Romanus and Sunderland, op. cit., p. 274.
8   BA/Box C247A.
9   Japanese divisions (although not Yamauchi's 15 Division) had, in addition to the
    divisional commander, a major general who commanded the divisional infantry.
10 The population of Japan in 1944 was about 70 million. Mutaguchi obviously
    enhanced the numbers to include those in client states of the Empire of Japan.
11 Quoted in Arthur Swinson, *The Battle of Kohima* (London: Cassell, 1962), p. 25.

CHAPTER 27

1   LHA/Wavell to CIGS July 1944, Alanbrooke Papers.
2   Ian Lyall Grant, *Burma: The Turning Point* (Chichester: The Zampi Press, 1993).
3   TNA/WO/172/4188.

4   Most histories follow the inaccurate account in the Official History, Lyall Grant being the honourable exception, following the clear evidence of the records in TNA that Scoones had been informed as early as 8 March of Japanese activity in the Tiddim area, and of Cowan's concern to initiate preparations for a withdrawal of his division at the earliest opportunity.

5   Collingridge and Cowan were old friends from 6 Gurkha Rifles.

6   John Randle, *Battle Tales from Burma* (Barnsley: Pen and Sword, 2004).

7   Japanese Monograph No. 134 (Headquarters US Army, Japan, 1952), No. 134, p. 107.

CHAPTER 28

1   Appreciation of the Situation by GOC IV Corps on 29 February 1944 in the Event of a Major Enemy Attack Materialising in the Next Two Months, TNA WO 172/418.

2   3/213 Battalion; two companies from 215 Regiment; 2/51 Battalion and 3/60 Battalion, supported by the 60 Type-95 tanks of 14 Tank Regiment, as well as sizeable numbers of artillery and combat engineers.

3   The Assam Regiment was formed in Shillong in 1941. Men from the Ahom, Naga, Mizo, Kuki, Khasi, Garo, Lushai and Manipur tribes were at first recruited, and these were followed by Adis, Nishis, Monpas and domiciled Gurkhas and Sikkhimese.

4   Many of these still exist, hidden in the jungle forward of the hill on which Sangshak is perched.

5   Eric Neild, *With Pegasus in India* (Singapore: Jay Birch and Co, 1970); Harry Seaman, *The Battle at Sangshak* (London: Leo Cooper, 1989).

6   Seaman, op. cit., p. 85.

7   File 1/23, Gracey Papers.

8   Major General John Grover.

9   6 Brigade had fought in the abortive Arakan campaign in 1943.

CHAPTER 29

1   The site of the tennis court is now marked out in the Commonwealth War Graves cemetery at Kohima.

2   See Arthur Campbell, *The Siege: A Story from Kohima* (London: George, Allen and Unwin, 1956); John Colvin, *Not Ordinary Men* (Barnsley: Pen and Sword, 1994); Leslie Edwards, *Kohima: The Furthest Battle* (Stroud: The History Press, 2009); Gordon Graham, *The Trees Are All Young on Garrison Hill* (Kohima Educational Trust, Marlow, 2006); Fergal Keane, *Road of Bones: The Siege of Kohima 1944* (London: Harper Collins, 2010); Michael Lowry, *An Infantry Commander in Arakan and Kohima* (Aldershot: Gale and Polden, 1950) and *Fighting through to Kohima* (Barnsley: Leo Cooper, 2003);

C.E. Lucas Philips, *Springboard to Victory: Battle for Kohima* (London: Heinemann, 1966).

3 123 Brigade (Brigadier G.C. Evans) and 9 Brigade (Brigadier J.A. Salomons) were flown into Imphal as planned.

4 Geoffrey Evans, op. cit., 166.

5 Peter Steyn, *History of the Assam Regiment* (Calcutta: Orient Longmans, 1959).

6 An account of the siege of Kohima by Brigadier Hugh Richards, in the possession of the author. On 19 February 1944, 1 Battalion (it was a two-battalion regiment) moved to 57 Reinforcement Camp at Kohima before making a three-day march over the 60-mile route through the Naga Hills to Jessami and Kharasom.

7 The exact number of fighting men able to bear arms on Garrison Hill at the start of the siege can only be approximated. The major units included 446 men of the Royal West Kents; about 200 men ('7 platoons' according to Hugh Richards) of the Assam Rifles and 260 men of the Assam Regiment recovered from Jessami and Kharasom. There were two composite companies (one Gurkha and one Indian) on GPT; two companies of Burma Rifles on Jail Hill; a company of the Shere Regiment on Garrison Hill; a handful of V-Force men at Kuki Piquet and the equivalent of a company of British NCOs and men from the reinforcement camp based at the DC's bungalow, along with a single 25-pounder. This gives an additional seven companies' worth to the Royal West Kents, Assam Rifles and Assam Regiment. Assuming that each was understrength, at say 80–90 men, this would have added up to 600 riflemen to the mix, giving Richards about 1,500 men able to fight. The remainder (about 1,000) were cooks, drivers, medical orderlies and bottlewashers.

8 Quoted in Swinson, *Four Samurai*, op. cit., pp. 248–249.

CHAPTER 30

1 Moon (ed.), *The Viceroy's Journal*, op. cit., p. 65.

2 There were in fact two roads, roughly parallel to each other, one for east-bound traffic and one for west-bound.

3 The Japanese named the hills after the officers who led the assault on them. The hill the British called Scraggy was named Ito, after Major Ito, of 213 Regiment.

4 See Hugh Toye, *Subhash Chandra Bose: The Springing Tiger* (Bombay: Jaico Publishing House, 1991); Gerald Corr, *The War of the Springing Tigers* (Osprey: London, 1975); Joyce Lebra, *Jungle Alliance* (Singapore: Asia Pacific Press, 1971) and *Japanese Trained Armies in Southeast Asia* (New York: Columbia, 1977).

5 Quoted in Allen, *Mutaguchi Renya*, op. cit., p. 220.

6 Quoted in Swinson, *Four Samurai*, op. cit., p. 129.

7 Jeremy Taylor, *The Devons: A History of the Devonshire Regiment 1685–1945* (Bristol: White Swan Press, 1951).

8 Terence Molloy, *The Silchar Track* (Ely: Melrose Books, 2006).

CHAPTER 31

1 Quoted in Swinson, op. cit., p. 142.
2 The location of the modern Catholic cathedral.
3 89 Brigade was now fighting with 5 Indian Division in Imphal, while Messervy's division was reinforced by Warren's 161 Brigade.
4 Arthur Swinson, *The Battle of Kohima* (London: Cassell, 1966), p. 199.
5 Ibid., p. 200.
6 Ibid., p. 230.
7 Ibid., p. 230. This series of messages are a paraphrased amalgam of a range of sources. There does not appear to be a single coherent account of this exchange.
8 Ibid., p. 231.

CHAPTER 32

1 Moon, op. cit., p. 72.
2 'Jungle Jinks', op. cit., Part 1.
3 Not to be confused with Colonel Tanaka Tetsujiro, 33 Division Chief of Staff, who was acting commander until Lieutenant General Tanaka Nobuo arrived from Thailand in late May.
4 Quoted in Barker, op. cit., p. 135.
5 Ibid., p. 142.
6 Quoted in Swinson, *Four Samurai*, op. cit., p. 141.

CHAPTER 33

1 Myitkyina rhymes with 'Kitchener'.
2 Told in Donovan Webster's *The Burma Road* (London: Macmillan, 2004).
3 Generals Liao Yao-shiang and Sun Lijen, respectively.
4 Kandy was chosen because it was anticipated at the time that naval (specifically amphibious) operations would predominate in the war against Japan. They didn't. This meant that SEAC was too far from the source of the fighting, in Assam and Burma, 1,300 air miles from Calcutta, the centre for what had become a joint air and land, rather than a naval, campaign. Calcutta (Barrackpore) was HQ for both Eastern Air Command and Giffard's 11 Army Group and later for Leese's ALFSEA.
5 S. Woodburn Kirby, *The War Against Japan*, Vol. III (London: HMSO, 1961), Appendices 17 and 18.
6 Wingate's concept of strongholds with 'floater columns' to protect them was actually Scoones' idea for IV Corps. Slim suggested that this might usefully be employed by Special Force. Wingate subsequently claimed that the idea had been his and this view is repeated by many. See, for example, Sykes, op. cit., p. 543. For Slim's view see *Defeat into Victory*, op. cit., p. 220.
7 Accounts of the start of Operation *Thursday* at Lalaghat airfield have caused heated controversy. For a good assessment of this incident, and its subsequent

reporting, see S. Bidwell, *The Chindit War: The Campaign in Burma, 1944* (London: Hodder and Stoughton, 1979), p. 106. Some have contended that Slim's account in *Defeat into Victory* was untrustworthy because it was written so long after the event. Slim, however, submitted a full account of this incident to Mountbatten on 13 September 1944, and it was this account that was subsequently placed in *Defeat into Victory*. See BA/Box C247A.

8   Quoted in Sykes, op. cit., p. 502.

9   Slim never knew that Brodie's brigade had not supported Fergusson's attack on Indaw: even in *Defeat into Victory* he did not realize that Fergusson had attacked the town entirely unsupported.

10 There is considerable confusion on this point. Wingate, for instance, appeared to have decided not to use 14 Brigade in support of 16 Brigade's attack on Indaw, and despatched him to his guerrilla task along the Chindwin instead. He did not, however, tell Fergusson of this change of plan. Nevertheless, it appears clear that Slim accepted this new role of one of Wingate's four deployed brigades, if only for a season.

11 SEAC Interrogation Records of Japanese Officers, p. 18, quoted in Romanus and Sunderland, op. cit., p. 222. See p. 475 for the provenance of these records.

12 Bidwell, op. cit., p. 252.

13 BA/S145, Mountbatten Archives.

14 Sykes, op. cit., p. 536.

15 TNA, CAB 106/111

16 Callahan, *Burma 1942–45*, op. cit., p. 138.

17 An excellent account of the Mogaung battle and the relationship with Stilwell was written by one of the column commanders, Brigadier Michael Calvert, in *Prisoners of Hope* (London: Jonathan Cape, 1952), pp. 174–253 and again in *Fighting Mad* (London: The Adventurers Club, 1964), pp. 190–203. John Masters, another of the column commanders involved, recorded his story in *The Road Past Mandalay* (London: Michael Joseph, 1961). The story is covered well by David Rooney in *Mad Mike* (London: Leo Cooper, 1997).

18 Ian Fellows-Gordon, *The Magic War: The Battle for North Burma* (New York: Scribner's, 1971); Donovan Webster, *The Burma Road* (New York: Farrar, Straus and Giroux, 2003).

19 The phrase was Slim's.

20 Auchinleck, Despatch, op. cit., para 2665.

21 TNA/106/171.

22 Ibid.

CHAPTER 34

1   Winterbotham, op. cit., pp. 169–172. Stilwell and Chennault also received ULTRA intelligence from WEC and Bletchley Park through Mountbatten's HQ in Kandy.

2   Frederick Winterbotham, *The Ultra Secret* (London: HarperCollins, 1974).

3   32 Brigade remained attached to 17 Indian Division on the Tiddim Road.

4 The strength of 2 Division in June 1944 was 12,436 officers and men; that of 7 Indian Division 10,014, including 819 British other ranks.

5 Swinson, op. cit., p. 243.

6 See George Wilton, 'The Forgotten Chindits – 23 British Infantry Brigade' in *British Journal for Military History*, Vol. 6, Issue 3, November 2020.

7 Bisheshwar Prasad (ed.), *The Reconquest of Burma Volume I, Official History of the Indian Armed Forces in the Second World War 1939–1945* (June 1942–June 1944), p. 267.

8 Saburo Ienaga uses figures from Japanese sources of an army of 100,000 which suffered 30,000 killed, 20,000 dead of illness, and a further 25,000 wounded or ill. Saburo Ienaga, *Japan's Last War* (Oxford: Blackwell, 1979), p. 147.

9 Mountbatten Papers.

10 Kase Toshikazu, *Eclipse of the Rising Sun* (London: Jonathan Cape, 1951), p. 92.

11 8,000 casualties in Arakan, 4,000 at Kohima and 12,000 at Imphal.

12 Ziegler, *Mountbatten*, op. cit., p. 250.

13 BA/S145, 6 May 1944.

14 Jonathan Ritter, *Stilwell and Mountbatten in Burma: Allies at War 1943–1944* (Denton: University of North Texas, 2017).

15 Lieutenant General Albert C. Wedemeyer, *Wedemeyer Reports* (New York: Henry Holt, 1958).

16 Quoted in David Rooney, *Stilwell* (London: Pan, 1971), p. 105.

17 After Stilwell's departure, the NCAC was commanded by the American Lieutenant General Dan I. Sultan and consisted of 36 British Division (Maj Gen F.W. Festing), 1 and 6 Chinese Armies and the American 'Mars' Brigade. 36 British Division transferred to 14 Army on 1 April 1945.

CHAPTER 35

1 S. Woodburn Kirby, *The War Against Japan*, Vol. V (London: HMSO, 1969), p. 419.

2 Lewin, op. cit., p. 192.

3 Taylor, op. cit., p. 107.

4 Tom Carew's remarkable story is told by his daughter, Keggie Carew in *Dadland* (London: Chatto and Windus, 2016).

5 In addition to 28 East African Division, two independent East African Brigades were allocated to 11 Army Group. 22 (East Africa) Infantry Brigade served in the Arakan under command of XV Corps, while 28 (East Africa) Infantry Brigade served under IV Corps.

6 W.J. Slim, 'Campaign of the 14th Army 1944–45' in *Australian Army Journal* (Melbourne, 1950), p. 18.

7 Warren had replaced Geoffrey Evans, who moved on to command 7 Indian Division. Warren was killed shortly after, in February 1945, and replaced by Bob Mansergh during the Meiktila battle, who had briefly been GOC of 11 East Africa Division. Brigadier William Dimoline from 28 East Africa Brigade replaced Mansergh in 11 East Africa Division.

8   W.J. Slim, 'Higher Command in War' in *US Army Military Review* (May 1990), p. 13. See also Slim, *Unofficial History* (London: Cassell, 1959), p. 156.

9   To give a sense of the magnitude of this achievement, a C47 could carry 3 US tons; 4,000 tons in one day constituted 1,333 separate aircraft sorties. To carry 78,250 tons would have required 26,084 sorties over the 31 days of the month, an average of 842 per day.

10   IWM, Box 3, Leese Papers.

11   18 and 56 Divisions (together with a brigade each from 49 Division and 2 Division), numbering 25,500 troops.

12   15 Army contained, from north to south, 15, 53, 31 and 33 Divisions.

13   Masters, op. cit., pp. 292–322.

14   Father of Mervyn Rees, the British Labour politician and Home Secretary (1976 and 1979).

15   Now commanded by General Dan Sultan, the advance comprised 30, 38 and 50 Chinese divisions, the British 36 Division and the American 5332 Brigade, more commonly known as the MARS task force.

CHAPTER 36

1   General Sir Oliver Leese, *Brief History of the Operations in Burma 1 November 1944–3 May 1945* (TAC HQ, ALFSEA, May 1945), p. 17.

CHAPTER 37

1   This two-brigade division was reinforced during the operation by the two-brigade 82 West African Division, under command.

2   Barnaby Phillips, *Another Man's War: The Story of a Burma Boy in Britain's Forgotten African Army* (London: Oneworld, 2014).

3   No. 1 and No. 5 Commando (British Army), and No. 42 and 44 Commando (Royal Marines).

4   8/19 Hyderabad Regiment; 16/10 Baluch Regiment and 2/2 Punjab Regiment.

5   Commissioned from the Royal Military Academy Sandhurst in 1927 (along with Pran Nath Thapar), Thimayya was to become the sixth Chief of Army Staff of the Indian Army in 1957. Thapar was the fourth. Thimayya was the only Indian officer to command a brigade in the Second World War, a reflection of just how late the Indianization of the officer corps was to ensure that Indians were able to rise beyond command of a battalion during the war.

CHAPTER 38

1   Louis Allen, 'The Campaigns in Asia and the Pacific', in J. Gooch (ed.), *Decisive Campaigns of the Second World War* (London: Frank Cass, 1990), p. 168.

2   Evans, op. cit., p. 202.

CHAPTER 39

1   Philip Davies, *Lost Warriors: Seagrim and Pagani of Burma* (Croxley Green, Hertfordshire: Atlantic Publishing, 2017).

2   These were (1) SOE (Force 136); (2) Z Force; (3) SIS (the Inter-Services Liaison Department, ISLD); (4) Combined Operations Pilotage Parties (COPP); (5) Air Sea Rescue; (6) Psychological Warfare Division (PWD); (7) Deception Division; (8) E Group (POW escape); (9) Burma Intelligence Corps (BIC); (10) V Force; (11) Office of Strategic Services (OSS)(US); (12) Office of War Information (OWI) (US).

3   Duckett, op. cit., p. 12.

4   The Jedburgh idea was a successful concept borrowed from pre-D-Day experience in Occupied Europe. Three-man teams were responsible for training local resistance volunteers in guerrilla tactics, sabotage and intelligence gathering. Eight 'Jed' teams supported *Character*, and six teams supported Operation *Billet*.

5   Research undertaken by Richard Ducket (see *https://soeinburma.wordpress.com/2020/10/29/a-force-136-special-group-ferret/*) demonstrates how in 1945 ethnic Burmans dominated SOE operations into the Karenni. Of the 18 men, for example, in Team 'Ferret', 11 were Burman, four were Karen and one each were Kuki, Kachin and Chin. That over 60 per cent of Burmese operatives recruited for operations in 1945 were Burmans indicates something of the shift that had been made in Burma away from support to the Japanese since the early, heady days of 1942.

6   Reduced to four when operations began, 'Ferret' working as part of 'Otter'.

7   Terence O'Brien, *The Moonlight War* (London: Collins, 1987). One of the Force 136 officers, John Hedley, is referred to in Masters, op. cit., pp. 314–315, and told in his autobiography.

8   Charles Cruikshank, *SOE in the Far East* (Oxford: Oxford University Press), p. 190.

9   TNA/CAB 106/48 (Account of operations of Fourteenth Army 1944–1945).

10 Duckett, op. cit., pp. 147–148.

CHAPTER 40

1   Of this number, 2,499,909 were army, 28,972 navy and 52,845 in the air force. Bisheshwar Prasad (ed.), *India and the War*, Official History of the Indian Armed Forces in the Second World War 1939–1945 (New Delhi, 1966), p. 258.

2   K.S. Nair, *The Forgotten Few* (Noida, Utter Pradesh: Harper Collins, 2019).

3   The Allies massively outproduced Japan in every area of war materiel. Japan largely stagnated from 1942 and made nothing like the technical or technological effort of the Allies to improve their military capabilities, relying on the willingness of their soldiers, sailors and airmen to die for their emperor in lieu of better equipment or weapons.

4   F.C. Jones, *Japan's New Order in East Asia: Its Rise and Fall 1937–45* (Oxford: OUP, 1954); Mark Felton, *Japan's Gestapo* (Barnsley: Pen and Sword, 2009); Lord Russell, *The Knights of Bushido: A Short History of Japanese War Crimes* (London:

Cassell, 1958); Laurence Rees, *Horror in the East* (London: BBC, 2001) and Yuki Tanaka, *Hidden Horrors: Japanese War Crimes in World War II* (London: Roman and Littlefield, 1996).

5   Ienaga, op. cit., p. 180.

6   Karaka, op. cit., p. 29.

7   Masters, op. cit., p. 310.

8   Formed in November 1943, 11 Army Group within SEAC comprised 14 Army, Ceylon Army Command (82 West African and 11 East African Divisions, and 99 Infantry Brigade) and an array of infantry units and garrisons. A year later it became ALFSEA.

9   Raghavan, op. cit., p. 6.

10   Cohen, op. cit., p. 140.

11   This figure is from Bisheshwar Prasad (ed.), *Official History of the Indian Armed Forces in the Second World War, Expansion of the Armed Forces and Defence Organisation 1939–45* (New Delhi: Government of India, 1956), p. 406. Omissi, op. cit., p. 191. The term 'mercenary' is described by F.W. Perry to denote the fact that rather than being constituted for the defence of India, the 'Indian Army was a means of policing a dependency or acting as an Imperial Reserve and the martial class concept was one of identifying the groups from which mercenaries could be obtained.' Perry, op. cit., p. 115. The 'mercenary' status of the Indian Army was entirely accepted at the time in military circles. See Raghavan, op. cit., p. 64.

12   Cohen, op. cit., p. 143.

13   Jackson, *The British Empire and the Second World War*, op. cit., p. 351.

14   Karaka, op. cit., p. 35.

15   I cannot now find the source for this quotation, after noting it in my files. If anyone finds it, please send it to me to allow for recognition in subsequent editions.

16   Howard, op. cit., p. 125.

17   BA/C2.

18   Lewin, op. cit., p. 210.

19   Jackson, *The British Empire and the Second World War*, op. cit., p. 352.

20   See Cat Wilson, op. cit.

21   Jackson, *The British Empire and the Second World War*, op. cit., p. 352.

22   Angus Calder, *The People's War*, p. 288. For casualties see Appendix 4. The British Commonwealth suffered total casualties of 73,909, of whom 14,326 died (Louis Allen, *Burma*, op. cit., pp. 637–645). The Commonwealth War Graves Commission use a figure of 14,731 dead. Fewer than 5,000 of those who died were British. The total casualty figure of 73,909 includes 14,552 missing, most of whom were lost during the Retreat in 1942. See also TNA/WO/33/2843, 'Strength Return of the Defence Services in SEA and India Commands, January 1945'. Louis Allen wrongly calculates that of the entire 1.3m soldiers in SEAC, 13% British, 25% African and 62% Indian (*Burma*, op. cit., pp. 655–660). The numbers of African soldiers were far fewer.

23   This number of deaths represented 60% of the 308,582 men deployed to fight in Burma and India during the war. Louis Allen, *Burma*, op. cit., p. 640.

24   Daniel Marston, 'Learning from Defeat: The Burma Campaign' in Daniel Marston (ed.), *The Pacific War Companion* (Oxford: Osprey Publishing, 2007), p. 106.

25   R.J. Rummel, *China's Bloody Century* (New Brunswick, NJ: Transaction Publishers, 1991).

26   Masters, op. cit., pp. 312–313.

27   Bayley, '"The Nation Within": British India at War 1939–1947' in *Proceedings of the British Academy*, 125 (2004), p. 270.

28   The efforts made by the Indian Army to fatten up recruits was not evidence of malnourishment per se, but reflective of the demanding tasks that would be required of them as trained infantrymen.

29   Bayley, 'The Nation Within', op. cit., p. 275.

30   Beaumont, op. cit., p. 194.

31   Karaka, op. cit., p. 33.

APPENDICES

1   Letter from Auchinleck to Brooke, 9 September 1943.

2   Mountbatten's Report (1951), pp. 276–277 and Prasad (ed.), *Expansion of the Armed Forces*, op. cit., p. 406.

3   This included 4,545 British officers commissioned into the Indian Army.

Index

References to maps are in **bold**.